THE BATTLE
OF THE
SOMME

THE BATTLE OF THE SOMME

A Topographical History

(originally *When the Barrage Lifts*)

by

Gerald Gliddon

with a foreword
by
Correlli Barnett

SUTTON PUBLISHING

First published in 1987 by Gliddon Books
Republished in 1990 by Leo Cooper

First published in this corrected edition in 1994 by
Alan Sutton Publishing Limited, an imprint of Sutton Publishing Limited
Phoenix Mill · Thrupp · Stroud · Gloucestershire GL5 2BU

Reprinted in 1996, 1998

Originally published under the title *When the Barrage Lifts*

Reprinted in 1996 under the title *The Battle of the Somme*

A catalogue record for this book is available from the British Library

ISBN 0-7509-1344-4

Jacket photographs reproduced by permission of the Imperial War Museum,
London.

Printed in Great Britain by
WBC Limited, Bridgend, Mid-Glamorgan.

*This book is dedicated
to the memory of the late
Anthony Comerford*

Contents

List of Maps

Foreword

At 0730 hours on 1st July 1916, 14 British divisions climbed out of their trenches along an 18-mile front north of the Somme, and marched slowly on towards the German defences. They expected to find the enemy barbed wire, trench system, artillery and defenders all annihilated by the week-long preliminary bombardment by 1,350 guns. Instead they were massacred by the German gunfire and machine guns, first as they plodded across no man's land, and then as they bunched to struggle through gaps in the often still uncut barbed wire. By the end of the day no fewer than 57,000 men of the British army had fallen, 19,000 of them killed, and without gaining a permanent lodgement in the German defences except on the right of the line next to five attacking French divisions.

It was a catastrophe without parallel in British history; today, seventy year's later, it remains the cause of sorrow and bitter controversy. Yet the battle had to go on, for the first day of the Somme was the 132nd day of the Battle of Verdun, where the Germans were attempting to bleed the French army to death. So week by week, month by month the British army continued to slog forward through immensely strong defences manned by the German army at the peak of its efficiency and power. Fought over foot by foot, obscure patches of French woodland passed into the memory of a generation of British Empire fighting men – Delville Wood, Trônes Wood, High Wood. the names of villages that had been reduced to brick-coloured traces in the mud acquired an enduring resonance – Fricourt, Montauban, Gommecourt, Thiepval, Beaumont Hamel. On 15th September 1916 the weapon that was eventually to transform land warfare, the tank, made its debut, when 32 slow and clumsy monsters spearheaded the British capture of Flers and Courcelette. On 18th November, after four months, Field Marshal Sir Douglas Haig, the C-in-C, at last closed the battle down in a sea of mud. Four months of fighting had cost some 419,000 British Empire casualties, killed, wounded and missing and 204,000 French, while the German losses at least equalled the combined Allied total.

No wonder 'the Somme' was to pass into the British national memory as a tragedy of appalling scale. No wonder the terror and the suffering were to challenge a generation of soldier poets and novelists to find language capable of conveying the true realities of modern battle. No wonder historians have disputed ever since about the planning and conduct of the offensive. And no wonder the Battle of the Somme has been re-fought again and again in books right up to the present time.

To find a fresh approach is therefore by no means easy. Yet Gerald Gliddon in WHEN THE BARRAGE LIFTS has succeeded in writing a study of the battle that is entirely novel in its conception. Rather than write yet another narrative history, whether of the frontline fighting or from the command point of view, he has based his book on the topography of the battlefield itself. He has compiled a Somme 'dictionary' – with all the villages and towns, all the woods and copses, all the features of road, track and trench systems arranged in an easy-to-consult 'A to Z'.

Each entry comprises a fully documented account of the military significance of that particular place or feature in the conduct of the battle, and of the military units which were stationed there, or attacked from it, or which captured it. Each entry also comprises a brief but lucid historical account of the fighting there; accounts brought to life with apt quotations from eye-witnesses or from books by men who fought in the battle.

The merit of Gerald Gliddon's approach also lies in its objectivity, for each entry is limited to fact, whether the fact be geographical, military or the actual sequence of the events that happened there. The reader is left to make his own mind up on the strategic and tactical issues on the basis of the factual record.

WHEN THE BARRAGE LIFTS therefore provides a fascinating and fully documented reference book for families with relatives who fought on the Somme and for the general reader alike. In particular, it is indispensable for anyone who explores the battlefield and its war cemeteries today looking for the traces and places of the greatest battle ever fought by the soldiers of the British Empire.

Correlli Barnett, February 1987.

Preface to this Edition

After *When the Barrage Lifts* was first published in July 1987 I received letters from numerous readers who seemed to welcome a fresh approach to the most remembered battle of the First World War. Several people suggested minor alterations and on re-reading and using the book myself I also found some errors that needed attention.

For the Leo Cooper edition published in 1989 these changes were incorporated together with a ten-page index of formations and units. This edition went out of print in 1991 and *Barrage* has been unavailable ever since.

For this third printing, being issued by Alan Sutton Publishing Limited, I have made a further fifty small changes. So this latest version of the book is up to date and in including the new index to units it represents a considerably altered version to the self-published edition of 1987. Superscript numbers in the text refer to page 472, 'Additional Material to this Edition'.

The interest in the First World War and its battlefields has increased a great deal in the last seven years, and this fact is reflected in the number of tour operators offering trips to the Western Front and further afield. This increased interest is also reflected in the number of new books and reprints that have been published since 1987. There really seems no end to the steady flow of books to be written and published on this 'War to end All Wars'.

It is a sort of paradox that, as the last survivors 'fade away', the interest in the war has greatly increased and there seems to be a sense of urgency to commemorate the deeds of those who took part in it. This new interest is not just being concentrated on military units but is also very visible at local level. In many cases memorials, which were in danger of falling into decay, are now being actively looked after, and a national survey of such monuments is being carried out throughout the United Kingdom.

It is not just the stonework which is receiving attention, but the names of the men listed are providing work for a vast army of local historians who have simply asked themselves: 'Who are these men and what happened to them?' The number of British servicemen who were killed in the war exceeded three-quarters of a million, a figure which of course does not include the names of all those who survived. Indeed more is often known about a man who was killed in the war than one who survived. Computer technology has often been particularly helpful to researchers who wish to make a listing of all the men from one unit or county, for example, and in Northern Ireland the research carried out includes the names of the men who were killed as well as those who took part in the war and yet survived.

Many excellent booklets too have been published which have set out to record short biographies of men from individual parishes.

The Somme battlefield has also altered in the past seven years and there has been quite a lot of industrial building along with a new road to the north-east of Albert, but the main villages, woods and other sites have in the main escaped destruction or damage. The British have made their contribution to these changes and a rash of memorials has broken out. To mention just a few erected in the recent past there is one to the Accrington Pals at Sheffield Park in Serre, one to the Welsh Division opposite Mametz Wood, one to the Manchesters at Mametz village and at the Ulster Tower there are new memorials to the Ulstermen who won the Victoria Cross, and one to the Orangemen who took part in the battle. The Butte de Warelncourt has been purchased by the Western Front Association, which complements the crater at Lochnagar which is a mine crater owned by Richard Dunning and is a place of pilgrimage every 1st July at 7.30 a.m.

There is a new museum to the Somme in Albert called the Musée des Abris, and the excellent Museum at Delville Wood has had a facelift and now proudly displays South Africa's new national flag. In the early 1990s a new museum was opened at Peronne called the Historial de la Grande Guerre and is jointly funded by the French, British and Germans. The three-nation approach is reflected in the three language displays. It is a place much visited by schools and has an academic research centre. The Historial is also responsible for erecting many signs around the Somme battlefield which give information to visitors about where the Allied and German lines were at certain times of the Somme campaign. The Peronne Museum also recently supervised the unearthing of a German Command Headquarters at Pozieres.

So there have been quite a lot of changes to the Somme battlefield and they have mostly been to the good; in particular it has escaped from any major road-building schemes.

In a recent edition of *The Independent*, the writer, Mr Ross Davies, on visiting the Somme region, asked: 'Who goes to such places as the Somme and its museums?' Everybody, it seems, from schoolchildren to pensioners. The First World War is about family as much as about military or diplomatic history. More and more people are finding out they have a relation who served on the Somme, and who may be there still.

Gerald Gliddon, August 1994
Brooke.

Acknowledgements

During the preparation of this book there have been many people who have been very helpful, and I would like to thank in particular the following for their assistance and kindness. The staff of the Imperial War Museum in the Departments of Printed Books and Photographs; the Archivist at the Liddell Hart Centre, King's College, London; the Archivist at Churchill College, Cambridge; the Bodleian Library, Oxford; the Royal Artillery Institution, Woolwich; the National Army Museum; the Meteorological Office; the Public Records Office; the Commonwealth War Graves Commission; the RAF Museum, Hendon; Thorpe Road Branch Library, Norwich; Mr. Correlli Barnett; Mrs. Claire Blunden; Mr. Chaz Bowyer; Mr. Patrick Mahoney; Mr. Tony Spagnoly, whose knowledge of the period is encyclopaedic, and who could always be relied upon to check facts; and Mrs. Evelyn Smith, who typed the final draft of the manuscript and prepared the index.

I would like to express my especial appreciation to my wife, Winifred, who shared the task of proof checking with me; I alone am responsible for any errors which may have crept in, and which are inevitable in a work as long and detailed as this one; and daughter Eleanor, who had to live in a house with the spectre of the Battle of Somme hanging over it for so long while this book was being prepared.

I would also like to thank Her Majesty the Queen, for her gracious permission to use material from the Royal Archives; the Controller of HMSO for permission to reproduce maps from the *Official History of the War: Military Operations in France and Belgium, 1916* (1932 and 1938), and for Becke, A.F., *The Order of Battle Divisions* (HMSO 1935–1945), 4 volumes; the Oxford University Press for lines from 'Crucifix Corner', 'Of Grandcourt' and 'Ballad of the Three Spectres', from the *Collected Poems of Ivor Gurney*, edited by P.J. Kavanagh (1982); A.P. Watt, on behalf of the Executors of the Estate of Robert Graves, for using lines from 'A Dead Boche', published in *Goliath and David* and 'A Letter to S.S. from Mametz Wood', published in *Fairies and Fusiliers* (1917); George Sassoon for the use of 8 lines from the poem 'At Carnoy', by Siegfried Sassoon, 3rd July 1916; Michelin for the use of a section of their map 52, scale 1cm to 2km; Mr. Andrew Rawlinson and the Master, Fellows and Scholars of Churchill College, University of Cambridge, for permission to use material from General Lord Rawlinson's War Diary; Bodley Head on behalf of the Estate of F. Scott Fitzgerald for use of material from *Tender is the Night*, published in the Bodley Head Scott Fitzgerald 1959; the Trustees of the Liddell Hart Centre for Military Archives, King's College, London; the Imperial War Museum for permission to use material from interviews with Cpl. L.J. Ounsworth (332/12), Sgt. C.R. Quinnel 554/18 and Captain R.C. Cooney 494/6 from the Department of Sound Records; also from Mr. Christopher Skelton, for permission to quote from his father's papers deposited in the Department of Documents; Peter Liddle 1914–18, Personal Experience Archives.

Army Divisions

At the beginning of the War in 1914 a British Division contained over 18,000 men, and in each Division there were three Infantry Brigades which had four battalions each, four Artillery Brigades with their batteries and a heavy battery and a Cavalry Squadron. Later Field Engineer Companies were added along with a Cyclist Company, a Signals Company together with Medical and Supply Units. Later still the twelve Infantry Battalions were reduced to nine, but to compensate, trench-mortar and machine gun companies were added. The Divisions that took part in the battle were drawn from three groups, the Regular Army, the Territorial Army and the New Army which had been raised since the War began in 1914.

In the first group were the following: the Guards Division, followed by the 1st, 2nd, 3rd, 4th, 5th, 6th, 7th, 8th, and finally the 29th Division. In the Territorial Army the Divisions who took part in the first Somme battle were the 46th (North Midland), 47th (London), 48th (South Midland), 49th (West Midland), 50th (Northumberland), 51st (Highland), 55th (West Lancashire) and the 56th (London) Divisions. The New Army Divisions who took part were as follows: 9th (Scottish), 11th (Northern), 12th (Eastern), 14th (Light), 15th (Scottish), 16th (Irish), 17th (Northern), 18th (Eastern), 19th (Western), 20th (Light), 21st, 23rd, 24th, 25th, 30th, 31st, 32nd, 33rd, 34th, 35th (Bantam), 36th (Ulster), 37th, 38th (Welsh), 39th, 41st and 63rd (RN) Division).

It was the Third, Fourth and Reserve Armies which were associated with the first Battle of the Somme, during which the Reserve Army became the Fifth Army. In turn these were broken down into Corps that became Divisions made up of Brigades which broke down into Battalions. It is the last named that I have used in the main as the most useful for my purposes. I have attempted to include Brigade and Divisional numbers in the text itself on most occasions.

List of Abbreviations

List of abbreviations used in the text.

ADS: Advanced Dressing Station
A & SH: Argyll & Sutherland Highlanders.

Bde: Brigade.
Bedford: Bedfordshire Regiment.
Berks: Berkshire Regiment.
BW: Black Watch.
Border: Border Regiment.
Bucks: Buckinghamshire Regiment.
Buffs: Buffs (East Kent Regiment).

Cam. H: Cameron Highlanders.
CCS: Casualty Clearing Station.
Cheshire: Cheshire Regiment.
Coldst. Gds: Coldstream Guards.
CP: Collecting Post.
CO: Commanding Officer.
Conn. Rang: Connaught Rangers.
Cpl: Corporal.

Devon: Devonshire Regiment.
DMS: Director of Medical Services.
Div: Division.
Dorset: Dorsetshire Regiment.
DCLI: Duke of Cornwall's Light Infantry.
DWR: Duke of Wellington's (West Riding Regt.)
DLI: Durham Light Infantry.

E. Lancs: East Lancashire Regiment.
E. Surrey: East Surrey Regiment.
E. Yorks: East Yorkshire Regiment.
Essex: Essex Regiment.

FOO: Forward Observing Officer.

Glosters: Gloucestershire Regiment.
Gordons: Gordon Highlanders.
Green Howards: Green Howards (Alexandra,
    Princess of Wales' Own) Yorkshire Regt.
Gren Gds: Grenadier Guards.

Hampshire: Hampshire Regiment.
Herts: Hertfordshire Regiment.
HLI: Highland Light Infantry.
HQ: Headquarters.
HAC: Honourable Artillery Company.

Irish Gds: Irish Guards.

King's: King's (Liverpool Regiment).
King's Own: King's Own (Royal Lancaster Regt.).
KOSB: King's Own Scottish Borderers.
KOYLI: King's Own Yorkshire Light Infantry.
KRRC: King's Royal Rifle Corps.
KSLI: King's Shropshire Light Infantry.

Lancs. Fus: Lancashire Fusiliers.
Leicester: Leicestershire Regiment.
Leinster: Leinster Regiment.
Lincoln: Lincolnshire Regiment.
LRB: London Rifle Brigade.
LS: London Scottish.
L.N. Lancs: Loyal North Lancs.

Manchester: Manchester Regiment.
MDS: Main Dressing Station.
MO: Medical Officer.
Midd'x: Middlesex Regiment.
Mon: Monmouthshire Regiment.

Norfolk: Norfolk Regiment.
Northampton: Northamptonshire Regiment.
N. Staffs: North Staffordshire Regiment.
North'd Fus: Northumberland Fusiliers.

OP: Observation Post.
O & BLI: Oxfordshire & Buckinghamshire
    Light Infantry.

Queen's RW Kent: Queen's Own
    (Royal West Kent Regiment).
Queen's RWS: Queen's Royal Regiment (West
    Surreys)

RAP: Regimental Aid Post.
RDS: Relay Dressing Station.
Rif. Brig: Rifle Brigade.
RA: Royal Artillery.
R. Dub. Fus: Royal Dublin Fusiliers.
RFA: Royal Field Artillery.
RFC: Royal Flying Corps.
R. Fus: Royal Fusiliers.
R. Innis F: Royal Inniskilling Fusiliers.
R. Irish Fus: Royal Irish Fusiliers.
R. Irish: Royal Irish Regiment.
R. Irish Rif: Royal Irish Rifles.
RMF: Royal Munster Fusiliers.
R. Scots: Royal Scots.
R. Scots. Fus: Royal Scots Fusiliers.
R. Sussex: Royal Sussex Regiment.
R. Warwicks: Royal Warwickshire Regiment.
R. Welch Fus: Royal Welch Fusiliers.

Scot. Rif: The Cameronians (Scottish Rifles).
Scots. Gds: Scots. Guards.
Seaforth H: Seaforth Highlanders.
Sgt: Sergeant.
Sherwood For: Sherwood Foresters
    (Nottinghamshire & Derbyshire Regiment).
Somerset LI: Somerset Light Infantry.
SAI: South African Infantry.
S. Lancs: South Lancashire Regiment.
S. Staffs: South Staffordshire Regiment.
SWB: South Wales Borderers.
Suffolk: Suffolk Regiment.

TA: Territorial Army.

Welsh: Welsh Regiment.
Welsh Gds: Welsh Guards.
W. Yorks: West Yorkshire Regiment.
Wiltshire: Wiltshire Regiment.
Worc: Worcestershire Regiment.

Y & L: York and Lancaster Regiment.

Introduction

I first visited the Somme battlefields twenty years ago, and at that time took with me a large number of books and maps. I then began to make notes of events that had occurred during the battle, and decided to put these notes together, and to try and produce a book which would be of use to visitors to the battlefields, and to students of the First World War alike. The main idea was to gather together material which although available, was scattered over many sources. I therefore read nearly two hundred published memoirs of men who had been involved in the battle, and virtually every one of the Regimental or Divisional Histories which dealt with the battle. I also read many articles that were only available in journals and sifted through a great deal of unpublished material. I then decided to put all this information together in topographical order. The main part of this book therefore is this topographical section and in addition, I have included a potted history of the RFC Squadrons who took part in the battle. I have only included them if they were based in the region, and not if they took part in the battle whilst based in airfields out of the area. I have also compiled a chronology of the battle and a note on casualties of the three Armies involved. I have attempted to mention every Cemetery in the immediate Somme area providing that they contain the graves of men who were killed in the 1916 fighting. All dates used in the text refer to events that took place in 1916 unless otherwise stated.

Considering the number of Regiments who took part in the battle, there would be enough material for several volumes, but one has to stop somewhere, and I make no claim to completeness. If I mention one battalion in connection with a small village in the back area, I do not mean that they were the only battalion who stayed there, but rather that the village was used for billeting purposes, and the men who stayed there included men from this particular battalion.

The seeds of the Battle of the Somme were sown at the Allied Conference at Chantilly on 6th December 1915. The British Army was to continue, along with the French and Belgian Armies to endeavour to drive the German Army out of France and Belgium. Later a battle which would heavily involve the British was planned to take place in the Somme region in the summer of 1916, and this would release French Divisions, who in turn would try and defeat the enemy in the Verdun region. In Britain in the first six months of 1916 there was a very considerable build-up of both men and equipment, but unfortunately it was obvious to even a casual observer that the British Army was being prepared for a 'Big Push', and there is no doubt that the Germans knew that the British were planning to make a strong attack on their positions in the Somme region. The battle was planned to begin with several days of artillery bombardment, which owing to very wet weather was extended. Finally the Battle began on 1st July and what happened, will I hope emerge in the following pages.

Gerald Gliddon,
Shotesham St. Mary,
February 1987.   Norfolk.

THE SOMME, 1916.

THE ATTACK OF THE FOURTH ARMY ON THE 1ST JULY. THE SITUATION AT NIGHT.

1ST JULY 1916.

Front Line at Zero — British
Objectives for the 1st July
Positions gained & held at night

SCALE

Heights in metres

Ordnance Survey 1929

3100/31

Acheux

Acheux is a village on the main road between Albert and Doullens the D 938. It is between Forceville and Louvencourt. In 1916 the VIII Corps Collecting Station arrived here in readiness for the start of the Battle of the Somme. The existing light railway from Acheux and its spur of a field 60cm system was taken over from the French, in preparation for the dumping of vital materials. One line ran from Martinsart through Aveluy Wood to the north-east corner of Thiepval Wood and the other through the same wood to Authuille. Acheux became one of the principal railheads to be used by the Fourth Army for supplies, engineering stores and for the collection of walking wounded, as well as a station for Ambulance trains. The 29th Div. CCS as well as the 29th Divisional HQ was here at the beginning of the battle. South of the village was the site of No. 3 CCS close to the broad gauge railway at Varennes.

After their disastrous involvement on the first day of the battle, at Beaumont Hamel, the 1st Lancs. Fus. returned here on 4th July. It was also a rest camp for the Border Regiment, and for the 19th North'd Fus. who were in huts in Acheux Wood on 5th July. The 1st KOSB (87th Bde. 29th Div.) also returned to the village, on the 8th July. In the cemetery are the graves of men killed in July, August and September 1916. The Field Ambulance moved eastwards as the battle progressed and the cemetery was little used for the remainder of 1916. Towards the end of August the West Riding Regiment were also here and the 10th Essex were in the wood, described as a 'pleasant beech wood', seven miles west of Thiepval. However towards the end of the month the wood was described as 'having huts in a sea of mud connected by duckboard tracks together with abandoned railway platforms'. On 4th October the Hood Battalion (63rd RND) arrived on their way to Forceville before being involved with the 2nd Division in the Ancre Battle between 17th November and the 23rd.

In mid November Corporal Hellis of the 22nd Kensingtons 'picked his way through the sombre wood in which stood the leaky, moss-grown, canvas-roofed shelters, through which ran a track of slippery narrow duckboards over a perfectly ink like quagmire'. Until recent times the railway still existed between Doullens and Albert and the railway system was two kilometres to the south-west of the village, on the road to Léalvillers and the cemetery is between the village and the site of the former station, about 100 yards north of the main road. The railway line used to run close to Acheux Wood but there is little trace of it now nor little in the wood itself, of its past of 70 odd years ago.

Albert

This town of 1105 houses and a population of 8742 was known as 'Bert' to the Tommies and was the main town within the British sector of the Battle area. Although it was mainly used as a billeting and supply town it was by no means automatically safe, as stray shells were falling all the time, and there were many cases of newly settled troops being driven out by a sudden concentration of German shelling.

The town lies on the D 929 main road which leads straight in a north-easterly direction towards Bapaume. It is north-east of Amiens and is on the River Ancre. It has a railway service and is on the main Paris, Lille, Arras and Amiens line.

In September 1914 the town was held against the German advance by French forces, and in January 1915 a bomb exploded at the foot of the dome of the famous Basilique Notre Dame de Brebiéres whose 70 metre high tower was ornamented by a statue of the Virgin and the Infant Christ. The statue fell from its base and remained hanging at an angle of 45 degrees, and was secured by French Engineers. It was always said that its collapse would signal the end of the War. It became, along with the Angels of Mons one of the most famous symbols of the Great War. It finally fell in April 1918. The town passed into British hands in the summer of 1915.

There are very many references to Albert in Memoirs and Military Histories and I would like to just mention a few, and firstly and appropriately Henry Williamson's Novel called *The Golden Virgin*. His hero Phillip Maddison is an officer with the 8th Service Battalion of the 'Prince Regent's Own Regiment' and in the period around the 11th of June 1916 Williamson writes the following: 'The British Front line lay upon a plateau one hundred metres above sea level. It faced the German lines on the slope, rising imperceptibly it passed through the two fortified villages of Ovillers and la Boisselle, to the horizon of one hundred and forty metres. "Major Kingman's" HQ was in the support trenches six hundred yards behind the firing line at the cross-roads known as Ovillers Post'.

No. III Corps established a MDS at Albert which at the beginning of July also possessed a walking wounded post. A broad gauge rail line was established between Albert and Longeau with a 12″ Howitzer in a cutting to the north of Albert Station. When the Somme battle began the 19th Division was in reserve to the south-west of the town whilst the 34th Division was concentrating in the attacks towards la Boisselle. The Battle was a disastrous one for the Tyneside Division which attacked along the Albert–Bapaume Road and many Tynesiders' graves can be seen in Bapaume Post Military Cemetery which lies on the west side of Tara Hill and south-west of Usna Hill. La Boisselle fell to the 19th Division on 4th July.

In his book *Three Years with the 9th Division* W. D. Croft mentioned that his Brigade had arrived at Albert from Millencourt on 4th July and then went on to Bécourt Wood where they bivouacked. They later became involved in the fighting for the village of Contalmaision.

C. S. Collison wrote in his book *The 11th Royal Warwicks in France* that on 16th July their battalion was relieved by the 5th R. Fus. and that they returned to Albert, where they were billeted near the wrecked railway station. Here they rested on the 17th, but at midnight were ordered to the trench system called Heligoland in the former German line south-east of la Boisselle, as support to the 68th Bde., which was said to be about to attack Pozieres.

From 17th–19th July the 1/5 R. Warwicks were at the Red House in bivouac at Albert. Charles Carrington, author of *Soldier from the Wars Returning* and a member of that battalion was probably there at the time. On 19th July Croft's Brigade was relieved by an Australian Brigade and returned to Albert, arriving there at 4 am on 20th July. On 23rd July the 2nd KRRC marched back to Albert from Scotts Redoubt where they remained for two or three days. D. W. J. Cuddeford of the 12th Highland Infantry also mentions in his book *And All For What?* detraining at Albert as part of the Scottish Division. In August the back area around Albert presented a striking appearance; every hillside and hollow was marked by bivouacs and camps, bands played, bugles sounded, troops drilled, there were machine gun and rifle ranges, bombing pitches, and bayonet courses, the roads were black with the endless lines of horses, motor lorries, cars, troops, railways and metre tracks, carrying loads of ammunition and materials amongst which gangs of prisoners worked, unceasingly, on road repairs, while overhead an endless procession of aeroplanes buzzed to and fro.

In the period 13th/14th August the Northants Regiment were at Maxse's Redoubt just east of Albert. The 2nd KRRC moved to Black Wood nearby on 20th September from Lozenge Wood. Cuddeford wrote that at the end of September after the capture of Martinpuich his battalion had spent one night in Mametz Wood and then rejoined the Transport at Albert before marching to Franvillers. Brigade Reserve was then in Albert having been transferred from Lahoussoye. They were back in Albert again in mid October probably, after action at Prue Trench. In the history of the 2/5 Gloster Regiment A. F. Barnes wrote that the battalion, to which Ivor Gurney the poet belonged, had arrived at Albert on 20th November from Robecq where they had been since 27th October. They spent one night there and he described the weather as being very wet and reported the battlefields as being in a deplorable state. On the following day they met their guides who led them to the front line at Grandcourt at Tullocks Corner.

The town was taken by the Germans in their great advance of March 1918 but the British took it from them in August of the same year. Bapaume Post Military Cemetery is about a mile outside Albert on the main Bapaume Road. In June 1916 the British front line had crossed the road between the Cemetery and la Boisselle village and after the unsuccessful attack of the 1st July the Cemetery was begun almost at once. It was closed at the end of January 1917, and on 26th March 1918 fell into German hands. It was recovered during the Battle of Albert between the 21st and 23rd of August. After the Armistice further graves belonging to the 34th Div. and 38th (Welsh) Divisions were brought in. The latter graves were of victims of the 1918 fighting. During the 1916 Somme battle the site of the Cemetery was close to a Collecting Post which was at the bottom of Northumberland Avenue.

Albert Communal Cemetery is on the south-east side of the town, at the junction of the roads to Fricourt and Méaulte. An Extension was used by fighting units and Field Ambulances from August 1915 to November 1916, more particularly in and after November 1916, when Field Ambulances were concentrated here. The 2nd Field Company, Australian Engineers, and the 29th, 73rd and 102nd Canadian Infantry Battalions erected wooden memorials in the Extension to their dead. In the Autumn No. 5 CCS moved from Corbie to Albert but had to move to a site near the village of Bray, which was out of range of hostile fire. This site was used for two months. The Albert French National Cemetery is about half a mile out of the town, on the north side of the Fricourt Road, and the Memorial to the MGC is on the front of the Hotel de Ville building in the centre of the town.

Allonville

Allonville is a village to the north of the Amiens–Albert Road (D 929) and is to the north-west of Querrieu. During the course of the battle No. 35 CCS was brought here from St. Ouen and at the end of the battle a CCS was still in the village, and was used for cases of disease rather than battle wounds. Many of those who died were buried in the Communal Cemetery.

Amiens

Amiens was virtually the capital of the area behind the British and French lines and its famous Gothic Cathedral has several memorials in it to the various Allied countries involved in the battle, including one to Raymond Asquith the Prime Minister's son killed on 15th September 1916 when serving with the Guards. The Fourth Army HQ was just up the road at Querrieu and Liddell Hart described the area between Amiens and Rouen as having about three miles of railway sidings forming a huge distribution centre for the Fourth Army.

At the beginning of the battle the ASSI Dir. of Railway Transport was based at Amiens and the DMS of the Fourth Army was in direct contact with him regarding the number of trains needed for transporting casualties. These were initially too few because the DMS had failed to estimate the demand sufficiently. There was a resulting backlog of wounded and barges from here were used from the 2nd July to ease the situation. Amiens was a favourite town of the Royal Flying Corps who were able to visit its restaurants more frequently than the Army, although Siegfried Sassoon took some time off from the fighting and dined with some friends at the Godbert Restaurant on the 7th July and his companions included the prototype of Julian Durley who appears in Sassoon's *Memoirs of an Infantry Officer*. They were often joined by members of the Press Corps, who were staying at the Hotel du Rhin. C. E. Montagu the journalist who had enlisted in his forties and who, after a bomb mishap had been awarded a commission and had left for France on 10th July became an Intelligence Officer and was attached to GHQ and was quartered in Amiens with Lt. Col. A. N. Lee who was there to supervise the Press Corps. One of his main duties was to conduct distinguished visitors around the front. The visitors included J. M. Barrie, G. B. Shaw, H. G. Wells, John Masefield, Muirhead Bone and Frances Dodd. Bone was the first official war artist at the front and he met Montagu in August, possibly for the first time. Neville Lytton who had formerly been a colleague of Edmund Blunden's in the Sussex Regiment had become a liaison officer and was summoned to an interview with General Charteris at advanced HQ near Doullens. Lytton subsequently became a Major and was sent to Amiens to learn Press Censorship. The main idea presumably being not to allow information to appear in the Allied Press which would be of benefit to the German cause, and also one imagines to put the British Army in the best light. Philip Gibbs used to complain about restrictions but didn't go into great detail as to what form the censorship took.

In mid July the 33rd Div. was in the Amiens Area. During the battle patients at the 1/1 South Midland Station here had to be taken by ambulance car for entraining at Longeau to the south-east of Amiens and from Beauval and the Citadel to Gezaincourt. The 1/1 Midland CCS then moved to Vecquemont which was to the south-west of Corbie. At one time a Motor Ambulance Convoy was parked on the Amiens–Albert Road but was moved on to Lavieville. At the end of the Battle a Stationary Hospital in the town had been taken over by the New Zealanders. Casualties transported by canal were often taken to Abbeville.

On 8th September C. E. W. Bean the Australian Official Historian left Amiens for Calais, and arrived in the United Kingdom on the 10th September before returning to the Somme front, where he escorted amongst others, the Australian Prime Minister and Keith Murdoch, famous Australian journalist and father of the present newspaper tycoon Rupert Murdoch.

Henry Dundas is quoted in the book *Henry Dundas, Scots Guards* as being in a training area with the Scots Guards to the south-west of Amiens on 2nd October. On 19th October the 10th KRRC were north of Amiens at Cardouette. Graham Greenwell in *An Infant in Arms* wrote that he was in a wretched village full of Flying Corps personnel, and that motor lorries were never silent. He was hoping to get a lift into Amiens if he stayed in the area long enough. He describes the roads as being ankle-deep in mud. Just outside Amiens on the Albert Road is a large civilian cemetery with 676 British graves, dating from the 1915–18 fighting.

Ancre Valley

The River Ancre ran south-westwards from the direction of Bapaume through the German lines and then divided the Allied line between Hamel and Thiepval. It was very marshy and had several crossing points which the Germans were aware of. These included the famous Blackhorse Bridge, Authuille Bridge, Passerelle de Magenta, North and South Causeways and Hamel Bridge. Passerelle and Hamel Bridge were both subjected to severe machine gun fire in the period 30th June/1st July. On 1st July the 9th R. Irish Fus. and the 12th R. Irish Rif. were caught by machine gun fire from an emplacement on top of a shaft which the Germans had reached by tunnelling into the railway embankment on the edge of the river valley.

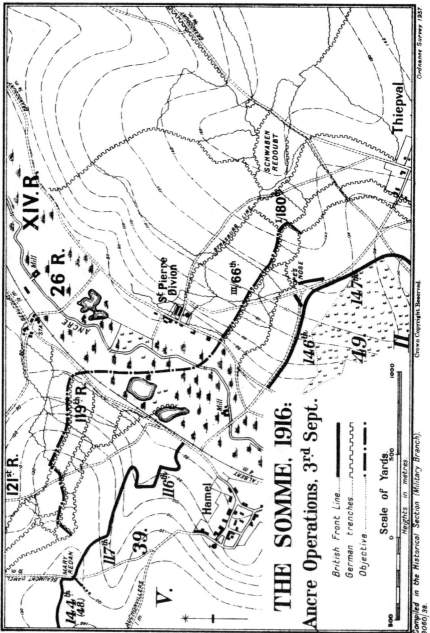

THE SOMME, 1916:
Ancre Operations, 3ʳᵈ Sept.

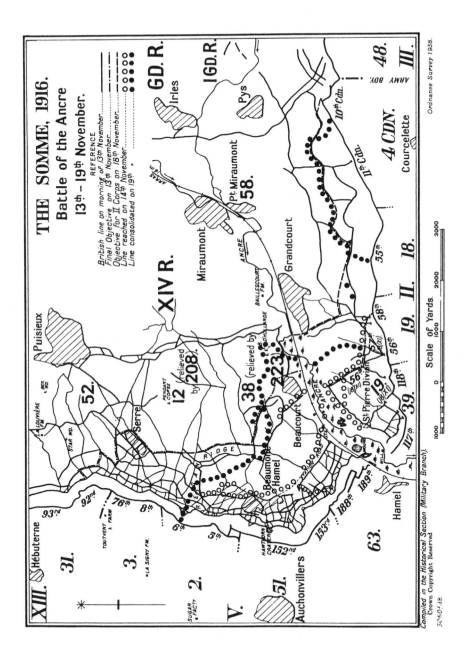

THE SOMME, 1916.
Battle of the Ancre
13th – 19th November.

REFERENCE

British line on morning of 13th November
Final Objective on 13th November
Objective for II Corps on 18th November
Line reached on 14th November
Line consolidated on 19th

Ordnance Survey 1938.

Compiled in the Historical Section (Military Branch).
Crown Copyright Reserved

Scale of Yards.

3060.18.

On 16th October the Hood Battalion who were part of the Royal Naval Division reached the Knightsbridge Sector and on the 18th October were relieved by the Howe Battalion. The company's right flank boundary was the road that wound along the flooded valley towards Beaucourt. On October 20th they were relieved by the Hawke Battalion and left for dry barns in the village of Engelbelmer.

Angle Wood

Angle Wood was in the centre of a three pronged ravine near Maltz Horn Farm and Falfemont Farm to the south-west of the village of Combles. In mid August the Germans held these positions in strength, and the plan was for the French to take the north end of the wood. Capt. O. Horsley of the 2nd Gordons (20th Bde. 7th Div.) was awarded the M.C. for an incident on 18th August when he led the first line of advance and consolidated his objective. Though wounded he directed from a shell hole until the position was safe. On 22nd August the 17th Lanc. Fus. took over from the French a section of the line which consisted of a chain of advance posts in front of Angle Wood and support reserve lines. In early September the 5th City of London battalion of the 56th Division were in reserve in this small valley living in shelters cut into the hillside or in trenches in Death Valley. In early to mid September, Farm Line was the HQ of the City of 1/2 Battalion. In the evening of 13th September the Queen's Westminsters were relieved by the London Rifle Brigade and moved back to Angle Wood Valley to re-organise.

In his memoir *Four Years on the Western Front* Aubrey Smith, a Rifleman, mentioned taking the water carts to Angle Wood over a mile beyond Death Valley. Up the Montauban road there was a large dressing station with several motor ambulances outside it. The far slope of Death Valley was very steep and muddy and at one moment it seemed as if they would come to a standstill. Smith took water there on alternate days. The Queen's Westminsters having been relieved by the Queen Victoria Rifles on the evening of 23rd September moved back to Falfemont Farm line and on the 24th went into Divisional Reserve in Casement Trench just north of Maricourt. Smith was involved in the attack of 25th September when the 168th Brigade stormed Bouleux Wood. They had to wait a couple of minutes while the fifteen inch railway gun at Maricourt prepared to fire.

Arrow Head Copse

Arrow Head Copse was east of Trônes Wood and south-west of Guillemont and had been taken by the Allies by mid July. It was between two roads coming out of Guillemont in a westerly direction, and is on the south side of the D 64 between Trônes Wood and the village.

On 20th July Lt. Col. Fraser–Tytler wrote in his book *Field Guns in France* that when his signals line broke down he went alone up the trench with the idea of reaching Arrow Head Copse, which was about four hundred yards ahead of his front line. When within twenty five yards he sensed it was unoccupied. At the far side of the copse he found himself almost behind the German trenches at Maltz Horn Farm and could see sixteen Germans asleep in the trench. He returned for reinforcements and they re-occupied the copse having given the Germans sixty rounds of rapid fire. In early August the Copse was used by the British as a strong point. During an advance on 8th August G. G. Coury attached to the 1/4 South Lancashire Regiment part of 164th Brigade was in command of two platoons, which were ordered to dig a communication trench from the old firing line to the position won. By his fine example and utter contempt of danger he kept up the spirits of his men and completed his task under intense fire. Later, after his battalion had suffered several casualties and the commanding officer had been wounded, he went out in front of the advanced position in broad daylight, and in full view of the enemy found his CO and brought him back to the new advanced trench over ground swept by machine gun fire; he not only carried out his original task, and saved his CO, but also assisted in rallying the attacking troops when they were shaken and in leading them forward. He was later awarded the VC. On 18th August F. C. Hitchcock in his book *'Stand To'* reported on Arrow Head Copse on his left flank as ceasing to exist, and Gilbert Frankau in his novel *Peter Jackson* said that his battery had been in continuous action for eighteen days and that some of the battery had been lost beyond Arrow Head Copse.

On 28th August one of W. H. Livens' unconventional weapons, a large projector was taken into the Copse and fired on September 3rd. Four others were fired in High Wood. In early September the Copse was used as a forward dump probably by the Irish and the Guards Division.

The 11th KRRC on the 26th September went to former trenches by Arrow Head Copse being in Div. reserve leaving next day for Carnoy.

Auchonvillers

Auchonvillers lies half way between Mailly Maillet and Beaumont Hamel with Hawthorn Ridge between it and Beaumont Hamel on the D 73 road, six miles north of Albert and ten miles west of Bapaume. In the summer of 1915 this part of the Ancre front was held by French troops some of whom are buried in the Communal Cemetery. An ADS or CP was established here. The village, which at the beginning of the battle was in the 29th Division sector, was a departure point for British troops, and during the battle was to be totally destroyed. During the early hours of 1st July the 16th Middlesex as part of the 29th Division's 86th Bde moved up from the Auchonvillers-Beaumont Hamel Road, their left rested on this road opposite the famous sunken road. The German guns wrought terrible havoc and the sunken road along with the ground opposite the Hawthorn Ridge became a death trap.

In November four months later 180 bodies were found, victims of northerly fire on 1st July. Many of them were buried in Hawthorn Cemetery

No. One south of the main road here on the north slope of the ridge, and near the 1st July front line. It was made by V Corps who cleared the Ancre battlefields in the spring of 1917. The cemetery includes many unidentified soldiers from the 29th Division, mainly soldiers who fell on 1st July or on 13th November. In the *Fighting Newfoundlanders* it is mentioned that the Newfoundland Battalions had been reinforced by the arrival of 127 other ranks and on 14th July they returned to trenches in the front line at a point over 450 yards east of Auchonvillers. The Battalion had numbered only a few officers and 260 rifles after its near annihilation on 1st July in the present day site of Newfoundland Park.

Hugh Bayley in his book *Triple Challenge* described his experiences in this sector during his time as an MO with the 1st Scots Gds. On 9th August the Guards went into the line here and he mentions being at the White City which was directly behind the sunken road. They alternated in the line with the 3rd Gren. Gds. Bayley also mentions that many of his colleagues were Old Etonians, which he was not; eventually they left for Bertrancourt.

In *Undertones of War* Edmund Blunden wrote that in early September his battalion, the 11th R. Sussex were reorganising the trenches in the Auchonvillers sector in front of Beaumont Hamel. Crossing the light railway, they had reached Auchonvillers. As Field Work's Officer he enjoyed his work which took him up and down from the dreary and mutilated front line where 'the little young poplars stood lightly at the extremity of Auchonvillers' orchards'. The long communication trenches had to be repaired daily, as it was a minewerfer sector, the front line being stubbonly pounded by them.

On 17th October the 51st Division took over the line from the RND spending their time mainly in preparation for the forthcoming Ancre Battle destined to be postponed many times. David Rorie, on the Medical Staff of this Division, wrote that one of the jobs that they carried out was to make an extra entrance to a Relay Bearer Post at Tenderloin, and make an entirely new one in Second Avenue and another at Uxbridge Road. They also had to pitprop a false roof at a CP at Auchonvillers in the stable of a farmyard there, and to prop, sandbag and fit stretcher racks into the cellars of the brasserie at Mailly as an ADS. During the battle a steady stream of motor transport slowly wound its way from Tenderloin along the much battered Auchonvillers–Beaumont Hamel Road.

Rorie also wrote in November that besides Auchonvillers ran a chemin creux in which were several dugouts where the Medical staff and the Division on their left had Battalion RAPs. An ADS or CP was in the village during November. On the 16th November Tenderloin in the White City became HQ for forward evacuation. On 17th November J. A. Whitehead who was with the 168th Bde. RFA. reported that they had moved to a position in front of Auchonvillers, the guns had been in Martinsart and the Wagon lines in Senlis.

The Military Cemetery is about 300 yards from the Church, at the end of a path leading north from the road to Mailly Maillet, it was used by Field Ambulances and fighting units. The graves are mainly from the 1916 and

1918 fighting. Further north is Serre, where there are very large French and British cemeteries, and where there were a great deal of Allied casualties. Auchonvillers Communal Cemetery is south of the village, and the gravestones are made from red sandstone, as in the Martinsart Cemetery.

Authuille

The village is on the D 151 road and is on the eastern bank of the River Ancre. The wood is on the south-east side of the village and Thiepval is to the north-west. In July 1916 the Allied line ran down roughly in a north south direction to the east of the village before turning in a more easterly direction that took it in the front of the wood. The village was just behind the British trenches in the 32nd Division sector. Blighty or Nab Valley ran from the wood in a north-easterly direction and was also the border line between X Corps and 111 Corps. The 32nd Division was assembled on the lower slopes of the Thiepval Spur from Authuille Wood to Thiepval Wood. At the beginning of the bombardment before the battle began the guns were standing wheel to wheel in the wood. An ADS was established here at the beginning of July. The three regiments that were initially involved in the attack towards the Leipzig Salient were the 1st Dorsets, the 11th Border (Lonsdales) and the 18th Lancs. Fusiliers.

We have been left a very clear description of the part that the Dorsets played, as their role is vividly described by Charles Douie in his book *The Weary Road*. He said that on emerging from either of two trenches including Hamilton Avenue they had the alternative of going along the main road to Authuille North Barricade or of following a safer track under the bank and on the edge of the stream to a ruined mill on the lower edge of the village. Here was a bridge just wide enough to take a trolley. Beyond the ruins of the village, was another high bank, honeycombed by dugouts and a long cause-way across the marshes known as Blackhorse Bridge. From here the way to the south lay along the bank of the river towards Aveluy. Passing this way he found a green meadow leading down to the Ancre. Across the river was a small chateau. Crucifix Corner lay ahead girdled by tall trees, before he turned aside to enter Authuille Wood. It was thronged with fatigue parties busily engaged on completing bridges, gun positions, and ammunition dumps. On the western edge he came upon the Allied front line.

Concealed gun emplacements held guns which were destined to fire over open sites at Leipzig Redoubt when the time came. He came to a bridge over a defile which the plan of attack required them to cross, and from a convenient machine gun emplacement one could survey Leipzig Redoubt and the long valley up which the advance was planned to sweep. At its far end he could see Mouquet Farm. The dugouts sheltering under the high bank of the Ancre at Blackhorse Bridge were the HQ of the battalion resting as Brigade Reserve in the sector Thiepval to Authuille Wood. Douie had many memories of days and nights spent under this high bank.

All this was before the battle and I have included it because it does tell us something about the geography of the sector and its situation before the battle actually began.

For the actual attack I have again leant on Douie for his account and also the Dorset Regimental history. On 29th June his Battalion was in camp at Senlis and moved off to Blackhorse Bridge at 8.30 p.m. on 30th June, and arrived at dugouts at 12.50 a.m. on 1st July. They moved slowly through the wooded valley, lined on each side by little streets of faintly illuminated canvas huts and passed through ghostly and barren country into Aveluy Wood and so to Blackhorse Bridge. They breakfasted at 6.30 a.m., a meal that was to be the last for so many of them. They then gathered under the high bank of the Ancre at Blackhorse Bridge. Under the bank they paraded at 7.10 a.m. and began to leave the Blackhorse Shelters, by platoons, at one hundred and fifty yard intervals; they went south-eastward heading through Authuille Wood, along Dumbarton Track. The 97th Brigade was to attack on the left with the 17th and 16th Highland Light Infantry. The 2nd KOYLI were to move in support and the 11th Borders were in reserve. The last named had Mouquet Farm as its special objective.

On the left the 17th HLI passed over the enemy's front trenches and were soon engaged in heavy fighting is the maze of trenches forming the Leipzig Redoubt, the right of the 16th HLI also gained the front line.

Meanwhile 7.30 a.m. having been planned as zero hour the Dorsets waited about for a quarter of an hour in Authuille Wood, when they received word that the 11th Borders were advancing. The Dorsets closely followed by the 19th Lancs. Fusiliers commenced to move. But the moment the leading platoon left the shelter of the wood it came under concentrated machine gun fire from the right. The distance from Dumbarton Trench at the edge of the wood to the front line was 100 yards but the track was a marked exit point from the wood. The inevitable massacre occurred and they became involved with the 11th Borders in front and the Lancs. Fusiliers behind. Indeed they were killed by machine guns in the wood before the advance even began. The same bridge over a defile which the plan of attack had required them to cross was heaped with dead and wounded as to be almost impassable. On reaching the exit of the wood they paused while a search was made for another way out. None was found; the wood was heavily wired. There was no alternative to a dash from the front line, and section by section the battalion crossed the bullet swept area. The fire came from a strong point on the south side of the valley which flanked Thiepval Ridge. It had also caught the Borders. Half the casualties of the day occurred when passing over this narrow stretch of open country to the front line. On reaching the front line trench, the remains of the Border Regiment were about 150 other ranks with no officers. In the British front line elements of the Dorsets were mixed up with the Borders. During the night it was reported that the 15th HLI would relieve the Dorsets, who by 2 a.m. on 2nd July were well clear of the front trench. They did not go far, only to the dugouts and trenches that formed the northern defences of Authuille.

The Lancashire Fusiliers had arrived at the edge of the wood and became held up by the congested trenches but they stood fast. At 1 a.m. on 2nd July they returned to dugouts at Authuille.

Vainly the 15th HLI sought to improve the position held in Leipzig Redoubt. The Dorsets were ordered up to the old British front line, between Tindrum Street and Chequerbent Street, during the night 2nd/3rd July and every man who could be spared was employed in carrying bombs and ammunition to the Highlanders.

On completion of relief the Battalion marched back to Senlis. The 11th Borders at 10 p.m. on 30th June moved from dugouts at Crucifix Corner north-east of Aveluy to assembly trenches which had been dug for them in the thickest part of Authuille Wood. The Battalion who were made up of men from the hills and dales of Cumberland and Westmoreland were under the patronage of the Earl of Lonsdale. They were to move northwards out of the wood and then swing due east. On leaving their trenches in the wood before even arriving at the British front line trench, the battalion came under terrific machine gun fire. They were to the left of the Dorsets and were due to emerge from the front trench on a strip almost opposite Leipzig Redoubt. On leaving their trenches they were gunned down. They suffered nearly 500 casualties out of 800 men including twenty five officers and 490 NCOs and other ranks. Very few got as far as the HLI had. Their CO Lt. Col. P. W. Machell was one of those killed.

The idea of the Earl of Lonsdale in forming this special battalion was that if given the opportunity men would join up with their friends rather than be placed just anywhere in the ranks of the British Army. They were drawn from amongst others, labourers, farm servants, shepherds, keepers, miners, industrial workers, clerks and small shopkeepers. They had carried out much of their basic training at a local racecourse at home. The casualties affected one small area of England which subsequently took several generations to recover.

The third battalion of the front line section was the 19th Lancs. Fus. (3rd Salford Battalion). On 30th June they had moved forward to dugouts at Blackhorse Bridge, which they reached at about 2.0 a.m. on 1st July. The 97th Brigade had its HQ in Authuille Wood and it was the right assaulting brigade of the 32nd Division. The Brigade's task was to capture the front line system at Leipzig Redoubt. After the 11th Borders were to pass through at 8.30 a.m. and supposedly on to the German trenches, the 14th Brigade including the Lancs. Fus., was to pass through and capture the German Intermediate Line. The left of the Brigade included the 19th Lancs. Fus. and the 1st Dorsets. At 7.10 a.m. they had moved off behind the Dorsets and marched south along the bank of the Ancre for a thousand yards, then turning eastwards into Authuille Wood, and moving slowly along one of the tracks leading through it. After the Borders and the Dorsets had been hit by the same fire from a German strong point, the Fusiliers were held up by the congested trenches and stood fast.

In the book *Artillery and Trench Mortar Memories 32nd Division* a contributor has the following to say 'the whole of the gun teams then went through the track in Blighty Wood to the main ammunition dump. Will any of us ever forget the journey that morning? Just to the right front of Rock Street gun pit the REs had cut a gap in the hedge on the edge of the wood, and through this gap marched our Infanteers – the 11th Borders and the 1st Dorsets – to be mown down like corn by Jerry's machine guns as fast as they marched through.' 'The wood was being heavily shelled, and clambering on to the Artillery Bridge we found a slaughter-house.' On the morning of 1st July the writer emerged from the gun pit at Rock Street. The OC had just come down the ravine and under Artillery Bridge over Rock Street. The bridge was littered with dead and wounded. Through the gap in the hedge could be seen men falling all over the field. The gap had turned brown and had formed a target for the German machine guns. The writer trekked to the dump in the wood. All down the track lay the dead and dying for the Germans had found that track with their 5.9s. He was never to forget that terrible scene of suffering and wounded that no one had time to attend to. These poor devils had crept together to die. Their eyes had a look that could not be described which the writer knew that he would never forget. The 2nd Manchesters were passing this group under the command of 'Corky' so named on account of his cork leg. The Manchesters went round Rock Street and attained their objective and by not going through the gap, had escaped the fire from the Nord Werk.

South-east of the attack on Leipzig Redoubt on the north-east side of the wood a similar tragedy had befallen the 70th Brigade of the 8th Division who were facing towards la Boisselle. The 8th Y & L and the 8th KOYLI were attacking with the 9th Y & L and the 11th Sherwood For. in support.

The 8th KOYLI and the 8th Y & L were in front of the wood on 29/30th June and after the disastrous 1st July attack were withdrawn to Long Valley along with the remnants of the 9th Y & L. The 11th Sherwood For. had come from Bouzincourt on 27th June and had gone up to their assembly trenches in Glasgow Street. After the two attacking battalions went forward two waves of Foresters went forward and were mown down. Their CO Lt. Col. Watson was wounded in the chest when trying to rally his men. A third and futile attempt was carried out by means of a sunken road, but to no avail. They had reached the German Second Line but were completely held up by the Third. When they were relieved they went by train and marched to Bruay via Dernancourt.

Blighty Valley was the name given by the Army to the lower part of the deep valley running south-westwards through Authuille Wood to join the river between Authuille and Aveluy. After 1st July a railway was carried along it. The upper part was called Nab Valley. The Cemetery is almost at the mouth of the valley a little way up its northern bank. It is partly in the communes of both Aveluy and Authuille. The Cemetery was begun early in July 1916 and used until the following November by the troops taking part on that front.

In an unpublished ms. at the Imperial War Museum W. R. Price wrote that 240th Bde. came from Hébuterne on 20th July and set up their new position

in Authuille Wood. On 21st July and 22nd the 6th Gloster and the Anzacs attacked through them encountering liquid fire. The Glosters reached and surmounted the Leipzig Salient. The Battery then concentrated in shelling Pozieres Ridge. On 11th August the E. Yorks. were billeted in Authuille Village. In mid August the 7th Somersets HQ was in the rectory in the village. On 26th September at Wood Post which was a main communication trench General Higginson wished the 10th Essex Regiment good luck. The accompanying tanks made the troops roar with laughter! On the 25th September the 17th KRRC went to Brigade Reserve. On the 25th September the 8th Norfolk proceeded to Wood Post in Authuille Wood in fighting order in preparation for the attack against Thiepval due to take place the next day. They were in Brigade support and the attack went well. On the 27th they were in support to the 7th Queen's and on the 29th were withdrawn to Forceville except for 'B' Company who were left at Crucifix Corner for burial duties.

On the 2nd October the 8th Norfolks replaced the 7th Queen's at North Bluff to the north of Authuille. Here there were dugouts as there were at South Bluff.

The 17th KRRC were moved to North Bluffs on the 10th October. On the 16th October the RND relieved the 11th R. Sussex the battalion that Edmund Blunden was part of and they immediately went into Authuille Wood in order to prepare for their attack against Stuff Trench. A Motor Ambulance Convoy operated from the village. On the 13th November one of the KRRC battalions after tours of duty at South Bluff was part of Divisional Reserve for an attack on the Hansa Line and the village of St. Pierre Divion.

In *Undertones of War* Blunden wrote that in November his battalion, the 11th R. Sussex came away for a couple of nights and billeted in Authuille built against the high bank called The Bluff, and there passed some pleasant hours. They were not being shelled. In another section he describes this period in the following way: 'we rested in cabinlike dugouts called Authuille Bluffs, on the steep rise from the Ancre inundations'.

Lonsdale Cemetery Number One: The present Lonsdale Cemetery originally contained 96 graves, the majority of whom were officers and men of the 1st Dorsets, 11th Borders and HLI.

Quarry Post Cemetery was on the south-east side of the wood and was formerly 70th Bde. Aid Post. It was used from July 1916 to February 1917 chiefly by units of the 12th (Eastern) Div.

Authuille Military Cemetery was used by Field Ambulances and fighting units from August to December 1916. It stands on a steep slope falling from east to west. It is on the south side of the village between Albert Road and the Ancre.

After the War Blunden wrote a novel with Sylvia Norman called *We'll Shift Our Ground*. He describes the village of Authuille in the book as being rambling and that once more the river had been recalled to its proper channels. He had revisited the area and had passed The Bluffs, apprehensive still that once over the rise he would be treading on dead bodies on dead land.

Aveluy

Aveluy Wood, being more than 1,500 metres in width, is much larger than Authuille Wood and is on the west side of the Ancre River. It is north-west of Aveluy and is on the D 50 road that runs north from Albert to Hamel. The village lies between the Ancre and the Albert—Arras railway. It was devastated in 1916 and served as a departure point for a new set of British trenches. The wood was one of the centres for the British Artillery.

In the book *Artillery and Trench Mortar Memories 32nd Division* Sgt. Prince wrote that in April when in Aveluy that the following names all had their own little history: The Strawberry Bed, The Rose Garden, The Rat Hole, Jacob's Well, Crucifix Corner, Honeysuckle Cottage and The Chalk Pit. At the end of June he refers to the 'Flying Pig' as being at Rock Street gun position and to a heavy gun team at Rock Street in Oban Avenue.

The wood at the beginning of the battle was shared by the 36th Division to the north and the 32nd Division to the south. The HQ of the 36th Div. was actually in the wood. Later on the 6th Division had its HQ here. Aveluy formed one of the three solid routes through the Ancre Valley, which had been flooded following the destruction of the river embankments. Lancashire Dump on the verge of the wood is now the site of Aveluy Wood Cemetery. The village was originally in the French sector and the British took it over from July 1915 onwards until March 1918.

On 27th June, 1916 the 19th Lancashire Fusiliers were at Shelter Trenches at the edge of the wood, prior to their attack on the Leipzig Redoubt on 1st July. This action is referred to in the section on Authuille.

On 30th June the 6th West Yorks. went to assembly trenches in Aveluy Wood at about midnight. During the march there they had followed lights which were laid out in 500 yard intervals. On 1st July they moved out of the wood across the river at Passerella de Magenta to their trenches in Thiepval Wood. On the same date the assembly positions of the 107th Bde. (less the 15th Rifles) were in slit trenches in Aveluy Wood. The battalions marched up by cross-country tracks, marked by red lanterns, the other by green. The night was a fine one.

From the book on the 32nd Div. Artillery Sgt. Price mentions that at Oban Avenue the gun began firing at about 7.30 p.m. on the night of 30th June, one round every fifteen minutes until 6.0 a.m. on 1st July when gunfire was ordered and the strafe began in real earnest. At 7.0 a.m. the gun ceased firing. At Rock Street 'nothing untoward' had happened and the French gun behaved remarkably well. They cooked their food in a ravine. In the 25th Div. at the end of June and on the 1st July the 7th Bde. moved into Xth Corps and proceeded to Aveluy Wood, and was held in Corps Reserve, the 75th Bde. moved to Martinsart.

There is a very detailed description of the fighting on the front by the 36th (Ulster) Division in Crozier's book *A Brass Hat in No Man's Land*. His Bde. was assembled in the wood on the evening of 30th June and he, 9th R. Irish Rif. and Col. Bernard 10th R. Irish Rif. were dubious about the possible

success of the assault on Thiepval Village by the 32nd Division on their right. 'If they fail?' 'Where are we on the flank?' They decided that on marching through Thiepval Wood if the village remained in German hands that they should meet in no man's land to alter their plans. If only one of them survived then it would be up to him to carry on for both battalions. If neither of them was to get as far, then the senior officers remaining would carry on. After a whistle had blown the men fell in in fours, in their companies on the Hamel–Albert road. At 7.30 a.m. they passed through Gordon Castle, in the centre of Thiepval Wood and picked up coils of wire and iron posts. Crozier glanced to the right and through a gap in the trees saw the 10th Rifles plodding on, it was the 32nd Division at its best. He later saw rows and rows of British soldiers lying dead, dying or wounded in no man's land, enough to convince him that Thiepval Village was still held by the Germans. It was then 8.0 a.m. and by 7.45 a.m. the village should have fallen to allow the 36th Div's. passage forward on its flank.

Also on 1st July the 15th HLI paraded at 6.40 a.m. on the Aveluy–Authuille road, which was packed with traffic, guns, limbers, carrying parties, troops and ambulance wagons. The day before they had sheltered at Brookers Pass which was between Crucifix Corner and Aveluy Wood.

In his book *With a Machine Gun to Cambrai* George Coppard mentions that on the afternoon of 1st July he was number two in a machine gun team and climbing Coniston Steps which were cut into a steep bank, he entered Aveluy Wood. It was being shelled heavily by lachrymatory shells or tear shells which drenched the wood. He said that the issued gas masks were of no use and that men staggered about like blind men. A winding track led through the wood, and many wounded and dying men lay on either side of it. When at nightfall they were at last clear of the wood they mounted a Vickers gun near la Boisselle. On 2nd July hundreds of dead, many from the 37th Bde. were strung out like wreckage washed up to a high water mark. Quite as many dead on the enemy wire as on the ground. The wire was so dense that daylight could be barely seen through it.

In early July the 104th Bde. bivouacked in the wood and in the period 4/5th July the 75th Bde. withdrew here. In mid July companies of Gloster Regiment were in reserve in quarries just north of the village. This would have been near Crucifix Corner. Bernard Montgomery who was to command the British Eighth Army in the Second War was at this time on the staff of 104th Bde. and on 12th July wrote home from Bouzincourt saying that his Brigade had marched to Aveluy about a mile west of la Boisselle, then on to Ovillers. Montgomery was not at all reticent about the use of place names in his correspondence home!

In W. R. Price's manuscript *Gunner on the Somme* it is stated that 240 Battery was at Crucifix Corner and had taken over from a unit of the 12th Division, on a steep chalk bank at a junction of the Arras–Bapaume roads near Aveluy. They were there, until relieved on 28th August by the 25th Division Artillery. In early September the 7th S. Staffs., probably on the 4th

September went via the ruined village of Aveluy and across the much shelled bridge over the swollen River Ancre, past Crucifix Corner, and up the hill past the guns to Ovillers Post. On their right as they went forward there were several rows of guns of all calibres lined up in Nab Valley. On 9th September the 6th E. Yorks. were based at the chateau at Aveluy. On 26th September the cross roads at the west end of the village were very 'unhealthy', this was the period when Thiepval fell finally to the British. In early October companies of the Cambridge Battalion were in tents in the wood and Blunden in talking about the wood in *Undertones of War* describes it as having moss which is rimy and that its red leaves made a carpet 'not a thread less fine than those in kings' houses'. He saw a sign-post pointing between the trees Ride to Black Horse Bridge, and others, both French and English. But they turned along a road unmolested which led to a chasm of light between the trees, and then saw on the left a downland cliff or quarry on the right and a valley in trees. But then they had to leave the road and file along the railway track, which despite all the incurable entanglements of its telegraph wires, 'might yet be doing its duty'. Below 'among mighty trees of golden leaf' there was a track across the lagooned Ancre. A trolley line crossed it as well, but disjointedly. Then they passed the last muddy pool and derailed truck and came into a maze of trenches which was formerly the old British system and which looked up towards lofty Thiepval. Thiepval Wood was 200 yards away scowling, but at that moment dumb; disjointed, burnt, unchartable. They were looking for Gordon House a Company HQ and they crawled along the wood edge and entered the earthy cave with its bunk beds and squatting figures.

During the action of Stuff Redoubt on 21st October the battalion was again holding the line at Thiepval Wood and stayed thereabouts being shelled and carrying out digging and carrying duties. On or around 22nd October at midnight after they had taken or seized Stuff Trench the 'portents of Aveluy Wood' seemed to Blunden remarkably comfortable. The 11th R. Sussex were again holding the line on 25th October at Thiepval Wood. A rail line ran through Aveluy Wood from the direction of Martinsart.

In fact Blunden mentions that they were still working in the Aveluy Region around 7th November when there was a severe winter storm. It seems that the enemy missed a golden opportunity in not shelling Lancashire Dump on the Albert–Hamel Road in Aveluy Wood. In November there was an ADS or CP close to the wood. Marlborough Huts was the name of dugouts at Crucifix Corner close to Aveluy and they were used by amongst other units the 8th N. Staffs. around 9th November.

Aveluy was captured by the Germans on 26th March 1918 who were in turn driven out on 6th April but minor fighting occurred in June and a raid was carried out by the Germans on 20th July. The Germans were finally cleared out of the wood area on 25th July 1918.

The Communal Cemetery is in Aveluy village and the Extension is on the south side of it, the French had begun the Extension and it was continued by British units and Field Ambulances from August 1915 until March 1917. It slopes down to the north, away from the village, and a long stretch of the

Ancre Valley can be seen from it.

After the War in *Goodbye to the Battlefields* H. A. Taylor wrote that one looked in vain for some remnant of the old sawmills by the railway at Aveluy, where during 'rest periods' tired battalions whiled away the time making duck boards for the trenches while shells screamed their way over the valley in an effort to find one or other of the many dumps about the railway.

Blunden revisited the area after the War several times and commented on one occasion that 'he never knew that Aveluy Wood was purple before – wild flowers were encouraged by great wars'.

In *The Wet Flanders Plain* Henry Williamson wrote that during a visit after the war 'the rain drove across the undulating Somme country, and the Ulster Memorial Tower at Thiepval, on my left beyond the marsh was sometimes washed out by a grey mist. I walked on with head bowed to the remembered rain' – 'now the wood is green, and the new growth was twelve feet high' – 'The verdant waves rear against the black stumps of the trees which knew the lost generation that toiled along the road. The trees were sapless and stark; only crows perch on them; the graves of the lost generation near. In this pilgrimage there were loving thoughts for all things which suffered grieviously.'

The British trenches can still be easily traced in the wood today (1985) as well as many shell holes.

Bailiff Wood

The wood is north-west of Peake Woods, south-west from Contalmaison Wood and due west of the village of Contalmaison.

Before July there were two stretches of rail line there, one which ran south towards Peake Woods and the other which crossed from Contalmaison itself. They were both probably used by the Germans for bringing up ammunition and supplies.

Around 7th July the 12th DLI (68th Bde. 23rd Div.) had to attack the German line which ran eastwards from the cross roads west of the wood to the outskirts of Contalmaison. Peake Woods was reached by a platoon. The trench along the Contalmaison road was occupied as far as the remains of the German light railway and a block was made beyond. The eastern edge of Bailiff Wood was reached.

In brief the *Official History* says that on 9th July that the 10th DWR who at the time were attached to the 24th Bde. sent forward bombing parties which established a post south of Contalmaison from which machine gun fire could sweep nearly the whole area. Patrols of the 12th DLI entered Bailiff Wood which was then a newly planted spinney of saplings only a few feet high, but could not remain there because of British Artillery fire. the British plan was to seize the wood by an advance of two companies from the west. Behind the wood were found four damaged field guns with 300 rounds of ammunition.

On 10th July the 11th W. Yorks. were due to attack the wood; they

progressed and wheeled round northwards from the eastern exit of the wood to capture a trench running east and west.

In the 1920s children used to play on the remains of the light railway which in turn had been improved by the British. Beyond the wood towards the chalk pit at Pozieres is a British dugout which at the time of writing (1983) is in superb condition. Close to the wood is a memorial to Capt. F. Dodgson (8th Green Howards) who was killed on 10th July 1916 and whose body is now in Serre Road No. 2 Cemetery.

Bailleulmont

Bailleulmont is north-west of Humbercamps and was a village used for training in and resting.

In early July the 6th Sherwood For. (139 Bde. 46th Div.) was in the area. Four Forester Battalions came to rest in the village every 18 days, and each battalion in turn spent six days in the line, six days in support at Bellacourt and so on. Battalion HQ was alternatively in the Chateau or at a farm house by the church at Grosville. The village was on the reverse slope of a crest, and close to the Arras–Doullens Road. There are several graves of men in the Village Communal Cemetery of men who were court-martialled and executed. They include members of the Manchester Regiment and the Irish Guards.

Baizieux

This village is north of Corbie, south of Warloy–Baillon and west of Hénencourt. The chateau is to the north-east of the village.

On 30th June the 12th Div. HQ moved here, and the infantry, marching after dark, reached Hénencourt and Millencourt by 10.0 a.m. on 1st July. The 7th R. Sussex and the 8th R. Fus. bivouacked here on 1st July. A Divisional Rest Station was established here.

On 20th July the 11th Sherwood For. bivouacked here with the rest of 20th Bde. In mid August as well as being in tents, they had shelters, mainly of brushwood and had dug holes into the sides of the banks. The village had been 'much used'. At the end of August there had been a lot of rain and dry billets in the village were used by the 8th DLI.

The 2nd KRRC were here on or about 13th September where they trained until the 19th when they bivouacked in Lozenge Wood.

On 19th September the 15th Div. HQ was at the chateau. On 4th October the 149th Bde. came back here from Eaucourt. In the wood in early November was a tented camp when the 10th Cameronians were inspected by Haig. Battalions used the wood for bivouacs; it was about three quarters of a mile west of the village.

Bapaume

The town is twelve miles north-east of Albert on the D 929. As early as August 1914 it was in the battle line and after the German push westwards remained in their hands until March 1917 when it was occupied by the

Australian 2nd Division. All the old buildings had by then been destroyed but a barn remained on the very outskirts of the town. Opposite is a water tower which is on the site of one which fell in the 1917 battle and was later used as a warm and dry billet for troops. The Germans made use of underground bastions during their time there and had left many buildings booby trapped or mined. They came back during the March Offensive of 1918 and were driven out again on 29th August by the New Zealand Division.

Captain Lord Lucas whilst flying with 22 Sq. was shot through the neck and as a result crashed at Mory Abbey north-west of the town and was buried at HAC Cemetery Ecoust.

Basin Wood

Basin Wood which was south-west of Matthew Copse which in turn was west of Serre, was adjacent to the communication trench named Sackville Street. It was also east of La Signy Farm. In mid-May the E. Yorks. established themselves in a dell here which was sheltered by a few tree stumps. The wood was established as a Casualty Clearing Station and on the eve of the battle the 12th KOYLI had dug a large communal grave close to it. From 1st July to 3rd, the CCS was very busy and stretcher cases were taken from there to Euston Dump, the ambulance collecting point.

Bavincourt

Bavincourt is to the north-west of Humbercamps on the north side of the Doullens–Arras Road. After being involved in the Gommecourt battle the 5th Lincolns (138 Bde. 46th Div.) marched back by platoons to rest billets immediately to the north of here. They rested on the 12th July and the next day moved on to Saulty to the south-west where they were inspected by a new Divisional Commander.

Bayencourt

The village is to the west of Hébuterne, north-west of Sailly-au-Bois and east of Coigneux.

Aubrey Smith in his book wrote that on 28th May his London Rifle Brigade Battalion (169th Bde. 56th Div.) was relieved after a week in the trenches. Bayencourt was beset by Artillery on all sides and it was decided to move the horse lines. Smith drove his limber to a sheltered valley near Coigneux about a mile away. Dolden is his book *Cannon Fodder* wrote that the London Scottish (168th Bde. 56th Div.) of which he was a member, left Souastre for Hébuterne on 2nd June. Dolden a battalion cook, followed on later with the cookers after having picked up the company rations at Bayencourt.

From Aubrey Smith we learnt that his Bde. required them to furnish a G.S. Wagon at an unknown dump at Bayencourt, to collect pit props and take them to Hébuterne with other vehicles from the Bde. at night.

The Queen's Westminsters (169th Bde. 56th Div.) moved on 3rd June to the village and its transport went to Coigneux. Two days later the Battalion was once again in the front line after being in Hébuterne. On 16th June the whole battalion was relieved by the London Rifle Bde. and moved back to Bayencourt. On 27th June Dolden moved up with the cookers from Pas in advance of the 1st L.S. to Bayencourt. The place was 'bristling with guns'.

At the end of June Aubrey Smith also mentioned the guns as well as those at Bienvillers, St. Amand and Souastre as all firing their hardest. In Bayencourt a battery of 9.2 Howitzers was firing every five minutes at Gommecourt Wood. The road to Sailly was 'screened' towards the end of June. 168th Bde. Dump was here.

Frank Hawkins in his book *From Ypres to Cambrai* mentions, as an infantry man with the Queen Victoria Rifles (169th Bde. 56th Div.) marching on 30th June via Souastre and Bayencourt before reaching Hébuterne at 8.0 p.m. They had left their packs at Souastre.

Bazentin le Petit and Bazentin le Grand

Bazentin le Petit is the larger of the two villages and is north-east of Mametz Wood and adjacent to the D 20 road that runs between Longueval and Contalmaison. The wood and village are north of the road and a little further to the south-east across the road is the village of Bazentin le Grand, with in turn, its wood. In 1916 the two villages with their woods were part of the German second line which at this point guarded High Wood which was not to fall to the British for two months. In Bazentin le Petit was a cemetery which was to feature strongly in the fighting and due east of it was a windmill which became equally famous. Two communication trenches beyond the northern edge of the wood were called New Trench and Ait Alley. A walking wounded collecting post was here during the battle.

In Raleigh/Jones *The War in the Air* it is noted that on 2nd July when the mist cleared north of le Petit that a new trench was observed which the Germans had thrown up several hundred yards in advance of the Switch Line, roughly parallel to the British forward positions between le Petit and High Wood. The intermediate line, which was connected with the Switch Line by a communication trench along the Martinpuich–Bazentin road, was seen to be strongly manned by the enemy.

No man's land in this area was over 1,000 yards in width and where the second German line ran through the wood it was known as Circus Trench.

Corporal Robertson says in his Diary that on 13th July their Division (3rd) had been ordered to storm and hold the heights from le Grand to Longueval. The 10th R. Welch Fus. and 1st Gordons were to be the 76th Bde. supports and 3rd Divisional Reserve.

On 14th July at 9.0 a.m. they moved on again. The edge of Bazentin Wood was a mess but not many dead were lying about, many men must have escaped from being in the pitch of the battle. At 10.0 a.m. more drum fire was heard from the French 75s on the right.

After capturing Contalmaison and Mametz Wood the British had soon

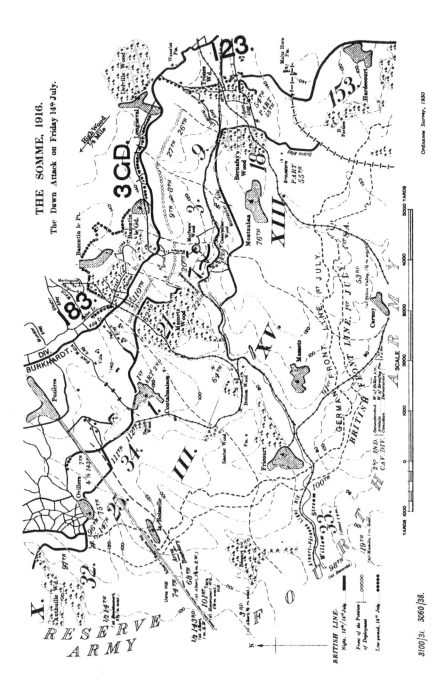

THE SOMME, 1916.

The Dawn Attack on Friday 14th July.

Ordnance Survey, 1930

3/00/31. 3060/38.

reached the Bazentins and le Grand was in German hands until 14th July when the 3rd and 7th Divs. captured both villages and the Communal Cemetery and held out against counter-attacks, and the 21st Div. captured le Petit Wood. The 7th Div. erected a commemorative oak cross at the end of le Petit. *The War in the Air* notes that a desperate struggle began on 14th July before le Petit, when the British attacked the German entrenchments, captured and lost the village several times, and finally remained masters of it. To consolidate the conquered line they immediately advanced beyond it. Penetrating into the German third line, they gained a footing in High Wood and on the slopes of Hill 155.

Haig noted on 14th July that the Germans had retaken le Petit but that it had been retaken by the 7th Div. In the evening High Wood was taken and connected up with le Petit in the evening.

Sec. Lt. H. J. Brooks of the 21st Manchesters who was on the staff of the 7th Div. wrote that on 13th July they were bivouacked near Mametz Halt and on 14th July that they went past Mametz Wood to Sabot Copse and were involved in an attempt to take le Grand Wood. In the defensive flank of the 91st Bde. in the direction of Longueval and Delville Wood, at nightfall established in the lower half of High Wood (Liddle), Noel Compton-Burnett who was the brother of Ivy the novelist and a member of the 7th Leicesters of the 110th Bde. of the 37th Div. was killed in the initial attack in the small hours of 14th July.

In Masefield's *The Battle of the Somme* he said that on the left the British broke over the line into le Petit Wood, which was defended much as Mametz Wood had been.

The British stormed its trenches, cleared out the machine guns and heavy guns hidden in it, and worked right through it, emerging at the northern end with many prisoners and much material by 8 o'clock. In the centre the British got into le Grand Wood and also into le Grand village. They chased the enemy down the hill beyond and up the opposite slope, they got into le Petit and made it theirs.

The 4th Suffolks moved up through Bécordel to a position between Fricourt and Mametz where they bivouacked during the night 14/15th July. The battle of Bazentin Ridge was raging in all its fury and the Suffolks became involved at dawn. The Battalion went into reserve in Shell (Death) Valley and dug itself into road side trenches for the night. After a day of heavy shelling they returned to the front line trenches, and an old German bombstore was found in the north-east corner of le Petit Wood. The store subsequently became used as a Battalion HQ instead of a deep dugout.

In the *Official History* it says of the dawn assault of 14th July that in spite of machine gun fire from the houses at le Grand the British troops went forward after topping the ridge, and captured the village. Large numbers of Germans could be seen making up the slope towards High Wood. Bazentin le Grand Wood was taken on schedule. In le Petit there was a counter-attack on the Royal Irish but the cemetery on the eastern side was held. The village was consolidated.

The two Bazentin villages, their woods as well as other woods such as Flat Iron Copse, were the scene of very fierce fighting, fighting which had gone on for several days before the Allies were to finally establish their new line securely. It should also be stressed that the Allied Artillery played a particularly important role on this occasion and that the villages and woods had been virtually pulverised by the very considerable number of guns that were in action.

Liddell Hart in an unpublished ms. (LH7/1916/23) said that the plan of attack was that the Fourth Army was to attack the German's second system of defence from Waterlot Farm to the west end of Bazentin le Petit Wood, the first objective being the main second line trenches and the second objective being from the north end of Bazentin le Petit Wood and village to the north of Delville Wood and Longueval. XIII Corps was to attack the right and XV Corps the left. Of the XV Corps the 7th Div. were to attack Bazentin le Grand Wood and the village and the 21st Div. were to attack Bazentin le Petit Wood and village. The cavalry was to go through at all costs and the way was to be made for them by the infantry. The attack was to begin at 3.25 a.m. on 14th July, shortly before dawn, from the north border of Mametz Wood. The 10th KOYLI was in Quadrangle Trench, the 9th in Bottom Wood and the 15th DLI in Lonely Copse, whilst the 1st E. Yorks. were to protect the flank from Pearl Wood along the west border of Bazentin le Petit Wood. Hart's battalion, the 9th KOYLI had come up from Ville and drawn bombs and stores outside Méaulte. They then went up the Fricourt Road and stopped near the cross roads just east of Bécordel for tea. At about 6.0 p.m. they moved off in platoons towards the cemetery. They noticed that guns were standing out in the open in rows along the line of the water-course. They were heavy guns, the field ones being further forward along the line of the hedge from Shelter Wood to Bottom Wood and in the valley behind. Here the guns were standing almost wheel to wheel and the artillery of three Divs., some 200 guns were in an area of about a square mile. They went through Fricourt and passed Rose Cottage via the east edge of Fricourt Wood and then down the hill across the railway and further up to Bottom Wood.

The attack duly began at 3.25 a.m. on 14th July and the first line of trenches known as Flat Iron Trenches and Villa Trenches were taken with little loss. Contalmaison Villa which might have threatened their progress was also taken. The rations came as far as railway copse. The battalion moved off alongside the railway at the base of the cliff and to the south-east of Mametz Wood.

The 10th KOYLI were ordered up to le Petit Village and lost 200 men within an hour. Hart's Batt., the 9th KOYLI were dug in on the edge of Mametz Wood, in many places the dead were ten deep, and fifty yards into the wood was a shambles. Hart went up to visit Brigade HQ at the west corner of the wood and went up via the railway which ran through Mametz Wood. On the night of the 17th/18th they were relieved and Hart was gassed close to Mametz Wood.

2nd Lt. L. A. Crook of the 2nd Queen's (91st Bde. 7th Div.) was awarded

the MC for bravery close to Bazentin between 15th and 21st July when setting a fine example under heavy fire and displaying great powers of leadership until he was wounded.

Capt. Sir Archibald Edward Dunbar was awarded the MC for work at Bazentin le Grand on 14th July and at Longueval on 23rd July. He was a member of the 12th W. Yorks. (9th Bde. of the 3rd Div.) He led his company in an attack with great dash, and skilfully consolidated its position. During the Longueval incident he handled his company with great skill under heavy shell fire.

A railway from Bazentin as far as Martinpuich existed in mid July. A. A. Milne, the writer who served with the 11th R. Warwicks on attachment and who had been trained as a Signals Officer had a swift introduction to the battle, when in order to gain experience he went into action with Harrison the already recently appointed Signals Officer. The attack was timed for midnight and the objective was the Switch Line at Bazentin le Petit and the day before Harrison was wounded, with the result that Milne had to take his place. HQ was in a German dugout, which faced the wrong way. In an adjoining dugout was the HQ of the E. Lancs. who were sharing the attack. In the space between these two underground rooms were Milne's Signallers. The attack was a complete failure.

Lt. Ellenberger who was in the same Regiment as Liddell Hart said that the 9th KOYLI was up at Bazentin on the 14th and Gerald Brenan in his book *A Life of One's Own* said that after mid-July the fighting in the direction of Bazentin le Grand had been very heavy. Both sides had dug themselves in and around one hastily scraped up gun emplacement which commanded a drive through the trees, the khaki bodies lay in heaps, and all across the battlefield, corpses of men, dead horses and mules, hand grenades, gas masks, the German spiked parade helmets, water bottles, were scattered like debris on a beach.

In his Memoirs Hart wrote that on 16th July he was sent up with his company to fill a gap that had arisen in the new front line on the front edge of Bazentin le Petit Wood. The German harrassing fire was very unpleasant because their shells often hit the branches of trees and then exploded with a shower of falling splinters.

In *The War the Infantry Knew* it is mentioned that on 17th July their Division (33rd) was relieving the 21st Div. in the village cemetery. At midnight the 2nd R. Welch Fus. moved through a light barrage of explosives and bromine shells to relieve the 4th King's between the Cemetery and the Martinpuich road.

In *The Machine Gunner* Arthur Russell wrote that the rest of the 33rd Div. including three sections of his company of machine gunners were to attack the German positions beyond the village of Bazentin le Petit and the approaches to High Wood and had already moved ahead. Mametz Valley was behind them and because of the very heavy enemy shelling it was called the 'Valley of Death'. Whilst they were still in reserve Russell had the job of section runner between section officer and Company HQ. On the morning of

17th July, the section had to take two guns to some forward position in the direction of Bazentin le Grand and to reach them they has to go round what was named Caterpillar Wood. This wood and the ground at the rear was often under heavy enemy shell fire and was one maze of shell craters.

The War the Infantry Knew records that 2nd RWF had become support brigade and French 75s had arrived in their rear. The Indian Cavalry were placed behind these guns and were reached by German reply. Batteries rolled all day into Happy Valley and onto the slight rise of Caterpillar Wood until the area was stiff with batteries. On 17th July the Division relieved the 21st Div. north of Bazentin le Petit, it had already relieved the 7th Div. in the Cemetery. On 18th July they came under heavy bombardment. On the same day Robert Graves reported that his 19th Bde. was a reserve Bde. of the 33rd Div. and that they advanced to a position just north of Bazentin le Petit. They relieved a badly shaken Tyneside Company. Frank Richards (2nd RWF) reported that his company took over a position on the east of Bazentin le Petit, they were in a shallow trench which ran into a cemetery. High Wood was about 700 yards in front of them. In his part of the trench the shells fell in front and behind.

In the evening they were relieved and returned to Mametz Wood. News of a proposed attack on High Wood was received.

Arthur Russell noted that on 18th July before midnight he set off with a guide at a slow pace between the woods of Mametz and Bazentin le Petit and that the guide lost his way and had to return for further directions. They then entered a sunken road along the side of Bazentin le Petit Wood. This roadway was a German target for their artillery. The gun positions which Russell's party took were a little in front of Bazentin le Petit Wood, and when dawn broke they saw that they were on slightly higher ground overlooking German positions some three hundred yards away.

Quoting from one of Hart's letters (LH1/327/35) to Robert Graves he said that presumably in the early hours of 18th July Graves moved up to relieve an Irish Battalion just north of Bazentin le Petit Wood. On the way Graves ran into the new phosgene gas shells. Hart ran into them too, with worse results, on his way back through Mametz Wood after being relieved. His Company had been sent up there to fill a gap left by a battalion that had lost itself. Hart had got slightly wounded on the way up. When the missing units turned up later in the day, Hart's company was kept as an immediate reserve just behind Bazentin le Petit Wood for a couple of days, and so got the benefit of the first heavy dose of the new gas shell, which burst all along the light railway to Mametz Wood while they were marching down it in the dark.

On July 19th Richards said that the enemy shelled them heavily, the other end of the company was not so lucky as they were, the shells burst on the parapet, blowing trenches and men to pieces. In the cemetery the shells were throwing corpses and coffins out of graves, and some of the dead were lying alongside them.

In the history of the 7th Div. it is said that by this time (19th July) the Germans barraged the depression north of Bazentin le Grand Wood persistently.

Graves was posted to D Company and they were gassed while going up through the ruins of Bazentin le Petit Village. D Company trenches were scooped beside the road. They got into contact with C Company behind them on the right and the 4th Suffolks fifty yards to the left. They began to widen their trenches. Two strong points were built and were to be held with Lewis guns. He visited one of the points and went along the Bazentin High Wood road, where the Public School Battalion were wandering about! They were a constant embarrassment to the Bde. On the 19th the 2nd RWFs were relieved and told that they were to attack High Wood. The French called it Raven Wood and Graves took command of B Company who were to relieve the Cameronians. They were in Bazentin Churchyard on the reverse slope of a slight ridge, about half a mile from the wood. They were to be in reserve to the CO of the Fifth Scottish Rifles with the Public Schools in support.

Graves was wounded before the attack by a splinter of marble, perhaps from a headstone in Bazentin Cemetery which lodged itself in his body, and this together with other wounds, one of which was in his chest and one in his thigh were the most serious of eight wounds that he received. He was transported via Heilly and Rouen to London where he was put in hospital and 'renounced his death' which had been reported in error. Sassoon had been under the impression that his friend had been killed on 20th July.

In *The War the Infantry Knew* a contributor who must be Frank Richards said that he was detailed with some signallers to use Bazentin le Petit Windmill, 200 yards east of the cemetery, as the forward post of a relay system. The windmill had been the target of their artillery, then in turn that of the Germans, and then the RWF captured it.

The assembly positions north-east of the village were on ground that rose fairly steeply and was covered with coarse grass or standing corn and gave some cover in the first stage of the advance towards High Wood.

D. J. Price of the 12th R. Fus. (Liddle) was in mid-July, with his battalion in front of Bazentin le Petit and he was involved in a dawn attack on 20th July. There were terrible casualties, and for a time he became separated from his comrades. The battalion later returned to the rear of Mametz Wood.

Richards wrote in his autobiography *Old Soldiers Never Die* that on 20th July when he was a Bde. Signaller together with seven others he formed a transmitting station between High Wood and Bde. HQ. which was situated on the fringe of Mametz Wood. The system to be used was the flag system and their position was a large mill that was about 600 yards this side of High Wood. It was on rising ground which gave them a good view. The Germans shelled them continuously. Five of the signalling team were sheltering in a hole nearby and were useless! On the right front of the Mill a battalion of the Manchesters from another Division were in some shallow trenches. A dressing station was in the valley below. Signalling was abandoned and instead the signallers became runners between Bde. and High Wood, below which a company of A & SH were in some shell holes and shallow trenches. They were treated to fifteen minutes of concentrated fire which destroyed them. At 10.0 p.m. the Bde. was relieved, the Public School Battalion was practically annihilated, and the RWF were not much better off. The Public School Battalion sent across their 'spare' parcels, and the RWF went back to a village south of Albert to re-organise.

In *The War The Infantry Knew* it was written that the 2nd RWF was relieved amid confusion, and held in reserve among the shell holes between Longueval–Contalmaison road and Flat Iron Copse. The massed artillery was behind them. Traffic was mostly through Montauban. The attacking troops of the Bde. in artillery formation were caught in a barrage.

The 5th Scot. Rif. and the 20th R. Fus. pushed on to the other side of High Wood. Three battalions were mixed up in the wood, and the northern part was still in German hands. Advanced Bde. of the 2nd RWF was in a quarry by the cemetery roadside. On the 21st they were relieved by the 1st Queens and a company of the 16th KRRC and they bivouacked on the south-east side of Mametz Wood. At 3.0 p.m. they marched back to Buire with the transport. The N. Staffs. took over the line from the cemetery to the windmill and their battalion HQ was in a chalk pit in German dugouts.

On the evening of the 21st the 9th R. Scots. Fus. marched through Fricourt and Mametz to take over the front line in the vicinity of Bazentin le Grand.

Russell reported that the 1st Battalion of the Middlesex Regt. was holding a section of the Bazentin front and during four days (17th to 21st July) that they had suffered very heavy casualties in their advance from Mametz Valley. Early in the afternoon he had to take a message down to Company HQ, and instead of returning to the gun position he was told to stay back and get his leg seen to. Moving as fast as he could down the shell torn track down the side of Bazentin le Petit Wood, and across the more open ground into Mametz Valley after delivering his message, he now took the opportunity of going to the 98th Bde. ADS at the far side of the valley about 500 yards away, passing close to several batteries of Field Artillery on the way. He entered the Dressing Station dugout excavated into the bank of a stone quarry (Quarry Post?) with a kind of covered verandah of corrugated iron and sandbags in front of it. On the night of 21st July there were a lot of poison gas shells and next morning they went back to rest.

As I have previously mentioned on 20th July Graves had become a casualty when a third of his Battalion had become casualties before the attack had even begun. Dr. J. C. Dunn (Btn. MO) had been responsible for getting him down to the old German dressing station at the north end of Mametz Wood. He was thought to have been mortally wounded but on 21st July he was found to be still alive and was sent to Heilly the nearest Field Hospital. The pain of being jolted down Happy Valley made him wake up screaming.

D. J. Price of the 20th R. Fus. had enlisted under age and on 21st July was told to report, as his mother had managed to get him withdrawn, but only temporarily, from the Army. He rejoined the Battalion in January, 1918.

By 25th July Bazentin le Petit Wood had become carpeted with corpses.

At Bazentin le Grand between 20th and 30th July the field artillery of four divisions was in action but they were not co-ordinated. When a Division was in the Bazentin section telephone exchanges north of Mametz were established for infantry and one for artillery with a cross connection between them. At the end of July the Military Cemetery was begun, outside the western wall in a German dugout.

During 30th-31st July James Miller of the 7th King's Own Royal Lancaster Batt. won the VC at Bazentin le Petit. His battalion was consolidating a position after its capture by assault, and he was ordered to take an important message under heavy shell and rifle fire, and to bring back a reply at all costs. He was compelled to cross the open and on leaving the trench was shot almost immediately in the back, the bullet emerging from his abdomen. In spite of this, with heroic courage and self sacrifice, he delivered his message, staggered back with the answer, and fell at the feet of the officer to whom the message was to be delivered. He was taking part in the advanced fighting on 30th July. His memorial is at Dartmoor Cemetery.

On 3rd August Collison of the 11th R. Warwicks. wrote that the 34th Div. held the part of the front from about the western edge of High Wood to a line of trenches running east and west, and about 300 yards north of Bazentin le Petit. Two Battalions of the 11th Bde. and two of the 101st Bde. were in the front line, their supports in the woods of Mametz and Bazentin le Petit. The 6th Bedfords. and 8th E. Lancs. of his Bde., were in reserve near Bottom Wood, the 10th LN Lancs. and themselves being for the present in bivouacs about Bécourt Wood. On 5th August he went forward via Quadrangle Trench and Mametz Wood to arrange for the relief of the 11th Suffolks. who were entrenched on the southern outskirts of Bazentin le Petit Wood, and also in the north-western part of the Mametz Wood.

The 4th Suffolks moved on 13th August from Fricourt Wood to support trenches in Bazentin le Grand Wood. The former German line ran south of Bazentin le Petit Wood. Edge Trench was on the northern edge of the wood and was still in German hands.

According to *The War The Infantry Knew*, on 18th August the 2nd RWF moved forward and arrived in the dark on the Longueval–Bazentin road below High Wood where they waited.

The 2nd Munsters Commanding Officer Lt. Col. W. B. Lyons was mortally wounded whilst making a personal reconnaissance. On 27th August Edge Trench fell into British hands.

According to L/Cpl. B. W. Whayman (Liddle) of the 2/6 Norfolks, he was involved in fatigue carrying parties and mine laying in High Wood and in carrying trench mortar shells known as toffee apples. The main communication trench at the time was in front of Bazentin le Grand, and was known as High Alley. It was about 80 yards long. They relieved the 1st Black Watch and were shelled by both sides. On relief they went to Albert.

On 9th September the 2/6 Norfolks relieved the Munsters of whom only 20 men were left out of 60. They bivouacked at Bazentin for a week.

On 20th September shelters and dugouts were built at Mill Road near Bazentin le Petit. The road ran east of a quarry where Bde. HQ was positioned. The two villages contained CPs for the wounded. N. Gladden of the North'd Fus. reported that in late September at 6.30 a.m. armed with shovel or pick they left for the reserve position, for such it was, and moved out of the wood and passed Bazentin le Petit, an immense rubbish heap of sheltered buildings which had been cordoned off and boldly signposted. As they skirted the windward side the horrible stench of the unburied dead filled their nostrils. The sickly smell of rotting humanity, which they were to come to know too well, so that it almost seeped into their dreams, overhung the pulverised village, like a pall above a communal tomb, as it indeed was.

The HQ of the 149th and 150th Bdes. was here on 23rd/24th October. In November they entrained, a weak and weary collection of human wrecks, at the railhead which had now been brought as far forward as Bazentin le Petit. Here abouts, the landscape was acquiring a shipshape look with new living quarters springing up like mushrooms in the form of neatly arranged hutments and other amenities.

The Communal Cemetery Extension had been begun immediately after the capture of the village in mid-July and was used until December as a front line cemetery. It was enlarged after the armistice. The graves include 59 members of the 1st Northamptons who are unidentified. The ground rises to the north-west and east and falls to the south towards Caterpillar Valley. The Communal Cemetery Extension joins the north of the Communal Cemetery. The Military Cemetery is behind a group of cottages on the west side of the village. It had been begun in July and was used until May 1917, as a front line cemetery. At the end of the battle the wood was almost impassable and the villages here were full of old trenches and the wreckage of strong points. The two villages were lost by the British in March 1918 and then retaken after the fall of Thiepval on 25th August 1918. There is a memorial to the RE 82nd Field Company just outside Bazentin le Petit, and one to Capt. Houston Stewart Hamilton Wallace (10th Worcs.) down a track in the direction of High Wood. He was killed on 22nd July 1916 and is commemorated on the Thiepval Memorial.

Beaucourt

Beaucourt sur l'Ancre is a village to the east of Beaumont Hamel, and north-east of Hamel on the D 50, and in the Ancre Valley. It was situated on the boundary of the German lines. At the beginning of the battle, it was a very strong defensive position that received relief and support from the villages of Grandcourt and Miraumont and from behind the occupied area.

The Battle for Beaumont Hamel and Beaucourt had been planned for October but had been postponed several times because of unfavourable weather conditions. In the end it was fought between the 13th and 19th November and Beaucourt itself was mostly involved on the first two days.

In brief the first British objective was the strong line of German trenches, the second Station Road, running from Beaumont Hamel to the Albert–Lille Railway, third the trenches on the outskirts of Beaucourt, and fourth the village itself.

Beaucourt is mostly associated with the 63rd Naval Division and the writer

Douglas Jerrold who was a member of that Division, became the main authority on the battle and it is from his books *The Hawke Battalion* and the history of the *Royal Naval Division* that I have based my short history of the battle.

This Division had been assigned to Vth Corps for the planned attack on the battle front to the north of the River Ancre. The front of the Naval Division was to be 1,200 yards in width and was immediately north of the river and at right angles to the river valley, which at this point ran almost due east to Beaucourt, whilst the German trenches ran roughly from north to south.

To expand on the plan I have already said that the objectives of the Division was the village of Beaucourt itself and the intervening positions opposite the British front. At a distance of from 150 to 250 yards from the British assembly trenches, on higher ground, was the German front line system consisting of as usual, three lines of trenches which formed the first objective, and was known for that purpose, as the Dotted Green Line. Behind the front line system and separated from it by a valley, through which the road known as Station Road, was a second ridge running from Beaumont Hamel to Beaucourt Station. On this ridge was a strongly fortified position, called the Green Line. This was the second defined objective. The country immediately behind this line was featureless, except for the right front of the Divisional Sector, where it sloped up to the hill immediately in front of the village, which commanded the enemy's communications with his forward system on this part of the line. On the western face of this hill was a trench, which continued parallel to the front across the more level ground on the left. The trench was known as the Yellow Line and formed the Division's third objective. The final objective known as the Red Line was a roughly defined position to be taken up beyond Beaucourt, the capture of which would be for the Naval Division a real proof of success.

The first and third objectives were to be attacked by the 1st Royal Marines, the Howe, Hawke and Hood Battalions each advancing in four waves. The first four battalions would then rest on the first objective which was the German front line trench and reorganise. The second and fourth objectives were to be attacked by the 2nd Royal Marines, the Anson, Nelson and Drake Battalions. These battalions were to pass through the lines and capture Station Road Valley, and the Green Line. They in their turn would rest and reorganise, while the first four battalions were to pass through to the Yellow Line. The final assault on the village was then, after another pause to be carried out by the battalions who reorganised on the Green Line. With each battalion was to go a sub-section of the Bde. Machine Gun Company, and trench mortars were to follow as soon as possible.

Jerrold wrote in *The Hawke Battalion* that in the early morning of the 13th November the main difficulty initially was that the Hawke and the Hood Battalions who were to lead the frontal attack of the Brigade with Hawke on the left and Hood on the right, were having to line up on the forward slope of the Allied position, since the reverse slope of the very steep crest of the ridge was needed to hide the supporting battalions.

Further back still, in what was normally the reserve and support trenches, were packed two battalions of the 190th Bde. On the 12th November the day before all surplus personnel had gone back to the transport lines at Hedarville. Of the four Hawke Companies 'B' was on the left, next to Commander Fairfax's Howe Battalion.

The creeping barrage had been used and Jerrold wrote that the full strength of the British Artillery was opened on the narrow divisional front. He also said that the morning was very misty and was abnormally dark. The first wave of the Hawke Battalion moved off at 5.45 a.m. into the mist and were soon out of sight when they were still only 70 yards away. Soon the fourth wave fifty yards behind the others, was itself out of sight. Through the mist and deafened by the explosions of guns, almost choked by lyddite, the battalion disappeared. Less than 20 of the men and none of the officers were to come back unhurt. They had gone into action with 20 officers and 415 other ranks. The Official casualties were 23 officers and 396 men. The whole stretch of the front line could be seen to be in the possession of the enemy but it was the infamous Beaucourt Redoubt which had brought about their downfall with heavy fire which had been directed against their battalion who had had the misfortune to attack directly opposite it. On the left of the Redoubt, in touch with the right of the Howe Battalion Lt. Tudor-Vere Harmsworth, son of Lord Rothermere and nephew of Lord Northcliffe was wounded in no man's land as he led the remains of his company to the second line. Here the last of them was hit and Harmsworth himself was mortally wounded by machine gun fire from the direction of the Redoubt. He was later buried in the Ancre Cemetery.

On the right of the line the Hood Battalion, perhaps because they kept closer to the barrage, reached the German front line, and passed through it without a devastating number of casualties. They proceeded with the destruction of the dugouts in the railway cutting to their right, which were part of a vast system of underground works running from the Ancre to Beaumont Hamel.

The Commander of the Hood Battalion, Colonel Freyberg decided to throw the whole weight of his battalion into the next advance, instead of endeavouring to reorganise in the mist and darkness. The combined attack was brilliantly successful, the dugouts in Station Road yielding some 400 prisoners. The Hawke and Nelson Battalions which had been so devastated by fire from the Redoubt were put under the command of Freyberg for the remainder of the battle. The Nelson Battalion had been attempting to assault the Station Road when they were enfiladed from the Redoubt.

Next to the Hawke and Nelson Battalions were the Howe and Anson Battalions and their flank was uncovered because of the failure of the attack against the Redoubt. On the extreme left of the attack the 1st and 2nd Marines met with disaster at the start, from enemy artillery, and the 51st Division on the left, engaged in an historic and ultimately successful assault on Beaumont Hamel the adjoining village.

There were two parties on the Green Line and Colonel Freyberg's alone was secure in its communications, adequate in numbers and adequately officered. Freyberg and Lt. Commander Gilliland led two independent assaults on the Yellow Line. Because communication problems increased General Shute would not let Freyberg carry on to the Red Line. The Germans still remained in the centre of their old front system.

One of the casualties of the Hood Battalion on the 13th November was F. S. Kelly who was born in 1881 and was an Oarsman and Musician, and had been educated at Eton and Balliol College, Oxford. He was also a contemporary of Rupert Brooke and was one of Brooke's pallbearers when he was buried at Skyros. Lt. Commander Kelly himself was buried in Martinsart Cemetery.

Lt. H. Cecil (RFA) was awarded the MC for laying and repairing a line under fire on the 13th, and RND Commander Sterndale-Bennett gained the DSO. He assumed command of his battalion and collected a party and bombed the enemy out of the second line which had threatened to hold up the attack. A connection with the London Stage and the Beaucourt battle was made through the son of Mrs. Patrick Campbell, actress and friend of George Bernard Shaw, in that her son was in charge of a Trench Mortar battery until his guns were knocked out. He then carried on in the battle as an infantry officer. On the 14th November Allied artillery fire was opened on the first objective the Beaucourt Trench on the front of the 63rd Div. and on Munich Trench which was opposite the 51st Div. and the 2nd Div. The 111th Bde. had been sent to help out in the battle from the 37th Div. In this brigade were the 13th R. Fus. and one of the officers who was probably with them was Guy Chapman who was later to publish a book of war memoirs called *A Passionate Prodigality.*

The attack of the 63rd Div. was made from Station Road by the 13th R. Fus. and also the 13th Rif. Bde. who had their right on Redoubt Valley. A loss of direction at the beginning of the advance was partially corrected by the sound of machine gun fire from the village and Muck Trench then formed the second objective. About 480 men were collected at Beaucourt Station and came under heavy machine gun and rifle fire and then reached Freyberg's position. The latter led the mixed force into the village of Beaucourt whilst the 13th KRRC also of the 111th Bde. pressed forward south-eastward through the village. Prisoners were captured from cellars and dugouts and a line was established around the eastern edge of Beaucourt. The village fell by mid-morning. In *The Royal Naval Division* Jerrold wrote that Freyberg had arranged to assault the village with the help of the 13th KRRC and the 1st HAC and had left the Hood and Drake Battalions in support. However there had been at the last minute considerable confusion by the unlooked for arrival behind the Yellow Line of the 7th R. Fus. It was at this point that a separate battle was being fought by the tanks against the enemy who had still been occupying trenches around the Redoubt. The tanks which had come from Auchonvillers got stuck. The whole garrison (600 strong) were marched back to the British lines. The Redoubt and the village had been captured and it only remained to consolidate the hold on the village and to clear up the situation on the flanks of the position. Freyberg was wounded for the third time and this time severely. He was awarded the VC for his leadership on these two days.

The *Official History* noted that at 1.0 p.m. on the 14th that the German infantry was seen massing near Baillescourt Farm, south-east of the village. The bridge over the river was held by the HAC. The counter-attack against Beaucourt didn't materialise, and the Naval Division was relieved and the remains of the different battalions assembled and reorganised in the captured front line system. They joined together at Engelbelmer from where they were taken in buses to Arquéves well behind the fighting zone. The story of the ill-fated Hawke Battalion which had virtually ceased to exist on the 13th November has already been told. And yet it played its part while the German machine gunners, untouched by the Allied barrage took toll of the eight lines of the Hawke and Nelson Battalions who were up against the redoubt. There was a point of controversy about the immunity of the garrison of the redoubt from the effects of the artillery barrage. The only possible explanation was that the exact position of the Redoubt was simply not known to the attackers and that no special artillery was requested.

A. P. Herbert who doesn't seem to have been involved in the fighting on the 13th as he was with the cadre left behind in support reported to Major Norris in the evening to join the front force of Colonel Freyberg. It is unlikely that he would have survived if he had taken part in the battle on the 13th. Herbert was born in 1890 and had joined the Battalion at a camp at Abbeville that summer after the Gallipoli campaign. The Royal Naval Division occupied a unique position and the possibility of relegation from Naval to Army status was anathema to both Herbert and Jerrold. Herbert had been made Assistant Adjutant and was one of two officers from the Battalion who had emerged unscathed. During the attack though there had occurred a failure of morale that resulted in the court martial and execution of Sub. Lt. E. Dyett of the Nelson Battalion. Herbert may have known the circumstances, as well as knowing the individual concerned. Certainly he used aspects of the case in his book *The Secret Battle* which he began to write in 1918.

There is a Memorial to the 63rd Naval Division in the village itself.

After reorganisation in 1916–1917 the Division ceased to be 'a semi-naval, semi-civilian force'; it was integrated into the Army as the 63rd (Royal Naval) Division. When it went into the line in February 1917 Herbert was on leave. On his return according to Jerrold, Herbert revitalised Battalion HQ. By this time he had been made Adjutant. In September 1917 Herbert published a poem called *Beaucourt Revisited* and it is written seemingly as a result of a return visit to this part of the Somme battlefield. In it he refers to Suicide Corner, Kentish Caves and the place where Harmsworth was shot. He also mentions 'young James' and 'William' these can be identified as two friends of Herbert's, James Cook and William Ker. Herbert died in 1971 and his biography was written by Reginald Pound. Douglas Jerrold upon whose writings for this section on Beaucourt I have drawn considerably was severely wounded on the Somme and, after the war he became a writer and publisher, dying in 1964.

Beaumont Hamel

Beaumont Hamel is a village on the D 163 road between Beaucourt and Auchonvillers; it is on the west bank of the River Ancre. There are three spurs, named Auchonvillers, Beaucourt and Grandcourt and between them there are shallow valleys separating the villages. The village of Beaumont Hamel connects with the road that runs eastwards from Auchonvillers. The valley called Y Ravine cuts into the south side of Hawthorn Ridge. The remaining valley was known as Beaucourt Valley and was marked by the Beaucourt–Puisieux Road and past south of Serre. The Colincamps–Beaucourt Spur was known as the Redan Ridge where it crossed the front line. The German front line first ran on the eastern slope of the Auchonvillers spur and then passed around the head of Y Ravine to Hawthorn Ridge and then crossed the shallow Beaumont Hamel Valley and continued across to the Redan Bridge (Beaucourt Spur) and over to where Serre stood. The Intermediate line was known as Munich Trench and began from Beaucourt Redoubt and went north and included the village of Serre, the second position ran from Grandcourt to Puisieux.

At the beginning of the battle in July 1916 the village had about 162 houses and was the third largest on the Somme. The village had a system of caves and underground passages which had been excavated in order to obtain hard chalk for building purposes. The German position known as The Bergwerk was on the Beaucourt Ridge immediately behind the northern end of Beaumont Hamel.

Later John Masefield described the village of Beaumont Hamel as being unrecognisable by its former occupants.

The 1st July battle of Beaumont Hamel was fought on the British side mainly by the 29th Division belonging to VIII Corps. To their right was the 36th (Ulster) Division of X Corps and to their left was the 4th Division facing towards Redan Ridge. In addition there were also two battalions of the 143rd Bde. of the 48th (South Midland) Division on the extreme left who were involved in the attack on the German Quadrilateral towards Pendant Copse. These were the 8th R. Warwicks. and the 6th R. Warwicks. (12th Bde.) and they were attached to the Division at this time. The ground had a series of deep chalk pits which gave every advantage to the defender and the Quadrilateral gave a flanking fire along the whole position. There were a great many machine guns.

The frontage of the Quadrilateral was about 400 yards and there was little cover between the German and the British trenches but there was a slight rise in the German direction. The objective was Pendant Copse to the south-east of Serre village which was the target of the 31st Division. On the 1st the 8th R. Warwicks. moved off at 7.30 a.m. and the first four lines of enemy trench were taken by 7.50 a.m. and small groups penetrated Serre and the outskirts of Beaumont Hamel. Troops even reached as far as Pendant Copse but were driven back. The position was held tenaciously until 1.30 p.m. but as the neighbouring divisions, the 29th and the 31st were making little or no progress the 4th Division was ordered to retire. Brigadier Prowse was killed early in the action when he was moving his Bde. HQ forward from the former British line to the German trenches which had been taken by the 8th R. Warwicks. The Germans counter-attacked later in the afternoon and large numbers of R. Warwicks. wounded were left in the German lines. The 6th R. Warwicks. were meant to take the fifth and sixth lines but this was not to be, as they were decimated before they reached the higher ground in front of Serre. In the evening the troops had retired and the casualties of the 8th R. Warwicks. were 573 out of 600 men. They withdrew to Mailly and for ten days rested in Couin Woods.

Behind the two Warwickshire battalions was the 1st King's Own and at 7.20 a.m. they moved off under artillery fire and were faced with uncut wire. Casualties were very considerable and by evening they were back in their own lines. They also were withdrawn to Mailly, on 7th July. Their casualties included their commanding officer Lt. Col. J. A. Thicknesse. They were supporting the 1st Rif. Bde. in the attack on the Redan Ridge.

On the right of the 12th Bde. came the 11th Bde. of the 4th Division. The plan was to attack astride Redan Ridge. The 11th Bde. was to attack with the 1st. Rif. Bde. and the 1st E. Lancs. The 1st Rif. Bde. moved off at 7.29 a.m. and the East Lancs immediately came under fire from Ridge Redoubt and also from Beaumont Hamel. The German wire was uncut and the Rif. Bde. Battalion were between the Quadrilateral and the Ridge Redoubt from which murderous machine gun fire came. They managed to bomb their way to their objective but were themselves bombed out and relieved by the 1st. R. Irish Fus. the next morning, casualties were 474.

Behind the 1st Rif. Bde. were the 1st Somerset LI and they moved off at 7.30 a.m. and very soon along with other members of the 11th Bde. came under heavy rifle and machine gun fire from both flanks. We have an eye witness account of what happened from A. H. Cook's book *A Soldier's War*.

The 1st Somersets had got their scaling ladders in position to get out of the trenches. There were also bridges for following troops to use. They breakfasted at 5.30 a.m. and at this time the bombardment was very considerable and the German lines were one cloud of smoke from the Allied bombardment.

The guns then quietened and they thought that their part in the attack was going to be a cakewalk. At 7.20 a.m. the mine exploded to the south, under Hawthorn Redoubt and the force of the explosion shook the Somerset trenches. However just before the forward troops reached the German lines the enemy opened up with murderous machine gun fire. The Somersets were supposed to follow the 1st Rif. Bde. at 7.40 a.m. but they were keen to be off and followed up in a few minutes. They had not gone far before the German guns opened up and they found themselves caught in no man's land. Men began to fall all around but the attackers had to go on despite the whole front being covered by strategically placed guns. They swung to the left as to approach their objective direct, meant that they would be going over some rising ground swept by machine gun fire. The British guns had made a mess of the German trenches but there were few German dead to be seen, only the bodies of the British attackers. The Germans had been stowed away safely in deep dugouts during the bombardment, some of the dugouts were over 30 feet deep. Later the Somersets got some support from the 10th and 12th Bdes. but they were met with withering fire. The only hope was to consolidate their meagre gains. The 2nd Seaforth H. came up at 9.0 a.m. with reinforcements and small parties on the left had begun to bomb forward towards Munich Trench, but gradually Cook and his group were driven back by the Germans through part of the Quadrilateral which was a defensive position to the left of Redan Ridge. They used their own as well as German bombs and were finally relieved at 11.00 a.m. Men from various battalions ended up in the Quadrilateral and after dark the Somersets were relieved by the R. Irish Fus. and withdrew to their own lines. At 10.0 p.m. they went back to Divisional reserve at Mailly. Casualties were very high especially amongst the officers. On the 3rd they went into huts at Bertrancourt.

To the right of the 1st Rif. Bde. came the 1st E. Lancs. who were in front of the 1st Hants. and on the right of the 1st E. Lancs. came the 1st Lancs. Fus. Immediately the British guns lifted from the German front line trenches there came heavy machine gun fire from that direction. One officer could see at least eight guns from either Ridge Redoubt or from Beaumont Hamel itself. Simultaneously the German artillery barrage came down in front of them. Many were killed on the uncut wire. They were relieved in the evening by the 1st R. Warwicks. and went on to Mailly before Bertrancourt on the 3rd July.

The 1st Hants. moved off after the 1st E. Lancs. who they found as having been almost wiped out by machine gun fire. Colonel Park fell before he could get half way across, and the majority of the battalion were brought down before they reached the wire. The battalion had their worst experience of the war with 321 killed and 265 wounded. The survivors went back to Mailly on relief.

Mention was just made of the 2nd Seaforth H. as being involved in the attack and it was probably during this time that Drummer W. P. Ritchie in order to encourage men of various regiments who were retreating jumped up repeatedly on the parapet of a German Trench and sounded the charge, this action plus further gallant action in the day gained him the VC. He was probably close to Cook of the Somersets when the action took place. Throughout the day he carried messages over fire swept ground and showed the greatest devotion to duty.

Next to the 1st E. Lancs. were the 1st Lancs. Fus. who had been carrying out their training in Mailly Wood. They took up their positions the night before the attack in the famous Sunken Road which ran in a northerly direction from the Auchonvillers–Beaumont road just outside the latter. The sunken road was between ten and fifteen feet deep and was shallow at the northern end and overhung with trees at the southern end. Tunnels had been dug from the British front line to this natural trench which was actually in front of the British front line. One of the tunnels was opened before the attack at 3.30 a.m. B & D Companies and the Bde. bombing company with eight Stokes mortars then occupied the Sunken Road. Battalion HQ moved there at 7.0 a.m. They were in front of The Bowery, the White City and Jacob's Ladder.

We have a vivid description of the Sunken Road from John Masefield's book *The Old Front Line*. Masefield described it as being five hundred yards long. From its start in the valley road to a point about two hundred yards up the spur it is below the level of the fields to each side of it. It was the deep part which was like a broad natural trench which was known to the troops as the Sunken Road. The men had built up walls of sandbags in the road itself to reduce the effects of shell fire. Defences that were cut into the chalk of the bank led to the field above where machine gun pits were positioned. The field in front of the Sunken Road was a fairly smooth slope for about fifty yards. Then there was a lynchet like a steep cliff from three to twelve feet high, hardly to be noticed until almost upon it.

From the Sunken Road the troops could not see the sudden dip down but rather a continuous grassy field, at first flat and then rising towards the enemy. The enemy had a small salient thrusting out here and to reach it the British were going to have to run across the field from the Sunken Road, slide down the bank of the lynchet, and then run up the glacis to the parapet. The Sunken Road was an advanced post or jumping off point. Another name for the Sunken Road was Hunters Lane and the whole point of using this advanced position was that precious advantage time could be gained when the attack commenced. However, mainly because of the unknown geographical hazards mentioned above, the attack by the 1st Lancs. Fus. was to be a disaster.

Geoffrey Malins who was the official war photographer had as his destination before the battle began the position called the White City. When the British arrived on this front in the summer of 1915 they had called this spur slightly north of the Auchonvillers–Beaumont Hamel road The White City, due to the chalky texture of the ground with its trenches, dugouts, headquarters and aid posts. The western edge of it was steep and was virtually a reverse slope which gave protection from German shelling. Barricades of sandbags were erected here and the construction of communication trenches to the front line begun. To this day the area that was formerly the White City can still be traced in outline at the rear of the plateau.

Malins said in his book *How I Filmed the War* that on his way to the White City that he went down a trench called Tenderloin Street. About one hundred yards on his right at the junction of King Street and St. Helena Street his guide pointed out the Bde. dugout. They continued on by way of King Street to Lanwick Street at the end of which was an artillery observer officer correcting the range of his guns. Malins carried out some filming and then the Germans began to use gas shells. He returned to the White City and when it was dark an officer took him to Jacob's Ladder. They retraced the earlier journey to King Street and followed it to Jacob's Ladder. It was a sudden open space as if the trench had been sliced off and it left a clear view of the British front line trenches and also beyond them. He was on the bank of a small valley and leading down from the position were about twenty five steps hence the name of Jacob's Ladder. This seemed to Malins to be a very good position from a photographer's point of view. The German lines could be seen some seventy yards away and the plan was for the Stoke guns to barrage the German second line from the Sunken Road. They returned to the White City and the Colonel invited Malins to film the 1st Lancs. Fus. in the Sunken Road. They occupied it during the night by tunnelling for about fifty yards through the parapet and under no man's land then sapped up into the road. Malins went to the Sunken Road and came across the Battalion who had bayonets fixed and were crouching as close to the bank as possible. He set his camera going. Time was getting on and at 6.30 a.m. on 1st July he prepared to return. The attack was timed for 7.20 a.m. He wanted to obtain some footage there before filming the mine explosion under Hawthorn Ridge. The Fusiliers were cut down as soon as they left the Sunken Road as were the companies who had come to join them in the attack. Malins returned to Jacob's Ladder but most of it had been blown down by now. He found a new place for his camera on the side of a small bank, this side of the British firing trench. He pointed his lens towards Hawthorn Redoubt which was due to be exploded. This position was well protected by sandbags and led off from a trench called the Moving Staircase.

After noon the attack was called off and there were left over a hundred men lying wounded in the Sunken Road. At 6.0 p.m. the road was evacuated, apart from a small holding party, snipers and shelling having caused havoc. On the 4th the remains of the Battalion marched to Acheux Wood.

It is now time to tell the story of the background to this planned mine explosion. I have depended mainly on the history of the Royal Engineers and the *Official History.* The attacking plan included provision to destroy the Hawthorn Ridge with a mine. The ridge or redoubt was part of the German front line defence of Beaumont Hamel and is just to the left of the road when one comes from the village itself on the Auchonvillers road. The mine was coded H 3 mine and work was begun in the spring of 1916. It was 75 feet deep and was directed towards the Ridge which was 1,050 feet distant. By the end of May the mine gallery had been driven 900 feet, and was giving considerable trouble because of the hard chalk and also because of the number of flints in the face. Silence was of course paramount and the face was softened by the application of water. The material had to be carefully dug out in order not to disclose what was going on, to the Germans. South of H 3 mine were two saps named First Avenue and Mary; both had emplacements for Stokes guns, and were well forward into no man's land. Russian Saps usually were named after the communication trenches which led into them. The large mine under Hawthorn Redoubt was laid by the 252nd Tunnelling Company but there was to be a great mistake at the last minute, as there was disagreement over when the mine should be blown. The VIIIth Corps Commander Lt. Gen. Sir Aylmer Hunter-Weston (late RE) wanted to fire it four hours before zero at 7.30 a.m. This would result in the crater being occupied and possibly consolidated before zero hour. The German alarm would then have subsided. The views of GHQ were however against this plan, on the grounds that it was more likely that the enemy would occupy the crater first and therefore have the advantage. In the end a compromise was made which was probably the worst of the alternatives. The mine was to be fired ten minutes early i.e. at 7.20 a.m. This was therefore against the advice of the Engineers and it resulted in the very situation occurring that initially was planned to be avoided. The Germans were to have ten minutes warning of the attack and they were to make full use of this time. It is difficult to believe that they did not know that the actual beginning of the attack was other than 7.30 a.m., there had been enough signs and captured Allied prisoners and other intelligence would surely have indicated this time to the other side.

The explosion of the mine was to begin the battle and also provide the first objective. The 2nd R. Fus. were the battalion of the 86th Bde. who were to seize the Ridge and in support were the 1st R. Dub. Fus. and to their left were the 16th Middlesex Battalion. Their left rested on the Auchonvillers road and opposite were the 1st Lancs. Fus. in the Sunken Road. The Fusiliers lay just north of the River Ancre and were in position at 5.15 a.m. as the bombardment was reaching a crescendo. Later a smoke barrage was put down. The artillery had to lift ten minutes early because of the early blowing of the mine. This alerted the Germans even more. Malins has given us a graphic description of the actual explosion and says that the ground where he stood with his camera working gave a mighty convulsion and rocked and swayed. The earth rose in the air to the height of hundreds of feet and with a grinding roar fell back upon itself. All that was left was a mountain of smoke. He was filming during all this period and produced what is possibly the most famous image of the War, and one that is reproduced in countless books.

The crater itself was 130 feet across and 40 feet deep. The Redoubt was completely destroyed with three sections of the German garrison with it. Many neighbouring dugouts were blocked. Despite all this devastation the Germans were able to recover and to man their remaining positions and even stand on their parapets in order to fire at their attackers.

It was D Company of the R. Fus. who were first into action and they rushed forward with machine guns to occupy the craters but were met by a German barrage together with machine gun fire. Five minutes later it was zero hour and the whole line began to advance. D Company when they reached the crater were only able to occupy the nearest lip as the Germans had already occupied the other side. The attack was a complete fiasco and not only were the Fusiliers and the Middlesex Battalion cut down but also the Lancs. Fus. advancing from the Sunken Road, John Masefield described Hawthorn Ridge as being littered with the Middlesex dead.

The 2nd R. Fus. were relieved on the 4th July by two battalions of the 4th Division. Lt. Col. A. V. Johnson of the 2nd R. Fus. had been wounded at Hawthorn Redoubt. Later after the battle Masefield visited the area and said that 'Right up on top, well behind our front line and close to one of our communication trenches, there is a good big hawthorn bush, in which a magpie had built her nest'. The crater now marked with a group of trees can be easily reached by a footpath which runs between two fields and is the highest point in the area.

Next to the 1st Lancs. Fus. in the attacking line were as I have said, the 16th Middlesex Btn. and their objective was to support the Fusiliers and also to provide a left flank to the 2nd R. Fus. who were advancing on Hawthorn Ridge to take advantage of the great mine explosion. The 16th Middlesex were part of the 86th Bde. of the 29th Div. and had been in Acheux Wood from the 23rd June until they marched to Auchonvillers on 30th June where they bivouacked having arrived at 10.30 p.m. The battalion was mainly made up of men from Public Schools and in the early hours of the 1st July they moved up to assembly positions namely to Cripp's Cut and Cardiff Street. The Bde. was to assault the German trenches from a point about 100 yards west of Hawthorn Redoubt to the northern edge of Beaumont Hamel. The attack was stopped by machine gun fire and not by German artillery and there was terrible havoc. It was a death trap that the Middlesex Battalion found themselves in, being enfiladed by machine gun fire from the north and very few men got beyond this point. The survivors were relieved at noon on the 3rd and moved back to 88 Trench and Auchonvillers and on the 4th they went back to Engelbelmer and Mailly Woods. In November 180 bodies of the battalion were found in the Sunken Road.

The 1st R. Dublin Fus. were part of the 86th Bde. in support to the 2nd R. Fus. who were attacking against Hawthorn Ridge, but their departure was held up by the failure of the Fusiliers to progress and at noon the attack was abandoned. The Battalion remained in the area for three weeks and then withdrew to reserve about Mailly Wood. They provided working parties and consolidation teams.

On the right of the Dublin and Royal Fusiliers were the 2nd SWB and they were to attack towards Y Ravine but the story was once again the same as all along this front on this terrible day and they lost over 400 men in casualties. They remained in the Somme line until nearly the end of July. Mixed in with the SWB were the 1st Borders and they attacked through the same line having formed up just beyond St. John's Road, a Sunken Road which ran from Auchonvillers to Hamel. Thurles Dump was to their left on the road itself. The actual objective for the battalion had been the Beaucourt Trenches which seems a very optimistic objective to have. Anyway they made little progress, and on the 8th were back in camp at Acheux. The battalion most written about was the 1st Newfoundlanders. The men had been in France for three months and had made the village of Louvencourt their home having by the end of June spent 34 days in billets there. They therefore had a special relationship with the local villagers. The plan for 1st July was for them to form up in Hamel Road which was renamed St. John's Road and to simply follow in the steps of the attacking Bdes. They were to begin their progress at 8.45 a.m. They would use bridges placed for them by the 87th Bde. and proceed on to Station Road where they would pause to reform, and then continue . . . This was the plan.

On 30th June they left Louvencourt heavily laden and marched via the east of Acheux, by-passing Mailly; they struck out across open fields south of the village in single file for nearly half a mile. They were temporarily held up at Tipperary Avenue which was a deep communication trench which they had helped to dig and it was 2.0 a.m. before they reached their destination and were in deep dugouts in St. John's Road support trench. Their 750 yard section was directly opposite Y Ravine. Behind them to the left were the 4th Worc. and to their right were the 1st Essex. The last named were supported by the 2nd Hampshires. Battle HQ was established in Fethard Trench about 150 yards in front of the Newfoundlanders and to their right.

The attack was a total disaster and not helped by the artillery keeping to a pre-arranged timetable. Instead of bringing down fire on the German trenches, they were keeping to their plan of lifting their fire every two minutes and were now shelling to the east of Station Road whilst troops were pinned down in no man's land. The Aid Post was in St. John's Road but the battalion was virtually annihilated with 14 officers and 219 other ranks dead or died of wounds and 12 officer and 374 ranks wounded. There were also 91 other ranks missing. The officers had been dressed like the men but each officer had gone into action carrying a walking stick and pistol and was without a rifle.

On the right of the 2nd SWB were the 1st KOSB who were to advance towards Station Road. They left their communication trenches on the northeast side of St. John's Road, and were to the right of the Newfoundlanders; they reached trenches to the north of Mary Redan and faced towards Beaucourt Station, in a parallel to Y Ravine. They were here until 4.0 p.m. when they withdrew to Fort Jackson which was a defensive redoubt in the rear of their support line. Here they passed the night and many casualties had been saved by falling back into the point of Mary Redan, where no man's land was at its narrowest. Fort Jackson was where their Corps Boundary lay. To the rear of the 1st KOSB were the 1st Essex who began their assault at 8.45 a.m. and held the line Mary Redan–New Trench Regent Street. At 5.0 a.m. on 2nd July they were back at the Thurles Dump position with Piccadilly on their right. The next day they were relieved by the 5th Glosters.

The last battalion to be mentioned for the action on 1st July is the 1st R. Innis. Fus. who advanced towards Station Road, but were mainly gunned down by German machine gunners firing from Y Ravine, they suffered 568 casualties in a few minutes of whom 246 were killed.

The casualties of the 1st Newfoundlanders were the same as those of the 10th W. Yorks. at Fricourt on the same day.

In his history of the 1/8th Worc. Battalion Edward Corbett says that at Beaumont Hamel that the caves and quarries should have been occupied and not the lines, and the defeat caused a complete breakdown in morale and discipline and that the men had helped themselves to the emergency rations and rum.

Behind the Essex Bat. were the 2nd Hampshires who had comparatively few casualties and spent their time in the Mary Redan front line sector, and

THE SOMME, 1916.
VIII. CORPS ATTACK ON THE 1ST JULY.
BEAUMONT HAMEL & SERRE.

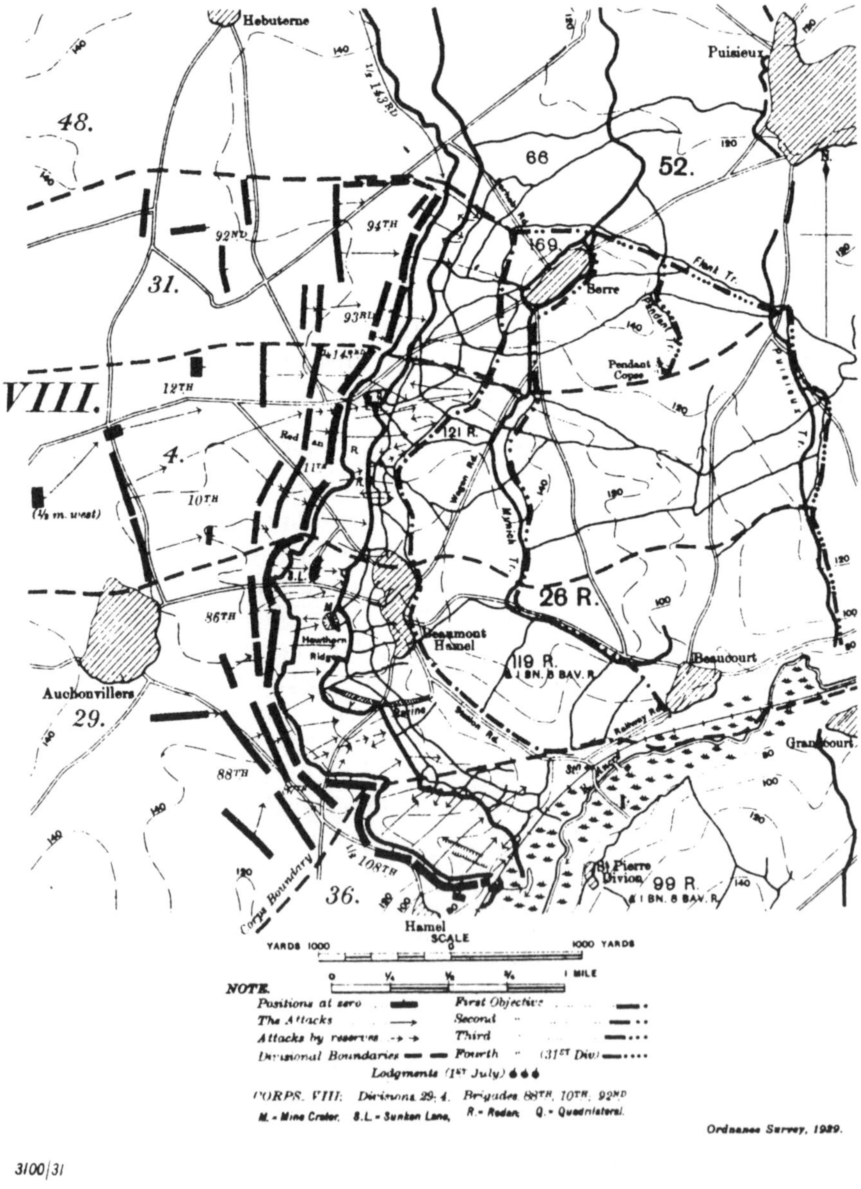

Ordnance Survey, 1929.

3100/31

came out of the line on 10th July.

A. H. Cook of the 1st Somerset LI Regiment said in his book *A Soldier's War* that on the 2nd July that they found their Brigade reserve at Mailly Maillet and at the roll call none of the 26 officers who had gone into action had returned and the casualties amongst the other ranks were 478. It seemed to him that the previous day's battle had been a test of the respective merits of heavy artillery and machine guns and the machine guns had won. Strategically the result of the attack had been absolutely nil. Lord Strang who was a Sec. Lt. with the 4th Worc. and who was in the Hawthorn Ridge sector to the left of the 48th Div. said that the show on the 2nd had been called off. (Liddle).

Pte. J. Sandiford who was a stretcher bearer on the night 1st/2nd July mentions gas shelling at the Sucrerie, and on the 3rd he was still involved in bringing in the very many wounded.

On 8th July the 1st KOSB returned to Acheux from the front.

On 29th July the 20th Div. relieved the 38th in the hilly country between Beaumont Hamel and Hébuterne.

The right of the line rested about half a mile north-west of Beaumont Hamel on the south side of the Redan Ridge spur and overlooking the village, which lay in a narrow valley some hundred feet below. From the crest of Redan Ridge the line ran rather east of north into some lower ground, facing Serre and extending to a point 1,200 yards north-west of it. There it formed a salient and turned back, rising to the Divisional left flank at a place known as Sixteen Poplars. At a crossroads lay a sugar refinery which at the end of July was in ruins, shelled by the enemy. An avenue of elm trees ran back from there which at night concealed batteries.

H. D. Paviere was Sec. Lt. with the 3rd Glosters and was seconded to the 61st MGC Brigade. (Liddle). At the end of July he entered the line in the area of Beaumont Hamel and took part in a machine gun barrage of 14,000 rounds which appeared to be of little effect.

David Rorie in his book *A Medico's Luck in the War* said that in early August his Division was taking over the line at Beaumont Hamel in preparation for the next battle which was put off until mid-November.

In his Memoirs Harold Macmillan when serving with the Gren. Guards said that his battalion moved up into the right sub-sector of the Beaumont Hamel line and were greeted with some pretty heavy shelling, and suffered a great number of casualties.

On 3rd September a further attack was delivered between Hamel and Beaumont Hamel.

In his book *Mind's Eye* Edmund Blunden wrote that Beaumont Hamel was a fortress and a masterpiece of German brainwork, spadework and ironwork. He was serving with the Sussex Regt. and they were restricted to trenches a little apart from its western tree stumps. He describes them as beautiful trenches except for an ugly corner or two. Over them the September sun burned and a young line of aspens 'silvered with musical restlessness' at their western entry.

Behind the trenches they lived in a sort of log cabin which was annexed to Second Avenue Trench. To the north they could see the grey structures of the White City another local headquarters position. Blunden's position was just above the old Beaumont Road, a cave existed under a hill with a crevice in the roof, through which a heavy trench mortar shot up 'flying pigs'.

From the *Artillery & Trench Mortar Memories 32nd Div.* we have the following extract: 'On 22nd October they reached Mailly Wood which was full of Scottish troops who belonged to the 51st Highland Division. They had suffered 46 casualties the night before through German shelling. The 32nd Div's new positions were in Hunters Trench, a front line position looking into Beaumont Hamel, which was only about 500 yards; Clive Trench which was about 100 yards in the rear of the British front line but more exposed to the enemy. The trench was only a trench in parts; it was really the back of a steep hillock and ladders were placed against it for the infantry to see over the top, it must have been 11 or 12 feet high. Their chief object was to cut the enemy front and support line wire on both sides of the Beaumont Hamel–Auchonvillers road. On 25th October the rain fell in torrents in the morning and the planned attack was postponed. On 26th October in the afternoon there was a great aeroplane fight, this took place slightly north of Mailly Maillet. This village was continuously shelled during this period. The Trench Mortar Batteries were billeted behind Mailly in huts and at the end of the month the batteries were between Mailly and Engelbelmer 161 Battery was at the last named.'

Lt. W. H. Livens had been experimenting with gas near Gough's HQ at Toutencourt and under his supervision they let go 2,300 lbs of gas on the night of 28th October into the enemy's position near Beaumont Hamel. The cylinders were make shift things and were launched out of extemporised mortars which could only throw a short distance, but on bursting, the cylinders emitted a high concentration of gas, and thus caught the Germans before they had time to put on their masks.

From *Artillery & Trench Mortar Memories 32nd Div.* we learn that on 1st November a Capt. Dyson was at the HQ at the windmill and on 7th November one of the contributors to this book noted that it seemed very hard to keep 155 Battery in such a horrible place as the White City when they had nothing on earth to do except sit still and be shelled. The White City was described at this time as being a long row of dugouts in the chalk with open ground behind them. On 11th November tanks moved up to the White City ready for the 13th November battle. At this time the Germans were retaliating with gas and high explosive against Mailly.

A. A. Milne in his autobiography described the battalion objective as being the Beauregard Dovecote; he was with the 11th R. Warwicks. The attack was postponed however because of continuous rain. He was sent home in November with a mystery illness and a very high temperature. It made him almost physically sick to think of the nightmare of mental and moral degredation . . . it seemed impossible to him that any sensitive man could live through another war.

General Gough had been preparing an attack against Beaumont Hamel, Beaucourt and Serre for some time and a brief improvement in the weather had allowed it to be finally planned for the morning of 13th November. The gains to the south of the River Ancre had put the troops in a position to take the German positions in enfilade. They were in the marshy ground around the river itself though the attacking troops would have to concentrate at the few points where the marshes could be crossed and the Germans could cause havoc because they commanded the Thiepval heights. The line actually crossed the marshes and at St. Pierre Divion the marsh could be covered by enfilade fire from three sides.

The valley led up from the River Ancre to the ruins of Beaumont Hamel which formed a natural stronghold by the junction of several uplands and as a result the area was broken and more difficult to fight over then most parts of the western front. The ruins of the village had provided the Germans with very good facilities for its defences and it was honeycombed with extensive caves.

We learn, in the accounts of the battle, a lot about these caves and I wonder if their importance has not been slighty exaggerated. Anyway we are told that they were capable of sheltering several battalions from the effects of shell fire and that they ran along the whole of the village of Beaumont Hamel. There was also of course the very famous Y Ravine which ran along the southern edge of the village. It had virtually precipitous banks, from which two arms emerged from the main stem in the direction of the British lines, it bristled with dugouts and was intersected by several trenches. It could contain a garrison and could easily be reinforced from the trenches or from Station Road which was behind it and connected to the village with the Ancre. The sunken roads too lent themselves to being ideal for troop shelter and these included Hunters Lane and Waggon Road. Cave entrances were in both of these. Waggon Road ran in a north-westerly direction from the village across Redan Ridge and was deeply sunken and riddled with dugouts. On the north side of the village was a valley flanked by Beaumont Hamel that ran parallel to the Y Ravine, the whole of the high ground between the ravine and the valley was thickly defended by thickly wired defences. As usual the Germans had the best of the ground and therefore had good reason with all these advantages to think that the place was impregnable.

The battle of the Ancre was to last from 13th November until the 18th, it is also known to some as the second battle for Beaumont Hamel. Those involved were 111 Corps: the 48th Div. from the Fourth Army and 11th Corps which contained the 18th, 19th and 4th Canadian Divs. V. Corps which included the 2nd, 3rd, 32nd, 37th, 51st and 63rd Divs. XIII Corps from which the 31st Div. was represented and finally the 120 Bde. of the 40th Div. who were under the command of the 31st Div. The 32nd Div. were involved between the 17th and 19th November and the others from 13th November until the 18th.

For reasons of space I am only to cover in any detail the actions of the 2nd and 51st Highland Divs. The actions of the 63rd (Naval) Div. is in the section on Beaucourt.

The Sixth Bde. of the 2nd Div. was on the line where the Serre front became the Beaumont Hamel one, and to their front was the German stronghold called the Quadrilateral. This was the northern part of their Redan Ridge defences. To the north-east was Beaumont Trench and beyond that Waggon Road. The 13th Essex were to be on the right of the attack and the 2nd S. Staffs. on the left. To their rear were the 17th Midd'x and the King's. The Essex went into the trenches on 11th November facing the Quadrilateral. The attack became a stalemate in the mud and they were relieved by the 1st Dorsets on the 16th and returned to Mailly and then went by lorry to Vauchelles-les-Authie.

To their left the 2nd Staffs. entered the assembly trenches south of Serre on the 12th and after being involved in the fighting were relieved by the 4th R. Fus. on the 15th and returned to Ellis Square and into rest billets at Louvencourt and then by bus to Mailly.

The 17th Midd'x left Mailly at 11.16 p.m. on the 12th and their objective on the 13th was to be Pendant Copse, which was to the rear of the adjoining village of Serre, and which had been one of the objectives on 1st July. There was confusion and muddle in the fog as much of the wire was uncut. Legend Trench was held and on the 15th they were relieved by the 4th R. Fus. and returned to the support trench in Ellis Square area and then to Mailly. On the 16th they bussed to billets at Louvencourt. The 4th R. Fus. marched up to their assembly point one mile south-east of Engelbelmer on the 15th to act as Bde. Reserve and up to Station Road arriving there at about 2 a.m. They were there until the 18th. An attack was planned to attack the junction of Puisieux and River Trenches with Miraumont Alley north of the river. On the 20th they were relieved and went back to the German Third Line and on the 26th went to billets at Mailly. On the 13th the 1st King's moved up to support the 13th Essex and on the 15th parties of King's were involved in cutting off the Quadrilateral position.

Still in the 2nd Div. but next Bde. down the line to the south came the 5th Bde. who also faced Redan Ridge. The facing battalions were the 24th R. Fus. and the 2nd. HLI. Behind came the 17th R. Fus. and the 2nd O & BLI. The 17th R. Fus. was the right support battalion. The 24th R. Fus. was the only one of the four Fusilier Batts. that were part of the 2nd Div. which was to take part in the initial attack. The 2nd HLI had come up the night before the attack and began using tapes which had been laid out in no man's land because over the months the trenches had become so deep. Within six minutes of their attack the enemy line had been captured together with many prisoners. Two companies of the 23rd R. Fus. were sent up to support the 2nd HLI in an unsuccessful attack on Munich Trench. The 2nd HLI were relieved on the 14th and went back to Mailly before embussing for Bertrancourt.

The 17th R. Fus. had left Mailly Wood at 10.15 p.m. on the 12th and had passed through the lines and with the 2nd O & BLI had attempted to advance from the German Third line to Munich Trench and Frankfurt Trench. After 10.30 a.m. the front was reorganised with the Battalion holding Crater Lane

Trench. Small parties penetrated Munich Trench which was part of the German front line, but in general their part of the attack failed. The 17th R. Fus. were relieved on 16th/17th November.

The 2nd O & BLI had taken over the Hotel de Ville area of Mailly on the 11th and after dark on the 12th had moved forward to assembly trenches. 'A' Company was at Valade Trench north of Sixth Avenue. 'D' Company thence southwards. They formed the first two waves of the Regimental attack. 'C' Company was in the north end of Mountjoy Trench and 'B' Company thence towards the White City. Regt. HQ moved to join with the 24th R. Fus. in Buster Trench from the White City. 6th Bde. failed to progress on the left and the O & BLI were withdrawn with the 17th R. Fus. to Mailly on the 17th.

The 22nd R. Fus. were part of the 99th Bde. of the 2nd Div. and assembled at Bertrancourt on the 12th and at 1.30 a.m. on the 13th began their march to the trenches near Mailly. The battalion moved up into Sixth Avenue and waited for the 5th Bde. to move. At 5.45 a.m. amidst a terrible bombardment they moved into the old British front and support lines. HQ went to the White City. They were in a defensive position on the south side of the Quadrilateral. On the 14th two other companies joined in. The Germans were holding on to the Quadrilateral which was a cluster of trenches on high ground to the north. On the 15th it was taken and on the 16th they were relieved by the 15th HLI and went into billets at Mailly. During this fighting the writer H. H. Munro, better known as Saki, had been killed by a sniper. He was a Lance Sergeant with the 22nd R. Fus. aged 45. His last words were said to have been "Put that bloody cigarette out". Munro had written many stories, including one called *Birds of the Western Front*.

The 2nd Div. between Beaumont Hamel and Serre did not share the success of further down the line. German defences were broken into in places but nowhere on a sufficiently wide front to make a serious gap, so that by nightfall those who got through had either to retire or be taken prisoner. The German line was restored intact.

The 153rd Bde. of the 51st Div. had the whole of Y Ravine within its objective and beyond Munich Trench and beyond it Frankfurt Trench. The Bde. consisted of the 6th Black Watch and the 7th Gordons who were attacking battalions supported by the 5th Gordons with the 7th B. Watch in reserve. The 6th B. Watch were in Mailly Wood on the 11th and their own objective was to be Y Ravine and they were to enter it from the north and bomb their way southwards instead of using the frontal attack method used on 1st July with disastrous results. On the 12th they left Mailly Wood. The mine explosion in front of them was the signal for the beginning of the attack at 5.45 a.m. on the 13th and this was accompanied by a tremendous barrage. At 9.0 p.m. the battalion was established on the Green Line. In the forenoon of the 14th the battalion was to hand over to the 4th Gordons. After two days fighting they marched back to camp behind Mailly Wood.

The other assaulting battalion was the 7th Gordons and they had taken four hours to reach the line in appalling and muddy conditions. It was also very foggy. However the right of the battalion took several lines and reached its objective which was Station Road known as the Green Line. The left side fared less well but many German prisoners were taken. The 7th had to fall back on Station Road. The 6th Gordons in Bde. reserve battled forward. The advance then continued into Beaumont Hamel. It was stubborn work clearing out the enemy from the underground positions. In addition to there being deep cellars and mined dugouts there were also the limestone caves. The deep tunnels and catacombs had been places of refuge in the Wars of Religion and the Germans enlarged them and made an underground network of them, using strong points and redoubts like Redan Redoubt.

The Germans set up rockets to signal their artillery to open fire on the Allied positions but the mist hampered the defenders. The 6th B. Watch and 7th Gordons had entered the German barrage area and the first signs of the progress of the attackers to the enemy was a series of long continuous 'hurrahs' that came through the mist from the direction of Beaumont Hamel. The enemy knew then that the British had broken through their defences. The bombing parties of the BW had effected an entrance into the German trench from the western end of Y Ravine. The right of the 51st Div. was held up but the left succeeded in pushing through on a wide front into the village. The capture of Frankfurt Trench was not attempted.

The 5th Gordons who were the supporting battalion helped in capturing the southern end of Beaumont Hamel and reached the second line. The 7th B. Watch had come up from Mailly Wood and reached the reserve trenches in St. John's Road by 1.30 a.m. on the 13th. Their objective was also Station Road (the Green Line) and Beaumont Hamel. In Y Ravine they were mainly providing carrying parties. The attack succeeded and on the 15th the Bde. were relieved and returned to bivouacs at Mailly Wood until the 18th. It was frosty during this time which would have greatly improved conditions in the battle where it was so muddy. A word should be at least put in for the artillery, on the 13th there were more guns firing in the rear around Beaumont Hamel than there were on the whole 1st July front. It was a predominate factor at Beaumont Hamel. The capture of the stronghold of Beaumont Hamel by the 51st Div. must have surprised the Germans because they had thought it to be impregnable. The number of prisoners numbered over 7,000. However to the north Serre had proved to be as difficult to capture as it had proved on 1st July. The final line at the end of the battle took in the Quadrilateral, part of Redan Ridge across Lager Alley and Waggon Road and then downwards to Beaucourt Trench and Beaucourt itself. Beaumont Hamel itself had fallen early in the November battle.

Initially the 51st Div. attack consisted of using the 152nd and 153rd Bdes. The land in front of them included Y Ravine and to the left the southern section of Waggon Road and to the right the end of Station Trench and Station Road. In the middle was the village of Beaumont Hamel itself. The 152nd Bde. consisted of the 5th Seaforth H, 6th Seaforth H, 6th Gordons and the 8th A & SH. An underground mine signalled the start of the battle and many machine gun bullets were discharged into the mist followed by the assaulting troops. At 5.45 a.m. on the 13th the 5th SH had led the attack with their left flank on the Auchonvillers–Beaumont Hamel road. Their final objective being a German trench 200 yards east of the village. There was uncut wire and dense fog, and the British barrage went too far ahead. But despite this, the German line was mainly carried. The seond line was also carried but the third line was more stubborn. In the evening the battalion went through Beaumont Hamel and consolidated the final objective. They captured 600 prisoners out of 1,700. The Battalion remained in the line until the night of 14th/15th November during which time they repelled several enemy counter-attacks. Their casualties of missing wounded or killed during these two days were 292. On the 19th they were back in the line after a short rest.

South of the Hawthorn Crater were the 8th A & SH who had suffered from machine gun fire before the front was carried. Eventually the German line was carried and the advance continued into Beaumont Hamel. The enemy was slowly cleared from dugouts and cellars and a line established on the eastern edge. Booty included machine guns, mortars, ammunition, bombs, grenades and an armourer's shop. Two tanks came up the road from Auchonvillers but became bogged down.

The 6th SH left their camp at 9.30 p.m. on the 12th and marched towards the trenches. On the 15th having been successful they returned to camp at Mailly and buried their dead at Mailly Military Cemetery.

On the night of the 13th/14th the 6th Gordons of the 152nd Bde. and the 4th Gordons of the 153 Bde. took over the Green Line.

After the battle was over the 20th Bde. of the 7th Div. arrived in the area and they used as a Batt. HQ a deep German dugout on the south-west spur. It was a most elaborate affair with separate dining and sleeping facilities. The left Bde. was badly off as it was further back in the White City which was always wet and most unhealthy. Later on the dugout north of Mailly known as Apple Trees was used. This not being in chalk was drier and much better. An ADS or CP was in the village in November.

The Cemeteries:

The Ancre British Cemetery is on land a quarter of a mile south of the village on the west side of the Albert–Miraumont road, a little west of the railway and the river. The great majority of officers and men who are buried in this cemetery fell on 1st July, 3rd September or on the 13th November.

Beaumont Hamel Military Cemetery is about 500 yards north-west of the village close to the Auchonvillers Road, the cemetery rises from near the road in two rows. The graves are mainly those of Lancashire Fusiliers and of casualties from the November battles. A little west of this cemetery is the memorial to the 8th A & SH almost on the site of their Batt. HQ. At Beaucourt is that of the 63rd Naval Div. which took part in the same victory and in the Newfoundland Park, west of the village are those memorials to the 29th Div. and the 51st which included the 8th A & SH who captured the village itself and Y Ravine in November.

Frankfurt Trench British Cemetery is named after a German trench about a mile north-east of the village which remained in German hands until the German retreat in 1917. It contains graves of 161 soldiers from the United Kingdom who fell in November 1916 or in January 1917. The cemetery is approached by a long path leading north from the road between Beaumont Hamel and Beaucourt. It commands wide views in all directions over the battlefields of 1916–1918.

New Munich Trench which like Frankfurt Trench is named after a former German trench is about 150 yards west of Waggon Road and stands on high ground. It is approached by the same path as that to Frankfurt Trench. Munich Trench was occupied by the 51st Div. on 15th November. New Munich Trench was dug on the previous night by the 2/2 Highland Field Company and a company of the 8th R. Scots. Fus. It contains the graves of 146 soldiers. Munich Trench Cemetery is about 150 yards west of Waggon Road and stands on high ground. It contains the graves of 126 men from the United Kingdom. Waggon Road Cemetery contains 195 graves of which 49 belong to soldiers of the Border Regt. (11th Lonsdales) who attacked on the Ancre between July and November 1916.

Redan Ridge Cemeteries: Redan Ridge lies to the north of Beaumont Hamel village and was named from The Redan a group of British front line trenches of 1916. The first one contains the graves of 154 men from the United Kingdom who mostly belonged to the 4th Div. which attacked between Beaumont Hamel and Serre on 1st July and the 2nd Div. who fought here on 13th November.

Redan Ridge No. 2 Cemetery is on lower ground about 100 yards west of the old German front line and contains the graves of 279 soldiers from the UK who mostly fell in July or November and who belonged to the 4th, 29th and 2nd Divs., men from the Lancashire and Hampshire Battalions. Redan Ridge No. 3 Cemetery is on the line of the old German front and contains the graves of 67 soldiers mostly from the 2nd Div. who fell in November.

Y Ravine Cemetery was made in the spring of 1917 and contains the graves of 328 soldiers or sailors of the Marines of the RND from the UK and 38 from Newfoundland. They mostly fell on 1st July or 13th November respectively belonging to the 29th Div., the 51st, and Royal Naval Divs. The Cemetery is within Newfoundland Park, just south of the southern fork of the ravine. After the War the village was helped in its recovery by the town of Winchester in Hampshire and a new road with poplars flanking it was built. In the nineteen thirties a decayed pill box was still there as well as some old nissen huts which French peasants still lived in.

Newfoundland Park or the Parc de Terre–Neuvien is on the D 73 road between Thiepval and Auchonvillers. It is north-west of the Ancre river and valley. It is also north-west of Hamel, south of Beaumont Hamel and south-west of Beaucourt.

The Park was named after the Newfoundland Regiment who had been formed at the outbreak of the War as a result of 'popular feeling in the Dominion'. The battalion had reached France via Egypt and in March 1916 was sent to the Somme region. On 1st July it took part in the attack on

Beaumont Hamel which was a total disaster and cost the regiment 715 casualties. The attackers were virtually decimated after the explosion on Hawthorn Ridge.

After the War H. A. Taylor in his *Goodbye to the Battlefields* wrote that a little west of the railway was a strange building (which was later replaced) and which had not been there before the War, or during it. It was built of logs, on a slight eminence, it came as a great relief from the monotony of new red brick. This was the lodge of the Park and was a replica of the log cabin of the oldest settlers of Britain's oldest colony. The modern house of the Park Superintendent can be seen towards Thiepval, and below, over the same ridge where the skeletons of the 'Tree of Death' rises in front of the former German trenches, is the ridge where the kilted Scotsman Memorial to the 51st Highland Division stands. Tall fir trees grow around the statue, the sweep of which is interrupted in the hollow by Y Ravine Cemetery. This ravine was a German position from which their machine guns wrought devastating fire; obstacles to dugouts were cut in the ravine sides. Between Hawthorn Ridge Cemetery No. 2, hidden over to the left, and the 51st Divisional Memorial, is the smallest of the Park cemeteries; Hunter's Cemetery. A small wall encircles the Cross of Sacrifice around the base of which are the headstones of 46 men, mostly of the Black Watch and Gordon Highland Fus., who died there when the area was captured by the 51st Div. in November 1916. It stands at the upper end of Y Ravine.

Hawthorn Ridge No. 2 is 460 metres south of No. 1, a little west of the top of Y Ravine. It was made by 'V' Corps, as V Corps No. 12, in spring 1917, and seven isolated graves were brought in after the Armistice. It contains the graves of 190 soldiers from the United Kingdom, mainly of the 29th Div. of whom the great majority fell on 1st July. The Park covers more than 80 acres of which some 40 acres are in the original sector of the Newfoundland Regiment of the 29th Div. attack on the 1st July.

The 29th Div. Memorial stands at the entrance to the Park and all around are the grass covered trenches of the battlefields as left in 1918. At the base of the great bronze Caribou is the Memorial to the Newfoundland missing, on land and sea; the names of over 800 men are listed on the bronze panels. The site of the Caribou marks the site where they left for the attack on 1st July.

The ground which the Park occupied fell into German hands in March 1918 and was retaken on 26th August of the same year on the same day as Thiepval Ridge. The grass covered trenches are clearly and well preserved in the approximate state that they were in 1918. If anything they are much shallower than originally because the ground levels have altered. It is an excellent place for a visitor to try and interpret at least part of the Somme battlefield, and the American novelist F. Scott Fitzgerald probably visited it in 1924 and published the following description in his novel *Tender is the Night* (1934). 'Dick turned the corner of the traverse and continued along the trench walking on the duckboard. He came to a periscope, looked through it a moment, then he got up on the step and peered over the parapet. In front of him beneath a dingy sky was Beaumont Hamel; to his left the tragic hill of

Thiepval. Dick stared through his field-glasses, his throat straining with sadness. He went along the trench, and found the others waiting for him . . . – "This land here cost twenty lives a foot that summer", he said to Rosemary. She looked out obediently at the rather green plain with its low trees of six year's growth . . . "See that little stream – we could walk to it in two minutes. It took the British a month to walk it – a whole Empire walking very slowly, dying in front and pushing forward behind. And another Empire walked very slowly backward a few inches a day, leaving the dead like a million bloody rugs. No Europeans will ever do that again in this generation" . . . "this western-front business couldn't be done again, not for a long time, the young men think they could do it but they couldn't. They could fight the first Marne, but not this. This took religion and years of plenty and tremendous sureties and exact relation that existed between the classes . . . You had to have a whole souled sentimental equipment going back further than you could remember. You had to remember Christmas, and postcards of the Crown Prince and his fiancée, and little cafés in Valence and beer gardens in Unter den Linden . . . They came out of a restored trench, and faced a memorial to the Newfoundland dead . . . After that they got in their car and started back towards Amiens. A thin warm rain was falling on the new scrubby woods and underbush and they passed great funeral pyres of sorted duds, shells, bombs, grenades and equipment, helmets, bayonets, gun stocks and rotten leather abandoned six years in the ground . . ." '

Beaussart

The village is to the north-west of Mailly–Maillet on the Bertrancourt road and it was here that Edmund Blunden of the 11th R. Sussex Battalion (116 Bde. 39th Div.) noted in the autumn that the personnel of the Battalion had vastly changed since the start of the battle. Of the original four hundred very many were either dead or wounded.

Beauquesne

The village is to the north-west of Puchevillers on the D 23 road and is close to Vert–Galant. It was chiefly known for its association with Sir Douglas Haig who moved his advanced HQ here on 27th June. It is ten miles from Querrieu where Rawlinson had his HQ and General Gough's HQ was between the two, at Toutencourt.

Beauval

Beauval is a village to the south of Doullens and was a medical centre in that several CCS were established there during the battle. There was also a Motor Ambulance Convoy and an Advanced Depot of medical stores in the village. Casualties were taken by motor to the railhead at Gézaincourt a village to the north-west. The 9th Norfolks (71st Bde. 6th Div.) were in the area on 28th August.

Bécordel–Bécourt

This is a village on the north side of the D 64 road from Méaulte to Fricourt. It was a well used departure place during the battle and supplies were brought up from the main railway line at Dernancourt via Méautle. Battalions used to frequently bivouac on the hill south of the village. The Allies also centred a huge artillery depot in this area of sunken woods. The troops used them and were protected by deep shelters. Villages were flattened and much of the ground was uprooted several times.

Dartmoor Cemetery was begun as the Bécordel–Bécourt Military Cemetery in August 1915. It is immediately north of the village, on the road to Bécourt, and is opposite the communal one. It was used by battalions holding that part of the line. In May 1916 the name of it had been changed at the request of the 8th and 9th Devon Battalions.

Siegfried Sassoon was in the district on the 27th March and wrote 'and in the foreground Bécourt Church tower peeped above a shoulder of hill like a broken tooth'.

At the beginning of the battle the 14th Field Ambulance was established in the village and XV Corps had a walking wounded post here and an ADS. On the 2nd July the 7th Y & Ls who were Pioneers to the 17th Northern Div. bivouacked in fields to the east of Méaulte which might have been at the Sandpits Camp, and then they moved to a deep ravine by the adjoining village of Bécordel–Bécourt. The valley was packed with guns and the battalion spent several days there in dugouts. In early July Sassoon recorded in his diary that they (the 1st R. Welch Fus.) reached the hill above Bécordel at 1.45 a.m. and slept for an hour in the long grass with guns bombing and flashing all around in the valley below. The battalion later reached Heilly at about 7.45 a.m. on the 6th. On the night of 14th/15th July the 4th Suffolks (98th Bde. 33rd Div.) moved up through Bécordel to the position between Fricourt and Mametz, the battle of Bazentin Ridge was raging in all its fury.

On the 17th July the 1st E. Surreys (95th Bde. 5th Div.) bivouacked on the slopes of the hill just south of the village.

Norfolk Cemetery is on the east side of the road to Bécourt and to the north of Dartmoor Cemetery. Units left for the front line from behind where the Norfolk Cemetery is situated. It was begun by the 1st Norfolks in August 1915 and was used by other units including the 8th Norfolks until August 1916. It lies in a valley running north and south and on the roadside has a brick wall and is surrounded on three sides by a hornbeam hedge. It contains the graves of many men of the 21st Div. who had successfully captured the Divisional objectives between Sausage Valley and Fricourt, including the grave of Major Stewart Loudoun-Shand VC (see the Fricourt entry). On the 6th August the 2nd R. Welch Fus. marched to the hillside behind Bécordel where they remained for a week. On the 13th August they moved to Fricourt Wood. For most of the week there the weather was very hot.

On 30th August they marched in a downpour on busy roads to their former bivouac, the sun baked slope had now become a slough up which two horses couldn't drag a messcart. A camp had to be improvised. At this time it was rumoured that there were as many as 9,000 horses and mules in the vicinity and 17,000 at Méaulte.

The 21st Manchesters camped in the village from the 31st August before moving to Albert on the 8th September.

Dartmoor Cemetery was designed by Edwin Lutyens and had a Dressing Station next to it at the beginning of the battle. Buried there are Lt. Col. Allardice – an Indian Army officer who commanded the 13th North'd Fus. and Lt. H. Webber a sixty-eight year old officer as well as Sgt. Lee and Cpl. Lee, a father and son serving in the 10th London Artillery unit, who were killed on the same day in September. The Cemetery contains 773 graves. In September XV Corps MDS was established in the neighbourhood. A mention is made of tented bivouacs as being there in mid September.

The 9th KRRC (42nd Bde. 14th Div.) moved to their old camp at Bécordel on the 17th September before going to Buire the next day.

Alexander Aitken in his book *Gallipoli to the Somme* says that in either September or October the New Zealand Infantry camped on a ridge near Bécordel overlooking Fricourt in the zone of heavy artillery. Batteries were all around, a battery of six inchers, in cages of netting, two six inch naval guns, long nosed monsters, contrasting with the stubby howitzers whose cough was heard from Bécourt Wood on the opposite slope. The French 75s were far away on the right camped on a crest commanding a view of a six mile radius from Thiepval to Longueval. In front of the left hand slope of the valley were the ruined bricks of Fricourt. The valley rose suddenly on the right to a chalk spur named King George's Hill, with a great mine crater gouged in its side. On the lower slope of this spur was the old British front line and nearer Aitken's camp, the old support lines now tumbled in.

From Fricourt a line of white road ran behind the hill to Mametz and Montauban hidden from view. The stages of the battle were clearly and visibly marked by a rising series of woods: Fricourt Wood topping Fricourt and some distance beyond the larger and infamous Mametz Wood; and above again and much further away the straggling trees of High Wood on the left; the more extensive Delville Wood on the right, where the opposing lines faced each other. To the left across the valley between Fricourt and Albert the ground rose to the ridge of Thiepval–Pozieres, with the wood of Bécourt in the foreground. In 1917 Dartmoor Cemetery was hardly used. The New Zealand Division erected a memorial to their officers and men who fell near Flers in September and October 1916. The 100th MGC also erected a memorial to their losses in July 1916.

Bécourt

South of la Boisselle was a valley which ran from Bécourt in a north-easterly direction crossing no man's land and continuing through the German trench system in the direction of Contalmaison Wood, it was known as Sausage Valley. Bécourt is separated from Bécordel–Bécourt by Bécourt Wood.

The Military Cemetery is on the west side of Bécourt Wood and on the south side of the road to Albert. It was begun on August 1915 by the 51st Highland Division and carried on by the 18th and other Divisions in the line until the Battle of the Somme. It continued in use chiefly by Field Ambulances until April 1917. It is surrounded on three sides by Bécourt Wood. Bécourt Village and the nearby chateau were in the British lines from which units moved off to the front.

At the end of June the Tyneside Scottish lines included Bécourt Wood in which the chateau was almost hidden. It was their HQ. The Bde. HQ at the time was in a small two roomed house which was part of the farm called Bellevue about a mile to the rear of the village. On 30th June the 11th Suffolks were in the wood part of which was used for its HQ. They were part of the 34th Div.

George Butterworth the British composer served with the 13th DLI and the 68th Bde. which in the latter part of June had been sent south to Amiens. After marching by easy stages, they bivouacked at Millencourt, and moved up to Albert, where they lay in trenches one night. On the 4th July the battalion marched to Bécourt Wood (The Divisional objective was Contalmaison village to a point just west of Bailiff Wood both inclusive). From the 7th to the 10th July the Bde. took part in the fighting on the Contalmaison front. The 2nd KRRC (2nd Bde. 1st Div.) bivouacked in the wood before going to Scotts Redoubt near Contalmaison on the 17th. On 19th July a Gloster Battalion bivouacked in Bécourt Wood and due to the fine weather found it 'agreeable'.

C. E. W. Bean the Australian Historian arrived at Pozieres on 31st July and camped on the edge of Bécourt Wood.

On 31st July also the 11th R. Warwicks. moved to a reserve position about Bécourt Wood. The battalion itself occupied the wood, and battalion HQ was also there. The traffic rolled continuously onward, past the chateau, and raised clouds of dust which hung about in the hot, sultry air, and mantled everybody and everything with garments of white. The chateau had become a hospital, and many of its rooms were in good condition, whilst the heavy shade of the wood surrounding protected it from the broiling sun and dusty thoroughfares. Several trenches ran through the wood and the enemy shelled it with resulting casualties. When not engaged the 11th R. Warwicks. spent time in examining the captured German defences and in particular those of the crushed and battered village of Fricourt, the scene of especially heavy fighting. During the nights the artillery displayed great activity, and after dinner it was customary to mount the opposite rise, where a wonderful view could be had of the line of bursting shells. Several howitzers were domiciled in the vicinity and added their voices to the clamour. On 3rd August the 34th Div. held a front from the western edge of High Wood to a line of trenches running east and west and about 300 yards north of Bazentin le Petit. On the 13th August the 2nd KRRC were back again for one night in the wood before joining Divisional Reserve at Mametz Wood. The 2nd KRRC were back yet again in the wood between the 21st and 26th August and then again to

Mametz Wood and back on the 11th and 12th September.

In September the chateau was still hardly damaged when it was used as a dressing station. Graves had been made in the former gardens.

On 22nd September the CO of the 9th Y & Ls was buried in the wood, he was Lt. Col. A. J. B. Addison, aged 49, son of General Addison, and had been killed on 1st July.

On 26th October the camp was 'churned up'. In mid November next to the dressing station in the chateau was a huge cemetery where padres were busy burying the dead. There was a wireless station also at the chateau that possibly connected with Bde. HQ at Mametz Wood in map reference S 13 b 3.9.

Bellevue Farm

The farm was to the south-east of Albert on the Méaulte road. At the beginning of July it was the home of the Royal Engineers and also of the Tyneside Scottish Brigade (34th Div.). The 9th Green Howards (69th Bde. 23rd Div.) returned to the vicinity of the farm on 11th July and later in the battle a cinema was established there for troop entertainment.

Bernafay Wood

Bernafay Wood is on the northern side of the D 64 Montauban–Guillemont Road or on the eastern side of the road to Longueval D 197 from Maricourt. The wood was very nearly captured by the British on 1st July the first day of the Somme battle, after Montauban village had fallen. Beyond it is Trônes Wood which is some 300 metres distant. In following the battle the two woods should really be considered together rather than separately. The line reached on 1st July and also maintained, ran from the eastern outskirts of Montauban south-west through the Briqueterie to the Bois Faviere. Patrols had been sent out and the wood was found to be empty except for a few Germans who were made prisoners.

I have depended a lot on material from *The Other Side of the Hill* which first appeared in the Army Quarterly in 1927. On 1st July and close to the front of the new British line along the northern slope of the Montauben Ridge and Caterpillar Valley, the bed of a small winding stream that rose in Trônes Wood flowed westward to the River Ancre. On the far side of the stream the ground rose fairly steeply, 150 feet in 1,000 yards, and reached the German second line trench that was on top of the slope between Bazentin le Grand and Langueval. On the right Trônes Wood lay across the head of the valley, the German second line then swung round southwards from Longueval on the high ground beyond the wood through Guillemont and then towards Maurepas. Its capture would threaten the rear of the Germans who were still holding on around Ovillers and Thiepval. The capture of Contalmaison and Mametz wood on the left flank was to be carried out simultaneously with the advance through Trônes and Bernafay Woods on the right.

In the afternoon of 1st July the remaining German defenders of their front trenches on the Montauban Ridge, the left of the 28th Reserve Division and the right of the 12th Division, together with the 6th Bavarian Reserve Regt. (10th Bavarian Division) were back in the German second line – Bazentin le Grand–Longueval–Guillemont, having abandoned several of their battery positions along Caterpillar Valley and in the two woods. It was at this point that the British should have followed up their success as both woods were almost completely devoid of enemy troops.

In the evening the German 12th Reserve Division arrived in the area in great haste, and at 6.45 p.m. came under the command of 28th Reserve Division. It was ordered to advance eastwards and to regain a footing on the Montauban Ridge near to Montauban village and Favière Wood. The last named was held by the French. This advance was planned to be made with the right, the 51st Reserve Infantry Regiment, past the north of Combles and then north of Guillemont and on towards the north-east corner of the village of Montauban. The 38th Reserve Infantry Regt. were to attack Favière Wood in the centre, and to the left the 23rd Reserve Regt. was to advance between Maurepas and Curlu, on the north bank of the Somme.

It was the eastern front of the new Montauban salient which was the target and on the 2nd July, north of Bernafay Wood the leading companies of the 16th Bavarian Regt. moved up from Caterpillar Valley and came across an advance post of the 17th Manchesters in Triangle Point, to the north of Montauban on the road to Bazentin le Grand. This post was annihilated and about a hundred German troops entered Montauban Alley at this point. British artillery fire helped to push the attackers back to the dead ground of Caterpillar Valley. The 20th King's (89th Bde. 30th Div.) repelled the 51st Reserve Regt. at the Briqueterie and they fell back into Bernafay Wood or back into the dead ground between the wood and Maltz Horn Farm.

During the same day, the 2nd July, the 20th King's sent out patrols into Bernafay Wood and found it unoccupied. Orders were given to occupy the wood at 9 p.m. on the 3rd.

In *The Other Side of the Hill* the 27th Bde. (6th KOSB on the right and 12th R. Scots. on the left) advanced from the front of the Briqueterie–Montauban which was due south on the Maricourt Road. They captured isolated pockets of Germans and the wood was claimed by the 9th Scottish Div.

Fraser-Tytler said that on the night of 2nd July two battalions had captured the wood and so the British held everything up to the the skyline except Trônes Wood. Troops on the right walked into Bernafay Wood almost without any opposition but were restrained fron advancing further.

There had been a brief bombardment and the few Germans in the wood made no attempt to fight. The 12th R. Scots. discovered four deserted field guns and one machine gun, but the wood once in British hands proved to be a dismal prize, for the Germans continuously shelled it with considerable violence, thus causing numerous casualties. After a week the wood presented a woeful spectacle. Before 3rd July a man on the firing line could only see a few yards in front of him, but after two or three days of shelling he could see the far end with little difficulty, a formidable strongpoint was dug in the centre of the wood. The two Scottish battalions had only six casualties.

In early July R. B. Talbot Kelly wrote that as FOO in the RFA that he was aware of a German field gun battery as being captured in Bernafay Wood. It had splendid dugouts for its personnel.

In *We Band of Brothers* G. W. Warwick wrote that on 8th July that they (the South Africans) saw Bernafay Wood come under very heavy German fire, huge explosions and columns of smoke, and he knew that the 2nd South African Regt. was in the wood.

Trônes Wood was reached during the fighting between 2nd July and 13th July and taken in the second advance of 14th July. The line of the second advance ran in part from the east of Delville Wood down to the south of Trônes Wood. Guillemont, Ginchy and the complete capture of Delville Wood were the next objectives. But it was two months before they were to be in the hands of the Allies.

Warwick reported that they marched up to Bernafay Wood with a guide in the lead, the wood was under heavy shell fire and the guide was killed. They were thus ordered to about turn and on reaching the road again they went forward to the front line trench which crossed the road that was held by the 10th A & SH (26th Bde. 9th Scottish Div.). They then relieved the 2nd SAI in the wood and Warwick's half of 14 Platoon occupied a large dugout whose entrances faced the Germans. Parties of six men from this dugout were posted on the edge of the wood facing Delville Wood.

On 11th July he was posted with five others to a listening post on the edge of the wood which again was facing towards Delville Wood. They came under heavy machine gun fire as well as violent shell fire that was bringing down the trees in the wood. On the 12th the Germans concentrated their artillery on the wood and every square yard was shelled. Sergeant Bubce took six of them to set a guard at the post. As they emerged from the entrance to the dugout they raced through the shelling, to be met with rifle and machine gune fire from the Delville Wood direction. At 9.0 p.m. a shell burst over the six men and Warwick was hit by pieces of shrapnel but was able to drag himself back. His wounds were attended to and he was given plenty of rum. That was the end of his share of the fighting for the time being. On 13th July he was carried from the Regt. Aid Post in Bernafay Wood through a trench held by the A & SH. On reaching Maricourt–Montauban–Longueval Road his stretcher was placed on a two wheeled limber which trundelled him along. At a point sufficiently far enough behind the line the stretcher was lifted into a small motor ambulance, which took him to a dressing station at Maricourt. When in hospital he was told that the 2nd SAI had captured and held Delville Wood. On 14th July the 2nd Suffolks were again in the line and were occupying the line on the eastern side of the wood.

In his book *Field Guns in France* Fraser-Tytler said that on 23rd July he was given orders to enfilade a hidden ravine which was strongly held by the Germans in the French sector opposite Hardecourt. This consisted of moving howitzers right forward with their trails towards the Germans, and shooting back over the salient into the ravine. The site was not far from the north-west corner of Bernafay Wood. On 24th July he went to Hardecourt laying the communication lines as he went. From there a distance of about 6,000 yards from the gun he measured and managed to register the ravine, which proved to be a principal stumbling block in an abortive attack that the French had made a few days before and thus they were very keen to heavily shell it before the next attack. The howitzer was close to the main road to Longueval and was continuously shelled.

On 28th July Fraser-Tytler went up to the advance gun again, and found a French 75 team nearby whose objective was the same ravine as his. They had found some wonderful dugouts in a deep quarry and he advised the British team to share it with them. He located the French battery and finding their line had been broken, he ran a line to his own battery. The French shelled the ravine vigourously all day.

Insidious communication trenches led from Bernafay Wood to Waterlot Farm which would probably be Longueval Alley. The 2nd HLI Batt. HQ was here at the end of July. The 8th KRRC (41 Bde. 14th Div.) moved to the quarry from Delville Wood for a couple of days, the 22nd/23rd August, before returning to Delville Wood. The 2nd S. Staffs. Battalion HQ was here on 8th August as part of the attack on Guillemont and General Jack in his Diary wrote that when he was Commanding Officer of the 2nd W. Yorks. from 27th August they were in positions at the north-east of the skeleton of Bernafay Wood. His bivouac was described as Camp D. The Camp however consisted of nothing more than a few shell holes and a few bits of derelict trenches which the men had covered with their waterproof sheets, a couple of tarpaulin and several sheets of corrugated iron. Batt HQ was in a small German trench which was made more inhabitable by the discovery of an old door and a small piece of metal sheeting for a roof; a small disused shed and stove that had been found added to the amenities. Another battalion who had their Batt. HQ in the quarry at the north end of Bernafay Wood was the 21st Manchester (91st Bde. 7th Div.). The battalion was gassed whilst there, before moving on to Pommiers Trench with their HQ moving to the top of Trônes Wood. After being in the limelight for the first part of July Bernafay Wood hardly receives a mention in August but does come to life again in September. By 5th September Falfemont Farm and Leuze Wood both near the village of Combles had fallen to the Allies and the artillery of the 35th and 56th Divisions who had covered the Divisional front, by their bombardment and barrage had rendered the success possible. Their gun positions had been in Chimpanzee Valley and the area south-east of Bernafay Wood had been subjected to heavy bombardments and considerable gas shelling. The Prince of Wales at the time on the staff of XIV Corps was a frequent visitor to the Division and Bde. HQ in the forward area as well as to the rest bivouacs and transport lines.

On September 3rd the 9th Devons drew detonated bombs at the quarry to the north of Bernafay Wood and the Welsh Guards stayed briefly at the wood in the period 11th/13th September. A forward depot had been established in the wood for the 15th September battle containing sufficient RE stores for the purpose of the initial assault. During the days before the attack the REs laid out and marked several routes for horse-transport leading to the wood, and began the heavy task of clearing from the northern end of the wood through Trônes Wood to Ginchy.

In *Turning Point* H. P. Robinson wrote that around the middle of September Bernafay Wood that had been captured at the outset of the battle and where there was comparatively little resistance, was less utterly stripped of all semblance of a wood than many others in the area. Of course there were no leaves on the trees, no signs of Autumn foliage anywhere; but the wood still stood reasonably compact, with a regular outline and enough bare poles standing to make it still a wood of moderate density.

On 16th September the 1st Lincolns were part of Brigade Reserve in a valley bordering the edge of the wood. A Camp X was mentioned as being the Bernafay Wood Camp.

Hugh Wansey Bayley author of *Triple Challenge* who was at the time an MO with the 1st Scots Guards wrote that having left Happy Valley and seen tanks for the first time they had moved forward to Bernafay Wood on the 12th September. They relieved the 1st Welsh Guards at Ginchy. They had previously rested at Carnoy in a deep little valley where a howitzer was at work and the Cavalry were collecting. He refers to a Lt. E. Holland as being killed by a German sniper around 13th September and on the night before the battle he takes part in a champagne supper in the HQ dugout in Bernafay Wood. This would have been the night of 15th September and he says that there were about 15 men there several of whom were to be killed on the next day. Sir Iain Colquhoun was there. They moved off soon after midnight for the 6.20 a.m. start. Their assembly area was the apex of a shallow salient immediately in front of Ginchy. About 750 yards on the right flank was the German Quadrilateral. They went down the western edge of Bernafay Wood turning right handed along the northern margins of Bernafay Wood and Trônes Wood and on into Guillemont and so by the Ginchy–Guillemont Road to their assembly trenches on the right front of Ginchy.

In *Other Ranks* W. V. Tilsley wrote that a communication trench which was named Hop Alley ran down to a point of Bernafay Wood, ending by the roadside. Cookers came down the slope to Bernafay and soon they were munching ravenously at thick slices of bacon. German observation balloons confined them to a trench and a battery of 5.9s barked away in broad daylight from the starkness of Trônes. An ambulance crept into view behind the cookers and pulled up at the dressing station. (It should be remembered that the book quoted here is a novel.)

On 25th September the 9th Norfolk Regt. were billeted in the area. The 61st Bde. as part of 20th Div. held the area on their own for a week at the end of September. The 60th Bde. was in support near Trônes Wood and the 59th remained at Carnoy in reserve. The Div. HQ returned to Bernafay Wood. On the 29th September the Divisional Artillery HQ was also established here. The actual batteries were in a valley about 800 yards to the north-east of

Delville Wood, known from its map reference as Toc 7 Valley. The 20th Division had been one of the more successful Divisions and had done good work in the battle to take Guillemont.

In early October Aubrey Smith of the LRB who was stationed at Méaulte said that the battalion was bivouacked near the wood. The big guns had moved much farther down the slope and a broad gauge railway was being laid down close to Guillemont. On one occasion he had to take a water cart beyond the wood.

The 10th KRRC (59th Bde. 20th Div.) were in the wood for six days from the 2nd October to the 8th, they had come up from Carnoy and were on their way to Méaulte.

During 1st/2nd October the 35th Bde. of the 12th Division was in reserve in the wood and on the 2nd the 7th Norfolk Service Bt. marched up to the wood. On the 10th the Norfolks held the front line with other battalions. On the 12th there was an attack on Bayonet Trench around 5.0 p.m. this trench ran from the north-west of Guedecourt across the Ligny–Thilloy Road and then slightly south-west. The objectives were Bayonet Trench and Scabbard Trench and secondly, to capture Luisenhorf Farm which was adjacent to the Flers Road on the east side. The left of the Norfolks secured 100 to 200 yards of Scabbard Trench. This was part of the battle for the Transloy Ridges. On 20th October the Div. HQ of the 8th Div. opened at the wood and on 22nd October at a short conference of battery commanders on the march General Fagan announced to General Jack's horror that the 8th Div. were to assault presently. The W. Yorks. were to act in close support to their Bde. on 23rd October. So in the afternoon accompanied by McLaren his second in command Hawley and some orderlies set off on foot to the valley beyond Ginchy–Flers Ridge to select the best position for the battalion which was to march at dusk. The Prince of Wales visited the Div. HQ of the 17th Div. at this period.

On 30th October the 9th North'd Fus. were at D Camp near to Bernafay Wood which they described as being a sea of mud and without tents. The roads en route had been full of mud and shellholes.

On the same day the 2nd RWF withdrew to reserve between Trônes and Bernafay Woods and conditions were described as being wretched for all. 'Tents that leaked were issued and during heavy showers it looked as if the bellying tarpaulin roof of H.W's. crazy shack would release a flood.' After a while they made a short move to the Briqueterie which was south-west of the wood. Here the tents were in another sea of mud but there were blankets for the men. At the beginning of November rain fell in torrents and the wretched shelters between Trônes and Bernafay Woods were just mud holes.

Bernafay Wood North Cemetery was opposite the northern edge of the wood, a little east of the Longueval–Maricourt Road. It was begun by an ADS and used from July to October. It then became a front-line cemetery which was used until April 1917. Lt. Col. C. S. Taylor of the 28th Heavy Artillery Group RGA was buried there having been killed on 6th November.

In 1935 according to the *Ypres Times* there were five giant trees (old scarred trees) that stood out in the 'new' Bernafay Wood like so many grotesque aerial masts. The wood could still be seen right through.

Postscript:

The communication trench that connected the northern parts of each of the two woods was called Longueval Alley. Another CT was called Irish Alley. The terrible crossroads at the south-west corner of the wood was on one occasion the scene of destruction of a whole Bde. who were on their way to Delville Wood.

A sunken road from Hardecourt joined up beyond the Briqueterie just before the 'terrible crossroads'. A railway ran at some time from Guillemont through Trônes Wood across the south-west part of Bernafay Wood to the Briqueterie.

Bertrancourt

The village is south-west of Courcelles au Bois and north-east of Acheux (D 114) where a railway used to be. The British took over the sector from the French in July 1915 and the first burials in the cemetery date from shortly after that time. On 13th June 1916 the 2nd Essex were here on Brigade relief and were involved in cable laying. On 26th June shells fell in the village and especially on the cross roads.

On 30th June the 2nd Lancs. Fus. (12th Bde. 4th Div.) left their camp in the village at 11.30 p.m. and crossed the Mailly–Serre road. At 9.0 a.m. on the 1st July, they had reached the Roman road which ran north-west from Beaumont Hamel and there was much cross fire coming from that village and also from Serre.

At this time there was a MDS in the Bertrancourt village.

From the 11th until the 16th of July the 2nd LF were back in the village again in what was described as a 'pleasant camp'. When on 20th July the 12th Div. relieved the 4th Div. in the line close to Beaumont Hamel their HQ was also at Bertrancourt Camp. Hugh Bayley in his book *Triple Challenge* which covers his period as MO with the 1st Scots Gds. mentions that they camped at Bertrancourt and went into the line at Hébuterne on the 16th August.

The last 1916 burials in the cemetery were after the capture of Beaumont Hamel at the end of November. Eighty graves belonged to soldiers of the Y & L Regiments and one hundred and seventeen to the Lancashire Territorial Battalions, these dated from the 2nd July. In Frederic Manning's book *The Middle Parts of Fortune* he wrote without indicating when, that they marched by the Divisional Artillery HQ at Bertrancourt to Courcelles. They had come from Mailly.

Field Ambulances used the cemetery in 1916 and also in 1917. Also Corps and Divisional burial parties used it in the months of June to August 1918.

Bienvillers-au-Bois

The village is north-west of Foncquevillers on the D 8 Pommier–Hannescamps road and immediately west of Monchy au Bois. There is a road here that also runs south-westwards to Souastre.

The 5th Lincolns (138 Bde. 46 Div.) were here on 20th May. At that time the village was two miles behind the front line and opposite Gommecourt. From then until early June the battalion was occupied building assembly trenches and communication trenches leading to Foncquevillers, which was directly in front of Bienvillers. They also worked on Midland Trench which was an assembly trench to the rear of Foncquevillers.

On 18th June the Sherwood For. were here and at that time guns were everywhere, and in many of the orchards on the outskirts of the village were wheel to wheel. A temporary field hospital had been erected near Saulty Station. Aubrey Smith mentioned in his book that the London Rifle Bde. reported that the guns here, as well as at Bayencourt, St. Amand and Souastre were firing their hardest at the end of June during the pre-battle bombardment. There was an ADS or CP in the village.

At the beginning of the battle Signaller H. G. R. Williams of the 5th City of London Battalion of the 56th Div. noted in his manuscript *Saturday Afternoon Soldiers* (Liddle) that he was in 'C' Company and that they had trenches in the Bienvillers–Foncquevillers district. The Signalmen were billeted at the village school in Bienvillers.

The 11th R. Warwicks. on 3rd July after 16 days in the trenches passed a night at Bienvillers. After standing in the streets of Halloy for two and a half hours waiting for motor lorries, their procession moved off at 8.30 a.m. on 6th July and passed through Amiens reaching Millencourt at 4.0 p.m. At the end of July Bienvillers was Batt. HQ either for the 1/4 Lincolns or 1/5 Lincolns (138 Bde. 46 Div.).

On the evening of the 22nd July the 1/5th Lincolns (138 Bde. 46th Div.) were relieved by the 1/4 Lincolns of the same Division by 7.15 p.m. and returned to Bienvillers, where they were billeted as Bde. Reserve. Brigade HQ was in the village. Having been out of the line for some time they returned to the trenches on the 9th August. During this particular tour gas cylinders were installed in a large number of front trenches to the great disgust of the garrison as they were a constant source of annoyance owing to possible leakage. They could also explode if hit by a German shell!

The 2nd R. Welch Fus. (19th Bde. 33rd Div.) were in billets in the village on the 21st September.

The Military Cemetery is south-west of the village, on the north side of the road to Souastre. There are many graves there from the Ancre battlefield.

Billon Farm, Billon Copse, Billon Valley

The Farm is south of Carnoy and just off the road from Maricourt to Bray. The copse is to the south-west across the road, and the Wood is to the west of

the Farm and Billon Valley leads into it from the south. At the beginning of
the battle the 9th Div. was in Corps Reserve assembled in Billon Wood which
was then two miles behind the front. Trigger Wood and localities where they
sheltered were hidden from enemy view by the crest of Maricourt Wood.

At the end of June the 2nd R. Scots Fus. ADS was at the Farm.

On 27th June the 10th Essex were in the Wood near the French gun
positions which were composed of 1872 howitzers on wooden platforms,
which were on the sloping chalk bank on the south side of the Valley. On 14th
July an Essex Battalion was in the Valley when the Indian Cavalry thronged
the road near their camp. On 18th August the advanced HQ of the 35th Div.
was established at the Farm. The two Bde. HQs were in Chimpanzee Trench.
On the 26th, Divisional HQ of the 5th Div. was in dugouts near the Farm
when the Division itself was on the Maltz Horn Ridge. On 6th September the
1st Norfolks after being at Falfemont Farm were resting at the Farm. And on
18th September the 14th R. Warwicks were at the Farm close to a 12 inch gun
on the railway.

Birch Tree Wood

The wood is north of Fricourt, south-east of Scotts Redoubt and east of
Round Wood.

On 1st July the *Official History* notes that the German machine guns caused
some loss before the leading lines of the 1st Lincolns (2nd Bde. 21st Div.)
reached the edge of Shelter Wood and the much smaller Birch Tree Wood
just beyond it to the north-west. A large number of Germans emerged from
dugouts and engaged the 12th North'd. Fus. The wood was captured but a
strong bombing attack from the right delayed the entry into Shelter Wood.

Birch Tree Avenue which ran towards Peake Woods to the north-east was
occupied by the 13th DLI (68th Bde. 23rd Div.) on 8th July as far as a
captured strong point.

Black Road

According to the *Official History* on 20th July the 5th and 7th Divs'. first
objective was Black Road the track which ran north-north-west to the
southern corner of High Wood. The second objective some 300 yards beyond
and parallel to the first was a track called Wood Lane, which reached High
Wood at its eastern corner.

The 33rd Div. were to cope with High Wood itself. Wood Lane was
untenable but Black Road, was consolidated.

Black Wood

Black Wood was less than a mile from Albert, on the south side of the
Albert–Bécourt Wood Road. It was also south of the Tara Valley and due
west of Bécourt Wood. The 1st Glosters (3rd Bde. 1st Div.) bivouacked here

between 16th August and 20th August. To the south, bivouacs, transport lines, supply depots and dumps of stores were spread over the country as far as the eyes could see, and the strains of other people's bands and drums were heard all day and the greater part of the night. There was also much activity in the air, and batches of German prisoners passed the bivouac daily on their way to Albert.

The 2nd KRRC on 5th September went via Black Wood to the west side of Mametz Wood. On 20th September they returned to Black Wood and marched to Millencourt on the 30th, where they rested.

Black Horse Bridge

Black Horse Bridge led from the central track which ran through Aveluy Wood from Martinsart and over the D 50 road to the west of the wood. It continued over the Ancre and on to the marshes. The Shelters were 150 yards south of Authuille and 1½ miles south of Thiepval. Amongst other battalions the 15th HLI spent rest periods here before the battle. There were massive dugouts and the north south causeway is still there. It is one of the most interesting places to explore in the whole Somme battlefield.

From 23rd to 26th June the 16th Lancs. Fus. were in dugouts here at the south end of Authuille. On the night of 30th June the 14th Bde. moved into assembly positions at the Shelters and at Crucifix Corner, which was to the south. On their way there, the 1st Dorsets on the same day had found the roads thronged with transport, and they passed through battery lines of massed artillery, behind convenient ridges the guns were almost wheel to wheel. The chalk pits were crowded with picketed gorses. They came via Aveluy Wood at 6.30 a.m. on 1st July and then left the Black Horse shelters and went along the Dumbarton Track through Authuille Wood.

The section on Authuille Wood covers this ground.

On 2nd July the 2nd S. Lancs. reached its assembly positions east of the Ancre, crossing the river by Black Horse Bridge.

On 2nd/3rd September bombs and other battle equipment could be drawn at the bottom of Black Horse Road before the troops began crossing the Ancre. On 24th September buses met here and one got away with part of the 1/4 DWR's. One description of it was 'sinister march to Black Horse Bridge on the well known track to Bouzincourt'.

Blighty Valley

Blighty Wood is just south of Authuille village on the east side of the D 51 road between Aveluy and Authuille. T. Slane joined the Y/32 Battery here on 1st June when one gun was positioned at the top of Blighty Wood where 'Bill Jackson' the notorious German machine gunner used to 'play the dickens'. For the following information I have drawn on an unpublished diary of the Worcester Regt. by Brigadier A. C. Johnstone.

On 18th August they went down to their old HQ in Blighty Valley near Authuille Wood in the morning. He also referred to an attack on the right which had gone awfully well as the objective was reached and 500 prisoners had been taken. On the next day he complained about the condition of the trenches that has been handed over to them. On 20th August General Bainbridge inspected the trenches and in the morning the Allied Artillery was causing a lot of harm by falling short. This was the Heavy Artillery who as usual were shooting off the map and had observers miles behind the line. He said that the Field Gunners were much more accurate.

Gunner Price (240 Battery) was positioned at Pozieres at the end of September and noted that he went to a spot near Blighty Wood and for the rest of the battle spent his time as part of a relieving battalion.

Blighty Valley Cemetery is almost at the head of the valley, a small way up its northern bank. It was begun in early July and was used until the following November. It then contained the graves of 212 soldiers. It was later expanded after the Armistice. The Register has 1001 names in it, about half of whom are casualties from 1st July. It can be reached by travelling between Aveluy and Thiepval, it is on the eastern side of the road.

In P. Longworth's book on the War Graves Commission *The Unending Vigil* he mentions that Blighty Valley was ploughed up during the Second World War.

Bois des Tailles

The wood runs along the side of the valley and stretches across the Morlancourt to Bray road (D 1). It is south of Méaulte. On 1st June the 8th Lincolns (21st Div.) arrived here and worked on the railway at Bray as well as carrying on with their training. At the end of May Sassoon described the wood as being full of men from the Devons and Border Regiments. A new Dressing Station was set up between there and Corbie and the tents camouflaged.

On the 28th June the 21st Manchester were here and on the night of the 30th took up positions opposite Mametz Village.

On 14th July H. M. Davson an artilleryman reported that they marched to the wood in inclement weather and the camp, which had been used previously by the French reserves had been left unclean!

On 19th July the whole of 54 Bde. was in the wood, and on 2nd August the 15th and 16th Cheshires from the 35th Division (Bantam) arrived here on the edge of the wood − there were no tents.

From *Andrew R. Buxton a memoir,* edited by E. S. Woods, we learn that after a fortnight spent training they arrived at Bois des Tailles, from Méricourt Station.

I have no date for when the 24th Manchester (Pioneers to the 7th Div.) were in the wood, but when they were there they listened to a concert. In Gilbert Frankau's novel *Peter Jackson* he wrote that his battery had arrived at the wood from Hangest and had bivouacked there. The horses were tethered between the limbers on the red sandy floor of the valley below. They were in action for 18 days and lost some of the battery around Arrowhead Copse.

The 10th KRRC (59th Bde. 20th Div.) were here on 6th September from the Guillemont area, and again on the 11th and 16th September before going up to relieve the 2nd Gren. Gds. in the support line before Lesboeufs.

Bois Français

Bois Français was the name given to the part of the front line that lay opposite the village of Fricourt. To the east of it was a small quarry and to the west, it continued into what was known as Aeroplane Trench as it resembled the shape of an aeroplane with its branching saps.

To the north-west was Wing Corner and the village of Fricourt itself. Bois Français is most known in its connection with Bernard Adams and Siegfried Sassoon of the 1st R. Welch Fus. Adams wrote a book called *Nothing of Importance* which was a record of eight months at the front with his Welsh Battalion, which was published by Methuen in 1917. The book contains maps that show considerable detail of this part of the Somme front and in part deals with the period of the build up to the Somme battle. In the book the names of battalion members were changed by Adams, and Sassoon was known as Scott. We know this from an annotated copy of the book which is in the Faculty Library at Oxford. Sassoon had made the annotations himself.

In his book Adams said that they held the trenches at Bois Français for over four months from February to June. One could have an uninterrupted view not only of both front lines running down into Fricourt Valley but of both lines running up onto the high ground north of Fricourt, with a very good view of Fricourt itself as well as Fricourt Wood. It was also clear that the Germans were able to have a similar clear view of the British lines and communications in the valley. They could not see however the Allied trenches to the east of Bois Français nor had they an enfilade view as the British communications were on the reverse slope of the shoulder of high ground. The British therefore had the advantage. The British could in addition get an amount of enfilade observation of the opposing trenches from a work called Bonté Redoubt or point 87, which was also an artillery OP (observation post) it was about a thousand yards to the west of the Bois Français trenches. A battery of field artillery was at the same time stationed in the gully called Gibraltar, at the head of Happy Valley which was immediately to the south, close to the village of Bray. Another was positioned just west of Albert and these were able to bring enfilade fire on the German trenches. Adams also mentions that howitzers were positioned in all sorts of places, some as far back as at Morlancourt. The woods also contained many batteries and especially the Bois des Tailles. And as the year progressed the woods grew fuller and fuller. When they were out of the line Adams said that they invariably supplied working-parties which could last as long as nine hours. They used to relieve in the daytime and for a time they always used to go up the line via Méaulte until the Germans took to shelling the road. They then began to use an alternative route via the Bois des Tailles and Gibraltar. They had for either route, to cross high ground south-west of Point 71 by way of the trench, but subsequently became out of observation once more. Adams mentioned that there were a series of dugouts along this road, and companies in reserve, headquarters of the RE, a dressing station, stores and field kitchens etc. The rations came up every evening to here from Bray. The position could not be seen by the enemy but they did begin to shell it, after a time. Adams wrote that he thought that the dugouts called 71 North were the best. The maps show these to have been just off the Bray–Fricourt road on the eastern side, and to the south-west of Bois Français. Here the bank sloped up very suddenly from the road and this gave the dugouts security except from shellfire of high trajectory. However it was dangerous to go along the road and turn the next corner, as one was then in full view of Fricourt itself. Adams mentioned that his company which was 'B' held part of Bois Français trenches whilst 'C' Company which included Sassoon held 71 North. Maple Redoubt which was three hundred yards to the south of Bois Français and was the Battalion HQ, contained the RSM bombers, medical staff and stretcher bearers.

The Company HQ was to the south of the Bois Français Quarry at a place named Trafalgar Square which was later changed to a position half way up 76 Street. At Trafalgar Square there were also two signallers and a permanent wiring party. This consisted of a Corporal with five men and they worked by day on concertina or gooseberry wire and at night were out for three or four hours putting it up.

Within the position at Bois Français were several mine craters and these were constantly being explored by either side. To this day the craters can be identified with only cattle now to occupy them. The trench lines were in places only as much as 60 yards apart.

For the next section I have relied heavily on the diaries of Sassoon and include information taken from them which relates fairly directly to the experience of the 1st R. Welch Fus. at this time. In February Sassoon states that Lewis guns and steel hats had reached the battalion, and on 5th February he rode up from Bray and over the hill to the Citadel. The Citadel was a camp further to the south on the road to Bray. On the 21st Major Stockwell became the Battalion Commander. Sassoon in his fictionalised memoirs gives him the name of 'Kinjack'. On the 23rd Sassoon went home on leave and in the Memoirs 'Sherston' brought back smoked salmon for his colleagues. The diary has him back in France on 6th March and on the 16th he is back at the village of Morlancourt. He described the village as being approached from five different roads which converged in a friendly fashion with a little crop of houses. There was a church with a slated tower and a giant vane, round which birds wheeled and cackled. In the hollow ground in the middle, where the five roads met, there was a congregation of farm buildings, round an open space with a pond on one side of it. The long lines of high ground hid the rest of the world. At this period Sassoon was Transport Officer and therefore slept in canvas huts close to the Transport.

In the Memoirs 'Sherston' went up to the front line using a communication trench called Canterbury Trench and then looked for Watling Street. There was a trench of this name and Canterbury Trench was in fact Canterbury Avenue. He passed the support company dugouts at Maple Redoubt which we have already noted above as existing, and then went down to the Company HQ dugouts. There were twenty steps down and this occasion there had been snow. 'Kinjack' wanted the whole of their front re-wired. The return journey was made down Canterbury Avenue to Morlancourt village. According to his diary Sassoon heard on 19th March that his and Robert Graves' great friend David Thomas had died of wounds. In the Memoirs he was buried near the Ration Dump. In reality Thomas is buried at Point 110 Cemetery. On that day Sassoon mentioned that he had escaped to the woods above Sailly–Laurette to be alone with his grief for his dead friend.

Both Graves and Sassoon attended the burial and Sassoon describes it in his diary 'In the half clouded moonlight the parson stood above the graves, and everything was dim but the striped flag laid across them. Robert Graves, beside me, with his white whimsical face twisted and grieving. Once we could not hear the solemn words for the noise of a machine gun along the line; when all was finished a canister fell a few hundred yards away to burst with a crash'.

On 27th March Sassoon began six days in the trenches with 'C' Company which he had joined from the Transport. In the Memoirs he was known as 'Kangaroo' and described a fine afternoon in the wood above Méaulte where there were anemones and bluebells, and also some wild cherry in blossom. He said that the rural spirit of the area had been affected by the presence of supply sheds and RE stores and the sound of distant artillery. He described Bécourt Church as being in the foreground. He also describes their steel dugout as being very hot and that his colleagues Greave and Stockwell were asleep on their beds and the servants were singing and joking next door.

On 30th of March Sassoon explored no man's land with his friend Corporal O'Brien and disturbed the Germans by lobbing bombs at them in the mine crater area. He described the craters as having pools of water in them and that nothing grew near them. Snags of iron jutted from their sides and there was trench refuse in the form of tin cans and coils of wire etc.

On 31st March he carried out more crater bombing and on 2nd April went out of the line. On 10th April he was at 71 North and mentioned further crater bombing. On 14th April he rode near Heilly through a strip of woodland on the hill above Treux and Mericourt. On 22nd April he was back in trenches that were waterlogged!

In the Memoirs he left Morlancourt after Easter and went to the Fourth Army School for a month's refresher course. He left the village on 23rd April and saw supply convoys, artillery horse-lines, dirty white tents of the Red Cross etc.

Spring had arrived. Once at Flixécourt, which was between Abbeville and Amiens he attended lectures and was trained for open warfare, on gas, the bayonet etc. He also got some reading done which included *Mr. Sponge's Sporting Tour* and Lamb's *Essays* and Hardy's *Far From the Madding Crowd*. On 22nd May he returned to Morlancourt at the end of a hot Saturday afternoon. The bus turned off the bumpy road from the town of Corbie and crawled up the steep winding lane. He was introduced to 'Fewnings' and hears that a raid was being planned. In the evening of 23rd May he was on Crawley Ridge which is to the south-west of Bois Français and in looking across to Fricourt saw trench mortars bursting in the village cemetery. Fricourt was a huddle of reddish roofs with an almost demolished church tower, the whiteness of the village was contrasted against the sombre green of Fricourt Wood which was full of German batteries. White seams and heapings of trenches dug in the chalk stretched away up the hill. The sky was full of skylarks.

In the Memoirs on 25th May he took a raiding party to 'Kinjack's' HQ at Maple Redoubt. The raiding party went up to the support trench. The raid's objectives was to enter the enemy lip on the edge of the crater, to enter Kiel Trench at two points and to examine the section of trench thus isolated. Furthermore they were to capture prisoners, bomb dugouts and kill some Germans. They went across the craters and Kiel Trench was quiet. They found that they couldn't force their way through a second belt of wire and 14 men scrambled back. 'Mansfield' was hit and Sassoon carried in a wounded Lance Corporal. Sassoon searched for a Corporal who was down in one of the craters and found him in the second crater with a colleague at his side. A rope was sent for and they got the wounded man back to the parapet. Two men were killed on the raid and ten were wounded.

The diary tells the story.

25th May: The day when the raid took place, the idea being to capture a Boche or two. Twenty seven men including one Officer and Corporal O'Brien took part in the raid. Bombs were exchanged with the enemy and Sassoon who was not officially on the raid counted the men back, when they got to sixteen, he went in search of O'Brien who was said to be wounded. He found him in the right hand crater and despite the Germans firing into the crater at point blank range he went about the preparations to get him out. O'Brien was seriously wounded and being over six foot was difficult to move. Sassoon went back for help and eventually O'Brien was brought back, but was found to be dead. Sassoon went back to 71 North. For his action Sassoon was awarded the MC but the raid was not a success and the CO was pretty sick about the whole business.

In the diary at the end of May he described the Bois des Tailles as being full of men from the Border and Devon Regiments and when walking home he saw Morlancourt looking peaceful in a basin with smoke going up from it. On 31st May he was at the Bluff above Sailly–Laurette and looked at the Somme river with its chain of lakes. On 1st June a Divisional Concert was held in which Basil Radford took part. On 2nd June Sassoon was up at the redoubt and in the evening was in charge of a working party at Bécordel–Bécourt.

On 4th June he was on duty at 71 North. On 9th June his leave came through and he rode to Morlancourt with the Quarter Master in a perfect sunset, the muddy road as they walked away from the Citadel was red in front of them. He drove down to Mericourt Station, probably on 10th June. On

19th June he returned, when the battalion was at Bussy on the Ancre. Bull frogs croaked continuously.

On 26th June in the diary he said that Morlancourt was full of troops and supply columns and that he had passed a large new dressing station halfway between Corbie and the Bois des Tailles. The tents were mostly camouflage colours. On 27th June in a remark on the Allied bombardment he said that the Germans had not retaliated much. As he went along Kingston Road Trench, Fricourt was being shelled. Men of the R. Irish Rif. were going along 71 North. The attack had been postponed and the men were at concert pitch. They were due to enter the trenches in front of the cemetery by Fricourt Station. They marched up to Bois des Tailles and were due to relieve the 7th Borders. In the Memoirs he writes that 'New Trench' had been a good deal knocked about and that they were opposite Sunken Road Trench.

In the Diary on 28th June he was reading Hardy's *Tess of the D'Urbervilles* in 85 Street dugouts. On 29th June there was a steady bombarbment and on 30th June he went down Kingston Road. This was about 500 yards behind the front trench where Sandown Avenue met Kingston Road. The Manchesters were to the right on the edge of Fricourt. In the Memoirs he wrote that the gun at Wing Corner had been silent.

On 1st July he watched the 21st Division advancing about three quarters of a mile away on the left.

Bernard Adams whose book contributed so much to this entry, died of wounds at Serre on 27th February 1917 and was buried at Couin Military Cemetery.

Bonnay

The village is to the north of Corbie and is where the Cavalry waited during the first few days of July. On the 4th they moved to the Merélissart–Allery area.

Bottom Wood

Bottom Wood is to the south-west of Mametz wood and a couple of thousand yards south of Contalmaison. It is adjacent to the Mametz–Contalmaison road. It was taken by the British in the fighting between 2nd and 13th July. John Masefield in his book *The Old Front Line* described it as an oblong wood, and that just above it running diagonally across the spur, was a linchet, once lined with trees. Beyond this was a half sunken track running parallel with the linchet.

In the *History of the 17th Northern Division* it is stated that on 3rd July the leading company of 7th Borders passed on from Railway Alley into the western side of Bottom Wood. They met with obstinate resistance. The Germans held the trench running north and south inside the margin of the wood, where they had their machine guns, and cross fire of other guns came on the left from Quadrangle Trench, a little higher up the slope towards Contalmaison. An immense quantity of stores and material had been captured, particularly in a huge dugout a little south of Shelter Wood, an underground barrack, close to Bottom Wood.

Hedge lines ran from the wood to both Lozenge Wood and Shelter Wood towards Fricourt and from Lozenge Wood battalions used to form up behind the hedge. Shelter Wood was a battalion change over place.

Bouleux Wood

This wood is just off to the right when coming from Combles on the D 20 road to Ginchy and Guillemont. It is long and narrow in shape. For the battle, it cannot be studied without being related to Leuze Wood, which is across the road, and also Combles itself. The period when it was prominent in the fighting was between 12th and 27th September. Ginchy had fallen and the line from Lesboeufs via Morval and Combles was the one that the Allied were attempting to achieve. The fighting was at its most intense in the approaches to Combles which in part were guarded by the Quadrilateral, a German strong point about a thousand yards from Ginchy on the Morval road.

A German railway ran from the direction of Combles around the back of the wood in the direction of Trônes Wood. On 12th September a trench ran through the wood as far as Middle Copse to the west of the wood. On 20th September a new trench was dug by the 5th Cheshires (Pioneers to 56th Div.) and was named Gropi Trench which was the unit's code name. A new trench on the eastern side of the wood was named Ranger Trench. I think the Gropi Trench stretched for about one thousand yards in front of the wood. On 22nd September the 7th Middlesex HQ (167th Bde. 56th Div.) was in a little dell on the right of the line here. The German gunpits were north of the railway embankment to the east of the wood. In Malins' book *How I Filmed the War* he wrote that on a date around 25th September he saw British troops pouring forward over open ground. He says that he raced towards them as fast as possible and filmed them going across first one section and then the other. German shells were falling near them but missing most of them.

Philip Gibbs in writing about the wood after the battle in his book *The Battle of the Somme* said that there had been fierce hand to hand fighting in the wood, and in the centre of it an unfortunate tank was crippled. He says that instead of attacking the wood itself, where the Germans were in great force, the British were ordered to take two lines of trenches to the west of it, and to establish a flank there. The Germans who massed at the wood couldn't there-fore put their machine guns to full use.

The 56th Division held the line in the wood and on the left were the 5th Division. The 6th Division held a short line to their left and then came the Guards Division who were in front of Lesboeufs.

Bouzincourt

This village is to the east of Senlis, west of Aveluy and two miles north-west of Albert. The road to Aveluy is the D 104. The village was used as a Field Ambulance Station from early 1916. The Communal Cemetery was used from March to July 1916. The Extension was begun in May and in the early part of July it was used not only for burials from the Field Ambulances but also for the burial of soldiers killed in action and brought back from the line. It lies in a shallow depression of cultivated land. A MDS was established here at the beginning of July.

Both before and during the battle the road from Bouzincourt to Black Horse Ridge near Authuille Wood was very often used. On 24th June the 15th HLI (14th Bde. 32nd Div.) slept at Knights Redoubt close to the village in bivouacs. The 9th NF (52nd Bde. 17th Div.) were here on 27th June. On 1st July the 1/3 Mon. (Pioneers for 49th Div.) watched the progress of the battle from the high ground or ridge near the village. The 17th HLI moved off from here on the same day on their way up to the line. The 25th Div. during the night 3/4th July relieved the 32nd Div. in the line, with the 7th Bde. on the right and the 75th Bde. on the left. The 74th Bde. at the same time moved from Warloy to Bouzincourt.

On the 4th the 11th Lancs. Fus. (74th Bde. 25th Div.) reached here where they bivouacked in huts. At night on 9th July the 9th Essex (35th Bde. 12th Div.) were in hutments on the western edge of the village. It was a well used camp. Bernard Montgomery (Monty) in a letter to his mother when he was part of 104th Bde. wrote that they were taken in buses to Bouzincourt and from there marched to Aveluy, about a mile west of la Boisselle. One of the Dorset Batts. went back to Bouzincourt and on 14th July was in the line relieving the 96th Bde. The battalion gained ground by digging a trench from their right and joining hands with the 75th Bde. east of the church or where the church used to be. On 17th July the 1/4 O & BLI (145th Bde. 48th Div.) were in huts on the west side of the village with transport in Senlis. They were brought to the village in 36 lorries. On 27th July the 12th Div. HQ was here having previously been at Bertrancourt. On 9th August the 1/4 R. Berks. (145th Bde. 48th Div.) bivouacked outside the village on the Senlis road. The cellars of Bouzincourt were full of men as there was constant long range shelling going on.

Many casualties had occurred in billets that troops occupied outside the village. I should think that the west side was dangerous at this time as troops are more often reported to be camped on the east of the village. The 1/7 Worcesters (144th Bde. 48th Div.) were in Bde. reserve on 13th August and Divisional reserve was camped by the cross roads between the village and Senlis.

The Guards were also camped here in early August. On 18th August the 'Brass Hats' watched the battle from the ridge and these included Generals Gough, Jacob and Birdwood. They were watching a barrage on Leipzig Redoubt. On 28th August W. V. Tilsley in his book *Other Ranks* wrote that they camped here for a week before marching towards the front, the sound of guns getting stronger and stronger. They learnt at this time that Guillemont had at last fallen.

Brigadier Johnstone in his diary of the Worcester Regt. said that he had been given command of the 10th Cheshires whom he joined when the Bde. moved to Bouzincourt. On the next day they moved out to billets about a mile outside. On the 30th which was a 'perfectly vile' day, blowing and pouring with rain he managed to get the Bde. back to Bouzincourt where the men could at least be put under a roof. On the 31st at a little after 10.0 p.m. they suddenly received orders to relieve the 8th Borders in the trenches in the Leipzig Salient.

On 2nd September they moved back except for one company which they left in dugouts at Crucifix Corner. On the 3rd there was a disastrous attack. On the 4th it came on to rain very hard in the afternoon, the trenches had become a sea of mud. On the 5th Johnstone went down to the reserve companies in Authuille in the afternoon. On the 7th they were relieved by the 9th W. Yorks. (32nd Bde. 11th Div.) during the morning and moved back to Bouzincourt. Edmund Blunden also mentions a high velocity gun firing at Bouzincourt and this is probably the same as the above. The Field Ambulance Station ceased to be used in February 1917 when the British line went forward from the Ancre.

Bouzincourt Communal Cemetery and Extension is on the D 104 road. The graves include those of an Irish Chaplain who was Chaplain to the forces and was killed on 5th July. He is buried close to French civilians and his name is Rev. D. O'Sullivan. There are a number of men from the Highland Light Inf. buried here from the early July attacks. There is another cemetery at Bouzincourt which is called Bouzincourt Ridge, which rises north-west of Albert in the Department of the Somme. It was partly in German hands after March 1918 and was re-taken at the end of August by the Allies. The Cemetery stands alongside a track that leads from Albert to Bouzincourt and contains 708 graves.

Bray

Bray is a town which stands on the northen bank of a loop in the Somme river. It is five miles south-east of Albert, due south of Fricourt and south-west of Maricourt. It has a railway station on a local line from Albert to Montdidier. From February to June it was shelled regularly almost every day. Bray Military Cemetery was begun in April by fighting units and Field Ambulances.

G. D. Fairley (Liddle) reported that when he was an MO with the 2nd R. Scots that they were in billets at Bray on 2nd June and that when the beginning of the battle was postponed on 28th June Bray was crowded with camps and horse lines. XIII Corps MDS moved from Dive Copse to a site on the Bray–Maricourt road during the battle and the No. 5 CCS moved here from Corbie via Albert.

The 1st Gordons (76th Bde. 3rd Div.) reached the outskirts of Bray on 5th July at 7.0 p.m. Corporal Robertson of the Worcesters wrote that they were 'getting amongst it now', 'no more quietness'. There were batteries of French guns within 200 yards of them which made a nerve-racking din. He talked with some of the French gunners who showed him all the points of beauty about the famous '75s'. He said that there was a terrific bombardment going on and that a wood near Fricourt was getting pure hell from the Artillery. On 9th July he reported that the wood had not yet been taken and that there wasn't much of it left, just twisted stumps. He heard that they were not going in until it was taken. One of the gun crew told him that three of them flattened the whole village of Fricourt. He said that he could believe it too with the terrible concussion of them. At 5.0 p.m. their sister battalion arrived back from the line and there was great excitement in talking to them, the fighting was described as pure murder. They were only 250 strong having lost 650 men at Fricourt.

On 13th July there was a Corps advance HQ in a steep bank about one mile north-west of Bray. In early September there was a camp called Forked Tree Camp on the Bray–Albert road, and the 6th Division had its HQ in the village. In September the front line having pushed further east, the Bray Military Cemetery was used by XIV Corps MDS. French Observers used the church as an OP until it was flushed out by the enemy. In 1917 the 5th, 38th and 48th CCSs came forward and used it. The cemetery is north of the town, and within Bray itself is a German cemetery with about 1,000 graves. Bray Hill British Cemetery is on the west side of the road from Bray to Fricourt on the southern slope of a high plateau, a little north of a chalk pit. It was made in August 1918. Bray Vale Cemetery is on the east side of the road to Albert, below the steepest part of the hill and it too was made in August 1918.

Bresle

Bresle is a village to the south-west of Albert between Laviéville and Franvillers. During the battle there was a camp here that stood on high ground just out of the village. On 10th November General Haig inspected part of the 15th Scottish Division here.

Bronfay Farm and Bronfay Wood

Bronfay Farm is on the road from Maricourt to Bray, the buildings being on the eastern side of the road. Across the road to the east is a small copse called Bronfay Wood. It is south-west of Billon Wood. The whole area was in the area of the 9th Division at the beginning of the battle. G. D. Fairley (Liddle) MO with the 2nd R. Scots. said that the Battalion on 11th June passed Bronfay Farm on the way up to the trenches. B. Copse was Batt. HQ and U Works (Ludgate Hill) Aid Post was established in West Avenue Communication Trench. On 12th June he mentioned the CP was at the farm. On 27th

June he mentioned that hollows and banks were honeycombed with emplacements. The ADS was at the crest of the hill. It was of corridor dugouts with room for 72 stretcher cases. 12 feet of sandbags were on top of the dugouts.

In early July the 8th Suffolks (53rd Bde. 18th Div.) who were in Brigade Reserve didn't take an active part as they were not called on to support the attack, instead they helped with carrying up ammunition and water. On 7th July when they were passing the farm they met the 2nd Suffolks (76th Bde. 3rd Div.) who were going up the line. The latter played the Regimental March on its drums as each company went by.

XIV CCS and Walking Wounded Post was established from 6th July and the farm at this time was a rest camp surrounded by Bell Tents and on 7th July was the home of the 10th Essex Batt. (53rd Bde. 18th Div.). The wood accommodated the 12th Midd'x (54th Bde. 18th Div.) on 6th July who had marched here from Beetle and Maple Alleys. Ravine Copse was due south of Bronfay Wood and adjacent to Trigger Wood. In mid July the HQ of the 35th Div. (Bantam) was there during their involvement in the battle for Bazentin Ridge. The 1st KRRC (99th Bde. 2nd Div.) were here on the 8th August about 300 yards west of the Farm.

On 26th August the 1st Norfolks (15th Bde. 5th Div.) after training at le Quesnoy bivouacked near the farm and at this time were employed in digging. The 10th KRRC (59th Bde. 20th Div.) bivouacked here on the 15th September. Bronfay Farm Military Cemetery is further along the road to Maricourt from Bray, on the right hand side and just before Billon Farm. It was begun by the French troops in October 1914 but little used by them. It was used by British Troops from August 1915 to February 1917, particularly in the Somme Battle when XIV Corps MDS was at the farm. After the Armistice in 1918 42 graves from March, August and September 1918 were brought in from fields between Bronfay Farm and Bray. The cemetery stands on high ground, commanding wide views on all sides except the east.

Buire

The village is north-west of Treux and south-west of Dernancourt on the D 52 road and was much used by battalions who camped here during the battle. On the 12th July there were horse lines here which extended in every direction, cavalry tracks wound round each end of the village, along which each morning an apparent unending stream of cavalry, both British and Indian with mounted machine gun attachments, horse gunners and signal sections moved up towards the battle. Each evening they returned to wait for what the next day would bring.

In his book *Goodbye to All That* Robert Graves wrote that the 2nd R. Welch Fus. came by easy stages to Buire reaching here on the 14th July. At the time they were close to the original front line where some of his friends had been killed earlier in the year; Thomas, Richardson and Pritchard. On the 7th August the 5th O & BLI (42nd Bde. 14th Div.) were camping in the village and their Battalion HQ was in a house close to the church. After their disastrous time in the fighting for the capture of Mametz Wood the 38th Division came here and many of the men camped in tents in an old orchard.

Half a mile to the east of Buire a supply siding was laid and named Edge Hill.

On the 18th September the 9th KRRC (42nd Bde. 14th Div.) moved to a camp south of Albert which was about a mile to the north of Buire and on the 22nd they moved off with the rest of the Division and used French buses as their transport. On the 11th November the 2nd RWF moved to Buire again and then moved out of the Somme area altogether. The village was often used as a Divisional Rest Station.

Bus-les-Artois

The village is on the D 176 road with the Bois de Bus to the north of it. It is north-west of Bertrancourt and south of Couin and Coigneux. In May the 10th E. Yorks. were camped here in an orchard amongst trees laden with apple and pear blossom. The village was a hot bed of working parties, and the wood at the beginning of June was alive with huts and bivouacs. On 6th June the 5th Sherwood For. (139th Bde. 46th Div.) had excellent billets here amidst beautiful scenery, but the hard training affected their leisure! They spent several days felling trees in Lucheux Forest and were entertained by a concert party called 'The Whizz Bangs'. At the sugar factory a water supply was set up and in mid-June a great ammunition dump had been established here.

On and around 1st July a detachment of the Indian Cavalry were resting their horses in the village. The 12th Div. HQ had moved to Bus, transferred from VIII Corps. In mid July the 7th R. Sussex were in huts and tents in the wood. At the end of July J. S. Ewart of the Scots Gds. noted that they were in camp here, deeply hidden among young oak woods, on the top of a hill. During their stay here they were visited by the King and Prince of Wales. On 13th August they went up to the front line. However Ewart was ill at the time and therefore missed the action at Ginchy Station and at Lesboeufs. On 19th August the 2nd O & BLI relieved the 1st Colst. Gds. in new billets here with HQ under canvas just outside the village. On 21st August the 1st Scots Gds. recuperated at Bus les Artois. There was a MDS in the village. Probably in September the 1/4 R. Berks. were here whilst General Fanshawe was at the White Chateau with his Div. HQ. In November the old huts in Bus Wood were very muddy, the Ancre battle was continuously being postponed and camp conditions deteriorated. Basil Hallam Radford (Gilbert the Filbert) who had fallen to his death from a balloon near Bus and Bertrancourt was buried at Couin.

In November a MDS was still in the village.

Bus Wood in 1985 when I last visited it had a friendly atmosphere with many tracks or rides running through it. I could not find any trace of the Great War Huts.

Bussy

The village is due east of Amiens and south of Querrieu. The 1st R. Welch Fus. (22nd Bde. 7th Div.) were stationed here with Siegfried Sassoon as one of their number on 9th June close to a tributary of the River Ancre. The 6th Cavalry Brigade were here on 15th September.

Butte de Warlencourt

The Butte is just off the main Albert-Bapaume road to the right after the village of le Sars, if coming from the direction of Albert. It is bordered to the south by a narrow road towards Guedecourt and is north of Eaucourt l'Abbaye.

In 1916 the Butte was a chalk covered eminence some fifty or sixty feet high and of Roman origin. It was on the slope of the spur overlooking the Bapaume Road where the Gird Line crossed it. At this time it was higher than it is today and stood out above the rest of the battlefield. It was an unofficial mound which had played a prominent part in the war of 1871 and was honey-combed with many tunnels, even before the Germans fortified it so strongly that it became almost impossible to capture. It gave excellent observation of the low ground to the south-west and also in the opposite direction towards Bapaume in which there were many battery positions. Its possession was important to both sides.

In mid September on the waste torn earth where the front lines lay invisible there was according to D. Boyd *Salute of Guns* no recognisable landmark between the Butte, described as a chalk mound soaring over the fold of land from the left front, and the ruins of Flers. In addition to having a warren of tunnels and strong MG posts it was surrounded by enormously thick belts of wire.

On the 6th October The Tangle trenches on the eastern side of le Sars were occupied but the company was later withdrawn. According to the *Official History* on the 7th the remainder of le Sars was captured when the attack was resumed against the Butte and Gird Lines as far west as the junction of the Gird and Flers systems.

On 9th October, R. Derry who was normally a bandsman with the 3/8 City of London was acting as a stretcher bearer and he himself became wounded. There had been no artillery or tank support to the attack and many troops were killed even as they left their trenches.

Boyd stated that the infantry were to attack the Butte across a thousand yards of country under view through its whole length. The guns were in the open and the slope was dreary beyond description. The attack was in broad daylight just before two o'clock. The infantry moved forward in perfect formation and were mown down piecemeal as they advanced. Again the guns moved forward, to the crest, and were directed on to the German lines to support another futile attack on the Butte.

The *Official History* notes that on 12th October the 9th Div. was to capture firstly Snag Trench and then the Butte and the Warlencourt Line. Included in these objectives was a trench named The Tail, located as running back from Snag Trench towards the Butte, also a mound known as The Pimple at the western end of Snag Trench.

From a Transcript in the IWM, a Mr. R. C. Cooney says, that on the 12th they had to attack up a reverse slope where they were quite protected from the Germans, and then they were to go over the hill where the Germans had their lines with a very powerful machine gun barrage rigged, up which the preliminary bombardment didn't disturb. They attacked in four lines, one after the other, and as each one went over the top it got caught by their MGs and pretty well wiped out. In the last line Cooney found himself the only one on his feet as far as he could see, and so he got down into a hole and stayed there until it was dark. He had bullets through his hat, and he had a belt with a pistol, and a bullet had got inside the belt and out through the buckle; through his trousers and all over the place. But he wasn't wounded.

Boyd noted that on the night of 13th October they pulled out the guns and brought them slowly down the crater field. W. D. Croft wrote that after taking Snag Trench they pushed forward a bit on the high ground confronting the Butte, which he described as a great white cone about 400 yards away. That night they 'dug like beavers'.

The *Official History* of 5th November says the left of the 1/6 DLI (151st Bde. 50th Div.), entered the German position with the 1/9 (151st Bde. 50th Div.), and they later broke through two lines of German trenches reaching the Butte, and established a post on the Bapaume Road, some parties even entering the Warlencourt line. Durham men were seen on the Butte itself but the advanced posts were established in the afternoon. At 10 p.m. the quarry west of the Butte was still held, and 500 yards of the German line, but at about midnight German counter-attacks forced the Durhams out and to a withdrawal.

In *The Machine Gunner* it says that the Durham Bde. of the Territorials attacked the Butte on the 5th November as part of the Fifth Army's preparation for the attack north of the Ancre on the 12th, over ground that was not devastated by heavy shelling. The Butte stood in the way of this offensive, a fortified hill which gave the Germans full observation of the entire Ancre sector. It was imperative that this hill fortress be captured before the main attack took place. The three infantry batts. who were assigned to the task were the 6th, 8th and 9th Durhams and were supported by the 151st MGC and 151st Trench Mortar Battery. Zero hour was 9.10 a.m. The weather was vile, wet, windy and foggy. A ten minute bombardment was intended to soften up the enemy and destroy the barbed wire surrounding the Butte. An Australian Bde. was to assist on the right flank of the 8th DLI but the Bde. along with the 8th DLI was bogged down in no man's land. They found themselves knee-deep in thick gluey mud; many unable to move were shot down. The 6th DLI fared little better. The 9th DLI captured the Butte and its garrison. Late that night the Germans counter-attacked and the 151st Inf. Bde. now decimated had to retire to the original front line where it was relieved by the 150th Bde. On the 5th the Quarry was taken and this was held with Butte Alley. For the 8th and 9th DLI this day was the most disastrous day in the war.

In Haig's *Great Push* the day is thus described: In the morning the Allies gained a footing on the western face of the Butte which the enemy had equipped with a bristling armoury of machine guns, many of which were in concrete emplacements; there was a sunken road leading back to the German support positions.

Several times in October and November the British had attempted to achieve the impossible and each time their attacks failed against the formidable defences. In J. Glubb's book *Into Battle* in an entry dated 25th October–13th November he says that 'A week ago the 8th and 9th DLI attacked the Butte, and they took it, held it all day under heavy shelling and lost it again the next night.'

The period 13–18th November marked the limit of the attack on the Butte. Glubb also says that after a Bde. refit that the 149th Bde. the North'd, repeated the Durham's attack of the previous week. They took over 200 yards of the enemy trenches, but didn't attempt the Butte itself. The *Michelin Guide to the Battlefield* says of the Butte that the Warlencourt Ridge proper consisted of two superimposed eminences; bare plateau about two thirds of a mile in width – now covered with graves – and a chalky torn hillock, which was the centre of the German position. Pierced with subterranean galleries, furrowed with successive lines of trenches, surrounded by a triple belt of entrenchments bristling with barbed wire entanglements and flanked at every angle by redoubts with innumerable mortars and machine guns, such was the ridge like an impregnable fortress which faced the British trenches throughout the winter of 1916–17. Although the Butte was overrun several times by British units the defenders from below ground counter-attacked and drove the attackers off, until February 1917 when the Butte fell into British hands as the Germans withdrew to their new line.

The 6th, 8th and 9th DLI erected crosses on the Butte, the 9th wanting top spot. The 151st Bde. put up a Bde. cross to prevent rivalry. After the War all four crosses were brought back home to Durham.

Charles Carrington in his book *Soldier from the Wars Returning* describes the Butte as 'a dome of gleaming white chalk from which all vegetation had been blown away by shell fire, it was most conspicuous object in the landscape'. It seemed to tower over you with its hidden machine gun posts, which he now believed to be quite imaginary. He had observed the Durhams in their unsuccessful attack from a reserve position far down the forward slope at Prue Trench.

In the summer of 1917 William Orpen in his book *An Onlooker in France* wrote that the Butte stood out on the right, a heap of chalky mud, not a blade of grass round it, nothing but mud, with a white cross on top. On the left the Crown Prince's dugout and Gibraltar. He supposed that these had all gone by then and le Sars and Grevillers were at that time the HQ of General Birdwood. The Butte looked very beautiful in the afternoon light in the summer. Pale golden against the eastern sky, with the mangled remains of trees and houses, which was once le Sars; on the left. But what must it have looked like when the Somme was covered with snow, and the white garmented Tommies used to raid it at night.

In Stephen Graham's book *The Challenge of the Dead* published in 1921 he wrote that one could walk up the Butte as one could walk upstairs, and that there were wooden monuments to the Durham Battalions and also the 2nd South African Infantry. From the top there was a complete circle of view and one could see a light railway from it towards Eaucourt lined with desperate trees.

In the Warlencourt British Cemetery register it notes that the cemetery bears witness to the very fierce fighting. The cemetery is on the south-east side of the Albert–Bapaume road, to the north of the Butte, the gatehouse was designed by Edwin Lutyens and King George V visited the cemetery on 12th May 1922.

At the time of writing there is still a cross on the top of the Butte, and a French memorial in the design of a sword.

Caftet Wood

Caftet Wood is south-west of Carnoy and on the left of the turning off from the Maricourt–Fricourt road, number D 938. Its northern edge faced on to the railway line between Guillemont and Mametz. In 1916, at the beginning of the battle the wood was just within the Allied lines. On 19th July the 35th Div. (Bantam) had its HQ in the wood which also contained its reserve battalions. The wood was to be 'home' for the 106th Bde. of the Division for the rest of the month. In November the 22nd DLI, Pioneers to the 8th Division were camped in the wood and they were involved in making fascines as well as being involved in working on improving communication trenches.

A Second Lt. A. V. Burbery had been observing from a balloon in mid September when the cable of the balloon was cut by a shell, when it was 3000 feet up. He destroyed his papers ripped the balloon and reached the ground close to the wood by parachute. He was awarded the MC.

Cappy

The village of Cappy is on the D 1 road to the south-east of Bray on the south bank of the loop of the Somme river. At the beginning of the battle it was some way behind the Allied line and in fact lay just in the French lines, the boundary between the two Armies passed through Bray. The village suffered very little artillery damage.

Carnoy

Carnoy is south-west of Montauban, north-west of Maricourt and south-east of Mametz. It was just within the Allied lines in 1916 and the objective for this front on 1st July for the 18th Division was the ground to the north of the Montauban–Mametz Road including Pommiers Redoubt and Loop Redoubt. Also if possible, patrols were to be pushed out towards Caterpillar Wood which was to the south-east of Mametz Wood. Carnoy is six miles east-south-east of Albert and formerly contained a light railway that ran between Peronne and Albert. The 18th Division whose sector it was, spread out in front of Carnoy with the 55th Bde. to the right. Then came the 53rd Bde. and on the left the 54th Bde. The flanking Division were the 30th who were due to capture Montauban on the right and the 7th Division who were to take Mametz and to reach a line overlooking Mametz Wood.

The 18th Division was part of XIII Corps and in July had a front of 2,500 yards. The main objective of the 55th Bde. was a trench line about 200 yards to the north of the Montauban–Mametz Road and also the western end of Montauban. The 8th E. Surreys were the extreme right battalion. Their first objective was Breslau Trench and it was during this action that one of the most famous Somme battle incidents took place. Captain Wilfred Nevill, originally of the E. Yorks. who was Commander of B Company 8th E. Surreys had sought permission from his CO to bring back some footballs from leave for the attacking troops to literally 'kick-off' with. He had presented each platoon with a football and offered a prize to the first platoon to reach the German line dribbling their football. At 7.30 a.m. Nevill himself 'kicked off' having been the first to leave the Company trench. One version of what happened next was that he was shot before he had gone twenty yards and another says that he reached the German wire before being killed, which meant that he would have covered about 400 yards. J. R. Ackerley, a brother officer in the East Surreys who after the War was to become a writer, was wounded in the same action and his close colleague Bobby Soames was killed along with Nevill. Ackerley described Nevill as a battalion buffoon and that because he had loose dentures he could make terrifying grimaces! Ackerley is one of those who said that Nevill was killed immediately which I think was likely in the circumstances. Ackerley himself was wounded, but was more concerned over a 'Victory' bottle of whisky that he had on him, which had been smashed and that might suggest to anyone who was to take him back to the British lines that he had been drinking. He therefore endeavoured to hide it from his rescuers. Ackerley wrote in his memoirs that he had no taste for battle at all but he nevertheless became a Company Commander simply, he says, because there was no one else left to carry out the job. Everyone else had been killed. Many of Nevill's letters have been deposited at the IWM by his younger brother as well as his identity disk. One of the footballs is an exhibit the Regimental Museum of the Queen's. Nevill's body lies in Carnoy Military Cemetery. The E. Surreys seem to have made very little progress and at dawn on the 2nd July they were relieved and returned to huts at Carnoy. Five of their officers had been killed.

On the left of the E. Surreys the 7th Queen's were to attack northwards. In support were the 7th Queen's RW Kents and the 7th Buffs. The Buffs had the objective of a trench to the north of the Montauban–Mametz Road but first

'Football charge'
hero's letters saved

THE Battle of the Somme was kicked off by a young English captain from a Surrey regiment – dribbling a football marked "East Surreys v Barbarians" across no-man's land.

Capt. Wilfred Nevill, 22, went over the top into German machine-gun and shell fire kicking a football "to give my men something to chase after."

Minutes later he was dead at the German wire, shot through the head by a sniper. But the troops had found a hero as the "East Surreys football charge" thrilled the British public in 1916.

Now the records of Capt. Nevill's action have been given to the Imperial War Museum, Lambeth, by his younger brother, the Rev. T. S. Nevill, 77, of Graham Rd. Malvern.

Boost morale

They include more than 100 letters that the young officer wrote to his family from the summer of 1915 to almost the eve of the Battle of the Somme.

Yesterday Mr. Nevill recalled how he heard at the age of 14 that the brother he worshipped had died trying to boost his men's morale.

"My sister was nursing at Abbeville at the time of the Battle of the Somme. Many of the people from the Surrey Regiment were sent back to her hospital.

She got the news even before my mother that he had almost certainly been killed.

She wrote to me at school, not knowing I had not yet heard. She only said: 'I am sorry I can't be with you now,' and I knew she meant that my brother was dead.

Rum Ration

He had done a year at Cambridge, and had been at the top of the school. He had been captain of cricket, was four years in the hockey team, and a rugger player.

The football was not a stunt. My brother always felt it was wrong to load the chaps up with ration rum before they went over the top. The football was to give them something to take their minds off it without a drink."

Capt. Nevill was "not handsome, but he was good-looking, more than 6ft. tall, a good athlete with a good brain".

The Nevill papers came to light when Mr. Malcolm Brown, an author, appealed for personal papers on the Battle of the Somme for his book, "Tommy Goes to War".

Biggest attack

Mr. Brown wrote of Captain Nevill: "There was no better example of the kind of man who went bravely to his death.

He wanted to give the men something homely and familiar to concentrate on."

But the Germans saw the feat as evidence that the British were a race of idiots, and publicised the kick-off as "an English absurdity".

According to Mr. Roderick Suddaby, Keeper of the Department of Documents at the Museum, footballs had been kicked before in September, 1915 on the battlefields at Loos, but he said, "Nevill was launching the biggest British attack of the war".

The football was recovered and is still owned by the East Surrey Regiment.

(Daily Telegraph)

---

had the special task of clearing Carnoy Craters which took them six hours to do. They remained in front trenches until the night of 4/5th July and during this time they were heavily shelled. Steadily the advance continued and by 1.30 p.m. the 55th Bde. were at the final objective, and aided by three companies of the 8th Suffolks (53rd Bde. 18th Div.) were working their way along Montauban Alley towards Loop Trench. On the 53rd Brigade front with the 8th Norfolks on the right and the 6th R. Berks. on the left; the Norfolks were to bomb their way up Loop Trench. The 6th R. Berks. reached a line in front of Mine Trench which was the most advanced of the German defences and at the west end of this trench was Casino Point under which the British had exploded a mine with disastrous results for the enemy.

Mine Trench was captured by two advancing battalions and by 7.50 a.m. the Berks. had taken Bund Support Trench and had gone forward to Pommiers Trench.

At 3.15 p.m. the right of the Berkshires was held up and they had to be assisted by the bombers of the 10th Essex (53rd Bde. 18th Div.) and it was not until 6.30 p.m. that the final objective on a line running east and west was reached in front of Caterpillar Wood. The Loop had been handed over to the 8th Norfolks when they had come up.

The extreme left of the 54th Bde. attack was in the hands of the 11th Royal Fus. whose first involvement in battle this was. At 7 a.m. a thick mist had shrouded the foreground but by 7.30 a.m. this had cleared and they began their advance towards Pommiers Redoubt which was almost due north of their assembly position. Firstly they dealt with an attempt to check them at Austrian Support Trench when a machine gun was taken between Bund Trench and Pommiers Trench. The battalion on their right the 6th Northamptons, had been held up by uncut wire, and the Germans in Mametz village used this time to strike against the battalion's left flank. A small party bombed up Black Alley which ran parallel to the Fusiliers' advance and led to Pommiers Trench. Pommiers Redoubt at this time was still to be taken. However after hard fighting in the area of Black and Beetle Alleys the advance continued, and by 9.30 a.m. the obstacle had been gained. The Fusiliers were actually in advance of their flanking battalions and in the afternoon they were still 1,000 yards ahead and reached White Trench which was below Mametz Wood. A line of strong points were made later in the day. The enemy had been driven back from a depth of about 2,000 yards. The night of 1st July was spent in Montauban Alley and they had seen the German gunners rushing up with their teams immediately beyond Caterpillar Wood in order to get them away. At 3 a.m. on 2nd July the R. Berks. went back to Pommiers Trench and on relief by the 8th Suffolks, to Carnoy until 7th July.

The 10th Essex behind the R. Berks. were to suffer from falling debris from the Kasino Point explosion. They held and consolidated the Pommiers Line. The Brigade had its main dumps on the Carnoy/Montauban road. The 7th Beds. were to the left of the 6th R. Berks. The 12th Middlesex was the reserve battalion of the 54th Bde. which went into action with the 7th Beds. on the right, and the 11th R. Fus. on the left, with the 6th Northamptons in support.

The 12th Middlesex were in deep dugouts at zero hour on 1st July and at 8.30 a.m. F. A. Maxwell their senior officer moved to Battalion HQ at Piccadilly in the old British front line. At 12.45 p.m. they moved up with men in Bund Trench and in Emden Trench, on the right of the Triangle. They were also in Austrian Support Trench. They remained in these positions for the rest of the day and at 8.30 p.m. on 2nd July were relieved in the advance positions by the 11th. R. Fus. Maxwell's HQ was then in Black Alley. On 2/3 July they relieved the 11th R. Fus. and at night on the 6th July were relieved themselves by the 7th Beds. and marched back to bivouacs west of Bronfay Wood.

Siegfried Sassoon of the 1st R. Welch Fus. (22nd Bde. 7th Div.) wrote the following poem dated 3rd July 1916.

At Carnoy

Down in the hollow there's the whole Brigade
Camped in four groups: through twilight falling slow
I hear a sound of mouth-organs, ill-played,
And murmur of voices, gruff, confused, and low.
Crouched among thistle-tufts I've watched the glow
Of a blurred orange sunset flare and fade;
And I'm content. To-morrow we must go
To take some cursèd Wood . . . O world God made!

In early July the Official War Office Photographer Geoffrey Malins took his car to the top of Carnoy Valley and left it at Minden Post which was XV Corps MDS next to Caftet Wood at the head of the valley above Carnoy. It was just off the Mametz–Maricourt Road, and was to become probably the most famous dressing station on the Somme. All the Corps wounded passed through there after receiving attention at the ADS. Malins was advised to move his car as it was likely to be destroyed by German artillery, which despite a large red cross lying on the ground still treated the Dressing Station as a legitimate target. Malins filmed some scenes here before attempting to film in the Bernafay/Montauban direction but Trônes Wood proved too 'hot' for him.

There was a military camp at Carnoy and in early July it consisted of dugouts, shacks and bivouacs, here too there was plenty of shelling. The valley of Carnoy had a military track and also a light railway and in addition was thickly populated with trench lines. Ammunition limbers made a continuous stream in both directions. Often men and horses were blown up but the traffic never ceased. Carnoy had the name sometimes of Death Valley as shells rained down so frequently. On 8/9 July the 2nd Suffolks (76th Bde. 3rd Div.) bivouacked here. As did the 7th KSLI (8th Bde. 3rd Div.) on 7th July and the 18th King's on the 9th. The artillery used to mass here and at the end of July one artillery Bde. increased from six batteries to twenty in one night, and the heavy stuff, 8 inch and 9.2s began firing at 10 p.m. Each battery was given about 50 or 60 yards of road and in half a mile there could be found 80 guns. This information is from L. J. Ounsworth (IWM) and was on the fighting between Longueval and Flers. We have a description of the conditions at Carnoy from a member of 166 MGC.

From *The Machine Gunner* written by an ex-gunner of 166th MGC: The 166 MGC found themselves in trench dugouts in Carnoy Valley during the Somme offensive. The trench, like the valley itself, was in enfilade (or end on) from the German line about 1½ to 2 miles away. The dugouts were 'baby elephants' being half loops of channelled steel bolted together to form an arched protection from the weather and also from the small shell-bursts they were covered with earth about a couple of sandbags thick. The 'baby elephants' were adjacent to each other, and were open-ended into the enfiladed trench. The men were in reserve in this position for a week or so, and some mornings they had to do physical exercises in the valley at 7 a.m. in the full view of the German observation balloon. They were 'registered' and the company who relieved them were decimated. At the end of July the 6th KSLI (60th Bde. 20th Div.) were in craters close to the Carnoy/Montauban road. On 22nd August the HQ of the 20th Light Div. was at Minden Post and the 60th Bde. was in reserve at the craters which were about 1,000 yards from Carnoy itself.

H. L. N. Dundas as recorded in the book *Henry Dundas, Scots Guards* noted that on the 4th September the 2nd Guards Bde. moved to Carnoy. He himself was with the 1st Scots Guards but at the time was ill at Corbie. The Guards Bde. had previously been at Happy Valley.

Aubrey Smith a London Rifleman, was with the transport at Carnoy between 4th September and the 9th and described it as a ruined village which had harboured the Battalion HQ and aid posts of one or two units that had charged near this spot on 1st July. Down the hill he went, with camps to the left, horse lines to the right, British 9.2s on one side, water troughs on the other, and two lines of convoy splashing in the mud. The battalion had left by now, carrying on towards the front, whilst the transport plodded on to the prescribed area and the horse lines on the far side of the village. Lewis gun limbers, cookers, water carts, mess carts, and medical carts were told not to unhook. They were shortly in an inferno, not of enemy fire but of Allied fire. Here in Death Valley where guns of all calibres were massed.

Several writers remark on the presence of artillery and one described the scene on 9th September as Carnoy having enormous clumps of guns in rows. The 3rd Guards Bde. was relieving the 47th and 48th Bdes. The 4th Gren. Gds. were to relieve the 47th Bde. on the right. The 1st Welsh Gds. were to take over the front at the south-east of Ginchy from the 48th Bde. The Irish Gds. were in support at Bernafay Wood, whilst the 2nd Scots Gds. remained bivouacked in reserve north of Carnoy. On the 10th two companies of the 2nd Scots Gds. were sent up to Bernafay Wood followed in the afternoon by the rest of the battalion. On the 16th September the Welsh Gds. of the 3rd Guards Bde. were resting on the slope of a hill near Carnoy. In the valley was a line of 9.2s howitzers and on the opposite slope were the cavalry lines with their horses knees in deep mud. All the transport for miles around watered their horses at a well in Carnoy Valley. On the 17th the 12th King's were based at Carnoy Craters. The 6th KSLI were involved in the Battle of Guillemont on 7th September and on the 8th were at Corbie for a rest. They next moved to Carnoy and on the 16th back to the trenches in front of Waterlot Farm. The Germans attacked on the 17th and 18th but Guillemont fell to the Allies and the 20th Light Division went for a short rest.

Later in the month the battalion was back again briefly at Carnoy. On the 19th the 1st Scots Gds. were ordered to move nearer the line and marched to Carnoy on the 20th. On the 24th orders were received for them to move up next day. However they returned the same evening from Trônes Wood. Meanwhile the 2nd Scots Gds. had been resting at Carnoy and re-fitting. On the 21st the 3rd Bde. was to relieve the 59th Bde. of the 20th Light Div. The

4th Gren. Gds. who were on the left shared battalion HQ with the 2nd Scots Gds. on whose right were the 3rd Coldstream Gds. The attack had been postponed until the 25th because of bad weather. After the battle, on the 26th the 1st and 3rd Guards Bdes. were relieved in the evening by the 2nd Scots Bde. and the 2nd and 3rd Coldst. Gds. moved to bivouac at Carnoy. On the 27th September the 11th KRRC (59th Bde. 20th Div.) camped here and provided working parties. On the 9th October they went in to the back areas. The 2nd RWF (19th Bde. 33rd Div.) were here on the 22nd October on their way to Trônes Wood via Guillemont and Ginchy.

As the weeks went by the conditions at Carnoy grew worse until towards the end of October the whole area was one expanse of mud. Mention is made of a hutted camp in November and also of H. Camp being situated in the village. In January 1917 Max Plowman wrote that after being at Flers they just had time to clean up and look around the town of hutments that was Carnoy before going back into the line, where he was wounded in the head. The village had been used as a collecting place for the wounded. Work on Carnoy Military Cemetery had begun in August 1915 by the 2nd KOSB and the 2nd KOYLI when the village was immediately south of the line. It is on the south side of the village alongside the railway halt and was closed in March 1917.

I would like to add a couple of postscripts to the Carnoy entry and they concern the role of the 18th Division. In early July W. H. Livens organised the use of gas projectors on the Divisional front. He had been recruited from the Royal Engineers in order to combat the threat of German gas warfare. He was really an inventor and was to design several types of gas projector. On the same front was a Major Alan Brooke who was to become one of the top British military leaders in the Second World War. He was a member of the Artillery which served with the 18th Division and was an early supporter of the 'creeping barrage'. He was more interested in destroying 'selected' enemy strong points rather than just attempting to destroy the whole of the enemy line, and not succeeding. The Military Cemetery was begun in August 1915 and used by Field Ambulances to the north of the village in July 1916.

Caterpillar Valley and Caterpillar Wood

Caterpillar Valley is between the village of Mametz and Mametz Wood. It lies south-east of Contalmaison and north-west of Montauban. The Valley extends from west to east in front of Mametz Wood across the Montauban–Longueval Road and across the north or top of Bernafay Wood towards Trônes Wood and Guillemont. Caterpillar Wood which is in the eastern end of the valley is south of Flat Iron Copse and Sabot Copse. The name given to the valley by the Army was presumably because it is Caterpillar in shape and outline. It is deep and made of chalk and runs from Longueval to Guillemont. The part of the valley or low ground in front of Mametz Wood is sometimes incorrectly called Happy Valley. The real Happy Valley is near Bray to the south.

Caterpillar Wood was on a steep chalk bank and the Germans had made it into a strong redoubt to defend the flanks of the valley. Just to the north-east of it was a small fortified copse or dingle known as Marlborough Wood. Men advancing northwards from Montauban would have to seize the wood before they could reach the valley and proceed against the hill beyond. The wood was the 'haunt' of German artillery.

On 1st July the troops of the 18th and 7th Divs. did not reach their final objectives for the first day but they did succeed in taking Pommiers Redoubt and the village of Mametz which meant that they were in sight of, and in contact with, Caterpillar Wood and Valley. The wood was in front of the 18th Div. and the western section of the valley was in front of the 7th Division. The progress of the two British Divs. was so good on the first day of the battle that across the valley could be seen several hundreds of Germans streaming northwards along the Bazentin le Grand Road. Many gunners of the German artillery were also forced to leave their guns behind. It seems that the view that the Allies possessed was as much as they were to achieve for several days.

Early on the 11th July the 9th Devons of the 20th Bde. of the 7th Div. reached the valley on the far bank of a depression, which wasn't steep enough as protection against howitzer fire.

Caterpillar Trench which ran south-eastwards towards the Allied lines was in full view of the Germans at this time and could only be used at night. H. P. Robinson in *The Turning Point* wrote that in early July the fighting in this area had been of the toughest kind and that the Germans had to be driven from Caterpillar Valley almost yard by yard and forced way up the slope to a line that was practically level with the middle of Mametz Wood. Further to the east Bernafay Wood had been cleared without great loss, but then a desperate struggle ensued for the possession of Trônes Wood. Liddell Hart who was with the 9th KOYLI (64th Bde. 21st Div.) noted that on 14th July soon after midnight the battalion assembled in the shelter of Caterpillar Valley, moving up in long worm like lines of companies or platoons in single file. At 3.20 a.m. the barrage fell on the German trenches, this was the night attack against Bazentin. Five minutes later the whole line moved forward and the whole of the German second line was rapidly overrun, and the attacking troops passed beyond. The 21st Div. passed through Bazentin le Petit Wood to the village, the 7th Div. cleared Bazentin le Grand Wood and pushed up the slopes towards High Wood, the 3rd Div. captured Bazentin le Grand village and the 9th fought their way, with difficulty through Longueval to the outskirts of Delville Wood.

The 2nd Suffolks of the 76th Bde. of the 3rd Div. on 14th July moved to the southern end of the wood. The Cavalry were concentrating in the valley for High Wood which was to be attacked and captured. The Cavalry included detachments of the Indian Horse. The 15th Bde. RFA took up positions to support the infantry in the valley which lay between Pommiers Ridge and Mametz Wood. The 21st Manchesters after the Cavalry had ridden through towards High Wood and were withdrawn 400 yards to the rear of High Wood. Their HQ was a former German battery and they were badly shelled.

They had been involved with the 1st S. Staffs. who were in the same Brigade in fighting actually in High Wood itself. There had been a panic withdrawal. Battalion Aid Post was in Sabot Copse and Bde. HQ (91st) was at Caterpillar Wood. The situation was untenable and they withdrew to Mametz Halt. On 18th July the Germans counter-attacked and forced their way with fine courage but at great loss, and on 19th July the valley was crammed with field artillery, because it was the only possible site for the more forward batteries. In addition to the Allied guns presenting easy targets, the German artillery also caught Dressing Stations and Field Kitchens which by necessity were also in the valley. The 15th R. Warwicks. (13th Bde. 4th Div.) were in trenches in front of the north section of cross-roads (from Montauban to Bazentin). The present Quarry Cemetery was then used as a Dressing Station.

When the 5th Div. Artillery came into the valley to take up their positions they thought it to be a most 'unhealthy' area. It was packed from end to end with guns of every sort, 9.2s, 8 inch, 6 inch, 4.5 howitzers, 60 pdrs, anti-aircraft guns and literally hundreds of 18 pdr. guns, which kept up an almost continuous roar by day and by night. They were overlooked by German positions at Ginchy to the east. There was hardly any cover for detachments, which were kept as small as possible in order to keep losses to the minimum. The troops dug holes in the ground and covered them if possible with corrugated iron and earth, which afforded scant protection against the 'Caterpillar Valley Barrage', which swept relentlessly down the valley at intervals during the day and night. In addition to the gun positions, a number of units had formed horse-lines towards the Fricourt end of the valley, and almost every square yard was occupied some way or other. As the line for approaching reliefs or for ration and fatigue parties, lay across Caterpillar Valley and over the slopes south and south-west of Longueval, the difficulties which had to be faced may be imagined. On the 22nd of July the danger of the valley as a site for horse lines was brought home to those who had used it as such. In the afternoon the Germans opened a sudden concentrated fire on them, and in order to prevent appalling losses, the horses were cut loose and they stampeded terrified down the valley towards Fricourt in a cloud of dust and shell smoke; it took several hours to collect them up again, but not many were lost. The guns remained in Caterpillar Valley until 1st September when they moved forward to Bernafay Wood to support the attacks on Ginchy and Guillemont and afterwards to positions around Delville Wood for the attack on the Switch Trench and Guedecourt positions.

M. E. S. Laws who was an Artillery Section Commander described the situation in the valley after the initial attack and wrote that the valley had formerly been a German gun position and they had built excellent dugouts which later the British were to use. Unfortunately it was the very German familiarity with their former positions which led to considerable British casualties. In addition to continuous German shelling there were also phosgene gas shells. Another hazard was that there was no water to be had and it had to be brought up by lorry in buckets, and each man received a very small allowance. One bucket only for the Officers' Mess for example.

H. E. Harvey of the 22nd R. Fus. (Kensingtons) in July wrote that they went on across the road that led to the Quarry and Caterpillar Valley, on past the uprooted orchard on the south side, down the broad road to Bernafay Wood with its snapping batteries of French 75s. The ground was captured only after very fierce fighting in the latter part of July. Between mid August and 10th September the 47th Div. batteries were in position in Bottom Wood with some further east near Montauban and in front of Caterpillar Valley. Further forward in the valley heavy howitzers stood in the open, lobbing their shells over a target miles away. Direct hits on either guns themselves or dugouts were not unknown. F. C. Hitchcock in 'Stand To' wrote that prior to the attack on Delville Wood due west of Montauban when they struck off for Caterpillar Valley. It was raining and the going was terribly heavy. The valley was waterlogged and they all became caked in mud. 'It was a miserable place, muddy, and all churned up by shell craters of all sizes that were now filled with water. The few trees there had been reduced to blackened stumps, and not a blade of grass was visible either in the valley or on the rising slopes. It was a valley of the dead and no one stayed in it longer than was necessary. The light railway which led up to Guillemont was completely torn up, lengths of it were standing up for ten feet in the air, with great shell craters under them. All along the valley were abandoned stores, boxes of SAA and the long shaped blue boxes which contained Mills Bombs. After a tiring tramp along the valley, they arrived at a dump called Green Dump; which was close to Longueval Trench and was always an unhealthy place.'

D. Boyd in *Salute of Guns* had arrived on the Somme at the end of August and wrote that the reconnoitering parties went up to Dead Mans Gulch to learn the position of the batteries that they were to relieve, but theirs was known, and they were told to go and search for it near Caterpillar Valley. 'The lips of shell craters overlapped. Enormous speckled horse flies buzzed and darted about the sweat running off their faces. On the left of the track lay several small shattered woods from which rose a sickening hum, as though all the flies in France were meeting over the bodies whose decay pervaded the battlefield. The hill on the right was broken by a cleft, Caterpillar Valley. Its black walls were full of shell holes and in places regularly grooved by the scraping of the infantry entrenching tool.'

Alexander Aitken who was with the NZ Infantry noted in his book *Gallipoli to the Somme* that in early September there was road mending and repairing in the valley. The valley road was so congested with traffic and limbers, that they were forced to walk along the sleepers of the railways from which siding after siding led off to the wood on the left. Each siding had a howitzer among the trees, the largest being a 12 incher which fired every few minutes. The road turned left at a corner and ran up to Bazentin. On this corner a German high velocity gun registered with accuracy at five minute intervals, and here they were amazed at the courage of the limber drivers who had to pass this point. Evidence of the July fighting lay all around. In addition to the ground being pitted with craters, there were dud shells all about, piles of anti-aircraft shells hurriedly abandoned, up on the wooded slope, sunk deep in to the chalky earth, German dugouts, their entrances half concealed by trees, many containing machine guns not yet cleared away, some facing so as to shoot over attackers in the back. Aitken says that they filled in the craters and levelled and topped off. The Germans all the time kept up their shelling of the corner. The New Zealand Infantry had entered the Battles of the Somme on the 11th September when their Div. took over the line between Delville Wood and High Wood. They were due to take part in the Fourth Army attack of 15th September which was to penetrate north and east towards Bapaume. It was on the 15th that the tanks lumbered into action and came along Caterpillar Valley. On 1st October the Fifth Div. guns again moved forward to positions in the vicinity of Switch Trench.

Fraser-Tytler wrote that in early November 'At night Caterpillar Valley is a wonderful sight. A perfect blaze of lights, extending 14 miles, as the valley contains the wagon lines of about three Corps.' Because of the water shortage scouts were detailed to report if water was running into any particular group of troughs, and when it did everyone hurried to it. The troughs could only water about 200 horses at a time. No one could approach them dismounted as the mud was almost waist deep. Towards the end of November a broad gauge line up the valley was nearing completion as were two hutted camps between High Wood and Bazentin le Petit and another just south of le Petit.

The area having been taken by the Allies in July 1916 was lost to the Germans in March 1918.

On the south side of the road to Longueval is Caterpillar Valley Cemetery and near the east side of it is the Memorial to those New Zealanders who fell in the Somme battles and whose graves are not known. There are also three Memorials to soldiers whose graves in McCormick's Post Cemetery near Flers were destroyed by shell fire. H. Baker was the architect of this Cemetery which stands on a ridge from which Longueval and other villages, High Wood, Delville Wood and other woods are visible.

Celestins Wood

These woods are to the north-west of Chipilly which is on the north bank of the Somme river and to the south-east of Morlancourt. In mid June the woods were the home of the 10th A & SH (26th Bde. 9th Scottish Div.). On 25th/26th June G. W. Warwick of the South African Bde. recorded that they left Welcome Woods at 9 p.m. and marched through Sailly-le-Sec to Celestins Woods where they arrived at 2 o'clock on the 27th and rested there in tents. However after only five hours they were on the move again, this time marching to Etinhem, Bray and Suzanne. They set off again from the camp at Grove Town and returned once more to Celestins Woods, arriving this time at

1 p.m. on the 29th. Warwick noted the considerable air activity with many aeroplanes and balloons in the skies overhead. On 8th July the 8th E. Surreys (55th Bde. 18th Div.) were in the wood and at the time it was described as being a 'dirty camp' which was however prettily situated overlooking the valley of the Somme. The French Army were close by.

Chimpanzee Trench

The trench was south of Bernafay Wood and adjacent to the brickworks and on the Montauban Road. In early August a S. Lancs. Battalion was sheltering in the neighbourhood and on the 19th two Brigades of the 35th Div. (Bantam) were here including the 105th Bde. who also occupied Arrow Head Copse which was to the north-east of Guillemont. An attack was planned for the 17th September but had to be cancelled owing to the muddy conditions. The 14th R. Warwicks (13th Bde. 4th Div.) were here on the 19th and were relieved by the Guards Bde.

Chipilly

Chipilly is a village on the north bank of the Somme river and is south-east of Morlancourt. It is 17 miles from Amiens and in 1916 was used by Field Ambulances. In March 1918 the village fell to the Germans in their great advance. Opposite the church is an 'interesting' drinking trough and at the north end of the Communal Cemetery there is a British plot. It was begun in August 1915 and was used until March 1916 and then again between July and October 1916. The Communal Extension was made by the British in the period between March 1916 and February 1917. It overlooks the village and the Somme Valley.

Citadel New Military Cemetery (Fricourt)

There are two roads that lead southwards from the Fricourt–Carnoy Road and the eastern one leads firstly to Pt. 110 Old Military Cemetery and then a little further on to the Pt. 110 New Military Cemetery Fricourt. A little further south and on the other road (D 147) to the west is the Citadel New Military Cemetery. The whole area is steeped in literary associations through the memoirs of Siegfried Sassoon, Robert Graves and Bernard Adams who were all members of the R. Welch Fus. and were in this sector before the battle began. The 'sites' to seek out on a visit include Wellington Redoubt, which is at the junction of the Maricourt Road, Maple Redoubt on the Fricourt–Méaulte Road, Reduit A which is where the artillery had their guns and of course the Citadel itself.

The Cemetery which was formerly Citadel Camp is just beyond the two points that were 71 metres above sea level and were known as 71 North and 71

South. It is about 150 yards north-east of the Fricourt–Bray road and about 5 miles from Albert. It was begun by French troops, and from August 1915 when the first British burials were made, it was known as the Citadel Military Cemetery (Point 71). The great majority of the burials were carried out from Field Ambulances before the Somme battle began. One of these pre-battle burials was that of Corporal O'Brien of the 1st RWF who was rescued by Sassoon in a raid that went wrong at Bois Français Craters to the north on the front line. O'Brien had died even before he was rescued and the register at the cemetery gives his date of death as 26th May 1916.

In his book *Nothing of Importance* Bernard Adams wrote that after he had been wounded he had been attended to by a RAMC Doctor who had given him tea and a second 'label'. He had also been given an injection against Tetanus. This was probably in June.

At the beginning of the battle the sector was in the 7th Div. area of the XVth Corps. 'A' Comp. of the 1st RWF was at 71 South, 'B' Comp. at 71 North and D. Comp at the Bois Français Quarry. The 20th Manchesters were to their right. The objectives were Mametz and Fricourt. In early July the battle moved slowly forward but the Citadel was in continuous use for billeting purposes. In his *Memoirs of an Infantry Officer* Siegfried Sassoon wrote that his battalion, the 1st RWF arrived here from Morlancourt and bivouacked on the hill behind the Citadel. After going up the line they returned and fell asleep to the sound of guns and rattling limbers on the Citadel Road. At the same time Frenchman were at work on the rail road at the Citadel. There were also crowds of guns in the neighbourhood. The 21st Manchesters of the 91st Bde. 7th Div. arrived at the Citadel from Buire on the 11th July and two days later they bivouacked at Mametz Wood. The exhausted 5th Div. were here in early August and were later relieved by the 17th Div.

During his August visit to the front King George V motored past the billets of the 22nd R. Fus. (Service) Batt. and on 10th August the 2nd Div. HQ and the HQ of the 105th Bde. of the 35th Div. (Bantam) were here. Another Bantam Bde. the 104th came here on 25th August, and the 10th KRRC (59th Bde. 20th Div.) were at the camp in Brigade Reserve 22/23rd August.

An observer described the Camp at the end of August as follows. 'The camp was situated in a vast plain, devoid of landmarks and bare and desert-like. They sheltered in contraptions like chicken hutches, with rabbit wire walls. The ground was badly smashed up, and covered with horselines and transports of other units. A huge French gun mounted on railway lines would arrive and fire a shell, immediately pulling away to some place further back by a steam engine.'

By early September the roads towards the Citadel were deep in mud and at this time the camp covered an enormous area on the rolling hillside and presented an astounding spectacle of numbers of units from every arm of the services, these included the 1/5 Cheshire Pioneers to the 56th Div. on the 5th September. On the 9th the Welsh Guards dumped their packs here with the transport on their way to Guillemont. After being involved in the fighting for Leuze Wood near Combles the Queen's Westminsters of the 56th Div. spent

11th and 12th September here in huts and tents, and after a short rest of some thirty hours, moved forward on 13th September to the old German trench system near the Crucifix to the north of Hardecourt.

Kipling in his history of the Irish Guards wrote that after their failure in the fighting of 15th September that no one seemed to recall accurately the order of events between the gathering in Bernafay Wood and the arrival of the shadow of the battalion at Citadel Camp.

Quite a number of the men who are buried at the Cemetery are famous or have high rank or come from aristocratic backgrounds and part of the cemetery reads like a page out of *Who's Who*. The main reason being the close association that the area had with the Guards Bdes. during their role in the September battles. On 18th September Guy Baring (Conservative MP) Colonel of the 1st Cold. Gds was buried there in a service which took place in pouring rain. Henry Dundas of the Scots Gds. was at the burial. Others include Brig. Gen. Phillpotts of the 2th Div. RA HQ who was killed on 8th September. Sec. Lt. Wernher of the Welsh Gds. on 10th September, also Sec. Lt. Cazalet of the Welsh Gds. on the same day. Also Major Bailie of the 1st Irish Gds. on 15th September. On 25th September Lt. Arbuthnot who was the son of a General, had been killed while with the 2nd Gren. Gds., as was Capt. Cunningham also of the 2nd Gren. Gds. who was killed in action at Lesboeufs. He had been the last survivor of the original battalion. And so the list goes on.

Kipling wrote that the 1st Irish Gds. were relieved on the evening of 26th September by its sister battalion the 2nd, who took over the whole of the Lesboeufs ruins from the Bde. and the 1st Irish Gds. went back with others through Bernafay Wood, where they fed, and returned to the Citadel.

Aubrey Smith of the London Rifle Bde. wrote that his transport section moved its lines on 26th September to the neighbourhood of the Citadel, the name given to several camps and huts used by the infantry. On this day the LRB Patrols had worked their way into Combles where they had joined up with the French.

Troops of the 5th Div. arrived at the Citadel Camp at this time and the 1st Bedfords lost some of their troops to German night bombers. After being involved in the battle for Eaucourt l'Abbaye the Queen's Westminsters handed over to the Kensingtons, then the whole battalion was withdrawn to the Citadel.

One battalion while at the Citadel had been issued with spotlessly white new tents which had to be smeared with 'cutch' to stain them brown. They were given to the infantry. The Pioneers cleared away a lot of furze on the opposite slope which allowed for the camp to be enlarged. The 2nd RWF (19th Bde. 33rd Div.) were in tents at the camp on the 21st October, and on 2nd November the Prince of Wales visited the 2nd Rifle Bde. here, in his capacity as their Colonel in Chief.

Our last source comes from Sidney Rogerson's *Twelve Days* and he wrote that on the evening of 7th November, when the offensive was spluttering out in a sea of mud, they were at the Citadel Camp. He described it as being a dreary collection of bell tents perched insecurely on the hillside near the one time village of Fricourt. His unit was the 2nd W. Yorks. Although he was an Officer Commanding 'B' Company he had less experience of France than his two officer colleagues who both wore the 1914 Star. On the 10th they were to leave the camp and move to a map reference in the 'particularly salubrious' locality between Bernafay Wood, and that on the morrow they were to move back again to the Citadel, whence they had set out a week before. On 15th November the Battalion fell in by companies outside their tents to drag themselves and their Lewis gun carts across the five and a half miles that separated la Briqueterie from the Citadel. The carts were described as 'lunatic vehicles' that resembled a species of shortened coffin; they were mounted on two wheels and provided with handles which were so near to the ground that the wretched pusher had almost to double up to grip them. At long last they came into sight of the familiar dirty bell tents and the high bank.

Clairfaye

Clairfaye is between Léalvillers and Forceville and is north-west of Varennes. It housed a Motor Ambulance Convoy attached to the Fifth Army during the later stages of the battle. It was also a Divisional Rest Station and provided a walking wounded collecting station and collecting post for X Corps. Clairfaye Farm was a farm close to Léalvillers and Harponville and 108th Bde. 36th (Ulster) Div. carried out pre-battle training there over an elaborate system of dummy trenches that had been marked out with plough and spade. The dummy trenches represented the German ones that were to be attacked.

Coigneux

Is a village south-west of Souastre and between Couin and Sailly au Bois. It was behind the lines during the battle and to the south-west of the village is the Bois de Coigneux. At the end of May, Aubrey Smith wrote that his London Rifle Bde. moved their horselines from Bayencourt about a mile to a sheltered valley near to Coigneux; this would be on the western side of the road north-east to Souastre. Whilst here companies who were close at hand, went up to the line each night to carry out digging and other fatigues. A. Stuart Dolden wrote of the London Scottish on 30th June at 9 p.m., that the battalion having gone to take up positions at Hébuterne ready for the 1st July, the cookers were taken by horse transport to the Transport Line at Happy Valley which lay between Coigneux and Souastre. This would be the same valley as mentioned above.

On 11th July the 38th Div. after being relieved at Mametz Wood came to Coigneuz where it relieved the 48th Div. which was taking over the line south of Hébuterne and Gommecourt. On 7th August the 61st Bde. of the 20th Div. was relieved by the 71st Bde. of the 25th Div. In early September the 2nd

O & BLI of the 5th Bde. of the 2nd Div. were in huts in the wood in Divisional Reserve and the 4th O & BLI of the 145th Bde. of the 48th Div. moved by Jena Track and Valley Road to bivouac between the Dell and Coigneux. In November there was a MDS in the village as well as a ADS or CP.

Colincamps

Colincamps is a village seven miles north-west of Albert, south-east of Courcelles and north of Mailly Maillet. It is also south-east of Hébuterne. From Hébuterne there stretched as far as Mailly an undulating common called Colincamps Plain and midway there stood the village from which it derived its name. In a straight depression to the east, were the Allied defences, an intermediate city with streets, lanes, alleys, woods, copses, avenues and the like.

The village had been battered before the battle began in July, and a CP or ADS was established here. The Hébuterne and Colincamps sectors were of great importance, for in large measure they commanded the valleys and spurs which ran from Hébuterne in the south and south-easterly directions, along which both sides made their lines of defence and placed their artillery. The Plain was full of battery positions both heavy and field. Similarly the Germans had large numbers of guns defending the Gommecourt Salient to the north and they were active towards the British lines and also Hébuterne and Colincamps. Except on the Hébuterne–Gommecourt ridge where the two sides were on equal terms the ground sloped down towards the German lines.

In April the Sucrerie or Sugar Factory to the south-east of the village of Colincamps which faced the Serre road, and was close to the Hébuterne–Auchonvillers cross-roads was already a heap of ruins. It was just south of the famous Euston Dump. From this corner the road leads directly to Serre and the road to Auchonvillers is sunken. Euston Dump was the main dump for amongst other battalions the 10th E. Yorks. and was also a main exit point from the line.

At the beginning of the battle the village was in the territory of the 31st Division. The 93rd and 94th Bdes. were to attempt to take Serre on 1st July with the 92nd Bde. in support. On the eve of the battle the 16th W. Yorks. (1st Bradford Pals) and 18th W. Yorks. (2nd Bradford Pals) who were both in the 93rd Bde. were camped in an orchard to the north-west of Colincamps where they ate bully beef for supper. The HQ of the 12th Y & L (Sheffield Pals) of the 94th Bde. was in an oblong schoolroom built of chalk with a slate roof. Later many men marched past the sugar factory on their way up to the line and passed the massed graves that had been made ready for the battle. Gerald Brenan mentions these graves in a harrowing extract from his autobiography which concerns events around early July. He had received orders to take his platoon to Colincamps a mile or two along the ridge from Hébuterne, for a burial party. The bodies, hundreds of them were brought up on a trench railway from the front line, and bundled out onto the ground. Legs had broken off from trunks, heads rolled off at a touch and horrible liquids oozed out of the cavities. A sickening stench filled the air and obscene flies crept and buzzed, not to speak of the worms that wriggled in the putre-fication. Brenan's Platoon's job was to cut the identity numbers from the corpses and then shovel them into shallow trenches which they had dug nearby. After three days of this he took a shovel and worked himself and found that his morale completely vanished; he knew that if they were asked to go over the top the next morning that he would be unable to do so. The stench had brought the fear of death 'to his very bones'.

Frederic Manning in his autobiograhical novel mentioned that after they had left Courcelles for Colincamps, mounting the hill they came under direct enemy observation for about 300 yards, so the road had been camouflaged with netting. At the top of the hill was a bend, and commanding the road, as well as another lesser road, was a more than usually substantial barn, a kind of bastion to the outskirts of Colincamps itself. The street at Colincamps ended, and the houses with it, on a meeting road with Mailly Maillet to the right, and on the left continuing to the sugar factory, where it joined the main road from Mailly to Serre. They turned left down the hill road curving into the valley, and there was another military control. Leaving the road and picking their way between the gunpits and dugouts, they came again to Southern Avenue. When 'Bourne' returned to Colincamps he met up with some Gordon Highlanders in order to obtain some Brigade messages. He thought that it would be better to use Railway Avenue, as the Germans seemed to have got the Southern Avenue pretty taped. He wrote that the shelling was worse in the corner in the direction of Courcelles, and to have extended on this side further along the Mailly road. He made for the corner of Colincamps doubling up the short rise with difficulty and arrived at a relay post in a cellar. Only a few shells came into Courcelles said the runner but they knew that the village and the dump were 'getting it'. After three days in the trenches the battalion was relieved and moved to Courcelles. Unfortunately we have no date for this extract.

In mid August the village was described as having a variety of rest huts, ruins and trenches and on 8th October the 4th Sea. H. were billeted in the village. The village contained an ADS or CP in November.

The Sucrerie Military Cemetery is a mile east of the village and 300 yards north of the road to Serre from Mailly. It stands on the south side of a private avenue leading from Colincamps to the site of the sugar factory; but is approached from the other side of the path. The Cemetery was begun by French Troops when they occupied the sector in early summer 1915 and was extended by the British from July 1915. It stands on a wide plateau among cornfields. The Euston Road Cemetery is close to the former dump and road junction. It is particularly associated with the Serre attack of 1st July, the capture of Beaumont Hamel on 13th November, and the attack on 5th April 1918 on the 3rd New Zealand (Rifle) Bde. trenches before Colincamps. Two Lieutenant Colonels are buried here, J.A. Thicknesse

(Som. L.I.) and the Hon. L.C.W. Palk (Hampshire). They were said to have been killed with two other senior officers, D. Wood (Rifle Bde.) and E.A. Innes (1/8th R. Warwicks) but these two men have their names on the Thiepval Memorial, as having no known grave. All four men were Lieutenant Colonels in the 4th Division.

Combles

Combles is ten miles east of Albert and eight miles south of Bapaume, on the D 20 Rancourt–Guillemont Road. It is in the north-east of the Somme battlefield, south of Morval, west of Guillemont and north-east of Falfemont Farm.

The original Falfemont Farm was near the Bois de Falfemont which is close by. The foundations can still be seen. The new Falfemont Farm building is further down the slope and closer to the town.

The Germans had turned Combles into a redoubt or fortified stronghold. Opposite their position was a junction between the British and French lines. The town did not suffer to the same degree as neighbouring villages as it was protected by the surrounding hills. It was an exceedingly strong position as in addition to the hills giving it protection it was enclosed at the bottom of a valley, and was out of reach of the Allied Artillery. The Germans had been in occupation for two and a half years and had built formidable entrenchments and extensive subterranean defences both in and around the town.

The battle for the central ridge raged all through August. Longueval and Delville Wood were still in German hands at this time and most of Guillemont too. Combles was not just in a valley but was also protected by the high ground to the west. There was a wedge pointing in a south-westerly direction towards Falfemont Farm. The town was so well fortified and immune to artillery that it would be better to 'enter it by the back door rather than by the front'.

A battalion of the 2nd KOSB (13th Bde. 5th Div.) remained in reserve before occupying trenches opposite Falfemont Farm and on 3rd September an attack failed, owing to the damage inflicted by the German machine guns. On the 4th the 1st Norfolks (15th Bde. 5th Div.) came up from Bronfay Farm and attacked Falfemont Farm, at 3.10 p.m. By the next day the whole of the objective was taken. Combles Trench was a German trench which ran along the south-west face of Combles but it was not appreciated by the attackers that it was protected by strong uncut wire entanglements which in turn were hidden by standing corn and weeds. It was also under heavy machine gun protection from Bouleux Wood to the north.

The 7th R. Irish Fus. was one of the battalions who had to wade through the corn with the belts of wire 'sown' in it.

The capture of Combles was to be part of the Battle of Morval, which also included the taking of Lesboeufs and Guedecourt. The Allies made progress in the first half of September in the whole region and the following villages fell during this period: Forest, Maurepas, Guillemont and Ginchy.

There is a German article on their defence of Combles called 'Im Felde Unbesiegt' by General Balck. It appeared in Vol. LXX of the *RUSI Journal* and the relevant passage says that 'from 12th to 16th September the Allies, although they had worked well forward on both sides of Combles had still failed to compel its evacuation. They therefore, determined to devote their next operations to the capture of the town and its garrison, in the same way that they had invested and secured Guillemont a few days previously, despite all efforts to relieve it. Each Regiment of the German Division had one battalion in the line, one in reserve, and one resting. On the right in touch with the left of the 52nd Res. Div., the 236 Res. Reg. held Morval, then came the 235th and 234th Res. Reg; the latter in Combles. There were very few machine guns available and there were about 1,200 rifles in line. Opposed to this thin line were five French and British Divs. all good troops; among the latter were Guards, Canadians and Scotch, with others in reserve, and Cavalry behind'.

Balck was at the time Commander of the 51st Reserve Div. who had been in a quiet part of Flanders since August 1914 but who came to the Somme in September 1916. The ground around Combles at this time was nothing but a 'field of craters', though shelters might be found in the deep catacombs beneath the houses of the town.

In all this sector, trenches, dugouts, wire, communications, had been blown out of existence; the infantry in order to conceal their positions from hostile aircraft and artillery observation, had to establish themselves as best they could in lines of shell holes. Rear lines of defence did not exist, supplies and ammunition owing to the constant hostile barrage, could be brought up only by night. The GOC recommended that they pay close attention to co-operation with their neighbours and also with the artillery; and immediate counter-strokes should be carried out in order to recover any lost position. He also asked for reports to be sent back as frequently as possible by all available means. The 51st Reserve Div. took over the reserve line on 3rd September and the front line on the fourth night after the issue of the first orders for their move.

Balck wrote that they were outnumbered by six men to one at least. All day long the hostile fire, skilfully directed from the air, continued against the German positions; the artillery at the latter's disposal (18 field batteries and 56 heavy guns) was insufficient to counter it effectively. The infantry of the defence therefore, could only work at night, and were exposed throughout the daylight hours to the destructive effect of hostile bombardment. The British and French, who were kept far back and only brought up shortly before the opening of their attacks, thus had both morally and materially a great advantage.

The ridge of high ground which had been the object of the Allied attack was cleft towards its southern end by a broad and deep valley known as Combles Valley. Immediately to the north of the town the valley widened out into a basin and then forked, running north-east and skirting the spur which Morval stands on.

In Kipling's book on the Irish Guards he wrote that the Allied advance held the main ridge of land in the Combles sector (in mid-September) but had not gone beyond it. The French left was almost equally restricted by the valley where Combles, among its quarries and hidden shelters, squatted and dealt death, with all the heights to the north, Morval, Lesboeufs and le Transloy joined, with Sailly Saillisel and St. Pierre Vaast in the east, to make sure. It was necessary then, to free the ground at the junction of the two armies in the direction of Morval, which commanded far too complete a fire; also beyond Ginchy towards Lesboeufs where the outlying spurs of high land raked Leuze Wood. This wood was to the north-west of Combles and opposite Bouleux Wood.

By mid September the village had become untenable to the Germans because it was dominated by the British right at Leuze Wood and by the French on the opposite heights. Balck wrote that on 20th September the British captured and consolidated a portion of the line held by the 52nd Res. Div. and on the 22nd the French drove the 213 Div. (on the left) of the 51st Reserve from the sugar factory south of Combles. Early on 25th September it became clear that the expected large scale attack was about to take place. The advance was accomplished and assisted by swarms of low flying aeroplanes. South of Combles the French stormed Priez Farm driving back the 213 Div. continued their advance and occupied Rancourt. In the *Official History* it notes that it was reported that the Germans were going to evacuate Combles on the night of 25th September. Subsequently a detachment of the 1/14th London (Lon. Scottish) began to push southward along the light railway track and before dawn on the 26th were within 500 yards of Combles. Patrols of the 1/4th London (R. Fus.) of 56th Div. had worked through the northern half of Bouleux Wood finding no Germans whilst the 1/1 London (R. Fus.) of the 167th Bde. 56th Div. did likewise through the southern half. Patrols of the last named reached as far as the orchard and one had entered Combles and joined up with the French. Further south the 1/5th London (LRB) of the 169th Bde. was working steadily forward down Combles Trench and joined hands with the French at the light railway track. The 1/1st London (R. Fus.) then pushed into the village on the Ginchy road. Most of the enemy had indeed left the town already.

In the *Michelin Guide to the Somme Battlefields* we have the following account: 'A fresh Anglo/French attack was launched on 25th September, after a terrific bombardment, with the object of encircling the fortress by the capture of the strong points which still protected it on the east and north. On the south-east the French started from their trenches in the old German positions at le Priez Farm – a powerful redoubt protected by six lines of defences which they had carried by assault on 14th September and captured the hamlet of Fregicourt. On the east they carried Rancourt village, and all intermediary positions between these two points, advancing as far as the north-west corner of St Pierre Vaast Wood. On the north the British took the fortified villages of Morval and Lesboeufs and nearly joined hands with the French – traces of German occupation including concrete shelters, strongpoints for machine guns, underground passages, chambers etc. The tunnels excavated out of solid rock under Lamotte Castle, which had already existed before the war, were the most important of the subterranean organisations. The Germans utilised them as posts of commandment, dressing stations, mustering places etc. They were large enough to shelter several companies at a time and were sufficiently proof against the heaviest projectiles. Opposite the 'ruined' church was the entrance to the underground passages and chambers to Lamotte Castle'.

In *Haig's Great Push* it says that for the Allies Tuesday, 26th September was perhaps the greatest day in the whole of the Battle of the Somme. In the early dawn the French forced their way into the cemetery and south-east part of Combles, while simultaneously the British broke the last of the trenches into the village from the west. The German garrison though, by this time reduced to about two battalions, offered stout resistance, but by 10.30 a.m. the British and French advance parties had come in touch near the railway station, where they saluted one another and shook hands over the 'la Belle Alliance'. A concerted assault was then delivered, and by noon the whole of the town was in Allied hands.

In a book called *The Somme* a novel written by A. D. Gristwood, he says that the 26th was a gloriously sunny day in September. The 'Loamshires' were in newly won trenches outside Combles. The town had fallen that morning, not a hundred yards away to the left lay Leuze Wood, captured by the battalion a fortnight ago (i.e. 12th September). Little progress had been made since then.

Jack Tucker who wrote *Johnny Get Your Gun* was in the 1/13 London (Kensington) Batt. of the 56th Div. and wrote that after being unsuccessful in the joint Allied operation they decided to attack the town of Combles on each flank. The 1/14 London Scottish and the 1/14 London (R. Fus.) led the fighting around Bouleux Wood, the French attacking the other side of Combles. The Quadrilateral strong point had been captured by the Guards, thus protecting the British left flank from enfilading fire which had held up previous assaults. Four tanks were also due to take part, but three of them broke down at the start and the fourth was soon hit by a shell. The Kensingtons were in support. This time everything went well, the British and the French broke through on each side, forcing the Germans to withdraw from the town, the London Scottish joining up with the French in Combles. Tucker himself was detailed with one other man to go to Leuze Wood, where they 'chanced it' and scampered forward to the low parapet and into a clearing some 50 yards square, which had been dug out about six feet below the surrounding ground inside the corner of the remains of Leuze Wood. Aubrey Smith still with the transport of the London Rifle Bde. or 1/5 London wrote that patrols worked their way into Combles where they met the French from the other side. This 'pinching out' process had been successful, for the attack of the preceding day had forced the Germans to evacuate the town – some hundreds of prisoners trooping along past the Citadel in the evening as a result of the fighting. They set to work to build a bivouac near the Sandpits on the Albert–Bray road. He presumably means near Méaulte.

For the German view again we have General Balck: The town itself had been heavily shelled throughout the night of 24/25th September, and only with great difficulty could food and water be got up to the German garrison. A wide gap had opened up between the flanks of the 52nd and 51st Reserve Divs. and the garrison at Combles. Therefore the withdrawal of troops from the town began at about 8.30 p.m. and the front lines were evacuated at about 10 p.m. The Germans re-established a fighting front west of Sailly which, however, had no great power of resistance; fortunately the Allies only occupied Combles at midday of the 26th. On the 27th, part of the front of the 213th Div. in front of Rancourt was carried by the French; Sailly, which at one time seemed endangered held firm, despite continued Allied efforts to capture it both on 27th September and the 28th. On the evening of the latter day the 51st Res. Div. was relieved and sent back to rest behind the lines.

In his memoirs General Ludendorff had the following to say: 'Great were our losses, Theenymtok, Rancourt, Morval, Guedecourt, and the hotly contested Combles'.

Twelve hundred prisoners were taken by the Allies and enormous quantities of war material fell into their hands. The sunken road to Sailly–Saillisel was the only line of communication left to the Germans and it was shelled by both sides which resulted in very heavy losses for the Germans.

In the March retirement Combles was the scene of more fierce fighting and the South Africans and New Zealand troops along with the British attempted a stand here but were driven out on the 24th March 1918. The Allies regained the town on the 29th August with the Germans this time being routed by the 18th Division. Combles had become a pile of bricks and the narrow gauge railway in the valley a mass of twisted metal.

One can get an excellent view of the battlefield of 1916 and also 1918 from the Guards Cemetery at Lesboeufs. It is on the south-west outskirts, 74 yards from a by-road towards Maurepas. It was begun by the Guards Division in September 1916 and carried on by other units until March 1917. Combles Communal Cemetery is a triangular piece of ground on the north-east side of the town, at the parting of the roads to Fregicourt and le Transloy. The Extension is at the back or north-east, of the Communal Cemetery. It was begun in October 1916 by French troops, but the 94 French graves made in that year have since been moved to another cemetery. The following burial grounds were brought into the Extension:

Fregicourt Communal Cemetery in a hamlet between Combles and Saillisel.

Leuze Wood Cemetery, at the north-east corner of Leuze Wood.

Longtree Dump Military Cemetery, Sailly Saillisel, a little south of the road Morval to Sailly–Saillisel.

Maurepas Military Cemetery on the south-west side of Maurepas village.

Contalmaison

Contalmaison is four miles north-east of Albert on the D 104 road between la Boisselle and Longueval. North-west of Mametz Wood, and south of Pozieres, it had a dominating position at the junction of several roads and was surrounded with redoubts, and defended by the Prussian Guard. Masefield described it as lying on the top of a spur some 500 yards to the north-east of Horseshoe Trench. It had a perfect field of fire in all directions and was trenched with a wired line, which was strongly held. The chateau was just to the north of the church and slightly above the rest of the village. There was a chalk pit near the village which at the beginning of the war possessed 72 houses which made it the seventh largest village on the Somme. The Cutting was along the northern edge of the village, with posts in Pearl Wood. Contalmaison Villa was situated at the northern point of a fault to the ridge whose crest sloped gently downwards for a distance of 800 yards, when it descended more steeply towards Fricourt.

It was planned that the 34th Div. should take the village and establish a line in front of the German second line, in the evening of 1st July. This was not to be, but small parties from this Division did in fact reach the village on that day.

Masefield wrote that rain hindered the advance throughout the next three days, and attacks on the approaches to the village and Mametz Wood proceeded. On the west side of the Contalmaison spur the Army carried the fortified copses and Horseshoe Trench after three days of most bloody and determined fighting.

On the east side of the spur the British attacked the Quadrangle, and on gaining three sides of it, attacked the fourth side. This fourth side known as Quadrangle support could be reinforced from the village and from Mametz Wood, and could be observed and fired into from both places, the British got into it and took it in a night attack but couldn't hold it.

When the Horseshoe fell early on 7th July, a big attack was put in against the whole of the two spurs, beginning with a very heavy bombardment upon the ruins of the village and the wood. The British reached the village, took part of it, and found and released in one of the dugouts there, a party of Fusiliers who had been captured by the Germans on the 2nd. The only 'easy approach' to the village was from the west, near to the Horseshoe, where the slope is gentler than it is to the south or south-west. The eastern approach was still blocked by Quadrangle Support. The 'easy approach' was not without its difficuties. Troops using it had to go down a slope into Shelter Valley. This was open and in fact without shelter, and was in full view of the enemy entrenched above him.

The British line 'bulged out' towards Contalmaison village but a wood called Bailiff Wood was between the British and the mainly German held village. The Durhams belonging to 68th Bde. of the 23rd Div. sent out patrols and found that the wood was occupied on its southern face and they came under heavy machine gun fire from it, Contalmaison and Quadrangle

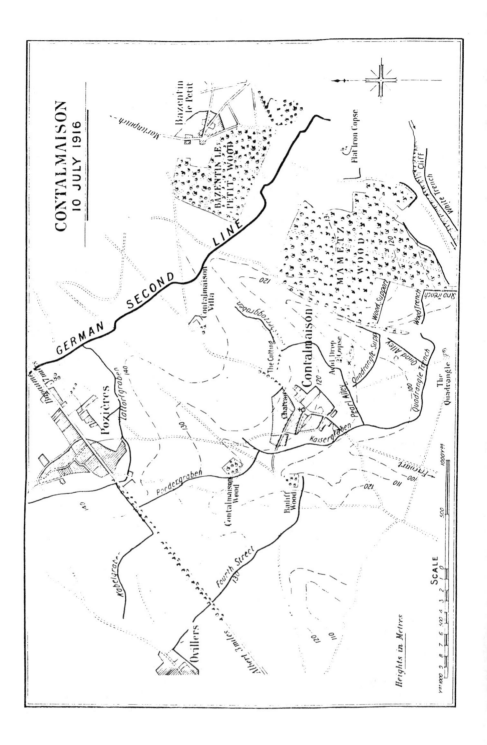

CONTALMAISON
10 JULY 1916

Support. However later the Durhams did in fact capture the wood, consolidated its eastern face, and reached a point 50 yards to the north-west of the village where they came under heavy machine gun fire. The Germans counter-attacked and pushed the Durhams back, who then retaliated. A German gun position and four guns were abandoned by the Germans and the Durhams pushed northwards until they overlooked Pozieres. Machine guns had been established in the north end of Bailiff Wood. Contalmaison on the right still had not been taken and it was decided that because of the exposure, to try again from the east when the troops could reach their positions without being observed.

At midnight (7th/8th July) companies of the 11th R. Warwicks (34th Div.) were to occupy the Work in the German line known as 'Heligoland'. The remainder of the battalion passed the night on the Tara–Usna Ridge. The Warwicks had received orders to relieve the 58th Bde. of the 19th Div. in the positions between la Boisselle and Contalmaison that had been taken on the 7th. At 8.45 p.m. on a fine evening the battalion passed the south end of the ridge, crossed the old front line, and thence went up Sausage Valley into the battle zone. HQ was established about 300 yards south-west of the lines in an extensive dugout. The previous day it had been the battle centre of the German Regimental Commander. It was two stories deep and fitted up in the most complete and elaborate way with all modern conveniences. Here the Warwicks installed the First Aid Post, the HQ Signallers and orderlies and a section of the Bde. MGC.

Brigadier Croft wrote that on 7th July his 68th Bde. which had been at Bécourt Wood in bivouac set off to take part of Contalmaison Village. They had been heavily enfiladed from Quadrangle Trench and also by fire from Bailiff Wood. Because of their exposure they were not assisted by reinforcements being sent up. The DLI were in the vacated assembly trenches. Croft concentrated on the left, which was less exposed and after dark the German Redoubt at Point 81 was taken and posts were put out. On the west side there was open ground, which was swept by the German guns, across which there were only two lines of approach. One, by inadequate communication trenches, from which it was impossible to debauch. Two, by the direct approach from the south which was completely at the mercy of the German artillery in the Pozieres direction.

Philip Gibbs in his book on the Somme wrote that 'Our guns were concentrating their fire along a line north of Birch Tree Wood from Horseshoe Trench, now in our hands, across Peake Woods and Quadrangle Trench away to Mametz Wood on the right. We were also putting a terrific barrage around the village of Contalmaison and Acid Drop Copse'. On the left of Contalmaison was Bailiff Wood, north-eastwards of the Horseshoe Redoubt – away to the right of Contalmaison was Mametz Wood, even more important both in size and position, with Bernafay Wood still further eastwards and Trônes Wood on the right again. Other small woods or copses south of Contalmaison were strong fighting points, from Shelter Wood to Round Wood and Birch Wood at the top of the sunken road and Peake Woods to the left of the Quadrangle Trench. Some of these places were but a few shell-slashed trees serving as land marks, but Bailiff Wood, Mametz Wood, Bernafay Wood and Trônes Wood were still dense thickets under heavy foliage hiding the enemy's troops and our own, but giving no protection from shell-fire.

The main trench leading up to Contalmaison was the sunken road which went up between Round Wood and Birch Wood, and this was being heavily barraged by the enemy's guns sweeping down from Pozieres. Farther up and slanting right to Pearl Alley was a shallow trench. A curious affair was happening in a trench called Old Jaeger Trench, running out of Horseshoe towards a German redoubt to the west of Peake Woods. Part of this trench was held by the troops on the left and partly by the troops on the right, and both reported and believed that they held all of it. The truth was that a gap in the middle was still held by a party of Germans, who had machine guns and bombs with which, presently, they made themselves unpleasant. Orders were sent to clear the trench of these 'ugly customers' and it was done by the troops on the left. Then orders were given to clear forward to a triangle to the right of the Old Jaeger. It was a strong redoubt – it yielded finally when the troops on the right fought their way up to Peake Woods, captured it, and enfiladed the enemy with machine gun fire.

The 12th DLI of the 68th Bde. of the 23rd Div. consolidated ground from which the 69th Bde. attacked Contalmaison on 10th July. The 8th R. Berks. (1st Bde. 1st Div.) marched to Albert and took over two trenches from the 10th Glosters. (1st Bde. 1st Div.) who had relieved the 24th Bde. (8th Div.) in the afternoon. Batt. HQ were in shelter on the main road from Fricourt to Contalmaison. The 13th DLI of the 68th Bde. was relieved on 11th July. The new trenches were near Lozenge Wood. At 9.15 p.m. the 8th Yorks. who had taken Contalmaison the previous night were relieved. The 8th R. Berks. established themselves in the chateau grounds with the 1st Black Watch on the left. In the chateau were cellars which were occupied by a German Medical Officer in charge of 110 wounded Germans. The battalion was to take before morning the cutting north-east of the chateau.

Geoffrey Malins the War Office Official Photographer filmed in the village soon after its capture in the period 9/10th July. The 7th, 17th and 23rd Divs. had attempted to capture the village since the 3rd and in the end it was captured by the 17th and 38th Divs.

Capt. G. K. Thompson of the 9th Yorks. was awarded a bar to his MC when he led the first line, and though wounded stuck to his duty. He was ordered back at midnight with a message and was sent to hospital.

H. P. Robinson in his book *The Turning Point* noted that by 10th July the British had worked their way up on the left, or west side into Bailiff Wood, which, while we had penetrated it before, was higher than at any point that they had formerly occupied. The 11th R. Warwicks. at 4.30 p.m. on the 10th assembled in outer trenches and launched an attack against the village from the west. An attempt to counter-attack by the Prussian Guard was bloodily repulsed, and the disordered elements of that force were caught by the Lewis guns as they emerged from the outskirts of the village. At 7.35 p.m. more orders arrived; this time to seize Bailiff Wood, in conjunction with a Battalion of the 11th Bde. of the 4th Div.

The Germans were shelled out of Quadrangle Trench and the village was heavily bombarded as well. Horseshoe Trench was captured and Donald Bell was killed in repelling Germans from entering the village.

In *Haig's Great Push* Bailiff Wood had been carried it says by a 'dashing assault' and the prospects on the western side were so good that it was decided to make the effort there, instead of from the south, in spite of the distance to be covered. The Germans had expected the attack from the south, and most of the machine guns were trained that way, when towards five o'clock on the morning of the 11th the British advanced upon them from the east. They had to traverse some 1,100 yards of open ground, and the infantry advanced in four waves, in extended order, leaving their packs behind them in order to push forward more rapidly, by seven o'clock the whole of the village was in their possession. The artillery had materially contributed to the success.

The 11th R. Warwicks. were relieved by the 10th L.N. Lancs. (112th Bde. 34th Div.) and returned to the Tara-Usna Ridge, where it became Bde. Reserve. The Battalion was now bivouacked on the reverse slope of the Tara-Usna Ridge, the enemy shelled the position with 5.9s. On the 13th the Battalion was relieved and went back into close support but on the 16th were ordered up again to support the 111th Bde. of the same division and moved to the chalk pit carrying spare ammunition and bombs to form a dump there.

At midnight on the 12th/13th July Pearl Wood was taken by a patrol and at the same time the Black Watch captured Contalmaison Wood to the left of the chateau. At 3 p.m. on the 13th the Battalion was moved from the chateau so that its left was now at the Cutting, and its centre in the sunken road to the right of the 1st Division. The 8th R. Berks. were ordered to move up to get into the German second line. In the late afternoon of the 14th the 1st Glosters (3rd Bde. 1st Div.) were given instructions to take over the line to the north of Contalmaison. The line lay just north of the village, along the road to Longueval, and continued westward of the junction of the latter with the road leading to Martinpuich. On either side of their point of union the roads had high banks, and this was the area known as the Cutting. 'D' Company held the trenches on the right and 'B' held the Cutting and its continuation westward. 'A' and 'C' were in support in lengths of trench among the ruins of the village, at the western edge of which HQ was lodged in a cellar. The site of the former church was marked by a great white stone; all that remained of the chateau was its vast cellars, now used as a dressing station, the other houses flimsily built had vanished. There were dugouts in the Cutting, and south of the village on the road that led to Mametz Wood was a cemetery. Close to it was a very large dugout which had a wonderful view of the ground over which the attackers were to advance. Close to the entrance lay a machine gun with its crew of Germans dead around it. On the 15th a long sap called Pearl Alley which ran forward from near the right of the Glosters' line, was found to be unoccupied and steps were taken to prevent the Germans from getting hold of it. In addition Contalmaison Villa, nearly half a mile forward on the Martinpuich road was found to be empty and was occupied. The small copse called Pearl Wood was secured as well. During the night of the 15th/16th the 3rd Bde. were involved in a successful night attack. The 1st Glosters had 450 yards of enemy line to capture. The 2nd RMF on the left were equally successful. The Glosters attacked and took the German positions which appeared to be more or less parallel with a line drawn from Contalmaison to Pearl Wood south-south-east of the Villa. A signalling lamp was placed in Pearl Wood so that it could be seen from the Villa. The Glosters also took part in the evicting of the enemy from Bazentin Wood. Late in the evening of the 17th the Battalion was relieved and went out to Scotts Redoubt to rest. I have depended on A. W. Pagan's book *Infantry* in the main for this account of the doings of the 1st Glosters.

On the 17th at 8 p.m. the 12th Durhams (68th Bde.) attacked and were heavily caught by machine gun fire and subsequently the attack planned for the 18th was cancelled. Over the next two days they dug trenches and consolidated. Croft's Brigade HQ was in Sausage Valley in a deep German dugout. There was a gas bombardment on the 19th which was very heavy. His Brigade were relieved by an Australian Bde. and they returned to Albert. A few days later they joined the right of an Australian Div. and the dividing line was Munster Alley. It had been the scene of heavy fighting both by the British and the Australians. They in turn relieved the Australians on 26th/27th July. The chateau had an ADS and another post was at the edge of Mametz Wood. On the 27th the Durhams, after a heavy bomb fight first gained 70 yards and 'locked' the trench. That night they deepened a ditch called Lancashire Trench. On the 28th no progress was made in the Alley and that night they were relieved.

Private William Short of the 8th York. Regt. (Alexandra, Princess of Wales' Own) was to be awarded the VC for an action on 6th August at Munster Alley, near which George Butterworth the British Composer had been killed previously. Short had been born in Middlesborough. He was foremost in the attack, bombing the Germans with great gallantry when he was severely wounded in the foot. He was urged to go back, but refused and lay in the trench adjusting detonators and straightening the pins of bombs for his comrades. He died before he could be carried out of the trench. For the previous eleven months he had always volunteered for dangerous enterprises, and had always set a magnificent example of bravery and devotion to duty. His grave is in Contalmaison.

D. W. J. Cuddeford arrived from the 15th Div. detail near Corbie with another officer of the 12th HLI and occupied a recently captured German trench near Villa Wood, Contalmaison. He was part of 'C' Company of the 12th HLI which was part of the 46th Bde. On 12th August the battalion had gone over the top for the first time in that sector against a strong system of trenches known as the Switch Line in front of Bazentin le Petit and a little to the left of High Wood. The attack was unsuccessful but a second attack on 25th August succeeded. The battalion then withdrew into reserve but went into the line again in early September. Having been in the line again, on 13th September they were withdrawn to reserve trenches in the neighbourhood of Villa Wood. Their battalion was to act as reserve to the Brigade and also supply ammunition carrying parties. Cuddeford was in charge of one of these. They were relieved by the 8th/10th Gordons of the 44th Bde. of the 15th Div. and went back to the dugouts near Villa Wood. These were between Contalmaison and Bazentin le Petit close to Mametz Wood.

On 14th September battalions supplied working parties for road mending based at the Cutting. Nissen huts were built on either side of the Fricourt–Contalmaison road.

The chateau was HQ of the Field Ambulance towards the end of September. Canon F. G. Scott in his book *The Great War As I Saw It* in which he describes his experiences as a member of the Canadian forces, wrote that in September at the corner of a branch road just above the ruins of Contalmaison their engineers had put up a little shack which was used by Army Chaplains and there coffee and biscuits were distributed. It was called Casualty Corner and had been started by the Australians. The once fine chateau was now a heap of bricks, and as already mentioned the Germans had used the cellars as a dressing station which was very large and had dugouts branching off from it. The road which turned to the left led down to a waste of weary ground in a wide valley where many different units were stationed in dugouts and holes in the ground. Towards Pozieres road was the famous Chalk Pit. In the hillside were large dugouts used when the battalions were out of the line. There was also a light railway.

C. E. Montague on one of his 'tours' took Muirhead Bone to Contalmaison and showed him the dressing station there; the chateau itself at this time had been destroyed. Later they went back down the slope to eat their lunch and below them was the battle. Despite Montague's calm elation at the scene Bone wrote that the sandwiches and his teeth didn't seem to keep proper time together!

In October there were many camps around the village and these were regularly shelled by the enemy. One camp was at Acid Drop Copse which caught the German barrage. On 2nd November the 1/4 O & BLI (1st Bucks.) (145th Bde. 48th Div.) were in support between le Sars and Martinpuich. They moved via Tramway and the Corduroy Track. In a letter of that day Graham Greenwell who was in this battalion wrote 'a hurried line amidst filthiest surroundings to let you know that we are just off to the trenches. Last night we camped on what was German ground before 1st July, in a filthy, muddy camp of tents and bivouacs; outside the remains of what had been a famous village during the 'Push'. The mud is perfectly ghastly, never have I seen anything like it: men and horses are caked in it from head to foot. It takes ten horses to get the smallest guns out.'

Charles Carrington of the R. Warwicks. said that in November he went to a new raw camp made of Elephant Huts at Scotts Redoubt near Contalmaison in the devastated area, a commanding height from which one could obtain a view for about 4 or 5 miles in any direction over a landscape entirely composed of mud. The Germans were seven miles away and they were safe except from very long range shell fire.

One camp was known as Contalmaison Villa Camp and another near the village was called Pioneer Camp. At the end of November the village was 'flatter' than ever, but the deep machine gun dugouts were still there intact. After the war a Memorial to the Tyneside Scottish and Irish Bdes. was unveiled by Marshall Foch. It was designed as a semicircular seat and is on the Albert road at a point where it branches off to Contalmaison.

Contalmaison Chateau Cemetery is within the chateau grounds on the north side of the main street. It was begun by fighting units on the evening of 14th July and used from September 1916 to March 1917 by Field Ambulances, and the pathway to it passes the ruins of the chateau.

The Sunken Road Cemeteries are in fields a little east of the Contalmaison–Pozieres Road, and 124 metres apart. The site was formerly wooded and the Sunken Road Cemetery is in the Bois Défrichés and the 2nd Canadian Cemetery is in the valley du Bois Derrieux. They were made in July–October 1916 during the middle fighting in the Somme offensive. Sunken Road Cemetery contains the graves of 148 Canadians and 61 Australian soldiers and five men of the Royal Artillery. It has no access road. The 2nd Canadian Cemetery contains the graves of 44 soldiers of the 2nd Canadian Infantry Battalion who died in September and October 1916.

Contay Village and Wood

Contay is a village on the main road from Amiens to Arras, about 11 miles north-east of Amiens and seven miles west of Albert. It is south of the village of Toutencourt on the D 919 road and was one of the principal railheads for ammunition at the start of the battle. The British Cemetery lies on the left or north-east side of the road to Franvillers, beside a quarry. The site was chosen in August 1916 for the 49th CCS, which arrived here at the end of that month and was joined by the 9th CCS in September. The German withdrawal on the Somme front took the medical units further east. On 3rd July the 2nd KOYLI (97th Bde. 32nd Div.) were in huts in the wood, and on the same night the remainder of the 11th Border Batt. (Lonsdales) marched here. The 16th HLI (97th Bde.) were also here in hutments having come from dugouts at Crucifix Corner. On 9th July the 32nd Div. HQ moved to Contay. On 10th August King George V left Querrieu (HQ of the Fourth Army) for Contay where General Gough of the Reserve Army and General Birdwood of the 1st Anzac Corps were waiting. He motored through the Australian lines and they 'cheered tremendously' according to the King's diary entry. The King's party went on to Warloy–Baillon. In early September the 4th Cheshires, Pioneers to the 56th Div. were in bivouacs in the wood. The CCS that had been established in the village was used by Ambulance Trains that ran on the Contay–Vecquemont Line. The latter named station was due south of Contay and close to the Somme river valley. To the north-east of Contay at Vadencourt XV Corps had a CP for wounded.

Contay Cemetery is one of the most beautifully designed in the Somme battlefield and based on the side of a hill, it was built in a stepped style that takes full advantage of the sloping nature of the ground. It is very much an 'English Garden'. Contay Wood can be seen from it.

Copse Valley

Copse Valley was to the south of the Peronne road between Carnoy and Maricourt (D 938 road) and at the beginning of the battle the boundary between the British and French Armies ran across it from north to south. Also at the beginning of the battle a canvas camp was in the valley which had been assembled by the 8th R. Sussex who were Pioneers to the 18th Div. In mid July the 2nd Wiltshires (21st Bde. 30th Div.) were billeted there for one night during their involvement in the Trônes Wood fighting.

Corbie

Corbie is small town at the junction of the Rivers Somme and Ancre, fourteen and a half kilometres east of Amiens and south-west of Albert, on the north bank of the Somme river. La Neuville is a sort of suburb of Corbie and they are separated by the railway line from Amiens to Albert. When the British took over the area from Berles-au-Bois southward to the Somme in July 1915 the town was about twenty-one kilometres behind the front trenches.

It was part of the Third Army Sector, and at once became an important medical centre. No. 5 CCS was set up there and was followed by the 21st CCS coming to la Neuville, across the Ancre. There were caves in Corbie which were similar to those at Beaumont Hamel and Naours. Presumably these were associated with the famous Abbey, part of which still stands and is still used. Before the battle began there is a mention of Corbie in *Gas* by C. H. Foulkes and he mentioned that four large flame projectors and sixteen portable machines were unloaded at Corbie on 26th June. The purpose of their presence was to set up three of the larger machines on the front of the 18th Div., at the head of existing mine galleries. They were discharged at separate times during the early hours of 30th June, twenty-four hours before the battle began. Corbie was also, at the beginning of the battle, one of the principal railheads for ammunition.

The 15th Field Ambulance had charge of the arrangements for evacuating casualties from the forward area, the ADS being in the Mametz–Montauban road. The 14th Field Ambulance was at Bécordel and the 13th at Corbie.

G. W. Warwick of the 4th SAI recorded that they stayed at a lemonade factory very briefly on 24th June, for breakfast, rifle inspection, dinner and then on to Welcome Woods. In *People at War* the Rev. J. M. S. Walker wrote that he was a member of the staff of the 21st CCS which he described as being converted from a partly burnt down motor car factory, its grounds dotted with huts, marquees and tents. Its function was to provide immediate treatment for casualties from the nearby front line, before they were moved by ambulance train or specially fitted barges down the Somme river, to base hospitals at Rouen, le Havre, and elsewhere. Prior to the start of the battle the staff of the CCS included six surgeons, three physicians, a dentist and eight sisters. There were two Hospitals in the Somme area which were exclusively for the use of officers, one was at Gezaincourt and the other was at Corbie.

Siegfried Sassoon in his memoirs said that on the 9th July he rode over to Corbie and visited Norman Loder (Denis Milden) 'in a garden in a splendid billet'. Riding back home he 'let his mare gaze in the still pools'.

Warwick was wounded in mid July and a motor ambulance took him and other casualties to the Dressing Station at Corbie which he says was a school. He was operated on on 14th July and on the 15th was taken by motor ambulance to a railway station a few miles away. The stretchers were placed on the platform with the faces of the casualties towards the sun. The hospital train arrived at 1 p.m. and they travelled via Amiens to Etaples and on to 'Blighty'.

On 21st July William La Touche Congreve, Brevet Major of the Rifle Brigade was buried at Corbie Cemetery. He was awarded a posthumous VC. His grave is next to that of Lt. Col. H. Bircham who was formerly CO of the 2nd KRRC of the 2nd Div. who had been killed by a shell on the 23rd July when at the Switch Line Trench, Pozieres. (See *Somme Harvest*). Bircham who had been educated at Eton and Sandhurst was a veteran of the South African War and had gained a DSO at Hooge Chateau near Ypres in March 1915. He had previously been badly wounded and twice mentioned in despatches.

There is a note that the 104th Bde. 35th Div. (Bantam) enjoyed 'splendid bathing' at Corbie, this could have been in the River Ancre or the River Somme. The Bantam Div. HQ was at Corbie on 10th August having moved from Cavillon and later the 15th Scottish Div. had a detail camp in the area which was midway on the road between Mericourt and Ribemont. On 3rd September the town was full of British wounded and also of German prisoners. In *Triple Challenge* by Hugh Bayly who at the time was with the 1st Scots Guards says that whilst at Morlancourt their bombing officer, a man called Leach, was killed in a bombing accident on 3rd September and that he had been recommended for a posthumous Albert Medal for the way that he sacrificed his own life and saved those of others. He was buried at Corbie Cemetery.

Aubrey Smith of the London Rifle Bde. wrote that in early September the town was crowded out with the four battalions of his Bde. who settled down in billets with a feeling that their training would be continued for a few days. All the familiar signs of a battle area were there: endless lorry convoys passing in both directions, French transport followed by British, French lorries, French artillery, British ambulances, British heavy guns drawn by tractors. There were also he says colossal dumps and myriads of horses. The Bde. lined up in the street and moved off, he squeezed into his allotted position in the convoy with the transport and they headed off up the road towards Bray and and Morlancourt.

Henry Dundas was with the Scots Guards, and in early September when they were at Carnoy he was at Corbie at a Corps Rest Station with some stomach trouble. He described the Rest Station as being a sort of chateau place in the middle of the town. On the 13th he left the town to rejoin his battalion and meanwhile had missed the attack of the 2nd Guards Bde. on 15th September.

G. A. Prideaux in *A Soldier's Diary* wrote that the Bde. HQ of the Somersets and Hants. was at Corbie, which he described as being a nice clean town with fine houses. The town was also the HQ of the Army Graves Registration Service and later International War Graves. The Commission were responsible for the work on the cemeteries which, even during the war, were in many cases flower gardens, where the troops used to go for a peaceful hour or two. No. 5 CCS remained at Corbie until October. The Newfoundlanders were billeted at Corbie in early October only to hear that they were to go into the line on the night of 10th October. It had been decided that for the attack by the Fourth Army the 88th Bde. of the 29th Div. should be temporarily attached to the 12th Div. which was in position at Guedecourt.

On the 19th October the 16th KRRC (100 Bde. 33 Div.) were billeted here before going on to Méaulte and Mansel Camp. The 21st CCS remained at Corbie throughout the battle until the spring of 1917.

Corbie Communal Cemetery lies to the north of the town between the roads to Bray and Vaux, and the British Extension is to the east of it. The graves are mainly of men from the No. 5 and 21 CCS, and the Extension was begun in May when the British plot was full. Plot 1 and most of Plot 2 of the Extension contain the bodies of men who died of wounds in the first Battle of the Somme. In 1918 with the Germans only 9 kilometres away the Cemetery was used again, this time by the Field Ambulances of the 47th Div. and later by the 12th Australian Field Ambulance.

La Neuville British Cemetery is on the west of la Neuville on the road to Bonnay. It is square in shape on level ground on the edge of the Somme marshes, surrounded by poplars and willows. It contains the graves of 886 men. La Neuville Communal Cemetery is on the north side of la Neuville, and forms one long row on the east side of the cemetery with 186 graves. Casualties from No. 21 CCS were buried in both of these cemeteries. In Corbie Abbey there is a memorial tablet to Congreve which was designed by Edwin Lutyens. La Neuville near Corbie was close to the broad gauge lines so that trains could come up direct to the CCS and evacuate them without using the motor ambulances.

Cough Drop and Drop Alley

The Cough Drop was to the north of High Wood and to quote from the 47th London Division History for the attack which began on 1st October, the Cough Drop, now accessible by day and providing excellent shelter, was selected for an ADS. There was a wonderful German dugout built as an aid post, with three entrances in the side of the bank. It provided accommodation for some seventy stretcher cases. The dugout was destroyed owing to a chapter of accidents on 2nd October, which began with someone 'mucking about' with a primus stove. The well timbered dugout caught fire but everyone escaped. An immense quantity of stores was destroyed, but far worse was that this precious haven, where, in emergency, so many wounded could be housed out of harm's way, had 'gone west' for good.

In his book *The Somme, 1916* Norman Gladden wrote that the company found its position in reserve in a trench known as Cough Drop Alley. In front of them was a low rise, behind which lay the shattered village of Flers, which had been captured when tanks were used for the first time. Their trench cut across towards the ridge while others zigzagged to left and right. Towards the horizon further to the right there was a fringe of trees with rolling country just discernable beyond. Somewhere on this side of the trees the Germans were entrenched and in that direction shells were continuously bursting.

Couin

Couin is a village and commune in the Department of the Pas de Calais, nine miles east of Doullens, in the valley of Authie. The village is on the D 2 road and is between Souastre and Authie. The chateau was used by the French Army and from 1915 by the British Army, as a Divisional HQ. At the bottom of the hill before the village, one of the few original military notices can still be seen, on a brick barn wall. This direction sign was there in 1916, when the 63rd Div. were assembling. It is thought to have been put there by the 94th Bde. who were members of the 31st Div.

There is a record of the 1/6 R. Warwicks. (140th Bde. 48th Div.) as coming to Couin Woods around 24th May and of using the woods and the hills between Couin and Authie for battle training. In mid June the 1/5 R. Warwicks. camped in the park here and Charles Carrington may have been with them. The pre-battle artillery bombardment which lasted from 24th June to 1st July was watched from the hill at the top of Couin. At the end of the month the 1/4 R. Berks. (145th Bde. 48th Div.) were in huts in the village, and the 1st Bucks. of the same brigade were in the woods around this time. In mid-July the 1/6 Glosters (143rd Bde. 48th Div.) were relieved and marched back to billets on the south side of the Couin-St. Leger Road. The 1/4 O & BLI (145th Bde. 48th Div.) in mid-July were in bivouac between Couin and St. Leger. The Pioneers to the 20th Div. the 11th DLI arrived in the village on 26th July and came to 'filthy billets'. Two days later they left for the nearby Dell. At this time the HQ of the 20th Div. was at Couin Chateau, they having returned to XIV Corps. On 7th August the 7th Somerset LI (61st Bde. 20th Div.) who were in Divisional reserve camped in tents in a field along the side of the wood.

Basil Hallam Radford, better known as 'Gilbert the Filbert', was in the Kite Balloon Section of the RFC. On 30th August he took Lt. P.B. Moxon up in his balloon from which they looked across the hills and railway stations of the Ancre Valley into Thiepval. Unfortunately the balloon ran into difficulties and Moxon had to jump out with a parachute. Hallam stayed on the edge of the basket and fell to his death on the Acheux Road. He was found without his parachute. Raymond Asquith who could be called a rival of his for Diana Cooper's affections said rather brutally in a letter to her, that Hallam 'was dreadfully forshortened and that he was only recognised by his cigarette case'. Hallam, who also used the name of Radford, fell between Bus and Bertrancourt and is buried at Couin British Cemetery.

The 2nd O & BLI of the 5th Bde. 2nd Div. practised co-operation in the area with the RFC around 12th September. In November the Motor Ambulance Convoy was transferred from the Fourth Army to Couin.

The British and New British Cemeteries are a little to the north of the village, and face each other across the road to Souastre at its junction with the road to Hénu. The British Cemetery was begun in May 1916 by the Field Ambulances of the 48th Div. and was used by units and Field Ambulances during the Battle.

In Couin New Military Cemetery across the road from Couin British Cemetery is buried Sgt. R. C. Travis of the 2nd Octago, New Zealand Army. He had gained the VC at Rossignol Wood close to Gommecourt and was killed on the 25th July 1918.

Courcelles

Courcelles-au-Bois is a village and commune in the Department of the Somme, and is about eight miles north of Albert, in the hilly country west of the Ancre. The village is north-west of Colincamps and east of Bus-lès-Artois. Whilst staying at Bertrancourt Geoffrey Malins, the Official War Office Photographer described the village of Courcelles as being mostly derelict and I do not have any entries until September when on the 1st of that month the 2nd O & BLI (5th Bde. 2nd Div.) were in huts and tents here with one company, another being at Colincamps. The 2nd Suffolks (76th Bde. 3rd Div.) marched through Bus to Courcelles around 17th October and reported that there was considerable shelling there and that a pair of 9.2s were behind their mess! All around the village the guns were being hauled into position and aeroplanes overhead were heavily shelled.

On 23rd October a party from HQ went up to Dunmow Trench in preparation for a Battalion attack against Serre which was due to take place on 25th October. That day their positions were taken over by the King's Own and they returned to Courcelles, as the attack had been indefinitely post-posted. This time the Suffolk's mess was in a chateau. After three more days they left for Bus.

In his book *The Middle Parts of Fortune* which is a novel, Frederic Manning wrote without giving a date, the following description; one should remember that Manning himself was in the 7th KSLI. 'After three days in the trenches, the battalion was relieved, and moved to Courcelles, where they were to remain for one night on their way to rest-billets at Bus. The village had been shelled from time to time, but had not been damaged to quite the same extent as Colincamps, which offered, on the crest of the hill, a more conspicuous target. Courcelles was uncovered at one end, but screened partially by rising ground on two sides. As Corporal Williams had said of Mailly-Maillet, it was simply lousy with guns.' – 'Monster guns, too, were secreted somehow in the courtyards of houses in the village itself.' – 'Battalion HQ in Courcelles was a small chateau, which stood, with its farm buildings, on a little hill practically encircled by a road.' – 'The rain continued, broken only by intervals of mist or fog, and spells of cold, which became more intense as the weeks drew on into November. The relay-post at Colincamps was abandoned; and they took their messages direct from the trenches to Courcelles.'

Now this may well be from a novel, but nevertheless it sounds pretty authentic to me and it is clear that the area was full of considerable artillery activity and this encouraged German retaliation.

The Communal Cemetery and the Extension on the north of the village is at the junction of the roads to Coigneux and Sailly-au-Bois. It contains the graves of British soldiers who were buried in September 1916; and in the following month the Extension was opened. This ties in with our first mention of activity as being as late as 1st September. Many of the graves are of soldiers from the KSLI who were killed in October to December period of 1916. This was Manning's Regiment. Like the Cemetery at Martinsart the stones are of the unusual red variety. The Extension was used by Field Ambulances and fighting units until March 1917, when the German Army retreated from the Ancre.

Courcelette

Courcelette is a village just off the D 929 main Albert–Bapaume road, it is seven miles north-east of Albert, north-east of Pozieres and south-west of le Sars. It is mainly associated with the Canadian Army.

The battle of Flers–Courcelette included the capture of Martinpuich which is a village to the south-east, and also of High Wood. The date of the attack was 15th September. The troops that were to be involved in the battle belonged to the 6th Bde. of the 2nd Canadian Div. The battalions were the 27th, 28th and 31st with the 29th in Bde. reserve. It was understood that the 27th Battalion was to attack the right sector and the 28th the left sector, and the 31st were to act as moppers up to both battalions, though on the day the 31st went ahead on their own and made greater progress than their sister battalions. The Bde. frontage was about 1,800 yards and the objectives were up to a mile away and involved Sugar Trench, Sugar Refinery and Ridge. On the right the 4th Bde. 18th, 20th and 21st Battalions were to advance straight through to their objective. Three tanks began behind the 6th Bde. at the mill and made their way slowly towards the Sugar Factory, also three more tanks left a point to the north-west in order to go round the back of the Refinery and link up. Two further tanks left from the south-east of Pozieres to get to a point to the north-west of the village of Martinpuich.

In his book *The Fifth Army* General Gough wrote that the direction of the

Allied advance had been altered on this occasion and instead of being generally northwards against Mouquet Farm and Thiepval, the Army was to attack eastwards and north-eastwards towards Courcelette with the right on the Albert–Bapaume road. The Fourth Army extended the attack south of this road, thus including Martinpuich in the sphere of its operations. As far as the Reserve Army was concerned, the attack on Courcelette on 15th September was the first occasion on which tanks were employed, six tanks co-operating with the Canadians. About fifty tanks were available at this time, and the majority of these were under the Fourth Army, seven only being allotted to the Reserve Army. Of this number a total of seventeen were destined not to reach their starting points, and the ones that were working with the Canadians began half an hour after the infantry. Many were ditched or knocked down and were unable to reach the German points of resistance such as the Sugar Refinery near the village. The remaining tanks had an immediate and decisive effect on the enemy, who in many cases simply ran away. Although it was to be the tanks who carried the day it should not be overlooked that the Canadian Infantry had a very tough day of fighting despite the success of the tanks. The fighting was to become desperate and the assaulting troops broke against the double line of German trenches, flanked by redoubts and salients armed with mortars and machine guns. Further artillery preparation was necessary. The assault was hard and costly and the German fire was withering from rifles and machine guns. They had dug new trenches in preparation which were called Fabeck Graben. They were north-west of Mouquet Farm and the Zollern Graben which was to the north of the Fabeck. These trenches had not been destroyed by the Allied artillery and it was not until six o'clock in the evening after fighting had been going on for 12 hours that Courcelette was finally taken by the Allies. A tank immediately set about clearing the streets. At the Sugar Factory a tank knocked down the walls, crushed machine guns that were hidden behind them, destroyed all the defence works and quickly overcame the German resistance. The name of the tank was Crème de Menthe.

In *The War in the Air* it is said that flares had been lit in semicircles around the village to indicate that it was wholly in Allied hands. Observers of No. 7 Squadron watched the Canadians move down the slope on the western face of the village and the flares were seen at 7.30 p.m. and were reported to be burning in a line as far as Martinpuich. The latter village had been virtually battered to pulp before being captured. The success against Courcelette and Martinpuich followed on the success earlier in the day against Flers where the first tank had gone into action. The wounded were carried on trolleys to Pozieres and then transported. On 16th September Private Kerr of the 49th (Edmonton) Battalion carried out the action that gained him the VC. His battalion was to advance through the 7th Canadian Bde. which was on the left of the Canadian attack, and was to then occupy a forward line within assaulting distance of the Zollern Graben. This the battalion failed to accomplish, being handicapped by ground difficulties and exposure to accurate machine gun fire; but the two companies took and held the Chalk Pit in advance of the Fabeck Graben, to which communication was dug. His citation reads in part 'During a bombing attack he was acting bayonet man, and, knowing that bombs were running short, he ran along the parados under heavy fire until he was in close contact with the enemy, when he opened fire on them at point blank range, and inflicted heavy loss. The enemy thinking that they were surrounded, surrendered. Sixty two prisoners were taken, and 250 yards of enemy trench captured. Before carrying out this very plucky act Kerr's fingers had been blown off by a bomb. Later with two other men, he escorted back prisoners under fire, then returned to report himself for duty before having his wounds dressed'. The 49th Battalion took up battle positions at a point near the sunken road, before and to the left of Courcelette with other battalions of the same Bde. The 49th supported the Princess Patricia's and the 42nd Battalion was on the extreme left of the frontage of operations.

C. E. Montagu who used to show important visitors round the Western Front came to Courcelette Sugar Factory ruins with a party, on 1st October. They were shelled there for some time with high explosive and were showered with earth and shrapnel. They then went back to the artillery lines, where they waited during an attack on the front. They set out homewards at 4.30 p.m. across the shelled area; none came very close but his 'flock' were very nervous and apt to scatter. They went 'home' by dark roads, arriving at Amiens at 8.15 p.m.

Canon Scott in his book *The Great War as I Saw It* wrote that after Courcelette was taken the Canadian front line lay beyond it past Death Valley on the slope leading down to Regina Trench which ran across the ridge. Over all this stretch of country waste and dreary as it got towards the end of September their various fighting units were scattered. He referred to a Piper who won the VC in the attack on Regina Trench and says that several tanks were knocked out near the village. One lay partly in the ditch by the road. On 26th September Scott spent some time in the Dressing Station in the sunken road close to Courcelette. He had walked from Pozieres down the railway track. The station had once been the dugout of an enemy battery and its openings were on the side of the road facing the Germans who knew its location perfectly. There was a large dressing station in the cellars of the Red Chateau in the village. The wounded who were waiting for the ambulance were in a dugout and shelter by the road. It was Dead Man's Trench and contained many German bodies. The village remained very close to the front line until the German retreat in the following February.

The British Cemetery is half a mile south-west of the village and was begun in the November as Mouquet Road or Sunken Road Cemetery. It was greatly enlarged after the Armistice by the concentration of graves of men who had fallen in 1916 around Courcelette and Pozieres. It stands in a hollow surrounded by cultivated land.

The Canadian Cemetery commemorates the Canadian action in October, when they took amongst other positions the longest trench built by the Germans on the Western Front, namely Regina Trench.

H. A. Taylor in *Goodbye to the Battlefields* wrote that after the War a black fragment of the old sugar factory was built into the long wall of a new farmhouse. One of the cellars in the main street was known to the soldiers as Number Ten dugout. One used to pass this spot on the way to Regina Trench and Dyke Valley. Nearby was Manchester Dump and two ground features known as Pope's Nose and Lady's Leg. In winter the line ran from Courcelette to Grandcourt and Miraumont. Many dead Germans had been found in the village presumably killed in the bombardment which preceded its capture on 15th September. The sunken road yielded up 100 bodies when the road was being cleaned and widened. Kitchener's Wood farm stock, had in December 1931, been gassed by leaking German gas cylinders. The old sugar refinery had been replaced by another building by 1931. On the right hand side of the D 929 road coming from Albert is the famous Tank Memorial.

Crucifix Corner

Crucifix Corner was on the cross roads close to Authuille Wood on the D 50 road out of Aveluy. Across the road was a quarry and just beyond it on the beginning of the road to Ovillers was the site of Crucifix Corner. There are many places on the Western Front with this name and this one was also known as Quarry Dugouts and consisted of a series of shelters in the chalk cliff. The dugouts here were reserve ones and on 25th September the 10th Essex of the 53rd Bde. 18th East Div. saw their first tanks while here, they were on their way up to concealed positions in Blighty Valley. Ivor Gurney who was with the Gloster Regt. has left a poem called Crucifix Corner; he was probably there in November or after.

Crucifix Corner

'There was a water dump there and regimental
Carts came every day to line up and fill full
These rolling tanks with chlorinated clay mixture
And curse the mud with vain terrible vexture
Aveluy across the valley, billets, shacks, ruins'.

Gurney was reminded by the Ancre marshes of the River Severn near his home in Gloucestershire.

Curlu

H. M. Davson of the Royal Artillery found an ideal spot as an OP on Curlu Ridge but it turned out to be too far from the guns. It was south of Hardecourt.

Danzig Alley

Danzig Alley was a German Trench which ran just north of the D 938 road south-west of the village of Mametz, through the village and out along parallel with the road to Montauban. To its east and also adjacent to the road was Pommiers Redoubt. The Montauban road is the D 64. Mametz Wood was due north of the eastern section of the Alley and the village of Contalmaison was to the north-west. The Alley was part of the objectives of the 7th Div. on 1st July. The Division had the following Bdes: the 20th, 22nd and 91st.

In *Haig's Great Push* it says that 'on the ridge by Mametz, their machine-guns had been so effectively hidden as to escape our bombardment, for no artillery can destroy every cache; and here the Germans offered a desperate resistance, emerging from the enormously deep dug-outs, such as are easily excavated in this hilly and chalky country, in which they had remained secure, and working their machine-guns with the utmost skill and determination.'

The 22nd Manch. of the 91st Bde. had reached the Alley soon after 8 a.m. on 1st July and there is a note in *The War in the Air* that a Captain Hawkins who was in charge of No. 3 Kite Balloon Section was responsible for some observation on this front which proved of direct help to the infantry. The 22nd Manch. had been pushed out again by the Germans from Fritz Trench which was just to the north-east of Danzig Alley. Hawkins directed a Siege Battery on to this trench so effectively that the 2nd Queen's who were also part of the attacking 91st Bde. were able to take the Alley in the afternoon with only small losses.

Philip Gibbs wrote that in the part of the Alley to the south-west of Mametz the 2nd Gordons of the 20th Bde. rushed forward with great enthusiasm until they reached one end of the village, and then quite suddenly they faced rapid machine gun fire and a storm of bombs. They flung themselves on the Danzig Alley position and had some difficulty in clearing it of the enemy.

Between the 2nd Gordons the 22nd Manchesters and the 2nd Queen's were the 1/S Staffs. who quickly reached Bunny Alley which was to the north-west of the Danzig and connected with Fritz Trench. All this fighting had been done by the 7th Div. who were able to boast at the end of the first day that they had not only taken the Alley, and Mametz village, but that they had almost reached their original planned objective in front of Mametz Wood. In the Danzig Alley Cemetery, which is sited on the former trench which had been captured by the right hand battalions of the 7th Div., are the graves of the first of July and not just from the 7th Div. but also from the 18th and 30th Divs. who were working successfully to the east of them. The Cemetery was begun in July and was used by Field Ambulances and fighting units until November 1916. After the Armistice it was greatly increased by the concentration of 1,782 graves, most of them from the 1916 battles which came from smaller burial grounds and from battlefields both north and east of the village. The Cemetery stands on high ground, amongst cultivated fields. From it there is a panoramic view of the battlefield with Mametz Wood in the centre. Within the Cemetery there is a memorial seat dedicated to the memory of the 38th Welsh Division who lost so many men in the fighting for the possession of Mametz Wood in early July 1916.

Daours

Daours is a small village in the Department of the Somme to the south of Querrieu on the D 115 road and on the east side of the Hallue river. It is to the west of la Neuville. The first British burial in the Communal Cemetery took place in February. The preparations for the offensive involved a grouping of Casualty Clearing Stations, the 1st/1st South Midland, 21st, 34th, 45th and Lucknow, section 'B', and later an Extension (it was designed by Edwin Lutyens) was begun on the south side of the Communal Cemetery. As the Allied advance progressed then the hospitals went forward with it. However the Germans were back in the Spring of 1918 when burials recommenced. From the east of the cemetery a commanding view of the Somme Valley can be had. There are 1,227 burials recorded in the two cemeteries combined. According to the *Ypres Times* in a report in 1935 every house in the village of Daours at that time still carried it's original billeting notice, so many men, so many horses.

Death Valley

The Valley ran between Montauban and Longueval to the north-east, and just in front of Delville Wood. It was often deluged with German shells. The Communication Trench was called Y & L Alley and it was littered with remains from the trenches of both sides, as well as the dead bodies of mules and horses.

In *Boy David* which is the Journal of the MGC it says that in the early days of the Somme battle the losses in Death Valley were truly terrible until our Pioneers, the Notts. and the Jocks, made a communication trench, over 1,000 yards long in a single night. It was so narrow that they could only just pass each other in it, but more important it was very deep and saved many lives.

In early September Aubrey Smith of the London Rifle Bde. of the 56th Div. says that beyond Carnoy they were shortly in an inferno, not of enemy fire but of the British fire: here in Death Valley guns of all calibres were massed in such numbers that one fired almost every second. After delivering his cookers he returned home to be held up by a traffic jam. In the evening some of the battalions moved up from Death Valley to the neighbourhood of Falfemont Farm. That meant that they were going to be put in an attack. On 8th September there was an exceptionally heavy bombardment; the Allied guns stood out boldly in the open – no better proof of British aerial supremacy was required – they were transferred to Happy Valley again on 9th September. On the 9th he wrote that he set out for Death Valley at daylight after dinner there, driving a water cart – 'Now I could see all those batteries which had startled me so much upon the first nightly trip, 9.2s, six inch howitzers, 8 inch guns and French artillery. However I had to stop at Death Valley, for from that point water would have to be taken up in petrol cans on pack ponies. The sun was low in the heavens as I stood in Death Valley and looked around at the scene of desolation. Dead horses, smashed limbers, and numerous stray shell cases lay about, the whole place hopeless. The reek from the guns, the dead horses, the foul soil and the lachrymatory shells made the place repulsive and horrible.' In his novel *The Somme* A. D. Gristwood wrote that sometime in September the cookers lay in a deep hollow a mile to the rear of the line (outside Combles was the line). The place was known as Death Valley by no means without reason. There the foremost batteries and fatigue parties waited until dark in a whirlpool of hurry. Always new guns were arriving, ration wagons, water-carts, field kitchens, mules, Royal Engineers, camouflage materials, corrugated iron, timber, barbed wire, sandbags in thousands. No lorries or ambulances could reach Death Valley however, which lay far from paved roads among the uplands of the Somme. The first sight of the 'Loamshires' of the Somme battlefield was gained from the Crucifix above Death Valley. This ancient iron cross, rusty, bent and ominous, yet remained as a notorious landmark on the hillside and from the shattered trenches near by they looked forward across the valley to a hideous welter of dust and smoke and intolerable noise. From Death Valley the 'Loamshires' marched over the hills to Méaulte.

S. Dolden of the 1/14th Lon. Scot. (168th Bde. 56th Div.) was resting at Angle Wood. Up on the ridge there were many French and German bodies covered in bluebottle flies. He took up his position in Death Valley slightly behind the line. The battalion was later relieved by the 1/13th London (Kensingtons) and then took up positions on the top of the ridge just above their cooker in Death Valley.

In the same way that there was more than one Happy Valley there was more than one Death Valley, and the other one in the Somme area apart from the one between Montauban and Longueval was south-west of Mametz Wood. Its other name is Valley of Death or Mametz Valley. It ran from the west of Mametz Wood in an easterly direction towards Caterpillar Valley. There is a description of it at the end of July as being a perfect inferno of bursting shells that concentrated on a narrow valley and road, the gun limbers went steadily up and down carrying their precious and necessary loads of shells to the guns which were banked almost wheel to wheel on the slope behind Bazentin Wood and were firing at this time all afternoon and evening, in the attack on High Wood.

In A. Russell's book *The Machine Gunner* he says that having gone up the line again they eventually came to a halt in the reserve lines half way down that all too familiar Valley of Death. They were in reserve for five days and on 10th August moved up to the front line in front of High Wood. The 33rd Div. was holding the southern half of the partly captured wood which was a German stronghold. There was a well dug communication trench up the gentle slope beyond Bazentin le Grand and then on to High Wood itself. However they were given orders to return as they had gone too far forward and a section had been hit.

In the diary of C. C. S. Gibbs MC, kept at the Suffolk Regimental Museum he wrote that in mid-August Death Valley had in it decaying dumps of barbed wire, boots, tin hats and shell holes, alongside the farm track that ran along its southern side – three hundred yards to the borders of Mametz Wood. On the south side of the track was a hill rising in a series of terraces of some thirty feet, and in these terraces were old German dugouts and disused Aid Posts.

Delville Wood

Delville Wood is north of the D 20 road to the west of Ginchy and its north-west edge is adjacent to the D 197 road to Flers. The Cemetery Register sets the wood's situation extremely well and it says that Delville Wood was a tract of woodland nearly half a mile square, the western edge of which touched the village of Longueval, while its eastern edge marked the boundary of the commune of Ginchy. It was to become famous in July and August 1916 for a battle that in the end lasted seven weeks. Originally the German front line ran from the south of Bazentin le Grand to the southern edge of Longueval village and then bent south-eastwards past Waterlot Farm just behind the front of Guillemont. Their intermediate line ran correspondingly behind the wood. The British front line ran from the north of Montauban, skirting the north of Bernafay Wood to Trônes Wood where it turned south alongside the eastern edge of Trônes Wood and on reaching the southern edge turned in a south-easterly direction. In Delville Wood the rides running in a north-westerly direction were Buchanan Street, which ran into the Strand, Campbell Street which ran into Regent Street and King Street which became Bond Street. going from west to east the rides were Princes Street, Rotten Row and Haymarket. Other names, mainly associated with London were given to other trenches and tracks such as High Holborn which led south-eastwards, Sloane Street which was to the south-west of Longueval, Dover Street which was south of the village, South Street which was the road from the village to Ginchy, Duke Street etc. etc. Flers Road led out of the north of the wood and North Street on its west side led to the Switch Trench after crossing Orchard Trench which connected the track to High Wood. In addition to the above there were many trench names which were chosen with mostly beer in mind and they included Hop, Beer, Vat, Stout, Pilsen, Bitter, Ale, Pint and several others.

H. P. Robinson in *The Turning Point* wrote that one speaks of Longueval and Delville Wood as if they were two separate positions; but, as a matter of fact, the wood engulfs the village, or the village is so embowed in trees that it is part of the wood. At the place where the two meet together, or where the building of the village ceases and the wood proper begins, the Germans had made some particularly strongly fortified positions, with machine guns and two field guns, which fired at point blank range from about 150 yards as British troops reached the edge of the ruins.

The *Stafford Knot* a regimental journal, described the wood as standing on a slight ridge extending eastwards from the village of Longueval, while about half a mile from its south-east corner lay the village of Ginchy, the intervening ground being, in 1916, covered by a system of trenches to which were given names reminding them of their national drink. The whole area

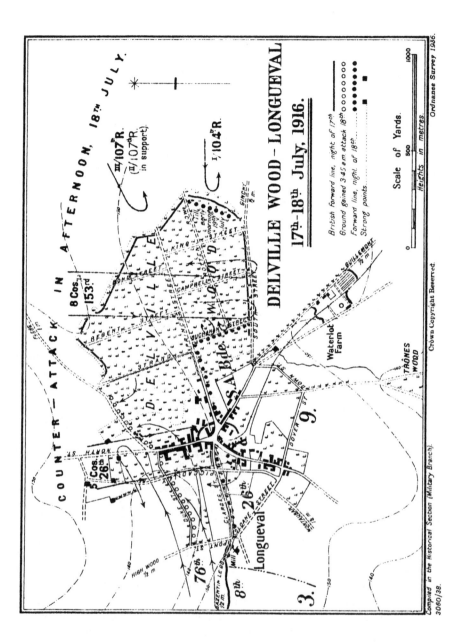

DELVILLE WOOD – LONGUEVAL
17th-18th July, 1916.

British forward line, night of 17th
Ground gained 3.45 a.m. attack 18th
Forward line, night of 18th
Strong points

Scale of Yards.

Heights in metres.

Crown Copyright Reserved.

Ordnance Survey 1936.

Compiled in the Historical Section (Military Branch).

3060/38.

originally formed part of the German second line defences.

In the *South African Forces in France* it notes that the sector Longueval to Trônes Wood was the most difficult in the battlefield because of (1) It was a salient under fire from three sides (2) The land sloped upwards from Bernafay Wood and Trônes Wood to Longueval (3) Both Delville Wood and Longueval were criss-crossed by trenches and machine gun nests and neither place could be held while the other was in enemy hands.

According to the DRH Springbok (September 1933) on the 14th July the greater part of the village of Longueval had been taken by the 9th Scottish Div. and on the 15th the South African Bde. of that Division captured the north-west corner of the wood, which at this time was a salient in the right angle corner of the lone Waterlot Farm and Mons Wood.

The battle was to rage from 15th July until 3rd September, the advantage was continuously to change from one side to the other and then back again. The Divisions involved in the fighting were the 2nd, 3rd, 7th 9th, 14th, 20th, 24th. Also the 53rd Bde. of the 18th Div. In his book *With the New Army on the Somme* F. Palmer wrote that the occupation of Mametz Wood and Trônes Woods left the British free to attack Delville Wood. In the course of that brilliant attack on 14th July the two Bazentin Woods and villages were captured and held 'at the first instance' by our left and centre: and the right wing began with equal dash and fortune. The South African troops swept across the wood but despite their success this turned out to be a prelude of the seven week struggle.

G. W. Warwick in his book *We Band of Brothers* wrote that the South African Bde. consisted of four regiments, the 1st, 2nd, 3rd and 4th South African Infantry from Cape Province, Natal, and Orange Free State, Transvaal and the 4th better known as the South African Scottish, were referred to by other members of the Bde. as 'Our Jocks'. Among the older men were those who had fought in the South African War some on the Boer side and others on the side of the British.

The South Africans had moved forward from Maricourt to Montauban and during a fury of action held part of Trônes Wood and Bernafay Wood. The task of the South African Bde. was to capture Longueval and clear Delville Wood and hold it against counter-attacks. The Bde. had a strength of 121 officers and 3,032 NCO's and men. On 14th July they had been in reserve at Montauban, less one battalion sent to assist the clearing of Longueval, The Bde. went into action on the morning of the 15th July.

After Delville Wood had almost been taken by the Allies, the Germans counter-attacked with lachrymatory and asphyxiating gas shells, forcing the attackers to fall back a few days later. However the Allies soon returned to the attack and a terrible struggle, which was to last for five days and nights without intermission began. Owing to the height of the trees no close artillery support was possible. In clearing the village the South Africans had had to face a murderous fire which was a test of the highest order. In the face of counter-attacks and murderous withering fire the South Africans held onto the village.

There is an extract from a diary of John Hay of the 4th SAI which was published in *The Springbok* of March 1936. Hay said that on going up the line, in a shed in Fricourt, they had picked up 45lb. mortar bombs which were three feet long with 'footballs' on them. They were already carrying full packs and subsequently had numerous stops and finally they left their packs behind at Montauban (14th July). They left Trônes Wood on their right flank, having previously fought over this ground on 10th July and defended the wood and entered the German second line position. The bombs were left at the rear of Longueval. They went back to Montauban and had breakfast, and then returned towards the line and came across the captured German trenches just where the road led up to High Wood. Following the road up, they came across, on the right of the road, a German sniper's post made of concrete. From the slits almost the whole of the Somme Valley could be seen and they saw the British Cavalry return from High Wood. By 7 a.m. on the 16th all the wood south of Princes Street had been captured, but after this initial success the advance was halted by a bombardment, which continued with only short lulls until the evening of the 17th, when Longueval village burst into flames; the whole wood was enveloped in smoke, and the name Devil's Wood was felt by many to be more appropriate. All except the south-west corner was re-taken by the Germans and attacks were made on Princes Street and Buchanan Street. Men of the 3rd South African Regiment on the eastern side of the wood were practically cut off and after a night of hand to hand fighting under appalling conditions, they were forced at dawn on the 18th to surrender for lack of ammunition. Between the 15th and 17th the South Africans despite the heavy bombardment had fought their way into the wood and despite heavy losses, had taken all the wood except the south-west corner by the 17th. The 3rd Battalion was cut off and had to surrender – three officers and 150 men. The Colonel of the 2nd Battalion gathered together 140 men of all ranks from the four battalions and fought his way through to rejoin the Bde. At 6 o'clock on the 20th, the Bde. was behind the Voortrekkers double cross, and the tree is the only surviving original tree and is full of shrapnel.

On 18th July what remained of the three battalions was forced back to Buchanan Street. The German artillery had begun a barrage for their great counter-attack and many huge trees fell as a result. The Germans counter-attacked successfully but at a great cost in men. Despite the Allies losing the greater part of the wood, their line held fairly well and it was possible to keep Group informed (according to Fraser-Tytler) and to shoot five or six batteries on various good targets around Guillemont. He returned to Group HQ at Maricourt and was to keep the Trônes Wood communication line going. This was the only means of Divisional communication with the front line, but it was an expensive luxury and needed eight to ten men continually mending it and his signallers were naturally becoming slightly tired.

Private Faulds of the 1st Batt. SAI was awarded the VC for his actions on 18th July. He was born in 1895, and the citation in brief was 'For most conspicuous bravery and devotion to duty'. A bombing party under Lt. Craig attempted to rush over 40 yards of ground which lay between the British and the enemy trenches. Coming under very heavy fire and machine-gune fire the officer and the majority were killed or wounded. Unable to move, Lt. Craig lay midway between the two lines of trench, the ground being quite open. In full daylight Private Faulds, accompanied by two other men, climbed over the parapet, ran out, picked up the officer, and carried him back, one man being severely wounded in so doing. Two days later Private Faulds again showed most conspicuous bravery in going out alone to bring in a wounded man and carrying him nearly half a mile to a dressing station; subsequently he rejoined his platoon. The artillery fire was at the time so intense that stretcher bearers and others considered that any attempt to bring in the wounded men meant certain death. This risk Private Faulds faced unflinchingly and his bravery was crowned with success. He died in 1950.

The South African Bde. retired on the 19th/20th July, and on their return to Montauban only one third of the Bde. was left to answer the roll call. For three days the fight had gone on and the Bde. had stood its ground. Tired, hungry and exhausted, the men held on and went forward, clearing the wood bit by bit. When the South Africans assembled at Happy Valley after Talus Boisé, they had lost 2,400 of their number. The battle had begun on the 15th and already the Bde. had fought through a fortnight's continuous action. When they were relieved Colonel Thackeray marched out with two officers, both of whom were wounded, and 140 other ranks, made up of details from all Regiments of the Bde. On the morning of 18th July Thackeray was holding the wood with nine and a half companies, a strength of about 1,500 men; two days later he had 140. (From *South African Forces in France*.)

In the *History of the Royal Fusiliers* it says that on the 19th they were occupied by the struggle to clear the wood once again; and it was in the lull after the fighting had temporarily died down that the 4th R. Fusiliers took over from the Essex, Suffolks and Welch Fusiliers in the south-east of the wood. There were many casualties in the 4th Batt. who weren't even taking part in the attack! In the *History of the Norfolk Regt.* we learn that the 8th Norfolks (53rd Bde. the 18th Div.) were ordered up the valley north-east of Carnoy to relieve the South Africans, and to prepare for a counter-attack on the wood. Reaching the valley at 4.30 a.m. they were ordered to be in position by 6.15 a.m. The Bde. orders required the battalion to take the whole southern portion of the wood but it was impossible to make progress. The attacks of the other battalions in Longueval and the northern parts of the wood could make but little progress, and they had to dig themselves in, as had the Norfolk men in the southern positions. Here from the afternoon of the 19th till the early morning of the 22nd, when it was relieved, the 53rd Bde. had to hold on to the captured portion of the wood against a tremendous bombardment, a perpetual fire from snipers, and innumerable attacks by small parties of Germans in the tangled undergrowth and amongst the ruined trees.

Two men gained the VC on the same day from the same battalion (20th July), firstly Corporal J. J. Davies of the 10th R. Welch Fus., who was born on 28th April 1889 and was a Regular soldier. 'For conspicuous bravery.' Prior to an attack on the enemy in Delville Wood he became separated with eight men from the rest of the company. When the enemy delivered their second counter-attack his party was completely surrounded, but he got them into a shell-hole and by throwing bombs and opening rapid fire succeeded in routing the attackers. Not content with this, he followed them up in their retreat, and bayoneted several of them. Corporal Davies set a magnificent example of pluck and determination. He had done very gallant work and was to be badly wounded in the second battle of Ypres.

The other VC winner of this day was Private A. Hill of the 10th R. Welch Fus. at Delville Wood. He was born on 24th May 1895. When his battalion had deployed under very heavy fire for an attack on the enemy in Delville Wood he dashed forward when the order to charge was given and meeting two of the enemy suddenly bayoneted them both. He was later sent by his Platoon Sergeant to get in touch with his company, and finding himself cut off and almost surrounded by some twenty of the enemy, attacked them with bombs, killing and wounding many and scattering the remainder. He joined the sergeant of his company, and helped him to fight their way back to the lines. When he got back, hearing that his company officer and scout were lying out wounded, he went out and assisted to bring in the wounded officers, two other men bringing in the scout. Finally he himself captured and brought in two of the enemy. His conduct throughout was magnificent.

Corporal Robertson of the Worcesters wrote that on 21st July they were off again to Delville Wood. 'Gee that wood will drive me mad – had enough of it on the 18th. We go through the remains of Longueval. Take up our positions in the remains of a trench running along the edge of Delville Wood, this is the bit we suffered for three days ago. Imagine sacrificing 800 men for about 200 yards of ground.' On 22nd July he could see about five miles back into German ground. They were on the ridge. That is why the place was contested so often. The remaining men of the South African Bde. who had been recovering at Happy Valley moved from there on 23rd July via Méaulte to Maricourt. There they were set upon by a 'plague' of War Correspondents.

In his book *Battle-line Narratives, 1915–1918* H. E. Harvey of the 22nd R. Fus. (99th Bde. 2nd Div.) wrote that after passing through Fricourt they were told to draw extra rounds and bombs and advanced eventually arriving in the 'odious' destruction of Delville Wood. A little after 7 a.m. on 27th July, their Bde. made the final assault to clear the enemy from the wood. The 1st R. Berks., 1st KRRC, and the 23rd R. Fus. led the attack, driving the enemy to the further fringe of the deadly area. Every man of the 22nd and the 17th Middlesex Battalion, and other men of various units was rounded up by Lt. Col. Arthur Grenfell, in charge of cavalry reserves at Montauban. Delville Wood was captured and held. Over the next few days they went in and out of the wood.

A member of the 1st KRRC was to gain the VC on 27th and his name was Sergeant A. Gill. He was born in 1880 and his award was for conspicuous bravery. The enemy made a very strong counter-attack on the right flank of the battalion, and reached the bombing post, after killing all the company bombers. Gill rallied the remnants of his platoon, none of whom were skilled bombers, and reorganised his defences, a most difficult and dangerous task, the trenches being very shallow and much damaged. Soon afterwards the enemy nearly surrounded his platoon by creeping up through the thick undergrowth, and commenced sniping at about 20 yards' range. Although it was almost certain death, Sergeant Gill stood boldly up in order to direct the fire of his men. He was killed almost at once, but not before he had shown his men where the enemy were, and thus enabled them to hold up their advance. By his supreme devotion and self sacrifice he saved a very dangerous situation. He was buried at Delville Wood Cemetery. The 2nd Div. retook the wood later in the day and held it until 4th August when the 17th Div. took it over.

From the *History of the Royal Fusiliers* it is stated that on 27th July the wood was again over-run. Four battalions of the R. Fus. had their share in the exploit, and the place of honour was given to the 23rd (99th Bde. 2nd Div.). They had had a comfortable time at Bernafay Wood prior to the attack and had formed up in a trench at the edge of the wood with the 1st KRRC on the right, and the 1st R. Berks. in support. The 17th R. Fus. of the 5th Bde. lay south of the wood with the 22nd R. Fus forward on the left. In the afternoon two companies of the 17th R. Fus. moved up to the wood and before the end of the day every available man of the 22nd R. Fus. had been thrown into the struggle on the right. On 28th July the wood was finally cleared of its last German occupants. On both sides the losses had been very heavy. Three German Regiments were completely annihilated. On the 30th 'C' Company of the 24th R. Fus. was engaged and had taken over the front line from the southern edge of the wood to Waterlot Farm on the previous day. On the 30th they advanced against a German trench some 600 yards east of Waterlot Farm. Fighting was still continuing about Delville Wood. General Gough noted in his *The Fifth Army* that although the Germans had counter-attacked with the assistance of flammenwerfer the British never made a general practice of this form of warfare, though it was used once in Delville Wood by the Fourth Army.

By 1st/2nd August the wood was a vast tangle of trees which had fallen, full of fragments of crumped trenches and 'scrapes' which were full of dead soldiers. The enemy still held the front edge of the wood. J. Delaney a noted boxer had been killed in the attack of the 23rd R. Fus. (99th Bde. 2nd Div.). From the 11th August the 7th, 8th and 9th Rif. Brig. of the 14th Light Div. were in reserve in the Delville Wood area. The Light Div. were to clear the wood of enemy resistance.

In mid-August according to the diary of C. C. S. Gibbs MC, a working party was to meet a guide from the Royal Engineers and they were to dig a trench half a mile from the front line near Bazentin le Grand.

On the 22nd August the 9th Rif. Brig. were in the Delville Wood locality and were to assist the advance of the 9th KRRC who were also part of the 14th Div. whilst the 61st Bde. of the 20th Light Div. had a battalion and a half in front trenches, continuing the line to a point south of the south-east corner of the wood. Bde. HQ was north-east of Bernafay Wood.

On 24th August the situation had much improved because of an attack in which the 20th R. Fus. (19th Bde. 33rd Div.) took part. The wood was finally and completely won on 24th August after six weeks of fighting.

In the *Stafford Knot* it notes that the 1st N. Staffs. had come out of the line on 25th August after spending just over a fortnight in the Guillemont sector, where they had had an unpleasant time and suffered some 150 casualties, but had not actually been committed to an assault.

The 22nd Bde. of the 7th Div. had relieved portions of the 14th Light Div. on 26th August on the eastern edge of Delville Wood and parts of the 20th facing Ginchy. At that time the Germans had been dislodged from all but a small corner of Delville Wood and were holding several trenches that ran into the wood and this had prevented the British from establishing more than a slight hold on them. These trenches ran across the top of the ridge leading from the wood eastward and flanked the approaches to Ginchy from the west, their capture was therefore essential; and early on the morning of 27th August the bombers of the R. Welch Fus. began fighting for the possession of Ale Alley, which entered the wood from the north-east corner. The attack went on for several days and involved the South Staffs., the Queen's and the Manchesters. This would be the 91st Bde. of the 7th Div. Conditions within what remained of the wood were quite ghastly, no foliage was left and the stumps of trees were twisted in all directions. One particular difficulty was that the trees tended to change their shape after each bombardment and guides who had been in the area for some days would become lost as they tried to locate their landmarks. Heavy rain and shell-fire had reduced the ground to a quagmire, and the so-called trenches, often mere ditches connecting shell-holes were sometimes in liquid mud. The most horrible thing though, was the presence of hundreds of unburied corpses belonging to both sides, some of which had been there for several weeks. The sight of these decaying bodies was bad enough, but worse still was the stench, for the sickly smell of death pervaded everything. It was in these conditions on 29th August that the 1st S. Staffs. moved into the wood, as the left forward battalion of the 7th Div. to occupy the trenches facing the direction of Gichy. Two companies were forward in Beer Trench, between Hop Alley and Pilsen Lane, with a detached strong point in Ale Alley. Another company was in support in Diagonal Trench and another in reserve just south-west of the wood. The old 38th had been out of the line for five weeks recovering from their July experiences, when they had suffered over 300 casualties in the attacks on Mametz Wood. On 30th August the 1st N. Staffs. (72nd Bde. 24th Div.) took over the sector on their left as the right forward battalion of the Div. Two companies held Edge and Inner trenches, while another company was in support in Devil's Trench and another in reserve (*Stafford Knot*).

F. C. Hitchcock of the 2nd Leinsters (73rd Bde. 24th Div.) was detailed to bring up his platoon on 30th/31st August, and support the 9th R. Sussex. Hitchcock's way lay up a slope on top of which they scrambled into a shallow communication trench, as they were quite visible to the enemy, who was then sniping at them. They made their way to due west of Delville Wood. The exact position was at the junction of Plum Street with Chesney Walk. His platoon was ordered up Plum Street and was to bomb the enemy, who had a position at the T Junction formed by Orchard Trench, which they knew as being held by the enemy in strength. To quote Hitchcock 'In broad daylight I was ordered to advance up an exposed communication trench with my platoon in file'. The objective being to capture the enemy post at Orchard Trench 'and with bent heads we turned into Plum Street, which was at right angles to Chesney Walk. We advanced very cautiously, as 150 yards ahead of us, on commanding ground, was the Boche post. Along the left-hand side of Plum Street were the shattered stumps of trees, and when we had advanced some 20 yards only,' – 'bombs rained down all around us. My bombers retaliated, and after a short exchange, the Boches whom we could see quite distinctly wearing their coal-shuttle shaped helmets, retired. We again advanced, but crawling on hands and knees, as the trench was completely obliterated. Enemy snipers now started to worry us, as our screen of smoke from the bombs cleared off. Some men were hit behind me.'

In the *Stafford Knot* it says that at the end of August the fighting having swayed to and fro, the Germans were finally expelled. Among the units involved had been the 2nd S. Staffs., who had positions against the German attacks for four days at the end of July, incurring over 300 casualties. The 1st RB (11th Bde. 4th Div.) had gone to trenches that were east of Delville Wood having come up via Montauban. Again I quote from the *Stafford Knot*. The next morning the whole wood was heavily shelled and at about 11 a.m. the bombardment became intensive. At about 12.30 p.m. the assault came in. The Germans in the South Staffs. sector tried to bomb their way forward along Ale Alley and from the right, into Bitter Trench, but they were held up and no ground was lost. The North Staffs. lost a little ground. In the afternoon one South Staffs. Company was led forward from the almost obliterated Diagonal Trench, then in a second enemy counter-attack were reduced to less than half strength and ran out of grenades. In the early evening the Germans broke through near the junction of Hop Alley and Bitter Trench. Meanwhile the pressure on the North Staffs other flank had been successfully held. Had they not held their ground there was real danger of the whole defence of Delville Wood crumbling; however the South Staffs. were relieved during the night by the 2nd Queen's. Reserves were brought up for the North Staffs. The next night the 64th were relieved by the 9th East Surreys of (72nd Bde. 24th Div.) Major Dugmore (North Staffs.) was to take over command of the East Surreys whose CO and 2nd in command had both been killed. The 12th RF (17th Bde. 24th Div.) were suddenly ordered up to the front on 1st September. On the way up they were delayed for two hours in Caterpillar Valley owing to a very heavy gas barrage. The guides had gone astray, and it was not until 3.30 a.m. that the battalion was in Carlton Trench, which lay between Delville Wood and High Wood. At midday the whole line advanced, the sector between High Wood and Delville Wood was obstinately defended. The Buffs' (17th Bde. 24th Div.) main objective was the strong point at the junction of the Wood Lane Trench and Tea Trench in the north-west corner of Delville Wood. 4th September was fairly quiet and on the night of 5th/6th September the 1st North Staffs. (72nd Bde. 34th Div.) and the 9th E. Surreys were both relieved. The battle of Delville Wood officially ended on 3rd September, after lasting seven weeks.

The two Staffordshire Regiments could claim that they had met and blunted the last German effort to regain this vital feature. The 38th suffered 270 casualties and the 64th 214. Ginchy fell a week later and the German Second Line in this part of the front was finally broken. On 7th September Lt. Col. Burnaby of the 11th Queen's RW Kents was killed while reconnoitering Delville Wood, and buried at Danzig Alley.

W. V. Tilsley in his book *Other Ranks* wrote that on their way to the front on 7th September the path wheeled at the edge of the gutted Delville Wood. The black mass of the wood receded on the left rear, but still they lunged on behind some 'wonderful brave' in front. On 9th September the Irish Guards were attempting to capture Ginchy.

H. W. Bayly a Medical Officer with the Scots Guards having recently treated Raymond Asquith and 'Sloper' Mackenzie of the Gren. Gds. was himself wounded in the leg and on 16th September was taken from the Field Ambulance near Delville Wood to the CCS. Hugh Ross was in the next bed in hospital and he learnt from him that Guy Baring had been killed.

According to the *History of the Royal Fusiliers*, in mid-September the Londoners left; sharing in the honour of the capture of Flers, was the Light Infantry Division which had recently come to the line on the Somme after spending nine months in the Ypres Salient. They had in all to make an advance from positions at the eastern end of Delville Wood of some 2,500 yards, carrying four successive German lines, the Switch Line, Brown, Tea, Support and Gap Trenches. On 21st September a salvage party was requisitioned to aid in widening and deepening an old track through Delville Wood.

Fraser-Tytler in his book *Field Guns in France* said that in early November that they were taking over an empty gun position in Delville Wood and as soon as they collected some new guns they were to 'open shop'. All along the road to the wood there were 'Archies' mounted on motor lorries. In making his position and planning dugouts it always appeared to be sited on top of several buried huns!

During the Allied advance in 1918 there was more heavy fighting in the area. In the introduction to the Cemetery Register it says that 'on Buchanan Street just north of the cross of Rotten Row, a monument marks the site of the South African Bde. dugout.' Several trenches can be followed away from it into the wood. The Cemetery is immediately to the south of the wood, on the south side of the road from Longueval to Ginchy. It was made after the Armistice, by the concentration of a few small cemeteries and of isolated graves, almost all from July, August and September 1916. It covers an area of 17,900 square yards and is on the south-west of the village.

The South African Memorial stands opposite the Cemetery and together they form one architectural theme. The Central Avenue of the Cemetery is continued across the Longueval–Ginchy road by a grass road, in a wide clearing, running northward into Delville Wood, and across the clearing, at the top of a low rise, is the Memorial to those South Africans who died in the Great War. It is a flint and stone screen, with a shelter at each end and in the middle an arch surmounted by figures of a horse and two men (representing the two races of the Union) in bronze. It was unveiled by the widow of General Louis Botha on the 10th October, 1926, a day otherwise memorable in South African history. This Memorial does not bear the names of any of the dead; those of the South African dead are recorded in the same cemeteries, or on the same memorials as those of the Corps and Regiments from the United Kingdom.

Many of the original tree trunks had been preserved in the wood, and we have a post war description of the wood from *Ypres Times* (in the 1930's). 'The old drives that intersected "Devils" are back, too, and little cairns perpetuating the war-time nomenclature bestowed upon them. Thus you come upon Campbell Street and your Rotten Row, your Princes Street and Regent Street. At the foot of these bournes are rusted machine gun tripods' – 'Scores of South African oaks, dressed in regular "parade ground" lines, have been planted, in that magnificent expanse of turf linking the Longueval–Ginchy road with the Union's memorial' – 'From the summit of the twin turrets, approached by short winding stairways, a wonderful panorama of the new Somme is gained, with the lone New Zealanders' Memorial chiselled out in the centre of the canvas' – 'as many as 42 villages can be seen from this monument.' There are Arrow head signs pointing to famous 'warm corners'. At the time there was a house built in the English style standing on the Longueval side of the wood bordering the wide drive. There was a rest room for tourists there. At the time of writing there is a Museum being built in the grounds, which was due to be opened in November 1986.

Dernancourt

Dernancourt is a village just off the D 52 road between Ville-sur-Ancre and Albert. It is south-west of Méaulte and due north of Morlancourt. It is in the Ancre Valley and the main rail route runs through it. General Rawlinson in charge of the Fourth Army had told the Director of Railways that there must be a metre gauge line laid from Dernancourt to Bontay Farm. Dumps were fed by this line but even so the majority of ammunition was carried forward by lorry or wagon.

The whole area was used for camping or bivouacking, and on 13th June there is a note of the 8th N. Staffs. (57th Bde. 19th Div.) as being here. They were camped in tents in a hollow close to the railway line between the village and Albert. Other battalions camped on the hillside here, and around 20th July the 2nd Gordons H. (20th Bde. 7th Div.) rested here after being in action at High Wood. Their commanding officer Lt. Col. B. G. R. Gordon had been killed in the relief.

The Dernancourt Branch Railway line was carried to the terminus called Loop, just east of the Bray–Fricourt road with sidings at Ford Spur, Grove Town and Happy Valley. This line led towards the point of junction of the British and French Armies and a short branch off it from Pilla Junction led southwards to a 'breezy' railhead aptly named Bell Air. Ambulance Trains used the Dernancourt–Loop branch line and the village was a walking wounded and collecting station. Xth Corps used the Dernancourt–Maricourt line for the clearing of lightly wounded cases from Corps Collecting Posts in the neighbourhood of Carnoy and Maricourt.

Siegfried Sassoon noted in his diary on the 21st July that his battalion transport (1st R. Welch Fus.) moved to a hill south-west of Dernancourt on the evening of the 20th July. The battalion was expected to return from the trenches at about midnight, and finally arrived at 5.45 a.m. Sassoon and the transport waited for six hours at the crossroads.

In his book *Subaltern on the Somme* Max Plowman of the 10th W. Yorks. (50th Bde. 17th Div.) said that they were at Dernancourt in August and the field where they slept by the crossroads in the open was called Belle Vue Farm, though Plowman saw no farm! Albert lay below them to the north. Hardy, a fellow lieutenant went on one occasion with Plowman on an expedition to Pommiers Redoubt close to Mametz village.

On the 8th August the 8th KRRC (41st Bde. 14th Div.) moved to the village and after a week, left for Pommiers Redoubt. The 7th KRRC of the same brigade also arrived on the 8th, by train and left for Pommiers Redoubt on the 11th August. They returned on the 27th August.

At the end of August XV Corps MDS was formed in the village on the right bank of the Ancre between Dernancourt and Buire, and the Extension to the Cemetery was opened. On the 24th August the 2nd KOSB (13th Bde. 5th Div.) having first marched and them spent a lot of time in a train that 'crawled' arrived finally at Dernancourt Camp from Mericourt Station to the south-west. Also on that day the 5th Div. after a rest moved by rail to the Dernancourt area and joined Cavan's XIVth Corps. On the next day the 25th, the 2nd KOSB marched to Happy Valley, west of Bronfay Farm, where in quieter times the Battalion HQ used to be.

The 18th KRRC (122 Bde. 41st Div.) moved to the village around the 6th September and carried out training in the area before moving to Fricourt on the 12th. During this period the 7th Div. had two of their Brigades, the 22nd and 91st in the area and at the time the billets were thought to be most unsatisfactory and also absolutely filthy. The 22nd Bde. cleaned them up and also the village too and burnt mountains of refuse. They also transformed the sanitary arrangements.

Between the 9th and the 11th the 9th King's bivouacked outside the village, and they had to move after a while, as a long range gun 'shelled them out of it'. On the 11th the 9th KRRC (42nd Bde. 14th Div.) arrived here, and camped in a field north of the railway. Another of the KRRC battalions was back in the area on the 10th having been out of the battle area for ten days. They left the village for Fricourt the next day. On the 17th, the 7th or 9th KRRC (41st

Bde. 14th Div.) arrived here for a stay that lasted until the 22nd. The 8th KRRC of the same brigade arrived on the 17th September. On the 19th the 18th KRRC arrived and were in the village until the 2nd October, when they left for Mametz Wood for one night. The village was used also by the 47th, 48th and 55th CCS under the name of Edgehill which was to the north-west of the village and took its name from its situation on rising ground.

In the second half of September the 11th King's who were Pioneers to the 14th Light Div. were billeted in huts here at Number One Camp. It was a curious sight to see from this hill at night the camp fires burning all around the countryside, it gave very much the appearance of a victorious army. This was before night bombing began. On 24th October the Germans were still firing long range shells into the village.

The Communal Cemetery is a little west of the village, across the railway line and the Extension is on the north-west side. The Communal Cemetery was used for British burials from September 1915 to August 1916 and again in the March 1918 retreat. It contains the graves of soldiers who were buried from Field Ambulances at Dernancourt. The Extension Cemetery was designed by Lutyens and contains the graves of 2,134 men.

Destremont Farm

Destremont Farm is now no more but was on the site of the modern le Château Ferme which is on the left of the D 929 Albert–Bapaume Road. Eaucourt l'Abbaye is due east and the Butte de Warlencourt is to the north-east. The next village is Courcelette to the south-west. The farm was eventually captured on 29th September early in the morning. It had been a strongly defended group of buildings and the taking of it assisted the attack on the Flers line on the left flank. It had been captured at 5.30 a.m. by a company of the 8th Y & L (70th Bde. 23rd Div.) who having stormed the Farm buildings had made contact with the Canadians on the left later in the day.

There were assembly trenches behind the farm buildings in October and the farm itself had two large cellars which couldn't be touched by shells, and platoons were able to shelter here.

Dewdrop Trench

Just out of the village of Lesboeufs on the road to le Transloy was Rainy Trench on the east side of the road and just beyond that came Dewdrop Trench which went across the road on both sides. It was captured by the 33rd Div. at the end of October.

During the night of 5th November 'C' Company of the 2nd R. Welch Fus. of the 19th Bde. of this Division was ordered up into Dewdrop. The condition of the ground was very bad.

S. Rogerson of the 2nd W. Yorks. (23rd Bde. 8th Div.) wrote in his book *Twelve Days* that they crossed a low valley where the shell ploughed ground was carpeted with dead, the khaki outnumbering the field-grey by three to one. There must have been two or three hundred bodies lying in an area of a few hundred yards around Dewdrop Trench, once a substantial German reserve line, but now a shamble of corpses, smashed dugouts, twisted iron and wire. The two companies were both posted on the ridge which had been but newly captured, and though their fronts were touching, their flanks were both entirely in the air. The only approximation to a trench was the one in which they were sitting, already christened Autumn Trench, which was merely a narrow, unrevetted channel, without shelters, or fire-steps, and in which 'A' Company had its HQ some 150 yards to the left − Fall Trench was the Communication Trench but the German position was unclear − The day passed slowly, with the sun doing its best to cheer the bruised landscape, won at the cost of so many thousands of lives, which could be seen stretching away for miles behind. Below in the valley ran Dewdrop Trench with its piles of dead. Beyond it the ground climbed slightly to where the remains of Lesboeufs Wood poked jagged, splintered fingers at the sky. Somewhere to the left was Sailly Saillisel and to the right Ginchy and Morval. What a view it was? The middle distance was as featureless as the ground to the rear, save where on a slope a tumbled outline of masonry was recognisable as Cemetery Circle, supposed to be an enemy strong point − This fragment was all that remained of Zenith Trench which, with the help of the mud, had resisted the 'Full Dress' attack which had cost the British so heavily last time they had been in the line.

Dive Copse

No. XIII MDS was established at Dive Copse named after a Captain Dive and was close to the Treux crossroads on the Ancre−Sailly Laurette crossing. Later it was moved to a site on the Bray−Maricourt road. There was also a Motor Ambulance Convoy based here as well as a Divisional Rest Station. Across the road from the Copse is a Cemetery which contains 597 graves.

Doullens

Doullens is a town between St. Pol and Amiens and was always well behind the lines. Although it was a town where many battalions were billeted it was famous for its medical role in the battle. There was always a medical unit in the town and the Third Army had their 19th and 41st CCS in the town, also on the Arras road they had taken over a chateau close to the village of Solerneau. After the first day of the battle many of the casualties from the Gommecourt battlefield were taken to the railway halt at Doullens as well as to Warlincourt. A line had been built from Candas to Acheux.

Later in the battle No. 19 CCS was placed at the disposal of the Reserve Army for the Ancre battle.

Eaucourt l'Abbaye

L'Abbaye is north-west of Martinpuich, south-east of le Sars, due south of the Butte de Warlencourt and due west of Guedecourt. It is also north-west of Flers. It is a complex of farm buildings and is down a short road from the main Albert–Bapaume road coming from le Sars. Destremont Farm was south-west of le Sars and had been converted by the Germans into a fortress, as had an old quarry just south of l'Abbaye. These formed a series of extremely strong positions which were to delay the British for several days from the end of September until early October. Further to the east where a shallow sunken road that ran north from High Wood crossed the German third line, was a group of fortified positions that was intersected by two trenches known as Drop Trench and Goose Alley. They formed a quadilateral. Further to the north-east was another series of formidable positions that were known as Factory Corner. The 2nd KRRC (2nd Bde. 1st Div.) went into trenches here on the 25th September and relieved the 1st Black Watch (1st Bde. 1st Div.) and were involved in an attack on the Flers line on 25th/26th September. According to *The War in the Air* on 27th September Fourth Army Observers spotted progress towards the line between l'Abbaye and le Sars on which the Germans had fallen back, after a successful attack on part of the line north-west of Guedecourt on the same afternoon.

By dawn on the 29th, the 47th Div. who were to capture l'Abbaye eventually, sent up their 141st Bde. to take over the line from the 1st Div. A further advance was intended, in which the objective was the village of Eaucourt l'Abbaye itself which was made up of a group of houses round the old Abbaye buildings which were reputed to possess extensive cellars. Lying low at the point where a short valley from the High Wood direction turns at a right angle north-west of the main Albert–Bapaume road, l'Abbaye is therefore commanded by higher ground on each side except from the north-west. It was important before the attack was to begin to push forward along the Flers line on the high ground to the south-west of the village. The 1/18th (London Irish Rifles) of the 141st Bde. were ordered to achieve this, and the first attempt on 29th September was unsuccessful, but on the 30th they gained the ground required. 2nd Lt. E. G. Steel of the 20th London 141st Bde. was awarded the MC for leading his platoon to their final objective and for maintaining the position for four days 1st-4th October. The 1/15th (London) Civil Service Rifles of the 140th Bde. after their involvement at High Wood had occupied some disused trenches that were entirely devoid of dugouts in the Quadrangle close to Mametz Wood. Here they waited for news of the attack of the 141st Bde. on Eaucourt village. They spent several days there and the relief took place on the night of 4th October. The 1/18th (London) had been held up on 1st October by continuous machine gun fire from the west corner of l'Abbaye complex. Later the tanks were to silence these particular guns whereupon the 19th and 20th London Batts. rushed through the village, and established a line to the north of it.

The 50th Division to the left of the 47th Div. were also involved in the fighting on 1st October and Lt. Col. R. B. T. Bradford of the 9th Durhams of the 141st Bde. was awarded the VC for his fine leadership at l'Abbaye. In brief, the citation for the award reads: 'For most conspicuous bravery and good leadership in attack, whereby he saved the situation on the right flank of his Bde. and of the Division'. Bradford's battalion was in support. A leading battalion having suffered very severe casualties and the Commanding Officer having been wounded, its flank became dangerously exposed at close quarters to the enemy. Raked by machine gun fire the situation of the Battalion was critical. At the request of the wounded Commander, Bradford asked permission to command the exposed battalion in addition to his own. Permission was granted, and he at once proceeded to the foremost lines. By his fearless energy under fire of all descriptions, and his skilful leadership of the two battalions, regardless of all danger, he succeeded in rallying the attack, capturing the objective and securing the flank. It was the second objective of the Durhams.

In *Haig's Great Push* it says that the second trench in front of l'Abbaye was easily carried as were the double line of trenches away on the left of the attack outside le Sars. There was, however, a piece of ground on the right of the advance to Eaucourt, where machine guns, skilfully placed and protected by a stretch of barbed wire which the British Artillery had failed to destroy, caused the British not a few casualties, until the tanks came up and flattened the entanglements, rolled down the sand bag defences, and wiped out machine guns and gunners. This was the group of entanglements named the Circus.

Four Divisions were involved in the attack on 1st October and the tanks advanced on either side of the l'Abbaye–Flers line. The British attack on this day achieved the capture of a front that was 3,000 yards long and I am including a note on the operations as seen from the air signed by Major J. Chammier, commander of the 3rd RFC Squadron. It mentions that the 47th Division had not been close enough up to the artillery barrage and Rawlinson also mentions this fact in his diary. Despite the success of the British on this day they were to lose ground over the next few days before securing the l'Abbaye and le Sars permanently.

REPORT ON OPERATIONS ON THE 1st INST AS SEEN FROM THE AIR

At 3.15 p.m. the steady bombardment changed into a most magnificent barrage. The timing of this was extremely good. Guns opened simultaneously and the effect was that of many machine guns opening fire on the same order. As seen from the air the barrage appeared to be a most perfect wall of fire in which it was inconceivable that anything could live. The first troops to extend from the forming up places appeared to be the 50th Division who were seen to spread out from the sap heads and forming up trenches and advance close up under the barrage, apparently some 50 yards away from it. They appeared to capture their objective very rapidly and with practically no losses while crossing the open.

The 23rd Division I did not see so much of owing to their being at the moment of zero at the tail end of the machine.

The 47th Division took more looking for than the 50th, and it was my impression at the time that they were having some difficulty in getting into formation for attack from their forming up places, with the result that they appeared to be very late and to be some distance behind the barrage when it lifted off the German front line at Eaucourt l'Abbaye, and immediately to the west of it. It was plain that here there was a good chance of failure and this actually came about, for the men had hardly advanced a couple of hundred yards apparently, when they were seen to fall and take cover among shell holes, being presumably held up by machine gun and rifle fire. It was not possible to verify this owing to the extraordinary noise of the bursting shells of our barrage.

The tanks were obviously too far behind, owing to lack of covered approaches, to be able to take part in the original attack, but they were soon seen advancing on either side of the Eaucourt l'Abbaye–Flers line continuously in action and doing splendid work. They did not seem to be a target of much enemy shell fire.

The enemy barrage appeared to open late, quite 5 minutes after the commencement of our own barrage, and when it came it bore no resemblance to the wall of fire which we were putting up. I should have described it as a heavy shelling of an area some 3 to 400 yards in depth from our original jumping off places.

Some large shells were falling in Destremont Farm but these again were too late to catch the first line of the attack, although they must have caused some losses to the supports.

30 minutes after zero the first British patrols were soon entering le Sars. They appeared to be meeting with little or no opposition, and at this time no German shells were falling in the village. Our own shells were falling in the northern half.

To sum up: the most startling feature of the operations as viewed from the air was the extraordinary volume of fire of our barrage and the straight line kept by it.

(2) The apparent ease with which the attack succeeded where troops were enabled to go forward close under it.

(3) The promiscuous character and comparative lack of volume of enemy's counter-barrage.

6th October, 1916　　　　　　　　　　　　(Sd.) J. CHAMMIER, Major,
LH/MM/48/23　　　　　　　　　　　Commanding, 3rd Squadron, RFC.

On the 2nd October the Germans regained a footing in Eaucourt and le Sars was not held. In the history of the 47th Div. it notes that two companies of the 18th Batt. London of the 140th Bde. attacked up the Flers line successfully, got through Eaucourt l'Abbaye and completed the circuit of British troops around the village. The capture of the village brought several of the batteries over from High Wood into a little valley beyond the Starfish, where they maintained a precarious existence for the remainder of their stay on the Somme, and helped to cover the gallant but unsuccessful attacks of the 47th Div., and later of the 9th Div. on the Butte de Warlencourt. On 3rd October the 47th Div. regained Eaucourt and on the 4th the Germans were driven out. The 1/15 London (Civil Service Rifles) of the 140th Bde. were relieved on the night of the 4th by the 1/17 London (Poplar and Stepney Rifles) in the Flers line at l'Abbaye. This relief was an ordeal almost as trying as a battle. There was a struggle through the mud and through High Wood in the pitch dark. They eventually reached the Flers line in a very exhausted condition. On the 5th the 6th London of the 140th Bde. gained an important point by occupying the old mill 500 yards west of l'Abbaye. Philip Gibbs wrote of this incident 'Yesterday the sky cleared and the men who had taken l'Abbaye by such gallant struggle pushed out and seized the mill house to the west of those ruins between it and the tanks, from which the Germans had been maintaining heavy machine gun fire!' In *Haig's Great Push* it is said that on the night of the 5th the British advanced their position north-east of l'Abbaye. On the northern part of their front they discharged gas at two points against the enemy's trenches, and carried out several successful raids.

According to the 47th Div. history on 7th October 'the main German line of defence opposite was the Gird Line, running north-west from Guedecourt to Warlencourt, and including the Butte de Warlencourt. Anticipating an attack on this important line, the Germans had dug a new trench across the Allied front over the high ground north of Eaucourt l'Abbaye, westward in the valley. This trench named Diagonal was the first objective of the 14th Bde. of the 32nd Div.; their final objective was the Gird Line, including the Butte itself'. On the right some progress was made, and a line was established along the sunken road leading north-west from l'Abbaye to le Barque. On the left companies of the 8th, followed by the 7th Battalions tried to advance down the slope, forward of the mill, and met, in addition to fire from Diagonal Trench, the full force of the enemy artillery and machine gun fire, cleverly sited in depth, so as to bring a withering fire to bear along the western slopes leading up to the Butte and the high ground to the south of it. From across the valley the enemy had magnificent observation of the ground leading to the British objective, and made full use of it. Although attacked by four divisions the Butte was not captured until the enemy left it in his general retirement at the end of February 1917.

We have the following account from the history of the Civil Service rifles. They were part of the 140th Bde. of the 47th Div. and their number was 1/15 London. On 7th October they learnt that they were to attack the Butte de Warlencourt line, an objective some 2,800 yards distant. Zero hour was 2 p.m., and other companies occupied the same relative positions as at High Wood, 'A' Company again being on the right. The three companies on the left were unfortunate once more, for they had to file through the village of Eaucourt l'Abbaye soon after leaving their assembly trenches and had to extend their right into waves again after negotiating the village. They were caught by the full fury of the German artillery barrage and those men who got through the village were swept down by a most intense machine gun fire. 'A' company on the right made some little progress, and crossing the Eaucourt—le Barque Road dug a new line alongside the remnant of other divisions, all of whom had met a similar fate. There was an artillery creeping barrage on this occasion, it is true, but as it moved at the rate of 100 yards per minute and there were 2,800 yards between the jumping off trenches and the objective, the advancing waves of infantry soon got badly left behind. The losses of the 7th October amounted to five officers, 344 other ranks, and it should be remembered that on this occasion the Battalion was not more than 500 strong at the outset. The relief by the 7th Seaforth H. (26th Bde. 9th Scottish Div.) took place on the 9th and was a welcome contrast to the previous one in this section; the men quickly finding their way out and before midnight reaching the transport lines in Bottom Wood.

We have another description from C. P. Clayton of the 2nd Welch (3rd Bde. 1st Div.) in the October/November period. His battalion was in support and they had had long nights of digging and carrying, under wretched conditions. Just half a mile to their left was the ruined monastery of l'Abbaye. They were told that the Glosters were mostly living in the cellars under the ruins, and, he received his Bde. orders to send a company to clear trenches which led from l'Abbaye to the rear. The Trench was shown on the map and had been covered in places with sheet iron lightly covered with earth to conceal it from aerial observation. Suddenly, right at his feet he saw a ray of light, and found that the trench entered l'Abbaye by a flight of steep steps. At the foot of the steps were a section of the Glosters taking their rest and from one room to another his party were directed until they came to the Company Commander in a tiny office of his own.

In Gird Trench by the main road to Eaucourt there still exists some elephant hutting on the north bend used by the New Zealanders and British when attacking the Gird System.

Norman Gladden in his book on the Somme described the conditions of his battalion the 7th North'd Fus. (149th Bde. 50th Div.). The morning of 6th November was cold and wet, and drizzle continued as they filed along the light railway track towards the line. Heavy clouds hung low in the sky. They approached a low ridge and a line of trees, where, the guide told them, the dressing station was situated. Heavy shells were falling away to the right and these made them hurry as the path turned into a sort of cutting. They came across a pile of shattered brickwork which marked the former hamlet of Eaucourt, as shown by a notice board! A little further on they came upon the cabin and shelters that formed the dressing station in what seemed to them to be a very exposed position and under a row of tall trees, which had suggested its name of Seven Elms – stretchers which bore those who had received attention were loaded onto the light railway which was to convey them to the rear. As they loitered under cover of the cutting beneath the broken elms Gladden found it difficult to understand why this forward dressing station hadn't been discovered by the enemy gunners and blown to hell. It was in a very exposed position for such an activity.

Edgehill

Edgehill was a railway siding to the north of the village of Dernancourt, it took its name from its situation on rising ground. At the beginning of the battle it was one of the principal railheads used for supplies and the siding had been built in a field between Dernancourt and Buire. The 5th Seaforth H. (152nd Bde. 51st Div.) bivouacked here on the 7th August and on the 15th November the 12th Manchesters (52nd Bde. 17th North Div.) entrained there for the village of Hangest. In the same month a CCS was in the area.

Engelbelmer

Engelbelmer is on the D 129 road south-east of Mailly–Maillet north-west of Mesnil, south-west of Auchonvillers, due west of Thiepval, and four and a half miles north-west of Albert. It was behind the lines during the whole of the war and was used as a Field Ambulance Station until the Autumn of 1916. On the eve of the battle on 30th June the 1st KOSB of the (87th Bde. 29th Div.) marched up from Acheux Wood on their way to the front, which lay along a communication trench called Gabion Avenue, which began almost as soon as Engelbelmer was left.

The Newfoundlanders in the period 30th June/1st July had their Regimental Cookers assembled in a wood near the village, and in the early hours of the 1st July the Newfoundlanders' 'ten per cent', who had moved up to the wood, supplied carrying parties to bring the troops in the dugouts their hot breakfast. On 6th July the battalion after their crippling losses at Beaumont Hamel on 1st July were back in the village and stayed there amidst continuous shelling. Early on 8th July they withdrew to tents at Mailly Wood to the north-west.

The poet Edmund Blunden mentions being billeted at Engelbelmer. He was with 11th R. Sussex (116th Bde. 39th Div.) and in his *Somme Overflows* and *Mind's Eye* has the following to say. After several postponements we made our first appearance in the fighting. In the cold early mist of 3rd September (5.10 a.m.) our Division went over and later the shattered battalions withdrew from the valleys and ridges still echoing with bombardment and the pounding of machine guns. The Somme pulled us under once, and we emerged gasping − and once in, appeared unlikely ever to get out − In these trenches we worked hard and were gas shelled and trench mortared not too violently most days; but the minewerfers caused casualties. The battalion relieved by the Cheshires assembled in a trench along Hamel village street and in the setting sun arrived at Engelbelmer, three hundred fewer in number then when it passed through earlier.

On 4th October Blunden wrote that under a burst of gas shelling they were relieved, but only that they might make a circuit through Engelbelmer Wood and Martinsart Wood, on their way up to the Hamel trenches. In mid September they had already taken over the extensive trenches before Beaumont Hamel. Neville Lytton who had been with Blunden whilst in training in England with the R. Sussex seems to have been in the same area around 3rd September but not a fellow participant in trench duties. I think that he was probably based at Engelbelmer but in Bde. HQ. He wrote a book called *The Press and the General Staff.*

There were Trench Mortar batteries around 21st October in the area of

Mailly and Engelbelmer and 161 Battery was at the latter village around 30th October. The Hood Battalion of the 63rd (Naval Div.) had been relieved and were billeted in barns in Engelbelmer until 23rd October when they went to Mesnil to the south-east. On 4th November they were back there again for the final Somme battles, having been to Puchevillers. The Hawke Battalion of the same Division derived some comfort from the village in the period before the battle began on 13th November, though very little safety. Here by day men could walk about or sit above ground with at least a roof over their heads. When the battalion was there however they were required to supply working parties and digging parties to their total strength and a good deal beyond it every night. These parties began with a march of three miles or more to the Hamel trenches, which were due east of the village, and due west of Thiepval. this led to the battalion losing 150 men even before going into action. The Field Ambulance Station was used again in the summer of 1918 and had been liable to occasional shelling.

The Communal Cemetery was used for British burials from June to September. There are the graves there of 51 soldiers and sailors from the 63rd Naval Div. The Extension is at the south-west corner of the Communal Cemetery away from the road and was begun in October 1916. After the Armistice, graves were brought into it from Beaussart Communal Cemetery Extension and from the battlefields immediately north and east of the village. It commands extensive views to the west and south.

Falfemont Farm

The original farm which is not to be confused with the one on the present site was a German fortified strong point. It was to the south-east of Wedge Wood and Guillemont and south-west of Leuze Wood. It was also south of Combles. It was situated on high ground which overlooked the Allied positions and was rectangular in shape.

The ground between Malzhorn Farm and Falfemont Farm was broken by a three pronged ravine that had Angle Wood in its centre. On 24th August the 17th Lancs. Fus. 104th Bde. (35th Div. Bantam) were to be involved in an attack to be carried out against Falfemont Ridge, whilst the French were to attack Oakhanger Wood which was to the south-east of the Farm. The attack was postponed. The French were under the impression that the farm was deserted in this period but it wasn't!

On the 3rd September it was planned to attack the farm together with Wedge Wood. German reinforcements could be seen emerging from Leuze Wood on their way to the farm. The Allied Division involved was the 5th and the 2nd KOSB, 14th and 15th R. Warwicks. of the 13th Bde. were the units involved. On this day the farm had not been bombarded as had been planned, owing to some mistake. Machine gun fire from the Germans at the wood broke up the 13th Bde. attack, but the farm was finally taken in the early hours of the 5th September by the 1st Ches. and 1st Beds. after the 1st

Norfolks had been held up in the front. No part of the farm was left standing by this time and there were no dugouts or trenches. The battalions therefore had to spend the night in the open. A few bricks were all that was left of what had been a vital part of the German defence system. The 16th R. Warwicks. had established a line down the slope of the ravine which linked the 95th Bde. of the 5th Div. in Leuze Wood with the French left which was now in Savernake Wood.

In the history of the 5th Div. there is a special tribute to the artillery of the 35th and 56th Divs. who covered this Divisional front. Their bombardment and barrage fire had rendered the success of taking the farm possible. Their gun positions in Chimpanzee Valley and the area south-east of Bernafay Wood were subjected to heavy bombardments and much gas shelling. On 10th September the 1st. E. Surreys (95th Bde. 5th Div.) had two companies in trenches half way up the slope to the farm in the Bois de Falfemont. Amidst the farm crops is a three man grave which contains the bodies of Capt. Heumann of the 2nd London (R. Fus.) (169th Bde. 56th Div.) Sgt. Major Mills (known of course as Bertram) and Sgt. Torrance. I have to thank Mr. A. Spagnoly for the account of how the men got to be in this small grave, which is quite separate from an official cemetery. He says that 'Heumann was killed in a abortive attack by A & B Companies of the 2nd London (R. Fus.). The 169th Bde. was endeavouring to get into the sunken road behind Combles and Loop Trench, and thus loosen the grip on Combles. 'A' Company bombed across the wood to Loop Trench and the Germans massed for a counter-attack. 'B' Company under Heumann was at a spot south-east of the wood called 'Lone Tree'. He was ordered to attack 'Q' Trench or Leugemake Trench running from the wood and divert or dissipate the counter-attack: he was sitting in a shell hole at 'Lone Tree' − briefing his officers − and a shell burst overhead killing both him and Mills. Both men were quickly buried where they fell and just how Sgt. Torrance who was killed on the same day at the wood came to be with them, only stretcher bearers cleaning up that night could say. The attack went in under another officer, and was partially success-ful: − but they did manage to get into 'Q' Trench: four officer and 23 other ranks died in the action. The ground gained was 50 metres. There were also 98 wounded'.

Jack Tucker who wrote *Johnny Get Your Gun* and served in the 13th Kensingtons of the 168th Bde. of the 56th Div. has written vividly of the action at the Bois de Falfemont which actually contained the Farm buildings in 1916. He mentions in particular coming across a trench full of dead Prussian Guards in white vests! There were also many dead of the Royal Irish Rifles. He also mentions the death of Major C.C. Dickens, grandson of the famous novelist, and member of the same battalion. At the Liddle collection at Sunderland Polytechnic there is a mention by L/Cpl. H. G. R. Williams of the 5th City of London of the 56th Div. that when going up the line, he came across the bodies of Kensingtons who had been killed in a recent attack on Falfemont Farm. He also says that there were no actual dugouts or shelters in the area of the Farm and that his battalion was shelled by a French battery!

Faviere Wood

This wood is north-east of Maricourt and due south of Bernafay and Trônes Woods, or the gap between. It had been a German Dressing Station. The British reached the edge of the wood running north-south on 1st July and captured it between 2nd July and the 13th. On the 1st several German trench lines were taken.

Masefield in his book *The Battle of the Somme* wrote that one of the thrusts of the attack had been towards the romantic dingle of Faviere Wood. At the end of July there was a French Bde. HQ at the wood. Battalions used to bivouac in the trenches there and in mid-September there were some French 75s in front of the wood as well as an old French Howitzer. A new fire trench was dug which was called Cheshire Trench.

Flers

Flers is a village and commune in the Department of the Somme, nine miles north-east of Albert and four miles south of Bapaume, east of Martinpuich, west of Lesboeufs and north-east of Delville Wood. It is on the D 197 road between Longueval and Ligny Thilloy. Flers was the object of XV Corps of the Fourth Army on 15th September. The Divisions in this Corps were the 14th, 21st, 41st, 55th and the New Zealand Divisions. The 15th of September was to be the first occasion on which tanks were used. The tanks had recently come from England and had been transported to the Loop which was north of Bray and a railway 'station', and were then moved on the 14th September to the Green Dump Valley in readiness. The British front line was in front of the north and north-east of Delville Wood. The first objective was the Switch Line, the second Flers Trench which was just before the village, and Bulls Road was the third which was at the end of the village. Beyond Flers were German positions called Flea Trench and Box and Cox. And beyond all these lines and objectives were the Gird Lines (which was actually the fourth objective) and the village of Guedecourt. The brunt of the attack was to be carried out by the 14th (Light Div.) the 41st Div. and the New Zealand Division. The 14th Div. was to deal with the Germans who were in a 'pocket' east of Delville Wood. This was to be before the planned zero hour and they had the use of one tank. The tank began from Pilsen Lane and having crossed Hop Alley was knocked out. Switch Line was captured at about 7 a.m. At about 9 a.m. Gap Trench was passed over and the third objective was within sight. The 9th Rifle Bde. (42nd Bde. 14th Div.) in particular was hit by enfilade machine gun fire as it approached Bulls Road.

The 41st Div. was in the middle of the Corps front and was meant to capture the village in the course of its advance to the third objective (Bulls Road). Most of the tanks were kept for this part of the attack. Four began from Longueval–Flers Road, and six started from the northern end of Longueval village. Others too, were to be part of the New Zealand attack towards Guedecourt. Seven got to the start line but probably none of them actually

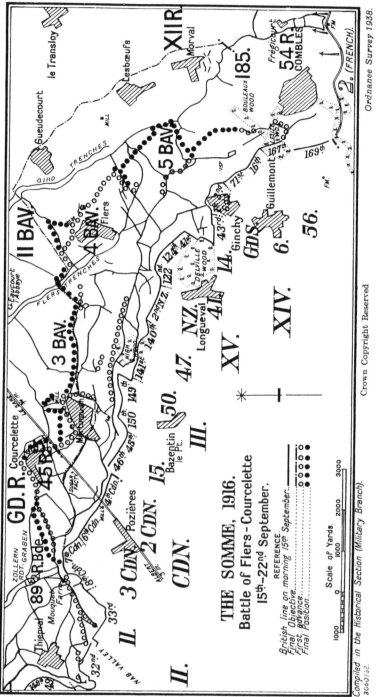

THE SOMME, 1916.
Battle of Flers–Courcelette
15th–22nd September.

REFERENCE.
British line on morning 15th September.
Final Objective.
First advance.
Final Position.

Scale of Yards.
1000   0   1000   2000   3000

Compiled in the Historical Section (Military Branch).
3060/32.

Crown Copyright Reserved

Ordnance Survey 1938.

began in front of the infantry. The 41st Div. began with two Bdes. the 124th on the right with the 10th Queen's and 21st KRRC at the front end and the other two battalions who were the 26th and 32nd R. Fus. at the second line. The Switch Line was reached by 7 a.m. and the advance to the second line was successful half an hour later. The 21st KRRC took part in the attack to the east of the village in which they carried three lines of trenches. The battalion lost heavily though, including its Commanding Officer Lord Feversham. The battalion had been made up from men predominantly from Northumberland and Durham. The senior officer of the 10th Queen's of the same Brigade Lt. Col. A. F. Townsend was also a casualty being mortally wounded by shrapnel in the attack on Flers Trench.

The 122nd Bde. also of the 41st Div. had attacked Flers and one tank went forward into the village arriving by 8.20 a.m. Three more were on the east side of the village and broke into houses and German strongpoints, the enemy fled towards Guedecourt. The 12th E. Surreys were the first battalion actually into Flers and the main opposition at the time was a German machine gun at the crossroads in the centre of the village which was eventually dealt with by a tank. The 15th Hampshires were with the 18th KRRC in the leading line, their objective being Flers Trench. The supporting battalions including the 11th RW Kents who went through their lines. The Hampshires were quickly into Tea Support which was also the German front line. They mastered the Switch Line and also reached Flers. After dark having suffered very heavy casualties they returned to York Trench in reserve.

The whole of the forward crest of the main ridge on a section of five miles from Delville Wood to Mouquet Farm was now in Allied hands with very valuable observation. As has already been said the 26th and 32nd R. Fus. Batts. were both in support, the 32nd on the right and the 26th on the left following the 10th Queen's and the 21st KRRC. Three tanks had been allotted to the Bde.

The 32nd met with little resistance in Tea Support and the Switch Trench. Box and Cox were a sort of double or twin German redoubt and when the Londoners came to clear them out they found them full of German dead and six machine guns were captured.

A note on the tanks on this day 15th September. Forty nine were employed of which 32 reached the starting point. Of these nine pushed ahead with the infantry, nine failed to catch the infantry but nevertheless helped in clearing captured ground, nine broke down and five were ditched in the centre of the battlefield. The first nine were especially useful in capturing Flers.

In *The War in the Air* there is a report by an observer in the RFC who watched the infantry move over the open ground behind the creeping barrage. The objectives were taken fairly quickly and air reports showed that north of Flers the Allies were holding Box and Cox and the Flame, and to the north-east were strongly established in groups of trenches known as Flea Trench and Hogs Head, the latter being a strong point in Flers Wood. Elsewhere XV Corps were holding their objectives. Three tanks nearly reached Guedecourt but were hit and caught fire. Of the others two returned, six were ditched, the rest were hit, two others caught fire. They moved forward in 'lanes' left clear by the barrages, and tank tapers were laid out for them. Before they crossed the trenches, the trenches had to be filled in to enable them to proceed.

Flers had been captured by the 41st and the New Zealand Division and progress was to be made over the next few days. It was the first involvement in a Western Front attack for the New Zealanders having refitted and been reinforced after their 'blooding' on the Gallipoli Peninsula. There are graves of 120 of them in Bulls Road Cemetery east of Flers.

Anthony Eden served as a temporary officer with the 21st KRRC of the 124th Bde. of the 41st Div. on the Somme. He was under the command of Lord Feversham and Major Gerald Foljambe. The former was not a regular soldier but the latter was. Eden's early training had been at Duncombe Park and after service at 'Plug Street' Wood the battalion was transferred to the Somme. On the 14th September it was decided that Eden should form part of the cadre of men and officers who were to stay behind while the attack planned for 15th September took place. Eden was upset by this decision but was told that there would be plenty of time for fighting later on! The HQ of the Battalion was at the back of Delville Wood in an assembly trench. On the 15th Lord Feversham was killed leading his men in an attack on the Ridge. The position was to be east of Flers and it faced Gird Ridge. On the 16th a roll call took place when many able men were found to be missing, killed or wounded. The position of CO was taken over by Foljambe who immediately made Eden his Adjutant. Eden protested about being thrown in at the deep end but to no avail. The two used to go riding together and Feversham's horse was used on these occasions.

A Lancashire Battalion left Méaulte on the 16th and bivouacked under groundsheets leading up Flers way. On the same road 'dusky sons of India', facetiously known as Bengal Lights (they exchanged bully for chapatti, a sort of tasty pancake made from 'dog' biscuits) − moved up to a slippery reserve line behind Flers. A. Aitken (1st New Zealand Otago Battalion) says in his book *Gallipoli to the Somme* that he was in Fat Trench in front of Flers having been misled by the guides. It was a trench on the south-west of the village.

The next main attack after that of 15th September was to take place on the 25th, the weather had been poor and the 18th and 19th were very wet days and the 20th was a day of rainstorms. On the 18th Capt. W. G. Newton 1/Artists/23rd London was awarded the MC for placing a lamp in the open to guide the night assault. Later, although wounded he rallied his men and bombed the enemy with courage and determination. In the battle of 25th September which was known as the Battle of Morval the New Zealand Div. captured Factory Corner which is on the road between Guedecourt and Eaucourt l'Abbaye. They were to be between Flers and Martinpuich during the next three days.

In his book *39 Months* D. V. Kelly of the Leicestershire Regiment mentions that he had walked to Flers looking for a Bde. HQ to occupy after the imminent attack on the village of Guedecourt. He found a bank running roughly north to south, that was close to the Montauben–Longueval road and a few hundred yards from Flers. Nearby lay a tank and the site was marked on the map S.6d 8.2. It was close to the existing front line and a working party was soon digging a hole in the bank for accommodation. The HQ was at one corner of the ridge while on the left, Guedecourt village was lying right in front, and Lesboeufs and Morval were on the right. The attack was fixed for 12.35 p.m. on the 25th. Kelly was sitting in the Switch Line waiting for the attack to begin. The 8th and 9th Leicesters. (110th Bde. 37th Div.) rose out of their assembly trenches just below the crest of the ridge. While away to the right for miles one saw the irregular waves of the Allied infantry which included the Guards Div. That night the 6th Batt. also of the 110th 37th Bde. moved along the partly German trench that had given so much trouble the day before, and enabled Kelly's men to clean it up. The Bde. had now taken all of their objectives as they had also done at Bazentin in July. The casualties were believed to be about 1,400.

Fraser-Tytler mentions in his book that a big gain had been achieved beyond Flers. And on 30th September they began preparing the position that they were then occupying which was a sunken road, that ran into the south-west corner of Flers. He was allotted a position in Delville Wood which was south-west of Flers wedged in amongst a host of other batteries. He looked for and found a more forward position, which was close up to the Germans and well away from the other batteries. This was the Longueval position.

Major Ash who became a Lt. Colonel in June 1916 was in charge of the 23rd Middlesex (2nd Football Batt.) was wounded in the same attack as Lord Feversham. He died a fortnight later on the 29th.

By the 1st October the New Zealand Div. had taken the Gird Trench, Circus Trench, and Gird Support, to the north of the Guedecourt–l'Abbaye road. On the 2nd Fraser-Tytler had moved his guns forward from in front of Delville Wood trudging up the road from the wood to Flers which was much barraged. They were on a forward slope which was so close to the Germans that all the shelling went over their heads into the crowded Delville Valley.

From October Flers itself had become a deathtrap and l'Abbaye Road that went out of the village was the scene of frequent shelling.

In early October in reconnoitering the ground Foljambe and Eden of the 21st KRRC went close to Gird Ridge. The planned attack was postponed because of the very poor weather. Turk Lane was a communication trench that was much used and the attack was now due to take place on 7th October. On the 8th Battalion HQ was moved to Factory Corner which was then a battered building, with only cellars left that were intact. On 10th October they were about to be relieved when they received news that Feversham's body had been found. Eden was put in charge of the party who were to recover the body and give it a suitable burial. They found it on a forward slope of a lip in the ground. Feversham had been of middle height, thick set with bristling moustache. He was, in Eden's words, essentially a commander and was at his best and happiest on a horse. Eden was in charge of the burial which took place in a meadow close to Factory Corner. After the 22nd October the

2nd R. Welch Fus. arrived at Serpentine Trench which was part of the Flers line between Ginchy and Morval.

The New Zealand Div. went north on the 10th and 11th, but their artillery remained on the Somme for the rest of October. In the battle of the Somme the New Zealanders had fought for 23 consecutive days, had advanced more than two miles and had captured five miles of enemy front line. They had also taken nearly a thousand prisoners and many machine guns; but they brought back all the machine and Lewis guns, and lost under 20 prisoners themselves. Their casualties were 7,000 and of these 1,560 were killed in action or died of wounds.

The 4th Suffolks (98th Bde. 33rd Div.) moved back to Flers Line on 29th October after Dewdrop Trench.

In his book the *The Somme, 1916* Norman Gladden (149th Bde. 50th Div.) wrote that at the end of October they were sent to Flers village to bring back duckboards which had been dumped there. It was a weird deserted place, especially at that time of the day, dominated by the abandoned tank looking ridiculous in its early demise. On 31st October they moved forward to the Flers line support trench. The mud in places was so deep as to make movement almost impossible.

Gladden says that in mid-November Flers Switch was to be their billet for the night but later in the day they were withdrawn to reserve in Prue Trench, which had been altered out of all recognition since their earlier occupancy. It had been converted by the Royal Engineers into winter quarters with a row of neatly sandbagged dugouts under semicircular iron roofs which, if not exactly shell proof, provided the acme of comfort after their recent exposure.

In January 1917 Max Plowman in his book *Subaltern on the Somme* wrote that the 11th W. Yorks. (69th Bde. 23rd Div.) were occupying a large dugout, with officers at one end and the men at the other, at a spot near Flers called Bull Dump. Presumably this was near or in Bulls road, to the north of Flers. They came out in the rain and just had time to get clean and look round the town of hutments that was once Carnoy.

In 1935 from the *Ypres Times* it records that there was a notice that said 'This way to Lord Feversham's Grave' by the roadside. A quarter of a mile through thigh high crops brought you to a little lych gate built over a flagstone that was inscribed 'Charles William Reginald, 2nd Earl of Feversham, Lt. Col. Commanding 21st KRRC, killed in action on this spot, September 15th 1916'. The same writer said that recently (1935-ish) 40 bodies had been discovered in this area all in a cluster where they had fallen. Flers had built itself a brewery since the Great War and had been adopted by Portsmouth. At the end of the main street is the 41st Div. Memorial, a New Army Division with units from many parts of England; their badges decorate the enclosing pillars. The rifle of the bronze infantryman points in the direction of tanks coming from Pozieres. The memorial is a copy or duplicate of the one that stands in High Holborn.

There are two main cemeteries in Flers and the first is the AIF Burial Ground at Grass Lane. It is almost in the centre of the battlefield and about four miles south-west of Bapaume. It is a mile north-east of the village of Flers on the side of a track known to the Army in 1916 as 'Grass Lane'. Australian Medical Units stationed in caves in the neighbourhood began the Cemetery to receive the graves of soldiers killed in the fighting during the Autumn of 1916. The local name of the site is 'Aux Cavés'. The Cemetery was begun in the period November 1916– February 1917. It was greatly enlarged after the Armistice by the concentration of 3,842 British and French graves and afterwards from a wider area; the great majority of the graves date from the Autumn of 1916. After the Second World War Lord Feversham's body was transferred to this cemetery. The cemetery stands in open undulating farm land, Guedecourt is over the hill to the east, and beyond it is the New Zealand memorial, recalling a successful attack on 12th October.

The other cemetery is Bulls Road Cemetery which was begun on 19th September and was used by fighting units (mainly Australian until March 1917). More graves were brought in after the Armistice from the fields between Flers and Longueval. It stands on sloping ground, and Longueval and Ligny–Thilloy can be seen from it.

Flesselles

The village is due west of Villers Bocage on the D 113 road to Vignacourt, an ammunition dump had been established in the village and battalions trained in the area including the 9th Norfolks (71st Bde. 6th Div.) who were there between 29th August and 5th September.

Foncquevillers

Foncquevillers (Funkyvillas) is a village in the extreme south of the Pas-de-Calais. It is on the D 3 road south-west of Hannescamps, north-west of Gommecourt, south-east of Bienvillers and east of Souastre. It was in British hands in 1915 and 1916, and the Allied front ran between it and Gommecourt, and had been badly damaged by artillery. It was here that the last named village was turned into a defensive fortress by the Germans and the village protruded into a gap between Foncquevillers in the north and Hébuterne in the south. The village became the 'home' of the 46th (North Midland Division) for nearly a year. This Division was made up of regiments from Staffordshire, Leicestershire, Nottinghamshire, Lincolnshire and Derbyshire, and many of the communication trenches bore names of famous Midland towns. The Division was part of VII Corps.

Before the battle began Bruce Bairnsfather the creator of 'Old Bill' when he was with the 1/4 DWR was in shelters and dugouts on the road between Foncquevillers and Hébuterne. It was known as Thorpe Street and was a 'straight line' between the two villages. It was just behind the Allied front line. The most dangerous spot being at this time the western end of the village. To the north-west of the village was Bienvillers and a long communication trench named Berlin Street into the north-west of Foncquevillers, about 800 yards from the German line which faced the village from the south-east along the side of Gommecourt Wood. In May two important communication trenches in use were Crawl Boys Lane to the north of the sector and Roberts Avenue to the south of it.

The 5th Lincolns. (138th Bde. 46 Div.) were in the village in the period 3rd/4th June and they began to dig a new advance trench about 400 yards long which was completed by the 10th June. They were later in huts in Humbercamps, where there was a 15 inch gun close to their billets.

On 20th June the 5th Sherwood For. (139th Bde. 46th Div.) reached the village and drew supplies of bombs, grenades, barbed wire, picks, sandbags etc. They then had a short rest in the orchards which were to the north-east of the village. Many of them were to have what was to be their last meal there, which consisted of enormous bacon sandwiches!

At this time the Germans were putting down heavy stuff every night and it was especially hazardous to be on the roads or in communication trenches. Regent Street in the 5th Sherwood For. sector, commenced at the Brewery north of the village, and then ran due east before crossing the la Brayelle Road in a south-easterly direction meeting the Allied front line 150 yards from the road. Nearby Roberts Avenue ran practically parallel with la Brayelle Road and crossed Support Trench and met with the Russian Sap which was a tunnel as close to the start line as possible. The 5th Sherwood For. Battalion HQ was at the end of Rotten Row. Brushwood from Lucheux Forest had been used for the construction of communication trenches and in particular of Roberts Avenue and Stratford Avenue. Other trench names included Cape Avenue, Raymond Avenue, Lincoln Lane, Leicester Street, Derby Dyke, Nottingham Street, Brasserie Trench and St. Martin's Lane. In front of the Sherwood Foresters Section of the 138th Bde. was the strong German position called the Z and Little Z. They protruded into the line at the extreme left of the attack and were in front of Schwalben Nest.

On the first day of the battle, 1st July, the regiments of the 46th Div. who were involved mostly in this sector were the Sherwood Foresters, the two Staffordshire Regiments and the Lincolns. For a description of what happened to them the reader is referred to the section on Gommecourt. At the beginning of the battle an ADS or CP was established here.

Just off the road from Foncquevillers to Bayencourt was the Chateau de la Haie and in the *History of the 17th Northern Div.* it is mentioned that it had been the HQ of the 56th Div., and was then the HQ of the 52nd Bde. It stood on an eminence, a large semi-castellated country house, having a courtyard on its eastern front with extensive stabling on both sides. Though it stood on the skyline at a range of not more than 4,000 yards from the German batteries near Gommecourt Wood, it didn't seem that they ever made it a target. For right and left of the chateau the artillery of the 56th Div. was in position close by, a fact that made it all the more remarkable that the chateau had not attracted the enemy's fire. But around 18th August the enemy changed its mind and the HQ was subsequently moved to a larger house in the eastern outskirts of Souastre.

The 16th KRRC (100th Bde. 33rd Div.) took over the right sector on 19th September and a month later they were billeted at Corbie.

The Military Cemetery on the western outskirts of the village which had been made by French troops before being taken over by the British in the summer of 1915, was used by units and Field Ambulances until March 1917. The burials of July 1916 are especially numerous. Many officers and men of the Sherwood Foresters are also buried here. Capt. J. L. Green is commemorated at the Cemetery. He was in the RAMC and attached to the 1/5th Sherwood For. (139th Bde. 46th Div.) and was posthumously awarded the VC having been killed on 1st July. He was born in 1888 and his citation reads in brief – for most conspicuous devotion to duty. Although himself wounded, he went to the assistance of an officer who had been wounded and who was hung up in the enemy's wire entanglements, and succeeded in dragging him to a shell hole, where he dressed his wounds, notwithstanding that bombs and rifle grenades were thrown at him the whole time. He then endeavoured to bring the wounded officer into safe cover, and had nearly succeeded in doing so when he himself was killed.

Forceville

Forceville is a village which is 12½ miles from Doullens and six miles from Albert on the main road between these two places. The Fourth Army were in occupation in 1916 until 20th July when it was included in the area of the Reserve Army (Fifth Army). In February a Field Ambulance had been established in the village, and it was succeeded by others until the end of July 1916. There is an account written by Capt. Stevenson-Jones MC from Regt. Chron. of the South Lancs. Reg. Vol. 20 No. 2. 'Night of 30th June marched out of Talmas towards Albert, and turned left just short of that town down a road parallel to the front to Forceville getting a wonderful view of the preliminary bombardment. They were in huts in Forceville six miles back. They arrived at 2 a.m. On the 4th July a battalion of the HLI were billeted in the village and it was described as being a 'dirty' village.'

In the *Hawke Battalion: Some Personal Records* it says that the Battalion had left the training area on 7th October, and arrived that same evening at Forceville, a small town some four miles east of Thiepval Ridge, and one of the recognised centres for units arriving to take part in the Somme battles. The main pivots of the German defences north of the Ancre, from north to south, Serre, Beaumont Hamel and Beaucourt. The last named was some distance behind the German front line, but was the key position commanding the actual valley of the Ancre. A little way behind Beaucourt were two further ridges, which, if the British could capture them, would command the gun positions defending the German positions behind Serre, and even further north. The capture of these positions along the Ancre Valley was a matter of the highest consequence, for on this depended the possibility or otherwise of enforcing the long awaited German retreat. The task of capturing them was allotted to the Naval Div. To the 51st Div. fell the hardly less difficult task of capturing Beaumont Hamel. J. Murray in his book *Call To Arms* wrote that they arrived at Acheux with the Hood Battalion and on 4th October moved to Forceville. They were working up the line in the period 6th to 16th October. During this time they stayed in barns in the village and on the 16th they went to the Knightsbridge Sector in the Ancre Valley.

The Cemetery lies to the west of the village, on the right from Acheux. Until quite recently there was a railway line that ran near here to Albert.

A MDS was here at the beginning of July, the MDSs of X Corps were here and at Warloy.

Franvillers

Franvillers is south-west of Albert on the main Albert–Amiens Road, south of Baizieux and north-west of Heilly. It was therefore well behind the 1916 lines, and there was a Divisional Rest Station in the village from the beginning of the battle. W. D. Croft in his book says that the 27th Bde. reached Albert on 20th July and marched back the same day to the Franvillers area to rejoin their Division. On 26th July they marched back to Contalmaison and relieved a Bde. that was north-east of that village.

The most amount of information about the village is concerned with a royal visit. King George V came to Franvillers in order to meet up with General Rawlinson. The weather was overcast which caused some concern to Malins (the Official War Office Photographer) as on that day he especially wanted to obtain good film. The official cars pulled up on the main road in the village and they had about 15 minutes to wait. Malins fixed his camera ready to film the King's meeting with Rawlinson. Whilst waiting Rawlinson spoke to Malins and talked to him about his work, and in particular his filming of the 29th Div. at Beaumont Hamel on 1st July. Shortly after the King's party arrived, and the King alighted and greeted the General. These scenes were filmed by Malins. The General joined the King in his car and they went along the main Amiens–Albert road and turned off through Dernancourt and went across the river to Méaulte, on their way to the battlefield at Fricourt.

In mid-September after the fighting at Martinpuich the 12th HLI (46th Bde. 15th Scottish Div.) came via Albert and before that dugouts near Mametz Wood by marching to an open field about half a mile Franvillers. Next day they went to la Housoye.

Frechencourt

Frechencourt is to the north-east of Querrieu and was one of the principal railheads for supplies at the beginning of the battle. The III Corps received walking wounded casualties here and they too used the railway. The position was closed down in mid-September.

Fricourt

Fricourt is a village in the Department of the Somme and three miles east of Albert, north of Bray and east of Mametz. It is just off the D 938 road. It used to have a station on a light railway running from Albert to Montdidier and Peronne. Before 2nd July it was in German hands and was to be one of the main objectives for the Allies to capture on 1st July. In addition to the village itself there were several features that were to become well known, and these included Fricourt Wood to the north-east of the village, the chateau which bordered the village and wood, Rose Cottage which was to become a famous landmark on the east side, and the Tambour which was a series of craters on the west side and which were the scene of considerable mining and counter-mining. Then there was Lozenge Trench which in most accounts of the fighting became known as the Sunken Road.

Fricourt was the 'second' village of the Somme before the battle and had 176 houses. Rose Cottage was built of red brick and when its name appeared on trench maps in 1915 it was creeper covered, with a fine rose garden. One of the regiments which had considerable experience of this front before the battle began, were the Royal Welch Fusiliers, and the area to the south towards Bray became associated with Siegfried Sassoon, Robert Graves and Bernard Adams.

Adams was in the 1st R. Welch Fus. and has left in his book *Nothing of Importance* a very detailed account of the area. In the period February/March 1916 he says 'Fricourt lay in full view before me.' – 'In the centre stood the white ruin of the church, still higher than the houses around it,' – 'All around were houses; roof-less, wall-less skeletons all of them,' – 'On the extreme right was Rose Cottage, a well-known artillery mark; just to its left were some large park gates, with stone pillars, leading into Fricourt Wood;' – 'the extreme northern part of the village was invisible, as the ground fell away north of the church. I could see where the road disappeared from view; then beyond, clear of houses, the road re-appeared and ran straight up to the skyline, a mile further on. A communication trench crossed this road:' – 'With my glasses I could see every detail; beyond the communication trench were various small copses, and tracks running over the field; on the skyline, about three thousand yards away, was a long row of bushes.'

'And just to the left of it all ran, the two white lace-borders of chalk trenches, winding and wobbling along, up, up, up until they disappeared over the hill to la Boisselle.' – 'Due west of Fricourt Church they touched in a small crater chain'.

Robert Graves, was also with the 1st RWF having rejoined them in March when they were in and out of the trenches facing Fricourt with billets at Morlancourt. The trenches were cut in chalk, better in wet weather than clay. The opposing lines came close together in this sector. The greatest trial, he wrote, was the German canister, a two gallon drum with ammonal and a smell like marzipan. It was full of scrap metal and rubbish and had a demoralising effect, even on the deepest dugouts.

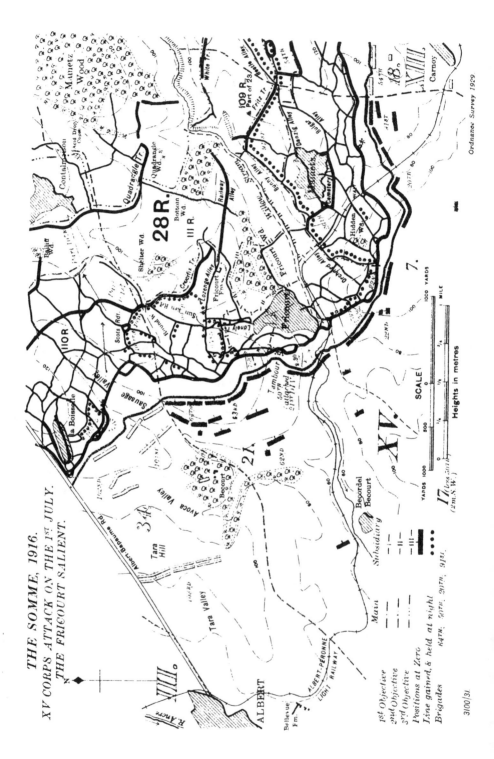

THE SOMME, 1916.
XV CORPS ATTACK ON THE 1ST JULY.
THE FRICOURT SALIENT.

In his book *The Old Front Line* John Masefield said that the ravine in front of the village was the gully between two spurs; it sheltered the sunken road to Contalmaison; a glance was enough to show that it was a strong position, that Fricourt was one of the boasts of the enemy on this front. Fricourt was strong in itself like Gommecourt and was perhaps the only place in the field that was as strong. It had, as at Gommecourt, a natural glacis up to the front line, which was deep, strong, and well wired. Behind the front line was a wired second line, and behind that, the rising spur on which the village stood, commanding both with machine gun emplacements. The Germans did indeed turn the village into a fortress during their stay which had begun in 1915, and in time the village became entirely ruined. It consisted of a series of block houses and redoubts, with numerous machine guns. Underneath the houses were deep comfortable shelters, some of which were 45 feet deep.

Buried in Point 110 New Military Cemetery south of Fricourt is David Thomas who was a friend of both Graves and Sassoon and who died of wounds in March before the battle began. Both men were distraught at the loss of this very dear friend and Graves wrote a poem called 'Goliath and David'. (For D.C.T. killed at Fricourt, March 1916.) In his diary Sassoon has described the moving night time burial: 'Everything was dim but the striped flag laid across the body. Robert Graves, beside men, with his white whimsical face twisted and grieving. Once we could not hear the solemn words for the noise of a machine gun along the line; when all was finished a canister fell a few hundred yards away to burst with a crash.' Also buried close to Thomas are Pritchard and Richardson of the RWF. In his diary entry of 23rd May Sassoon wrote that on Crawley Ridge in the evening when going across to Fricourt, trench mortars were bursting in the cemetery. Fricourt was a huddle of reddish roofs, skeleton village, church tower − white almost demolished, a patch of white against the sombre green of Fricourt Wood which was full of German batteries. Away up the hillside the white seams and heapings of trenches dug in the chalk. The sky was full of lark song. Sassoon wrote in his diary of the 23rd June that after a bombardment by the Allies the Germans had not retaliated much, although Fricourt was being shelled as he went along Kingston Road Trench, where the company was to go the next day the 24th. Men of the Royal Irish Rifles were scuffling along 71 North, the attack had been postponed, and the men, according to Sassoon, were at concert pitch. They were due to go into trenches in front of the cemetery by Fricourt Station. They marched up to the Bois des Tailles and relieved the 7th Borders. Conditions were muddy. On the 28th June Sassoon recorded that he was reading *Tess of the D'Urbervilles* in 85 Street Dugouts. On the 29th there was a continuous bombardment.

I record here an incident which took place at this time. The CO of the 9th KOYLI, Colonel C. W. D. Lynch, was very unpopular with his brother officers because of what had happened at Loos, and the way that he had subsequently treated them. As a result, six of them put in for a transfer including some to the Kite Balloon Section. Two days before the battle actually began, in the officers' mess it was suggested that the Regiment should be toasted, coupled with the name of the Commanding Officer. There was some dissent and several of the officers refused to take part in the ceremony, but Captain Haswell the senior officer present, stepped in and saved the situation, proposed the following toast 'Gentlemen, I give you the toast of the King's Own Yorkshire Light Infantry, and in particular the 9th Battalion of the Regiment' – a slight pause – 'Gentlemen, when the barrage lifts . . .' This toast appeared subsequently in the Memorium column of *The Times* for many years.

On 1st July though, twenty four KOYLI officers of the Regiment became casualties including Colonel Lynch, who was killed, probably by a shell, whilst leading his battalion.

To set the scene of the battle that was due to begin on 1st July after a two day postponement, I think that I cannot do better than use the *Official History*. On 1st July XV Corps on the left of XIII Corps faced the head of the Fricourt Salient, the corner stone of the German line between the Ancre and the Somme. The slopes of the Bazentin–Pozieres Ridge were broken through by the Willow Stream and its feeders. The centre valley ran up the western side of Mametz Wood with Caterpillar Way to the east and Contalmaison to the north-west. The Willow Stream made the boundary between the two Divisions of XV Corps in the front line, the 7th on the right facing north opposite Mametz village on the lower slopes of the Mametz Spur and the 21st on the east along the western slopes of the Fricourt Spur. The German defences about Fricourt were of exceptional strength and 1,200 yards in depth, and in the front line there were many salients and flanks. The front system was backed up by two intermediate lines; Fritz Trench – Railway Alley – Crucifix Trench and White Trench – Wood Trench – Quadrangle Trench. The two battalions who were to be involved on the part of the 7th Div. Front closest to Fricourt were the 20th Manchesters and the 1st R. Welch Fus. The other sections of this Division were more involved in the fighting on the Mametz side. Sassoon observed the progress of the battle on this section and said in his diary that the 20th Manchesters were in front of the R. Welch Fus. who were about 500 yards from the front trench where Sandown Road met Kingston Road. He said that the barrage was working to the right of Fricourt and beyond. He could see the Division advancing about three quarters of a mile away on the left. He could see our men advancing steadily on towards the German front line. He could also see some Yorkshiremen of the 50th Bde. 17th Division on the left watching the advance and cheering as if it was a football match. By 9.30 a.m. the 21st Div. were still going across on the left, apparently with no casualties. Trench Mortars were knocking hell out of Sunken Road Trench. This trench was close to Aeroplane Trench on the track at Fricourt. At 9.50 a.m. he said that Fricourt was half hidden by clouds of smoke and that our men were still advancing on the left in small parties. He mentions another huge explosion. At 10.05 a.m. he said that he could see the Manchesters in our front trench getting ready to go over. Two hundred shells burst close to our positions at 84 Street. The 21st Div. were still trotting along the skyline towards la Boisselle, which was the Division to the left. The barrage was going strong to the right of Contalmaison Ridge. And the Allies were shelling the Mametz area heavily. At 1.30 p.m. the Manchesters attacked and left New Trench and took the Sunken Road Trench. Sassoon could see about 400 of them, and about 25 casualties on the left from a machine gun at Fricourt. Then he says the 'swarm of ants' disappeared over the hill. At 2.50 p.m. no man's land was empty except for casualties. Later he says that the Manchesters had been held up behind the Sunken Road Trench. The RWF were holding the Rectangle and the Sunken Road and the Manchesters were holding Bois Français Support. And so on this section at the end of 1st July the Manchesters had got just beyond the Bois Français Craters to the Support line and the 1st RWF in a north-easterly direction had taken the Sunken Road Trench. They were poised to move beyond Fricourt which was due to be 'pinched out' by attacks on both sides of it.

Further to the north-west of the 1st RWF and between the Welch Battalion and the Tambour were some battalions of the 50th Bde. of the 17th Div. who at this time were attached to the 21st Division.

Firstly I shall deal with the 7th Green Howards who held the line from the Cemetery to the Tambour. The 10th W. Yorks. were in the line from the Tambour to the apex at Purfleet. The 7th E. Yorks. were in Bécordel Bécourt and Bonté Redoubt in support. The regimental history of the Green Howards says that the key to the taking of Fricourt was Wing Corner which was just to the north of where the 1st RWF were, where the Germans would be able to see on both sides of the attack coming towards them. The other strong point was thought to be Wicket Corner. The 7th Green Howards had been billeted in houses and barns in Ville on 27th June and at night had gone to trenches in front of Fricourt.

The German trenches were full of men who were pouring out of the left section which was the Tambour. The companies of the Green Howards had no chance and were literally mown down. At 6.15 p.m. the 6th Dorsets relieved them and the dead were thick on the ground. Total casualties were 352 including the wounded and missing.

At midday the Dorsets had filled their water bottles at Bonté Redoubt on their way from Bĉordel Bécourt to the front. The 50th Bde. attack had failed and was not renewed that day and the Dorsets spent the night near the Fricourt Cemetery and recovered many of the wounded, and at dawn on the 2nd moved back to Méaulte.

On the left of the 7th Green Howards and the 6th Dorsets were the 10th W. Yorks. In the attack two of the their leading companies made rapid progress in reaching Konig Trench and pressing on for the northern edge of the village. It was the third and fourth companies that caught the full brunt of the German machine gun fire which came mainly from the left flank. The Companies were cut down and virtually annihilated. They hadn't the advantage of the Tambour mines. Casualties included Lt. Col. Dickson and his second in command Major J. Knott who were both killed. Dickson lies with his men in the part of no man's land where they fell, in what is now Fricourt

New Military Cemetery.

The poet A. Victor Ratcliffe was a Lieutenant with the W. Yorks and he too became a casualty probably as a result of the machine gun fire from the Tambour. His work had been published in a volume entitled *Soldier Poets*. The 10th W. Yorks attacked in the morning and it was found later that their casualties were higher than those of any other battalion on 1st July.

The 7th E. Yorks of the same brigade as the W. Yorks had two companies at 9 a.m. moving up from Bonté Redoubt up to Kingston Road. Another company was in Surrey Street and two companies advanced towards the extreme of the village. They had attacked in the afternoon, but like the W. Yorks were met by murderous machine gun fire. During the night they were relieved and marched back to Heilly and Méaulte in order to reorganise.

There have been several references to the Tambour Mines. The purpose of the mines was to distract the enemy's attention and to form craters which would block enfilade fire against the 21st Division and the 50th Bde. of the 17th Div. from the northern face of the German Tambour. Three large mines against the Germans had been driven and these had been prepared by the 178th Tunnelling Company and were fired at about 7.27 a.m. on the 1st July. Two mines were exploded but not the third and the Germans established themselves pretty quickly, before the British Infantry could reach them. This is a similar story as at Hawthorn Redoubt a little earlier in the day at Beaumont Hamel. In addition to this activity three Russian Saps had been driven out in this sector for the purpose of having emplacements at their mouths or terminals which could accommodate flame throwers. Of these only Dinnet Street was used as the German line opposite the other two which were called Purfleet and Balmoral Street was not captured. Lt. A. J. Willis of the 10th Yorks. & Lancs. who was wounded on 1st July mentions the Matterhorn Crater as being in front of the Tambour and that it was about 50 feet deep. Today the bumped ground caused by all these operations is quite noticeable and only the cattle are now in occupation. Willis was sniped when going forward, from the direction of Fricourt Wood. (Liddle.)

The next battalion that I would like to deal briefly with is the 10th Green Howards who were in reserve behind the 10th W. Yorks. On the 29th June they had been in billets in Buire and on the night of 30th June they were in Queen's Redoubt which was in front of the wood south of Bécourt. Part of the battalion helped the 15th DLI pushing on to the sunken road that ran north and south through Fricourt and in support at Lozenge Alley. They consolidated. This was part of the taking of Fricourt by an encircling movement. One of the heroes of the 10th Green Howards was T/Major S. W. Loudoun-Shand who died near Fricourt on 1st July and is buried at the Norfolk Cemetery. The Citation for his Victoria Cross says that it was awarded for most conspicuous bravery. When his company attempted to climb over the parapet to attack the enemy's trenches, they were met by very fierce machine gun fire, which temporarily stopped their progress. Major Loudoun-Shand immediately leapt on to the parapet, helped the men over it, and encouraged them in every way until he fell mortally wounded. Even then he insisted on being propped up in the trench, and went on encouraging the NCO's and men until he died. He had previously fought in the Boer War.

Beyond the 10th W. Yorks were the 4th Middlesex who had moved up on the 30th June. On their left were the 8th Somerset LI. The supporting battalions were the 10th Y & L and the 8th Lincolns. At 7.30 a.m. after two mines had been exploded to the right of the Tambour they attempted to leave their trenches but were met by violent machine gun fire. It was decided to hold on to Empress Trench and consolidate. The Middlesex right flank was exposed and their left was held by scattered parties of the Somersets. By 9.15 a.m. supporting battalions had begun to arrive.

The 8th Lincolns in support had one company in the rear of the 8th Somerset LI and cleared the front line. The battalions worked their way down German communication trenches by bombing Dart Lane and Brandy Trench when Lozenge Alley were reached. This position was held at night. Their right flank was attacked from Fricourt up Lonely Trench but later that night the enemy retired.

The last two battalions of the 64th Bde. of the 21st Div. in this sector were the 9th and 10th KOYLI who were supported by the 15th DLI and the 1st E. Yorks. They were to lose Lt. Col. H. J. King of the 10th KOYLI who was wounded, and Lt. Col. M. B. Stow of the 1st E. Yorks. mortally so.

On 26th June the two KOYLI Battalions had moved up to Buire village, and on the 1st the 9th left from a Russian Sap and only five officers managed to get past even the first German trench and they included 2nd Lt. Ellenberger. They reached Crucifix Corner and the Bde. Commanding Officer Brig. Gen. Headlam had his HQ in the Sunken Road. At 8.45 a.m. Capt. L. Spicer reached the sunken road from reserve at Buire. Spicer's instructions were to reorganise the battalion and to take charge, and as they were relieved by the Reserve Bde. they were to go back to South Sausage Support. On his way Spicer had come across a lot of Lincolns and Green Howards who were obviously resting on the way to the Sunken Road. This was the Reserve Bde. which had been told to relieve the KOYLIs. Spicer was directed by them to the sunken road and he thought he was in Lozenge Alley which was too far over to the right. He hurried on and finally arrived at the end of the trench where they were digging a small sap onto the road. They were warned of sniper activity in Fricourt Farm because the enemy could see anyone getting out. Spicer dived across the road to the safety under an embankment on the far side of the road. The others joined him and they then proceeded up the Sunken Road which was full of men. Once they got to the German lines, the place had seemed full of English troops. He found Company Sgt. Major Warren and told him about the relief and that he was therefore to return the men to South Sausage Support. He found that Btn. HQ had been established at a large German dugout which was approached by a covered entrance, it had been converted into a temporary dressing station. When they were ready to move off the CO of the Lincolns gave orders that none of Spicer's Bde. were to leave the Sunken Road until the whole of the 62nd Bde. were in. During the night the enemy was quiet except for a certain amount of shelling. The dugout was a fine example of trench architecture. It was about 25 feet deep, with several rooms, both sleeping and living and it possessed a large oven. Forty German prisoners were taken at the dugout and it also accommodated wounded from both sides. There was a quantity of stores there which included cigars, cigarettes, chocolate and soda water. The latter was drunk by the British. R. C. Money of the 15th DLI says that on the 1st they followed the 9th KOYLI and that there were severe casualties and they went down Lozenge Alley, and found the remains of the battalion at the Sunken Road. He wrote that the men seemed to be sitting around waiting for orders. Their CO had become a casualty. The 64th Bde. was left in the air and they went back. He himself was wounded and returned home on a boat during 3/4th July. Bruce Bairnsfather was ill and travelled on the same boat home (Liddle).

To sum up then on the battle for Fricourt on the 1st July I do not think that I can do better than rely on the history of the 17th Div. The morning's attacks have been covered and in the afternoon the historian of the Division says that the advance of the 21st Div. had been brought to a standstill in front of the German trenches in Lozenge Wood on the Fricourt–Contalmaison Road. On the other side of the salient the 7th Div. was held up in the southern outskirts of Mametz. The plan of cutting off Fricourt by using two Divisions to join hands on the higher ground to the north of the village had failed. There was a gap of nearly two miles between them. During the afternoon the 7th Green Howards had been ordered to attack the west front of the village with the 7th E. Yorks. in close support. They were caught in a barrage fire, and along the margin of the village machine guns opened on them. The attack had failed. The remnants of the battalion struggled back to their trenches.

H. P. Robinson in his book *The Turning Point* wrote that Fricourt was of no strategic value but was a notoriously strong German Salient, in view of this there had been no original plan to take it by direct assault. Fricourt was to be pinched out.

In *Haig's Great Push* it is said that beyond the third line to the left of Fricourt lay a work called Crucifix Trench, the possession of which could greatly facilitate the capture of the village. It was against this that the Yorkshire troops advanced but they were heavily shelled and machine gunned. Further progress was impossible, since just beyond the captured trench was a wood called Shelter Wood, at the south-east corner of which the enemy erected a redoubt that bristled with machine guns.

Fricourt had turned out to be a particularly difficult village to take because of it being in a valley west of Mametz Wood but also because Fricourt Wood sloped up towards Mametz, the enemy who were entrenched could bring flanking fire to bear on Fricourt Wood. On the other side the British artillery was not able to inflict as much damage as it would have liked, again because of the sheltered position of the village.

One of the casualties of this day's fighting was Percy Lucas who was brother of the Essayist E. V. Lucas. He had a house near the Meynells at Greatham in Sussex and D. H. Lawrence had based a short story on an incident that had taken place there.

There is an article in *The Territorial* of July 1937 on the Battle of the Somme, which says that 'when the village was eventually entered they were swept by machine gun fire along the streets. The advance beyond Fricourt was even more difficult. Strongly defended woods and plantations up the slopes were honeycombed with enemy machine guns and snipers' posts, each of which had to be cleared by hand to hand fighting at bayonet point'.

The Germans despite the very considerable damage that they had inflicted upon the Allied attack on the village on the 1st July decided that the position was not tenable and therefore they planned to fall back on the village of Contalmaison to the north-east and make a stand there. This is not to say that they just presented Fricourt and Fricourt Wood to the British on a plate but rather that they made the Allies fight for every foot of the way.

The British plan had been for the 7th Div. on the right and the 21st Div. on the left to pinch out Fricourt with the 17th Div. pressing forward in the middle. It was to the 17th Div. that the capture of Fricourt or rather the fall of Fricourt is attributed.

In his diary Sassoon noted that on the 2nd Fricourt and Rose Trench were to be attacked again, although he was not involved in the fighting. At 2.30 p.m. the Adjutant reported that these two had been taken without resistance and that there hadn't been a bombardment. The 7th Division was reported as having taken many prisoners including 200 by the 1st RWF. Fricourt had become full of British troops and the 7th Div. had reached a line just short of Mametz Wood. Sassoon also adds that the 2nd Queen's of the 91st Bde. had 'legged it as usual'.

The 17th Division first had the inkling that the Germans were pulling out of the village when prisoners began to be brought back to the Allied line, for it was prisoners who gave the British the information about the German evacuation. The order was subsequently given for a Brigade to push forward to occupy the village, with Fricourt Farm and Wood for its second objective. Shortly after noon on the 2nd it was reported that the Bde. had pushed out northwards towards Fricourt Farm. The latter was to the north-east of the Wood and close to the Poodles and Lozenge Wood. At the Farm the 7th Lincolns were preparing to make an attack on the wood. They had already come under heavy machine gun fire from Fricourt Wood when they reached the north-east line of the village. According to the 17th Div. History, what was described on the maps as Fricourt Wood was at the time the park of the Fricourt Chateau, a building that was just outside the village. The enemy had abandoned it, and the 7th Lincolns used it as their HQ. But the Germans still held on to the park. From the park in front of the chateau was a wide clearing that stretched for about a quarter of a mile to a ride that traversed the wood from east to west. The clearing had been a grassy lawn and because of the bombardment and obstacles movement through it would be very slow. The Germans had machine guns amongst the trees, and more were hidden near the cross ride in order that the machine gunners could sweep the park's central clearing. The 7th Lincolns then advanced into the wood and pushed right through it. This was in the middle of the afternoon. On their left were the 8th S. Staffs. and the 10th Sherwood For. also of the 51st Bde. and these two battalions went forward along the northern edge of the wood. The advance had reached Fricourt Farm by now but the Germans still held not only a trench that ran from it nearly as far as the railway, but also a trench which was strongly wired that ran parallel to the margin of the wood and only about 150 yards from it. This was known as Crucifix Trench which was just to the north of the Poodles. It took its name from a roadside cross on the slope near its northern end. From here a heavy fire of machine guns and rifles was directed from the wood. At dusk there was still a lot of firing in front of Crucifix Trench and British 'Bombers' were fighting their way at the end of Railway Alley Trench which was near the farm.

The cellars of the chateau were used as a Bde. HQ, above ground the building was a ruin of fallen brick and rubble and only its southern wall was still standing. The strongly vaulted cellars had withstood the bombardments. According to *The War in the Air* at some time during the day a German battery was seen getting into position at Bernafay Wood. Subsequently though, they were knocked out by a French battery.

On the front of the 21st Div. who as we know were on the left of the 17th Div. we know that the 10th Y & L of the 63rd Bde. went up to join the 62nd Bde. and went up via the famous sunken road which ran virtually from north to south through the whole of the village. The occupied part of Dingle Trench which was to the north-west of Crucifix Alley and their HQ was part of the Sunken Road to the south of Round Wood.

The 9th KOYLIs of the 64th Bde. who were actively involved on the 1st were at 7 a.m. allowed to go at last, having been relieved and then been held up by the non-arrival of two and a half companies of the 12th North'd Fus. They filed down Patch Alley and then according to Spicer to positions in South Sausage Support. They established a Battalion HQ in a dugout at the junction of the Support and the front line. They spent the day consolidating and 'reversing' the trench. Their men had had no sleep for two nights having been in the trenches for four nights before that. They did manage to get some food and tea from Queen's Redoubt.

The 63rd Bde. which had been badly cut up took over a great German dugout which contained hundreds of beds and had been fitted with electric light. In his *War Letters to a Wife* R. Feilding describes a dugout which was possibly the same one although he is by no means the only commentor to remark on the dugouts of Fricourt indeed they became a centre of attraction, even to the King as we will see later on. Anyway Feilding reported 'This dugout beats all the ones that I had previously seen. It might almost be described as an underground house, where instead of going upstairs you went down, by one flight after another, to the different stories. There were three floors, the deepest being 60 feet or more from the door by which one entered. The entrance hall, so to speak was the brick cellar of a former house. There were two entrances, only one of which, however, could be recognised from the inside, since the doorway had been blown in. The other door, by which we entered, had been partly closed by a shell, a hole being left behind revealing heavy trench bombs, grenades, steel helmets, underclothing etc. Many rifles hung from the wooden walls of the first flight of stairs. Nooks and corners were occupied by sleeping bunks'.

Beyond Railway Alley was a small crescent shaped spinney on the left which was called Shelter Wood which had been full of Germans and which was captured by an attack from the west. The possession of the wood sub-sequently isolated the Germans who were in Railway Alley from support on that side. From the Alley though and from the Poodles and Railway Copse there was a withering fire from German machine guns and rifles as the British infantry advanced. The capture of these positions virtually finished off the German salient position between the two sections of the British advance so that a line from la Boisselle on the left to Montauban on the right was held. On the right, northwards from Montauban the British artillery bombarded the lines of Caterpillar Wood which reduced its resistance to the 18th Div. who were on the Montauban front.

In *Haig's Great Push* it notes that the capture of Fricourt was the supreme achievement of the day. The ground which had been won the previous day had been heavily shelled during the night, but the British had held on to it with splendid determination, and slowly the salient became contracted. The villages like Mametz and Montauban had been pounded to bits and were simply ruins.

In his book *The Battle of the Somme* Masefield wrote that Fricourt Wood was now (2nd July) outflanked on the east by our troops in Mametz, but it was still a strong enemy fortress − like all other parts of the salient, the wood was edged and crossed with deep and strong trenches of the usual enemy pattern − Above the highest, northern part of the wood the ground rises to a chalk tableland about as big as the wood and shaped rather like a boot raised to squash Fricourt flat. On this small boot-shaped plateau were more defences − At the heel is the deep valley of the Contalmaison road, the sole is the valley of Mametz, and the instep is a deep romantic curving valley, with the abrupt, sharply cut sides so often seen in a chalk country. This last valley, from its depth, steepness, and isolation, was known by our men as Shelter Valley.

The defences of the boot-shaped tableland were as follows: A line of trench known as Railway Alley, which ran (NE) from Fricourt Wood towards the toe; odds and ends about (1) a farm (2) a copse called the Poodles, and (3) a crucifix along the leg of the boot; a strong field fortress in the biggish copse called Shelter Wood which hangs like a curtain of shrubs and trees on the steep wall of the valley, at the top of the leg; the trenched copses Lozenge Wood and the Dingle, on the heel and the back. At dawn on the 2nd July our troops advanced to storm Fricourt Wood, the Contalmaison Road, Shelter Wood and as much of the boot-shaped plateau as they could take. As they advanced the massed guns in all the trenches and strongholds opened upon them. They got across the field of fire into Fricourt Wood − They climbed over fallen trees and were caught in branches, and were shot when caught. It took them all day to clear that jungle − and by dark they were almost out of the northern end, where Railway Alley lay in front of them on the roll of the hill. Further to the north, on the top of the leg of the boot, our men stormed the Shelter Wood – till the wood was heaped with corpses, but in our hands. The dugouts which had once been the HQ of a hidden battery in the gully, were taken over as dressing stations. In his diary entry for 3rd July Sassoon wrote that his battalion (1st RWF) assembled at 71 North and marched to a point north-west of Carnoy where the 22nd Bde. of the 7th Div. had concentrated. The four battalions piled arms and lay down in an open grassy hollow south of the Carnoy–Mametz Road, with a fine view of where the 91st Bde. had attacked on the 1st July, about 600 yards away. After lunch the commanding officer Brig. General J. R. Minshull-Ford rode round to congratulate the Bde. on what they had done in the previous few days. The 1st RWF were about 420 strong and the 20th Manchesters had been reduced to about 250 men. The 2nd R. Warwicks. and the 2nd R. Irish had not yet been in action. The four battalions were in four groups. A little smoke drifted from tiny bivouac fires. At the end of the hollow was the road to Mametz, where some captured guns had been recently brought along. Beyond that the ground rose towards the Bazentin Ridge. Sassoon wrote a poem which called 'At Carnoy' and whose first line is 'Down in the hollow there the whole Brigade'. (See Carnoy.)

Meanwhile on the left of Sassoon's 7th Division the 21st Div. were clearing Railway Alley and had secured the rest of the village of Fricourt by capturing the other fortresses, the Poodles and the Crucifix.

In his book *Letters from France 1915–1918* L. G. Spicer of the 9th KOYLIs of the 64th Bde. says that the 62nd Bde. had attacked Shelter Wood and had captured over 1,000 prisoners who had passed through the KOYLI trenches. At noon the battalion had received orders that the 21st Div. were going to take up a new line in support. Spicer's battalion occupied a small piece of line from the junction of Patch Alley and South Sausage Support to the left. The trenches were obliterated and despite shelling they carried out this work in order to be ready to hand over. Because there were so many men in this part of the line there was a lot of shelling and away above Contalmaison was a German kite balloon. They were relieved and marched out on 4th July straight to Dernancourt and from there they entrained for Picquigny.

On 3rd July the *Official History* records that Fricourt Wood was taken by an enveloping attack by the 13th North'd Fus. which was covered by Stokes/Mortar fire. Many prisoners were taken and a counter-attack against Bottom and Shelter Woods was repulsed.

In his book *The Turning Point* Robinson noted that on 5th July the British had forced their way for about 1,000 yards beyond Montauban which was to the right of Fricourt, to Marlborough Wood which had been captured after a short burst of fierce fighting. On this side this brought the British to almost abreast of Mametz Wood. On the further left there was prolonged fighting for the possession of a wood called Birch Tree and also Peake Woods, and of a formidable group of trenches that were close to Peake Woods which were known as the Horseshoes. The British attacked from two sides simultaneously. It was not until the Horseshoe was taken, that the situation was cleared, and this was done on the night of 6th/7th July. On the 7th the 110th Bde. of the 37th Div. was attached to the 21st Div. when they replaced the 63rd Bde. and in his book *39 Months* D. V. Kelly has written about this particular Bde. which was made up only of Leicestershire Battalions. On the 10th July Kelly went round the lines with the Bde. bombing officer and saw trenches that had been heaped with dead, mostly he thought to be Yorkshiremen. When Contalmaison was attacked the wounded came via Scott's Redoubt to Fricourt where the ADS was and they were then evacuated in Ambulance cars. Kelly also remembers that the 9th Leicesters HQ was in a deep dugout in a copse. By now Fricourt village was full of field guns and howitzers.

In a note in the *History of the Royal Engineers* it says that an elaborate plan for carrying water forward had been worked out by Major H. S. Rogers, for the Fourth Army. The careful arrangements proved of great value in subsequent operations. 'The most successful pipe-line in point of time was the extension of the Fricourt System, one water point had actually been established in Fricourt within 12 hours of the village being taken. The entire system had been completed in about ten days from then'.

In his book *Sagittarius Rising* Cecil Lewis mentions that on one occasion when the weather was bad for flying, a small party from his RFC Squadron set out in a tender for a visit to the front. Because of the state of the roads they were forced to leave their vehicle near the former front line at Fricourt. They then set out on foot towards Caterpillar Wood to visit a nine inch howitzer battery. The party passed through the formidable Fricourt defences and dugouts and noted its commanding position. They walked on past Mametz and up the valley, observing and taking in everything. There was little troop movement at the time. Batteries were perched below the crest of the rise. They discovered the battery that they had set out to visit, who were snug in a little valley and living in 'large tubular steel caissons, corrugated and shell proof'.

In *The War the Infantry Knew* (2nd RWF 58th Bde. 33rd Div.) one of its contributors wrote that on the 15th July the Battalion moved on down the Fricourt Road in heavy mist and that they went via Bécordel and then detoured to the right beyond Fricourt because of German shelling of 5.9s. At 8 o'clock the mist cleared and they found themselves amongst the dead of the Welsh Division and many friends were recognised and quickly buried. The objective of the Division was the Switch Line and High Wood.

The location of the 5th Div. on and around 19th July was at Rose Cottage in Fricourt. The peaceful beauty suggested by the name was not born out in actuality. The name being applied to a field that was pitted with shell holes, and covered with debris, the only cover consisted of a few tarpaulins that were stretched over poles, and also a Nissen hut. The ruins of a red brick cottage in one corner was the origin of the name.

Frank Richards in his book *Old Soldiers Never Die* of 2nd RWF wrote that they left Albert on the 20th July and moved in stages up to Fricourt Wood. He records that he camped in shacks in the wood which were shelled by the enemy.

On 21st July the 5th Seaforth H. of the 152nd Bde. of the 51st Highland Div. bivouacked on the edge of Fricourt Wood for the night. Across the valley lay Mametz village and in front of them was the dark mass of Mametz Wood. The whole of the 152nd Bde. was bivouacked in an open field on the south side of Fricourt Wood in Bécordel. In the valley ran the chief road which wound its way through Mametz past Mametz Wood to Bazentin le Grand. All along the side of the road were gun emplacements. Because of enemy shelling they had moved back to Méaulte. On the 24th July we have the following from Maurice Baring's book on the RFC in which he says that he went with Trenchard to Fricourt to see the ground wireless stations and mechanics.

The Australian Historian C. E. W. Bean visited Fricourt on the 3rd July and went north on the 10th and then visited Vignacourt. In an entry dated 4th August Capt. F. C. Hitchcock of the 2nd Leinsters wrote that he and some companions toured the old German front line at Fricourt and were surprised and amazed when they saw the stronghold on the commanding ground north of the village. It looked to them as if it was impregnable but the several mine craters told the tale of its capture. Masses of chevaux de Frise and barbed wire were heaped up all over the area. There was an Indian encampment close by – a Punjabi Regiment, employed on the lines of communication.

On 6th August the 4th Suffolks took over trenches in Fricourt Wood, and during the next few days furnished working parties for the construction of Thistle Alley communication trench.

In early August Max Plowman wrote in *Subaltern on the Somme* having left Dernancourt with his battalion the 10th W. Yorks. (50th Bde. 17th Div.) – 'We descended the long hill leading to Fricourt, dodging about the stream of traffic that stirs the dust of the road to a thick haze. Near the bottom of the hill we come upon the old front line of the 1st July. The country here is stricken waste:' – 'On the far side, in the face of a steep rise, we see the remains of what were deep, German dug-outs, but everything needs pointing out, for the general impression is a wilderness without verdure or growth of any kind. To our right, we noticed a ruined cemetery.'

Perhaps the high spot of Fricourt's history from the British Army's point of view was the visit of King George V on 10th August. We have several accounts of this visit including the King's own account from his diary which I will use first. 'We walked across no man's land and the German first line trenches and support trenches to an observation post just south and between the villages of Fricourt and Mametz. From there we got a fairly good view of the ground in front, but unfortunately the visibility was low, it was possible to make out Pozieres, Contalmaison, the Bois de Mametz, where all the fighting is going on now and there was plenty of shelling going on all the time, we were about three and a half miles from our front line. It was interesting seeing the trenches and every kind of thing lying about from shells to clothes and empty bottles. The masses of shell holes and lines of craters caused by mines are extraordinary. I went down into one German dugout about 30 feet deep, but I didn't stop long as I think a dead German was in it. I saw the grave of a French officer killed at the beginning of this year, before we took over the line, another of an unknown British soldier and a third of an English soldier with his steel helmet lying on the grave with a hole right through it which killed him and lastly a grave of a German with his boots sticking out of the ground. All very pathetic, which is war'.

Geoffrey Malins the Official War Office Photographer after filming at Franvillers noted that the news of the King's arrival and journey to Fricourt had spread, for everywhere numbers of troops were strewn along the roadside. The spot where the King alighted in Fricourt was arranged in a form of a circle with underground tunnels and dugouts of great depth. In various sections of the wall were machine gun emplacements, the whole being on top of a hill which had formed a formidable obstacle to the British troops. The hill is now known as King George's Hill. At a second stop the King was on a hill top and a General described the various movements of the attack and the fall of Fricourt. The guide for the party was a Lieutenant in the REs and he suddenly called attention to an old German Trench. The Prince of Wales first entered it and examined from above the depths of an old dugout. The party then halted at another dugout, the guide entered and for some moments did not re-appear whilst the King and the General stood gazing. The King walked over former mine craters and stood using his deer stalking glasses and watching the bombardment of Pozieres, at one point he picked up a piece of shrapnel as a souvenir. Malins' car had a flat tyre after the King's party had moved on and he made hurried tracks for a Casualty Clearing Station which the King was due to visit.

Philip Gibbs the famous journalist was another witness to the royal visit and when he was on what was named as King George's Hill, to the south of Fricourt Gibbs wrote that the King looked down on the white ghastliness of its ruins. Half a mile away lay Mametz and in front was Contalmaison with its ruins of its chateau, it stood amongst charred tree-trunks. Although the day was misty the King could see Montauban and Trônes Wood and a little way over to la Boisselle, and massed smoke clouds over Pozieres. Gibbs says that the King found the inscription on a cross that contained the bodies of two soldiers of the Border Regt. and that he went into a German dugout but did not go into the very depths of it.

In the book *At GHQ* by Brig. General John Charteris wrote that 'His Majesty's visit had been a great success. We took him to Fricourt and even a bit farther forward than that, so that he was very close to the fighting line. The King had been followed by cameras everywhere, and the whole visit is being well written up in a series of articles which will appear as soon as he is safely back in England'.

On 12th August the 9th KRRC marched to billets at Fricourt from Mericourt and on the 19th August they moved to Montauban. On the 13th the 2nd RWF moved from Bécordel to Fricourt Wood. The Brigade occupied a three storey dugout which was completely underground. They supplied working parties for digging a communication trench to High Wood and to carry materials from the Bazentin Dumps. Also on the 13th the 4th Suffolks. moved from Fricourt Wood to support trenches in Bazentin le Grand. On the 19th August they moved from a corner of High Wood back to Fricourt Wood and at sundown moved to a camp near Méaulte, near the Albert Road.

On 27th August the 2nd RWF relieved the 1st Black Watch and arrived at Fricourt Wood which was very muddy.

On 6th September, Fricourt was to receive further distinguished visitors, in fact once it had fallen to the Allies and providing it was safe to take visitors, the village had become a sort of Number One Tourist attraction. The main reason of course was to see the elaborate defences and dugouts that the always practical Germans had produced. Anyway on the 6th the Prime Minister Herbert Asquith together with Maurice Hankey who was the Secretary to the War Cabinet came to see the village to visit the British Army. Asquith had requested that his son Raymond who was with the Guards in the vicinity should meet the party at th crossroads close to the village. Once the party had arrived they had to shelter as the Germans were bombarding the village. They sheltered in the famous German dugout which at this time was the HQ of the 7th Div. Raymond Asquith wrote that he received a telegram whilst he was training which asked him to meet his father at the village, on the crossroads K6d at 10.45 a.m.. Raymond rode over on horseback and reached the rendezvous exactly on time, and waited for an hour on a very muddy road that was congested with lorries and troops and which was surrounded by barking guns. Then two handsome motors arrived from GHQ. His father the Prime Minister was in one with two Staff Officers, and in the other was Hankey, together with Maurice Bonham-Carter and 'one of those nondescripts who hang about the corridors of Downing Street in the twilight region between the civil and the domestic service'. They went up to see some of the captured German dugouts and just as they were arriving the Germans began to send over a few 4.2 shells from a field howitzer. The shells fell about 200 yards behind the party and they quickly sheltered in a large and commodious dugout for half an hour. The Prime Minister then drove off to lunch with the GOC of the Fourth Army, General Rawlinson, and Raymond rode back to re-join his unit. It was to be the last time that the two men met for shortly afterwards Raymond was mortally wounded. A few days after Asquith's visit, Lloyd George who was Secretary of War also visited Fricourt and the Welsh Division. He was to become Prime Minister three months later, in December 1916.

In the period 10th to 12th September the 47th London Div. was occupying a large area before going up to the line and the slopes were covered with transport of all kinds. The Cavalry also awaited once more its opportunity to 'break through'. On the 11th the 7th KRRC were in tents in Fricourt having come from Dernancourt, and on the 16th were back at the Transport Camp at Fricourt.

On the 12th September the 18th KRRC (122nd Bde. 41st Div.) moved to Fricourt from Dernancourt and on the night of the 14th September took up positions at Tea Trench prior to the Flers battle.

On 25th September Aubrey Smith of the London Rifle Bde. set off from Maricourt for Fricourt where the next water supply was situated. Smith it will be remembered was in the transport. Whilst they were looking for signs of drinking water at Fricourt their Transport Section moved its line to the neighbourhood of the Citadel, south of Fricourt on the road to Bray.

In early October the conditions at the Citadel were very muddy. The state of the countryside at this time was deplorable and the continuous rain of October in fact caused great hardship. According to the history of the 12th Div. the road from Fricourt to Montauban which was no wider than an ordinary country road and which at times had to take a double line of traffic, had an instruction to users that it was forbidden to proceed against the traffic. Also artillery limbers were unable to get across country. Shells were carried by using pack horses which often sank in the mud over their hocks. The conditions were of the worst and the 12th Div. made little progress at this time.

On the 8th November the 2nd RWF were relieved via Montauban, Fricourt and billets at Méaulte.

During the battle No. 25 CCS with the Fourth Army was at Fricourt with XIV Corps and the village was also a collecting station for walking wounded.

In November there was a Motor Ambulance Convoy in the village. There was also a rail line built of the British standard gauge towards Bazentin and Longueval which at the time was not in use.

At Fricourt was a camp named Mansell and towards the end of October the HQ of the 25th Div. was at Fricourt Farm.

I am going to mention several cemeteries, and not all of them are actually in Fricourt itself, but all are in the area.

Fricourt British Cemetery is out in the fields close to the Tambour Mine craters in the former no man's land and is associated especially with the men of the 7th Green Howards many of whom were killed on the morning of 1st July. Eighty-nine of the graves out of 132 belong to that battalion alone.

Fricourt New Military Cemetery is west off the north end of Fricourt on the former German front line. It is in fact four large graves made by the 10th Yorkshire Regiment after the capture of Fricourt and also contains the graves of a few who were killed in September 1916. 159 graves are of the 10th W. Yorks. and 38 of the E. Yorks.

One of the few German Cemeteries in the area is also at Fricourt and contains the resting places of about 5,000 men. After 1918 the Germans had no organisation equivalent to the Allied Imperial War Graves Commission and subsequently the German dead were buried in one large utilitarian cemetery which is a harsh contrast to the British Cemeteries of which there are about 100 in the area. Each metal cross on a grave carries at least two names. A high proportion of German dead were not recovered from the Somme.

Peake Woods Cemetery is on the north-west side of the road almost opposite the former copse of that name, about half a mile from Contalmaison, and four and a half miles from the centre of Albert. It was not begun until the later part of July 1916 and was used as a front line cemetery until February 1917. It stands on the side of a hill and Contalmaison and Pozieres can be seen from it. Peake Woods was the name given to the copse on the south-east side of the road to Contalmaison.

As already referred to, about a mile south of Fricourt on a track running between the roads from Fricourt and Mametz to Bray are two cemeteries both on or near the side of the track. Point 110 Old Military Cemetery was begun by French troops in February 1915 and continued by the 1st Dorsets and other British units from August in that year to September 1916. Point 110 New Military Cemetery was begun by the 403rd French Inf. Regt. in May–July 1915 and continued by the British units in February–July 1916. 110 as a name is taken from the map contour. And finally one thinks that the British have the monopoly of battlefield visiting, but there was a party of Germans who used to visit Fricourt in the 1930s every July and who gathered in a spot close to the village. In 1919 the body of von Richthofen was moved from Bertangles where his grave was being vandalised, to Fricourt, before it was taken six years later to Germany.[1]

German Road

At the end of August work on the this road was being carried out. It was to run from Fricourt through Death Valley, which was south of Mametz Wood and on to the Bazentin villages. It became the main track used by the 47th Div. in their actions at High Wood, and on the 14th September the road was packed with six inch Naval Guns and 9.2 Howitzers. Twelve and fifteen inch guns were mounted on railway mountings and on the next day, the day that High Wood fell, tanks used the German Road as well.

Gezaincourt

Gezaincourt is to the south-west of Doullens and from the 5th to the 12th of June the Sheffield Pals were billeted in the village before their disastrous involvement at Serre on 1st July. They were staying in a 'lovely valley'. No. 49 CCS was hastily set up to cope with the flood of wounded from the beginning of the battle and many of the casualties were brought here on the narrow gauge railway. The CCS was later replaced by No. 11 from the Citadel close to Doullens.

In the first 24 hours of the battle no fewer than five trains were waiting for casualties to arrive from the front, and one of the two hospitals which were especially set up for the use of officers was established in the village; the other at Corbie. The Communal Cemetery and Extension overlooks a small valley; the graves are mainly those of men killed in 1916 and 1918.

Ginchy

Ginchy is one and a half km north-east of Guillemont and is situated at the crossing of six roads. It stood on a high plain that defended Combles which is four km to the south-east. It was a forward position in the German defence line. The 7th Div. actually captured the village on 3rd September which was the day that Guillemont fell to the Allies. The final objective of the 7th Div. had been the high ground to the east of the village on a line that was approximately north and south through Ginchy Telegraph, which was the site of an old semaphor station. Ginchy was protected by a crescent shaped defence line that ran from north to south and 'wrapped' itself around the village. The trenches that were immediately in front of Ginchy were Porter Trench and Stout Trench. To the north of them was Beer Trench and to the south, and going towards Guillemont was ZZ Trench. The 91st Bde. bombers and two battalions of the 22nd Bde. and also the 1st R. Welch Fus. were involved in the 7th Division attack. A counter-attack pushed the 20th Manchesters who had reached the village back as far as Porter Trench. Later in the day the Manchesters retired and the Royal Irish were to re-occupy the village. German artillery was very heavy and by mid evening the enemy had re-occupied the village. On 4th September another attack was made on Ginchy by the 9th Devons with the help of a company from the 2nd Borders, both of the 20th Bde. of the 7th Div. They entered the village and later withdrew. Several more attacks were to be made on the village before it was finally captured on the 9th.

2nd Lt. F. E. S. Phillips RFC received the MC for work carried out on the 3rd. He had done fine contact patrol work. On one occasion he came down very low and his machine was hit by machine guns and rifle fire. He carried on and successfully put the British artillery on to the enemy who were massing for a counter-attack.

On the 5th the 16th Irish Div. had assaulted the village but had failed to capture it, together with a German strongpoint called The Quadrilateral which was on the Morval road. The 1st RMF (48th Bde. 16th Div.) relieved the 8th KRRC (41st Bde. 14th Div.) in trenches facing the village astride the railway to the south. On the 6th the 2nd Gordons (20th Bde. 7th Div.) tried three times to take the village and their casualties were very high and included three company commanders.

On 7th September the sunken road was reported as being full of German dead who had been caught by British artillery on the 3rd. On the 8th approach to the village was through quarries and Batt. HQ of the 7th R. Innis. F. (49th Bde. 16th Div.) was in Mount Street. Major W. Redmond MP was a member of the 6th R. Irish Rif. of the 47th Bde. On the 9th the left of the attack was to be delivered by the 16th Irish Div. and the 48th Bde. of that Div. was already weakened by previous fighting. On the left of the 56th Div. the 6th R. Irish and 8th RMF of the 47th Bde. with a detachment of the 6th Conn. Rangers received their instruction for the attack. The 48th Bde. moved off at 4.45 p.m., and the 47th Bde. were stopped by machine gun fire. The 7th R. Innis. F. were brought up as reinforcements. A wheel to the flank routed the nearest Germans and the Munsters pressed on beyond the Guillemont Road. The 7th R. Irish Rif. from the 49th Bde. who had met with slight opposition began to clear the western part of the village with men of the 8th R. Dub. Fus. who had followed the 1st RMF and carried on the attack through the village, and the 8th R. Innis Fus. from the 49th Bde. came in on the right. The 9th RDF (48th Bde. and the 7th R. Irish Rif. and some of the 7th R. Irish Fus. cleared the western part of Ginchy. Some Germans surrendered and some fled towards Flers and Lesboeufs. The 47th Bde. was checked in front of the Quadrilateral which was a strong point to the north-east of the village. On the right of the 47th Bde. the 56th Div. succeeded in forcing its way to Bouleux Wood, but could make no further progress owing to its left flank being uncovered as a result of the failure of the 47th Bde. to reach its objective. At 4 o'clock a heavy enemy barrage was put down on the assembly trenches of the 4th London in Leuze Wood, but the battalion went forward in six waves. In little over an hour they had captured their objectives and pushed out advance posts in positions overlooking Morval–Lesboeufs road. During the clearing of Ginchy T. M. Kettle, Irish Nationalist and poet was killed whilst fighting with the Dublin Fusiliers. He has no grave but his name appears on the Thiepval Memorial panels. The attack of the London RB further to the east failed.

And so the honour of capturing the village of Ginchy fell to the 48th Bde. together with two battalions of the 49th Bde. This was the end of several days of very heavy fighting. The Germans though did not give up and indeed entered the village once again during the next twenty-four hours, but were never to regain it in the 1916 battles. The new position though, formed an awkward salient which invited counter-attacks.

Casualties of the 16th Irish Div. were very high, in particular amongst the officers.

In John Buchan's words 'the British made good the old German second position, and had won the crest of the uplands, while the French section had advanced almost to the gates of Peronne. The moment was in a very real sense the end of a phase, the first and perhaps the most critical phase of the Somme battle.'

On the outskirts of Ginchy a road made of planks had been constructed over the original road which had been destroyed. It was a duckboard track from Ginchy to the top of 'Hogsback'. It extended for several kilometres. Apart from keeping the Germans from re-taking the village the next objective for the Allies was the Quadilateral which was behind Ginchy Telegraph on the road that led from Ginchy to Morval. It was at the top of the Ginchy–Leuze Wood spur just south of the railway and communication with the sunken road was a four-sided trench 300 × 150 yards, sited where the roads to Morval from Ginchy and Guillemont respectively meet. The Ginchy–Morval road as it approached the latter, is a sunken road and concealed anything in it, and just about halfway between the two villages a railway to the south of the sunken road almost touched. Where the road and railway most closely approached, the Germans had constructed a very 'strong work' which was in turn close to Bouleux Wood which guarded Combles.

In the period 9th/10th September the *Official History* notes that the 3rd Guards Bde. took over Ginchy from the 48th Bde. of the 16th Irish Div. Later

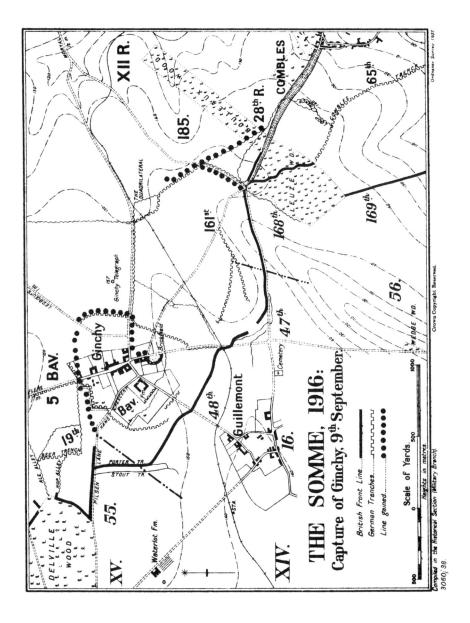

THE SOMME, 1916:
Capture of Ginchy, 9th September.

British Front Line	▬▬▬
German Trenches	⌐⌐⌐⌐⌐
Line gained	●●●●●

Scale of Yards.

Heights in metres

Compiled in the Historical Section (Military Branch)

Ordnance Survey 1937

Crown Copyright Reserved.

3060/38.

the 4th Gren. Gds. of the 3rd Guards Bde. relieved the 47th Bde. of the 16th Irish Div. in the angle formed by Wedge Wood–Ginchy Road and Leuze Wood–Guillemont Road. Contact with the 1st Welsh Gds. was lost until on the 10th the 1st Gren. Gds. of the 3rd Guards Bde. was sent up to fill the gap between the 1st Welsh Gds. and the 4th Gren. Gds. Fighting continued and was chiefly concerned in pushing forward the centre so as to include the Quadilateral and Ginchy Telegraph in the line before the big offensive. On the night of 11th/12th September the sector of the 3rd Guards Bde. was taken over by the 1st Gren Gds. and 2nd Scots. Gds. with orders to round up the Germans who were still occupying the re-entrance in the Bde. front. Prisoners were rounded up and at 6 a.m. on the 12th the 1st Gren. Gds. made a little ground towards Ginchy Telegraph and the 1/8 Middlesex (67th Bde. 56th Div.) did likewise south-east of the Quadrilateral. The movement failed though as a converging movement. By this time the 6th Div. had taken over from the 56th Div. and the right of the Guards, the centre of XIV Corps front from the Leuze Wood–Morval road to the outskirts of Ginchy. The line of the Leuze Wood–Ginchy Road was gained and held, but further advance was stopped by German machine guns. The 9th Suffolks and the 2nd. Sherwood For. lost heavily. The Quadrilateral which bristled with machine guns had been one of the pre 15th September objectives and remained in German hands. One of the officers of the Sherwood For. a Capt. J. F. Gibbons received the MC for bravery on the 13th. He reconnoitred the position under heavy fire and later organised and led his company in attack, but was severely wounded.

Harold Macmillan in his memoirs said that on the night of 12th September his battalion the 3rd Gren Gds. took over part of the line which had been occupied by the 3rd Guards Bde. He was told that it was likely that his Bde. and the 2nd Bde. would be leading the advance on the 15th, the 3rd Bde. being in reserve. In order to have a good jumping off place it was essential to gain certain ground, small in area but strongly held. They had to drive out a German machine gun hold on the Ginchy–Flers road. Two platoons were detailed for this work and they were very successful; the orchard was cleared of all Germans despite heavy fire. All the next day the 13th, his battalion, remained in the front line and was heavily shelled. There are many accounts of the action of the Guards Bdes. at Ginchy and for this account I have mainly drawn upon the *History of the Guards Division* and Harold Macmillan's Memoirs. In the former it says that during the night of 13th/14th September the 2nd Battalion of the Gren. Gds. advanced along the Ginchy–Flers Road and drove the enemy out of the orchard which was about 400 yards north of Ginchy and dug themselves in. On 14th September Divisional HQ moved forward to Bernafay Wood. During the night the men of the Guards Div. had gone to their various assembly positions. The front that they had to cover was 1,200 yards in length, and great emphasis was made, that the enemy should be driven out of any territory that they were occupying on the north-eastern out-skirts of Ginchy, pointing out that any opposition from this quarter could jeopardise the planned fighting for the following day's big battle, and would assuredly cause high casualties. Two particular places just north-east of Ginchy had been cleared of Germans before the 2nd Irish Gds. and the 2nd Gren. Gds. took over the line, in order to gain more ground for the launch of the attack on the right of the Guards; it was thought advisable to take possession of a trench east of Ginchy which actually formed part of the Quadrilateral. Artillery was used but it was hurriedly and inadequately organised, and it ended in failure on the night of the 13th using the Irish Guards.

Macmillan says that on the 15th in accordance with their orders they moved off just after dawn and advanced in platoons in artillery formation, about three to four hundred yards behind the Coldstreams. When they reached Ginchy there was a very heavy barrage raining down and they were almost blinded by the noise and confusion. Much of the bombardment was directed on the area a little to the south of Ginchy. They were also worried by heavy fire that came from the right and some was apparently coming from the rear. This was the dangerous part of the line where there was a junction between their Division and that of the neighbouring 6th Div. As Macmillan was going along with his platoon he was wounded in the knee just below the kneecap by a piece of shell. However he managed to continue and didn't feel much discomfort until later. They were going forward in accordance with their orders, with their right on the Ginchy–Lesboeufs Road. But the two Coldstream Battalions the 2nd and the 3rd were nowhere to be seen. What actually happened was that the whole of the leading attack had swerved to the left, and therefore the Coldstreams were no longer in front of the Gren. Gds. who they were meant to be supporting! Macmillan wrote that he remembered they halted for what seemed a long time, which in fact was about 20 minutes, and then the order was given to move on again to what they believed to be the first objective which they confidently expected to be in the hands of their friends the Coldstreams. But the objective was still held by the Germans. The creeping barrage had ceased and therefore they had no artillery support of any kind. All they could therefore do was to deploy and attack. They captured the line of trenches after fairly hard fighting and managed to make some contact with their own 3rd Battalion who were to their immediate right. Machine gun fire was going on on their left flank and Macmillan took a party in that direction in order to silence it. The enemy gunners were silenced but Macmillan was wounded again being shot at close range while half crawling, half crouching. This time he was hit in the left thigh by machine gun bullets, just below the hip. He rolled down into a large shell hole, where he lay dazed, but not unconscious. Being a literary man he read from a pocket edition of *Aeschylus's Prometheus* in Greek. At one point German soldiers ran around the lip of the shell hole but he lay 'doggo'. When it was dark he was brought back to the trenches that they were holding and was taken to where the CO had made his HQ. He was taken by stretcher to Ginchy and then left his bearers, to hobble on. He felt safer once he had left Ginchy as it was being continuously shelled. He was later picked up by a transport of the Sherwood Foresters. The casualties suffered by the 2nd Gren. Gds. in the operations of 13th-15th September were very severe.

From the *History of the Guards Division* we have the following account. On the right of the 2nd Guards Bde. the 3rd Gren. Gds. and the 1st Cold. Gds. took over the line from the 1st Royal Scots Guards. The trenches which were then occupied by the Grenadiers ran about 300 yards east of Ginchy, and those of the Coldstreams on their left were astride the Ginchy–Lesboeufs Road. The Scots. Gds. remained in the rear of the Gren. Gds. and the Irish Gds. in the rear of the Cold. Gds. The front of the 6th Division on the right of the 2nd Guards Bde. ran in a south-easterly direction along the Ginchy–Combles road about 300 yards behind the right flank of the 1st Scots. Gds.

Henry Dundas of the 1st Scots. Gds. of the 2nd Guards Bde. missed the 15th September fighting as he was ill at the time but he does say that the whole of his Bde. bivouacked on a hillside, as did six divisions of the Cavalry who were close by. He describes reports of the Ginchy fighting as being very severe and casualties as being very high. His battalion number was reduced from 750 to 142 and he mentions in particular the deaths of Alex Wernher a contemporary at Eton and Edward Cazalet of the Welsh Gds. We also know that Capt. 'Sloper' Mackenzie of the Gren. Gds. was mortally wounded in the same attack as was the most famous of that generation, Raymond Asquith on the 15th at Ginchy when leading his company. Asquith had joined the Queen's Westminsters in the early days of the war, but was later transferred to the Gren. Gds. Asquith had met his father, the Prime Minister in August, only a short time before (see Fricourt). This was to be their last meeting.

2nd Lt. N. F. Machin of the Cold. Gds. received the MC for rallying his men under heavy machine gun fire and brought them back under a heavy barrage until he fell wounded.

2nd Lt. I. Laing of the Cold. Gds. received the MC on the period 15th/16th September 'When he was the only officer left in his company he reorganised his men and rushed forward through a heavy barrage, and remained out, securing the front till ordered to withdraw'.

Hugh Wansey Bayley MC was MO to the 1st Scots. Gds. of the 2nd Guards Bde. and mentions that the assembly trenches were on the right front of Ginchy, north of Ginchy Telegraph. His aid post was in front of the Ginchy–Morval Road and about 200 yards east of the Ginchy–Lesboeufs Road. He saw three tanks advancing which drew German fire, and he heard Colonel Campbell's hunting horn when he was leading the 3rd Cold. Gds. on the extreme left of the Guards front. He gave morphia to Raymond Asquith and Captain 'Sloper' Mackenzie of the Grenadiers. They both had penetrating chest wounds and he sent them both down the line. Mark Tennant was killed on 16th September. He was a cousin of Edward Wyndham Tennant who was to be killed six days later on 22nd September. J. V. Campbell was born on 31st October, 1876, and was a Brevet Lt. Col. on 1st January, 1916, in brief part of his citation for his Victoria Cross for what he achieved on 15th September is as follows: Seeing that the first two waves of his battalion had been decimated by machine gun and rifle fire, he took personal command of the third line, rallied his men and led them against the enemy machine guns capturing the guns and killing personnel. Later in the day, after consultation with other unit commanders, he again rallied the survivors of his battalion and led them through a very hostile barrage against the objective. He was one of the first to enter the enemy trench.

Lance Sgt. F. McNess was in the 1st Scots Gds. and was born on 22nd January, 1892. During a severe engagement he led his men on with the greatest dash in face of heavy shelling and machine gun fire. The left flank was found to be exposed and the enemy was bombing down the trench. McNess organised a counter-attack and led it in person. He was severely wounded but passed through a barrage in order to bring up fresh supplies of bombs to his men. Finally he established a 'block' and continued encouraging his men and throwing bombs until he was exhausted by loss of blood. He too was to be awarded the VC.

Thomas M. Kettle born in 1880, a Lt. with the Dublin Fus. was killed on 9th September at Ginchy whilst clearing houses in the village. He was a writer of prose and poetry, barrister and professor at Dublin University. Previously he had been at Guillemont. His name is on the Memorial at Thiepval. He died for the Allied cause although he believed in a free and united Ireland. He had been an MP at Westminster but had resigned to give more time to his work of being a Professor of Economics.

The Quadrilateral: 18th September. According to the *Official History* the attack of the 6th Div. on the Quadilateral and Straight Trench resulted in a complete success and the establishment of a new line 500 yards beyond, over-looking the valley in front of Morval. After an accurate barrage the 1st KSLI advanced from the Ginchy–Combles road at 5.50 a.m. with its left on the railway track and keeping close behind the barrage swept into the Quadri-lateral. The Quadrilateral had fallen on 18th September which allowed the advance to go forward 1,000 yards to within half a mile from Morval and Lesboeufs. The Fifth Div. front now extended some 2,000 yards from the north edge of Bouleux Wood, and lay on the slope of Ginchy Telegraph.

The weather broke and little flying was therefore possible, but the Quadri-lateral was surrounded by the 6th Div. who took it in the morning. On 22nd September the Hon. Edward Wyndham Tennant (Bim) (son of Baron Glenconner) who was born in 1897 was killed. He was with the 4th Gren. Gds. and for a time was in the same company as Osbert Sitwell. He was buried near to his friend Raymond Asquith at Guillemont Road Cemetery. He was hit in Gas Alley, which was a trench that ran north-east of Ginchy towards Lesboeufs, and close to the present day Guards Memorial on the Ginchy–Lesboeufs Road.

In the period 26th–30th September the 2nd KOSB (13th Bde. 5th Div.) remained in trenches north-east of Ginchy and returned to Carnoy on 1st October. And on 7th October the Queen's Westminsters occupied a forward position south of Ginchy when they were 'on loan' to the 167th Bde. carrying stores and ammunition to the forward trenches.

The Carnoy Dressing Station was in early October situated between Ginchy and Lesboeufs.

In his book *Subaltern on the Somme* Max Plowman who was with the 11th West Yorks. (69th Bde. 23rd Div.) was on the eastern side of Ginchy and he describes being confronted with a wide rolling plain over which there was no road except for single 'duck walk' track. Slowly the battalion stretched itself out in single file along this track, and one by one the men followed each other, till the trail extended like a vertebrae of an endless snake! On either side lay the open plain – shell holes filled with water appeared in endless succession. In a letter he referred to being at Lesboeufs in October/November having nearly starved because communication lines across the morass between Ginchy and Lesboeufs were almost impassable. There was an ADS or CP in the village during November.

After the war Gen. Feilding unveiled the Guards Div. Memorial on the left of the Ginchy–Lesboeufs road at about the position where it had been crossed by the green line.

Gommecourt

Gommecourt is south-east of Foncquevillers and north-east of Hébuterne on the D 6 road to Puisieux. It is 15 km north of Albert and in 1915 and through to early 1916 the front line here, executed a sharp change of direction, to the north-east running up around Arras and northward to la Bassée. The resultant bend became known as the Gommecourt Salient.

In *The Old Front Line* John Masefield said that it was doubtful if any point on the Western Front in France was stronger than that of Gommecourt. Seen from the British front line at Hébuterne, it was little more than a few red buildings, standing in a woodland in a rise of ground, which hid the village to the north, the west, and the south-west. A big spur of woodlands, known as Gommecourt Park thrust boldy out from the village towards the plateau on which the English lines stood. This spur which was strongly fortified by the Germans made the greater part of the salient in the enemy lines. Apart from the Wood and Park the other very significant points were The Z, Little Z, Kern Redoubt, which was close to the Cemetery, the Quadrilateral, Nameless Farm and Sixteen Poplars. The Cemetery was in the village itself had been made into a formidable strongpoint but the Quadrilateral which was behind the village had been designed to be strong enough to drive the attackers back should they break through into the Park and village. It was 250 yards east of the village and there were many dugouts close to it which gave artillery protection. The outline of the Quadrilateral can still be traced (1983).

Masefield described the position as being immensely strong in itself, with a perfect field of fire for the defenders. In front of it was the usual system of barbed wire over a width of 50 yards and behind it, the first enemy line from which many communication trenches ran to the central fortress of the salient, which was known as the Kern Redoubt, and to the support line. The enemy had 12 machine guns both in and in front of this redoubt, the sites of which were continuously being changed to confuse the attackers.

There were two systems of trenches which were about 400 yards apart. The

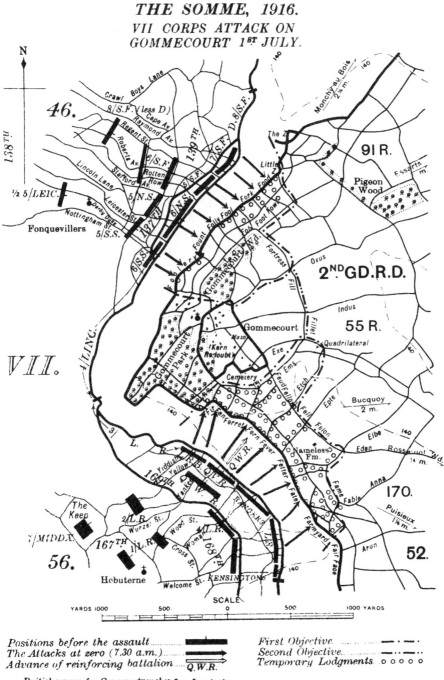

THE SOMME, 1916.
VII CORPS ATTACK ON
GOMMECOURT 1ST JULY.

N

46.

138TH

8/S.F. (less D)

½ 5/LEIC.

Fonquevillers

5/S.S.

The Z

91 R.

Little

Pigeon
Wood

Essarts
½ m.

Oxus

2ND GD.R.D.

Indus

Gommecourt   55 R.

Gommecourt
Park   Kern
Redoubt

Maze

Quadrilateral

Cemetery

Exe   Ems

Bucquoy
2 m.

Elbe   140

VII.

L.   R.

169TH

Yiddish Yellow

Ferret Fern Fever

Q.W.R.

Nameless
Fm.

Eden   Rossignol Wd.
¼ m.

Anna

170.

Puisieux
1¼ m.

The
Keep

7/MIDD.X.

167TH   1/L.R.

56.

2/L.R. St.
Wurzel

Wood St.

Woman

Cross St.

Welcome St.

168TH

4/L.R.

KENSINGTONS

Arun   52.

Hebuterne

SCALE

YARDS 1000   500   0   500   1000 YARDS

Positions before the assault
The Attacks at zero (7.30 a.m.)
Advance of reinforcing battalion   Q.W.R.

First Objective
Second Objective
Temporary Lodgments   o o o o o

British names for German trenches Fen, Ferret, etc.

3100/31

Ordnance Survey 1929.

front one was about 400 yards from the British line and ran in a south-easterly direction from the village, and consisted of three lines of trenches which were parallel with each other. The distance between the first and second lines was about 100 yards and between the second and third about 170 yards.

To the right of the 56th Div. front to be attacked by the 169th Bde. were the remains of the farm known as Nameless Farm and the road which ran parallel to the third German trench was known as Nameless Farm Road. The task of the Bde., to be carried out in four successive phases, was to capture the three lines of the first German trench system and link up with the 168th Bde. at a point in Fall Trench, fifty yards north-west of its junction with Epte Communication Trench; secondly to capture Ems and Etch communication trenches and the Quadilateral, thirdly to join hands with the 46th Div. on the ridge to the east of Gommecourt village, and fourthly to clear the village and Gommecourt Park. Thus the line would be straightened out from the point known as Sixteen Poplars in the south to The Z in the north by the 46th Div. If the plan was successful then the village would be surrounded and the final capture of the garrison was thought to be a relatively simple manner.

The *Official History* has this to say. The subsidiary offensive against Gommecourt was given to VII Corps. Between it and the left of the main attack against Beaumont Hamel and Serre carried out by VIII Corps there would be left a two mile gap from which no attack would be made owing to the lack of troops. The village stood at the juction of four low ridges; one arm stretching towards Essarts, Rossignol Wood, the western edge of Hébuterne and the eastern edge to Foncquevillers. On the south-west face of the salient almost as far south as Nameless Farm the British and German trenches were nearly on the same level with a dip that had a hedge between them beyond this point. Both were on the west side of the wide valley between Rossignol Wood and Hébuterne, the British line thus being on a forward and the German on a reverse slope.

The enemy artillery posts were on th eastern side of the valley. When the new line nearer to the enemy was dug, carts full of empty biscuit tins were driven up and down in Hébuterne in order to disguise the noise of the preparations.

In *Pilgrimage* G. Hutchison the author said that the terrain favoured the defenders, who had done so much to improve on it, but despite the German strength and the German artillery the London Battalions were confident that they could get into the German positions and secure them.

The 1/14 London Scottish of the 168th Bde. were at the south-west corner of the firing line, on their right was the 5th R. Warwicks and on their left were the 1/12 Rangers. Their objectives were German trenches to the right of Nameless Farm.

However I would like first to give brief details of what they had been doing before the 1st July attack. In May the 56th Div. had been moved at the beginning of the month to hold the line opposite Gommecourt positions. The London Scottish themselves were at St. Amand in reserve. On the 20th May they moved to Halloy for intensive training, at the time they were accommodated in huts. For training purposes they had a 'layout' of the position at Gommecourt which had been marked out complete with dugouts. It was laid out on undulating ground near Hurtebise Farm. After 'rehearsing the battle' here they left for the village of Souastre on 1st June. They then left the next day for the front at Hébuterne. They were involved with the Divisional task of digging new trenches which were 300 yards closer to the enemy and which drew enemy fire. On the 8th they were relieved by the 1/12 Rangers. The Battalion remained at Hébuterne and supplied working parties. On the 21st they marched to Pas-en-Artois and remained in huts there. On the 27th they moved to Bayencourt. In the village was a battery of 9.2 howitzers which were bombarding Gommecourt Wood, and firing every 5 minutes. On 30th June they moved to their assembly positions by 10 p.m. The new and hastily dug assembly trenches were of little use as they did not afford proper protection. They were on the extreme right of the attack with their right company almost on the line of the Hébuterne–Puisieux road. They left their trenches at 7.30 a.m. with the protection of a smoke screen and were immediately caught by an enemy barrage, but they pressed on despite this. They held the line in front of Fame Trench and the west end of Fable Trench. At around 9 a.m. the Rangers who were on their left were driven back by the enemy. This in turn exposed the left flank of the London Scottish. In the afternoon the situation deteriorated and they were joined by the Kensingtons, Victorias and Rangers. Howitzer fire poured down on them and they could see audacious German batteries boldly galloping up and opening fire from a slope close to Rossignol Wood which was to the north-east of their positions. A withdrawal was inevitable and they went back to the old British front line near Hébuterne, and just north of the road to Puisieux. The position was simply not tenable, it was exposed and enemy observation was complete. Also British counter-battery work was sadly lacking. The Battalion cookers were taken by horses to the Transport Line at Happy Valley which lay between Coigneux and Souastre. In the evening the remnants of the battalion moved to Sailly, the wounded having been taken to Hébuterne where RAMC bearers took them over. On the 2nd they were joined by Battalion reserves and then marched to Souastre where they stayed for a few hours. On the night of 2nd/3rd July they marched to Foncquevillers and were then sent into trenches that faced Gommecourt Park. They were here for four days and were then relieved by the QVRs, and returned to Souastre. For the next few weeks they were in and out of Hébuterne trenches and when they weren't in the front line they were billeted at Bayencourt and Sailly.

On the left of the London Scottish were the 1/12 Rangers and there is an excellent account from a Platoon Commander which is often quoted. His name was E. G. D. Liveing and we begin on the evening of 30th June when he says that in a little courtyard he called his old platoon to attention for the last time, shook hands with officers who were left in reserve, marched off up the road, and made a turning on to Blue Track. They had gone along about a quarter of the distance between Bayencourt and Sailly-au-Bois when a messenger caught up with them and they had to halt. On the left nearby was the spire of Bayencourt Church. On the right was Sailly-au-Bois in a girdle of trees. Along the side of the valley which ran out from behind Sailly-au-Bois arose numerous pillars of smoke from the wood fires and kitchens of artillery encampments. Going round Sailly they arrived in the middle of more battery positions in the level plain behind Hébuterne. Their destination was a Dump which was close to the ruined church there where they picked up materials. They entered a communication trench called Wood Street, and then turned sharp right into Boulevard Street and clattered along the brick floored trench. They arrived at a belt of trees which marked the orchard and turned right into Cross Street which was behind the trees and came to Woman Street. They were then directly in line with their front line and objective which was in the area of Nameless Farm. Liveing mentions that at one point a German search light from the direction of Serre Wood seemingly turned itself almost dead on him. They were to move off at 7.30 a.m. plus 45 seconds on the 1st July and he was in charge of No. 5 platoon who were part of the third wave. His life was to be spared by Rfl. C. S. Dennison who was his Platoon Observer but despite this he was still wounded badly in the thigh although they had reached as far as the German wire. Liveing's account then details his return and his treatment as a casualty. At Cross Street was a First Aid Post, he was then taken to an Advance Dressing Station which was a well sandbagged house reached through an archway and courtyard. A dugout had been tunnelled out beneath the courtyard and here surgical operations were performed. Liveing was taken by ambulance through the village of Sailly. At about 11.30 it arrived at Couin which was the HQ of the First Field Ambulance. From there they went to the CCS via Souastre where previously they had 'spent some pleasant evenings at the Divisional theatre'.

The CCS was situated in the grounds of a chateau in the area of the Arras–Doullens road.

To the left of the Rangers were the 1/9 Queen Victoria Rifles and their objective was enemy ground to the left of Nameless Farm. On 30th June they assembled for the march up the line and left their packs stored in old barns at Souastre. They then made their way up to the front via communication trenches. Frank Hawkins wrote about his experience with the QVRs in his book *From Ypres to Cambrai* but like Liveing he was quickly wounded and his account is less full than Liveing's. On 1st July they had about 500 yards of no man's land to cross as one of the leading battalions of the 56th Div., and smoke was discharged to assist them in their advance. They had erected ladders in the trenches and these were used as they climbed out into the open. The enemy barrage was very heavy and as they moved forward they could see the first line of the German infantry waiting for them through the drifting smoke. Parties of the QVR reached as far as Nameless Farm Road where they became muddled up with the Westminsters who in turn were on their left flank. They lined a steep bank which was about four and a half feet high on the side that was close to the enemy, the range of this bank was well known to the opposing machine gunners and was also under point blank rifle fire from Fellow Street which was a German line that continued on from Nameless Farm.

On the left flank of the 1/9 QVR was the battalion of the 1/6 Queen's Westminsters who have left possibly the most detailed account of the fighting of the 56th Division on this day. Their history also contains some useful photographs and a panoramic photograph of the ground that the London Division was to cover in its hopeless task of capturing this southern part of Gommecourt facing Gommecourt Park.

We have already noted that the 56th Div. came to this sector on 5th May and that several Battalions were used during the nights 25th to 27th May when nearly 3,000 men were involved in digging a new trench closer to the enemy's line. They also dug new communication trenches as well. During this time eight men were killed and 55 wounded. On 6th June a new trench was dug in Y Sector opposite the south-west corner of Gommecourt Park. The park was honeycombed with deep dugouts and the ground in front of it was known as the Mousetrap. The German front line ran along the edge of the park and remains of the trench line can still be easily seen (1985). The Queen's Westminsters had moved forward during the early hours of the night of 30th June/1st July from their billets at St. Amand and reached their assembly trenches at 2 a.m. on the 1st July. At zero hour they moved off and went steadily forward and found that the enemy lines of Feed and Feiln to the left of Nameless Farm, the German second line, to have been imperfectly destroyed by the Allied artillery, and that both were still strongly held. Both the Westminsters and the QVR had to wait under galling machine gun fire from the right, close to Nameless Farm, and also from Etch Trench which was close to the enemy front line. As noted the two battalions became mixed together when Nameless Farm Road was reached, and German machine gunners even emerged from their dugouts and fired into the rear of the advancing battalions. An attempt was made by the Westminsters to reach the German strongpoint the Quadrilateral using bombers but they were repelled.

From the moment that the attack of the 46th Div. on the northern face of the salient had failed, the fate of the assault of the 56th Div. Battalions was sealed, for it meant that the Germans could concentrate the fire from a large number of guns that they had behind the village of Gommecourt, on the area of the southern attack.

By the end of 1st July the Queen's Westminsters were bereft of officers. They, like the other London Territorial battalions, had been brought to a standstill by the concentration of enemy guns and the fact that they were cut off from reinforcements. There were 198 survivors and they marched from support trenches where they assembled after the day's fighting, to Bayencourt, where they billeted for the night. On 3rd July they moved to St. Amand and on the 4th they were reinforced by a draft of 268 men. On the 6th they went back to the trenches to relieve the 1/4th Londons (RF) in the late afternoon. The portion of the line that they took over lay to the north of the Gommecourt Salient, between Foncquevillers and Bienvillers, and was known as Z sector. Since 1st July there had been a lot of rain and in the communication trenches men stood waist deep in water. A large portion of the new draft were 'Bantams' and they probably had particular problems with these trench conditions. Very heavy rain fell on the 7th and on the 22nd the battalion was relieved by the QVR and they moved back to St. Amand for a week. They relieved the QVR on the 30th in the old trenches at Foncquevillers, and remained there until 7th August.

On the left of the Westminsters was the 1/5 London Rifle Bde. On the night of 23rd June the British bombardment had begun and on the 27th the LRB left Halloy and went into huts at Souastre. Souastre was where the Divisional Concert Party used to perform and in particular the 'Bow Bells Concert Party'. Aubrey Smith who was with the transport of this Battalion and wrote *Four Years on the Western Front* was one of those who waited all day for news of the attack. So much had been expected in the way of success that they were not just saddened by the appalling casualties and the destruction of a battalion, but also surprised at the complete failure. In brief he reported on what happened. The Allied bombardment had seemed to be successful and the LRB who were to attack the park, stood up and watched the wood being pulverised. The Germans put down a protective barrage and the LRB began under cover of numerous smoke bombs. They were to cover about 300 yards and the German machine gunners had a good view of them as they advanced towards them. They reached the first, second and even third lines but there were no reinforcement to take the place of the men who had already been killed or wounded. However Germans appeared from deep dugouts which the artillery had not penetrated and bombers were disgorged from them by the hundred. The advancing Riflemen were surrounded and cut off. In addition, the German barrage increased in intensity and reinforcements couldn't get through. The failure of the attack to the north brought German reinforcements to the southern part of the Salient. The Riflemen were simply cut down and Smith lists casualties as being 588, a figure that included 19 officers. The next day in the early afternoon a German Medical Officer came towards the British lines and an armistice was arranged that allowed wounded to be taken from the battlefield. Some men however were still lying out in the field as late as 6th July. The LRB had got as far as the trenches near the Gommecourt–Hébuterne Road, Signalman H. G. R. Williams of the LRB noted that on the 1st July because of the complete chaos no signals were actually received after the attack began. If this was so then it would explain the lack of reinforcements.

The last Regiment who were involved on this side of the Gommecourt battle and who were members of the 56th Div. was the Royal Fusiliers. They were to the left of the LRB in the Z Hedge area. On 1st July the 2nd London (R. Fus.) lay in the front line until 2.30 p.m. When D Company was ordered up to the German first line Ferret Trench, three unsuccessful attempts to cross the open ground in the face of artillery and machine gun fire had been made with the additional help of A and C Companies. Soon after noon the Germans showed a white flag in Ferret Trench and a formal truce took place which lasted for about an hour whilst the wounded were collected. The role of the 3rd London (R. Fus.) was to dig a communication trench from Z Hedge to the junction of Fir and Firm Trenches on the left of the point which C

Company attacked; but when this began at 10.10 a.m. the German barrage was so heavy that the attack had to be abandoned. Z Hedge was very heavily shelled.

The plan to take Gommecourt was a subsidiary one, a sort of distraction that VII Corps of the Third Army were to provide to the left of the main trust of the Fourth Army to the south of the Somme battlefield. The attack of the 46th Div. was to be carried out with two Midland Bdes. The 139th Bde. on the left were to attack between the northern edge of Gommecourt Wood and the Little Z, and the German first three lines were to be captured, and in conjunction with the attack of the 56th Div. on the right, the Allied lines were to be carried to a point just east of Gommecourt village. The aim of the two Divs. was not so much to capture Gommecourt as to prevent its defenders from being of use to their colleagues further south. The 46th and 56th Divs. were to 'join hands' having cut off the enemy.

The line on the front of the 46th Div. was half a mile to the north of Hébuterne just east of Foncquevillers, and it was held by the enemy northwards towards Monchy-au-Bois. Foncquevillers was the centre of the position. The chief work carried out before the start of the battle was the digging out of former communications trenches from Foncquevillers to the front line which was a distance of about 700 yards. There were about a dozen of these, several of which were named after the Midland Div. The main one was called Stafford Avenue, and others were called Lincoln Lane, Leicester Street, Nottingham Street, Derby Dyke, Roberts Avenue, Rotten Row etc. All of them had to be dug about two feet below their existing level, which made them about seven feet deep. In addition trenches for the support and reserve troops had to be prepared. There were also some Russian Saps made which were to allow troops to enter the line close to the front having been hidden with only a thin covering of earth to shield them. Dugouts had to be made for forward Battalion HQs and many miles of narrow cable trenches dug which had to be about six foot down for the protection of the wires from forward HQ to Bde. Division or Artillery. In addition to this, large quantities of stores and supplies had to be carried to dumps in the forward positions. This of course also included bombs and ammunition etc. The German position was very strongly fortified and indeed was along with Fricourt, one of the best defended of the German fortified villages. The trenches were very well constructed and also deep. The wire in front of them was almost impossible to get through and the dugouts were so deep that they were proof against any except the heaviest of Allied barrages.

There was also a long subterranean passage that had been built behind Gommecourt Wood that connected up with the German second line. Reinforcements could therefore be brought up quickly in case of a counter-attack. Some of the German wire protecting his trenches and lines was forty yards broad and built on iron stakes interlaced with barbed wire. In addition machine gun redoubts were built to protect specific points and behind all this was the artillery who knew to a foot their own and also the British trenches.

To the north of the line was Pigeon Wood and a small salient of trenches called the Z were opposite the left of the 46th Div. front, whilst in the middle of no man's land, which averaged about 400 yards in width was the ruins of Gommecourt Sucrerie, which was 20 yards from the main Foncque-villers–Gommecourt Road. Before the battle it was in reasonable condition and provided accommodation for the Battalion HQ and support companies and for baths and canteens.

A large full size model of the German lines was dug near to Lucheux Forest, where the attacking Bdes. were training and practising. Here the trenches were dug to the depth of two feet and tape lines were laid down for the troops to form up on, and the whole attack was rehearsed as a 'drill'. It was this sort of tactic that contributed to the lack of progress on the day. It was against this background with the odds overwhelming in favour of the defenders that the British was to make one of its most disastrous attacks of the first day of the Somme.

On the right of the 46th Div. attack at Gommecourt on 1st July was the 137th Bde. with the 1/6 S. Staffs. and the 1/6 N. Staffs. in the front with the 1/5 S. Staffs. and 1/5 N. Staffs. in support. The 1/5 Lincolns attached from the 138th Bde. was in reserve and supplied carrying parties.

The 1/6 S. Staffs. had been in the line in mid-June and were at Bus St. Leger for three days training, in the period 18th-21st June. On the 23rd June they returned to Souastre. When they were in the line their front was some 250 yards from the Germans on the flank close to the Foncque-villers–Gommecourt Road. A new assembly trench was built by them and also by the 6th N. Staffs. The Germans were aware of this new work and there were casualties as a result. On the evening of 30th June the 1/6 S. Staffs. moved up to their assembly positions. They moved off at 7.30 a.m. on 1st July but it was a hopeless task and they were severely affected by flanking fire from saps and shellholes to the south. Some of them reached the enemy wire but here they were mostly shot down and hit by hand grenades. A few men entered the front trenches but were driven out. Casualties were about 220/237. In the evening after they had been withdrawn, they assembled and proceeded to St. Amand where they spent the night. The 1/6 N. Staffs. being in the same frontal attack suffered in a similar fashion and they suffered 305 casualties. By 9 a.m. the Brigadier General of the 137th Bde. knew that the Bde. assault had failed and he endeavoured to organise a second attack using the 1/5 S. Staffs. and the 1/5 N. Staffs., but they were already very short of men and their officers had mostly become casualties and the general condi-tions up and down the trenches were chaotic. The troops had been trained to follow a certain plan of action of which this new attack was not part. The casualties on this day of the 1/5 S. Staffs. were 219, a figure that included 14 officers. The 1/5 N. Staffs. had taken up its position behind the 1/6th sister battalion in lines of attack. When the attack began they were overwhelmed by the German barrage which especially caught parties of men who were in com-munication trenches, and as a result they could not be of assistance to the 1/6th N. Staffs. who were being shot down by machine guns and rifles.

On the left of the 137th Bde. who had had such a disastrous time was the

139th Bde. which had done better. The 5th and 7th Sherwood For. were in the front line with one company of the 8th Sherwood For. on their left. In support were the 6th Sherwood For. and in reserve more companies of the 8th Sherwood For. Brigade line was roughly from la Brayelle Road on the north to the northern end of Gommecourt Wood on the south where the 139th Bde. joined up with the 6th N. Staffs. of the 137th Bde. The 139th Bde. front was from Little Z southwards to Gommecourt Wood. The communication trenches allocated to them included Regent Street, Roberts Avenue, Rotten Row and Stafford Avenue. Regent Street began at the brewery in Foncquevillers and then ran due east and crossed the la Brayelle Road in a south-easterly direction meeting the front line 150 yards to the south of the road. Roberts Avenue ran practically parallel with the la Brayelle Road, crossed Support Trench and met the front line at Russian Sap, which was a tunnel as close to the start line as possible. Fifth Batt. HQ was at the western end of Rotten Row and joined the front line about 100 yards south of Roberts Avenue. Stafford Avenue joined the front line 100 yards south of Rotten Row. Z and Little Z were jumping off trenches.

On 30th June the 5th Sherwood For. had arrived from Pommier in the evening at Foncquevillers. Batt. HQ was then in Crawl Boys Lane on the Foncquevillers–Gommecourt Road at the junction of Colonels Walk. Companies moved up at about midnight into the muddy trenches.

A note about the Sherwood Foresters:

When on the night before the battle they reached Foncquevillers their cookers were taken down the western edge of the wood behind the village, where the troops were issued with supper and rum at about 10 p.m. Each man carried in addition to the following day's ration, a bacon and bread sandwich. The *Official History* says that the first three waves of Sherwood Foresters suffered considerable casualties, but reached and broke into the German front trench; some parties advanced to the second, but there was some loss of direction on the left, as air observers reported British soldiers in the Z and Little Z. Succeeding waves were met by heavy fire and touch with the leading lines was lost. The Sherwood Foresters were also attacked by the enemy from the rear who had been in deep dugouts which should have been dealt with. The Germans also bombed men who were sheltering in the shell holes. Although a lodgement was made in the German line this could not be supported, although several attempts were made in the afternoon. The Sherwood For. had reached their assembly positions early on the 1st July and the British bombardment opened at 6.25 a.m. and the discharge of smoke from their front line began an hour later. Under cover of this the assaulting battalions moved from the advance trenches. A heavy and accurate barrage was immediately put down on the front line and support lines by the enemy, who were obviously aware in advance of the extent of the attack. At about 8 a.m. the forward trenches were cleared of troops. The trenches were in many parts deep in mud and water. Communication lines were often blocked by dead bodies or by wounded men, or were blown in. Little progress was possible. Little news came through but it soon became evident that the attack on their front had not succeeded. They later learned that owing to the difficulty experienced by the supporting waves in getting across their own water logged trenches they lost the advantage of the barrage, and that smoke had cleared long before the assaulting troops had got across no man's land. The long Allied bombardment had made little effect on the German trenches, dugouts and wire, and the attackers were met by rifle and machine gun fire, shellfire and uncut wire.

In *The War in the Air* it says that Observers had watched the leading waves of the Sherwood For. pass over the front line and make their way gradually towards the northern corner of what was left of Gommecourt Wood. Then they saw, as the waves passed on their way, the German infantry come scrambling from the shelter of their dugouts and re-occupy their front line trenches. The rear waves which had been given the task of clearing the dugouts, never got across no man's land owing to the heavy artillery and machine gun barrage. The men who had been cut off behind the German lines fought desperately all day. It proved impossible to develop fresh attacks to help them. It was hoped to renew the attack, but lack of smoke bomb protection, chaos in the communication trenches and the continued alertness of the enemy led to the eventual abandonment of the plan of attack again. A few men even returned as late as 9.30 p.m. In the evening the 8th Sherwood For. took over the remnants of the 5th and 7th Battalions and were later relieved by the 5th Lincolns. The 5th Sherwood For. marched back to Bienvillers. Casualties were 491 out of a total of 734 men. Lt. Colonels L. A. Hind and D. D. Winch were both numbered amongst the casualties. After 1st July they spent the next night and the following day in collecting up the wounded and tidying up the position, and were relieved by the Rangers on 3rd July.

In the history of the Sherwood For. it says that 'It must have been quite obvious to the enemy that their attack was to be the flank of the Somme attack, although some demonstration was made by the 37th Div. to their left. The enemy therefore were able to bring all their guns from the direction of Adinfer Wood to bear on no man's land on the Sherwood For. front'.

On the extreme left of the 46th Div. attack against Gommecourt Wood was a part of the 11th R. Warwicks of the 112th Bde. of the 37th Div. In the history of the 11th R. Warwicks it says that the slopes around Pigeon Wood, which was opposite the Z and Little Z position, and all the ground from the Z Trench up to Gommecourt, ground which had recently been more or less green, was now so thrown about and shattered that it appeared like waves and hillocks of brown earth, and every vestige of grass soon disappeared. The Warwicks were involved in the trenches for sixteen days and on the 3rd July they were relieved by the 5th Lincolns.

Behind the 137th Bde. (Staffordshires) attacking battalions were the 5th Leicester Batt. In June they had moved up to Foncquevillers and had relieved the 5th Sherwood For. in the right sector, opposite Gommecourt Park. A road and bank, ran parallel with the front line, and about 300 yards behind it, provided Battalion HQ. Behind this again, the Bluff, a steep bank, gave the support company a good home. The Staffordshires had so much work in the way of new trench digging and other duties that they were lent a battalion from the 5th Leicesters to help out. The 5th Leicesters were to advance as the ninth wave behind the attackers, while one company was to dig a trench joining the Sucrerie to the German front line a communication trench for use after the battle. The new assembly trenches which had been so recently dug became full of water because June was such a wet month. Soon after midnight on 30th June they moved up to Midland Trench, an assembly trench running north to south about 700 yards west of Foncquevillers Church. A & D Companies were in cellars and dugouts in the village, since they would be needed first. There were many communication trenches up which they could advance and at the last minute all of them were made 'up' trenches until after the attack. After the attack had begun and the fourth wave was advancing the smoke blew away and the whole of the attack was revealed. On the right the Staffords, passing the Sucrerie, found the German wire still too strong. The rear waves had no protection and the fifth wave was enfiladed by machine gun fire from the north, from the Z and from the front line. Two leading battalions of the Sherwood For. were seen crossing no man's land unscattered and had then entered the German lines complete and were never seen again. Other battalions lost their leading waves and sent back messages for smoke and reinforcements. Gallant efforts were made to take the wood. The situation became critical and they were still due to join hands with the 56th Div. attackers. The lines became congested and the Division did nothing in the way of counter-battery work. A further attack planned for mid-afternoon was abandoned and later the 5th Leicesters took over the front line from the Staffordshires and the 5th Lincolns came in on the left and relieved the Sherwood For.

In June the 5th Lincolns had been at Foncquevillers on the 18th. Afterwards they were at St. Amand, Humbercamps, Warlincourt and Souastre. On the morning of the 1st July the battalion advanced by platoons in artillery formation across the open ground between Souastre and Foncquevillers, and reached the Midland Trench in the rear of that village. There they spent the rest of the day. Some officers were instructed to reconnoitre the enemy front line trenches in front of Gommecourt Wood. There was the possibility that the battalions might be called upon to capture an enemy trench with uncut wire, which had not been taken in the day and the Germans would be on the alert. The plan was scrapped though. The 2nd July was spent mostly in getting the wounded in. On the 3rd July the 1/4 R. Fus. began to relieve them. The 5th Lincolns proceeded to Foncquevillers but instead of returning to billets they were told to relieve the 11th R. Warwick in a sector of the trenches immediately to the north of those previously occupied. Their right was on the la Brayelle Road. Rain fell heavily in the next few days and the trenches in places were in four feet of water. On the 9th two companies were relieved by the Queen's Westminsters and on the 11th the 8th Lincolns were relieved by a company of the 8th Somerset LI. On the nights of the 9th and 10th a strong carrying party was supported by the

Support Company to carry gas cylinders under supervision of the RE from Hannescamps to the front trenches held by the 1/4th Leicesters before Monchy, in preparation for the gas cloud attack on the German trenches.

Graham Hutchison in his book *Pilgrimage* has some pertinent things to say about the battle of Gommecourt on 1st July and wrote that the 1/6 N. Staffs. and the 1/6 S. Staffs. who were Territorial battalions from Wolverhampton and Hanley, had their leading companies caught by fire opposite uncut wire, on which most who arrived there were either shot or bombed by the defenders. The 46th Div. attack failed completely and one of the Bde. Commanders Brig. Gen. H. B. Williams who had seen these two battalions massacred declined to send forward their sister battalions later in the afternoon.

Hutchison also wrote that the first phase of the battle can best be studied by going to Foncquevillers, it was a village which although a mile behind the front line, had been immune from shellfire. He says that the attack was to emerge on 1st July from the lines in front of Hébuterne and then wrest the Park from the Germans, squeeze out the high ground at Beaumont Hamel and then force the Germans to retreat beyond the valley of the Ancre River. The attack completely failed and one German infantry regiment alone opposed an assault of ten thousand men. Comparatively few men reached the German lines and they found themselves unsupported and heavily bombed from both flanks and were finally overwhelmed by counter-attack and were killed or captured. The ravine which lay between the lines was heaped with dead who lay there for weeks, the prey of rats and of myriads of swollen flies. The extent of the failure appears to Hutchison as being unbelieveable. Superb battalions were reduced within a few minutes to but skeletons of their original strength.

In Dewar's *Sir Douglas Haig's Command* we have the following point of view voiced 'The failure of the subsidiary attack must be ascribed, in part at least, to the faulty handling of the supporting troops of the Division'. With the idea of securing protection and avoiding casualties, the attempt was made to bring these troops forward through communication trenches instead of across the open, with the results that the trenches became hopelessly blocked, the assault troops were left unsupported, and such of the support troops as succeeded at last in getting forward were met by withering fire from trenches and strong points which their slow advance had given the enemy time to re-occupy. So far as this Division was concerned the want of success was clearly due to a lack of knowledge of, and training in, the offensive tactics suited to the new type of fighting. On the other hand VII Corps Commander General Snow passed on this message to the troops. He said that he wished all ranks to understand that the attack on the Gommecourt Salient in co-operation with the 56th Division embraced two purposes: the capture of the position and the retaining of considerable numbers of German troops in the immediate front in order to prevent them taking part in resisting the advance of the Allied troops in the south. Although the first purpose was not achieved, the second was fulfilled, and there was no doubt that the action assisted the men of the

Fourth Army to the right and contributed to their success. In spite of this it was considered at least by the Sherwood For. (despite the comforting words of General Snow) that the action was a failure and this couldn't be denied. The retaining of enemy troops on the British front was done by the artillery, and other preparations, and the extra German Division was lured in to the line opposite the Midlanders at least three days before the battle. The actual assault made no difference to this. The object was to capture Gommecourt and this they failed to do. Obvious reasons were apparent to all: the rapid dispersal of the smoke barrage, the terrible enfilade bombardment from the left, consequent on the inactivity (the 37th) on the left, the failure of the artillery to smash up German posts, and in some cases German wire, and perhaps the fact that the pre-battle preparations were observed and known by the Germans who were therefore fully prepared for the attack when it came.

A document that was published by German sources entitled the *Defence of Gommecourt* is I think worth quoting from as it tells of the experiences of the German defenders at Gommecourt both on the 1st July and the period immediately before it. The document in turn is based on the War Diary of the German 55th Reserve Infantry Regiment of the 2nd Guards Reserve Division. The abbreviated extract tells of the severe effects of the Allied bombardment especially on Kern Redoubt. On one occasion it was partly blown in. Splinter shells destroyed emplacements of several trench mortars, a battery in Biez Wood received several direct hits. Despite the bombardment the telephone linesman succeeded in maintaining communication most of the time during the build up to 1st July.

On 1st July the bombardment shortly before the attack began succeeded in rendering the front sectors of GI, which was the ground in front of the Sherwood For. on the Wood section and G5 the section that contained the Cemetery ripe for assault. On the GI Sector the plan was presumably to help to cut off the garrison at Gommecourt. Strong British skirmishes were made from Pilier Farm and bombers and flame projectors were used. The British were repulsed and did not gain a footing in the sector. An energetic British attack was delivered against G5. The other sectors were kept under a heavy bombardment which was not followed by an infantry attack.

On the G5 sector many dug out entrances were blown in, trenches were flattened and wire destroyed. The front trench was enfiladed from the direction of Foncquevillers. Gommecourt Cemetery was overrun and the Kern Redoubt reached. Successive attacks advanced from Patrol Wood. The British were driven back to the cemetery with help from their colleagues holding Kern Redoubt, and by 4 p.m. portions of the G5 sector had been won back. An Allied prisoner stated that it was intended to cut off Gommecourt Village. The greatest danger, therefore, lay in G1 and G5 sectors and on the left flank of the Kern Redoubt. Communication was cut and not re-established until the evening. Regimental Command Post was at Point 147 where the situation could be observed. It is acknowledged that the equipment and preparation of the British attack were magnificent. The troops had been amply provided with machine guns, Lewis guns, trench mortars, and storming ladders. The officers were provided with excellent maps which gave the fullest details of the German positions and trench systems. Their losses on 1st July in this section were 708 men. This included those killed, missing or wounded. They had been able to live in their dugouts throughout the seven day bombardment. Prisoners had agreed that the German machine gun fire had been very effective.

Many of the British casualties on the 1st July were taken to the rail halts at Doullens and Warlincourt. Senior Officer casualties included Lt. Col. L. A. Hind (7th Sherwood For.), Lt. Col. C. E. Boote (5th N. Staffs.) and Lt. Col. D. D. Wilson (1/5 Sherwood For.), all of whom were killed. After 1st July Gommecourt is rarely mentioned in the history books and the British were never to capture it, and it was relinquished by the Germans on 27th February 1917, when they retreated to the Hindenburg Line.

Gommecourt Wood New Cemetery is on the south side of the road to Foncquevillers, west of the wood. It was made after the Armistice by the concentration of graves from certain smaller burial grounds and from the battle-fields of July 1916, including Bastion Cemetery of Foncquevillers. Lt. Col. Boote's grave is there.

Gommecourt British Cemetery Number One is a hundred yards north-west of Number Two. It contains the graves of soldiers mainly of the 56th Div. who fell on 1st July. It was concentrated into Number Two after the Armistice. Number Three was also concentrated with Number Two; it was at the south-west corner of the village and contained the graves of soldiers who fell, from the 56th Div. on 1st July; and 12th November Number Four as Number Three Gommecourt British Cemetery. Number Two is in open cultivated farmland three quarters of a mile south of Gommecourt village, sixty yards north of a road running from Hébuterne to Bucquoy.

Grandcourt

Grandcourt is on the south bank of the River Ancre between St. Pierre Divion and Miraumont. It is on the D 50 Road, north-east of Thiepval and north-west of Courcelette. It was part of the German entrenchment of the Ancre to St. Pierre Divion and the Germans were very well dug in here. Like Serre it was involved both at the beginning of the battle and at the end but little of note happened in between. On 1st July, the 36th (Ulster) Div. advancing from the direction of Thiepval Wood having begun the day at Aveluy Wood, actually reached as far as Grandcourt village having taken the immensely strong Schwaben Redoubt. This was a tremendous achievement but was not sustained because of lack of reinforcements and support.

It was the German 180th Inf. Bde. who faced the Irish Riflemen advancing from the eastern face of the Schwaben Redoubt. Some of the Irishmen reached the German Fifth Field Battery that was in a field in Battery Valley which ran from the south-west of Grandcourt in the direction of the Schwaben. Other members of the Ulster Division reached as far as the south of the Grandcourt/Thiepval Road crossing. The Germans enfiladed the

Ancre Valley with a high velocity gun that had been brought up at night on the Grandcourt–Beaucourt railway just far enough to fire southwards. Between Grandcourt and Courcelette which had been taken by the 2nd Canadian Div. on 15th September but closer to the latter is the Regina Trench Cemetery. This Cemetery was named after a German Work that was captured for a time on 1st October by the 5th Canadian Bde. and again by the 1st and 3rd Canadian Divs. on 8th October; taken by the 18th and 4th Canadian Divs. on 21st October and finally cleared on 11th November by the 4th Canadian. The Cemetery is on a side road called by the Army 'Twenty Three Road' and leading from Grandcourt Road to West Miraumont Road; the trench ran, roughly east and west, about 500 yards north of it.

In early November the Allied line still ran south of the Ancre and then in front of Grandcourt. After many struggles the whole of Regina Trench was at last in the hands of the Allies. It was planned to bring up the line north of the river, level with these positions, and to prepare for another attack on the village of Beaumont Hamel.

On 13th November the line ran down from a north-easterly direction and then took up the majority of Battery Valley which ran almost north to south. The Ancre Battle dates were from the 13th November to the 19th. To the south-east was Grandcourt Trench and to its south was Desire Trench and Support where the British line was consolidated at the end of the fighting. Behind Desire Trench and in front of Courcelette was Regina Trench. The famous Baillescourt Farm was just to the north of the River Ancre.

The 19th Div. was to attack from the south-west and the 11th Canadian Bde. were to the south-east.

On 17th November the 8th N. Staffs. were cut off at Grandcourt and their attack subsequently failed, they were part of 57th Bde. of the 19th Div. On the same date the 8th East Lancs. of the 37th Div. had been given the task of taking Baillescourt Farm which stood on a bank which was at least 30 feet high and sheer as well. The whole valley was commanded by the Germans on the hills beyond.

Owing to the nature of the boggy ground the Allies did not reach Grandcourt until 18th November 1916, and some heavy fighting took place during the following months but it was not until 14th February 1917 that the Allies were able to complete the capture of the village.

On the 18th Capt. C. G. Elkington of the 8th Glosters. of the 57th Bde. 19th Div. was in charge of an action that silenced an enemy machine gun and organised a defensive position. He was severely wounded and was awarded the DSO.

By the 21st Baillescourt Farm had been captured by the 63rd Naval Div. At one time the writer Henry Williamson was at the farm and used the ammunition boxes made of deal for heating, as they provided excellent fuel. Ever after he associated the smell of burning deal wood with the farm. It is now one of the largest farms on the Somme and is run as a Co-operative. On 21st November the poet Ivor Gurney arrived in the area with his battalion the 2/5 Glosters. They met their guides at Tullock's Corner and the battalion was for three or four days behind the Grandcourt Trenches, that stretched about 3,000 yards from Irving Post to Towse Burrows. The conditions were very primitive with men clinging to shell holes, and the mud was deep enough to completely submerge a gun team and limber. Masses of unburied dead were strewn over the surrounding battlefields and there was no sign of organised trenches, but merely shell holes that joined up to one another, and there were no landmarks anywhere. Gurney wrote a poem about the living conditions of the Canadians.

Of Grandcourt

Through miles of mud we travelled, and by sick valleys –
The Valley of Death at last – most evil alleys,
To Grandcourt trenches reserve – and the hell's name it did deserve.
Rain there was – tired and weak I was, glad for an end.

On 26th November the 2/5 Glosters. marched back to Wellington Huts.

Regina Trench Cemetery: the original part of the Cemetery was made in the winter of 1916–17 and was completed after the Armistice by the concentration of 2,086 graves from the battlefields of Courcelette, Grandcourt and Miraumont. The dates of death for the great majority of the dead are from October 1916 to February 1917 which was when the Germans left the village. The Cemetery stands in bleak open country, with considerable views to the north and east.

Grandcourt Road Cemetery is about a mile south of the village, on Stump Road which was the third objective of V Corps in the November Battle. Stump Road Cemetery is close by across some fields, but it is well worth a visit. Opposite Baillescourt Farm is the famous Boom Ravine which presumably got this name from its association with the German artillery. Early in 1917 it was 'found out' by the British artillery and both Philip Gibbs and John Masefield have commented on the utter destruction in the ravine and the number of German dead lying in the valley.

Grevillers

Grevillers is a village in the Pas de Calais and two miles to the west of Bapaume. On the north side of the Bapaume road there is a British Cemetery designed by Edwin Lutyens. It is not a 1916 one but Bayonet Trench Cemetery in Gueudecourt contains the graves of 19 men of the 1st AIF who were killed on 5th November and who are now buried in Grevillers British Cemetery.

Grove Town

Grove Town is south-east of Méaulte. It was the name given to a station on the Dernancourt–Loop–Plateau Line. There was not much there apart from sidings and its main use was for entraining or detraining.

G. Warwick in his book on the South Africans called *We Band of Brothers* wrote that after Suzanne they arrived at Grove Town Camp. This would presumably have been close to the station and also the present day cemetery. Warwick wrote in his book that the Camp had a high sounding name, and consisted of a wide open space with tents and barbed wire enclosures for German prisoners; there was no town! On 2nd July Warwick's battalion left the camp by companies and marched up to the trenches. On 3rd July they were put in proper dugouts which were in a narrow valley which was full of French 75s and other guns. The boundary of the two Armies was near and south-east of Grove Town. At 7.30 a.m. on the 4th they marched to an Engineers Dump and filled up trucks on a small tramline, with barbed wire and timber. They pushed the trucks along by hand and arrived eventually at a valley where the material was unloaded. On the return journey they had joy rides on the trucks and a group of Arg. & Suth. Highlanders passed them by. On the 5th they cleaned their rifles, packed up and marched to the old German trenches opposite Maricourt.

As the battle advanced in September/October new sites for CCS had to be found and at Grove Town by the side of the new railway 3 CCS the 2nd London was established from Heilly, 3 and 4 came from Vecquemont and 48 was also established in the period 10th to 12th September. In November a CCS was still in the village. In *Twelve Days* Rogerson also made some comments about Grove Town. He noted that it was a station only in the sense that special trains stopped there. It was not even worth the description of a siding, possessed no more shelter than it did platform. Sidney Rogerson was involved in a long wait for a 'missing' train and the troops began to wander further afield, and towards the dripping tents of the CCS whence one of his NCOs hurried back to Rogerson and informed him that behind one of the big marquees a dump of equipment from the wounded or dead had been made. Later on the station became a railhead for tanks as well.

Grove Town Cemetery designed by Edwin Lutyens is all that remains of the Grove Town connection and it is about half way along a secondary road leading from the main road to Bray, about three miles from Albert. In September 1916 the 34th and 2/2nd London Casualty Clearing Stations were established at this point which was called locally 'le demie-lieue'. The CCS were set up to deal with casualties from the Somme battlefields. The Cemetery stands on high ground overlooking Bray and the Somme Valley. One of the graves is of a journalist and poet Leslie Coulson who was an NCO and had been born in 1889. One of his poems which often appears in Anthologies is called *'From the Somme'*. He was wounded at Guedecourt and died on 7th October.

Gueudecourt

Gueudecourt is a village on the road between le Sars and le Transloy and is north-east of Flers and north-west of Lesboeufs. It was the centre of many actions in September 1916. It was protected to the south-west towards Flers by Gird Trench and beyond that by the Gird Support Trench. To the west along the road to Eaucourt were Seven Dials and Factory Corner. To the north-west on the road to Ligny Thilloy was Luisenhof Farm. When the Gird System was in German hands the lines were 500 yards apart. They ran from the north-west to the south-east across the Divisional front, but in the rear of the Butte de Warlencourt. Beyond the Gird Trenches lay a stretch of unspoilt open country with Bapaume clearly visible and midway almost hidden in a small valley was le Barque.

On the day that Flers had fallen, a Mark One Tank had actually reached as far as Gueudecourt and its very novelty struck terror into the enemy. It waddled into the village and engaged a whole battery of German guns, before it was hit and caught fire. The tanks had destroyed at least one German gun and perhaps two.

Anthony Eden who was with the 21st KRRC (124th Bde. 41st Div.) on the 15th September tells briefly in his book *Another World 1897–1917* the story of what happened in the direction of Gueudecourt on the day that Flers fell. Two battalions of the Bde. the 21st KRRC and the 10th Queen's were by the afternoon in a line on a position that was to the east of Flers and facing Gird Ridge. They appeared to be well in advance of the troops on either flank, but still capable of holding onto the ground that they had taken. Their next objective was the Gird Ridge, a formidable obstacle which the Germans had strongly entrenched with wire that was uncut. The Brigadier despite this wanted to proceed as a further advance might help the Divisions who were on the right and who were held up around Lesboeufs and Morval and had suffered heavy casualties. The attack took place without any more preparation and failed with heavy losses. Eden thought that maybe it was the success of the advance of the 41st Div. that had encouraged the Brigade to try and take the ridge when the defences were far too strong to be captured without effective artillery bombardment.

From Bulls Road that ran along the north-east front of Flers a clear view of German movements could be had and parties of them could be seen coming from the direction of le Transloy. The communication between the two lines was very shallow. The main approach to the front was down an open valley, into which shells dropped continuously, against the side of a sunken road to the east of Flers.

Part of the attack was coming from Gas Alley to the south-east of Gueudecourt. It was previously a German communication trench which the 1st Lincolns (62nd Bde. 21st Div.) began consolidating. They were however subjected to continuous fire and decimated.

On 16th September Lt. Ellenberger of the 9th KOYLIs wrote that they advanced nearly half a mile over no man's land, preceded by a tank which had straddled the German front trench and which subsequently burst into flames. None of them got nearer than 100 yards or so.

In his book *The Turning Point* H. P. Robinson wrote that the German artillery barraged the support trenches heavily and that Gueudecourt was very strongly defended. He meant that the Gird System was under bombardment. The road from Ginchy running due north, crossed the Gird System at a point just below the village in a deep ravine. The ravine itself, forked at this point, ran into two legs on the eastern and western sides of Gueudecourt and across these, a little higher up, the road from le Transloy to Eaucourt cut across through a deep gulley on both sides of the village. In the village itself were machine gun posts and in between these trenches and ravines lurked minor defended holes and hidden strongholds.

On 25th September the British front line ran along the southern edge of the village.

In his book *Gallipoli to the Somme* A. Aitken (1st Otago) in the 1st NZ Bde., wrote that on the 25th that they assembled in Grove Alley which ran in a south-westerly direction between the front of Gueudecourt and the front of Flers. The Alley was faced in a north-westerly direction and in a very carefully planned advance the New Zealanders entered the German trenches in Goose Alley which was a trench which ran towards the Gird system. The plan was that they should advance to the north-east and capture Gird Trench.

To paraphrase the *Official History* — A tank from Flers which was to assist in capturing Gird Trench in the plan for 26th September came up and was followed by bombers of the 7th Leicesters (110th Bde. 37th Div.) followed with two companies in support. The Germans were driven steadily south-eastwards towards the Guards Div. 370 Germans surrendered at this time and British losses were minimal. The Gird Trenches were then occupied by the 15th DLI (64th Bde. 21st Div.) Infantry patrols were instructed to enter the village and the Cavalry was called upon. A Squadron of the 19th Lancers (Sialkot Cavalry Bde. of the 1st Canadian Cavalry Div.) left Mametz and proceeded mostly at a trot up by a track east of Flers and then turned towards Gueudecourt and in the process they crossed two trenches full of British infantry. They were under artillery and machine gun fire from the right front and had to withdraw because of heavy shelling. Later they had another try at entering the village from the south-west at about 2.15 p.m. but this time they had dismounted. A troop of the South Irish Horse also had to resort to using its legs and dismounted as they too came under fire. The Cavalry withdrew at about 6 p.m., by which time the 110th Bde. had entered the village. Three battalions of the enemy had advanced from the direction of Thilloy and took cover in the long grass and standing crops a mile to the north of the village, but the Allied artillery 'searched' them out. British troops dug in on the far edge of the village.

In his book Aitken has this to say about what was a disastrous time for the New Zealanders, in an attack on Gird Trench. There was little cover for their advance as the ground sloped slightly down and they could be clearly seen by the Germans and would be machine gunned. Unlike the attack on the 25th when they had 23 minutes for crossing 700 yards they were only to be allowed a bare 8 minutes for the crossing of 1,000 yards which was far more exposed to fire, also there was little barrage protection. Aitken's platoon followed quickly up Goose Alley and climbed out on the right at the point where the sunken road from Flers to the Abbey at Eaucourt crossed it. As they reached the road that ran due west to east, the Abbey to Factory Corner, they came under fire from machine guns and from their own shells. The New Zealanders were virtually annihilated and Aitken himself was wounded. Nevertheless the trenches were reached by the next day, 28th September, when the village fell.

The 12th Div. relieved the 21st Div. on the night of 1st-2nd October, the 37th Bde. took over the right including the northern and eastern extremities of Gueudecourt and the 36th Bde. on the left, occupied Gird and Gird Support Trenches.

The next Somme battle in this area was to be the Battle of the Transloy Ridges and it was to last from 7th to the 20th of October, and as has been said the village was in the hands of the 37th Bde. at the time. To the north-east of the village there were many trenches with such names, reading from left to right, Bayonet, Hilt, Rainbow and beyond them Bacon, Grease, Mild and beyond them Barley, Bread, Stormy and Cloudy Trenches. All these were in the direction of the village of Beaulencourt. At this time the Fourth Army was occupying the whole front from Lesboeufs to Destremont Farm in support of the French advance at Sailly–Saillisel. The front on which the Royal Fusiliers were operating stretched roughly between the road from High Wood to le Barque and the road that ran north from Gueudecourt.

The 9th Batt. of the 36th Bde. was on the extreme right and the 26th Batt. on the extreme left. Before these battalions lay the trenches and strongpoints that formed the outer defences of Ligny Thilloy. On 7th October the 8th and 9th Batts. of the Royal Fusiliers (36th Bde.) were involved in an unsuccessful attack on the very strongly held positions towards Bayonet Trench.

In early October Leslie Coulson the poet was killed here and was buried at Grove Town Cemetery south of Méaulte.

Anthony Eden in the 21st KRRC (41st Div.) which at the beginning of the Transloy Ridges action was to left of the 12th Div. has this to say. 'The incline at Gird Ridge towards the front line was a gentle one into a valley of dead ground which extended for at least a hundred yards. It ended against a bank topped with some scruffy and shell torn bushes.' Eden's CO Major G. Foljambe decided that the foot of the bank should be their HQ from before zero hour. The attack was postponed for two days until 7th October and the weather grew rapidly worse. Turk Lane which was waterlogged in several places was the one and only communication trench. At 2 p.m. the British barrage came down which brought an immediate reply from the Germans who fired on the Gird Ridge and elsewhere. They could also hear the machine gun fire that the Fusiliers were enduring. Eden's 21st KRRC were meant to provide close support. The British preliminary bombardment had not silenced the machine guns and very soon the 21st KRRC came over the slope and down the ridge towards the Battalion HQ. Nothing went right, the plan was probably a mistake. The machine gunners took heavy toll of the Riflemen in addition to the Fusiliers. On the evening of 8th October the 21st KRRC moved their HQ to Factory Corner at a cross roads on the Gueudecourt–Eaucourt Road. Under this battered building of which nothing but rubble remained were some quite strong cellars which could just accommodate two battalion HQs with their staffs and signallers. The site was also well known to the Germans who had previously used the factory cellars themselves, and as a result kept up an almost continuous bombardment. Eden preferred the bank! They remained there through 9th October, and were relieved the next night by the 17th Manchesters and the 2nd R. Scots Fus. of the 90th Bde. of the 31st Div.

On the 9th October the Newfoundlanders had come via Corbie and Bernafay Wood and then Delville Wood in order to relieve the Royal Fusiliers. By 9.30 the battalion was manning a 500 yard section on the northern outskirts of Gueudecourt, immediately to the left of the road which ran north-eastwards to Beaulencourt. The 1st Essex were in positions of support to the rear. They were part of the 88th Bde. of the 29th Div. The Bde's. first objective was the Green Line about 400 yards from the British front line which would necessitate the capture of a part of Hilt Trench, whilst its extensions of Rainbow Trench to the south-east and Bayonet Trench to the north-east formed the main German position opposite the Fourth Army. Brown Line was about 400 yards beyond Green Line and was the second objective. Zero hour was set at 2.05 p.m. and during the night the 1st Essex had moved up to the left of the NFs. The 2nd Hants. took over from the 1st Essex in support. The 4th Worcesters, also members of the 88th Bde., had come up from Corbie. Owing to an excellent creeping barrage the two attacking battalions kept pace with the first part of the attack which was successful, and the German machine gunners were kept at bay, and Hilt Trench was taken. However the 1st Essex got into trouble as the 35th Bde. left an open flank next to them. This in turn of course depleted the flank of the NFs and bombing parties had to be quickly organised. Their trench lay in a small depression overlooking the German held ridge to the north-east. On the 13th the NFs handed over responsibility for Hilt Trench, and went back to a position close to Bull Trench at Flers. Between 10th October and their relief they had had 239 casualties.

In *Field Guns in France* the author Fraser-Tytler said that on 15th October to the north of Gueudecourt was a collection of German saps and strong points which were based on an old gun position, the whole lying in a curious salient surrounded on three sides by Allied trenches. As a consequence the Germans were immune from routine harrassing fire. He says that they continued laying their communication cables and reported to Bde. when they saw 'a host of German helmets'.

On the 16th October the 9th Norfolks (71st Bde. 6th Div.) were in front of trenches towards the enemy ridge east of Gueudecourt facing le Transloy. Batt. HQ was on a reverse slope. On 18th October the objective of the 12th Div. was Mild Trench approximately 1,000 yards out of Gueudecourt on the road to Beaulencourt, to the right. Part of Mild Trench was captured before their relief on the 19th October. The fighting was very costly on this day at Gueudecourt.

In the fighting between 23rd October and 5th November the 1st Australian and the 2nd Div. held the village. The 8th followed by the 17th Divs. were on their right. On 26th October Donald Hankey, brother of Maurice Hankey and author of *A Student in Arms* was killed here.

The 17th November line ran in front of the village south of Ligny Thilloy and west of le Transloy. On the outskirts of the village on the Beaulencourt road stands the Newfoundland Caribou Memorial above a former strong point with a curve of trenches and machine gun posts which had been the site of the regimental position.

Guillemont

Guillemont is on the D 20 going eastwards to Combles and on the D 64 road that goes south-west to Montauban. To the north-west is Longueval and Delville Wood and to the north-east is Ginchy. There was continuous fighting for the village from July 1916 until it was finally taken by the Allies on 3rd September. A main German line ran in a south-easterly direction from Longueval in front of it which took in the famous railway station and quarry. It continued behind Arrow Head Copse and went behind Wedge Wood towards the French lines beyond Maurepas.

To approach the village the way lay over perfectly bare country where the Germans had excellent observation from Leuze Wood and beyond. The quarry which was to the west of the village had been made into a strong redoubt and the ground to the south of it between Maltzhorn Farm and Falfemont Farm with Angle Wood in the centre was held by the enemy in strength. Brighton Road Trench was north of Guillemont Station.

According to Liddell Hart in his *History of the First World War* the village became a shambles of horror. The way to it from Trônes Wood was down a slope, up another slope, now only a few hundred yards of farm road, yet in July and August 1916 it seemed to be an infinite distance. On 23rd July the 21st Bde. of the 30th Div. tried to enter Guillemont but was let down by a lack of artillery support. The 19th Manchesters advanced from Trônes Wood and were aided by the 2nd Green Howards. Both had to withdraw and the Manchesters suffered many casualties. The 2nd R. Scots (8th Bde. 3rd Div.) tried later in the day without success and the 2nd R. Scots Fus. (90th Bde. 30th Div.) virtually disappeared as the enemy managed to appear behind them and cut them off.

The 30th of July was the date for the next attempt to take the village and this time it was planned that the 30th Div. would attack through the 35th Div. lines. The 89th Bde. of the former was to advance as far as the southern edge of the village and the 5th Bde. of the 2nd Div. was to take Guillemont Station and the German trenches to the north of it. During the night 29th/30th July the German artillery had bombarded the Trônes Wood area very heavily and in the morning there was a thick mist with visibility down to about 40 yards in places. Zero hour was 4.45 a.m. and Maltz Horn Farm was quickly taken and the advance carried on downhill in an easterly direction. The 2nd R. Scots. Fus. of the 90th Bde. advanced from Trônes Wood and entered the village from the south-west, and after waiting for the barrage to catch up, proceeded to the north-west of the village and joined up with the 18th Manchesters of their own Bde. The latter were severely hampered by crossfire of machine guns from both the Quarry and the Station. Uncut wire at the station held up companies of the 16th Manchesters. During the afternoon the Germans counter-attacked and the Allied barrage was hampered by the fact that three companies of the R. Scots. Fus. were holding out in the village. Communication was very difficult and Sgt. G. Evans of the 18th Manchesters was awarded the VC for his gallant service as a runner. Evans was born in 1876 and enlisted in 1915. He undertook under heavy rifle and machine gun fire, to take back an important message after five runners had been killed in previous attempts. He had to cover about 700 yards, the whole of which was under enemy observation. He delivered the message and though wounded re-joined his company. He returned, dodging from shell hole to shell hole and was taken prisoner some hours later. On previous occasions at Montauban and Trônes Wood he had also displayed great bravery and devotion to duty. The 2nd Div. also made an attempt on the village using the 2nd O & BLI and the 24th R. Fus. of the 5th Bde.

The *Official History* says that it was hardly surprising that the attack failed as did that of the 23rd of July for the tactics were the same. An attack from the west up the exposed shallow trough which marked the termination of Caterpillar Valley and from the south west over ground that was sloping and devoid of cover, had little chance of success.

It was planned that the village should be attacked once again, this time on 8th August. The 55th Div. was to attempt to take the village, except for the northern edge and the Railway Station which were both to be objectives of the 2nd Div. Zero hour was 4.20 a.m. and once again it was misty. Those battalions involved included the 1/5th King's of the 165th Bde., the 1/4th King's Own of the 164th Bde. and they were to be checked opposite the south-west village. The 1/8th King's or Liverpool Irish of the 164th Bde. got as far as the Quarry and fought its way into Guillemont.

Sec. Lt. G. G. Coury of the 3rd Lancs. who was attached to the 1/4th S. Lancs. who were Pioneers to the 55th Div. was awarded the VC for helping to bring in Major Swainson who died within minutes of being rescued. This action took place close to Arrow Head Copse.

The 2nd Div. attacked using two battalions of the 6th Bde. the 1st King's and the 17th Middlesex. They made little progress. The 166th Bde. was relieving the 164th Bde. and the 1/10th King's (Liverpool Scottish) lost heavily. The 1st/5th L.N. Lancs. and the 1/7th King's made little headway. The 2nd Div. put in the 13th Essex of the 6th Bde. together with the 17th Middlesex but they too failed. On the same day the 1/8th King's of the 55th Div. and the 1/King's of the 2nd Div. had been virtually cut off in the fight for the village. H. P. Robinson wrote in his book *The Turning Point* that the difficulty with Guillemont lay chiefly to the south of the village, in the region of Arrow Head Copse, by Maltz Horn Farm to the junction with the French Army near Angle Wood; the lie of the ground there, with the low wooded ravine which ran out from the last named place north-eastward, being particularly adapted to defence. The Machine Gun House also played a vital role in the German defences.

In the *History of the Royal Fusiliers* it says that three battalions of the Regiment played a part in these operations and the 1st Batt. were in the area from 8th August, when they took over trenches from Delville Wood to Trônes Wood.

Capt. N. G. Chavasse who was a member of the RAMC and attached to the 1/10th The King's (Liverpool) received the VC for his bravery on 9th August. He was son of the Bishop of Liverpool and was temporary Chaplain to the Forces. He was born in 1884 and had been a very accomplished athlete whilst studying at Oxford University. He joined the RAMC in 1913. Though severely wounded early in the attack whilst carrying a wounded soldier to the Dressing Station he refused to leave his post, and for two days not only continued to perform his duties but in addition went out repeatedly under heavy fire to search for and tend to the wounded who were lying out. During these searches, although practically without food, worn with fatigue and faint with his wounds, he assisted in carrying out a number of badly wounded men over heavy and difficult ground. By his extraordinary energy and inspiring example he was instrumental in rescuing many wounded men who would have otherwise undoubtedly succumed under the bad weather conditions. He was to be awarded a bar to his VC in February 1917. His twin sisters recently celebrated their 100th birthday (1986).

On 12th August the British were involved in a joint attack with the French and their roll was to capture a spur to the south of Guillemont. The attack again failed.

The 3rd Rifle Brigade (17th Bde. 24th Div.) were in reserve just to the west of Guillemont from the 12th to the 14th August. Andrew Buxton was a member of the 3rd Rifle Bde. and one of his fellow officers was Sec. Lt. R. E. Vernéde the French writer and poet. On the 8th Buxton had reported seeing masses of guns in the area, as he went up the west side of Bernafay Wood and Longueval Alley towards the top of Trônes Wood. On 12th August he was involved in working on trenches at Longueval. On the 15th there had been heavy rain and he observed Guillemont from Arrow Head Copse.

In the Imperial War Museum's Oral History collection there is a tape of Lt. E. K. Page who was an Artillery Section Commander. He had been posted to the 3rd Div. and then to the 6th Battery of the 40th Bde. and joined them in action on or about 15th/16th August near Maricourt. His Div. was next to the French, on the front Falfemont Farm–Guillemont. He was sent to man the night OP which was 'a very alarming experience' for a young officer. OP work was very unpleasant and it was hot August weather with many corpses remaining unburied.

On 17th August the HQ of the 1st Batt. R. Fus. was at Waterlot Farm. The next attack was to begin on 18th August at 2.45 p.m. on a broad front, with three other Divisions co-operating. The objective of the 3rd Rifle Bde. was Guillemont Station while the 8th Buffs. were directed against a trench some 200 yards from the front line in the direction of Ginchy. The station lying on a light railway just outside and to the north of the village, had become a tactical feature of some importance, and later in the month was to be the scene of a vigorous counter-attack. The 12th R. Fus. Batt. had been in reserve during the battle. On the 17th/18th the CO of the 7th Northamptons Lt. Col.

Mobbs was severely wounded.

The plan was to capture the village together with the help of the French and to spread the attack over two days. The objective on the 18th for XIV Corps was to be a line from Angle Wood to the spur south of Guillemont and then through the west side of the village to the railway station and the German front line further to the north. On the right of the village the 76th Bde. of the 3rd Div. attacked in the area of Lonely Trench. The attack failed. On the right section of the 24th Div. the 73rd Bde. attacked but were also checked. A section of the 7th Northants made a lodgement in the Quarry and they were reinforced by the 9th R. Sussex.

On the left the 3rd Rif. Bde. of the 17th Bde. had some success, and the 8th Buffs. were involved in a successful bombing attack on the ZZ trench. The two battalions joined hands and moved their way north-eastwards. However later in the day the German artillery counter-attacks regained the ground. During the night 19th/20th August the 3rd Div. was relieved by the 35th Div. A member of the 3rd Rif. Brig. (17th Bde. 24th Div.) was 2nd Lt. G.F. Marsden-Smedley who has a small memorial on the site of Guillemont station. This is probably on the site of the German front line trench dug in defence of the station which was such a bone of contention, between the two sides. He was killed on 18th August 1916 and is commemorated on the Thiepval Memorial. The Guillemont–Longueval Road was called High Holborn and the main ZZ trench was behind.

We have a detailed account of the fighting here at this time in Capt. F. C. Hitchcock's book *"Stand To"*. He was with the 2nd Leinsters of the 73rd Bde. of the 24th Div. Batt. HQ was at the Briqueterie. The ruins of Guillemont stood on the highest point of the ridge and dominated the surrounding countryside. The Germans were only too well aware of its importance and had already 'seen off' the Allied attacks on three occasions. Hitchcock viewed the attack from the Briqueterie, which was about a thousand yards as the crow flies from the jumping off trenches before Guillemont. The attack had got to within 30 yards of the objectives but when the barrage lifted, the Germans rushed up from deep dugouts and directed withering fire on the attackers. Machine guns had been concealed in a sunken road which ran between the advancing battalions and also enfiladed the two units. The Division failed. On the left, the 17th Bde. captured some small post near Waterlot Farm and a party of the 7th Northants captured a small post at the Quarries close to the station. They were relieved by the 1st N. Staffs. during the night. They went to sleep in funk holes. On waking they found that they were surrounded by dead of the 1st N. Staffs. who had been caught by the enemy when involved in a relief during the night.

Beyond the Cemetery was the sunken road, to the south where Ernst Jünger the German author of *The Storm of Steel* and Hitchcock faced each other, on 20th August. The road was where the trench lines formed just south-west of Guillemont and to the right of Arrow Head Copse.

Also 20th August Andrew Buxton remarks that there was a dugout with two entrances at Guillemont. On the 21st he mentions Brompton Road and Hill Street which was a continuation of High Holborn. A new line was being

Attack on GUILLEMONT
4-20 a.m., 8th August, 1916.

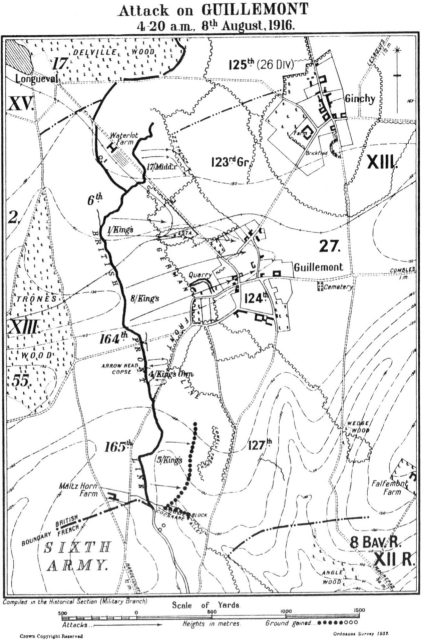

Compiled in the Historical Section (Military Branch)

Scale of Yards

Attacks........

Heights in metres.   Ground gained....●●●●●○○○

Crown Copyright Reserved
3060/38.

Ordnance Survey 1937.

established from the east end of the station to Brompton Road.

The *Official History* says that on 21st August that the 3rd Rif. Brig. and the 8th Buffs. of the 17th Bde. 24th Div. were occupying without fighting most of the portion of ZZ Trench in their sector but that further fighting later in the day was unsuccessful.

Between 18th and 22nd August the 3rd Rif. Brig. had maintained hold of the Station and had taken some prisoners on the 18th. On the 21st the Royal Fusiliers attacked in the rear of the enemy's position in the Quarries to the west of the village. The village was held so strongly as the Germans had very strong supports in tunnel dugouts. On the 21st the new front line was to the west of the Quarries. One of the minor excitements of the battle occurred on 21st August when continuous explosions came from the stokes mortar ammunition dump. The 1st R. Fus. advanced at 3.30 p.m. and their objectives were Hill Street and Brompton Road. On relief they went to Happy Valley near Bray as did Buxton with the 3rd Rif. Brig. on the 22nd of August. Also on 22nd August the 20th Div. relieved the 24th Div. in the sector north of the Guillemont–Montauban Road. The 6th Div. artillery which had been attached to the 20th Div. since 17th August, when it had replaced that of the Guards, also moved into the new area. The 11th KRRC of the 59th Bde. 20th Div. were in the area on 22nd August and were attacked by the Germans on the next day and relieved by the 11th Rif. Brig. on the 24th.

On the 25th the trenches were on low foreground in the valley south of Guillemont and the 20th Div. positions were six to eight hundred yards south-west of Falfemont Farm. At night a trench was being dug four hundred yards nearer the enemy lines which was to be used as a new jumping off place. The Germans were spotted in an old concrete gun pit some 300 yards beyond the Allied front line. A further attack was planned for 27th August but at this time bad weather set in and this, together with heavy hostile shelling in which gas shells were largely used made the work extremely difficult.

The trenches became waterlogged and were deep in mud. The state of the Carnoy–Montauban road was such that at one time on the 29th thirty-seven vehicles were either broken down there or stuck in the mud. The enemy's line ran a little to the west and north-west of the village, which being part of the German original line of defence, was strongly fortified. To the north high ground extended for about 3,000 yards, with the village of Ginchy at the highest point. Running more or less south from the south-west corner of the village were two sunken roads which gave more trouble than any other obstacle encountered both in this battle and in earlier attempts to capture the village. The plan on this occasion was to attack the village from the north side as well as from the west and south. To carry out this plan it was necessary to dig assembly trenches to the north of Guillemont Station. The 59th Bde. was to cover the right of the attack with its HQ at the Briqueterie, whilst the 47th Bde. of the 16th Irish Div. was to cover the left flank, its HQ being near the north-east corner of Bernafay Wood. Supporting battalions came from the 20th Div. and were to be two battalions of the 61st Bde.

GUILLEMONT
XIV Corps attack, 18ᵗʰ August, 1916.

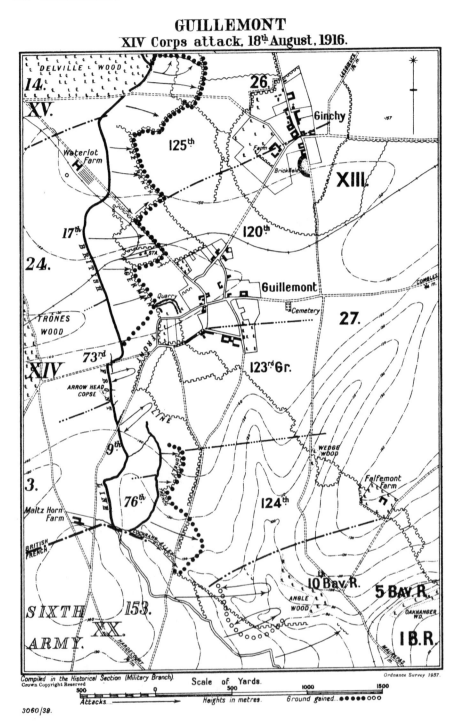

Compiled in the Historical Section (Military Branch).
Crown Copyright Reserved

Scale of Yards.

Heights in metres.

Attacks

Ground gained

Ordnance Survey 1937.

3060/38.

On 3rd September the 59th Bde. had the southern part of Guillemont as its objective. The 6th O & BLI (60th Bde.) and the 7th Somersets of the 61st Bde. came up to help with the assault. Between the 3rd and 5th September the 10th and 11th Rif. Brig. (59th Bde.) were very successful in the attacks on Guillemont, and 150 prisoners were captured.

The 47th Bde. of the 16th Irish Div. were brought up to replace the 60th Bde. in the attack on the northern part of the village. On the left of the 59th Bde. the 10th KRRC pressed forward and the 6th Connaughts of the 47th Bde. followed suit on the northern side of Mount Street. To confuse matters, in the Liddle collection at Sunderland, an observer of the role of the Connaught Rangers wrote that a part of them 'ran away like a rabble' despite the pleas of their officers. This same man Sec. Lt. H. D. Paviere of the 61st Bde. MGC also reports that on one occasion he sheltered in the tomb of the Waterlot Family in Guillemont Churchyard! At this time one of the Connaught Rangers was to win the VC. He was Private T. Hughes who was born in Ireland in May 1885. Part of the citation reads that he was wounded in an attack, but returned at once to the fighting after having his wounds dressed. Later, seeing a hostile machine gun he dashed out in front of his company, shot the gunner, and single handed captured the gun. Though again wounded he brought back three or four prisoners. These accounts of the doings of an Irish Battalion confirm the two aspects or characteristics of the 'fighting Irishman'. At midday the rest of the line advanced and the 10th and 11th Rif. Brig. and the 10th KRRC from right to left reached their objectives. The 10th KRRC had to mop up at the Quarry after the 6th Connaughts had rushed forward without consolidating the position. On the left of the Division the 7th Leinsters (47th Bde. 16th Div.) captured the trenches beyond Guillemont Station. A member of the 3rd Leinsters who was attached to the 7th Leinsters gained the VC for his bravery at this time. Lt. J. V. Holland was born in County Kildare in July 1889. He was involved during a heavy engagement when, not content with bombing hostile dugouts within the objective he fearlessly led his bombers through his own artillery barrage before the greater part of the village had been cleared. He had begun with 26 bombers and ended with only five after capturing 50 prisoners. By this gallant act he undoubtedly broke the spirit of the enemy and this saved many casualties when the battalion made a further advance. He was far from well at the time, and later had to go into hospital!

Advance to the second objective began at 12.50 p.m. In the 59th Bde. the leading battalions were reinforced by the 6th O & BLI (60th Bde.) and the 7th Somerset LI (61st Bde.). The 8th Royal Munsters (47th Bde. 16th Div.) passed through the Rangers' lines. During this fighting the MC was won by a Capt. C. S. Chandler of the 8th RMF when 'although wounded led his men and beat off repeated German attacks'. By 1.15 p.m. North and South Street were being consolidated.

In the 47th Bde. the 6th Royal Irish had taken up the attack and had reached a position to the north of the 59th Bde. Line. The Irish had held the sunken road and had suffered losses before reaching the road through shell fire.

Earlier in the day a 'push pipe' mine had been exploded with the object of destroying a German machine gun emplacement in the line of the sunken road that was opposite Arrow Head Copse. It didn't reach that far and gunfire destroyed it anyway!

The 59th Bde. ordered forward the 7th DCLI (61st Bde.) into Guillemont. Contact was made with the 95th Bde. of the 5th Div. and a Capt. A. K. Totton of the 1st DCLI was awarded the MC for his bravery. Although already wounded he led his men on to the first objective where he bombed the enemy dugouts and was again hit by a bomb. He then went on to the second objective being wounded a third time on the way. Meanwhile the 7th Div. had entered Ginchy but was soon forced out. At Guillemont the flanks were secured and the village was at last taken by the Allies. Sgt. David Jones of the 12th King's (Liverpool) Regt. was awarded the VC when he was in charge of a platoon well forward of the village towards Ginchy, Jones was born in 1891. His platoon was ordered forward and during the advance came under heavy machine gun fire, the officer in charge was killed and the platoon suffered heavy losses. Jones led the remainder forward and occupied this forward position for two days and nights without food or water. On the second day they drove back three counter-attacks and inflicted heavy losses. Jones himself was killed on 7th October, and is buried at Bancourt British Cemetery near to Bapaume.

During the period 3rd to 5th September the poet Vernéde was fighting with the 3rd Rifle Bde. and was to be killed in April 1917 when attacking a machine gun post on the edge of Havrincourt Wood and is buried at Lebuquierre Cemetery near Bapaume.

Gilbert Frankau (1884-1952) was another writer who was possibly involved in the battle. He had formerly been in the East Surreys and was transferred to the Royal Artillery in 1915. He wrote a book called *Peter Jackson Cigar Merchant* and fictionalised his experiences. For example he uses the name of The Chalkshires or The Fourthdowns. In the book the hero's battery sets off for the Somme with four guns, eight wagons, a water cart, 125 horses and 138 helmeted men. Heavy transport brought up the rear. At Guillemont 'Peter Jackson' was wounded and was taken back to London. He writes of the experiences of being a liaison officer and it is probably correct to suggest that Frankau was himself a Liaison Officer.

Still on the Artillery we have the following from the *Master of Belhaven*. The Master's name was Lt. Col. the Hon. R. G. A. Hamilton who was in charge of an Artillery Brigade. In 1917 he returned to the area and saw hundreds of white crosses in the long grass. In many cases rifles stuck in the ground and with a steel helmet on top. From Ginchy he made his way down the famous sunken road which was the final objective for 3rd September 1916 to what was left of Guillemont. He found the sunken road where his guns formerly were. He went along it to the Quarry. The hundreds of dead had gone. There was rank vegetation and a famous concrete machine gun emplacement which had defied the Artillery. He left his horse and walked to Arrow Head Copse. There was at the time a large railway junction at the corner of Trônes Wood.

And so to sum up on the fighting for Guillemont, the village which had been converted into a fortress with a chain of dugouts and tunnels that defied the heaviest artillery barrages had finally fallen to the 20th (Light) Div. and to part of the 16th (Irish) Div. John Buchan put it in the following way 'The British right, attacking in the afternoon, swept through Guillemont to the sunken road – 500 yards to the east. They captured Ginchy also but were forced later in the day to relinquish the eastern part of that village. Further south they fought to the east of Falfemont Farm, where they joined hands with the triumphant French.' 'So Guillemont was a triumph for the troops of Southern and Western Ireland. The men of Munster, Leinster, and Connaught broke through the intricate defences of the enemy as a torrent sweeps down rubble. The place was one of the strongest of all the many fortified villages in the German line, and its capture was the most important since the taking of Pozieres.'

In *The Turning Point* H. P. Robinson said that the result of the taking of Guillemont was that the lower corner of Delville Wood down to Angle Wood Ravine allowed the whole of our line to be pushed forward. The whole of what had been the German second main line was now British as far as the junction with the French. The labyrinth of tunnels explained the fates of the disappearing battalions, i.e. the 1st and 8th King's as well as the 2nd R. Scots. Fus. Liddell Hart commented that at last on the 3rd Guillemont was secured. Ginchy a few hundred yards further up the slope was a similar obstruction until 9th September.

During 4th/5th September Divisional orders instructed the 48th and 59th Bdes. of the 16th Irish Div. to relieve the 47th Bde. of the 16th Irish Div. and the 60th Bde. of the 20th Div.

On 9th September the Welsh Guards left Citadel Camp south of Fricourt and went to Guillemont. Their HQ was on the outskirts of the village. The 4th Gren. Gds. who were in the 3rd Guards Bde. was led to the incorrect line somewhere east of the village. Sec. Lt. Edward Cazalet of the Welsh Guards was killed by a shell on the 10th and is buried at the Citadel Cemetery. On 24th September Geoffrey Malins the Official War Office Photographer has this to say about the scene at Guillemont at this time. 'Before the 25th September attack the village of Guillemont did not exist, in fact, it was an absolute impossibility to tell where the fields ended and the village began. . . . It was one of the most awful specimens of the devastated track of war that existed on the Western Front. The village had been turned by the Germans into a veritable fortress; trenches and strongpoints, bristling with machine guns, commanded every point which gave vantage to the enemy'. Between the 26th and 27th of September the 10th and 11th Rif. Brig. (59th Bde. 20th Div.) were in reserve and handed over to the French on the 27th September. In early October Fraser-Tytler an Artilleryman wrote that the station in the village was a mass of craters and was the HQ of the Guards Bde.

On 16th November S. Rogerson wrote in *Twelve Days* that orders were brutally short. One item was enough. The Battalion was to find a working party of 6 officers and 300 men. The party was set to work till 4 p.m. and was required to supply labour for a Decauville railway track which the sappers were laying a Guillemont of all unhealthy places. In November the village was a walking wounded station.

In January 1917, after taking part in training courses etc. Max Plowman of the West Yorks said in his book *Subaltern on the Somme* 'this afternoon we marched to Guillemont, where we spent the night in shelters that were half dugouts. Shells dropped in Trônes Wood as we came by, but otherwise the march was uneventful. As a battalion we tramped the old duck boards again yesterday, and now we have two companies in the front line (this time to the right of Lesboeufs). The village was lost to the Allies in March 1918 but was later recaptured by the 17th Div.'

After the war a Memorial was erected in the village, to the Irish troops, next to the church. The 20th Div. erected a Memorial at the cross roads east of the village, which has been replaced by a monument close to the same spot; a Memorial to the 16th Div. has been erected between Guillemont and Ginchy.

Guillemont Road Cemetery: This cemetery is between the village and Trônes Wood, on the north side of the road to Montauban. Just inside the entrance is the grave of Raymond Asquith one of the sons of the Prime Minister. The cemetery was begun by fighting units of the Guards Div. and Field Ambulances after the battle of Guillemont. It was greatly increased after the Armistice by the construction of 2,139 graves, almost all from the period July–September 1916 from the battlefield surrounding the village. Asquith had been mortally wounded in charge of the first half number four Company of the 3rd Grenadier Guards (in the attack towards Lesboeufs). He was given morphia but died at the dressing station. A friend of Asquith's, the Hon. H. W. Tennant, is also buried in the Cemetery close by, he was a member of the 4th Gren. Gds. and a son of Baron Glenconner. He was killed on 22nd September. Behind the grave of Raymond Asquith is the grave of Lt Col J. C. Stormonth Darling, one of the 1st Cameronians, who was killed by a sniper east of the Trônes Wood on 1st November. At the time he was commanding the 9th HLI (Glasgow).

Halloy

Halloy is on the D 24 road just south of the Doullens–Arras Road and south of Lucheux Forest. It was due west of the Gommecourt lines. In the spring and early summer of 1916 it was very much a 56th Div. village and Stuart Dolden in his memoirs of his time with the London Scottish, who were part of that Division, wrote that on 20th May he arrived here with his cookers, and dispensed tea in an orchard and slept in a local barn. He said that the supply of water to the village was very bad and that he had to travel three miles to collect it. As the time for the battle of Gommecourt drew near the training was intensified and his battalion practised at Hurtebise Farm where a system of trenches had been laid out similar to those of the enemy between Gommecourt Wood and Hébuterne–Puisieux Road. They had been dug out and marked on the undulating ground. These rehearsals went on until the end of May.

L/Cpl. H. G. R. Williams who was a signaller with the 1/5 LRB mentions Z Hedge as providing cover and training near Halloy with Advanced HQ being in Elephant Huts in the old line.

Aubrey Smith who was also a member of the LRB wrote, that in early June they were at Halloy again and that his battalion were involved in battle rehearsals in the neighbouring wheat fields which were modelled exactly on the German defences as revealed by aerial photographs. The Bde. moved up to the firing line again while the transport, that Smith was with, made their quarters at Souastre.

The Queen's Westminsters (56th Div.) left Bayencourt for Halloy on 21st June to complete their final training and to rehearse their part in the forthcoming attack. The Rangers too, were in huts in the village at that time.

Smith mentioned the new gas masks that had been issued for use by the horses and described in his book attempts to fit the absurd respirators. They left the village on 27th June when the companies went into huts at Souastre, in the neighbourhood of a twelve inch gun! Transport made for St. Amand. During this time the Divisional Concert party called aptly the 'Bow Bells' used to give concerts in barns as well as in Souastre.

Hamel

Hamel together with Beaumont Hamel is a commune in the Department of the Somme, adjacent to the railway line on the D 50 road in the Ancre Valley. To the south-east is Thiepval and to the north Beaumont Hamel and also Beaucourt which is on the Ancre. Hamel was in British hands from 1915 until 27th March 1918. The German lines crossed the valley in a solid wave to the north of the village, which became the scene of terrible fighting in July 1916.

In *The Old Front Line* John Masefield wrote that the Church and the Churchyard made good posts from which British snipers could shoot across the river at the enemy, who were in the German stronghold the Schwaben Redoubt, which was almost due east of Hamel. One of the most used causeways on the Somme was in front of Hamel on the line of the road to the old Mill, which lay to the left of the causeway on a sort of green island. The mill which had not been destroyed at this time could still be seen amongst the ruins. The Germans had a dressing station there at some time. The foundations are still there (1986).

On 1st July Hamel was part of the 36th (Ulster) Div. attack. The section across the river formed the main thrust which was towards Thiepval and beyond. The 12th R. Irish. Rif. and the 9th R. Irish Fus. of the 108th Bde. were the main attacking troops but by the end of the day they had made little progress. They had been attacking north-easterly, to the left of the Ancre marshland. One member of each battalion was to gain the VC this day. Geoffrey St. George Shillington Cather T/Lt. with the R. Irish Rif. who had been born in 1890 and was the Battalion Adjutant won his for his courage near Hamel. The citation reads. 'For most conspicuous bravery.' From 7 p.m. until midnight he searched no man's land and brought in three wounded men; next morning at 8 a.m. he continued his search, brought in another wounded man and gave water to others, arranging for their rescue later. Finally at 10.30 a.m. he took water to another man and was proceeding further when he himself was killed. All this was carried out in full view of the enemy, and under their direct machine gun fire and intermittent artillery fire. His name is listed on the Thiepval Memorial.

The second VC was Private P. Quigg of the 12th R. Irish Rif. His citation in brief says that he advanced to the assault with his platoon three times. Early on the 2nd July, hearing rumour that his platoon officer was lying out wounded, he went out seven times to look for him, under heavy shell fire and machine gun fire, each time bringing back a wounded man. The last man he dragged in on a water proof sheet from within a few yards of the enemy wire. He was seven hours engaged in this most gallant work, and was finally so exhausted that he had to give it up.

The next time that Hamel is in the battle news is as part of the Ancre operations dated 3rd September, and we have an eyewitness to the pre-battle conditions and also to the battle itself in the writings of Edmund Blunden who was a Lieutenant with the 11th R. Sussex (116th Bde. 39th Div.). His battalion moved south to Hamel and detached some parties on 26th August and 27th, when they all moved to Mailly Maillet Wood which was viewed by German observation balloons and 'shelled unpleasantly'. The battalion shared the wood and suffered the shelling. Blunden was in charge of work at Hamel and had his good friend Sgt. Worley with him, to help him with getting an ammunition store ready. In his book Blunden talks of places in Hamel that become familiar to them and the troops such as the 'Cafe du Centre' which was all that was left of the level crossing keeper's house. In the direction of Thiepval, the enormous British Trench Mortar, the flying pig was discharging from a cellar in Hamel into the German lines.

On the evening of 2nd September the 11th R. Sussex moved cautiously from Mailly Maillet by cross-country tracks though Engelbelmer over the Downs of Mesnil and then assembled in the Hamel trenches to attack Beaucourt the next morning. They had used the long communication called Jacob's Ladder. They entered the assembly trenches at about midnight and Blunden stood at the junction of four advanced trenches directing several companies into them as had been planned. Every man remembered the practice attacks carried out at Monchy Breton. When the rum and coffee was duly on the way to these men, he then went on to his other duty. A carrying party from another battalion was to meet up with him in Hamel and for a time he and a fellow officer had nothing to do but wait. They walked along the river road and past a sandbagged dressing station that had been set up only one or two days earlier where the front line (Shanklin Terrace) crossed the road, and had already been battered in. They entered no man's land and saw some wounded troops of the Black Watch who were trailing down the road, they had been wading the marshes of the River Ancre trying to take a machine gun post called the Summer House (see Thiepval). The Ancre operations had been postponed several times but this had not especially affected the 39th

Div. as they had only recently come into the sector. On the 3rd September they were expected to capture three lines of hostile trenches on the spur south of Beaumont Hamel and, by an advance up the river valley, cover the flank of the 49th Div. to the right. In their positions to the north-west of the river the 116th and 117th Bdes. of 39th Div. began their advance at 5.10 a.m. The 14th Hampshires and the 11th R. Sussex made progress but the advance failed for a number of reasons, not least being the failure of the 49th Div. to their right, which allowed the enemy to enfilade his former trenches from the area of St. Pierre Divion. The 49th Div. had begun it's attack at 5.13 a.m. and had been withdrawn by 10 a.m. and was in no state to make a second attempt. The idea of a frontal attack against the Schwaben, however efficient the role of the artillery was, did not seem to have much chance of success.

Some parties of the Sussex Battalion were not back in their lines until nightfall and Blunden mentions that his battalion was relieved by the Cheshires, who were probably the 1/6 Cheshires of the 118th Bde. The Sussex battalion assembled in a trench along Hamel village street and in the setting sun arrived at Engelbelmer, 300 fewer in number than when it had passed through that village previously. Blunden described the battalion as being 'much impaired'. By the 6th they has received 400 reinforcements and on the 14th they took over the extensive trenches before Beaumont Hamel.

In early October the battalion HQ of the 1/1 Cambs. of the 118th Bde. was in dugouts burrowed out of the hillside. Below them they could see Hamel Mill which was 300 yards away with the German strong point in front of it called the Summer House. Further to the south was the Schwaben Redoubt. They could observe the German lines and especially the German Dressing Station at Miraumont. One of the Cambridge companies had sheltered in early October in Kentish Caves alternating in and out of the line for three weeks. Mill Road, along which ammunition and stores had to travel each day was always risky. The line was taken over in October by the 63rd Naval Div. It was just in front of the village on the reverse slope, the crest and forward slope of a ridge which faced up the Ancre Valley. The Ancre itself was the Divisional Boundary, and the valley defences were part of the left Division's sector. This was the section taken over by the 189th Bde. of the Naval Div. and on 19th October by the Hawke Batt. of this Bde.

From now on the sector was to be the territory of the 63rd Naval Div. and the battle for Beaumont Hamel and Beaucourt was postponed several times before finally beginning on 13th November just before the Somme fighting for 1916 stopped altogether.

The possible lines of communication on the lower slopes headed down into the Ancre Valley and had never been exploited because of the lack of adequate drainage.

Within the Naval Division at this time rumours were circulating that a scheme was afoot to replace the Naval Battalion Officers with Army ones. The Division Battalions took turn to go in and out of the line and in preparation for the battle the Hood Battalion went from Mesnil to Hamel in full battle order and on 6th November were in the firing line in the Hamel sector.

On the 10th November they were relieved by the Hawke Battalion, and returned to Mesnil.

On the 13th November the front of the Royal Naval Div. stretched for 1,200 yards north of the river. On the right of the 63rd Div. was the 189th Bde. next to the river. The Hood and Hawke Battalions were in front with the Drake and Nelson in the rear. Behind were the 1/HAC and the 7/R. Fus. of the 190th Bde. To the left was the 188th Bde. of the Naval Div. with the Howe and 1/Royal Marines in the van. The Anson and 2/Royal Marines were in the second line. In the rear were the 4/Beds. and the 10/R. Dub. Fus. of the 190th Bde. The commander of the Anson Batt. Lt. Col. F. J. Saunders was killed whilst waiting for the battle to begin. The left flank of the Bdes. was in touch with the 153rd Batt. of the 51st Highland Div. At 5.45 a.m. the Hood Battalion went forward and the Hawke Batt. on the left was held up by heavy machine gun fire from a redoubt which was midway between the German first and second lines. This redoubt had been missed by the British Artillery. Two Battalions of the Naval Div. were virtually destroyed in thirty minutes. Lt. Col. Freyberg led the remnants of the Hood Batt. to the next objective which was the trench in front of the sunken Station Road. There were many dugout entrances in Station road and plenty of prisoners were taken.

The 13th KRRC on 11th November had marched to Puchevillers from Gezaincourt and on the 13th had arrived at Engelbelmer, the advanced HQ of the Naval Div. to which they were attached as part of the 13th Rif. Brig. At about 2.30 p.m. they marched off to Mesnil and went up the Yellow Line. Their duties were to prolong the line which at that time was held by the remains of the Hood and Drake Battalions south of Beaucourt. The roads were congested by the number of motorised ambulances. From Hamel the 13th KRRC moved off in file along Railway Road in the Ancre Valley, and at 9.30 p.m. they halted at the junction of Beaucourt Trench and Railway Road. Freyberg and his troops were 150 yards in front and 150 yards from the edge of Beaucourt. The KRRC went in on the left of Freyberg's men, and cleared part of the line. The next day they advanced through the village and flushed out the enemy from its many dugouts. On the 15th they went to the shelter of Station Road Valley.

Hamel Military Cemetery which was designed by Edwin Lutyens, is on the south side of the village, 20 yards west of the road to Albert, and a mile south-west of Beaucourt–Hamel Station. It was begun by fighting units and Field Ambulances in August 1915 and carried on until June 1917. It was known at times by the names of Brook Street Trench and White City. It contains the graves of 487 soldiers and sailors of the Royal Naval Div. It is sheltered by rising ground on the south and west, but it looks to the east across the valley of the Ancre to the Ulster Tower and Thiepval Wood.

In *The Mind's Eye* Edmund Blunden wrote 'I find myself frequently living over again moments of experience on the Western Front – The mind suddenly yields to simple versions. Pale light striking through clouds in shafts like the sunrays of Rembrandt. Perhaps these moments occur according to the seasons, for it is now Autumn, and our share in the Somme fighting began towards the end of a splendid August'.

Blunden in one of his visits to the Ancre sector after the war wrote 'may as well take another view of Hamel from above, and of the Schwaben from somewhere by Hamel Church, a touch of John Crome'.

Hangest

The village of Hangest is to the west of Amiens on the D 218 road to Abbeville. In Gilbert Frankau's novel *Peter Jackson Cigar Merchant* the main character who was a member of the Artillery and also a liaison officer is with his battery when they march from Amiens to Hangest. It took three days to concentrate the four Bdes. of the 'Southdown' Artillery there and later they left the village one late summer morning and went up past 'the round fortress of the Citadel and on to the Bois des Tailles'.

Hannescamps

Hannescamps is a village in the Department of the Pas-de-Calais on the D 3 road north-east of Foncquevillers and between that village and Monchy-au-Bois. It is also south-east of Bienvillers and north of Gommecourt. The village though always behind the lines was often heavily bombarded. It was a 'behind the lines' village for the 46th Div. in their attempts to capture Gommecourt on the 1st July and battalion HQs were in dugouts near the crossroads in front of the village. On the 1st the village was one kilometre inside the British lines.

Aubrey Smith wrote that in the period around the first week of July the village was more famous for bullets than for 'whizz bangs' as the enemy directed overhead machine gun fire on to the road every minute or so. Other battalions were here in the line including the 2nd R. Welch Fus. who were here on 18th September. At the end of September the Battalion HQ of the 1/4 DWR was in shelters along the road just south of the village. The Churchyard is on the west side of the village, and the New Military Cemetery is in fact an extension of the Churchyard to the south-west. It was begun in March 1916 and used until February 1917 and again in March 1918. The village was not even reached by the German March breakthrough of 1918. The village chateau was also used as a Battalion HQ.

Happy Valley

There are several Happy Valleys which were far from being actually 'Happy'. The main one is close to Bray, but there is also one that ran close to Mametz Wood and was also known as Death Valley which was a more accurate title for it. However there were also many Death Valleys!

In mid July after the Bazentin and Mametz Wood fighting there was a serious attempt to take High Wood and the ridge on which it stood. At the same time there were many batteries in Happy Valley and they were aligned one behind another in the rear of the Bazentins. On 22nd July in addition to the many batteries there were several Bde. HQs here as well. The valley was often under fire from the direction of Leuze Wood, Guedecourt, Courcelette and also from behind Pozieres. The valley was the only line of communication through which every relief party, every round of ammunition and every ration had to pass on their way, not only for the Highland Div. but for several neighbouring Divs. Part of the valley was under observation from German balloons and the dust from the continuous wheeled traffic caused the enemy to concentrate their firing on the area day and night. The only protection were slits in the ground that were covered with waterproof sheets or corrugated iron. The dust and flies from half buried animals was also a constant factor which remained in the memories of men who had to be in the valley at that time.

At roughly the same time David Rorie who was with the RAMC attached to the 51st Highland Div. was in the area of Happy Valley according to his memoirs which he called *A Medico's Luck in the War*. His Div. was here having relieved the 33rd Div. after their attack on High Wood. There was an ADS in the valley and the MDS being in a large barn in Mericourt.

There was later a CP in Happy Valley and at Quarry Post which was further along the valley to the north of Montauban. Rorie describes Quarry Post as being on the route to High Wood and a most dangerous spot, enfiladed as it was by enemy fire and without proper dugouts. The only shelter in the quarry was the roof that was sandbagged and roofed with corrugated iron. The road was so cut up at the end of July by enemy shelling that it became impossible for the Ambulance motor cars to use it, and so horse Ambulance wagons worked past it and for three days and nights took casualties from the Quarry all the way to the top of the hill at Mametz where they were reloaded into motor ambulances to go back to the ADS at the File Factory at Bécordel. Rorie described Happy Valley as always an extraordinary scene of destruction and desolation. Going downwards the road hugged the sharp rise of the hill on the right, into which ran numerous small dugouts and shelters, while on the left of the road the flat ground ran for a hundred yards or so gradually sloping uphill again. On this ground guns were going up with their teams at a mad gallop. Dead men and dead horses and smashed timbers lay about in every direction, and a torn and twisted railway showed protruding strands. By 2nd August conditions at Quarry Post had improved and four dugouts had been made on the roadside beyond it. The cooks were in another dugout some 100 yards away. A South African Battery which was close by prevented sleep and the clouds of chalk dust pervaded everything. They were relieved a few days later and moved back to Dernancourt.

As we have seen Happy Valley was the name given to several valleys, but the one that is described next is the main one and is just north-west of Bray towards Méaulte. Today it is close to the old road which has provided a sort of layby. The Bois de Ricourt is on the site of Gibraltar, which was also the site of a military camp, and is adjacent to Happy Valley. Across the hill to the north-east in the direction of Fricourt is the Citadel and Point 71 South and North. Formerly the Plateau Railway Line ran in a loop around this valley towards Trônes Wood and Ginchy having come from the direction of Pilla Junction and Grove Town.

This Happy Valley was the reserve area for battalions of the reserve of the Fourth Army as was Sandpit Valley and the Bois des Tailles which were close by.

Liddell Hart who was with the 9th KOYLIs wrote that his Bde. which was the 64th of the 21st Div. and who had been in action at Fricourt had been part of the Divisional withdrawal at night on 3rd July. They reached Happy Valley which he described as being a sheltered hollow behind the original British front line. Hart who had been in reserve at the beginning of the battle says that the men of his Bde. were revived with panniers of tea which was laced with rum. Of his battalion there were fewer than 70 men left from a previous 800.

In mid July there were serried ranks of artillery guns in the valley and the writer H. M. Tomlinson describes the valley at the time as being a monstrous fairground with everybody going to the fair. The guns caused a continuous eruption blasting down the exit from the valley towards the north-east; Montauban, Longueval etc. The valley had become a desert, its surface had been pulverised by myriads of feet, hooves and wheels. Restless brown lakes could be seen in it, they were congestions of horses. All the trees of the valley were dead or dying because the horses had gnawed off their bark. The slopes of the valley were covered with canvas dwellings, surgeons, craftsmen etc. The broad valley crawled with human beings, cattle and machinery. The land around was terraced with massed batteries and howitzers.

A few days later amidst the Infantry, Cavalry and Artillery the Dominions were represented as well in that the South Africans after their mauling at Delville Wood occupied a sadly small area near that of the 2nd HLI (5th Bde. 21st Div.) Although the valley was out of the battle area the roar of the 13 inch guns which came up each night and were within a few hundred yards of the bivouacs made sleep impossible. These guns were mounted on railway platforms. In addition there were no wells in the valley or a water supply. The water had to be brought up from Bray by cart.

At the end of July Guy Chapman 13th R. Fus. (111th Bde. 37th Div.) in his book *A Passionate Prodigality* wrote that the brown banks of the valley seemed to hold a million men and animals. All day long the dust, brown and golden in the sunlight, rose and choked the blackening trees. All day long carts, wagons, men and horses, went by. All day long too a band of the Royal Scots practised the 'Broken Doll'. The valley was a meeting place, the market square of the Army. Broken Divisions coming back, paused here one night before release to quiet sectors. Fresh Divisions bivouacked on its stale earth before being sent up to their ordeal. Friends from other days strolled over as they waited, to ask the news, have a drink, and pass out into the 'rosy twilight dusk'.

In the beginning of August German prisoners were being kept at Gibraltar Camp, and at the time the weather was very hot and the camp plagued by flies. Troops used to bathe in the River Somme north of Bray in order to cool off!

On Minden Day, 1st August, the Lancashire Fusiliers had a parade in Happy Valley when the battalions wore red and white roses in their steel helmets. They paraded under their commander and were reviewed by their Brigadier.

In mid August the 35th Div. (Bantam) was in the area and left for Talus Boise on 18th August.

Lord Moran of the 1st R. Fus. who was later to become physician to Winston Churchill wrote in his book *The Anatomy of Courage* that one day two officers of the 20th Light Div. came into the dugout in August to take over. They looked so fresh and sleek and young that they might have stepped out of a hot bath after hunting. They seemed to listen for shells, though it was peaceful enough at the time. The relief took place that afternoon when Moran and his colleagues left for a camp at Happy Valley. They assembled at Carnoy where they met the cooks who provided them with tea. The horses were also there, for the use of the officers and some buses for the use of the men. On the road they passed a Kitchener Battalion going up. After tea the men clambered into the old buses with the novelty of being 'carriage folk', and the officers slowly mounted their chargers. On 23rd August there was a blue sky and peace, but all day the camp in Happy Valley appeared to be deserted and when you looked into tents you found that everybody in them was asleep. On the next day the men just sat about and enjoyed the sun. No-one did anything.

In early September the whole area was still stacked with troops on every side in addition to the camps there were also dumps here. Every road was congested with guns and vehicles of all kinds.

The Queen's Westminsters of the 56th Div. moved by rail on 3rd September to Corbie, and on the 4th marched to Happy Valley. The battalion reached it after dark on a cold and miserable night and the only shelter available consisted of a number of tents. Half of the Battalion managed to pack into them and the remainder had to lie out in the open. Also on 4th September the 1st Scots Gds. of the 2nd Gds. Bde. were here before moving to Carnoy. The 1st Coldst. Gds. and 2nd Irish Gds. of the same Bde. were here before going up the line.

In the period 4th to 9th September Aubrey Smith reported on the experience of being with the transport of the London Rifle Bde. of the 56th Div. At the time the eastern slopes of the valley were dotted with hundreds of tents, into which the LRB were ushered. The first night that they spent there was stormy and tempestuous and the rain came down in torrents. The wind came up the valley with a roar and the guns were going incessantly like a continuous thunderclap. After six o'clock they set off for the water troughs and they could see more than on the night before. The valley was as populated as before and half of the horses there, belonged to French units. Over one hill came a long stream of cavalry, over another an endless queue of artillery mules in addition to a procession of animals to the water troughs. It seemed to Smith that the whole of the transports of the British and French armies were congregated here on the ridges above Bray. Soon Smith was to go up to Carnoy and Death Valley with the transport and then return to Happy Valley briefly on 8th/9th September. He wrote that there was a disadvantage in that the Valley was some distance from the line, over three miles from Carnoy and five miles from Death Valley, as the crow flies.

The water problem was always difficult on the Somme for hundreds of thousands of men and animals had to be supplied in the devastated wastes, and there was a limited number of sources which had been opened up by the REs.

It seems that September was the 'high point' for Happy Valley, as once High Wood and Flers were taken in mid September, the battle zone moved away, however No. 4 CCS was brought here from Beauval in early October and the 3rd Australian CCS replaced the 11th CCS.

Hardecourt

The village of Hardecourt is north-east of Maricourt and south of Guillemont. In mid August the Allied objective was the road between the two villages. The French were to take the northern edge of Angle Wood. The 1st Cheshires (15th Bde. 5th Div.) were detailed to cross the forward slopes of the hill north-west of Hardecourt and on the 4th September they were in full view of the enemy and came under heavy shell fire. A barrage of 5.9s was 'playing' on the valley to the south of Angle Wood. On the 13th the Westminsters (56th Div.) moved up from the Citadel Camp to the former German trench system near to the Crucifix to the north of Hardecourt. During the morning the battalion who were in Divisional reserve, were moved up from Falfemont Farm to Angle Wood Valley to the north of the farm. They were not yet employed but it was the prelude to the fighting at Leuze Wood.

Harponville

The village is due east of Toutencourt and south-west of Acheux. Battalions billeted there including the 19th North'd Fus. who were Pioneers to the 35th Div. (Bantam). They were in the village during the night of 9th July and camped in an orchard.

Hébuterne

Hébuterne is a village in the southern part of the Pas de Calais, nine miles north of Albert, and immediately to the south of Gommecourt, behind the Allied lines but subject to enemy shellfire during the whole period of the battle. The village was the boundary between the Third Army and the Fourth Army. The British were to turn it into a fortress village and it is particularly associated at this time with the 56th London Div. who were to launch themselves from here against the Gommecourt position on 1st July.

The 56th Div. came to the area in May 1916 and the Hébuterne Plain became full of gun positions. The Germans however had artillery at Quesnoy Farm, the Bois de Biez which was beyond Rossignol Wood, and at Puisieux.

In addition they had more guns to the north in the area of Adinfer Wood. Gerald Brenan describes his experiences in the Spring of 1916 when they returned to Hébuterne, and he was put in charge of an OP just outside it. Every day new batteries would arrive and then begin registering, new light railways sprang up, new shell dumps and notice boards would appear. Through his telescope he could see mounds of white chalk appearing in the German support trenches; evidently they were building deep shell proof dugouts in preparation for the expected Allied attack. Brenan's OP was immediately opposite the hamlet of Serre which was a mile away.

On 5th June at night the Queen's supplied working parties to work on the new front line which was to be 300 yards in front of the previous line, to the east of the village. They were also to clear sapheads in preparation for the digging of the new line further forward. On 9th June the battalion moved to Hébuterne, relieving the 2nd London (R. Fus.) in Y Sector between Hébuterne and Gommecourt.

On 2nd June Dolden who was with the cooks of the London Scottish of the 56th Div. left Souastre for Hébuterne. The cooks followed separately and stopped at Bayencourt to pick up company rations. There was a very deep well in the village which supplied a plentiful water supply to the troops who were in occupation. They arrived at Hébuterne after dark. Part of the battalion was in the line; in front of the village and the rest was in Hébuterne itself. On the 8th June the Battalion was relieved by the 1/12th Rangers of the 56th Div. and moved up to the Keep which was in the north-west part of the village.

The roads and byways had been barricaded and defended by machine guns. On 13th June they went back to the position. They were later relieved by the Royal Fusiliers and marched to St. Amand. On the 16th the Queen's Westminsters were relieved by the LRB and they then moved back to Bayencourt. Aubrey Smith with the transport of the LRB as always is a good source for detail and he says that they had collected pit props from a dump at Bayencourt and taken them to Hébuterne with other vehicles from the Bde. having previously come from St. Amand. On 29th and 30th June they had to cross the plain from Sailly au Bois to Hébuterne, where they were supposed to be under observation from the right. Smith describes the topography of the front in the following way. The ground fell away gently for a few hundred yards and then rose again in a long slope towards the German position. To the right the white tower of the Church at Achiet le Petit was visible half hidden among the trees, while in the foreground the ruins of Nameless Farm stood up amongst the labyrinth of the enemy trenches. Further to the right the ground dipped sharply to the valley overlooking Serre, to the left on slightly higher ground stood Gommecourt. The Keep at the rear of Hébuterne was a system of trenches which were protected by barbed wire and commanded the flanks, front and rear. It was a tactical reserve place. Along the main street at intervals of about 100 yards were the entrances to communication trenches bearing such names as Yankee Street, Yellow Street, York Street and Yule Street. On the 30th the Rangers went from Bayencourt along the blue track leaving Bayencourt and kept to the right of the Bayencourt–Sailly road, which dipped into the valley behind Sailly au Bois and on to the plain between Sailly and Hébuterne.

There is a typescript at the Imperial War Museum which is by Gunner W. R. Price of the C/240 battery of the 48th Div. who were in the Second Army before they became part of the Third Army on 26th June. His battery used Boer War 15 pounders which were inefficient and they looked forward to replacing them with 18 pounders. The latter were light and easy to run forward and switch around. They had four positions at Hébuterne, one south-west of Foncquevillers, two on the Hébuterne–Auchonvillers Road and the fourth on the Colincamps road. The first Hébuterne position was on the Plain close behind an escarpment. Between Hébuterne and Colincamps was an old French position. Price became a layer for 'A' Gun. On the 20th July they were replaced by a Welsh Battery. On a lighter note Price mentions three songs that were especially popular at the time and that they were always singing; 'Again, Again and Again', 'Fred Karno's Army' and 'Grooming'. Jack Tucker of the 1/13th London Kensingtons describes in *Johnny Get Your Gun* at the end of June great activity in the fields behind Hébuterne, great gun pits were being dug and the number of artillery guns increased. Tucker described the transport who at this time were living in the open, the horses were tethered to a long rope line or lines in a large green field. They were ensconced in shacks made from oddments of timber and corrugated iron to pieces of tarpaulin. On 30th June they took most of the limbers, GS Wagons and pack ponies to Hébuterne, loaded with supplies of hand grenades, picks, spades, axes etc., and food and water. These supplies were unloaded in the main road leading to the front line and dumped them in a ruined brick shed.

On the first day of the battle, 1st July, the 5th R. Warwicks. who were holding the line in front of Hébuterne discharged a cloud of smoke and poison gas, so as to mask the fire of the concentrated artillery behind Gommecourt Wood, on the right the main attack was to be delivered on the 1st by the Fourth Army, while on the left a subsidiary attack was to be made by the Third Army. The remainder was held in reserve to exploit the gains of the attacking troops. This was the left hand battalion of VIII Corps and Rawlinson's Fourth Army. The 5th R. Warwicks. were to rejoin them when their special task was done.

(For a description as to what happened at Gommecourt on 1st July, I refer readers to that section.)

On 5th July Graham Greenwell who was with the 4th O & BLI (145th Bde. 48th Div.) wrote home from 'G' Sector at Hébuterne: 'Here we are again, back in the trenches, or rather canals, as the water is over our knees'. He was to be there until 8th July. 'Yesterday afternoon I had a good look at the battle-field of 1st July through the telescope at a splendid observation post. It was a very interesting sight; it lay just to the right of us; the whole plain sloping up to the village called Serre held by the Germans was visible. Our troops attacked it after six days bombardment, and after getting into the village were driven back to their original trenches. Heaps of bodies are still lying out there unburied, but the Germans and ourselves have been sending out stretcher parties each night. The three lines of German trenches in front of the village are absolutely shattered and are almost levelled; their thick wire is absolutely wrecked, but their machine guns did appalling damage in spite of everything. The village is one mass of ruins with a few gaunt trees standing up; before the battle it was thickly wooded and almost invisible. Far to the right I could see our guns shelling a large German railway centre behind the line – good sight.' On the 16th Greenwell wrote home and said 'This is tremendous news about Bazentin le Petit. If only we can hold these places against counter-attacks'.

The 5th Glosters were in the same Bde. as the 4th O & BLI and from the 4th to 18th July were in the Hébuterne sector. They found plenty of stores at Hébuterne when they arrived; biscuits, bully beef and pork and beans. The Scots had left them.

I expect that these two battalions took turns in and out of the line at this time. The 11th KRRC of the 59th Bde. 20th Div. were in the area about 24th July for three weeks, and the 10th, 11th and 12th KRRC also of the 20th Div. were in trenches south-east of Hébuterne in the period end of July until 16th August.

The 1st Scots Guards of the 2nd Guards Bde. left Bertrancourt and went into the line at Hébuterne on 16th August. The London Scottish of the 56th Div. were on their left. Hugh Wansey Bayley who was a Scots Gds. MO established a new aid post on the side of a communication trench. They sapped as far as Sixteen Poplars and they were in the line here until 21st August when they went into rest at Bus-les-Artois.

Max Plowman who was with the 11th West Yorks. of the 69th Bde. 23rd Div. wrote in *Subaltern on the Somme* that in August their Company HQ was in an imposing farmhouse and that on the previous day when on the march they had halted at Souastre, close to Hébuterne. The quickest way to the front line was under enemy observation from the rising ground at Gommecourt. They entered the village and came across the ruined church. The troops that they were relieving were the London Scots who told them that this had been a quiet sector since 1st July, when they buried half a battalion of men in a front line trench which had been abandoned. Plowman's line was the second line. There were no bays and so they posted men at various firing points at fairly wide intervals and put Lewis gunners out on both flanks. His dugout was not very deep but he says that it was a 'wonderful place'. At the bottom of the steps on the left were two canvas bunks that were extremely comfortable. Their trenches were just a little to the right of the trenches that the battalion had held previously, with the Royal Fusiliers on their right flank. The ground to the front sloped gently away for a few hundred yards, then rose again in a long sweep. To the left was Gommecourt, a sinister spot which was now a heap of ruins and contained the remains of a wood. The whole area suggested to him the sharpest contrast to the rough bayless chasm of St. Georges Hill that they had occupied the previous week. Plowman was probably in a dugout in Welcome Street which was a chalk dugout about thirty feet deep.

The 1st KRRC (99th Bde. 2nd Div.) relieved the 23rd R. Fus. on 25th August. The 16th KRRC of the 100th Bde. 33rd Div. were in reserve billets in mid September for the line to the north of Gommecourt. Jack Tucker of the 1/13th London (Kensingtons) 56th Div. wrote in his book that 'at the end of August they were relieved by a Yorkshire Bde. who were fresh from the Somme battlefield further south, where they were now to go. They marched via Corbie and Sailly le Sec to Bray where they spent the night before proceeding to Citadel Camp. The ground to the north of Hébuterne was in a dreadful state having been shelled since the end of June. The 56th Div. with the help of the Guards Bde. helped to clear up the battlefield. It was altogether a dreary village and the trenches were in a poor state. It was also a daily target for the German artillery'.

H. E. Harvey of the 22nd London (The Queen's) of the 47th Div. mentions at the end of September/beginning of October that the 'Gas Experts' were in the area. He describes them as affixing taps and gas piping along the parapet with rows of gas-jets, which were called 'pot hooks and hangers'. They had to wait for a favourable moment in the weather. With the appointed signal, a single white British rocket, the masked men standing by, turned the small circular cylinder ends, and with a frightful hiss like compressed steam from a 100 ton locomotive, the deadly green-yellow cloud spouted outwards from the line of jets. The long drifting cloud of gas, withering white the first few yards of green grass before it, carried slowly menacingly towards the post fifty yards away. Inevitably some of the gas blew back over the British lines.

In mid September the 17th Div. artillery was reinforced by bringing up several batteries of the Corps Heavy Artillery, which were concentrated on the high ground behind Hébuterne, and wire cutting by gun fire began. On the 20th September the 17th KRRC (117th Bde. 39th Div.) moved into the line at Hébuterne from Y Camp at Betrancourt where they returned on the 30th.

The Hébuterne–Sailly road (D 27) was subjected to a great deal of hostile fire. It was exposed to the enemy position at Gommecourt Park for about 600 yards halfway between the two villages, and was accurately ranged by the Germans.

The 18th W. Yorks. (93rd Bde. 31st Div.) had in their sector what was known at the time as Suicide Corner. It was a corner that was always busy and the code word 'Gasper' meant that there was a wind that was favourable to a gas discharge. This caused extra hardship i.e. turning around in the village and retreating, another reason why the village had a sinister reputation.

Private J. Cunningham of the 12th (Service) E. Yorks. Batt. was to receive the VC for his action on 13th November opposite Hébuterne. After the front line had been captured he proceeded with a bombing section up a communication trench, where there was much enemy opposition and the rest of his section became casualties. Collecting all the bombs from the casualties, Cunningham went on alone. Having expended all his bombs, he returned for a fresh supply, and again proceeded to the communication trench, where he met a party of ten Germans. These he killed, and chased up the trench to the enemy line. His conduct according to his citation 'was throughout the day magnificent'.

An ADS or CP was in the village during the battle.

Hébuterne Communal Cemetery contains graves mainly of men of the 20th (Light) Div. and of the 31st Div. The Military Cemetery is in a secluded position on the west side of the village. It was begun by the 48th South Midland Div. in August 1915, and used by fighting units and Field Ambulances particularly those of the 56th London Div. until the spring of 1917. Owl Trench Cemetery is one and a half miles east of the village, on the south side of the Gommecourt–Puisieux road. Owl Trench was a German cross trench before Rossignol Wood, raided by the 4th New Zealand Rifle Bde. on 15th July 1918. Hébuterne was in Allied hands from 1915 to March 1918, but the eastern part of the Commune was in German hands until February 1917.

Hedauville

The village is on the D 938 road south-east of Forceville and north-west of Senlis-le-Sec. The transport of the 1/4 DWR (147th Bde. 49th Div.) moved to the village on 3rd June. On 1st July the 1st E. Lancs. (11th Bde. 4th Div.) was here and a post constructed close to a burnt house named Lancashire Post. There were huts in the village that were used by the troops. There is a note that the Green Howards used the village for rest billets. At the end of October the Hood Battalion were billeted in barns in the village.

The Cemetery was used for burials only after 1918.

Heilly

Heilly is on the Ancre on the D 52 road to Albert south-west of Ribemont, north-west of Méricourt and south-east of Franvillers. Before 1st July the 102nd Bde. of the 34th Div. otherwise known as the Tyneside Scottish or Northumberland Fusiliers trained here and in the Franvillers area for their role in the Battle for la Boisselle. There was a camp here and the 9th North'd Fus. of the 17th Div. were camped on the banks of the Ancre. The village was one of the principal railheads used for supplies when the battle opened. There was also a Motor Ambulance Convoy established here. Later the 1st R. Welch Fus. (the battalion of Siegfried Sassoon) were camped in the village and left there at 4 p.m. on 10th July on their way to the Citadel which they reached by 9 p.m. During their march they had been passed by Haig between the villages of Maricourt and Treux. The Battalion had marched via Morlancourt.

Sassoon wrote in his diary they started back for Heilly which was about 12 miles away. When they came through Mametz they were heavily shelled. The total casualties of the 1st RWF for the previous 7 days had been 132 but only 14 dead. In mid July the 16th Cheshires of the 105th Bde. of the 35th Div.(Bantam) were camped in what was described as a 'wooden place in the marsh by the river'. In early August there was a large area around the cross roads to the north of the village which had close to it, ammunition dumps, refilling points, innumerable camps and also horse lines. The roads were full of vehicles, horses and men.

There were seven CCSs in the village at different times; No. 21 CCS of XV Corps. and the 27th CCS of the Fourth Army attached to the 1st Anzacs. The 36th there from 1st April 1916 to April 1917, was joined in May 1916 by the 38th CCS, and in July by the 2/2nd London. The last hospital left Heilly in June 1917, but the 20th CCS was still there in August and September 1918. A senior officer brought here wounded in the Flers attack in mid September was Colonel Walmisley-Dresser of the 12th E. Surreys. He died at the CCS and was buried in the cemetery which was begun in May 1916 and used by three medical units until April 1917. It was occasionally named from the Bois Hareng, which was behind it. Regimental badges numbering 117 are carved on the cloister wall on the north side. The cemetery stands on high ground that rises sharply to the south, commanding a wide view of the wooded valley of the Ancre.

It was designed by Edwin Lutyens and is a mile and a half south-west of the village of Méricourt, 100 yards south of the road to Corbie, and 500 yards south of Heilly Halt on the railway line. Hence it is known as Heilly Station Cemetery.

Hénencourt

Hénencourt is three and a half miles west of Albert on the D 91 Road. It is south-west of Senlis, west of Millencourt and north-east of Baizieux. There is a wood and a chateau in the village.

On the 27th June the 7th E. Lancs. (56th Bde. 19th Div.) were given permission to light fires in the wood which at the time was in full foliage and untouched by shell fire. In the heart of the wood as many as twenty great fires were lit, which almost reached the tops of the trees, and on the ground attempting to get dry from the heavy rain which fell before the battle began and which delayed the start by two days, were up to a thousand men. There were many groups of rival singers and wits and much yelling laughter and fooling. The Battalion marched off to the Intermediate Line south-west of Albert, and on 2nd July they were attached to the 34th Div. in the fight for la Boisselle, and on the 6th were involved in the fighting at Horseshoe Trench. At the end of the month during the bombardment the effect of the barrage was watched by crowds of troops on the high ground between Hénencourt, Bresle and Millencourt.

Infantry of the 12th Div. who had marched after dark reached Hénencourt and Millencourt by 10 a.m. on 1st July. On the same day the 7th Service Battalion of the Norfolk Regiment (35th Bde. 12th Div.) marched to the wood and at 6.50 p.m. they left to occupy the Intermediate Line south-west of Albert, for an attack planned for the 2nd which was later cancelled. They were then in reserve behind the embankments of the Albert–Arras Railway, and remained there until late at night on the 2nd when they moved up into trenches for the attack against Ovillers.

On 8th July the 25th Div. moved to the village and the 2nd KRRC bivouacked in Hénencourt Wood. It was described as a very pleasant camp surrounded by woods and a few hundred yards away was the HQ of the Third Corps under Gen. Sir W. B. Pulteney in the Louis XIV Chateau.

After their heavy involvement in the 15th September High Wood fighting the Civil Service Rifles (140th Bde. 47th Div.) arrived in Albert when they spent the night in billets. Next day the march continued to the tented camp in the wood just outside Hénencourt. Here the process of reorganising took place over the next two days. On the 30th September they were at the Quadrilateral close to Mametz Wood before going to Eaucourt. Other battalions used the village in the autumn and by coincidence they were often on their way to or from the fighting at Eaucourt l'Abbaye. Hénencourt was the site of a MDS. No. III Corps MDS was also here.

Hénu

The village is to the west of Souastre on the D 6 road. In May the HQ of the 56th Div. was in the village, in preparation for the assault against Gommecourt.

Hesdin

Hesdin is a village to the south of Doullens and No. 47 CCs was here at the end of June before being transferred to Beauval, No. 20 Field Ambulance was established in the local chateau and could accommodate up to 500 patients in tents.

High Wood

High Wood is on the D 107 Road between Martinpuich and Longueval. In July 1916 it was behind the German Second Line which ran in front of Bazentin le Grand and Bazentin le Petit. The defences ran through the Flers Ridge to Thiepval, and although the Ridge was scarcely more than a hundred feet in height, it nevertheless dominated the whole countryside for miles around. From the wood the Germans could observe any Allied attempt to take the wood and the summit ran from east to west through the northern part of the wood. At the time of the initial fighting the trees in the wood had not been damaged by shell fire and the country beyond it was not pockmarked by shell holes. From the high ground just west of the wood it would be able to enfilade any attacker.

The wood was known locally as the Bois des Fourcaux and had been turned into a German fortress. It had the usual grassy rides and a lot of young saplings which were to make progress difficult for any attacker. The 16th KRRC (100th Bde. 33rd Div.) were involved in an attempt on the wood and part of the Switch Line which ran through the northern part of the wood on the 6th July but it was unsuccessful, as was a similar attack on the 13th.

On the 14th July there was a chance for the 7th Div. to make an advance on the wood but they were held back by the Corps Commander General Horne who wanted to give the chance of taking the wood to the Cavalry. This seems with hindsight, to have been a fatal mistake as at the time patrols reported the wood as not being occupied. This delay allowed time for German reserves to be brought up, and not for two months was the German hold on the wood to be released.

The instructions to the Indian Cavalry in mid July were to seize the wood and the enemy's new line to the east and west of it, as a stepping stone to a further advance. The rest of the plan was for the 7th Div. to relieve the 2nd Indian Cavalry and the 21st Div. was to move northwards and clear the communication trenches between Bazentin le Petit and the light railway at Martinpuich. The 21st and the 1st Divs. were to provide a combined operation at 2.30 p.m. and at the same time the 34th Div. was to push forward strong patrols towards Pozieres to the west. At 7.40 a.m. the Cavalry went forward from its assembly place around Morlancourt but because of the slippery nature of the ground they did not arrive in the valley to the south of Montauban until early in the afternoon. Their advance was held back as Longueval had not been taken which was one of the conditions of the advance.

Meanwhile the 21st and the 1st Divs. didn't make progress either and the attack was postponed. The 62nd Bde. of the 21st Div. became severely depleted. They had been fighting in the afternoon for the north-west corner of Bazentin le Petit Wood which was not actually cleared until 7 p.m. False news of the fall of Longueval reached Corps HQ and the plan was for the 7th Div. to advance at 5.15 p.m. but these instructions never reached the Division until later on. The 91st Bde. which was the reserve Bde. of the 7th Div. lay to the east of Mametz Wood and was to be supported on the left by the leading Bde. of the 33rd Div. who would pass through the 21st. Finally the advance began at about 7 p.m. with the Cavalry and the 1st S. Staffs. and the 2nd Queen's (91st Bde. 7th Div.) who went into the wood but were unable to clear it because of being held up by the Switch Line but also by defences on the western side of the wood. The 33rd Div. according to the *Official History* does not ever seem to have received the order to support the 7th Div. I cannot let the role of the Cavalry be too brief because there is something both appalling and fascinating in the mere fact of using them in this situation and in conditions of modern warfare which clearly made them redundant. This is not to underestimate their pride and undoubted bravery. In the late afternoon a Squadron of the 7th Dragoon Guards, Secunderabad Bde. moved forward on the flanks of the 7th Div. and entered the wood at about 8 p.m. Other Squadrons patrolled the high ground between Delville Wood and High Wood, whilst the attempt to clear the wood was going on.

The Germans were waiting for the attack. The advance withered under machine guns and the two Cavalry Regiments had 102 men hit, some fatally.

130 horses became casualties, mostly killed. The Germans were well defended with the use of concrete positions which could be seen from the road in the trees.

British troops held on in the wood but next day were withdrawn to the general line of the Longueval–Bazentin Road.

Lt. Col. Graham Hutchison wrote two books in which he refers to the fighting at High Wood on 15th July and they are *Warrior* and *Pilgrimage*. In addition he wrote a *History of the 33rd Div. in France and Flanders 1915–1919*. Although he tends to repeat himself he does have a good story to tell in that he was there at the time. It is because of this I have depended on him quite a lot whereas the *Official History* is almost dismissive of the part played by the 33rd Div. on this day. On the evening of 14th July Hutchison wrote that patrols went out to make contact with the enemy and were fired upon from the edge of the wood and by the riflemen lying out in scrapes, and in narrow trenches south of the village. They discovered that the enemy had laid out several strands of wire which were uncut by the Artillery and hidden by the long grass. This formed a dangerous obstacle and requests for bombardment were not met.

At around the same time the 9th HLI (Glasgow Rangers) and the 1st Queen's took up positions between High Wood and Bazentin le Petit to the south-west. At dawn on 15th July a thick ground mist obscured completely both High Wood and the village of Martinpuich which was to the north of Bazentin and the north-west of High Wood itself. The 100th Bde. concentrated in the valley about 800 yards to the west of High Wood, and there was no cover to screen them across the area of no man's land. The 1st Queen's was ordered to attack on the left and the 9th HLI on the right. They were supported by the 16th KRRC, and the 2nd. Worcs. in reserve.

Each of the battalions in the forward wave was to be supported by one machine gun section which consisted of four guns. The MG Section with the Queen's was under Lt. Heseltine and that of the HLI under Lt. Huxley, according to the book *The Machine Gunner*. Under cover of the mist the transport was able to get forward to the area of concentration. At the same time the 98th Bde. of the 33rd Div. with its machine gun company was in position to the south-west on the outskirts of Bazentin le Petit. Hutchison's Bde. was deployed behind the 9th HLI and they lay down in the long grass awaiting the signal to assault. The mist was clearing and then rising rapidly. High Wood now seemed quite near and just up the hill. They could see the village of Martinpuich with its jagged ruins and rafters askew, broken walls and shattered fruit trees looking down on them. The men who crouched in the grass were probably visible to German observers in High Wood. Hutchison reported that he could see broad kilted buttocks and the bronzed thighs and knees of the Glasgow Rangers lining the slope in front of him. The attackers rose and swept forward under the cover of a weak bombardment. It was the first of several attempts that day to take the wood. There was an inferno of rifle and machine gun fire both from the edge of the wood and its trees all along the ridge to Martinpuich. To Hutchison's left he could see men of the Queen's passing up the slope towards Martinpuich and stumbling on a low wire entanglement. They were cut down and no one moved. The HLI too, were virtually annihilated. At the same time an enemy barrage of great intensity opened up. Hutchison's orders were to move forward in close support of the advancing waves and as his company rose, they too were cut down, by machine gun fire. Hutchison managed amidst the hottest fire to get two machine gun sections to within 150 yards of the wood, and engage the enemy who were posted in the trees. He could see them moving forward silhouetted against the skyline. The attack of the 16th KRRC and the 9th HLI failed. Hutchison meanwhile rushed forward two companies of the 16th KRRC as they had no officer left, in support of the guns. They were able to inflict damage on the enemy. Hutchison wrote a hurried note to Colonel Pardoe of the 2nd Worcs. who it will be remembered were in reserve. They were in a sunken road three hundred yards to the rear.

Meanwhile a field battery began to enfilade from the valley between Pozieres and Martinpuich and commenced shelling amongst the wounded. Hutchison turned his gun in the direction of the battery and claimed to have hit two of the gun loaders. By noon the Worcesters had obtained a footing in High Wood and the 98th Bde. began to come up on the left in order to fill the gap made by the 1st Queen's. The Bde. on the right was showing signs of weakness and began to dribble back. This exposed the right flank of the 100th Bde. on the south-east side of the wood. Hutchison said that he saw a Squadron of Indian cavalry with their dark faces under glistening helmets, galloping across the valley towards the slope. A few disappeared over the slope but never came back. During the advance he had noticed a small quarry which was screened by a small hedge and they dismantled their guns and began to retire to the safety of this quarry. He then found himself in charge of about 41 soldiers who were the remnants from three Battalions who had been involved in attacking the wood. They 'reversed' the former German trench and manned a German machine gun to ward off any counter-attacks. He could see men moving up to the wood.

Hutchison's party rushed over the lip of the quarry where they had retreated, towards the wood and took ammunition from the dead of earlier in the day. He then secured a position in High Wood and after dusk signalled for help and sent a runner back. After two hours he could see men moving up the valley towards the wood and was soon amongst men from the 2nd R. Welch Fus. (19th Bde. 33rd Div.) and on the left battalions of the 98th Bde. and other from Manchester, men fresh from Divisional reserve. Bde. by this time had sent orders to Hutchison to return with his men.

The complete teams of six guns of the 100th MGC had been casualties and Hutchison had gathered up the rest and got five into action as a battery that guarded the right of the Bde. whilst the remaining guns were disposed in groups covering the whole front. If Hutchison's company had not retired then the company to a man would have perished, according to *The Machine Gunner*.

Commenting on the day, the *Official History* says that there seemed to have been little co-operation between the 7th and 33rd Divs!

In *The War in the Air* it says that at 5 p.m. an aeroplane of No. 3 Squadron was sent out to find the exact situation and the Observer reported that the British were holding on to a trench to the west of the wood, and were also collecting south of Bazentin le Petit Road. From just inside the wood on the west side he could see flags being waved in reply to his signals, but on the east side the Germans were in strength and opened rapid fire on his aeroplane. The whole length of the troublesome Switch Line was seen to be full of German infantry. Until the Switch Line was taken the cost of hanging on to High Wood would be exceedingly heavy. The wood was wholly evacuated by 8 a.m. on the 16th July.

The above account is based mainly on the involvement of the 100th Bde. of the 33rd Div. but it would be churlish to forget that the 98th Bde. of the same Div. had been involved having come upon Bazentin le Petit in the early part of the morning of the 15th July. The 1st Middlesex led the way forming the left of the 33rd Div. attack on a frontage of 1,000 yards but on leaving Bazentin le Petit it too came under machine gun fire and shell fire. By mid-afternoon the attack had been abandoned. By 8 a.m. on the 16th July the 91st Bde. of the 7th Div. was concentrated behind Bazentin le Grand, having withdrawn from High Wood at 11.25 p.m. the night before. On succeeding days the preparations for a renewal of the attack was hampered by the bombardment of Caterpillar Valley with gas and lachrymatory shells.

In *The Machine Gunner* it says that the 19th Bde. relieved the 100th Bde. and what was left of them returned to defensive positions on the north side of Mametz Wood. Awards were given including an MC to Capt. Hutchison. Fighting of the bitterest nature followed, in which both the 19th and 98th Bdes. of the 33rd Div. were involved. The 1st Cameronians and the 5th Scots. Rif. of the 19th Bde. in particular suffered heavy losses. The attack was held up and holding on to the ground gained became ever more costly owing to the very heavy shellfire. Trenches were dug by the Pioneer Battalion the 18th Middlesex by night and were obliterated by day. It was possible to sit on the western edge of High Wood and actually see the shells in the air for about the last 40 feet of their descent. On the night of 17th/18th July the 21st Div. handed over its position in Bazentin le Petit to the 33rd Div. and withdrew to reserve. The 7th Div. relieved the 3rd Div. on 300 yards of front eastward from Bazentin le Grand Wood. High Wood was to be included in the objectives of the main operation now fixed for 18th July. It was to be a part of a main attack planned for the 19th and 20th with Anglo French co-operation in part.

On the 19th the eastern side of the wood was under machine gun fire apparently from Delville Wood. The 2nd KOSB of the 5th Div. marched up past Fricourt and Mametz and across country which was freely shelled, towards High Wood. After dark they were guided to the former German second line between Bazentin le Petit and Guillemont to take up positions there. Relief was completed by 2.30 a.m. The line extended from north of Bazentin le Petit to the south end of High Wood, whence it went in front of a

Q736   Lt.-Gen. Sir A. G. Hunter-Weston, GOC VIII Corps and Staff.
Marieux, 24th June, 1916

Q796   White City near Beaumont Hamel.

Q730   Warwickshires resting at Jacob's Ladder, Beaumont Hamel, July, 1916.

Q104   Eight inch Mark V Howitzer in a camouflaged emplacement, near Carnoy,
July 1916.

Q3998   Site of la Boisselle, July 1916. Small mine crater in foreground.

Q80572   Maj. S. W. Loudoun-Shand, VC.

Q79785   Pte. W. McFadzean, VC.

Q4087 Troops moving up through the ruins of Fricourt for the attack on Contalmaison, 10th July, 1916

Q882 RFA horses watering on the Fricourt–Mametz road, July 1916.

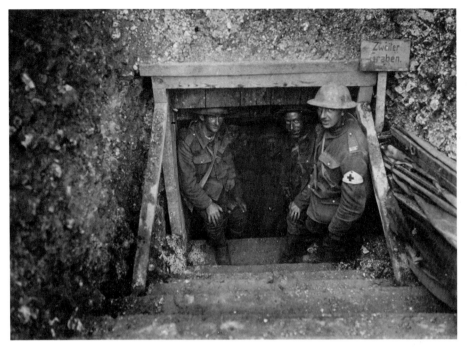

Q814 British troops at the entrance to a German dug-out in Danzig Alley, Fricourt, July 1916.

Q890 Captured German trenches, la Boisselle, July 1916.

Q164 Battle of Bazentin Ridge. Refreshment caravans for the use of walking wounded, 14th July, 1916. On left hand one is the sign of the 9th Scottish Division.

Q849 Convoy on a road near Albert, July 1916.

Q17490   Railway in Trônes Wood, 1916.

Q51814   Mametz Wood Howitzers.

Q3978   Southern road Mametz Wood.

Q3979   Troops digging in or resting at Mametz Wood, July 1916.

Q868 Brigadier General and Staff Officers studying a map in Mametz Wood, July, 1916.

Q1375 Men of the RAOC playing cards on a dump of trench mortar ammunition known to British troops as 'Toffee Apples'. Acheux, July 1916.

Q898 Australian transport passing through Bécourt Wood near Albert, August 1916.

Q4192 Mr. Asquith watching the return of a squadron of aeroplanes. General Trenchard is in the centre. Franvillers, RFC HQ, 7th August, 1916.

Q870   Captured German machine gun post near Mametz, August 1916.

Q913   British troops bathing near Aveluy Wood, August 1916.

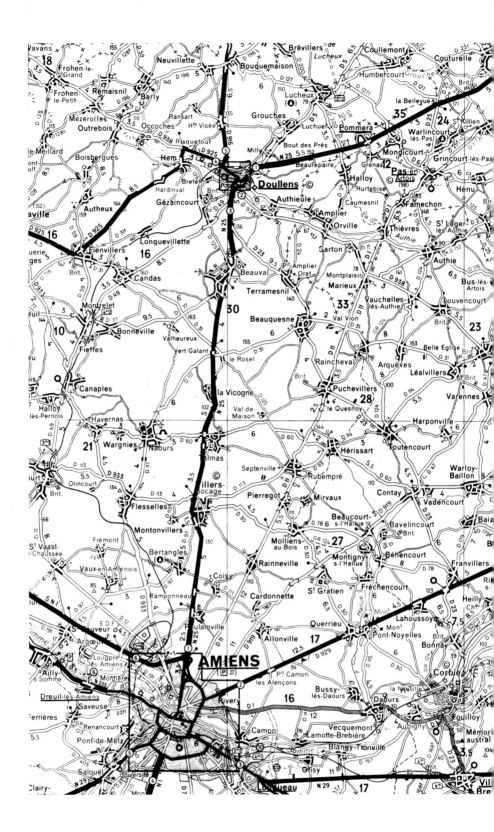

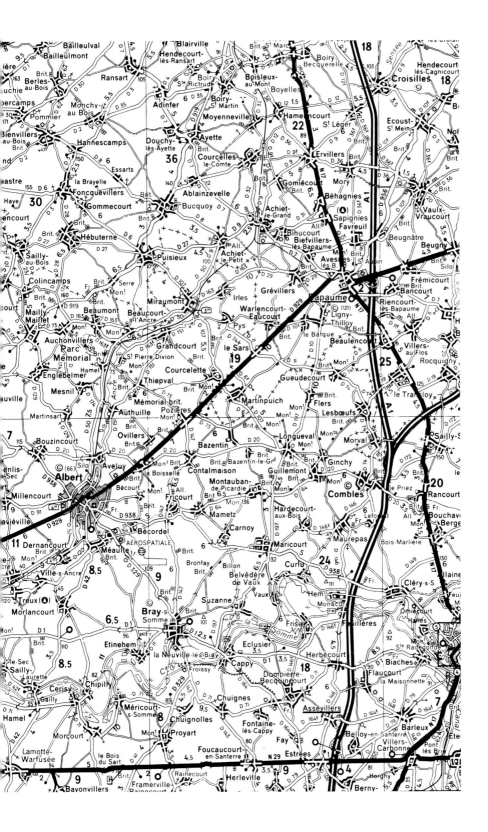

Q1163   The road leading to Guillemont, 11th September, 1916.

Q1196   Mr. Lloyd George with Lord Reading on King George's Hill, near Fricourt.
12th September, 1916.

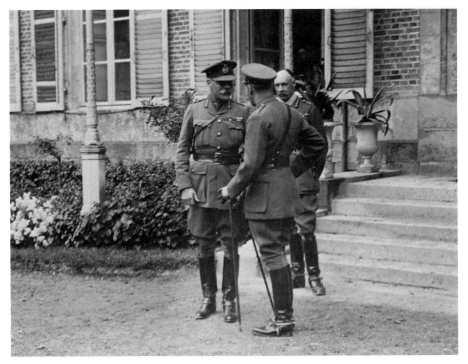

Q3922   HM King George Vth, Haig and Rawlinson, Querrieu Chateau.

Q4153   A BE2c Biplane flying over the mill Baizieux, 25th August 1916.

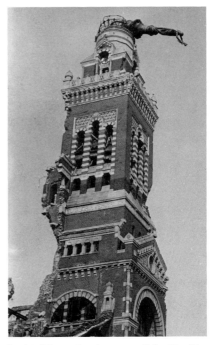

Q855   The ruined tower of the Basilica of Albert, September 1916.

Q5574   A 'C' Company Mark I Tank (C19 'Clan Leslie') Chimpanzee Valley,
15th September, 1916.

Q1209   Reserve troops waiting to move up to a forward area. Thiepval (early morning),
15th September, 1916.

Q1062 Mr. J. Irvine, 'Morning Post' and Mr. Philip Gibbs, 'Daily Chronicle' (right), watching an aerial combat from a trench, 20th September, 1916.

Q1089 Captured German pill-box, 'Gibraltar' Pozieres, 20th September, 1916.

Q1096   Dug-out in a trench being used as a canteen. Crucifix Corner, near Aveluy,
September, 1916.

Q1150   RAMC Officers of a special station received gassed cases near the Amiens
Road, five kilometres from Albert, September, 1916.

Q1259 Delville Wood, September 1916.

Q1456 Lt. E. Brooks, the official photographer with Mr. Malins, an official cinematographer at a coffee stall near the front, September, 1916.

Q4226 Battle of Ginchy, view of bombardment from Trônes Wood,
9th September, 1916.

Q4295 Ruins of Ginchy, September 1916.

Q1328   Remains of Thiepval Chateau (Battle of Thiepval Ridge),
26th-28th September, 1916.

E (Aus) 4043   Mouquet Farm.

Q1532   Officers of the Queen's Royal West Surrey Regiment in a captured German dug-out. Mr. Basil Clarke (War Correspondent) is seated on the right. Beaumont Hamel. November 1916.

Q4602   A working party about to start off in the rain, wearing waterproof sheets and trench waders, near St. Pierre Divion, November, 1916.

Q4600   Ration wagons on the muddy road, Montauban, November 1916.

Q49393   The Durham Light Infantry and the South African Memorials on the Butte de Warlencourt. 20th September, 1917.

Q51314 Gommecourt Park.

Q6202   Dugouts near Authuille on the Ancre, June 1917.

track leading south-west and then to Longueval. About 400 yards north-east of this latter position and roughly parallel to it, was a sunken road, lying invisible 50 yards down the reverse slope of the crest. The first task was the acquisition of the track as a jumping off place and this was given to the KOSB to accomplish. Divisional orders were for them to move immediately to reinforce the 7th Div. holding the line between High Wood and Longueval. The 13th Bde. was on the left of the 95th Bde. close to Longueval. From there the line was continued by XIII Corps past the cross-roads and church in the centre of the village, through the southern part of Delville Wood, and then due south past Waterlot Farm, to the west of Guillemont. The German Third Line or Switch Line was opposite them.

Robert Graves of the 2nd RWF (19th Bde. 33rd Div.) wrote that they were relieved at Bazentin le Petit and that they were to attack High Wood, which was a thousand yards away to the right at the top of the slope. The RWF at this time had been reduced by casualties to about 400 strong. They waited at Bazentin Cemetery on the reverse slope of a slight rise about half a mile from the wood. Their role in the attack was to be part of the Reserve. Graves reported that the 'Jocks' got into the wood and that the RWF were not called upon until 11 a.m. The Germans put down a heavy barrage on Bazentin Ridge and a third of the battalion was lost before the show had begun. Graves himself was wounded and was taken down to the old German Dressing Station at the north end of Mametz Wood.

According to Capt. C. H. Pigg of the 2nd Worcesters on the evening of 19th July orders had come through for them to move forward. They passed again through the front line to take up a covering position on the left flank of troops who were to make another attack on High Wood. Battalion HQ was at Bazentin Cemetery with their 'A' Company who were to be in reserve. 'C' Company was in support some 200 yards further forward whilst 'B' and 'D' Companies were in front and to the left of 'C' Company facing north-west-wards towards the Switch Line from which trouble might be expected. They dug in in pairs in slits, using shell holes and previously made excavations. Heavy firing went on through most of the night and especially around 3 a.m. when the 19th Bde. of the 33rd Div. attacked the wood. After the night had passed the hot sun rose in a cloudless sky and all that day they sat tight and casualties were few as the German artillery had not 'found' them. At around midday Pigg walked down the slope to report to HQ but there were no fresh orders of information. Having spent a day in this exposed position they finally received orders to withdraw which they did at dusk, to support trenches on Windmill Ridge. They returned in the darkness through German shelling which included gas shelling.

On 20th July on the right of the 5th and 7th Divs. the first objective was to be Black Road a track that ran NNW to the southern corner of High Wood. The 95th Bde. of the 5th Div. had already taken over Pont Street, whence the 3rd Div. attack began at 3.25 a.m. against Longueval and Delville Wood which was to coincide with this new attempt to take High Wood. The 13th Bde. 5th Div. was to advance in touch with the 7th Div. which then had to secure 800 yards of Black Road up to High Wood. Black Road and Wood Lane ran south-easterly towards Longueval and were parallel to the ridge that connected High Wood with Longueval and Delville Wood. Switch Trench was in turn behind them and was full of enemy machine gunners. The ground was also littered with the dead horses of the Secunderabad Cavalry Bde. The second objective 300 yards beyond Black Road was the track called Wood Lane which reached High Wood at its eastern corner. The task of capturing the wood itself was given to the 33rd Div. who were to advance from the south-west.

The planned advance was preceded by a bombardment at 3.25 a.m. and began with the 8th Devons and the 2nd Gordons (20th Bde. 7th Div.) They made progress and kept in touch with troops in the 5th Div. who were on their right. The Devons and the Gordons went on over the crest to Wood Lane and all the time they were under German shellfire. The British Artillery lifted at 3.25 a.m. However despite the hour the Germans were waiting for the attackers in full force concealed with their machine guns in the standing corn. Our men under heavy fire, the Gordons in particular from the rear. The two battalions dug in ground that was 25 yards short of Wood Lane but the position quickly became untenable and they had to crawl back to Black Wood and consolidate. As the Wood had not been taken the chance of a further attack was thought to be pointless, and after dark the 5th Div. relieved the troops of the 7th Div. on the Black Road. Lt. Col. B. G. R. Gordon of the Gordons was killed during this relief. Private T. W. H. Veale of the 8th Devons gained the award of the VC at the east end of High Wood on the 20th and in brief his citation says that – he was born in Devon in 1893. A wounded officer was lying out in front close to High Wood. Veale went out to look for him and found him amidst the growing corn some fifty yards from the enemy. He dragged the officer to a shell-hole and returned for water. Finding that he couldn't carry in the officer by himself he returned for assistance and took out two volunteers. One of the party was killed and shellfire drove them back. At dusk he went out again taking more volunteers and a Lewis gun to cover the carrying party. Thus the officer was carried to safety.

Meanwhile the 33rd Div. had been fighting hard in High Wood and indeed had made some progress at least in the southern part of the wood. On the 19th the 20th RF of the 19th Bde. had moved to battle positions in the valley about a mile from High Wood, and their company had dug in at the side of a small sunken road and they moved forward over open ground which was badly shelled. They went to a support position at the edge of the wood. At the same time on the previous evening the 2nd Worcesters of the 100th Bde. had pushed out a line of posts from Bazentin le Petit in the direction of the western corner of the wood to protect the flank of the assault of the 5th/6th Scots. Rif. who had been amalgamated the previous month and the 1st Cameron H. These battalions had been in reserve at Mametz on the 19th and after a march of three miles formed up near the windmill east of Bazentin le Petit facing the south-west side of the wood. The Scottish Batts. attacked with the help of the 11th Field Company of the REs and forced their way into the wood, and came under fire from the part of the Switch Line which was in the wood and also from a strong point on the western corner. The 20th R. Fus. in support followed close behind the attacking Scots and there was fierce and muddled fighting. At 9 a.m. the 2nd RWF were called up and on their way they were heavily shelled.

The very hard fighting in the wood necessitated the help of a relief Bde. and the 1st Queen's and the 16th KRRC of the 100th Bde. were then brought up. Before they arrived however after dusk, there was a gas and shell barrage, and this coupled with the British retreat to the southern half of the wood again brought the day's fighting to an end. The two sides consolidated. Frank Richards who wrote *Old Soldiers Never Die* and who was a member of the 2nd RWF says that his Bde. was hanging on to three parts of High Wood and was relieved at 10 p.m. Three quarters of them became casualties. Half of the Bde. according to Richards had been 'knocked over' before they even entered the wood.

In 1955 J. L. Hodson published a book called *Return to the Wood* and in it he described the experiences of a 'William Hargreaves'. In real life Hodson was with the 20th RF and was later commissioned with the Royal Naval Div. In this book their role in the attack on High Wood began at 12.40 p.m. two or three hours after the Cameronians. They advanced in open order and on their way up via Mametz Valley were exposed to a gas barrage. On the road side they saw dead soldiers with haversacks that were daubed with red paint to indicate their Bde. or Div. They could see the 'Scotties' streaming back from High Wood and they resembled a ragged football crowd. On 21st July Hodson said that they crossed the same 100 yards as the 'Scotties' had. When they reached the wood it was a mass of broken blazing trees and they were protected by a superb bombardment of French '75s'. They got into the wood without much loss although it was taped by either side's artillery to the yard. However in twenty four hours they lost two thirds of their battalion, mainly through being shelled.

Conditions in the wood were hellish and eventually they were relieved by the 16th KRRC. A. G. Skelton who left a Typescript of his experiences with the IWM and was with the 20th R. Fus. says that he escorted a Machine Gun party to the strong point at the north-west corner of the wood, which had been made by a Field Company.

On the night of the 21st the 33rd Div. in and about High Wood were finally relieved by the 51st Div.

The barrage lifted at 10 p.m., and the 1st Queen's RW Kents and the 14th R. Warwicks who were both in the 13th Bde. of the 5th Div. advanced and made some progress, until beyond the crest and in the lights of German flares they were enfiladed by enemy machine guns from the eastern corner of High Wood. The fire became very heavy and the attack turned into a disaster for the two battalions. The same strong point also defeated the 1/9 R. Scots and a platoon of the 1/4 Gordons who were both members of the 154th Bde. of the 51st Division. The 2nd KOSB and the 15th R. Warwicks (13th Bde. 5th Div.) were also ordered to advance towards the Switch Line but without any positive results.

In their time in the line the 33rd Div. had not adequately dealt with the strong machine gun positions in High Wood, and the 2nd KOSBs finished off their part in the attack by being called upon as a support, instead of being able to develop a success. The whole of the 5th Div. found themselves back where they has started and the 51st fared little better.

On 23rd July a trench was taped out in broad daylight from the windmill at Bazentin le Petit to High Wood and a communication trench known as High Alley which ran from Bazentin le Grand to High Wood was improved, and a new communication trench known as Thistle Alley was begun. A footing had been established in the wood which was sufficient to deprive the Germans of the wide observation that they had previously enjoyed. Nevertheless the position taken over by the 51st Div. was very dangerous to traverse. The route by which troops went up the line and by which all stores and rations were brought, was an indifferent path along the valley just south of Mametz Wood, and the Germans knew this. The road was never empty of men or vehicles, at any hour of the day or night and although the Germans didn't have direct observation they could see what was going on in Happy Valley by means of their observation balloons.

At 9 p.m. on the 23rd the 1st Norfolks of the 15th Bde. relieved the KOSBs who retired to Pommiers Redoubt.

On the night of the 28th July the HQ of the 5th Gordons (153rd Bde. 51st Div.) was in the south-east corner of High Wood. On 1st August a new device was used which was called a Bartlett Forcing Jack in order to help with trench digging. It was a mixture of ammonal and iron pipes that exploded in the ground which could be then used as trenches. On the night of 2nd August the line of the 51st Div. up to the western edge of High Wood was taken over by the 34th Div. and in the wood itself saps were pushed out as far as the German positions in advance of the Switch Line. In addition a new forward trench was dug closer to the German position along Wood Lane east of the wood. On the night of 6th August the 33rd Div. relieved the 51st Div. In the period 6th to 12th August there was patrol activity on both sides at High Wood. On 18th August the 98th Bde. of the 33rd Div. was ordered to take a portion of Wood Lane and some German positions in High Wood. Wood Lane itself was to be taken by the 4th King's of the 98th Bde. with the help of the 4th Suffolks (the 14th Div.). They were not successful. Flame throwers, burning oil drums and pipe-pushers were used on this occasion and the last named blew a crater in the lines of the 2nd A & SH of the 98th Bde. The 19th Bde. also of the 33rd Div. was later brought up to relieve the whole front line, until the morning of the 19th.

Frank Richards wrote that in mid August the 2nd RWF took over trenches in High Wood. The British trench ran just inside the wood to the centre of it. Richards, who was in Signals wrote that he dumped their telephone on the firestep and that they were in a bay by themselves. Anyone who left the centre of the wood would have to pass them to make their way to the communication trenches. Other duties of the 2nd RWF were to provide working parties in order to dig a communication trench to High Wood and to fetch and carry from the Bazentin Dumps. On 18th August an unsuccessful attack on the wood was made by the 1st Bde. of the 1st Div.

Towards the end of August the 33rd Div. was called upon once again to capture the Switch Line although they had already lost 799 men. They worked in preparation in Death Valley and loaded ammunition at Green Dump. Hutchison placed 10 Machine Guns in Savoy Trench over which they had a magnificent view of the German line at a range of about 2,000 yards. For two days they carried ammunition to the battery positions as well as great quantities of water for cooling purposes that was stored in empty petrol cans. It was planned that the 100th MGC was to stage a machine gun barrage under Hutchison. The fire was to be maintained for twelve hours in order to cover attacks and consolidation. The Vickers Guns proved their stamina and during the attack on the 24th August 250 rounds short of a million were fire by the ten guns. The attack was successful and the operation ended with the capture of Delville Wood but the north-east corner of High Wood still remained in German hands. The 19th and 98th Bde. had gained certain tactical advantages at High Wood in the re-capture of Orchard Trench, Black Watch Trench and the snipers east of Black Watch Trench. The 2nd A & SH were involved in a further attack through High Wood.

The 2nd RWF of the 33rd Div. returned to High Wood on 26th August and their Div. was marking time before the next attempt to take the wood. On 3rd September the 8th Buffs of the 17th Bde. 24th Div. made some progress west of Wood Lane by a frontal attack which was later checked. Also on the 3rd four pipes were used by the REs and fired when the infantry attacked, a tube of 21 pipes was successfully fired to the south-east of the wood, after great trouble and many casualties. The overall results of these and other mining experiments did not encourage further pipe pushing in High Wood.

It seems that around 7th September the German hold on the wood began to weaken because on this day there was found to be no opposition at Wood Lane and it was subsequently consolidated. On the 8th the 2nd Welch Gds. (3rd Bde. 1st Div.) made some progress in the western half of High Wood. The 1st Glosters too were in action and they also remarked on how few Germans were now in the wood, but nevertheless the Germans still kept up a steady machine gun fire from the north. The situation deteriorated and suddenly the whole area was 'alive with bullets' and was quickly strewn with British dead and wounded. The shelling too, became severe. The artillery support was inadequate. The 1st SWB also of the 3rd Bde. was the supporting battalion and Colonel Pritchard was much grieved at their losses. General Strickland began an enquiry as to why the 3rd Bde. was unable to take the wood. One would have thought that the wood being so strongly defended was sufficient reason.

On 9th September a second mine was blown which destroyed the enemy garrison holding the lip of the earlier mine crater and this time an advance proceeded unchecked. The combined craters were 135 feet by 35 feet deep. The 1st Div. tried to clear the wood. The 2nd KRRC and the 2nd R. Sussex assembled at Wood Lane and this time there was progress and contact with the Rifles was kept i.e. the 165th Bde. on the right. On 11th September the wood was just under half in British hands and was full of charred tree-stumps and bodies.

We now come to the time when the Wood finally fell into Allied hands and the Division chosen for the job was the 47th London Div. The Civil Service Rifles (1/15th London Batt.) left the village of Franvillers on the 12th September and after their training every man understood what he had to do and where he had to go in the battle plan.

Two tanks had been allotted to them in the place of an artillery barrage, the battalion marched to Bécourt Wood and relieved the 2nd R. Sussex (2nd Bde. 1st Div.) in what appeared to be a 'big rubbish tip'. They were to remain here until the 14th. A Corporal attached to the 140th Trench Mortar Battery wrote at the time they were camped in bivouacs on the crest of a ridge just behind the old front line, and to the left of Bécourt Wood. As far as the eye could see there were miles of tents, bivouacs, limbers and horse lines. Huge dumps of supplies and ammunition covered the ground, and between them in any old corner, were the big guns. The sky was continuously patrolled by Allied aircraft. In the dip below them lay Fricourt, and the Allied guns were continuously firing.

Although the 47th Div. were to take High Wood there were three Divisions involved in the battle and from the right to left they were the 47th, 50th and 15th. The objectives of the 47th and 50th Divs. ran from east to west along the reverse slope of the ridge and linking the Flers defences with Martinpuich. The 15th Div. were to wait until the High Wood flank was progressing and were then to press on to capture the whole of Martinpuich. The 47th Div. was also to cover the New Zealand left who were to attack with two Bdes. The Civil Service Rifles the 1/15th Battalion London were to be allotted the first German line in the wood itself, with the 1/7th City of London on the right and the 1/17th Poplar and Stepney on their left. They had had full dress rehearsals at Franvillers and these training 'shows' had been attended by the whole Division, and included artillery, trench mortars and contact aeroplanes attached to the Div. The second objective was to be the Starfish Line, down the forward slope and the third on the right was the strong Flers Line where the 140th Bde. were to join up with the New Zealanders, falling back to the 141st Bde. in a communication trench, Drop Alley when the final objective was progressed westerly along Pru Trench in the valley.

The 1/7 and 1/15 London Battalions were to be in the van after they had taken the first objective and were to include the Switch Line and north point of High Wood and the 1/8 Londons were to come through and secure the second line and the 1/6 were to take the final objective. In the first stage of the advance the 1/15 Battalion were to clear the enemy from High Wood in conjunction with its left and the 1/7 Londons of the 141st Bde. which allotted the first objective to this battalion and the 1/18 Londons. Four tanks were to pass through the wood and four were to be involved in the attack against Martinpuich.

The attack was to begin at 5.50 a.m. on the 15th September and troops of the Civil Service Rifles were assembled in Black Watch Trench where they were issued with their rum ration. At that time the tanks had not been seen or heard. The assembly trenches were irregular in formation and the men of 'B', 'C' and 'D' Companies were told to creep out before zero so that when the attack began they would be on the extreme right. These companies began to creep up soon after 3.30 a.m. The enemy soon retaliated with rifle and machine guns and even before zero hour these companies were already under murderous fire. At the same time the German artillery barraged the Allied assembly trenches. Casualties were not surprisingly very high. 'A' Company fared better as they left their assembly trenches later and the enemy were occupied with the other companies. 'A' Company carried the first and second German trenches outside High Wood with comparatively little loss. One of the tanks showed up late and then got stuck in a communication trench and the other got in front of 'D' Company's objective and caught fire. By 11 a.m. the 140th Inf. Bde. Stokes Mortar Battery had come to the rescue and as a result 'C' and 'D' Companies were able to go forward again. The tanks could make no headway over broken tree stumps and deeply pitted ground and were stuck before they could give the help expected of them.

The infantry were short of artillery coverage due to the expected assistance of the tanks. By 11.40 a.m. after the 140th TM Battery had fired 750 Stokes Mortar shells into High Wood the Germans began surrendering to bombing parties of the Londoners which worked forward around the flanks. Several hundred prisoners were taken along with machine guns and howitzers. By noon the whole of High Wood was in British possession together with the Switch Line beyond. Only 150 men of the four companies of the Civil Service Rifles reached the objective. The remnants of the Battalion advanced a little beyond the Switch Line and dug themselves in a new trench. The Starfish Line was still to be carried.

During the day the 6th London (City of London) and the 1/8th Post Office Rifles had pushed through to take trenches some distance beyond, known as the Flers Line which connected Flers with Eaucourt l'Abbaye with the Starfish Line which was the Intermediate Line. These operations were only partly successful and in the early evening of the 15th the 1st Surrey Rifles (1/21 London Battalion) who up to then were in reserve were sent up to attack the western part of the Starfish Line whose other name was the Cough Drop. The Civil Service Rifles were to take over the Starfish once the 1st Surreys had vacated it. The Surreys however were caught by intense artillery and machine gun fire when they emerged from High Wood to attack. The attack subsequently failed, but the Starfish Redoubt was taken.

In the history of the 47th Div. it says that the 17th and 18th London Battalions and half of the 1/15th had a desperate struggle in High Wood for every foot of the advance. The Germans met them with bombs and rifle fire, from their trenches and machine guns from his concrete emplacements, still undamaged, mowed them down. The 140th TM Battery certainly had its effect on the German garrison and by 1 o'clock the wood was reported clear of the enemy. On the flanks the progress had been faster and the wood was taken really because the troops on either side went forward and left High Wood behind. On the right the tanks had been a success and had caused dismay to the German garrison at Flers. They had gone forward with the New Zealanders, the 7th Batt. fighting their way to the Starfish Line and the 6th beyond this again. The objective was to make good a ridge running north-east from High wood to a point above the villages of Flers and Eaucourt l'Abbaye which involved the capture of the Cough Drop a group of trenches, lozenge in shape, that were just under this ridge, and a communication trench which was called Drop Alley which ran from it in a north-easterly direction to the Flers Line itself. It was thought to be imperative that a footing should be made where the Flers Line was joined by Drop Alley. In four days of fighting the 47th Div. lost 4,500 men in casualties. The battalions who suffered most were the ones which had been in the open and had suffered so much from German machine gun fire and from the artillery too, namely the 23rd, 21st and the 6th Londons.

The cause of these heavy losses according to the Divisional History and also the subsequent delays in the prosecution of the attack were due mainly to the decision regarding the disposition of the tanks in the front of High Wood, a decision that was made despite the opposite views of both the Divisional and Brigade Commanders who had made personal visits to the wood itself. The tanks which were unable to make progress in the conditions in the wood should have been placed outside it and the infantry would not then have been starved of artillery assistance. The communication between Divisions and Bdes. was very bad chiefly because Fricourt Farm had been prepared as an Advance HQ Divisional but HQ remained to the south-west of Albert.

Sgt. D. F. Brown of the 2nd Otago Inf. Regt. NZEF gained the VC for 'conspicuous bravery' and determination when the company he belonged to suffered very heavy casualties in officers and men from machine gun fire. At great personal risk he advanced with a comrade and succeeded in reaching a point within 30 yards of the enemy guns. Four of the gun crew were captured. The company continued their advance until they were held up by another machine gun. The two New Zealanders dealt with this in similar fashion and they then came under heavy shell fire. The Switch Line was carried with few prisoners.

The New Zealanders hurried on to the heavily protected Flers Line and endured five hours of fierce fighting. Brown's company was decimated and eventually came out with one officer and 49 men with Sgt. Brown and his colleague Sgt. Rogers in command. On another occasion too Brown captured a machine gun from the enemy. He was to be killed on 1st October during a second attack in the area close to Eaucourt l'Abbaye.

There is a vast amount of literature on High Wood and many are first hand accounts. Obviously there is a lot of overlap with many of these accounts, but I would like to quote from Beach Thomas who wrote a book called *With the British on the Somme*. He says that the wood might have been planted for the purposes of defence. On the further side it sloped down which offered a perfect artillery target from the north altogether cutting off guns from the south, the northern end being protected by the southern trees which caught and exploded even in the highest angled trees. The battlefield had to be imagined, he wrote, for he had seen nothing like it on earth: in desolation, horror, in pitifulness, in grimness. At the west corner were mine craters which were lined with fragments of kits, with helmets and masks, and half tunics and bones. Every tree was beheaded or maimed and at the door of the wood lay a lop sided tank in a shell hole with its nose against the base of a tree. One walked through the roots and pits and ditches that had supplanted the undergrowth; but there were worse things in the wood than the sights. The wood had been a target for any and every battery for over two months and the Germans had made no attempt during that time to bury their dead. It was also a difficult task for the British as the Germans almost always held the upper hand in the wood. Machine gun emplacements had been built by the enemy along with concrete blockhouses and wiring had been attempted quite close to the British trench, all the while that artillery fire was kept chasing up and down the wood and across it.

John Glubb who was with the REs 7th Field Company of the 50th Div. took part in the High Wood battle and wrote in his memoirs that the sappers worked all day and night on the 16th and 17th September together with the 1st and 2nd North'd Companies. They carted bricks from the ruins of Bazentin le Petit in order to fill the shell holes in the road up to High Wood. Boast Trench was dug which connected the right flank of their Div. with the left flank of the 47th Div. where there had been a gap for three days. Also his company hastily built a decauville light tramline from the left of High Wood towards Eaucourt l'Abbaye, which was later extended to Bazentin le Petit. The other tramlines ran from behind Contalmaison to Martinpuich and forward. These together with the railway reduced the need to use the ruins which had been demolished by shell fire and the weather. There were eight miles of tramlines. Glubb also commented that 'High Wood was quite the place for the tourist now with the following items of interest: Two derelict tanks dating from 15th September, two crosses commemorating the 1st Div., the 47th and his own North'd Fus., several very fine German dugouts and a concrete blockhouse and lastly one of the finest views, nearly all the Somme battlefield and the then German front line.'

Colonel Whitehead who at the time was attached to the Post Office Rifles (1/8th London) wrote home in a letter that there was nothing between the wood and Starfish Redoubt, not a single square foot of original surface. In mid September it was like a honeycomb.

R. Derry who was a Bandsman and stretcher bearer with the City of London Battalion said that on the 15th the objective had been a strong point. His company was at the edge of the wood and as the tanks arrived at daybreak, one was destroyed by a direct hit. The second one got mixed up with tree trunks and the third fell into a trench and was burnt out. They were a complete disaster and the fact that there was no artillery support at the time contributed to the overall failure. The further ridge was cleared except for one strong point, a large dugout cut into the side of the hill which was laid out like a field hospital. Mud was ankle deep. The next objective was to be the Butte de Warlencourt. The 2nd Welch were ordered up to take over the Starfish system of trenches on the slope beyond High Wood. C. P. Clayton an officer on their staff who later wrote his memoirs, found himself in command because of losses and his HQ was in a deep dugout in an old German reserve line close to Flers. They were later relieved by the 2nd Munsters. He had a new Colonel by this time and they went back to a hut camp close to Mametz Wood. There was to be a shadow that overhung the triumph of the 47th Div. at High Wood. Using the history of the Division which said that 'the heavy losses incurred in the capture of High Wood, and the delays occurred later in the prosecution of the attack by the 47th Division, as also by the Division on its left, were mainly due to the unfortunate decision regarding the disposition of the IIIrd Corps Tanks in the area of the 47th Division, a decision which was taken in opposition to the urgent representation, more than once expressed to higher authority by the Divisional Commander after personally visiting High Wood in conjunction with the Brigadier concerned, that the Tanks could not move through the wood, owing to the insurmountable nature of the obstacles inside it. Had the tanks been placed outside the wood, as urged by Sir C. Barter, they could have materially helped the attackers in the wood. As it was they were the cause of the infantry being obliged to attack the wood without artillery assistance'.

High Alley: The 47th London Div. while the post at High Alley became the MDS and HQ of the Field Ambulance. Here the horse transport, of necessity, had their lines by the side of four batteries of heavy howitzers, with a 9.2 battery in the rear. There was a Field Ambulance Post established on the side of High Alley, where tea could be obtained for the asking night and day. On 13th September and the 21st the 47th Div. buried 47 of their dead in a large shellhole opposite High Wood, on the west side of the road from Martinpuich to Longueval. Other burials were brought in later bringing the number to 101, mainly of soldiers who fell on 15th September. The little burial place was called London Cemetery.

On 18th September the Civil Service Rifles were given some reinforcements who arrived from a camp at Bottom Wood. A few officers were relieved on the 19th by the 1st Black Watch of the 1st Bde. 1st Div. The Rifles had to undertake two more operations and the first on the 18th was to advance into the Flers Line, which was achieved without loss because the enemy had evacuated this trench. But he still held the junction of Flers Line and Drop Alley, and that portion of the line west of the junction. On the 20th they were relieved and went down to Bottom Wood. Their losses amounted to 380 men.

On 28th September Barter was replaced as Commander of the 47th Div. by Maj. Gen. Sir George Gorringe. Barter was to appeal later against this dismissal but his plea for an investigation was ignored.

At this period much time was spent in filling up potholes and mending roads etc.

Norman Gladden of the 7th North'd Fus. 149th Bde. 50th Div. said in his book on the Somme that their resting place on 24th October was behind High Wood in bivouacs. The weather was poor but on the 25th the rain had stopped but everywhere was a quagmire. He inspected High Wood which was 'seared and torn', full of all kinds of rubbish. There was an abandoned tank amidst the tree stumps. A little way from the edge of the wood was a derelict German battery with guns of a light type. On rising ground behind the wood were the stark walls of a high building whose shape had survived. The Germans made a last stand in this ex factory.

Cecil Slack (E. Yorks) in his memoirs mentions a brief but miserable time at the wood on 24th October. He had been told to go there to wait for the rest of the battalion and he got to the wood after dark. He dismissed his men and they had to make the best of it. Later the rest of the battalion turned up and he was able to get some sleep. They had eight officers wiped out by one shell. They cleared out of the wood after that and made themselves 'homes' in some old trenches a few hundred yards away. It was raining almost continuously at this time and the conditions grew worse and muddier. At one time Slack's company was standing in mud over their knees for 18 hours. The landscape became so bleak that it was difficult to find a feature that remained static in it. When he saw High Wood for the first time he thought that the trees were covered in black tar. This tar turned out to be masses of great fat blue bottle flies. On another occasion one of his gumboots sank into something soft which turned out to be a 'very dead' stomach. In October/November the 2nd Welch were bivouacked in huts at a new camp that was called the High Wood West Camp. It was a group of huts and tents on the open part of the country between High Wood and Bazentin Camp. It was the nearest to the front of reserve camp.

In 1917 when William Orpen was painting scenes from the battlefield he visited the Cough Drop just beyond High Wood which he described as a large mine crater, with a stench coming from its watery bottom. He saw at the edge of the wood a German and Highlander locked in a deadly embrace.

High Wood Longueval London Cemetery and Extension: The small burial ground which in September was called London Cemetery was extended in 1934 and the original is between the entrance gates. The Cemetery is a little way south-west of the Martinpuich–Longueval Road, opposite High Wood. It now contains the graves of 3,870 men of whom 3,114 are unnamed. The Cemetery, one of five in Longueval which together contain the graves of more than 15,000 dead, is the third largest on the Somme. It is in Longueval although High Wood is part of Flers. It stands on high ground commanding extensive views over the countryside, and from it can be seen at least five churches. Opposite London Wood Cemetery is a memorial to the 47th Div. and a Cairn to the memory of the Glasgow Highlanders 9th HLI unveiled in 1972.

On the peak of a nearby hill can be seen an isolated monument in memory of the New Zealand Div. It is on the crest of the rise between High Wood and Delville Wood.

On the eastern flank of High Wood is a memorial to the Cameron Highlanders and Black Watch, who fought here when a large mine was blown by the REs. Originally a stone cross within a frame of stones from Verdun, stood on the south-west edge of the wood to replace the wooden memorial erected by the 47th Div. in 1916. Other temporary memorials were erected in the wood by the 1st and 51st Divs. the 1st North'd Fus, the Cameron H., the 1st SWB, the 10th Glosters and the 20th R. Fus.

Thistle Dump Cemetery stands in a field south of the southern apex of the wood. It was begun in August 1916, and used as a front line cemetery until February 1917. It was increased after the Armistice and contains the graves of soldiers from the UK, NZ and Australia, some Germans. It is surrounded by cultivated fields, in a valley running between Longueval and Bazentin.

High Wood was to have an often anthologised poem named after it by P. Johnstone, and another poet E. A. Mackintosh who served with the 5th Seaforth was wounded and gassed here. He was later killed at Cambrai in October 1917.

In 1935 the *Ypres Times* mentioned that bodies of men were still being found and that they were buried in the London Cemetery. The writer saw many wooden crosses awaiting replacement with white headstones. Of the 887 bodies recovered in France in 1934–35, 603 were recovered on the Somme. And in 1935–36 the proportion was even higher, 721 out of 821. The French people received ten francs at the time for each body found and reported. I have already referred to J. L. Hodson's book *Return to the Wood* and I would like to finish this piece on High Wood by quoting once again from this book. Hodson returned to the High Wood area in 1954 with some friends and they traced some of the places where he had been in 1916. They went to the place where they came that summer night or early morning in July, the wood that was a mass of broken blazing trees under the superb bombardment of the French 75s. This was the place with the noise and thunder where they lay down before the final rush into the wood. In 1916 they had got into the wood with little difficulty but they were to lose 2/3rds of the battalion mostly to shellfire. The trees in the wood were now youthful like the men who were killed there. They inspected the cemetery which was full of nameless graves. After a storm they entered the wood (in 1954) at the right hand corner. At the far end of the wood was a pond formerly a mine crater which now cattle drank from. They found bits of weapons etc. the remains of German machine gun posts of broken concrete. Also broken slabs which legend has it, covered the remains of seven officers who had had their heads cut off. The party walked around the wood and found the approximate place where their Lewis gun had fought a duel with a German machine gun. At the rear of the wood commanding the left was the strong point. They had sung 'In Summertime on Bredon' or 'My Old Shako' or 'Twelve are the Apostles'. Hodson said to his friends that if ghosts walk then they must parade in companies or even in brigades around this place. For there in three months thousands of men were slain. Hodson mused as to whether the ghosts were friendly and whether the two sides were friendly with one another. They wrote their names in the Cemetery Book and drove away from that place both of hideous and hallowed memory, away from their youth. When they had been relieved by the West Kents with their laconic Cockney voices the RFs had marched away from the wood to the Mametz Valley. As they marched they sung a farewell to those that they had lost and left behind.

Horseshoe Trench

This trench was south-west of Contalmaison, north-east of Bécourt and east of la Boisselle. It was part of the German line which ran from Ovillers la Boisselle through Round Wood and the Dingle to an area behind Fricourt Wood. It rested on Peake Woods. It was attacked simultaneously from two sides, from the southern end and also from the northern end, which was protected by a strongly fortified redoubt. On the further left there was a hard and prolonged struggle for possession of Birch Tree and Peake Woods. Horseshoe Trench and Lincolns Redoubt stood on high ground between Mametz Wood and la Boisselle, some 1,200 yards south-west of Contalmaison. The objective of the 69th Bde. of the 23rd Div. was Horseshoe Trench running from Lincoln Redoubt to Scotts Redoubt, the latter was slightly to the south-west. The line was curved. On 5th July the first attack failed. A gun to the left of the Trench had to be put out of action and 2nd Lt. Donald Bell of the 9th Green Howards 69th Bde. was the man responsible for taking it being awarded the VC as a result. The citation reads that during an attack a very heavy enfilade fire was opened up on the attacking company by a hostile machine gun. Bell immediately, and on his own initiative, crept up the communication trench, and then followed by Cpl. Colwill and Private Batey, rushed across the open under very heavy fire and attacked the machine gun, destroying it and its personnel with revolver fire and bombs. This very brave act saved many lives and ensured the success of the attack.

Lincoln Redoubt was taken and in the evening Horseshoe was cleared. On the 10th, five days later, Bell lost his life in a very similar act of bravery. He is buried at Gordon Dump. Subsequently Horseshoe Trench became known as Bell's Redoubt.

Humbercamps

Humbercamps is a village to the north-east of St. Amand and is 13 miles south-west of Arras. There is a Communal Cemetery Extension on the north-east side of the Communal Cemetery, in part of a former old orchard. It was used by Field Ambulances, from September 1915 until February 1917.

Jacob's Ladder

Jacob's Ladder was a communication trench which ran north-east from Mesnil to Hamel village, it then bent south-eastwards and connected up with Hamel Bridge across the Ancre. On the 1st July it was in the area of the 36th (Ulster) Div.

In mid August the miners of the 1st Lancs. (11th Bde. 4th Div.) were set to dig deep dugouts which became known as Kentish Caves. Edmund Blunden who was with the 11th R. Sussex (116th Bde. 39th Div.) says in his memoir that 'if ever there was to be a vile, unnerving and desperate place in the battle zone, it was the Mesnil end of Jacob's Ladder, among the heavy battery positions, and under perfect enemy observation.' This long communication trench was good in parts and apart from being unusually long also required a flight of stairs at one or two steep places. Leafy bushes and great green and yellow weeds looked into it as it dipped sharply into the green valley by Hamel, and hereabouts according to Blunden the aspect of peace and innocence was as yet prevailing. Further on was a small chalk cliff, facing the river, with a rambling but remarkable dugout called Kentish Caves. The front line was sculptured over this brow, and descended to the wooded marshes of the Ancre. Running across it towards the German line went the narrow Beaucourt Road, and the railway to Miraumont and Bapaume; in the railway bank was a look out post called Crow's Nest, with a large periscope, but none seemed very pleased to see the periscope. South of the Ancre was broad-backed high ground, and on that a black vapour of smoke and naked tree trunks or charcoal, an apparition which he found was Thiepval Wood.

La Boisselle

La Boisselle is a small village to the east just after emerging from Albert on the D 929 road to Bapaume. It is also on the D 104 to Contalmaison. On the other side of the road, to the north-west of the village is the village of Ovillers la Boisselle.

In 1916 the hamlet of la Boisselle had 35 houses and was the centre of a small but pronounced salient in the German lines, the apex of which was as little as 100 yards from the British lines. On the eastern or right hand side was Sausage Valley and various German strong points such as Heligoland, Kipper and Bloater Trenches were connected up to it. To the north-west and across the main road was another valley called appropriately Mash Valley. The village therefore stood on a spur between the two famous valleys and at this point the valley between the villages of la Boisselle and Ovillers la Boisselle resulted in no man's land being here very wide.

To set the scene I have depended heavily on the *Official History* which tells us that the position was in the territory of 111 Corps between Bécourt and Authuille to the west. The positions of the Corps lay on the forward slopes of a long low ridge that went from Albert to la Boisselle and was marked by Tara Valley on the right and Usna Valley on the left. They were a continuation of the spur of the main Ginchy–Pozieres Ridge. Behind this ridge the Divisional artillery were deployed in rows and were dug in on open ground, on both sides of the Amiens road just west of Albert. The right of the Corps faced the western slope of the long Fricourt spur and la Boisselle was at its centre. The distance between the opposing lines varied from 50 to 1,000 yards and any advance would have to pass over open land which could be covered by cross fire from both sides of the position and also from the Thiepval Spur which overlooked the position. The spurs themselves were covered with a network of trenches and machine gun nests.

The German defences consisted of a front system with four main strongpoints in its southern half. Sausage Redoubt (Heligoland) with Scotts Redoubt behind it; Schwaben Höhe just being the ground that was being made ready for a huge mine explosion and la Boisselle village itself. The fifth German defence was Ovillers la Boisselle to the north-west. Behind the German front defences were two intermediate lines, the first from Fricourt Farm to Ovillers and the second which was unfinished in front of Contalmaison and Pozieres. Behind these again, was the second position from Bazentin le Petit to Mouquet Farm that consisted of two lines. The front of the German line was not as completely exposed to fire as was the ground behind it.

The two Bdes. of the 34th Div. who were to provide the attack on the incredibly strongly held la Boisselle positions were, the 101st on the right and the 102nd (Tyneside Scottish) on the left. The positions to be captured included Sausage Redoubt, Heligoland, Bloater Trench, Scotts Redoubt and Gordon Post. I will deal firstly with the role of the 101st Bde. Their objectives for the first day of the battle were in a north-easterly direction across Sausage Valley towards Contalmaison and going across the top of Fricourt. A cluster of trees known as Round Wood and beyond it Peake Woods mounted a spur to Contalmaison village. The position of the 101st Bde. was to the north-east of Bécourt Wood and just beyond Chapes Spur to the south-east of la Boisselle. The 15th R. Scots, one of the Edinburgh Battalions was in the front line with the 16th R. Scots behind them. They had assembled at the bottom of the valley. On their left was the 10th Lincs. or Grimsby Pals and behind them were the 11th Suffolks (Cambridge). The British had made considerable preparations to destroy part of the German stronghold in extensive underground mining operations that were to come to fruition in time with the Allied advance on 1st July. The 179th Tunnelling Company had prepared two very large mines in an area where mining and counter-mining had been going on for months and in which the French were involved before the British took over the sector. One of the mines was charged with 60,000 lbs of ammonal and the other with 40,000 lbs. In addition three Russian Saps had also been dug on 111 Corps Front in order to provide a covered approach after the assault. The use of Russian Saps by assaulting troops was limited and impractical as only small numbers of men could emerge from them at one time, and once exit points were spotted by the enemy it would be no problem to cover the exit with machine guns and this would therefore bottle up men underground. The real use of these saps was for messengers and reinforcements after a capture of an enemy front line.

At Y Sap south of la Boisselle village two charges were set at a depth of about 52 feet and the charges were 60 feet apart but a single crater was to result to a depth lower than that of the original chambers and was formed with remarkably wide rims. It was fired a couple of minutes before 7.30 a.m. on 1st

July and it was the plan that the Allied infantry would be able to seize on the advantage from the 'dazed' defenders. The explosion caused a hollow 100 yards across and 30 yards deep. As desired the mine threw up a high lip that cut off the north of la Boisselle and accorded the infantry a little protection for their advance. However from the German point of view it appears that they had had advance warning of the explosion time, probably as a result of 'listening in' to a British telephone line. They therefore evacuated the position and had comparatively few casualties. However one of the German strongholds the Schwaben Höhe on the left of the crater was destroyed in the explosion. A Russian Sap called Kerriemuir Street which was connected with Y Sap was for some time the only means of crossing Sausage Redoubt.

The explosion of these mines was indeed very effective but was very local and on these occasions it always seemed that the defenders were well able to take advantage of the situation themselves rather than allow the advantage to remain with the attacker. On this occasion after the explosion which must have severely jolted the enemy he nevertheless, because of underground protection and early warning, was able to come up and to get himself into a position from which he could take toll of any advancing waves of attack. Once the mines had gone up the 15th R. Scots had climbed their parapets and advanced into no man's land. The explosion from which they had hoped so much had failed to demoralise the German garrison and the fight for village therefore surpassed their worst expectations.

The 15th R. Scots were in the words of their history 'buffeted by the storms of shells and bullets'; then came the 16th Battalion and it was probably at the exposed zone just in front of the parapets that so many of the officers and men were killed. Nevertheless the 15th did secure some of their objectives and were the only unit in the Division to do so. 'C' Company for example 'plodded grimly on' and, crossing Scotts Redoubt reached Peake Trench.

As already stated to the left of the Edinburgh battalions were the 10th Lincolns (Grimsby Pals) and behind them the 11th Suffolks These two battalions were caught by the same flanking fire and suffered very heavy casualties indeed, and although they reached the lip of the mine crater, they had not only been caught by machine gun fire but some were even burnt to death as when reaching the German lines they were repelled by flame throwers. According to John Keegan's *The Face of Battle*, an Artillery officer was later to come upon line after line of dead men lying where they had fallen with the various battalions. Lines of dead who had undergone a bizarre and pointless massacre.

To the left of the 101st Bde. attack was the 102nd Bde. or Tyneside Scottish who were battalions of the Northumberland Fusiliers. On the la Boisselle side of the road was the 21st Battalion with the 24th due to come through on their right and the 26th North'd Fus. who were due to attack on their left. Beyond them to the left and across the road were the 23rd and 25th Battalions. Their left flank bordered on the right flank of the 8th Div. who were to take Ovillers la Boisselle. The 102nd Bde. could make no progress in the face of fire that swept them from Ovillers la Boisselle. This failure in turn reacted on the

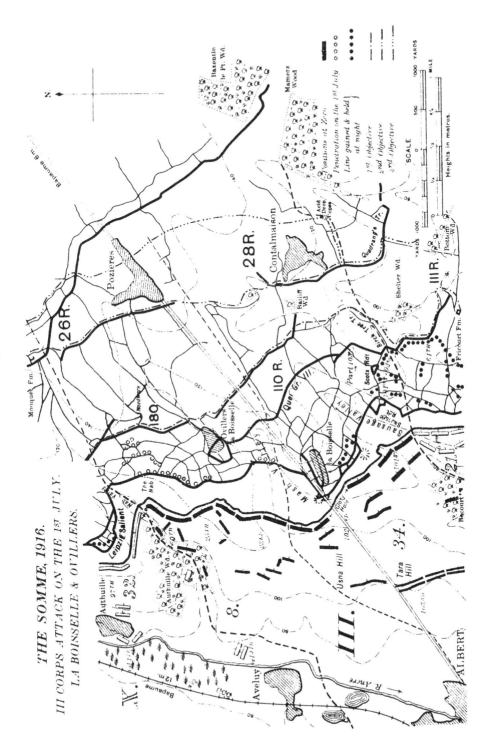

THE SOMME, 1916.
III CORPS ATTACK ON THE 1st JULY.
LA BOISSELLE & OVILLERS.

101st Bde. attack. From the time that the first wave of infantry had sprung from their trenches they also came under a very heavy barrage and many were killed before getting clear. The heaviest fire came from the concealed fortifications of la Boisselle and from the high ground to the left of the battalion, and only men who knew that they risked almost certain death would have made any progress.

The 103rd Bde. or Tyneside Irish were in support to the 102nd Bde. in front of Albert. The Tyneside Scottish had been in a new dugout in the Tara Usna Line which was north of the Albert road in front of that town, and each unit was in telephone contact with its Bde. or Division. It can be seen today how impossible the task of the Tyneside Battalions was when one sees that they had to come from the direction of the Tara Usna Line and go down into an open slope and across Avoca Valley. They presented a perfect target to the German machine gunners. A heavy Trench Mortar barrage was to be maintained on la Boisselle till such times as bombers from the 102nd Bde. had reached points from which they could attack the village from both the north and the south. The 34th Div. had decided to move all the Bde. Battalions forward simultaneously and this included the Tyneside Irish of the 103rd Bde. This decision taken before the battle assumed that the British Artillery would have destroyed the German defences, and as it hadn't and the German machine gunners were still very much in evidence, the simultaneous use of 3,000 men could only lead to a Divisional suicide. It was truly remarkable that any progress at all was made under such adverse conditions, parties of men were somehow able to make their way through the very heavy shell fire and the machine gun enfilade from la Boisselle and the ground beyond it. The attackers gained part of the village and it was not until the 4th that the village was finally taken by the Allies. All the time that the village held out then it followed that the 8th Division on the left of the main road would not be able to make progress up Mash Valley. The flanking fire from the enemy machine guns on the slopes of the la Boisselle side of the valley was sufficient to seal the fate of the attackers. In *The War in the Air* is the following account of the day. 'The 111 Corps with which the largest part of No. 3 Sqn. operated was held up by the strongly fortified villages of Ovillers and la Boisselle, but the 34th Div. penetrated as far as Peake Woods. This proved to be the point of the wedge into the line north of Fricourt. The artillery co-operation was provided by the pilots of the 3rd and 9th Sqns. The 8th Div. was caught partly by machine gunners placed in Leipzig Redoubt'.

All the commanding officers of the 102nd (Tyneside Scottish) Bde. were killed on 1st July. As already stated the Brigade was made up of four battalions of the North'd Fus. Three of the officers were Lt. Colonels A. P. A. Elphinstone (22nd), W. T. Lyle (23rd) and C. C. A. Sillery (20th). They were all killed at Usna Hill and it was said that General Ingouville-Williams (CO of 34th Div.) found the bodies of Lyle and Sillery at the head of their battalions. The three Lt. Colonels were buried at Bapaume Post Cemetery. The fourth senior officer to be killed was Lt. Col. F. C. Heneker (21st) whose grave is at Ovillers Military Cemetery. Ingouville-Williams himself was killed shortly afterwards at Queens Nullah close to Mametz Wood on the 22nd July. His nickname was 'Inky Bill'.

Other senior officer casualties of this tragic day were Lt. Col. Maddison of the Green Howards who was attached to the 8th Yorks. & Lancs. (70th Bde. 23rd Div.) as was Lt. Col. Addison of the 9th Yorks. & Lancs. of the same Brigade. Two Commanding Officers of the Tyneside Irish (North'd Fus.) of the 103rd Bde. were wounded namely Lt. Col. M. E. Richardson (3rd Tyneside), Lt. Col. J. H. M. Arden (2nd Tyneside) and a third, of the 1st Tyneside Irish Lt. Col. (or Major) L. M. Howard was killed.

A poet Bernard Charles de Boismaison White who had published a book of verse called *Remembrance and other Verses* was born in 1886 and had worked before the war with the Marconi Company and later was the Assistant Editor of *Wireless World* before joining the publishing firm of Hutchinsons. He was a member of the 1st Tyneside Scottish and became a casualty in the advance over Tara Hill.

A famous naturalist named John Charlton who was a Captain in the 2nd Tyneside Scottish was also killed whilst leading his company against the German third line.

The 34th Div. who had been so tragically cut down on the 1st were still in the line in front of la Boisselle on the 2nd. They were now supported by the 19th Div. The 101st Bde. and the 102nd (Tyneside Scottish) Bdes. 34th Div. were in the area of Scotts Redoubt.

It was two companies of the 7th E. Lancs. of the 56th Bde. who had been lent to the 34th Div. who captured the Redoubt in the afternoon of the 2nd July. To their right was the 56th Bde. 19th Div. and to their left and across the main road was the 57th Bde. of the same Div. The 34th Div. while still holding the right sector of 111 Corps had made unsuccessful attempts by bombing out from its forward position to link up with the 19th Div. but had failed to do so. When night fell on the 3rd the 23rd Div. began to relieve the 34th Div. and the 69th Bde. took over the captured trenches. The 8th N. Staffs. (57th Bde.) were involved in the fighting in la Boisselle and their ground included the large mine crater that had been blown on the 1st July. Their CO Major C. Wedgewood was killed on 3rd July, aged 53, and buried at Bapaume Post Cemetery. The CO of the 10th Worcesters (57th Bde.) was forward of his battalion and had reached the mine crater with his adjutant, when he too was killed. The 57th Bde. which consisted of the 10th R. Warwicks., 8th Glosters., 10th Worcesters and 8th N. Staffs. were fighting hard in la Boisselle on the 3rd July and in the end the Germans held a line that ran through the church ruins. The 57th Bde. was then reinforced by the 56th Bde. and after dark the 12th Div. dug a forward trench to connect its right with the flank of the 19th Div. Adrian Carton de Wiart who was a Temp. Lt. Col. attached to the 8th Glosters was in command of the 57th Bde. during the period 2nd/3rd July. He had been in the Army since 1899 and had lost an eye in Somali and a hand in Zonnebeke in addition to being wounded several times. He was awarded the VC for his work at la Boisselle. The citation notes that his inspiring example prevented a severe reverse, after three other battalion commanders had become casualties. He maintained that the ground won was to be held at all costs. The *Official History* says that he led the fight in person and pulled the pins from Mills grenades with his teeth. The same award was also made to Private T. G. Turrall of the 10th Worcesters who stayed out all day beyond the village with a wounded subaltern and brought him in after dark. The officer had been badly wounded. At one time both men were completely cut off from British troops but Turrall held the ground, and brought the officer in when a counter-attack made it possible.

The village had fallen to the 19th Div. in the period 3rd/4th July and a thunderstorm during the night filled the trenches with water. The 58th Bde. attacked from the south of la Boisselle and the 57th Bde. attacked from the north. At the same time across the road the adjoining Div. the 12th attacked towards Ovillers la Boisselle but barbed wire and machine guns from Mash Valley checked them.

In the 57th Bde. the 8th N. Staffs. had moved forward with the 10th Worcesters on their left. They fought their way to the south end of la Boisselle Salient in the small hours of the 3rd. Losses were very heavy. On the 4th the village was cleared and 111 Corps at last held the whole village. A third, but posthumous VC was awarded in this sector, to Lt. T. Wilkinson who was a Temp. Lt. with the 7th LNL (56th Bde. 19th Div.). During an attack when a party from another unit was retiring without their machine gun, he rushed forward and with two men got the gun into action, and held the enemy until they were relieved. Later when the advance was checked by a bombing attack, he forced his way forward and with the help of four or five men from other units they mounted a machine gun on top of a parapet and dispersed enemy bombers. Later he made two attempts to bring in a wounded man but during the second attempt was shot through the heart. His name is recorded on the Thiepval Memorial. The *Official History* says that the bombers of the 56th and 57th Bdes. met with little success.

In early July Geoffrey Malins, the War Office Photographer visited the area although he had been warned that it was not a 'healthy' area to be in. He talked with the troops of one battery and was told that the place was 'strafed' every day and as soon as he arrived there were crumps behind him, probably in the direction of Bécourt. After much dodging and twisting he halted the car close to a forward dressing station, and was told of a German battery of 77mm guns on the left hand side of the valley leading to Pozieres so he decided to make for it. He filmed from a place that was 800 yards from Pozieres.

On 5th July the 74th Bde. was detached from the 25th Div. and joined the 12th Div. and took over a sector of the line in la Boisselle which had been captured by the 19th Div. on the 4th. On the morning of the 7th it participated in an attack by the 12th Div. on Ovillers la Boisselle and the trenches to the right across the Pozieres Road.

The 13th Rif. Brig. (111th Bde. 37th Div.) spent some time in the trenches on 7th July and buried many of the dead from the beginning of the battle. There were scores of Tyneside Scottish and the great mine crater was virtually one vast tomb. One observer described the scene at Tara Usna Ridge on the 7th July as being like a vast crowded fun fair with bivouacs, dumps, horse lines, batteries, cookers, water carts, and French 75s. John Masefield said of la Boisselle that after being battered and taken by the British, it was destroyed by German fire. It was then cleared by the British who wished to use the roads, just outside it. Between the old lines, there was a spur, that was useful for observation purposes, and for which both sides had fought bitterly. For about 200 yards no man's land was a succession of pits in the chalk where the mines had been set off. The lines crossed this debated area, and went across a small and ill defined bulk of chalk which was known as Chapes Spur, on the top of which was a vast heap of dazzlingly white chalk, so bright that it was painful to look at.

One commentator says that the Germans who were from a Guards Battalion had held out in la Boisselle in the ruins for nearly a week. He said that they finally emerged as starving prisoners. The final number was 124 men and two officers, who surrendered on the 17th July.

In the next few weeks the fighting towards Pozieres was to be particularly associated with the Australian troops and apart from anything else they had a vast amount of artillery guns and batteries in the valley.

On the 18th July a Worcestershire Battalion was called upon to supply working parties to dig a communication trench along the Albert–Pozieres road in the neighbourhood of la Boisselle. The party was very severely hit by an unexpected bout of gas shelling. There were 500 casualties and they were brought back to Bouzincourt. Later the still very unfit battalion received a new draft of men whilst at Crucifix Corner. It was two weeks before the medical authorities sent home at least some of the men to convalescent camps. At the end of August they were still unfit.

William Orpen came across the great mine at la Boisselle when in 1917 he was touring the battlefield making sketches and paintings. He described it as a wonderful sight and a great wilderness of white chalk without a tuft of grass, no flowers, nothing but blazing chalk dotted thickly all over with bits of shrapnel. He walked up to the edge of the crater and he felt himself to be in another world. He remarked on there being another large crater just by the Bapaume Road. This is the one that has been built over in the last few years.

John Masefield was on a similar mission as Orpen, only he was a writer and poet rather than a painter. They both however probably obtained a unique intimacy and understanding of the 1916 Battle of the Somme, simply because they spent so much time in the study of the landscape attempting to grasp the significance of the various lines, hills, woods and fortified villages etc. Masefield like Orpen preferred to work on the spot and in the morning he would get a lift out from Amiens by lorry and work all day by himself, at some spot like la Boisselle for example. Later he would walk back to the bridge at Albert and thumb a lift for Amiens. The British lost la Boisselle in March 1918 and regained it in August 1918.

After the war on the other side of the road from the Grand Mine, was a famous cafe which was called the Cafe de la Grand Mine which at the time testified to the inhabitants the pride in the possession of the crater. In the nineteen thirties there were still many sunken roads and old trenches with their communication trenches still visible.

Beyond the village is a Memorial to the 34th Div. and on the green before the Church is a Memorial to the 19th Div. In the main road there is a memorial seat that commemorates the attack of the Tyneside Scottish and Irish, who fought to win the road here.

In recent years more and more of the numerous small craters have been filled in and it was only in the last few years that the Grand Mine Crater itself was protected by Mr. Richard Dunning who wished to save it from the ravages of youthful French motorcyclists. He has erected a cross and a memorial seat, and as already mentioned, it is virtually a tomb of hundreds of British troops. Each year there is a service at the crater on 1st July and one feels that even when all the survivors of the Great War have finally faded away that there will always be people to come to this spot to commemorate the great sacrifice that the 34th Div. made on the 1st July 1916.

Gordon Dump Cemetery is about half a mile due east of la Boisselle Village and about four miles from Albert Railway Station. 'Plot 1 of Gordon Dump Cemetery was made by fighting units after 10th July, 1916, and closed in September. It contained the graves of 95 soldiers, mainly Australian. It was called variously Gordon or Gordon's Dump Cemetery or Sausage Valley Cemetery. The remainder of the Cemetery was formed after the Armistice. The great majority of the soldiers thus reburied fell in July 1916. The wooden Memorial of the 10th Lancs. Fus. to their officers and men who fell on the 7th July 1916 in the capture of Quadrangle Trench was removed to this Cemetery which is sheltered by hills except on the south-west side, from which Bécourt and Bécordel can be seen'.

Lahoussoye

Lahoussoye is eight miles to the north-east of Amiens and was a village much used for billeting including the 12th HLI (46th Bde. 15th Div.) who arrived there in mid September from Franvillers.

No. 21 Motor Ambulance Convoy of 111 Corps was based on the village.

Laviéville

Laviéville is a small village to the north of the Albert–Amiens road (D 929) south-west of Millencourt and south-east of Hénencourt. The village was always behind the battle lines and was mainly known for dealing with casualties from the battle that raged just a few miles to the north-east of it. Troops also used to bivouac in the village. A MDS run by III Corps was here at the beginning of July and in addition there was a walking wounded post and a Motor Ambulance Convoy was established. At one point the 21st CCS was moved here from Lahoussoye.

Leipzig Salient

The site of Leipzig Salient is just north-east of the crossroads on the road from Ovillers la Boisselle to Authuille and the Thiepval–Aveluy Road.

The German front line bent round like a nose at this point and there were further defensive lines behind including the Hindenburg Trench and the Wonderwork, another strong point a few hundred yards beyond. Nab Valley or Blighty Valley as it was to become was to the east and Thiepval Village and Chateau to the north. The strongly held Mouquet Farm was in the north-east direction towards Pozieres.

John Masefield in his book *The Old Front Line* described the Salient as a long sloping spur which was wooded at one end. It was known as Thiepval Hill of Leipzig Salient. Masefield wrote that this hill was of the greatest importance to the enemy and that it was a sort of eyrie for the Schwaben Redoubt which was on the higher ground to the north. It was the key to the covered way to the plateau from which all the spurs in this area thrust southwards. There were two large enemy works on the Leipzig Spur which were well to the south of Thiepval. One being the Wonderwork which was a six angled star shaped redoubt and the other still further south-wards which was Leipzig Salient and which Masefield described as being a big, disused, and very evil looking quarry. It had another name which was the Hohenzollern from the trench of that name which ran straight across the spur about half way down the salient. The enemy could look down easily on the Allied line from these eyries and though the British Artillery in the end blasted the Germans off the hill it was to be a hugely costly place to hold onto in terms of casualties and suffering. Enemy fire could be directed from the rear above Hamel, from the hill itself or from the left flank towards Thiepval.

The 17th HLI (97th Bde. 32nd Div.) in preparation for the 1st July attack which was delayed for two days had made preparations in that they had taken water up to the line in petrol cans. These were stacked in dugouts and along the trench and formed their reserve water supply. Their route to the trenches had been via Aveluy and Authuille. The day before the battle began the 17th HLI were in Bouzincourt and spent the night in huts.

Bouzincourt stands on a hill and Lt. Bentley Meadows who was with the battalion described the battlefield as being stretched out like a map below. Near the Crucifix on the Aveluy Road a long naval gun barked. Just behind the HLI there were 15 inch howitzers and around Albert there was a long line of observation balloons. The air was thick with aeroplanes and the German lines looked like long ribbons of white fur. The air was also full of shrapnel balls, especially over the woods and the villages that were burning. The Germans were putting shrapnel into the woods that lay in the triangle between Hamel, Bouzincourt and Aveluy. Here the Allied guns were massed and despite the troops putting cotton wool in their ears they were deaf for days after 1st July. Meadows also wrote that they made a bonfire using boxes from the CQM's stores and destroyed their letters and had a sing-song the last that the old 17th HLI was to have.

The objectives for the 36th (Ulster) Div. and the 32nd Div. for 1st July was for the German held territory from Grandcourt in the north to Miraumont to the south, which seems with hindsight a hopelessly optimistic task. The 32nd Div. planned to use most of their battalions in the attack against Leipzig Salient in the morning of 1st July and from the right they were the 2nd Manchesters, 1st Dorsets and 19th Lancashire Fusiliers, these three being part of the 14th Bde. To their left were the 11th Borders (Lonsdales), the 2nd KOYLI and the 17th HLI all of the 97th Bde. And to the left again were the 16th HLI and more companies of the 2nd KOYLI both of the 97th Bde.

On the evening of 'Z' Day the 17th HLI marched off by platoons and Meadows described the very heavy concentration of 18 pounders on the way up. They entered Oban Avenue at the right end of the village of Authuille. It was the 'up' stretch for the advance and Campbell Avenue was the down. The line in which they spent the night had almost been blown out of existence. They took up their battle positions and at 6.25 a.m. on the 1st July the final bombardment began. At 7.25 a.m. they left their trench and walked over to within 60 yards of the barrage. At 7.30 a.m. the barrage lifted and they rushed up the front line defences, destroying the garrison in and out of the dugouts. The HLI overran the Salient gaining its summit that was known to the British as Leipzig Redoubt.

Meadows wrote that they were working up between two communication trenches and after two or three rushes further progress was impossible. They therefore waited for their own reserve waves and also the 11th Borders (Lonsdales). The Lonsdales had moved up on the 30th June from dugouts built in to a high bank at Crucifix Corner to their assembly trenches in the thickest part of Authuille Wood. The battalion subsequently moved out of the wood and swung to the east. On leaving their trenches they had come under terrific machine gun fire. They were cut down opposite the redoubt, and had been massacred by enfilade fire from the Nord Werk and machine gun fire from the Ovillers Spur. Their commanding officer Lt. Col. P. W. Machell was one of their casualties. He is buried at Warloy–Baillon Communal Cemetery Extension. He had virtually raised and trained the whole of the 11th Border Battalion himself only to have them tragically cut down in the one morning – the 1st July. Meadows wrote that they began to work towards the communication trench, but owing to the lie of the land they were badly exposed. At about noon Meadows managed to leap the parapet. Around this time an order came up the trench that the 17th HLI were to move to the left and support the 1st Dorsets. Lt. Col. J. V. Shute the CO of the 1st Dorsets was wounded in the fighting. The communication trench was chiefly manned at this time by the 2nd KOYLI who should have given support to the 16th HLI who had been held up by the German wire and cut down before being able to take the first line of defence. They had suffered heavy machine gun fire from Thiepval Chateau. A few of the Lonsdales who had not been casualties had come up through Blighty Wood but were not able to give the 17th HLI much support, along with a company of the Manchesters. The barbed wire was impossible to cut through. At 5 p.m. the Germans counter-attacked but were repulsed. 'B' Company of the 17th HLI were caught up in the wire and cut to pieces by machine gun fire and Meadows' own 'A' Company was by this time very low in numbers. The battalions on the flanks of the attack were unsuccessful in storming the enemy's front line defences and thus the flanks of the 17th HLI were exposed and therefore blockades had to be formed at the front lines forward to their advanced positions, which developed into a series of bombing posts. The nature of the Leipzig defences, a maze of trenches and underground saps made advancing into the salient extremely difficult. Sgt. James Young Turnbull was awarded a posthumous VC for conspicuous bravery and devotion to duty, when having his party capture a post of apparently great importance to the enemy, he was subjected to severe counter-attacks, which were continuous through the whole day. Although his party was wiped out and replaced several times, he never wavered in his determination to hold the post. Almost single handed he maintained the position. Later in the day he was killed whilst bombing in a counter-attack from the parados of the Allied Trench. He is buried at Lonsdale Cemetery, named after the 11th Border Battalion who had suffered so grievously on this day.

The 17th HLI had reached Hindenburg Trench which was 150 yards beyond the redoubt but were repulsed by machine guns at the Wonderwork which forced them back to the redoubt. With the 1st Dorsets there were the remnants of five battalions in the salient at the end of the day. The Quarry was full of corpses.

In *Haig's Great Push* the achievement of holding on in the Leipzig Salient was described as a brilliant success. Gough wrote that it was a wonder that the British managed to hang on to this small holding. But the troops were set to work at once to dig good communication trenches back to their own lines.

On the morning of the 2nd July the 17th HLI handed over the front line of attack to Divisional Reserve and went into support. At sunset they were relieved by a Cheshire Batt. and moved back to dugouts at Crucifix Corner. The northern end of the salient was the most northerly point permanently secured by the first day's fighting, and a small party of the 32nd Div. were in the redoubt. On 2nd July the Germans made unsuccessful bombing attacks towards the redoubt. The objective of the 32nd Div. was now a south-north line from the eastern end of the redoubt to the Wonderwork on Thiepval Spur which was a frontage of 800 yards. On the 3rd the attack on the right was to be made by the 14th Bde. (32nd Div.) who had relieved the 97th Bde. of the same Division in the tip of the salient and on the left by the 75th Bde. who were attached to the 25th Div. The 75th Bde. had arrived and were in Aveluy and Martinsart Woods by 3.30 p.m. on the 2nd.

On 3rd July the attack of the 14th Bde. consisted of two companies of the 15th HLI from the tip of the salient entering the enemy front trench at around 6.15 a.m. and being driven out. Three hours later the 75th Bde. repeated the exercise with the same negative result. On the 5th the 1st Wiltshires (7th Bde. 25th Div.) gained a foothold in the Hindenburg Trench which was the German front line position in the salient. On the 6th Capt. H. L. G. Hughes of the RAMC went out looking for seven men who had been wounded under heavy fire and brought them back at night through a barrage. On the 7th July two companies of the 1st Wiltshires completed the capture of the German front line in the salient and held it with the assistance of the 3rd Worcs. of the same Bde., under severe bombardment.

The *Michelin Guide* to the battlefield describes the action on the 7th in the following way. 'The British carried the greater part of the Leipzig Redoubt (Hill 141), a powerful stronghold which protected Thiepval from the south, and consisting of a system of small blockhouses connected up by a network of trenches. A wide breach opened by the Artillery enabled the troops to gain a footing in the position and conquer it trench by trench'. The 36th Bde. of the 12th Div. had been kept on the south side of the spur in order to avoid as much as possible the machine gun fire from the salient.

On 15th July the 49th Div. repelled attacks on the salient that were delivered with gas bombs and flame throwers. At this time the salient was held by the 1/6th W. Yorks. (14th Bde. 49th Div.) and the night of 14th/15th July was much quieter than usual as both sides were thoroughly tired after a series of bombing stunts for which the W. Yorks. were acting as carriers, for the 1/7th W. Yorks. At about 3.30 a.m. in the morning they heard the terrifying shrieks of the sentries who had been caught without any warning by the German liquid fire attack. However the W. Yorks. beat off the counterattack, which lasted about three hours.

Corporal Robertson of the Worc. Regt. wrote that on the 19th July at 11.00 a.m. he was having a look around when suddenly about two dozen gas shells arrived. They came quietly and burst quietly. Heavy gas bombardment followed and lasted for three hours. Everything was coated yellowish green including their food.

On 17th August the Worcesters heard that they were due to go into the trenches in and around the salient again on the 18th. Charles Carrington wrote that the Warwicks Bde. carried the redoubt by a sudden attack with a limited objective. The 5th and 6th R. Warwicks (143rd Bde.) with their flanks covered by the 7th R. Warwicks went over the top in waves that followed close behind the barrage, the first creeping barrage that they had seen. A concentration of fire by 18 batteries on this small front.

On 21st August another attack had been planned and in the Redoubt all day final arrangements were being made in which the 25th and 48th Divs. were to be involved. At 6 p.m. there was a three minute barrage onto the German trench under cover of which two companies of the 1st Wiltshires the (7th Bde. 25th Div.) entered the German positions very quickly. On the right where the troops were close up to the German trench in which the enemy had a block a 'push pipe' was used for the first time with great success. It was a contrivance which bored a pipe at the rate of 18 yards an hour underground under the German trench. The pipe was full of ammonal and as the boring was silent the Germans were unaware of its presence. When the 1st Wiltshires began their advance the pipe was 'touched off' and in addition to blowing up the German block it made a ready made communication trench in their line, up which British bombing parties could rush. The Wiltshires attacked eastwards and captured important points in the German front and support line of the redoubt.

The 1/4 Glosters had begun their advance from the Nab Trenches to the south of the salient and advanced to attack the south-east face of the salient, behind an excellent barrage. The 1/6 Glosters entered the Hindenburg Trench and virtually surrounded the salient.

2nd Lt. L. A. Bessant of the REs was awarded the MC for work achieved on this day when he laid out and superintended the work on 250 yards of communication trench up to the captured trenches under heavy shell fire. On 23rd August a further attack was postponed and the line was rearranged to take a bigger objective. On the 24th the 1st Wilts. and 3rd Worcs. with the aid of push pipes again assaulted the German positions. There was furious hand to hand fighting and the British battalions inflicted frightful losses on the enemy. On the 26th they were relieved by the 7th Bde. (25th Div.) except for the 8th Loyal North Lancs. who were to carry out a small attack in the left hand corner of the salient. This they did at 6 p.m. but without success. The 75th Bde. also of the 25th Div. was in Authuille Wood at this time. On the 31st August the 8th Borders (75th Bde. 25th Div.) in their trenches in the salient were relieved at daybreak.

On 2nd September the Germans shelled in every direction on all the communication trenches, bridges over the Ancre, Blighty Valley, Authuille etc. and the 3rd Worc. marched forward from Bouzincourt in order to have another crack at the salient. They went via Blackhorse Bridge near Authuille. This time they were to attack the western side of a small salient from the original line further down the slope. The attack was destroyed by the German artillery and Colonel Gibbs was killed.

Later in the month Blunden describes the captured German work called the Leipzig Redoubt, with its underworld comforts, from bakehouse to boudoir. Their companies (Royal Sussex) were accommodated there, while the Battalion HQ was at a spot called Tithe Barn in Authuille Wood which was made up of sandbags and tin.

The redoubt is now a disused chalk quarry which has been planted with poplars, and a visitor to the spot can very easily appreciate the tremendous advantage that the Germans had here, with the whole of the hill within their lines.

Le Sars

Le Sars is a small village that straddles the main Albert–Bapaume road. To the south is Courcelette, to the north-west Pys and Miraumont, to the south-east Eaucourt l'Abbaye. To the north-east is the Butte de Warlencourt and just off the main Albert road south-west of le Sars is the site of Destremont Farm.

In *The War in the Air* it was reported that on 6th July in the afternoon pilots of No. 21 Squadron had bombed enemy dumps at le Sars and on the 21st No.

4 Squadron reported that new entrenchments could be seen around le Sars and Courcelette, and No. 3 Squadron discovered a new line between le Transloy and Warlencourt and a doubling up of the third line between Eaucourt and Flers.

The ground slopes downwards from le Sars towards the village of Warlencourt. East of le Sars there was a sunken road and also a very strongly held quarry to the north-west of the village.

On 1st October a battalion of the Durhams attacked le Sars but were unable to consolidate. Norman Gladden who was in the area with the 7th North'd Fus. described the area as being of dirty brown slime and mud which was criss-crossed with trenches here and there. On the horizon beyond the German positions were trees and open country. In a recess just behind the North'd Fus. a Vickers machine gun had been set up to assist in the barrage which would protect the attackers.

On 4th October Sec. Lt. H. T. Kelly of the 10th Duke's gained the VC for his actions. He had been born in 1887 and his citation reads in part that he showed the utmost valour in an attack on the Flers Line, immediately to the south-west of le Sars. He twice rallied his company under the heaviest fire, and eventually led the only three available men left in his company into the enemy trench, there bombing until two of his men became casualties and enemy reinforcements arrived. He then carried his wounded Company Sergeant Major back to his trenches, a distance of 70 yards, and subsequently three others.

On 7th October, the 47th Div. to the right and the 23rd Div. to the front of le Sars were to first make an advance of 500 yards which would involve the capture of le Sars. The remains of the village was to be secured when the attack was resumed again, on the Butte and Gird Lines, known as the Warlencourt Line.

In his book *All Our Yesterdays*, H. M. Tomlinson described the area of le Sars. He wrote that the village was most foul and full of dreadful heaps that had once been a community. There was a track through it and the sound of machine gun fire was not far off. Batt. HQ was at le Coupe Queule. Beyond le Sars was Loupart Wood which was a wooded ridge beyond the German lines. It had been full of MGS because of its protection of Bapaume. A famous sign nearby was Via Dolorosa. Cut Throat Corner was an Aid Post in the district and was a deep cave where surgeons did their work. There was also a deep German dugout in the village which had two entrances to it. It was the bad weather as much as anything that ended the advance in this area as there was continuous rain. The crest of the rise that overlooked Bapaume was to mark the limit of the British advance. On 25th November rations were brought by limber to Destrement Farm when the 1/4 O & BLI (145th Bde. 48th Div.) were at le Sars.

Hexham Road that led from Warlencourt to Eaucourt gave its name to the Cemetery which is on the west side of l'Abbaye grounds.

Le Sars was lost in March 1918 and retaken by the New Zealand Infantry in August of the same year.

Lesboeufs

Lesboeufs is on the D 74 road between Morval and Guedecourt. To the north is Bapaume and to the north-west le Transloy.

On 15th September it was the plan for High Wood and Martinpuich to be taken, and also that to their right Flers, Guedecourt, Lesboeufs and Morval should be captured. It is the attempt to capture Lesboeufs that I am concerned with here. There are numerous accounts of the involvement of the Guards on this day including the histories of regiments, also in memoirs by Harold Macmillan and Oliver Lyttleton for example. The plan was that the Guards Brigades should take four lines of objectives which all had a different colour code, green, brown, blue and red. This would give them Flers Ridge which covered the approaches to Bapaume and Lesboeufs to the east of Flers. They were to be supported by ten tanks and then the Cavalry was to be brought up for the breakthrough.

On the night before, the Guards came up the line from bivouacs at Carnoy via Montauban, they saw there many artillery batteries who were firing on the German positions. In fact the barrage lasted for three days and became a 'creeping barrage' when the attack finally began.

Lyttleton who was with the 3rd Gren. Guards of the 2nd Guards Bde. as adjutant to its commanding officer Lt. Col. B. N. Sergison-Brooke (later to become a Lt. General) writes in his memoir, that they set off in the dark along the road through Montauban then crossed a wood and were not shelled and came to an area of ground which was like a 'rough sea', grassless and featureless. They made their way up a slope and there were a few salvoes of gas shells.

Rudyard Kipling says that the 1st Guards Bde. moved on the 14th to shellholes and fragments of trench that were to form their assembly positions which were on a front of about 500 yards between Delville Wood and the left or western side of Ginchy.

The Guards were in XIV Corps and the boundary line with XV Corps on the left ran from the junction of the Ginchy–Flers and the Ginchy–Guedecourt roads, a little to the north of Ginchy and along the latter road for about 800 yards.

To the right of the two Guards Brigades were the 56th Div. and on their left the 6th Div. who flanked the Guards. The 56th Div. were to establish themselves in Combles Ravine and move towards Bouleux Wood. The 6th Div. with the Guards were to advance in a north-easterly direction and to cover the highest part of the ridge to Morval and Lesboeufs. Three tanks were to take the Quadrilateral which was a German strongpoint to the north-east of Ginchy. To the right of the line the 169th Bde. was to almost reach its objectives for the day and the 6th Div. beginning at 6.20 a.m. which was zero hour for the battle to start, attacked the Quadrilateral that lay behind a crest of high ground, and was protected by wire which lay in a depression. On this front the 16th Bde. met deadly machine gun fire.

The Guards formed up amidst shell craters clear of Ginchy because the ruins were frequently bombarded by the enemy. On the right was the 2nd Guards Bde. under Brig. Gen. John Ponsonby (later General Sir John). The 3rd Gren. Guards and the 1st Coldst. Guards were in front and the 1st Scots Guards and the 2nd Irish Guards were behind them. To the left of the 2nd Guards Bde. was the 1st Guards Bde. under Brig. Gen. Pereira. The 2nd Coldst. Guards and the 3rd Coldst. Guards were in the front with the 1st Irish in the second line and the 2nd Gren. Guards in the rear. The Colst. Guards were to carry the advance as far as the third or blue line which was in front of Lesboeufs. Of the ten tanks only three turned up and these were not successful. They had moved up from the Loop. The 2nd Guards Bde. had its HQ in Dummy Trench west of Trônes Wood and the 1st Guards Bde. had theirs in Bernafay Wood.

The early morning was misty and the ground was still wet and slippery as there had been a lot of rain in the days before the 15th.

Battalion HQ of the 3rd Gren. Guards under its commanding officer Lt. Col. B. N. Sergison-Brooke, Lyttleton the Adjutant, the Signals Officer, the Sergeant Major, Drill Sergeant and HQ Signallers were established in a few shell holes between the first and second waves of the attack. The attackers themselves formed up in the open and at 6 p.m., the heavy guns barraged the enemy lines and the Germans barraged Ginchy, but the Guardsmen were just clear of the village, as already noted. At 6.20 a.m. the attackers set off under a creeping barrage but immediately they were met by withering fire from the direction of the Quadrilateral to the north-east which had clearly not been silenced by the Guards' flanking Brigades of the 6th Div. The Coldstreams who had three battalions in the front lines advanced too far over to the left, and the 3rd Grenadier Guards, the other front battalion, carried straight on towards their objectives. This resulted in a gap between it and the three Coldstream Battalions. The 2nd Gren. Gds. a supporting battalion of the 1st Guards Bde. lost sight of the Coldstreams and advanced with its right on the Ginchy–Lesboeufs Road and came across a trench full of Germans instead of Guardsmen. In the muddle the Coldstreamers assumed quite wrongly that they had reached at least their third objective when they had only reached their first, which was beyond a German strong point named The Triangle. The 1st Guards Bde. had been under fire from the junction of Pint Trench and the sunken part of the Flers road. The 1st Irish Guards who were in the second line of the 1st Guards Bde. were close up in the attack and suffered many casualties together with the Coldstreamers.

During the fighting Sergison-Brooke was wounded and Lt. Col. Guy Baring CO of the 1st Coldst. Guards was killed (to be later buried at the Citadel New Cemetery). The fighting was very confused and Oliver Lyttleton organised a party of Guardsmen from various Guards Battalions that totalled about a hundred men and put himself in command.

At one point Lyttleton recalls seeing Lt. Col John Campbell, CO of the 3rd Colst. Guards in a nearby shell-hole together with his famous hunting horn. Campbell was to receive the VC for his leadership during the battle. The outskirts of Lesboeufs was just in front of Lyttleton's party and he joined up with

Major Rocke down the hill towards the village. A large party of Germans attacked them and the two sides fought and became confused. At one point Lyttleton threw down a pistol which was devoid of ammunition and the German party mistakenly took it to be a bomb and retreated in good order. Casualties had been very heavy. The rapid fire of the party put paid to another counter-attack and Lyttleton was ordered to report to Brigadier John Ponsonby, whose HQ was in a trench which was covered by galvanised sheets and camouflage. Later Lyttleton met up with Cecil Boyd Rochfort of the Scots Guards who was marching with some details. They tramped across the Ginchy Valley using duckboards. The valley was being shelled heavily.

In mid afternoon the 1st and 2nd Bdes. had each been reinforced by a battalion from the 3rd Guards Bde. The 4th Gren. Guards moved up at about 5 p.m. and had reached the third objective in front of Lesboeufs. The attack was delayed until the next day, the 16th.

The Guards Bdes. were a sort of big happy family that in many cases combined the best qualities of the British Aristocracy, brains and leadership. To read their histories is like reading down a page of *Who's Who*. Casualties were very heavy and officer casualties particularly so, and these included Raymond Asquith (in command of the Fourth Company of the 3rd Gren. Guards) who was shot in the chest very soon after the battle began. One commentator sums up the days events on this part of the front in one very accurate sentence. 'The front of attack was too narrow, the objectives were too distant, and from the start the flanks were enfiladed'. This is why it was to be another ten days before Lesboeufs fell to the Allies. Asquith in letters home had rated his chances of survival to be very slim. Seventeen out of twenty officers in the 3rd Gren. Guards were either killed or wounded in the day's fighting.

Oliver Lyttleton who was not wounded in the day's fighting describes in his Memoirs, the Guards as being the 'best human organisation, the most efficient and the most closely knit'. Another commentator describes the 3rd Gren. Gds. as being the best Battalion in the Guards Division at that time. Harold Macmillan in his Memoirs voiced similar views. The Guards were undoubtedly something special. I have already mentioned John Campbell as receiving the VC for rallying the 2nd and 3rd Coldstream Guards with the aid of a hunting horn, the other VC holder from this same battle was Lance Sgt. F. McNess of the 1/Scots Guards who had led a bombing party even after being severely wounded. On the 16th September Lord Cavan who was XIV Corps Commander informed Lyttleton that he was to be awarded the DSO for his achievements on the day before. His Battalion was back at camp at the Citadel south of Fricourt. Orders for the 16th were that the third Objective and then Lesboeufs were to be taken. This would form a defensive flank towards Morval and would link up on the left. The Guards Bde. were to use the 61st Bde. of the 20th Div. and the 3rd Guards Bde. Zero hour was 9.25 a.m. and the 61st Bde. went forward behind a creeping barrage and were able to reach the original third objective, in front of Lesboeufs. On their left the 3rd Guards Bde. began late and made little headway. The 1st Gren Gds. and 1st Welsh Gds. had to dig in where they were facing, north instead of north-east.

The Guards Div. were relieved altogether on this front by the 60th and 59th Bdes. of the 20th Div. The 10th KRRC of the 59th Bde. who had come up from the Bois des Tailles relieved the 2nd Gren. Gds. in support. The 10th and 11th Rif. Bde. the 59th Bde. were unsuccessful in an attack and the 60th Bde. in the right sector of the 20th Div. attacked south of the Ginchy–Lesboeufs Road on the 17th. Mark Tennant was killed by a shell on the 18th.

On 19th September the remainder of the Guards Bde. attended a church service and were later thanked for what they had achieved by Brigadier John Ponsonby. During this time there was more rain which made conditions even more difficult for the men and for transport, roads and tracks got very slimy and increasingly difficult to negotiate. After two or three days rest the Guards were to relieve the 20th Div. in the line and had gone up via reserve trenches at Waterlot Farm close to Longueval.

In brief the plan for the 25th September was, from right to left, that the 56th Div. were to form the flank in front of Combles, for the 5th Div. on their left to take Morval, for the 6th Div. to occupy the southern part of Lesboeufs and for the Guards Div. to take the rest of Lesboeufs. This time the 1st and the 3rd Guards Bdes. were to be involved in the frontal advance. The 1st Guards Bde. was on the right and the 3rd Guards Bde. to their left. In the front of the 1st Guards Bde. were the 2nd Gren. Gds. and the 1st Irish Gds. and they were supported by the 2nd and 3rd Colds. Gds. On their left in the 3rd Guards Bde. the 4th Gren. Gds. and the 2nd Scots Gds. were to the front and were supported by the 1st Welsh Gds. The creeping barrage came down at 12.35 p.m. which was zero hour and it seems that the enemy were taken by surprise. Anyway whatever the reason, quick progress was made by the attacking Guardsmen. Unlike the situation on the 15th September, close contact was kept up beween the flanks and the 3rd Guards Bde. sent the 1st Gren. Gds. forward at 3.30 p.m. to enter the north part of Lesboeufs. Lesboeufs and Morval after they had both been captured were kept clear of troops and bombarded. There had only been one real hitch and that was that the 21st Div. on the left of the Guards attack was held up and the left flank of the Guards Div. was subsequently left in the air and the 4th Gren. Gds. had to throw out a defensive flank to the left.

Kipling in his history of the Irish Guards said that the plan for the 25th was much less ambitious than that of the 15th September. The distance to the first objective was 300 yards, to the second 700 yards and to the last 1,300 yards. In each case he says that the objective was a clearly defined one. Also the ground sloped down towards Lesboeufs. In addition the artillery did its work more accurately than on the 15th. The casualties were nevertheless very high and especially amongst the officers again.

On 26th September the 3rd Gren. Gds. moved up to Trônes Wood and the 1st Scots Guards were sent up as relief at Lesboeufs. On the 29th the 3rd Gren. Gds. relieved the 1st Scots Gds. in front of Lesboeufs. Henry Dundas who was with the Scots Gds. was temporary adjutant as well as bombing officer. They were 'beside' Lesboeufs. On the 29th they were in support line and on the 30th they went back to tents or billets, and to a training area south-west of Amiens on the 2nd October.

Lyttleton wrote that after the Guards Div. was relieved they were allotted the task of building a railway in the Somme Valley. They were close to the river and established themselves in a comfortable camp on one of the islands. He describes the valley as a place of great beauty and peace which was bathed in Autumn light.

On 4th October the London Scottish (168th Bde. 56th Div.) relieved the London Rifle Bde. (169th Bde. 56th Div.) to the east of at the bottom of the valley.

H. N. Todd who served with the Queen's Westminsters was killed in the fighting on 7th October, he had written verse that was published in a book called *Poems and Plays*. He was born in 1878 and was a schoolmaster before the war. He was killed near Dewdrop and Spectrum Trenches. Another poet who was killed near the village was Leslie Coulson of the 2nd London Royal Fusiliers. He was a former journalist and had published a volume called *From Outpost and Other Poems*. He was an NCO whereas Todd was a private. Coulson had seen fighting at Gallipoli and in April 1916 was attached to the 1/12th London Regiments (Rangers). He had been in the Somme fighting on 1st July. He is buried at Grove Town Cemetery near Bray.

On the 14th the 2nd Sher. For. (71st Bde. 6th Div.) were ordered to attack a certain gun in the north of the village and also some new German trenches. In supervising this operation their CO Colonel C. Hobbs was mortally wounded.

Between the 12th-18th October there were further attacks made to the east of the Lesboeufs–Guedecourt line. The trenches around Lesboeufs by this time were in a very poor state and battalions reported that they were up to their knees in mud. In the period 17th-19th October the 1st Rif. Bde. (11th Bde. 4th Div.) were involved in a night attack to the left of Lesboeufs and on 19th October the 2nd Rif. Bde. (25th Bde. 8th Div.) were in trenches to the east. During the day 23rd-24th October the 1st and 2nd Rif. Bde. Battalions were involved in an attack but made little progress.

Also around 23rd October the 2nd R. Welch Fus. which included the writer Frank Richards were lent to the 4th Div. for a time and took over trenches in front of Lesboeufs. The German trenches were directly facing them from in front of le Transloy, which was to the north-west. About sixty yards behind the front line was a small trench which they used as an advance Signal Station. Messages were brought by runners who used the old German communication trenches, to this station. They were transmitted back to Batt. HQ which was in a sunken road about 500 yards behind. It had been raining and it was like a sea of mud, the ground just a series of connected shell holes. They later returned to a sunken road on the edge of Trônes Wood, where they were billeted in huts.

On 23rd October Sgt. R. Downie of the 2nd R. Dub. Fus. (10th Bde. 4th Div.) gained the VC. He was born in 1894 and he was given the highest award for his bravery and devotion to duty in an attack, when most of the officers had become casualties. Downie took over and despite the heavy fire he re-organised the attack, which had been temporarily checked. The position which had resisted previous attempts to take it was won by his bravery, courage and initiative.

On 28th October the 4th Suffolks (98th Bde. 33rd Div.) occupied some poor front line trenches of newly gained ground in front of Lesboeufs and on the same day Dewdrop Trench fell to the 98th Bde.

By early November the mud in the area was appalling. On 2nd November the 2nd R. Welch Fus. (19th Bde.) were here with their HQ in a German chalk dugout in a bank facing the 'wrong way' in a sunken road about 800 yards north-west of Lesboeufs Church. On the 4th they knew that the cemetery at le Transloy was to be their objective, which was about a mile away perched on the highest ridge in the area.

Also in early November the 1st KOSB (8th Bde. 29th Div.) were in the line between Lesboeufs and le Transloy which was still in German hands. The line at this point faced north-eastwards and was also the extreme right of the British line. The French 152nd Div. touched the KOSB at this point. The Borderers took over the front trenches from the 2nd Lincs. (25th Bde. 8th Div.)

On 6th November Lt. E. P. Bennett of the 2nd Worc. Batt. (100th Bde. 33rd Div.) was awarded the VC for his involvement in the fighting towards le Transloy (see that entry). These attacks were still being pursued despite the very adverse conditions for an advance.

In the period 10th/11th November the 2nd W. Yorks. (23rd Bde.) relieved the 2nd Devons of the same Bde. in the front line. This sector taken over was at the apex of the salient formed by the offensive, a little to the left of Lesboeufs. Sidney Rogerson reported in his memoirs *Twelve Days* that the Citadel Camp was only about 6 miles behind the le Transloy Line yet the distance took a very long time to cover in the conditions. They had to wind their way along crazy duck-board tracks, past holes in the ground many of which were occupied by men, until as dawn was breaking they reached the HQ of the Devons, in a sunken road to the left of Lesboeufs Wood. On the 14th the 1st KOSB bussed to Buire sue Ancre and then marched to Lesboeufs.

In walking the battlefields in this area it is as well to appreciate the tremendous importance of the sunken roads many of which can still be easily traced, they virtually divide up the battlefield. One such road linked up with le Transloy. Thistle and High Alley were important communication trenches.

The Guards Cemetery is half a mile to the south-west of the village, on the north-west of the road to Ginchy. The 1916 fighting is commemorated by the Grenadier Guards Memorial, further along the road towards Ginchy. The cemetery itself was greatly increased by a concentration of graves from the battlefield and small cemeteries around Lesboeufs. At the time of the Armistice it contained only about forty graves of men from the 2nd Gren. Gds. who had fallen on the 25th September. Many of the dead were brought in from places such as Ginchy, ADS Cemetery, Needle Dump Cemetery, Lesboeufs Cemetery and Switch Trench Cemetery Flers where most of the graves were of Australian soldiers. The Guards Cemetery is an indication of the very great losses and sacrifice made by Britain's premier Division.

In *Goodbye to the Battlefields* H.A. Taylor wrote that a visit to this cemetery completed the story partly told by the Guillemont Road Cemetery of how dearly the Guards Brigades paid in the attack they launched against Lesboeufs; this is enhanced by the Guards Memorial on the Ginchy Road. He says also that standing near the cemetery, one can understand why the enemy clung so desperately to Lesboeufs, Guedecourt and Morval, as from the ridge one could see the Bapaume–Peronne Road, the best means of communication running parallel to the former German front. To the south-west of the Guards Cemetery is a memorial to Capt. H.P. Meakin (3rd Cold. Gds.) killed on 25th September 1916. He is commemorated on the Thiepval Memorial.

Le Transloy

Le Transloy is on the N 37 main road between Bapaume to the north-west and Sailly–Saillisel to the south-east. The name le Transloy was given to the battle for the Transloy Ridges whose official dates were 7th to the 20th of October, rather than to the village itself.

To the south-west is the village of Lesboeufs from which the battle on the extreme right of the line was to be launched, although the French were to be involved even further to the right in co-operation with the British and in the direction of Sailly. The trench names in the sector between Lesboeufs and le Transloy which appear again and again in the account of fighting on this front over the next two weeks include Rainy, Hazy, Cloudy, Spectrum, Misty and Rainbow.

The attack on the ridges was planned for the 5th and because of poor and wet weather, was postponed until the 7th October. A bombardment began from the British side at 3.15 p.m. on the 6th. Companies sheltered in the valley to the south of the Guedecourt–le Transloy Road. The task of the 56th Div. who were in the Lesboeufs sector included the capture of disconnected trenches known as Hazy, Spectrum and part of Rainbow and the second objective was to establish a line on the forward slope of the ridges from which the le Transloy system could be seen. The attack was to be in conjunction with the French to the right.

To the left of the 56th Div. front was the 20th Div. and their role was to establish a position on the top of the ridge that overlooked both le Transloy and the village of Beaulencourt which was to the north-west. This line might then serve as a point of departure for a further advance against these places. The first objective for the 20th Div. was Rainbow Trench which was on the near side of the crest; the next objective included Cloudy Trench and was about 1,200 yards of the Brown Line facing the original Divisional front.

The assault itself finally began at 1.45 p.m. on 7th October the 1/4 London and the 1/14th London Scottish (168th Bde.) and the 1/1 London and 1/7th Middlesex (167th Bde.) were involved. The London Scottish captured the southern group of gunpits and part of Hazy Trench beyond. The 1/12 London (Rangers) failed in front of Dewdrop Trench. The 1/10 London met with no success against Spectrum Trench. The battalions then had to withdraw that evening. To the left the 60th and 61st Bdes. (20th Div.) made some progress and held their trenches until the night of the 8th/9th when they were relieved by the 6th Div.

On the 8th the 56th Div. attacked again at 3.30 p.m. and the LRB of the 169th Bde. reached Hazy Trench but again that night there had to be a withdrawal. Between 8th and 11th October the 56th Div. was relieved by the 4th Div. On 12th October another attempt was made and zero hour was 2.05 p.m. The 10th Bde. (4th Div.) was to attack with the French on their right and the 12th Bde. of the 4th Div. was also to be also involved. To their left the three Bdes. of the 6th Div. were to assist namely the 16th, 71st and the 18th.

Lord Cavan, who was in command of XIV Corps in this sector, protested to Haig as to whether these continuous attacks through the mud towards le Transloy were necessary, just in order to help the left flank of the French, or was it a plan to sacrifice British lives just for this? Unfortunately, but hardly surprisingly there had been no real progress by mid October in achieving the original objectives of the 5th of October. On the 14th the 2nd Seaforths (10th Bde. 4th Div.) made a surprise attack but a counter-attack drove them back. The 2nd R. Dub. Fus. also made no progress. There was more heavy rain and the conditions grew worse and worse, and all hope of Allied progress had gone. The good news was that the French had reached and gained parts of Sailly–Saillisel by mid October.

Capt. E. R. Street, DSO, who was with the 2nd Sherwood For. (71st Bde. 6th Div.) and who had become a company commander was killed in action when involved in the fighting for the gunpits close to Hazy and Cloudy Trenches east of the Lesboeufs–Guedecourt Road.

Capt. R. Johnstone of the RFC was awarded the MC for turning Allied artillery on to columns of German infantry and on one occasion he carried out counter-battery work in cloud and mist at 800 feet under heavy fire from the ground.

On 18th October the attack continued with zero hour at 3.40 a.m. and with the conditions as bad as they could be, with water and mud in the trenches and shell holes, the attackers also had to begin their advance in the dark. It is not surprising that the 4th Div. made slow progress. It was to be the conditions that were to bring the battle to a close in this area as much as anything, and the historian of the 8th Div. describes the whole great enterprise as coming to an end, drowned in a sea of mud and rain. On 19th October the 24th and 25th Bde. (8th Div.) went forward from reserve positions in and around Trônes and Bernafay Woods, in order to relieve the 6th Div. in the line. It was another day of incessant rain. The roads or tracks were deep in liquid mud and crowded with traffic. The change over process was a lengthy one as a result but was completed during the night of 19th/20th October. At 9 a.m. on the 20th General Hudson took command of the Lesboeufs/Guedecourt front, being the left sector of XIV Corps. On the night of the 21st the 23rd Bde. also

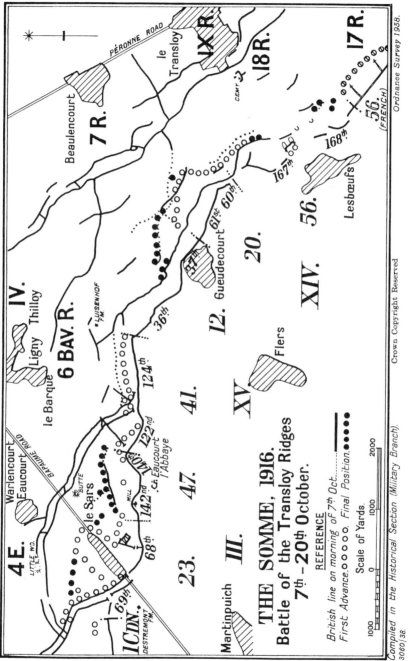

THE SOMME, 1916.
Battle of the Transloy Ridges
7th – 20th October.

REFERENCE

British line on morning of 7th Oct........
First Advance.ooooo. Final Position.•••••

Scale of Yards.

Ordnance Survey 1938.

Crown Copyright Reserved

Compiled in the Historical Section (Military Branch).
3060/38.

of the 8th Div. took over part of the 4th Div's front to the right of the 25th Bde., and the whole of the 8th Div. was once more in the line. With the arrival of the 8th Div. the weather took a turn for the better and the days were bright and the nights frosty which improved conditions. Preparations for a fresh assault were made for the 23rd October. The operation should prepare the way for a later attack on le Transloy from the south-west. The preliminary bombardment was in progress when the 8th Div. came into the line. On 23rd October the 25th Bde. was meant to capture the remainder of Zenith Trench midway between Guedecourt and le Transloy and them similarly establish a line beyond it with the 23rd Bde.

General Jack wrote in his diary that around 5 a.m. on the 23rd October that the 2nd West Yorks (23rd Bde.) reached Windmill and Shine Trenches. The late arrival of the battalion was due to its having been required by the staff, after Jack had gone on ahead the previous day, to carry stores of ammunition, of which duty he had received no notice. As it turned out they were not required for 'major exertions' that day. The attack on le Transloy was to be carried out by the extreme right of the 8th Div. with the 4th Div. to its right, the 25th Bde. on its left and the 24th Bde. further to the left of them. The 2nd Cameronians and the 2nd Middlesex carried out the 23rd Bde. attack and captured Zenith Trench which was in front of them and pushed on to Orion Trench. Unfortunately the neighbouring units were unable to keep abreast which prevented further advances and the subsequent counter-attacks meant that many gains were lost. On 27th October Jack was instructed to prepare for bombing attacks in order to clear out the enemy from the parts of Zenith Trench which were still in his hands. The *Official History* mentions that it was captured by the 17th Div. which had relieved the 8th Div. at the end of October. The part taken was the south-western face of the German salient midway between the two villages.

In early November Henry Dundas (Scots Guards) reported as being alternatively close to le Transloy or in a dugout by the side of a hill beside the road to Combles. Throughout October and well into November the French strove to take Saillisel, with the British co-operating with them. On 2nd November the 17th Div. captured the remaining section of Zenith Trench and a new trench was dug to connect with Misty Trench.

On the 4th November the 2nd R. Welch Fus. were warned to be ready for a three or four division attack planned for the 5th. The cemetery in front of le Transloy was to be the objective and they were to dig in about 200 yards beyond the crest of the ridge, but little progress was made because of the openness of the ground. On the 5th November some success was gained by the 2nd Worc. (100th Bde. 33rd Div.) who had concentrated in the French area and had struggled forward to their objective which was to be called Bennett Trench after Lt. E. P. Bennett. The position is described in *The Machine Gunner* as being opposite le Transloy the infantry squatting like ducks in the mud. They were accompanied by two machine guns from the 100th MGC. Bennett of the 2/Worcs. had been born in 1892 and was awarded the VC for what he did at this time when in command of the second wave of the attack. Finding that the first wave had suffered very heavy casualties, including its commander, he advanced at the head of the second wave and reached their objective with 60 men. His small party became isolated and he took steps to condolidate his position under heavy machine gun fire from both flanks and although he was wounded he remained in command and there was little doubt according to the citation that but for his courage the attack would have been checked at the outset.

Leuze Wood

Leuze Wood or Lousy Wood as the British inevitably called it, straddles the D 20 Road along with Bouleux Wood, as it enters the village of Combles from the direction of Guillemont. To the south is the site of Falfemont Farm which is in Falfemont Wood. During the second phase of the battle of the Somme the wood occupied a very commanding position, northwards and eastwards, though the view was partially restricted by the Morval Spur. It overlooked the basin and both branches of Combles Valley and the main valley, while southwards, it commanded all the low ground between Hardecourt and Guillemont.

The wood is roughly rectangular in shape, with a narrow extension to the north-east which takes the name of Bouleux Wood. The main road here as it leaves the cover of the trees, drops rapidly down the hill to Combles. This sunken road was a very marked feature and a source of trouble to the British in their several attacks. The wood itself consisted of bare stumps and was thickly entangled with barbed wire. Its southern face was lined by a number of German gun emplacements and in 1982 there was still a surviving German pillbox of the two man variety in existence in the south-west corner. Loop Trench was 300 yards to the east of Leuze Wood and ran parallel to its edge, the sunken road from Ginchy to Combles and the northern edge of the Wood. The capture and holding of this position was a prerequisite to the capture of Combles which was to fall to a combined 'pinching out' by the Allies. On the 4th September the Germans had delivered a counter-attack on the newly won British position in the vicinity of Mouquet Farm which was easily repulsed by the Australians. To the right of the battlefield Wedge Wood was captured and also ground to the north of Falfemont Farm was gained. On the 5th the British were nearly a mile to the east of Guillemont and had reached Leuze Wood. By the evening the whole of the wood had been taken which brought the British to less than a thousand yards from Combles. All the ground between Leuze Wood and Falfemont Farm had been taken, as had the ground between the wood and Ginchy.

According to the *Official History*, during the night 5th/6th September the 8th R. Irish Fus. relieved the 1st Devons (95th Bde. 5th Div.) and on the 6th they advanced in the morning across the Combles/Ginchy Road. On the right Bouleux Wood was entered, but all day a German barrage was maintained against the south-west corner of Leuze Wood. During the night patrols of the 56th Div. were to take over. Patrols from the left of the 16th Div. had tried to advance along the light railway track in the early morning of the 6th, but lost many men from fire at the Quadilateral, when they reached the higher ground and could not go further. The 49th Bde. of the 16th Div. advanced by swinging forward its left from the Guillemont–Leuze Wood to the north-east. The attack of the R. Irish Fus. had reached as far as a cornfield in front of Combles but they had to withdraw to shellholes in the area of Falfemont Farm.

The very best historian of the wood fighting was J. F. Tucker who served with the 13th London Batt. (Kensingtons) 168th Bde. 56th Div. and has only recently died. He wrote about it in his memoirs *Johnny Get Your Gun*. They had been at Maricourt and had travelled for about seven miles before reaching Angle Wood Valley. The top of the ridge on their left had shallow dugouts and strongpoints, which overlooked the valley that they had just come across. On the right was a steep embankment which faced the German lines, and half a mile along the ridge was Wedge Wood which was a small and by now, a shattered copse. The Kensingtons were on the extreme right of the British Army. At Wedge Wood Tucker's party entered a trench which was full of dead Prussian Guards clad in white vests and trousers. Apparently they had come from bathing at Combles and because of the heat of the day had been given permission to wear these clothes which they had paraded in. Further on Tucker was to come across more bodies of the R. Irish Fus. some had obviously been killed by concussion, and many unexploded bright steel shells lay about which he thought were either whizz bangs or even French 75s. Tucker later saw a battery of French 75s firing over Leuze Wood and noted that half of the shells were prematures. A few of the survivors of the Irish Fus. came by the Kensingtons and said that they had been only stopped by a wired trench which had been concealed in standing corn, probably Combles Trench. The Kensingtons emerged and took up positions in shellholes which they connected by digging a trench line between the southern corner of Leuze Wood to beyond Falfemont Farm. The battalion was in touch with the left flank of the French Army south of Falfemont Farm. Tucker also reported seeing the signs of a detachment of Daccan Horse, a cavalry patrol which had obviously been ambushed. Tucker tells us that they were relieved from time to time and went back into reserve trenches for a few hours or a day or so, but they were still under shell fire in places such as Maltzhorn Farm, Casement Trench, Chimpanzee Trench and Waterlot Farm. Frontal attacks were attempted by the 56th Div. but without success.

In *The Machine Gunner* Russell wrote that in early September that he was detailed to join the 13th MG Company which was attached to the 13th Bde. (5th Div.). He joined them in Leuze Wood on the 8th September. The wood had been a stronghold and had only recently been captured from the Germans by the 16th Irish Div. Russell saw tanks and also masses of Allied dead at Leuze Wood. Company HQ and those of the Infantry Batts. were in a large quarry half circular in shape, with numerous German constructed dugouts built into the high wall face. It was situated not 25 yards behind the infantry front line positions. At 11.30 p.m. on the 8th according to the history of the

Queen's Westminsters the London Rifle Bde. of the 169th Bde. and the QVRs of the same Bde. carried out a combined bombing attack, with the object of establishing a line along Loop Trench, the sunken road and the northern edge of Leuze Wood. The QVR succeeded in occupying a trench that ran close alongside the northern edge of the Ginchy–Combles Road, but about 5.15 a.m. on the 9th the LRB who had made some progress, were driven back into Leuze Wood by a strong counter-attack. The 56th Div. had relieved the right of the 168th Bde. by the 169th Bde., the LRB occupying the southern part of Leuze Wood. The 168th Bde. took over the ground to the left along the Leuze Wood–Guillemont Road thus relieving the 49th Bde. (16th Div.). At 11.30 p.m. on the 8th the 169th Bde. attempted to push south-east towards Combles, the LRB bombing down Combles Trench from Leuze Wood. A heavy counter-attack early next morning compelled withdrawal. On the 9th the 169th Bde. had the task of establishing a defence line along the slopes of Combles Ravine and the LRB advanced from the south-east edge of Leuze Wood against Loop Trench but was forced to retire. The Westminsters were sent up in the evening and they were to drive the Germans out of Leuze Wood if they made a foooting there. They had to move over very difficult ground, and went through a severe barrage in passing over the Falfemont Farm line. They reached Leuze Wood by 11 p.m. Loop Trench was to be taken. The night was a very dark one and the wood was full of barbed wire entanglements and the Germans were shelling the wood heavily.

The fighting here was very tough indeed and the Allied line was not to be straightened for three days. Before the Kensingtons were relieved Tucker saw a tall tree trunk that had been used as a German lookout and would have given a wonderful view for miles but had been abandoned once the British had got too close. The Kensingtons themselves could see beyond Death or Angle Wood Valley and towards Guillemont, Ginchy and Lesboeufs. The battalion was relieved and reformed and marched off past the Citadel Camp and on to Morlancourt.

On 10th September at 7 a.m. in heavy mist the Westminsters attacked south-eastwards from Leuze Wood under the cover of a weak barrage and no ground was covered whilst enemy machine guns in Loop Trench and along the sunken Combles Road were still in action. Another attempt was made in mid afternoon but without success. That evening the 169th Bde. was relieved by a composite Bde. from the 5th Div. L/Cpl. H. G. R. Williams of the 5th City of London 56th Div. 169th Bde. (Liddle) gives the following account: At the time the high ground in front of Combles was still in German hands. Leuze Wood was to the left and was shelled by both sides at the same time. Reserve was in a small valley called Angle Wood. They lived in shelters out in the hillsides or else in a trench in Death Valley. He mentions seeing the tanks and the Cavalry on the 15th September. The 168th Bde. was relieved by the 167th Bde. On the 12th the 1/8 Middlesex of the 167th Bde. 56th Div. formed up in the valley between the south end of Leuze Wood and Wedge Wood and on the 15th the 1/7 Middlesex of the same Bde. were brought to a standstill by the German rifle and machine gun fire from the road that led into Combles.

By this time a dressing station had been established in the wood.

On the 15th Bouleux Wood was carried by the British. Their attack actually coincided with a German counter-attack and the result was a very hard fight between the two sides. Once the redoubt to the east of the wood was captured the British were able to gradually outflank the Germans, and pressing them on all sides forced them to retire one kilometre northwards. Bouleux Wood was carried by assault.[2]

In *The War the Infantry Knew* it states that Leuze Wood was less mutilated than woods further to the rear and that it became a main feature in a wide and bare winter landscape of grey-green stubble stripped here and there with chrome grey shell holes, and scarred with trenches. In an issue of the *Ypres Times* of 1935 it was reported that the wood was green and dense again except for the shooting drive. They shoot rabbits and partridges there now!

Longueval

Longueval Village is planned around a crossroad. To the south-west is Montauban, to the east Ginchy, to the north Flers and to the west the two Bazentin villages. In 1916 it was the village that was the gateway to Delville Wood. In other words an attacker had to take the village before being able to take the Wood. The village itself was built along three roads and the cross roads or junction formed the centre of the village. The road that extended to meet a track midway between High Wood and Flers was called North Street. The second branch went in a south-westerly direction and skirted the west side of Bernafay Wood and the third went in a south-easterly direction towards Guillemont. From the main square itself the road branched westwards towards the Bazentins, and was known as Claridges Street. Parallel to it and to the north was Duke Street and these two roads were cut by a track called Piccadilly. Thus four roads formed a rectangle that enclosed the northern orchards of the village. These come into the story a little later on.

The German trench line skirted the south of Longueval and then turned south-eastwards going past Waterlot Farm in the direction of Guillemont. As usual the Germans had the advantage of the position in that their positions could not be precisely located. In addition they had a good view over the ground that any attacker would have to traverse. An important feature to the British was Longueval Alley which was to the south of the village and the quarry there was often used as a Battalion HQ.

Longueval makes its first appearance in the Battle of the Somme as part of General Rawlinson's plan to make a night attack against the Bazentin Ridge which included the villages of Bazentin and Longueval. The proposal was to form up two Divisions in the dark and to attack at dawn. Haig was worried about the possible confusion of troops forming up in the dark. However he did agree to the plan after certain modifications had been made and the battle turned out to be a brilliant success.

The 1st Div. on 14th July captured Contalmaison and Lower Wood. At 3.25 a.m. after an intense bombardment of five minutes the enemy's second line was attacked from the west of Bazentin le Petit Wood to Longueval with the 21st, 3rd and 9th Divs. The attackers reached their objectives without a hitch and by 9 a.m. Bazentin le Grand Village was being held by the British and also half of Longueval but not the strongly fortified northern end which encompassed the orchards. The 12th R. Scots (27th Bde. 9th Div.) were involved in the fighting here and their history describes the fortifications in the orchards as being of 'quite exceptional strength'. Nevertheless the 9th Div. had a firm hold on the southern end of Longueval and had made a lodgement in Delville Wood. The 22nd and 27th Bdes. of the 9th Div. continued in the village under a heavy bombardment as well. Machine gun fire and also that of German snipers was very fierce. The men who were in Longueval Alley were in touch with men of the 18th Div.

The historian of the 17th Div. wrote that the village and also Delville Wood itself were persistently shelled by the enemy who used guns of various calibres. The fire coming from three directions in front, from the rising ground of the Bapaume Ridge to the west of Flers, on the left from the ground north of High Wood and from the right around Ginchy. For the German artillery Longueval and Delville Wood were on the skyline as they stood on the crest of the Combles–Thiepval Ridge, the outlying high ground that ran parallel to Bapaume Ridge.

On the 15th there were several attempts to take Waterlot Farm which was part of the German second line, by a company of the 5th Cameron H. (26th Bde. 9th Div.) and also two companies of the 4th South African Regiment. The R. Scots made a further attempt to take the north of Longueval but these were unsuccessful and they became exhausted.

In *Haig's Great Push* it says that the village was garrisoned by Prussians and that though they fought fiercely they had no chance against the Scots! Many Germans had taken refuge in the houses in the village and they had to be winkled out.

W. D. Croft the historian of the 9th Div. says that there were subterannean passages that went right through the village which were difficult to penetrate. The enemy had entrances on his side of the village and could escape down the passages from the houses which had bolt hole entrances to the passages. A Company HQ of the Seaforths and Black Watch was nearly captured as a result of the enemy appearing unexpectedly!

On 16th July Talbot Kelly of the RFA described going up from Montauban as Bde. FOO to Longueval which he entered by a sunken road between the shattered orchards. He observed the fire of the British 9.2 Howitzers from the first floor of a house in the village square. Across the street were Germans who were crouched in houses as indeed he was. The distance was 20 yards or less. He was a witness to the fighting in the village and in particular the part played by the Cameron Highlanders.

On 18th July the 1st Gordon H. and the 8th King's Own of the 76th Bde. moved out from trenches near Bazentin Windmill and forming up to the right attacked Longueval from the west. Again the orchards were not carried but Longueval was occupied as far as Duke Street and a line taken up on the north-west edge of Delville Wood. They were in contact with the South African Bde.

On the 19th July the 95th Bde. (5th Div.) went up to the Longueval positions and at that time the front line ran along the road that led from the southern corner of High Wood to Longueval. The German artillery again shelled Longueval heavily and after close fighting the 27th Bde. (9th Div.) were forced back to the southern edge of the village. The 26th Bde. saved the situation and the centre of Longueval. That night the 3rd Div. began to relieve the 9th Div.

The plan for the 20th was to make another attempt to clear the village and Delville Wood in the morning. Brevet Major William la Touche Congreve of the Rifle Bde. was awarded the VC for his bravery between 6th and 20th July. The citation stated that he performed acts of gallantry and showed the greatest devotion to duty, and by his personal example inspired all those around him. In preliminary preparations for the attack he carried out personal reconnaissance of the enemy line and took out parties of officers and NCOs for over 1,000 yards in front of the Allied lines in order to acquaint them with the ground. On one occasion when Bde. HQ was heavily shelled resulting in heavy casualties, he went out to assist with moving the wounded, although he himself was wounded and suffering from the effects of gas. His Bde. was the 76th Bde. and one of its Battalions was the 2nd Suffolks whose CO was Major Stubbs. Congreve had talked to Stubbs at his HQ and they went up the line together where they entered a freshly dug trench along the side of Duke Street. Stubbs warned Congreve about the danger of snipers but at 10.55 a.m. on the 20th Congreve was shot in the throat and died in a few seconds. Congreve was a son of Lt. Gen. Walter Congreve who also had been awarded the VC. Congreve is buried in Corbie and there is a memorial to him in the Abbey there.

On 23rd July the 2nd R. Scots of the 8th Bde. were to attack and bomb down the trenches from Waterlot Farm and thus recapture Guillemont Station. The 3rd Div. attacked the northern part of Delville Wood and the northern part of the village. The 9th Bde. were to attack from the west side. The 95th Bde. were to clear the left flank and the 5th Div. was to deal with the strongpoint in the orchards. The 3rd Div. were involved in an unsuccessful attack.

The fighting for the possession of Longueval now entered its last week and intensified between 24th July to 31st. Haig was badly wanting the village and wood to be cleared.

On the 25th the relief of the 3rd Div. began and the village now became the objective of the 5th Div. The 1st Norfolks (15th Bde. 5th Div.) had been at Pommiers Redoubt to the south until late on the night of the 26th and it was their task to attack Longueval Village and part of the wood, and there was the usual heavy fighting. The capture of the north-west end of Delville Wood was made especially difficult by machine guns in High Wood, Switch Trench and many strong points in the open outside it. One of the officers of the 1st Norfolks, Captain H. J. R. Sibree was awarded the MC. His company was held up by machine gun fire and although he was wounded, he continued to re-organise until he was again wounded.

On the 27th the 15th Bde. was to advance on the left of the 99th Bde. with the 1st Norfolks in front and the 1st Beds. in support against Delville Wood. The enemy still held on the north of the village, fierce fighting continued in the orchards all day and in particular in the area of a German redoubt, called by the British, the Machine Gun House.

On the 28th Longueval was yet again shelled heavily and the Staffs. and the Middlesex were involved in a counter-attack. The 15th Bde. had been relieved by the 95th Bde. on the night of the 27th. On the 29th at 3.30 a.m. the 95th Bde. made some progress and on the 30th the 13th (5th Div.) made some progress. By the end of July the village was in Allied hands but the fighting from Delville Wood was to go on for another month. On the 31st and 1st August the 1st Norfolks of the 5th Div. were again in Longueval before going back to le Quesnoy on 2nd August for training.

The 8th Rif. Brig. (41st Bde. 14th Light Div.) were to the north of Longueval on the 14th August and were preparing on the 18th August for an attack on trenches at Longueval along with the 7th KRRC and 7th RB of the same Brigade. It was only partially successful. Between the 1st and 2nd of September the 3rd RB (17th Bde. 24th Div.) retook Orchard Trench.

Talbot Kelly of the RFA wrote that they were relieved from Longueval in August and that their column of a thousand or more horses with guns and ammunition wagons presented an extraordinary sight as they went through the valley below these chalk downs. Everybody except for the first few were shrouded in a great pall of white dust. On 24th the HQ of the 5th O. & BLI was in Crucifix Alley close to Longueval Church. The Medical Aid Post was in the shrine of the Alley.

On 9th September the sunken road between Longueval and High Wood was captured, and on the 16th/17th the 1st Norfolks moved forward to Waterlot Farm from Billon Farm. There were many bodies that remained un-buried from earlier battles. In early October the Longueval road to Flers was always busy with wheeled traffic and was frequently shelled. On the 16th C. E. Montague went up to Longueval with John Masefield and they walked around Delville Wood. Most of the bodies had been removed but the wood was still 'haggard and sinister'.

Fraser Tytler in his *Field Guns in France* wrote that up the road near Longueval one reached a 'big gun farmyard' which was full of vast guns that had seemingly been dumped anywhere close to the road, with the usual piles of shells, half buried in mud all around, and stacks of empty canisters and boxes which held charges.

On the 5th November C. E. Montagu was again doing one of his battlefield tours and on this occasion left his car and chauffeur Harris at the entrance to Longueval, with orders to go back a little and wait. When Montagu had gone about 250 yards a German shell pitched roughly where the car had been. Harris had in fact already moved the car and the shell destroyed a limber and its crew.

John Masefield described the site of the village in 1917 as being a reddish patch such was the destruction.

Longueval Road Cemetery is on the east side of the road from Longueval to Bernafay Wood and Maricourt, less than half a mile south of the village. It was begun in September 1915, near a Dressing Station known as 'Longueval Alley' or 'Longueval Water Point' and it was used until January 1917. It stands on relatively high ground, and in addition to Longueval other villages that can be seen from it include Guillemont, Montauban, Bernafay and Trônes Wood. The Cemetery was designed by Arthur Hutton.

In May 1986 a wooden cross was erected at the Longueval cross roads close to High Wood, it replaces one that was lost in the Second World War and is in memory of the 12th Glosters (95th Bde. 5th Div.) known as 'Bristol's Own.'

Louvencourt

Louvencourt is a village on the main road between Doullens and Albert, about 13 miles from each. The Military Cemetery is on the road to Acheux, the D 938. From July 1915 to August 1916 British Field Ambulances were established at Louvencourt which at the beginning of July 1916 was six miles behind the front line. The village housed a Corps MDS, shared with three other villages. The progress of the battle meant that these medical units moved further eastwards, until in April 1917, the German offensive pushed the British line back to its old position. Eight of the graves were brought from the Communal Extension at Vauchelles-les-Authie, a mile away on the road to Doullens. This Extension was opened in July 1916 for Field Ambulances at Vauchelles, but no more than eight burials took place in it. Authie is to the north-west, Bertrancourt to the east and Bus les Artois to the north-east. After their involvement at Serre on 1st July the 18th Durhams of the 31st Div. were in the area along with Brigade Reserve.

In August the 9th battalion of the Suffolk Regiment having been in the trenches in front of Mailly Wood had a week's intermission at Louvencourt. Whilst there they were allotted the task of clearing the battlefield where the Ulster Div. had fallen on 1st July in the Thiepval sector. On 27th August the 9th Norfolks (71st Bde. 6th Div.) were here for a day before going on to Beauval, and in early October tanks were assembled in the village.

Buried in the cemetery are Lt. Roland Aubrey Leighton who died of wounds on 23rd December 1915 at Hébuterne at the age of 19. He was a friend of Vera Brittain and features in her classic memoir of her generation *Testament of Youth*. Also buried in the cemetery is Brig. Gen. C. B. Prowse DSO of the 1st Somerset LI, 11th Bde. Commander. On 1st July he was mortally wounded when in search of information as to the progress of the battle. He was 47 and in May 1915 had made a stand with the Hampshire and Somersets at a place that was later named Prowse Farm. Prowse Point Cemetery is just in front of Ploegsteert Cemetery.

Lozenge Wood

The wood is just to the north of Fricourt on the eastern side of the D 147 Road to Contalmaison. To its east is The Poodles. Lozenge Wood was part of the line that was reached and maintained on 1st July. It had been protected by several lines of strong German trenches.

H. A. Taylor in his book *Goodbye to the Battlefields* described it in the following way 'Over to the left is Lozenge Wood, barely to be distinguished. At best it was nothing much of a wood, though a distinct trouble to our men when they sought to dislodge the enemy from it. And if Lozenge Wood can hardly be seen, what are we to expect of The Poodles. Two trees so proud and important that they were deemed worthy of special designation and a place on the trench map. But still, only two trees, and so much happened after they were put on the map.'

In August the 11th Sherwood For. (70th Bde. 23 Div.) buried their dead here whilst out of the line and on the 8th September the 5th North'd Fus. (149th Bde. 50th Div.) were in dugouts around the wood.

Lucheux

Battalions used to rest and train in this village which is north-east of Doullens. They included the 1st Scots Gds. who came here from Doullens at the end of July/beginning of August and the 2nd R. Welch Fus. who came here on 30th September and stayed eighteen days.

Luisenhof Farm

The farm was to the south of Ligny–Thilloy and to the north of Factory Corner. It was where Major Hawker VC crashed in mid November having been brought down by Von Richthofen in an 'epic duel'. There is no trace of Hawker's grave.

Mailly–Maillet

Mailly is a village above five and half miles north of Albert, south of Colincamps, north-west of Englebelmer and due west of Auchonvillers. It is on the D 919 road. It was behind the lines before 1st July and was a very 'busy' village. Like its neighbours it had many underground tunnels in the subterranean quarries from which the stone for building provided cover for the troops. The village boasts a church with a splendid Gothic carving on its western façade. During the war special measures similar to those adopted for the protection of Amiens Cathedral were taken to preserve it and the door was well sandbagged. Fortunately despite heavy bombardments in 1917 and 1918, the precautions were successful.

The village used to have a railway station on the light railway between Albert and Doullens and was to provide a continuous home for British troops both before and during the battle. The large wood to the south-west of the village was very often used for troops to bivouac and camp in.

On 25th June thirteen men of the 2nd Seaforth H. (10th Bde. 4th div.) were killed and buried in what was to be named Mailly Wood Cemetery. On 1st July the 48th Div. moved up to the village which at the time was two miles behind the front.

One observer mentions that on the 1st July there was a 15 inch gun in a plantation to the south-west of the village and it fired every half hour. Graham Greenwell's Battalion the 1/4th O & BLI (145th Bde. 48th Div.) were camped 400 yards from this gun. Greenwell reported that on the 1st July they moved to their allotted positions, a large field behind Mailly. He was able to ride with the battalion and was never so thankful for the use of a horse as the march was very hot and dusty. Part of VIII Corps Reserve were camped in the wood during the afternoon of 1st July.

On 8th July the Newfoundland Battalion after their involvement in the fighting at Beaumont Hamel on 1st July withdrew from Engelbelmer which was being shelled by the enemy and occupied tents in Mailly Wood. There is a note that towards the end of July the 7th Somerset LI (61st Bde. 20th Div.) had their HQ in a large house in the village on the corner of the square. The Signallers occupied outbuildings to the rear of the house. Headquarters of the 113th Bde. (38th Div.) was in the chateau and the 7th Durhams who were the Pioneer Battalion to the 50th Div. occupied cellars in the village. In early August the 7th Somersets made use of the church tower for an observation post. Mailly with its delightful orchards and gardens was also especially associated with the Artillery and there were many batteries in the area during the battle.

Around the 10th of August the Guards Bde. added their artillery and the Coldstream Guards were here on 14th August. The 9th Suffolks (71st Bde. 6th Div.) were in the area between 4th and 28th August and took over the trench in front of Mailly Wood with the intermission of a week at Louvencourt.

Edmund Blunden was in the village and has written about it in his *Undertones of War*. In August his battalion the 11th R. Sussex (116th Bde. 39th Div.) had moved forward to Mailly Wood which he described as a straggling wood called P18 from its map reference. They were three miles from the German guns camping in tents. Mailly according to Blunden had until recently been a delightful and flourishing place, but now it was in the 'sere and yellow'. Its long chateau wall had been broken down by trees which had fallen as a result of shellfire. Its church was protected by straw mats. Blunden wrote in his book 'Another postponement took me dustily back to the battalion in the wood watched by so many German observation balloons in the morning sun, the wood shelled deliberately because of its camps and accidently because of some conspicuous horse-lines, and silhouetted movements on the hill to the west, had frayed the men's keenness; there had been casualties. On the evening of 2nd September, the battalion moved cautiously from Mailly–Maillet by cross-battalion tracks, through pretty Engelbelmer, down over the downs to Mesnil, and assembled in the Hamel trenches to attack the Beaucourt Ridge next morning'.

At one time Blunden mentions being in the cellars of a house in Mailly which were concealed by an ingenious contrivance, opening into a subterranean passage which ran underground for several kilometres. The 17th KRRC Batt. were relieved at Auchonvillers on 12th September and moved to Mailly, and then to Y Camp at Bertrancourt on the 19th September. Frederic Manning who was the author of *The Middle Parts of Fortune* and who was in the 7th KSLI described their stay at Mailly. The wood in which they were encamped was just behind Mailly–Maillet, in an angle formed by two roads, one rising over the slope to Mailly–Maillet and the other skirting the foot of the hill to Hédauville. It was on a rather steep reverse slope, which gave some protection from shell fire and there were a few shelter trenches, which had been hastily and rather inefficiently dug, as a further protection. It was well screened from observation. A road running from Colincamps converged towards the road they had just left, to meet it at a point known as the sugar refinery. Just before striking the road, they came to a large dump called Euston, and halted there.

It can be seen at a glance at a map of the area that Manning was very accurate in his description of topographical features. This was probably around 8th October when they were preparing for the Ancre battle which finally took place in mid November. On the 9th October the 20th KRRC (3rd Div.) were involved in Pioneer duties and on the 29th they moved to Courcelles where they worked for the rest of the year.

One of the members of the 32nd Div. Trench Mortar Battery mentioned the batteries situated at Engelbelmer and at Mailly around 21st October and on the 22nd October he reported seeing about 30 tanks in a field close to the village. Everywhere was muddy after the continuous rain. The village housed an ADS or CP from November.

Mailly Wood Cemetery is about 400 yards south of the centre of the village, on the further edge of the wood which borders the road to Hédauville. It is close to the chateau with its walled garden, beyond which is the famous church. The cemetery was especially used by the 51st Highland Div. who buried in it many of their dead from the battle for Beaumont Hamel which took place in November 1916. It also contains the graves of many casualties from the July fighting. After the Armistice 101 graves from the battlefield immediately north-east of the village were brought into the cemetery. Included is the grave of Major H. G. Lush Wilson RHA who was killed on 21st July, formerly a fencing champion. Also the grave of Lt. the Hon. Sydney Trench, son of Baron Ashtown, who was an officer in the KRRC when he was killed. He had been born in Galway in 1894, educated at Eton and Magdalen College, and had taken part in the annual University Boat Race. He was wounded in Munich Trench at Beaumont Hamel on 14th November and died two days later.

The Communal Cemetery is about half a mile north of the village, a little west of the road to Courcelles-au-Bois, and the Extension is on the east side of it. The Extension was begun by French units who were mainly Engineers in June 1915. It was taken over by British troops in August of that year and used by Field Ambulances and fighting units until December 1916. The surrounding countryside is under cultivation. The village was a comparatively quiet place until the German March breakthrough in March 1918. It was to remain in Allied hands, but was severely shelled by the German artillery, when the British troops used the catacombs as shelter.

Maltz Horn Farm

The Farm was north of Hardecourt-aux-Bois south of Guillemont and almost equal distance from both villages. It was also due south of Arrow Head Copse and south-east of Trônes Wood. Before it was taken by the Allies it was a protruding point in the German defence line. The Farm was where the British and French line flanked one another. The German defence line or trenches then went in a south-easterly direction towards Maurepas and northwards towards Arrow Head Copse and Guillemont Village. Beyond Maltz Horn lay Falfemont Farm and the village of Combles which was the direction that the battle was to take.

The farm fell on 30th July, according to the *Official History*, to an Allied attack that began at 4.45 a.m. in the morning. The easterly objective was in fact Falfemont Farm. The 89th and 90th Bdes. of the 30th Div. were involved in the capture of the Farm and the 89th Bde. advanced keeping in touch with the French on the right. Simultaneously the 5th Bde. of the 2nd Div. were to take Guillemont Station and the trenches to the north-west of it. The 89th Bde. advanced from the direction of Trônes Wood and on the way were heavily shelled with high explosive and gas shells. The 90th Bde. was also affected. There had been a dawn fog which cleared later and the farm fell to an assault by the 2nd Beds. of the 89th Bde. who attacked from the west and to a company of the French Army from the south. The advance swept eastwards down hill.

The 20th King's captured the German front trenches and got as far as the Hardecourt–Guillemont road. The 2nd R. Scots of the 90th Bde. advanced across the Trônes Wood–Guillemont road and entered Guillemont from the south-west. A counter-attack from the direction of the cemetery was repulsed. The 18th Manchesters of the 90th Bde. advanced leaving its left on the Trônes Wood–Guillemont Railway but they were caught by cross fire from machine guns in the Station and Quarry at Guillemont. They had to withdraw and another attack was planned which was checked by uncut wire in the area of Guillemont Station.

In early August the valley on the right of the Farm known as Maltz Horn Valley was also known as the Valley of Death as there was continuous artillery shelling into it. In mid August whilst the Germans still held Angle Wood in strength, the 1st Gordons (76th Bde. 3rd Div.) were in positions in front of the farm. Their objective was the road from Angle Wood to Guillemont. The

French were also involved in this advance. However the Germans had organised a powerful resistance at the junction between the two Armies.

On 26th August the Fifth Army relieved the 35th Div. (Bantam) on Maltz Horn Ridge and their position covered the whole of the eastern slope on which stood the farm. Their advanced posts on the right were in the valley which ran from Maurepas to Combles. Opposite the right brigade front, rose the spur on which Leuze Wood and Bouleux Woods were situated, which ran diagonally across the Divisional front. It was to the south-west of this spur that the famous Falfemont Farm was situated. On 1st September the Battalion HQ of the 1/8 Middlesex Batt. (167th Bde. 56th Div.) was in a quarry on the east side of Maltz Horn Ridge and on the 3rd it was planned to blow up the farm road but the mine failed to explode.

The fighting continued in the direction of Combles, and until Falfemont Farm was taken the French Army would be unable to advance along the valley. The French artillery undertook the bombardment and barrage in early September and finally the Farm was taken, to be followed by Leuze Wood. Guillemont was also taken after several weeks of continuous British attacks.

Mametz Village

The village of Mametz is four miles east of Albert on the D 64 Fricourt–Guillemont Road. It is east of Fricourt, south of Contalmaison, south-west of Montauban and north-west of Carnoy and Maricourt. It was formerly a railway halt on the line from Albert to Peronne. The famous wood is a thousand yards to the north-west of the village and is in fact far closer to Contalmaison with which it was to be more associated in the fighting that was to follow. Before the war with about 120 houses Mametz was about the fifth largest village in the area. It was the objective of the 7th Div. for the 1st of July. The Brigade that was to be to the south-west of the village was the 91st and on their left was the 20th Brigade, then beyond was the 22nd Bde. To deal with the 91st Bde. and reading from right to left the attacking battalions were the 22nd Manchesters the 1st S. Staffs. with the 2/Queen's behind the 22nd Manchesters and the 21st Manchesters behind the 1st S. Staffs.

To the left of the 91st Bde. was the 20th Bde. and firstly there were the 2nd Gordons, the 9th Devons, which consisted of Devon men, Londoners and Midlanders, and the 2nd Borders. The 8th Devons were to the rear in Lucknow Redoubt with the 2nd R. Warwicks on their left. The 2nd R. Irish Rif. who were behind the 2nd R. Warwicks were to come up to the front via Minden Post in order to support the Manchester Battalions and the Queen's. The right and centre Brigades of the 7th Div. were to attack on a front of 1,800 yards between the Carnoy–Mametz track and the quarry to the south of Hidden Wood. The 1st S. Staffs were the first battalion to enter the village and had approached between two mined positions in the German Bulgar Trench which was the enemy front line. The assaulting troops had at least a thousand yards to cover. The Divisional Commander had kept the front and support lines empty and instead a new special assembly trench had been dug about 250 yards to the rear. It was from this new line that the S. Staffs. advanced. The Allied artillery were still shelling the German defensive positions in front of them. At 7.30 a.m. on the 1st July the S. Staffs began their advance which was met by a good deal of shrapnel and machine gun fire. They took many prisoners who had been sheltering in their dugouts and in half an hour the forward companies had reached the outskirts of the village which meant that they had covered 1,200 yards in thirty minutes. When they tried to enter the village they came under more severe machine gun fire from points on their right which had not been reached yet by the Manchesters. By about 10 a.m. these guns had been dealt with, and together with a company of the 21st Manchesters they penetrated the village. The Staffordshires pushed right through Danzig Alley and established themselves to the north of the village and there the rest of the battalion, which had been clearing Danzig Alley were able to join them. At midday the position was still not secure and the enemy were on either flank in Danzig Alley but cellars and strongpoints were being cleared by the battalion. At around 1 p.m. the leading companies moved on in order to secure Bunny Alley, which was to the north-west of the village, but their flanks were in the air and they were forced to withdraw to the village to consolidate Danzig Alley.

The 2nd Queen's the reserve battalion of the 91st Bde. was committed in the afternoon and both ends of Danzig Alley were secured while the Staffordshires continued to 'mop up' in the village and to consolidate. At about 5 p.m. Battalion HQ moved up to the village and a fresh attempt on Bunny Alley was successful. The Staffordshires had reached their 1st July objective. The 21st Manchesters on the night of the 30th June had taken up positions opposite Mametz and their Battalion HQ was in a deep dugout in Queen's Road Trench close to the Rat Hole. On the 1st July the 2nd Queen's and the 22nd Manchesters were to push through the lines of the 21st Manchesters who were in reserve though two of their companies helped the S. Staffs in their capture of the village. The Historian R. H. Tawney who was with the 22nd Manchesters as a Sergeant on the 1st July was wounded in the fight for Mametz.

On the 2nd July the Staffordshires were brought back into the village and were able to bring light machine gun and rifle fire on parties of retiring Germans. Together with the 21st Manchesters they put the village in a state of defence. On the 3rd they moved up to Bottom Wood which was north-westwards of Bunny Alley and they were then about 500 yards to the south-west of Mametz Wood. Here before being relieved they found themselves alongside a sister battalion the 8th S. Staffs. of the 17th Div. which had been involved in capturing Fricourt Farm. They were relieved on the 5th July.

The 21st Manchesters had been relieved on the 4th. Their Battalion HQ had been at Mametz Church which by then was a heap of white stone and patrols had pushed out to Bottom Wood without meeting any resistance. They occupied during their relief, billets in the village of Mametz except for 'C' Company who were at Minden Post.

To turn now to the 20th Brigade of the 7th Division which was a very different story from that of the 91st Bde. The right hand attacking battalion was the 2nd Gordons who were attacking down in the valley close to where the railway line was and they were cut down by machine gun fire from the direction of the Shrine to the south-west of Mametz. Their right company did reach as far as the German intermediate trench which was called Cemetery Trench but could go no further. Ninety nine men of this battalion are buried in Gordon Cemetery which is close to Mansell Copse. Brian Brooke, Capt. in the 2nd Gordons was wounded on the 1st July and died of wounds on the 25th July. He had published a book of poems with John Lane and came from a military family, and on the 1st was in charge of the right wing of B. Comp. 20th Bde. 7th Div.

On the left of the Gordons were the 9th Devons and their sister battalion the 8th Devons were to join up with them from reserve. At the end of June it was clearly known that Mametz was protected by the enemy by a network of trenches which were studded with strongpoints and redoubts which shielded many machine guns. A particularly well placed machine gun was in Shrine Alley to the south-west of the village with a clear field of vision that included Mansell Copse. On the 1st July there was also a steep bank with undergrowth full of dugouts which was also known to be a potentially very dangerous spot. The machine gun, at Shrine Alley about 800 yards away, caught the 9th Devons as they filed through and around Mansell Copse. A gap also opened up between them and the 2nd Gordons on their right flank. The 8th Devons fared better as the ground protected them from the destructive machine gun at the Shrine and they managed to cross as far as Danube Trench and to actually reach Shrine Alley. They pushed along Danzig Trench to the west of the railway from the village and were able to clear the high dugouts along Danzig Trench.

The 8th and 9th Devons had attacked from a point on the south-west of the Albert–Maricourt Road close to Mansell Copse and the disaster had been predicted by a Captain D. L. Martin of the Devons who had forecast that they would be caught by machine gun fire from the Shrine, which is exactly what happened. Normally in this book I put details of cemeteries at the end of each section, but I think that on this occasion that it would be more suitable to include details here. The Devonshire Cemetery as it was immediately called, contains the graves of one officer of the 8th Devons who fell on the 28th June, seven officers and 121 other ranks of the 9th Battalion, killed on 1st July, three officers and 29 other ranks of the 8th Devons who also fell on the 1st, and a Sergeant and a Driver of the B/92nd Bde. RFA, killed later in the Somme battle. Ten men of the 9th Devons were unidentified and on the 4th July 1916, a special service was held at Mansell Copse in the evening for the two battalions when the ten men were commemorated. The cemetery stands on the top of a high steep bank, containing dugouts and is bounded to the north-east side of Mansell Copse. The bodies of the Devons are buried in their original front trench, and the graves include those of Captain Martin and Lt. W. N. Hodgson, the poet.

Hodgson had taken a First Class Degree in Classical Mods. at Oxford in 1913 and was a contemporary of Rupert Brooke. During the war he had been mentioned in despatches as well as earning the MC. He had gained the latter in October 1915. His poem 'Before Action' tells of the period before the battle of the Somme began and was first published under the name of 'Edward Melbourne' in *New Witness* on 29th June. His book *Verse and Prose in Peace and War* was published postumously later in 1916. Mansell Copse Cemetery has become a particularly poignant one for visitors to the battlefield.

Across the road and a little further down from the copse is Gordon Cemetery which is the burial ground of six officers and 93 other ranks of the 2nd Gordons killed on 1st July and buried in their former trenches. Three artillerymen who fell on the 9th July are buried beside them. The cemetery stands on the level of the road and was formerly separated from it by a light railway. The headstones are ranged in two semi-circles round the Copse. It is one of the most moving cemeteries in the area.

There is another battalion who was involved in the frontal assault close to Mametz on the 1st July and who were on the left of the 9th and 8th Devons, and they were the 2nd Borders of the 20th Bde. Their particular objective was Apple Alley in the direction of Fricourt.

At 7.27 a.m. the battalion moved forward and reached Danube Support Trench and began to wheel further to the left on coming under indirect machine gun fire both from Mametz and Fricourt. But the advance continued to Hidden Lane where it was held up by machine gun fire from Hidden Wood on the right flank, and from the junction of Kiel Support and Bois Français Support.

In the late afternoon the battalion had made their final objective with two companies reaching Apple Alley. A party of the 8th Devons were to their right, and two other Border Battalion companies were in support in Hidden Lane Trench. Battalion HQ was established in a dugout in Support Trench. The Border Battalion casualties were 334 officers and men. Later in the battle the Battalion was in deployment to the rear of Caterpillar Wood, and on the 13th July in the area of Flat Iron Copse before being withdrawn to Pommiers Redoubt on the 15th July until the 19th. Although there had been a lot of casualties in the taking of Mametz it was nevertheless a considerable success as indeed was the taking of the village of Montauban as well as the land in between. Most of the original objectives had been taken on a day when there had been little or no progress elsewhere.

To the north of the Albert–Bapaume road the only gain maintained at the end of the 1st July was a footing in Leipzig Salient.

There is not a great deal more to say about what happened in the village of Mametz after its successful capture by the British on the 1st July. On the 2nd the Germans conceded defeat at Fricourt, the neighbouring village to the west, and the Allied line was pushed forward on to rising ground facing the south-west of Contalmaison to the north-west of Mametz Wood. At the same period a position on the right was established along the Mametz Valley which included Caterpillar Wood as well as Bernafay Wood. Haig was going to push on where there had been some success with the Allied advance as opposed to his original plan which was to attack across the Thiepval Plateau.

On the 24th July Maurice Baring who was on the staff of General Trenchard of the RFC described Mametz as having nothing left in it but crumbling stones. The village had been annihilated. On the next day the 25th, a Divisional Ammunition dump near the village containing some 100,000 rounds of trench mortar and artillery ammunition and a large quantity of bombs and rifle ammunition, was set on fire by a shell and the whole dump exploded. Max Plowman of the 10th W. Yorks (50th Bde. 17th Div.) described Mametz in early August 'now as we near Mametz, we come upon guns hidden under the banks of the roadside and camouflaged above by netting. The road through Mametz is still under enemy observation; so we turn sharply to the right to go round the back of the rising ground that faces us – '. They went on to Fricourt.

John Masefield on his first visit to Mametz described it as 'eight feet of brick'. Danzig Alley British Cemetery is in the commune in the Department of the Somme, and its name was taken from the German trench of that name. It is a little to the east of the village on the north side of the road to Montauban. As we know Mametz was carried by the 7th Division on the 1st July, after hard fighting at Danzig Alley and at other points in the village. The Division erected a memorial in Mametz Village to their dead.

Mametz Wood (Quadrangle)

The Quadrangle was the name given to the strong point 500 yards to the south-west of Mametz Wood. It was part of a German defensive line which ran down from Ovillers-la-Boisselle to a position in front of Mametz Wood. It consisted of Quadrangle Trench and some distance behind it the Quadrangle Support. Quadrangle Alley ran into it from the outskirts of Mametz Wood just behind Wood Support. As the trench reached towards Mametz Wood it became known as Wood Trench which in turn came out at a right angle and was named Strip Trench.

John Masefield wrote that it was sited so that men approaching it from the south could be seen and fired on from both flanks, and from the rear. Well hidden supports linked it with the village of Contalmaison as well as Mametz Wood. The work defended the spur on the eastern side. On the west it was defended by the work in Shelter Wood just beyond the Poodles on the Fricourt–Contalmaison Road, by two fortified copses to the north of Shelter Wood and thirdly by a field work to the north of these copses known as the Horseshoe. H. P. Robinson wrote in *The Turning Point* that the position was a formidable one and that the Quadrangle Trench was the longest side, the Quadrangle Support was the shortest, but that both had extremely strong positions at their two ends. It was in fact commanded on the one hand by Contalmaison and the other by Mametz Wood whence it could be easily reinforced. The Support looked down on a bare natural glacis which was without a scrap of cover, except for a few shell holes.

Two battalions of the 7th Div. were detailed by General Steele to carry out an attack on the position namely the 1st R. Welch Fus. and the 2nd R. Irish both of the 22nd Bde. They left the Halt at Mametz soon after midnight on the 3rd/4th July, but the Welch Fusiliers' guide lost his way and as a result the battalion did not reach its place of deployment until daybreak and by then it was too late to attack. Subsequently the 2nd R. Irish had to go it alone, and a bombing attack up Strip Trench to the right, was organised towards the Quadrangle Trench which reports said was unoccupied! This was not the case and a counter-attack pushed the bombers back to the southern edge of the wood where a stand was made. The position was clearly untenable and the R. Irish had to withdraw.

An attack was planned by the 17th Div. for 12.45 a.m. on 5th July and after the barrage had lifted two battalions advanced. The night was dark and the ground had become heavy and slippery after the recent rain. The Welch Fusiliers managed to get into the left of Quadrangle Trench and gained touch with the 9th North'd Fus. of the 52nd Bde. and promptly began bombing to their right. Bombers then started to bomb along the trench to its eastern end, a little distance short of a light railway, and according to the 17th Div. history a party went across the 70 yard gap which separated Quadrangle Trench from Wood Trench. They made a lodgement there, but could not contact the R. Irish because they in turn had been caught by enfilade fire from the right and had lost heavily, when on reaching Wood Trench the wire was found to be uncut. Just before dawn the Irishmen were withdrawn and the R. Welch Fus. party which had reached Wood Trench had to get back to Quadrangle Trench and then the Artillery barraged Wood Trench and the south part of the Wood. On the other flank the Welch Fusiliers' bombers pushed along Quadrangle Alley till nearly halfway to the Support Trench. They made a 'block' and were twice counter-attacked by the Germans who worked down from Quadrangle Alley and Support. However they hung on and were relieved that evening by units of the 38th Div.

During the above fighting Siegfried Sassoon had been involved and, on the 4th at 2.30 a.m. he was with the 'C' Company of the 1st R. Welch Fus. at Bottom Wood, their attack having been cancelled. He went up on his own towards Mametz Wood and in the words of Robert Graves he captured a trench by himself without signalling for reinforcements and sat down and read a book of poetry in the German trench instead. He was not popular with his Colonel who told him that he had held up the attack on Mametz Wood for two hours! On the 5th Sassoon had been heavily involved in the fighting against the Quadrangle Position and was recommended for a further decoration. Although Quadrangle Trench was secure the Support did not fall until a few days later.

Mametz Wood

Possibly more has been written about Mametz Wood, than any other wood, feature or village in the Somme area. The reasons being perhaps, that it was a very hard position to capture, but then so were other places, like Trônes or High Wood. Also battalions were continuously 'fed into the position' under conditions that were very unfavourable to any attacker. Maybe it is because of its literary associations that it has become so well known, these associations are mostly connected with the R. Welch Fus. and include Siegfried Sassoon, David Jones, Wyn Griffith and Robert Graves. The text of David Jones' long poem *In Parenthesis* has the poet's involvement in the wood as its central theme. Certainly any present day visitor to the area is aware of something special about the wood and especially at dusk when the day becomes night! The wood was the next objective after Mametz Village, and is due north of that village, east of Contalmaison and south-west of the Bazentin villages.

The German Second Line ran in a south-easterly direction from Pozieres through the gap between the top of Mametz Wood and the front of Bazentin le Petit Wood. Its capture was essential in order to avoid a salient in the Allied lines, and to enable the Allied Artillery to be brought for use in an attempt to take the German Second Line. In his book *The Battle of the Somme* Masefield wrote that the spur was covered with the bogwood of Mametz which was divided into three prongs of woodland in a gradual northwards facing ascent. The highest part of the wood was at its northern limit and then the land broke into a natural scarp or disused quarry, which is where the Second Line ran, with a redoubt of machine guns and trench mortars. The trees in the wood included hornbeams, limes, oaks and a few beeches. The undergrowth having been neglected for two and a half years was very wild and thick especially to the north, where there was bramble as well as hazel. Allied shelling had brought down many of the trees which was going to add to the hazards of the attackers in the forthcoming battle, as they had fallen in full growth. The Germans had built machine gun posts in some of the trees, which were camouflaged with the use of green paint. There were also heavy guns in the wood, as well as field gun batteries to its rear in the Second Line. Barbed wire was strung from tree to tree in the southern section and machine gun pits were also dotted here and there to command some of the clearings.

After the Poodles and Shelter Wood had been taken along with the villages of Mametz and Fricourt the way was clear for attacks towards Mametz Wood. The German 3rd Guard relieved the remnants of the 28th Reserve Division that had its right on the Albert–Bapaume Road and its left on Flat Iron Copse which along with Sabot Copse were to the north-west of Mametz Wood. Their territory also included the wood. After the advance on the 1st July the Germans continued to hold various positions across the spur of the ridge reaching out into the Mametz–Montauban Valley. The main point taken up by the 3rd Guards was the Kaisergraben which protected Contalmaison on the south-west. This trench had been made a few months previously and was almost complete, well wired and possessed dugouts in the chalk which were twenty feet deep. On its right it was connected with Ovillers using Fourth Street which ran in front of Bailiff Wood, its left end connected to Mametz Wood by Wood Trench, which ran into the southern section.

Haig wanted the capture of Mametz Wood and Contalmaison in order to secure the British left flank, whilst on the right Trônes Wood was to be captured. One has the feeling that Haig became impatient, but one also thinks that had he seen the conditions confronting the attackers he would not have been so impatient. If only the Allies had known at the time that the wood was virtually undefended on the 3rd July!

On the night of the 4th/5th July the 17th Div. captured part of the Kaisergraben between the Contalmaison–Fricourt road and Wood Trench, named Quadrangle Trench. They also captured part of Wood Trench. On the 5th July the 7th Division was in front of Mametz Wood with the 91st Bde. On the right flank was the 18th Div. after their progress in the area between Montauban and Mametz and on the left the 17th Div. were still in the front line.

The 38th (Welsh) Division, was to become most associated with the wood, the fighting and the final capture. Its 113th Bde. marched through the old front line up to Mametz Village and then entered the former German communication trench that led to what some called Happy or Death Valley, which ran along the front of the wood, and the Quadrangle which was a small copse to the south-west of the wood. The communication trench was Danzig Alley and there were no duckboards. The Brigade occupied positions to the south-west of the wood on the night of 4th July.

According to Siegfried Sassoon the 1st R. Welch Fus. (22nd Bde. 7th Div.) had started out at 9.15 p.m. on the 4th and had gone up a communication trench and come down across the open hillside that looked towards the wood. They found that the 2nd R. Irish of the same brigade had been bombed and machine gunned by Germans in the wood itself. It was a still and grey morning. At 12.30 p.m. Sassoon saw 30 dead from the 1st R. Welch Fus. laid out in two rows by the Mametz–Carnoy Road. The R. Welch Fus. and the R. Irish had both been sent up to consolidate trenches close by and were meant to clear the outskirts of the wood.

The Irish were first on the scene and found German machine gunners, bombers and snipers in the wood. 'A' Company of the 1st R. Welch Fus. went to help out but were caught by snipers and took shelter in a quarry. The Irish had tried to bomb the wood and had suffered casualties. After that, the Allied artillery helped out with a barrage that enabled the Irish Batt. to escape. It had been assumed by the staff that the nearside of the wood was unoccupied. It was during an attack against Wood Trench in the south corner of the wood that Lt. Moore-Brabazon in 'B' Company of the 2nd R. Irish was wounded in the foot. They were out for 11 hours before returning to their 'field' at 8.30 a.m. on the 5th July. Later the 1st R. Welch Fus. moved off again for an attack on the Quadrangle position close to the wood. They attacked rather undermanned on a front of 600 yards from Bottom Wood. They struggled up to Mametz and Bottom Wood in awful mud after a short bombardment and had to cross 500 yards of open ground. Quadrangle Trench had some wire in front but was also quite shallow and roughly dug. The Germans were bombing up a communication from the wood and the 2nd R. Irish were to attack on their right but failed to get into the enemy trench called Strip Trench.

The 1st R. Welch Fus. established a bombing point on the right where the

Quadrangle Trench came to a sudden end. The Germans continued to snipe from the wood and Sassoon went to a bombing post and frightened 50 or 60 Germans into running back into the wood. A Lewis gun followed the enemy and Quadrangle Trench had fallen. Sassoon was recommended for a decoration which was not proceeded with as the attack had not been 'official'.

On the 6th July the 116th Bde. 38th Div. was to the right and the 113th to the left of the position in front of the wood. The 115th Bde. was to replace the 116th Bde. on the 7th and on the 6th July the 11th SWB halted with the 10th SWB behind Mametz Village. They were both to attack the wood as part of the 115th Bde. attack. At 8 p.m. on the 6th July they had moved to a position in Happy/Death Valley from which to make their attack. They were loaded with bombs, sandbags, steel stakes etc. The communication trench ran through Caterpillar Wood and they came across timber line dugouts and even some German allotments.

On the night of the 6th/7th July a party from the 10th Lancs. Fus. (52nd Bde. 17th Div.) pushed out from Quadrangle Trench and reached the southern end of Contalmaison Village but were unable to hold it. The section of the Kaisergraben in front of the western end of Contalmaison, north of the Contalmaison–Fricourt road was still in enemy hands.

According to *The War in the Air*, No. 3 Squadron was ordered to reconnoitre Mametz Wood and the German positions to the west of it and especially Quadrangle Support Trench which connected the wood with Acid Drop Copse to the north-east of the trench. The copse had been levelled with shell fire, but the majority of trees in the wood were seen to be still standing, not enough of them had been blown over to form a barrier reported one Observer. Quadrangle Support Trench was strongly manned on the 7th July when the next attacks on the wood were due to take place.

The 7th began with heavy showers and there was also a variable wind. It was planned to attack the two German trenches Quadrangle Support Trench, which was about 500 yards north of Quadrangle Trench and the point of Pearl Alley running forward from it. The ground was quite open though. The 17th Division were to take these trenches, although it was thought that the attack would be enfiladed from the wood which is exactly what happened. The enemy counter-attacked followed by another attack by the 52nd Bde. which failed. There was a heavy bombardment as well as fire from the wood and in addition, the attacking troops were slightly late in arriving which didn't help with Artillery co-operation. There was little or no hope of reaching the Quadrangle Support over open ground. On the right bombers of the 50th Bde. were sent to work up Quadrangle Alley but they were driven back, and a company of the 6th Dorsets was decimated by machine gun fire from Strip Trench.

The 38th Div. attacked the wood again at 8.30 a.m., when the 115th Bde. advanced across the valley from the line Marlborough Wood–Western end of Caterpillar Wood. The 16th Welch and the 11th SWB were held up by machine gun fire and the CO of the Borderers was killed. Two more attempts were made during the day but the Welshmen could get no closer than 250 yards from the wood. They were particularly affected by machine gun fire which didn't just come from the wood itself but also from the valley higher up to the north-east (from Flat Iron and Sabot Copses). The operation was abandoned with the loss of 400 men. The 115th Bde. withdrew and two companies of the 17th R. Welch Fus. were left behind to hold the Marlborough Wood–Caterpillar Wood position.

The advance of the 23rd Div. to the left of the 38th and 17th Divisions was held up by the lack of support on their right flank and was forced back from Contalmaison.

During the night of 7th/8th July in the German positions the 122 Reserve Infantry Regiment took over from the 163rd Infantry Regiment between the south-west corner of Mametz Wood and the village of Contalmaison. A section of the 3rd Guards Division the Lehr Regiment which had been holding the southern edge of the wood and about Flat Iron Copse was not relieved. The HQ of the 122 Reserve Infantry Regiment was in Contalmaison Chateau and that of the Lehr Regiment in Mametz Wood itself.

The battle situation on the 8th July was as follows: the 38th Div. was still south of the wood with the 3rd Division on their right and the 17th on their left. The two Brigades to the front of the Welsh Division facing the wood were the 114th Bde. to the right and the 113th Bde. on their left. Quadrangle Support Trench was again attacked at around 5.30 p.m. and the enemy had been quickly alerted, rockets were seen going up behind Contalmaison which was the signal for a heavy German barrage to be brought down on the attackers. The German artillery was in the position of Bailiff Wood to the west of Contalmaison. Not surprisingly the British attack once more failed. The fighting for the wood over the next few days was to be ceaseless.

On the 9th the 38th Div. was closely supported by the 7th Div. in front of the wood and the 3rd Div. was still to the right. On the left of the 38th Div. however the 17th Div. was now supported by the 21st Div. On the morning of the 9th July no attack towards the wood took place and the 17th Div. attacked towards Contalmaison from a starting point at Quadrangle Trench. The 8th S. Staffs. and the 7th Lincolns advanced to the village from the western end of Quadrangle Support and parties did reach as far as Acid Drop Copse and Pearl Alley. But they were unsupported and had to return to Quadrangle Trench, leaving behind them a S. Staffs. machine gun crew at the Copse.

Also on the 9th July a large artillery telescope was found in the cliff between White Trench and Mametz Wood, it had been obviously used by the enemy for observation purposes earlier in the battle. On the same day the German 28th Reserve Division was relieved by units of the 10th Bavarian Division, who were the only reserve of the XIV Reserve Corps.

An account of how the Germans had been faring during this time of intense Allied pressure on the wood has been left by Lt. Köstlin which is worth referring to. He was a member of the 2nd Batt. of the 122 Reserve Infantry and they were ordered to reinforce the 3rd Battalion who occupied the wood. He had taken his company to an ammunition depot at Martinpuich to collect hand grenades and other ammunition and also to have a square meal. The

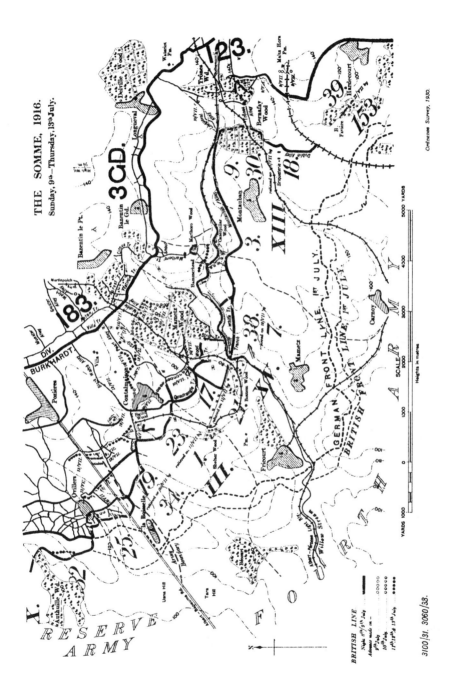

THE SOMME, 1916.
Sunday, 9th–Thursday, 13th July.

Ordnance Survey, 1930.

3/00/31. 3060/38.

meal was interrupted by a shell that hit the field kitchen cart and frightened the horse away! Köstlin took his company across the open land between Contalmaison and Mametz Wood and they were harrassed by the darkness of the night and also by British shelling. In the small hours on reaching the German front positions, he was told that the British had broken through the western end of a trench close to the wood. The Germans were ordered to act on their own initiative and Köstlin took charge, being the senior officer present. The British bombardment began at 3.30 p.m. on the 10th. The wood was difficult to defend apart from a few machine guns in shelter pits. Köstlin concentrated his men on the trench along the southern edge of the wood, with support lines in the open ground on both sides half way up to it, Wood Trench and Wood Support on the west and a line of trench around Flat Iron Copse on the east. The 38th Div. took a direct assault against the southern edge of the wood. They assembled at both corners of the southern and narrow strip of the wood which reached out some 200 yards towards the bed of Mametz Valley. The accuracy of the artillery bombardment allowed the attack on the right and left to make progress but the centre part was held up because of the distance of open ground that companies had to cover. There are several accounts of the fighting both towards and within Mametz Wood which are so well written and seemingly historically accurate that it is very difficult not to draw considerably upon them. However I do recommend readers to get hold of copies of at least three books that cover the fighting for Mametz Wood and they are Wyn Griffith's *Up to Mametz*, David Jones' *In Parenthesis* and Guy Chapman's anthology *Vain Glory*. Wyn Griffith and Jones were both in the 15th R. Welch Fus. (Carmarthen) Welsh although Jones was a private, and Griffith was a Lieutenant on the staff. They did not meet during this period and in fact it was unusual for men from the 'other ranks' to have much of a relationship with anyone who was commissioned.

Griffith described the attempts of the 38th Div. to take the wood in the period 9th/10th July and the build up and delays of the days before the main battle. He was with Lt. Taylor the Brigade Signalling Officer and they were on their way to Pommiers Redoubt which is to the east of Mametz Village and looks towards the wood. They saw in preparation for the big attack lines of batteries, ammunition dumps, wagons and stores. He slept in what was previously a German dugout. At this time it was Contalmaison to the west of Mametz Wood which was due to be barraged and captured, as a prelude to the taking of Mametz Wood. From Pommiers Redoubt they scanned the wood with their field glasses and Griffith wrote that it seemed 'as thick as a virgin forest', there was seemingly no sign of life in it, though there could have been ten machine guns concealed in it or ten thousand men! The wood's edges were clean cut, much as they are 70 odd years later and the ground between Pommiers Redoubt and the wood was completely bare of cover.

The men of the 38th Div. were assembled in trenches above a dip in the ground. The plan was to advance and then descend into the hollow before crossing the bare slope which was bound to be covered by machine guns. On their right as they advanced they would be exposed to enfilade fire from the direction of Flat Iron Copse. The General then arrived with his Brigade Major and Staff Captain and they established their HQ in the signaller's dugout. The shelling of Contalmaison continued and after a while the artillery bombarded the edge of the wood. The infantry were to go forward in three stages, and then to penetrate the wood. A few minutes after 8 a.m. the wires to the battalions were cut by the enemy artillery, there was also no smoke screen to give the advance protection. Runners brought bad news about the attack, in particular that the artillery had made no real difference to the German defences. The attack went on towards the wood and the artillery were to begin another bombardment. The operation was in isolation without support from either flank. The second attack began, but a frontal attack towards the wood in such conditions was doomed to failure. Griffith and the General set off to Caterpillar Wood to make contact with the battalions. On their way Griffith came across a disused trench after passing through Caterpillar Wood and asked an Artillery Officer in it if his telephone line was still working, which it was. He was in touch with the Heavy Artillery beyond Pommiers Redoubt. Griffith joined the General and they dropped down into the Nullah between Caterpillar Wood and Mametz Wood. In a bank close to the Nullah there were scores of stretchers on the ground because it was an ADS. On the bare ridge beyond, the Welsh Battalions were burrowing into the open ground with their entrenching tools. The Nullah was out of sight of the enemy. The time for the third attack towards the wood drew near, and the General and Griffith planned to cancel it, as to go on was a senseless waste of men's lives. The General had thought that the best approach had been to creep up to the edge of the wood at night and to rush it in the morning. Griffith remembered the Artillery Officer's telephone and the General used it to call off the attack and to save the total annihilation of the Brigade. Six weeks later the General, Major Gen. I. Philips, went home to England 'under a cloud'.

On the 9th July the two remaining Brigades of the 38th Div. were to attack Mametz Wood once more and Griffith's Bde. were to take over the defence of the wood if the attack was successful. This time the front was to be narrower and there was to be greater artillery support, but at the last moment the attack was called off and postponed for twelve hours. Griffith wrote that it was not until dawn of the 10th July that the 'flower of young Wales stood up to machine guns with a success that astonished all those who knew the ground'. Griffith had on the 10th assumed the duties of a Staff Captain.

From the 9th July Maj. Gen. H. E. Watts was put in temporary command of the 38th Div. for three days, the period during which the wood was finally to fall into Allied hands.

The full 38th Div. planned to attack at 4.15 a.m. on the 10th July, the task of the 114th Bde. was the eastern portion of the wood and the 113th Bde. were allocated the western portion. The central ride which ran through the wood was the dividing line. (The wood was divided into sections by various rides.) The 115th Bde. was in reserve near Minden Post and Mametz. Three quarters of an hour before the attack was due to start a heavy barrage was concentrated on the southern edge of the wood and a smoke cover was provided at the eastern end and at the south-west of the wood. The activity at the south-west of the wood drew the German fire whilst the main thrust was to be carried out to the east of these positions. The infantry began to advance at 4.15 a.m. with the 13th R. Welch Fus. to the right, the 14th R. Welch in the centre and the 16th R. Welch on the left. The 16th on the left suffered very heavy casualties including their Commanding Officer and were repulsed by German machine gun fire. The 14th speedily cleared their portion in the centre of the line. The 13th on the right had to be reinforced by the 15th and David Jones was one of their number being in 'B' Company of the 6th Platoon. Eventually the 13th, 14th and 15th Batts. were able to form a line just south of the most southern cross ride eastwards, from its junction with the main ride. On the south-west side of the wood the Germans still held Wood Support Trench, and their enfilading fire held up the advance in the Wood itself. There was a gap between the R. Welch Fus. Battalions which was filled by the 10th Welch of the 114th Bde. The 19th Welch Battalion, Pioneer Battalion to the 38th Div. were ordered up to dig a trench all along the southern side and to wire it. By early afternoon Wood Support Trench was taken by the 13th R. Welch Fus. under Lt. Col. O. Flower who was later killed by a shell. The wood was now partly in Allied hands and troops from the 115th Bde. were sent up from Minden Post to reinforce the 114th Bde. At 4 p.m. on the 11th July a further advance took the 38th Div. to the northern end of the wood. The eastern side of the wood was taken and the Germans fled to Sabot Copse away in the direction of Bazentin le Grand Wood. Allied machine gun fire from both Caterpillar and Marlborough Woods caused many casualties amongst the German defenders. The 15th Welch east of the central ride in the wood and the 17th and 15th R. Welch Fus. to the west of it fought to up to 40 yards from the northern edge of the wood and the remainder of the 115th Bde. were brought up and the 113th and 114th Bdes. were relieved.

During the fighting David Jones was wounded, in the southern part of the wood and in his book *In Parenthesis* he describes in poetic form what happened to him and his colleagues. He describes the wood, which is one of the largest on the Somme, as the 'Queen of the Woods'. The whole experience of his fighting with the 15th R. Welch Fus. is brilliantly portrayed, and it was an experience that was to become an obsession with him for the rest of his life as it did for Wyn Griffith. Jones found that with his wound he could neither walk nor stand, and so he crawled towards the British line and hoped that he would meet up with a RAMC man. He still had his rifle with its bayonet in the fixed position and somehow it fouled his helmet. It was with feelings of guilt that Jones abandoned his rifle although he kept hold on his gas mask. A corporal came across him and carried him to safety on his back until a major told the corporal to set him down. Jones recalls being in a large marquee with other casualties and it being very hot. He had what was called a 'beautiful blighty'. Some of the men in David Jones' poem, if not all, were based on real persons. Thus there was a Major referred to as 'that shit Major Lillywhite' who was killed in the wood, and Aunty Bebbridge was based on Brig. Gen. Price Davies VC. Colonel Bell is 'Well Dell', and Reg Allen, in the dedication, was a Lewis gunner.

This then describes briefly the taking of the wood on 10th/11th July but there are other accounts which are worth considering and to find out what happened to Wyn Griffith we turn once more to his book *Up To Mametz*. Just before dawn on the 10th General Watts and the Brigade Major went up towards the wood leaving Griffith to follow at noon. However the major was wounded which meant that Griffith had to be up at the wood at 7 a.m. having passed through two barrages. He saw dead from his old battalion the 15th R. Welch Fus. with the distinctive yellow band on their sleeves. Before the division actually attacked the wood it was known that it was full of dense undergrowth and had a labyrinth of trenches and dugouts as well as wire stretched across from tree to tree. The central ride led to a communication trench which led to the German second line to the north of the wood. This was useful for enemy reinforcements and it also meant that the wood could at any time be quickly evacuated and subsequently bombarded. Griffith found that all the time he was on a ride that he could make progress but it was very difficult to struggle through the undergrowth to the left and right. There were other horrors, not just dead soldiers but bits of soldiers, mutilated trunks, detached heads and splashes of blood on the green leaves. It was these sort of horrible sights that were to give the wood its sinister reputation to troops who passed this way once that it had been taken by the British. Griffith recalled vividly the smell of 'green' timber and in later life when he smelt this smell again it recalled the horrors that he witnessed in 1916. He reached a cross ride in the wood where four lanes broadened and near this ring was a group of officers. The Brigadier was talking to one of his Battalion Commanders and to Lt. Taylor the Signals Officer as well as the Intelligence Officer. At that time the line held was about 300 yards south of the northern edge of the wood. The units were very mixed up and Griffith was responsible to give them their boundaries. They were attempting to dig themselves in in the undergrowth. The battalions in the wood were relieved at dawn. The 162nd Bde. of the 21st Div. completed the job of reaching the northern edge of the wood, and consolidated it. Their line was linked up with 7th Div. on the right and the 1st Div. on the left.

Lt. Köstlin had been defending Quadrangle Support Trench to the west of the wood which should have been captured the night before thus making the German position untenable. He shot down many bombers at the Sap Head including those of the 7th E. Yorks (50th Bde. 17th Div.) a flanking Division, but at the time was not aware that the Welsh Division had reached the centre of the wood although he could see khaki figures behind him who were probably from the 6th Dorsets (50th Bde. 17th Div.). The Germans were able to shoot down many of the British troops who had appeared in the large clearing south of the wood across which was Wood Support.

Liddell Hart wrote in his memoirs that his Division, the 21st, moved up on the 10th July. He said that it was astonishing to see how 'trench warfare had vanished for the moment, with lines of guns standing out in the open almost wheel to wheel'.

On the 10th the Allied attack had reached to within forty yards of the northern edge of the wood and on the same day Contalmaison had been taken for the third time, by the 23rd Division and this time it was held. The remaining strip of Mametz Wood was taken by the 21st Division who had relieved the 38th Div. who eventually moved to Coigneux where it relieved the 48th Div. taking over the line to the south of Hébuterne and Gommecourt.

Wyn Griffith was to write about his experiences in Mametz Wood not only in his book *Up to Mametz* but also in his piece *The Pattern of One Man's Remembering.* 'I can only call it a kind of emotional explosion inside me, and under its impetus I wrote on and on until I came towards a kind of climax, the Battle of Mametz Wood in July 1916, where so many of my countrymen, including my own brother, were killed. There I stopped, because I was afraid of my own memories and dreaded their coming to life' — 'But the challenge was still there, in Mametz Wood, and I found that there was no peace within me until I had faced and recorded this high point of the war where for me and so many other Welshmen the tragedy reached its culmination. The words had to be torn out of me, hurt as it must. The events are mere history, to be found in many books, but my own reactions, as I recorded them, turned remembering into a surgical operation. And, as happens with the body, there came afterward a kind of peace within. I had spent my emotional capital, in this detailed recovery of what I thought to have been buried beneath years of happiness, and I was left in what I can only call a neutral state. This kind of remembering had done its work, and I was purged of the pain of war, untroubled, confident that I had nothing more to fear from its recurrence in the years ahead'.

To get back to the battle the 7th and 21st Divisions had taken over from the 38th Division and the immediate objective of the 7th Div. was the trench that ran south of Bazentin le Grand Wood known here as Flat Iron Trench, which the 2nd Queen's (91st Bde.) reached and overran on the 13th and 14th. The Division's final objective was the establishment of a line from the north-east corner of that wood to the northern edge of Bazentin le Petit. As stated the main task of taking the wood had been carried out on the 10th when the Welsh Division was virtually brought to a standstill by the conditions in the wood. Apart from all the horrors of wood fighting and the continuous German shelling there was also an acute shortage of water. It was not until the early morning of the 12th July however that the wood was completely in British hands. When it was finally cleared hundreds of dead Germans were found and also 13 heavy guns just beyond it including two batteries of old French fortress guns from Mauberge on high overback carriages.

On the 13th July the 62nd Bde. 21st Div. had their HQ on the western edge of the wood which was HQ of one the Leicester Batts. as well of the 21st Division. They found the wood littered with dead and the rides blocked by fallen trees. Before dawn the Brigade exchanged with the 63rd Bde. 21st Div. and the 6th and 7th Leicesters 21st Div. carried the German second line trench to the north of Mametz Wood. Seven enemy machine guns alone were captured in this trench. Colonel Haigh of the 9th Leicesters (110th Bde. 37th Div.) was in Forest Trench and he gave instructions for the troops to go forward to occupy the north side of the wood. The attack had been very costly, partly because co-operation between the artillery and infantry was still in its infancy and it was hard for the infantry always to keep up with their own barrage.

The 7th Leicesters lost 14 officers in the attack. However they had the satisfaction of seeing the enemy routed as from an orchard near Bazentin Village they could see the Germans running back. During this time though the Germans were still shelling the north-west part of the wood, which cost a lot of casualties. On the 14th July they were ordered to withdraw although as it happened there was no one on hand to relieve them. One company of the 1st E. Yorks (64th Bde. 21st Div.) was left behind who had come up to reinforce the line. Brigade casualties were about 2,000 out of 3,000 with high officer casualties. Communication had been very poor which contributed to the carnage.

The scheme to capture the rest of the German Second Line had been worked out by General Rawlinson in co-operation with his Corps and Divisional Commanders. The Commander in Chief was at first reluctant to grant permission to carry it out as he thought that there would be greater risk in the attack as planned which was to be a night attack. However it finally began at 3.25 a.m. on the 14th July. The task of XV Corps was to give cover for XIII Corps under which assaulting lines could form. In the wood at this time flies had settled thicky. There was sticky sediment at the bottom of the shell holes and another horror in the wood at this time was the wreckage of an Allied aeroplane.

In a letter dated 10th July 1941 written by Hart to Robert Graves (King's College LH 1/327/35) he mentions that his battalion the 9th KOYLIs had moved up from Fricourt in order to take up position in support in Bottom Wood just by the Quadrangle which the 1st R. Welch Fus. had taken. And in the early hours of the 14th July they had moved slightly forward and flank-wise up to the fringe of Mametz Wood, where they found themselves amongst the dead of the Welsh battalions that had attacked it earlier.

In Hart's memoirs he described the 64th Bde. as moving forward, in case it was needed, and that they lay on the edge of Mametz Wood under a hot sun amid rows of decaying and strongly smelling corpses. In pushing on into the wood the dead were even thicker and often German and Briton were locked in a death grapple. In Hart's letter already referred to above he also told Graves that he would have marched up the Méaulte–Fricourt Road in the early hours of 15th July and that his battalion (Hart's) had gone up the same road on the afternoon of the 12th or 13th July, having been out of the line since 1st July in order to recuperate.

Indeed in *Goodbye to All That*, Graves wrote that on 15th July they struck the Méaulte–Fricourt–Bazentin road which ran through Happy Valley. Just beyond Fricourt a German barrage made progress on the road impassable and so they left it. They arrived at Mametz Wood at 8 a.m. Although he himself was still with the transport, Siegfried Sassoon's battalion the 2nd R. Welch Fus. was involved in the Mametz Wood fighting from the 14th to the 17th of July and on the 14th he had managed to meet up with his friend Robert Graves who before going up to Mametz Wood had been bivouacked by the Bécordel Road, and they had managed to have a long talk.

Robert Graves who was in the same battalion as Frank Richards mentions in his autobiography on the 16th that they were amongst the dead of their own New Army Battalion who had helped to capture it. They had halted in thick mist which had been caused by the Germans using lachrymatory shells. They spent two days in bivouac outside the wood and like Richards he went into the wood and took greatcoats from the bodies of dead Prussians who lay there. In addition to there being dead from the Royal Welch New Army Battalion there were also the dead from the South Wales Borderers who Graves describes as being small New Army men.

Graves wrote at least three poems as a result of this experience and one is called 'Letter to S.S. from Mametz Wood' in which he describes what they will do after the war. He talks of them living in North Wales in a country seat, a sort of 'Morlancourtish Billet' and the final line is 'And God, what poetry we'll write'.

Another dialogue poem between him and Sassoon begins:
'Back from the Somme two Fusiliers
Limped painfully home; the elder said,
S. "Robert, I've lived three thousand years
This Summer, and I'm nine parts dead".'

In 1917 Graves published a collection of poems which he dedicated to his Regiment. The volume is called *Fairies and Fusiliers*. One of the poems is called 'A Dead Boche' and part of it is as follows:
'Today I found in Mametz Wood
A certain cure for lust of blood:
where, propped against a sheltered trunk,
In a great mess of things unclean,
Sat a dead Boche; he scowled and stunk
with clothes and face a sodden green,
Big-bellied, spectacled, crop-haired,
Dribbling black blood from nose to beard'.

Frank Richards (2nd R. Welch Fus.) wrote a book called *Old Soldiers Never Die*, and he was also a contributor to *The War the Infantry Knew*, which was a book on the history of the same battalion. In his own book he noted that they had arrived from a railhead, and that on the 15th July had passed through Fricourt where their first battalion had broken through on 1st July. He had been transferred to 'A' Company and after Fricourt they reached Mametz Wood. He described the valley as being thick with guns, and that there were small howitzers on the ridge behind them.

The Germans had been sending over tear gas, and the valley was thick with it, and the ground all around was covered with the bodies of the men who had been killed during the taking of the wood. The battle was going on about threequarters of a mile ahead and a few hours later his battalion moved round the corner of Mametz Wood and Richards' company occupied a shallow tench which was only knee deep. The majority of the company then went 'on the scrounge' in the wood for food and German top coats. It was at this time that the German artillery was firing with pin point accuracy, and this had been made possible by a German officer who had stayed behind and with the use of a communications cable which stretched from Bazentin le Petit as far back as High Wood had directed the German artillery. He was later discovered and captured by a patrol of a Middlesex Battalion on the 17th July.

On the 15th July Liddell Hart wrote home to his parents (LH7/1916/15) and told them that he was on his way up from the rest position to take up residence in a line of rough shelter trenches which had been dug on the north side of Mametz Wood. The artillery he told them was from three divisions and was subsequently very noisy and was grouped around Hart's position. This artillery also attracted enemy retaliation. Hart's battalion which was the 9th KOYLI moved up towards the front line via the east side of Mametz Wood and was relieved three days later when Liddell Hart was wounded.

In his book *The Machine Gunner* Arthur Russell wrote that in mid July he was within four miles of the forward infantry positions and he and his colleagues spent a night on the slopes of a ridge beyond Mametz Village, prior to going up the line the next morning. He reported 15 inch, 12 inch, 9.2 inch howitzers and 6 inch long naval guns situated all around the area where they were bivouacked. The next day the machine gun teams moved off with the infantry platoons. As 'A' Section of the 98th Company Machine Gun Corps together with the 4th King's of the 98th Bde. 33rd Div. reached a point some three hundred yards behind the Allied line they were ordered to dig in along a ridge of high ground at the end of Mametz Valley close to Bazentin le Petit Wood. Their Company Commander was in his dugout on the edge of Mametz Wood. Their job was to sit tight and await orders. They were to support the 33rd Div. who were involved in the fighting beyond the Bazentin villages and in the vicinity of High Wood.

The author Gerald Brenan who was a member of the 48th Div., who in mid July were involved in the battle for Bazentin Ridge describes the scene in Mametz Wood at this time. 'Its trees were torn and shattered, its leaves had turned brown, and there was a shell hole every three yards. This was a place where something almost unheard of had taken place – fierce hand-to-hand fighting in the open with bombs and bayonets. What seemed extraordinary was that all the dead bodies there lay just as they had fallen in their original places as though they were being kept as an exhibit for a war museum. German in their field-grey uniforms, British in their khaki, lying side by side, their faces and their hands a pale waxy green, the colour of rare marble. Heads covered with flat mushroom helmets next to heads in domed steel helmets that came down behind the ears. Some of these figures still sat with their bare backs against a tree and two of them – this had to be seen to be believed – stood locked together by their bayonets, which had pierced one another's bodies and sustained in that position by the tree trunk against which they had fallen.'

On the 16th July 19th Bde. Transport which had followed the infantry of the 2nd R. Welch Fus. of the 33rd Div. was dismissed. Battery after battery was rolling into Mametz Valley and onto the slight rise of Caterpillar Wood, until the site was stiff not just with guns but with batteries. Whole brigades sat down en masse in a field, and they bivouacked there for several nights. The 'whole show' was in the open guns and all.

Captain C. H. Pigg of the 2nd Worc. (100th Bde. 33rd Div.) has left a diary and wrote 'Early on 16th July we reached the Bazentins, reformed and marched back a short distance to the south-eastern side of Mametz Wood, where the remnants of the Bde. re-assembled and rested. Water was scarce we couldn't shave ourselves. As the day wore on the shell fire became incessant, and presently we saw coming up the valley beside Mametz Wood a long and curious caravan containing guns. Nothing less like war could have been imagined; but the word to halt was given, the caravan deployed and, in less time than it takes to write, a battery of French 75s was in action. Their precision and speed was beautiful to watch, and equally was the skill with which they went to ground. It was the only time I saw these superb gunners in action. We sat down to tea on ammunition boxes by the track in the open. There were about a dozen officers surviving, and we had reached that last stage when bullets and shell fire became meaningless; some part of the creature was numb, and we seemed immune to fear. On our left lay Mametz Wood, torn by shell fire and strewn with dead of both armies; in the open there still lay some of the men who had fallen in the assault; on our right lay the main track leading up to the front, crowded with traffic of all kinds, and lined by dead mules and horses. The brigade was busy beside us going to ground (they began to be shelled) – Soon after dark we had orders to move into Mametz Wood to occupy the old front line trenches on its northern face. We moved into and up the wood in single file with a bright moon filtering through the shattered trees; a few shells broke the eerie stillness. Along our path lay many Boches frightfully bloated and distorted by death – We reached our position along its northern edge and fixed company headquarters in a deep German dugout near a howitzer gun which they had been unable to remove. Here the enemy must have lived for many months, and, though the dugout was fairly clean, its typical Boche-stench was nauseating. But we had no greatcoats or blankets and were glad of some cover.'

It was about the 17th July when Liddell Hart moving back with the 9th KOYLI after relief was passing through Mametz Wood, suddenly heard a lot of shells falling around them, but they didn't explode and then there was a strong smell of gas. Hart began to cough violently and stayed on to warn platoons of the danger, and he then led his company back to battalion bivouac. On the 18th he reported to the nearest Field Ambuance to get his earlier wound seen to and on examining his chest the doctor immediately put him on stretcher. Hart was on his way to the King Edward VII's Hospital for Officers in London. Frank Richards who was with the signals of the 2nd

R. Welch Fus. of the 33rd Div. wrote in his book that during the period 19th/20th July after being shelled at Bazentin le Petit they were relieved and returned to Mametz Wood. Eight of them and the Brigade Signalling Corporal were detailed off to form a transmitting station for visual signallers between High Wood and Brigade HQ, presumably 19th Bde. which was situated on the fringe of Mametz Wood. No telephones could be carried and their station would receive messages by flag and from the signallers with the attacking force, which they would transmit by heliograph or flag. The position that they had to take was by a large mill this side of High Wood (this mill was at Bazentin G.G.). It was built on some rising ground which made it a very important landmark. They fixed up the heliograph and the telescope and at 8 a.m. were in communication with brigade. The enemy then started a terrific barrage and the mill seemed to be in the middle of it. One message said that the wood would be taken and another gave news of a counter-attack. As the Signallers in the wood were knocked out messages later came by runners. The enemy then turned a machine gun on the mill as their flag waving had attracted their attention.

On the 20th July the 2nd R. Welch Fus. were relieved in confusion, and held in reserve in shell holes between Longueval–Contalmaison Road and Flat Iron Copse. Any exit point from Mametz Valley was a busy traffic route and subsequently a favourite target of the German gunners. Artillery was behind the Welch Battalion and HQ and details were under the muzzles of two batteries. Brigade was in poor quarters, a thinly roofed trench in the south-east of Mametz Wood.

On the 21st some of the battalion, even the most hard bitten, were beginning to show the strain through which they had been passing.

On the 22nd July the Commanding Officer Maj. Gen. Ingouville-Williams of the 34th Div. who had been reconnoitering the ground in the vicinity of Mametz Wood was killed on the bank at Queen's Nullah after having walked back from Contalmaison round the south side of the wood to meet his car. He was buried at Warloy–Baillon Cemetery. Dumps were stored at the south-east corner of the wood which were used to get material forward to High Wood. The wood at this time had two shallow trenches and very insecure dugouts. All around the guns continued almost incessantly and along the road was an almost endless stream of transport of all kinds, water wagons, motors, and horse ambulances, cyclists and officers on horseback. Many gunners slept beside their guns during this period of the battle.

On 23rd July the 10th Worcesters (57th Bde. 19th Div.) rested at Flat Iron Copse in a reserve position close to the strong point called the Snout, which was projected in the form of a triangle.

On the 5th August C. S. Collison of the 11th R. Warwicks (112th Bde. 37th Div.) went forward with a brother officer via Quadrangle Trench, on the south-west side and into the wood itself, to arrange for the relief of the 11th Suffolks (101th Bde. 34th Div.) who were entrenched in the southern outskirts of Bazentin le Petit Wood, and also in the north-western section of Mametz Wood. The Battalion left Bécourt by half platoons on the afternoon of the 6th August, and established itself in its new positions, two companies being in Mametz Wood. The 10th LN Lancs. (112th Bde. 37th Div.) occupied the north-eastern border of the wood, whilst the 6th Bedfords and the 8th E. Lancs. held the trenches to the north of Bazentin le Petit. The space that divided Bazentin and Mametz Woods was ploughed and furrowed by shell fire and in many places arms and legs were to be seen protruding from the ground. At 7.30 p.m. on the 10th the 11th R. Warwicks relieved the 6th Bedfords in the line to the north of the village, and the 10th LN Lancs. took over the ground to the right, in relief of the 8th E. Lancs. The British troops were now approaching the summit of the great ridge, whose southern slopes were marked by the villages of Bazentin le Petit, Pozieres and Thiepval. In the evening of the 14th August the 11th R. Warwicks were relieved by the 10th Lincolns (101th Bde. 34th Div.) and moved to the northern and north-western border of Mametz Wood. On relief they proceeded through the desolation by the 'Quadrangle' of trenches, Fricourt Farm, to Bécourt wood, where the battalion bivouacked. Collison was fortunate to get a small room to himself in Bécourt Chateau.

Also on the 14th August the 2nd KRRC (2nd Bde. 2st Div.) were positioned in Mametz Wood as part of the 1st Divisional Reserve. They were frequently shelled whilst there, and they supplied working parties during this period. On the 19th August they moved off to the north-west of High Wood. Towards the end of the month and also briefly in early September they were back in Mametz Wood for a brief time. The 2nd KRRC arrived at the wood on 26th August from Bécourt Wood and on their way to a trench in part of High Wood.

On the 6th September the author of the novel *Other Ranks* – W. V. Tilsley said that on the way to the front line in the dusk 'C' Company was turned into a saturated cornfield near Mametz. On the crest behind them there was an amazingly long Naval Gun, on stupendous mountings. Still further behind, in a deep basin between the ridges, a dimunutive battalion of the Guards Brigade paraded. Along the road to Happy Valley wormed a toylike procession of transports. In mid September after an unsuccessful attack on High Wood the 2nd Welch with the 1st Glosters returned to dugouts at the upper end of Mametz Wood. They had lost 193 men in the attack. They then marched back to Millencourt. The New Zealand Brigade had bivouacked in Mametz Wood in mid September before going up to the ridge between Delville Wood and High Wood.

John Glubb who was with the Royal Engineers wrote in *Into Battle* that they marched with the sappers to some dugouts behind Mametz Wood, for the attack on High Wood which was to begin again on the 15th September at 6.20 a.m. The Cavalry were stationed at Bécourt and long streams of troops and wagons poured up the Mametz Road. He first saw tanks at this time having had no prior knowledge of them. Also on the 15th the sappers left with their forage carts at 6 a.m. to mend the road from Bazentin le Petit to High Wood, as soon as the latter was taken. Glubb had to spend the day in Mametz Wood in case messages came in for Company HQ. The sappers were not disturbed for the first few hours, as the German guns were concentrated on the infantry instead.

The 47th Div. were up near the line by Flat Iron Copse, and the ground was 'alive' with field guns, many of them were hidden by the roadside and startled the unwary. This was prior to the 15th September attack and the 5th London Field Ambulance was set up at the Copse which was shared with the New Zealand and 2/3 North'd Field Ambulance.

The 142nd Bde. 47th Div. were about Mametz Wood in reserve on the 15th September and were ready to move forward to Bazentin le Grand where it would be in support to the attacking Brigade.

The 18th KRRC of the 122nd Bde. 41st Div. were in the wood on 2nd October for one night and on the 12th were at Mametz Wood Camp.

Around 7th October the 11th RW Kents (122nd Bde. 41st Div.) left bivouacs near the wood and entrained at the local siding , which the REs had built.

The 10th and 11th R. Scots (27th Bde. 9th Div.) were bivouacked at the wood on 10th October.

In mid October the Germans had begun to night bomb which was another disturbing element to add to the artillery shelling. The Allied guns were still very much in evidence in the area of the wood and in Mametz Valley. Towards the end of October the 151st Bde. (50th Div.) were in the wood as Divisional Reserve. A CP was here at the end of the battle. At the end of November after the battle had 'officially finished' there was the work of repairs and consolidation still to be done as well as to prepare for a winter stay for the infantry. In addition plank roads were built in Mametz Wood.

Flat Iron Copse Cemetery is at the southern end of the Copse which is to the north-east of the wood. The ground was cleared by the 3rd and 7th Divs. on the 14th July, and an ADS was established at the Copse. The Cemetery was begun about the 20th July according to the Register, and it remained in use until April 1917. After the Armistice 1,149 graves were brought in from smaller cemeteries in the neighbouring battlefields and these former cemeteries included Caterpillar Cemetery, Montauban, Cross Roads Cemetery, Bazentin, Mametz Wood Cemetery which had been on the western outskirts of the wood, Quadrangle Cemetery between Bottom Wood and Mametz Wood, Valley Cemetery between the Montauban Brickworks and Maltzhorn Farm and lastly Villa Wood Cemeteries which were close to a small copse to the north of Mametz Wood.

Originally the 7th Division erected a memorial in Mametz Village itself and the 14th and 16th R. Welch Fus. erected memorials in the wood to commemorate their involvement. The 38th Div. with whose name the wood will be always most associated, ironically captured the wood again after the German breakthrough in the Spring of 1918.

Today the wood is very much the same outward shape of 70 years ago and the only sign of life at the southern edge over the open ground that the Welshmen had to attack are the quietly chewing cows! It is pretty dense, though one can easily retrace the rides that were such a feature of the fighting as well as discover equipment and former elephant hutting shelters. In July 1987 a memorial to the 38th (Welsh) is due to be unveiled in front of the wood.

Mansell Copse

The Copse was the wood that the 9th Devons (20th Bde. 7th Div.) were to penetrate on 1st July in the attack on the village of Mametz. The Battalion assembled some 250 yards behind the front trench and went forward on what was the steep side of a valley. From the moment its first lines entered no man's land they were hit by devastating machine gun fire not only from trenches south of Mametz village but also long range from Fricourt Wood. In attempting to move past the Copse the Devons and in particular the 'A' Company had suffered appallingly high casualties. Many of the Battalion dead are buried close by. (See Mametz Village entry.)

Max Plowman author of *Subaltern on the Somme* was in tents in the copse with the 11th W. Yorks in September and remarked that they looked down on the no man's land of the 1st July. His battalion later moved on to Trônes Wood. The 16th KRRC camped at Mansell Camp and Briqueteries Camp in the period 20th October to 5th November.

Maple Redoubt

Maple Redoubt was behind the British lines due south of Bois Français Trenches at Fricourt. It was adjacent to the track that led to the rear of Point 71 South.

The Redoubt was a strong point that had been built in case the enemy attacked the British front line and pierced it. Orders were that the Redoubt in such an eventuality was to be held at all costs and to the last man, even if the Germans were to get right past and down the hill towards Bray. There was a dugout there which was provisioned with enough bully beef and water in petrol cans for such an emergency. There was also a certain amount of barbed wire that was erected to the east and north-west of the position supported by two Lewis guns. There was another store of provisions at 71 North. It was unlikely that the Germans would have made an attack as they had a perfectly good position on the ridge, which they had been making into a strong line of defence for two years.

The main source of information on the life behind the British lines south of Fricourt in the late winter and spring of 1916 is Bernard Adams of the 1st R. Welch Fus. in his book *Nothing of Importance*. In February he wrote 'We are in support in a place called Maple Redoubt, on the reverse slope of a big ridge. Good dug-outs, and a view behind, over a big expanse of chalk downs, which is most exhilarating. A day of blue sky and a tingle of frost. Being on the reverse slope, you can walk about anywhere, and so can see everything.'

On another occasion in early February he wrote that 'I sat up in "the fort" most of the day, watching the bombardment'. On the hundred metre contour line Adams wrote that there was a small quarry and 'there was a disused support trench running west from the Quarry, – It ran just along the crest of the hill, and commanded even a better view of Fricourt than the Quarry itself.'

Another writer who was in the same area was Siegfried Sassoon who often refers to these same redoubts and trenches in his autobiography and diary. In his *Memoirs of an Infantry Officer* he mentions going up the line and using Canterbury Trench and passing the dugouts of the support company of the R. Welch Fus. at Maple Redoubt on his way to the Company HQ dugouts. On 1st July the battalions in the area were the 20th Manchesters and the 1st R. Welch Fus. of the 7th Division and Fricourt village which had been over-looked for so long by the British was evacuated by the Germans during the night of 1st/2nd July. Sassoon mentions that he talked to men of the 7th Division on 12th July and also saw the French 75s at Maple Redoubt. On the 13th he noted that he was reading novels of Thomas Hardy such as *Tess of the D'Urbervilles* and *The Return of the Native*.

Maricourt

Maricourt is on the D 938 Albert–Peronne Road. It is north of Vaux on the River Somme, south of Montauban and east of Carnoy and Mametz. It was just behind the Allied front line before 1st July and marked the junction of the British and French forces. The boundary line went south-westwards through the village in the direction of Cappy. Southwards in the British and the French lines were several more copses that gave shelter to batteries. A XIII Corps ADS was established here at the beginning of the battle on the road between the village and Bray. At the end of June assembly trenches were in front of Oxford Copse in a hollow. Both Oxford and Cambridge Copses were south of the Maricourt–Carnoy road to the west of the last named village. The objective for the 30th Div. was to be Montauban on 1st July. Machine Gun Wood was to the north-west of the village just behind the 1st July front line.

One observer of the situation in this area before the battle began was R. B. Talbot Kelly who was busy taking up supplies of ammunition to the spur behind Maricourt where battle positions were being prepared. Because of the closeness of the British and French lines the two Armies shared many tracks and roads, and the French used some of the 1870 mortar guns. Kelly was busy for two or three days in helping to prepare a more advanced position in the British second line trenches and helping to register the guns from an OP in the hedge in front of the village. On the 23rd June they had begun to cut the wire in front of Glatz Redoubt which was south-west of the famous Briqueterie at Montauban. The British guns fell steeply away on the right into Suzanne Valley and across the valley there were four lines of French batteries, firing at right angles to the British line. At 5 a.m. on the 1st July

Talbot Kelly set out through a white mist for the OP in Maricourt. In front of him stretched a little valley on the left by a small battered coppice on the edge of which he could just pick out the uneasy twistings of the British front line trench.

Maricourt Ridge contained masses of artillery both heavy and field partly because it was a reverse slope towards the enemy. There was also excellent observation from the ridge towards the Montauban–Mametz Road.

The 30th Div. set off towards Montauban and I refer readers to the Montauban entry for further details of the action. The 19th King's of the 89th Bde. 30th Div. were in reserve in the north-west corner of the village. The battle went well and after lunch Talbot Kelly together with his Major and two signallers walked across the battlefield towards Montauban the Divisional objective.

John Masefield said that in modern war wet weather favours defence as so much depends on the roads being hard enough to bear the advancing cannon in order to secure a conquered strip. The success between Ovillers and Maricourt had made it necessary to advance the British guns along a front of six miles, which meant that the British had to put suddenly on little country roads, a great traffic of horse, gun, caissons, and mechanical transport. When the weather broke, as it broke on 4th July the holes and trenches that had been filled in became canals and pools, and the surface of the earth a rottenness.

During the attack towards Montaban when the 2nd R. Scots were part of the 90th Bde. their MO G. D. Fairley was wounded in the right arm. Although he fainted, and was far from well, he worked on with attending both British and German casualties before being evacuated to hospital. He described the Germans as either being young or towards middle age. This account is in the Peter Liddle collection at Sunderland.

The *Official History* describes the situation at Maricourt Salient as being embarrassingly congested with both French and British troops.

G. W. Warwick who wrote *We Band of Brothers* in which he told of his experience fighting with the South Africans wrote that on the 5th July they marched to the old German trenches opposite Maricourt. He was involved in digging new trenches under machine gun fire at Glatz Redoubt. They camped at Montauban. During this time he was wounded and was taken by a small motor ambulance to the Maricourt Dressing Station. His kilt had been badly torn and he was made comfortable at the Dressing Station.

On 8th July Lt. Col. E.H. Trotter, the CO of the 18th King's, was killed at the HQ of the 21st Bde. HQ at Train Alley to the west of Glatz Redoubt, south-west of Montauban, as was Lt. Col. W.A. Smith of the 18th Manchesters 90th Bde. 30th Div. A shell had hit Brigade HQ.

The *Official History* says that on the 18th July the French were allotted a larger area behind the battle front which resulted in moving some of the British HQs and positions of reserve communications. The new boundary gave the whole of Maricourt to the French and the boundary line passed to the north of the Bronfay Farm–Maricourt Road but it didn't include the Bray–Fricourt road at a point one and a quarter miles north of Bray. At that time the Fourth Army had a right of passage for up to 150 lorries per day from Maricourt to Bray via Bronfay Farm.

Brigade HQ was often situated at Stanley's Hole which was described by one observer as an evil smelling dugout about 400 yards south-west of Maricourt. In *Memoirs of the Great War* H. M. Davson who was with the artillery described how he had moved his artillery Bde. into action between Maricourt and Trônes Wood. He had his HQ in an old French trench, close to Oxford Copse with one battery in the chateau grounds and another further in advance. He also had a Howitzer Bde. the 157th under him as well. On the 30th July he moved his Brigade position because of communication problems. The enemy had simply got too accurate with their shelling.

John Tucker in his Memoir *Johnny Get Your Gun* in which he told of his experiences with the Kensingtons (168th Bde. 56th Div.) wrote that on 10th August that they marched a short distance to a camp of nissen huts at either Fricourt or Maricourt Siding. This camp was at the edge of a plateau with a main road that ran past at the bottom of a cliff-like bank. They spent some time in huts and on the next afternoon they moved off and crossed a road and entered what appeared to be a valley or large quarry, where they dumped their packs and overcoats and changed into 'battle order'. They were to relieve the 7th R. Irish Fus. (49th Bde. 16th Div.) in trenches close to Falfemont Farm and Leuze Wood. Tucker described the landscape there onwards for about seven miles as being entirely bare and devastated. No greenery and covered with shell holes which merged one with another. The 1st KRRC were here on the 11th August having come from Bronfay Farm.

At the beginning of September Maricourt was bristling with French Batteries of all sizes.

On the 15th September the journalist C. E. Montagu made one of his front line visits and went to a point between Maricourt and Hardecourt to the north-east, close to Nameless Copse. He set out at 5 a.m. in moonlight and mentioned seeing the Cavalry with their lances against the dawn twilight in fields beside the road. They were waiting to be used in the 'breakthrough' which had been planned for that day.

On 24th September the Queen's Westminsters (169th Bde. 56th Div.) went into Divisional Reserve in Casement Trench which was just north of Maricourt. Aubrey Smith who was with the transport of the 56th Div. and who was a member of the LRB was involved in the attack when the 168th Bde. stormed Bouleux Wood. They had to wait for a couple of minutes whilst the 15 inch railway gun at Maricourt prepared to fire. The 14th R. Warwicks were at a copse here on the 26th September.

Peronne Road Cemetery which at one time had been called Maricourt Military Cemetery No. 3 is on the north side of the road to Albert, on the western outskirts of the village. It was begun by fighting units and Field Ambulances in 1916 and used until August 1917. It was completed after the Armistice by the concentration of 1,146 graves from the battlefields in the neighbourhood. It stands above the level of the road, looking over the valley towards the River Somme.

Marlborough Wood

Marlborough Wood is a small copse to the north-west of Montauban, due south of Bazentin le Grand Wood and to the east of Mametz Wood. It is also five hundred yards in front of Caterpillar Wood. During the period 4/5th July it was in the line of the 18th Division who were attacking between Montauban on the right and Mametz village on the left.

Parties of the Division occupied the wood unopposed and it was used as an advance post in the attacks towards Mametz Wood. On 9th July two machine guns were placed there and two more in Caterpillar Wood. Together they were able to sweep the ground to the north-west between the wood and the German second line.

Martinpuich

If one takes a road off to the right of the main Albert–Bapaume road opposite Courcelette one comes to the village of Martinpuich. The village is south of le Sars, west of Flers and north-west of High Wood. It was a strongly fortified village in the German defences and according to H. P. Robinson in his book *The Turning Point* was the hinge and key of the whole German front.

There were several trench names of lines which were in front or south of the village and they included Hook Trench to the right, The Tangles Trenches, and Bottom Trench. Running into Martinpuich from the west was Factory Lane. In early September the new British line was just beyond the crest of the rising ground south of Martinpuich which was the next objective. The jumping off trenches included such names as Bacon, Ham, Egg and Liver. Martinpuich was the centre of the German line beyond which the ground sloped, and 15th September was the date chosen for the attack which was the same date that High Wood and Flers were to be taken.

The 50th Northumbrian Bde. were to the south-east of the village and on their right were the 45th and 46th Bde. of the 15th Scottish Division. In addition the attackers were to be assisted by the presence of four tanks, two for each division. The outskirts of the village were quickly taken in the morning of the 15th and the following trenches quickly fell into British hands: Cutting, Tangle South, Tangle Trench and Gunpit Trench. Then a line of posts were placed to the north of Gunpit Trench, west of the Martinpuich–Eaucourt l'Abbaye Road. Also a further chain of posts was established eastwards of Gunpit Trench. The taking of the village had nevertheless been more difficult than this swift progress makes it appear as the village was full of dugouts and was manned by troops of the Bavarian Division. The four tanks diverged right and left in pairs. The pair to the right reached as far as a dump near Starfish Line to the northeast of the village towards Prue Trench. *The Michelin Battlefield Guide* says that the tanks crashed down the walls of the village which had still been standing and behind which were hidden machine guns. Geoffrey Malins the Official War Office

Photographer filmed the advancing tanks from the position of the Scottish Rifles opposite Martinpuich. He was a witness to the Royal Scots (45th Bde. 15th Div.) going through the village towards Prue Trench.

In his book *And All for What?* D. W. J. Cuddeford who was with the 12th HLI (46th Bde. 15th Div.) wrote that on the 14th September he was in charge of making a bomb base at the head of a communication trench called Highland Alley. Brigade HQ dugout was at Contalmaison. The communication trenches used from there to Martinpuich were Gordon Alley and Highland Alley. He said that the 7/8 KOSB were to the right and the 10th Scottish Rifles were to the left with the 10th/11th HLI in support. Cuddeford also mentioned in his book that he heard two tanks clanking up in the small hours of the 15th September. Once the front German positions had been carried then it was possible to establish a forward ammunition dump in an enemy position in Bacon Trench whilst the attack was pushed on into and through the village. Cuddeford saw many dead Germans in the part of Factory Lane where it crossed the sunken road leading out of the village. They had presumably been 'caught' by the British artillery. Cuddeford later joined 'C' Company of the 12th HLI after his task had been done.

In the afternoon according to the *Official History* the 150th Bde. of the 50th Div. at 1.50 p.m. had been ordered to push patrols into the northern end of Martinpuich in order to link up with the 15th Div. who were already in possession of the village and at 3 p.m. the 6th Cameron H. (45th Bde. 15th Div.) had advanced driving the enemy from the north-east sector of the village. Forward troops of the 46th Bde. 15th Div. took over the remaining ruins of the village which had been virtually flattened before the battle began. German prisoners, a field battery and a 5.9 inch howitzer were taken.

On the 16th September Cuddeford wrote that at about 2 a.m. he started off with half a company to take over a section of Gun Pit Trench. The village was under continuous German shelling. A little to the right and just where the road cleared Martinpuich was a temporary causeway that had been constructed by the enemy for their artillery and wheeled traffic crossing the road from bank to bank. But the German artillery shelled and destroyed it. The 12th HLI were relieved by the 8/10 Gordons (44th Bde. 15th Div.) and the Highlanders went back to old German dugouts near to Villa Wood on Old German Trench One or OGI.

At around this time C. E. Montague the writer and journalist visited Martinpuich and reported that there were many dead on the ridge, and more Germans in the sunken lane under trees. As a result there were millions of flies swarming around and the bodies had blackened faces with open staring eyes!

At the end of the battle an ADS or CP was in the village.

Later in the year a Tramway 16 lb Decauville was put into working order from the village to Peake Woods. Sidings were built and a regular service operated. Thus the petrol locomotive was able to run right up to Gun Pit Road. The rail track was also chalk ballasted and provision was made for pedestrian troops.

The village was lost to the Germans in April 1918 and retaken in August of that year by V Corps.

Martinpuich Communal Cemetery is on the south side of the village and contains the graves of five men from the United Kingdom.

Martinpuich British Cemetery also on the south side was begun in November, and used by fighting units and Field Ambulances until June 1917, and again at the end of August 1918. The school playground in the village was designed and presented by the 47th Div. who took High Wood on the 15th September 1916 as a living Memorial to their Division.

The *Ypres Times* says that in 1935 the village still had rows of filled in dugouts clearly visible in the bank of the sunken road as one dropped down from the direction of Courcelette.

Martinsart

Martinsart is a village on the D 129 road between Aveluy to the south-east and Engelbelmer to the north-west, south-west of Mesnil and north of Bouzincourt. Aveluy Wood is between the village and the valley of the Ancre.

Martinsart's own wood is on the south-western and western side of the village which was close to the British front line in 1916 and at the end of June it was in the territory of the 36th (Ulster) Div. The Divisional border with the 32nd Division ran through the lower portion of Aveluy Wood. Behind the 36th Div. was the 49th Div.

On the 27th June the troops of the 36th (Ulster) Div. as a result of the postponement of the Battle were billeted in huts in Martinsart Wood. The huts at that time according to one witness trembled and creaked as a result of the terrific roar of Siege Howitzers that fired close by, day and night. The wood was to be used by troops for the remainder of the Battle of the Somme. After their involvement in the attempt to take Thiepval the 6th Yorks (146th Bde. 49th Div.) were billeted in empty houses in the village and on the 11th July the 1/4 Y & L were in huts in the wood and they too remarked on the howitzers that were in their midst and were called 'Lucky Jims'. They were kept awake by them and also their candles were blown out by them!

In early October when a Sherwood Foresters Battalion was in the wood they had a plague of rats which were becoming more and more numerous. In mid October there was a camp on the reverse slope of the spur which runs north from the village. A week before, Edmund Blunden of the 11th R. Sussex mentions in his *Undertones of War* that they made a circuit through Engelbelmer Wood and Martinsart Wood on their way up to the Hamel trenches, he too remarked on the howitzers, the mud and the 'confusion' of hutments and adds a poetical touch when he wrote 'and yet its sylvan genius lingering in one or two steep thorny thickets'. They crossed the Nab sunken road on their way to Hamel. Blunden was very aware of the changing seasons and after the war he was continuously reminded of the Somme battle in the period between August and November as it came around each year.

An ADS or CP was here in November in the village.

Martinsart British Cemetery is on the south of the village, beside the road to Aveluy. It was begun at the end of June 1916 when fourteen men of the 13th RIR (198th Bde. 36th Div.) were killed by a shell close to the church on 28th June. It was used as a front line cemetery until October 1916 and again in 1918, and enlarged by the concentration of 346 graves from the area north, east and south of the village. The gravestones are unusual, being a reddish colour instead of the usual white. There is at least one other cemetery in the Somme battlefield which shares this distinction. Those buried in the Cemetery include Lt. Col. H.C. Bernard, the commanding officer of the 10th RIR (107th Bde. 36th Div.) He was killed in Thiepval Wood on 1st July when he should according to orders have remained at battle HQ. Also Lt. Commander F.S. Kelly of the Hood Battalion, who was a contemporary of Rupert Brooke and was killed on 13th November. For details I refer readers to F.P. Crozier's *A Brasshat in No Man's Land*. For years after the war, the village in the words of one visitor 'abounded as an old war ground'.

Maurepas

Maurepas is a village that is due east of Hardecourt and south-west of Combles, on the D 146 road.

At the beginning of the battle the Germans had strongly fortified it as it protected the ground towards the village of Combles where there was a junction of roads that came into it from several directions. According to the *Michelin Battlefield Guide* the village was made up of a group of large farms each of which possessed a meadow surrounded by trees. The farms had to be captured one at a time and the subsequent advance was therefore slow.

It was in the French Army territory and they led the first attack against it which took place on the 12th August, with troops who had advanced westwards from Hardecourt. Only the southern and western parts of the village were carried and these included the fortified cemetery and church. The northern part of the village was captured a few days later and on the 24th August the last centre of resistance fell. It was notably the houses along the side of the roads that led towards Combles that had been holding out until then. The main German defence line was a line that bent round on the western side of the village. As a prelude to the complete capture of the village the French had taken Angle Wood to the north-east the day before with the assistance of the 17th Lancs. Fus.

Méaulte

Méaulte is south of Albert between the two main roads that converge on Albert from the south-east which are the D 329 from Bray and the D 42 from the direction of Morlancourt. To the south-west is Dernancourt and to the north-east the village of Bécordel–Bécourt and then Fricourt.

Méaulte was occupied by British troops from 1915, and was also occupied by three quarters of its peacetime population! The mixture of the two nationalities did not always harmonise and it certainly seems strange for the French civilian population to be allowed to be so close to the front line. During the spring and early summer of 1916 brigades were billeted in Bray and Méaulte and both villages were regularly shelled by the enemy. At the end of June there was a ration dump on the north side of the village. At the beginning of the battle the boundary between the 111 Corps and the XVth Corps ran just outside the north-west side of the village and on the 1st July the 13th Northumberland Fusiliers moved off to the front line along with the 1st Lincoln (62nd Bde. 21st Div.) and the 6th Dorsets (50th Bde. 17th Div.). The Dorsets went past Carcaillot Farm on their way up to Fricourt, after they had been billeted around Méaulte.

In the words of Sidney Rogerson in his book *Twelve Days* the village was one of the bottlenecks through which was fed the flood of men and munitions for the offensive. Here hundreds of Regiments and Batteries had spent a last night's rest before moving on nearer the line.

Beyond the village was a forward slope over which German balloons observed.

Siegfried Sassoon (1st R. Welch Fus.) says in his diary that they were in reserve lines close to Méaulte on the 12th July and that in the morning he rode up to the Citadel Camp. He saw the Indian Cavalry on their way up to High Wood on the 13th/14th. On 14th July at 11 a.m. the 2nd R. Welch Fus. moved to Méaulte, which is described as a squalid and only slightly damaged village, where they had a haversack lunch. Then the whole Bde. bivouacked on a forward slope nearby.

The 20th R. Fus. (19th Bde. 33rd Div.) were bivouacked in mid July on the high ground above the village and were under groundsheets. The whole village was swarming with troops and after being involved in the High Wood battles the 29th R. Fus. marched back to Méaulte. The 21st Manchesters (21st Bde. 7th Div.) were bivouacked in the village from the 16th July until the 18th when they entrained at Mericourt for Hangest. The 22nd R. Fus. (99th Bde. 2nd Div.) who had been heavily involved in the Delville Wood fighting towards the end of July were also in Méaulte after their ordeal. Here General Walker told the battalion which was 'diminished and badly battered' of his pride in their achievement.

Rogerson wrote that night after night unit had succeeded unit since the battle began. Morning after morning they had been pitchforked towards the battle. He also noted that a bakery had become the office of the French Mission and that some farm buildings round a midden sheltered the mobile workshops of a brigade of heavy artillery, and eight inch howitzers stood to have their recoil buffers repaired, where previously a Percheron plough waited to be unharnessed.

King George V in his August visit to the Somme front arrived at the village on the 10th August where he met General Congreve VC, Commander of the XIII Corps who escorted him to the original 1st July line.

Harold Macmillan who was with the Grenadier Guards wrote in his Memoirs that they came to Méaulte from Courcelles around the 25th August.

Méaulte was to be the base for their September involvement in the battle.

In A. D. Gristwood's fictionalised account of the battle he wrote that in September, 'from Death Valley the Loamshires marched over the hills to Méaulte. – Méaulte lies on the edge of "the old front line" and, to normal eyes, was hideous enough.'

In *Other Ranks* W. V. Tilsley wrote that on the 14th September they arrived at Méaulte which was a well worn many times second hand village known to most infantrymen. The tanks passed through.

After the Queen's Westminsters (169th Bde. 56th Div.) had been involved in the clearing of Combles their Brigade was withdrawn during the day and evening from the line to billets at Méaulte. On the night of the 30th September they relieved the 9th Suffolks (71st Bde. 6th Div.). The 1st R. Welch Fus. were back at Méaulte on 8th October.

In *The Middle Parts of Fortune* Frederic Manning who was with the 7th KSLI wrote that they moved back about two miles to another camp at Sandpits, which was a camp close to the village. The next day they moved to the 'sordid squalor' of Méaulte where they spent two nights in stables, and the draft ceased to have a separate existence, being absorbed by the various companies.

During October Max Plowman of the 11th W. Yorks (69th Bde. 23rd Div.) was billeted in Méaulte and wrote 'I hate this place. It lies low, near the Ancre, and has the dejected utilitarian air of a poor industrial town. It is one of those waste places that are neither in or out of the line. Méaulte has a hang dog look. Almost every house is used by troops for one purpose or another, and all the country round is strewn with dumps and the refuse of an army scrapheap. On its churned-up roads, over which the stream of traffic never ceases to pass, pitifully miserable-looking German prisoners work, scraping and sweeping'. They later made another move forward and bivouacked in Mansell Copse.

Aubrey Smith was in the transport attached to the London Rifle Bde. (169th Bde. 56th Div.) and described the civilians as extraordinarily hostile, they would not lift a finger to help the men, and profiteered most shamefully. The battalion was at Bernafay Wood at the time.

Sidney Rogerson mentioned in his book that at the end of the village there was a Foden disinfector, or to use the vernacular a 'delousing machine', whose function was to receive the highly populated under-garments of men coming out of the line, and fumigate these so that, it was hoped that all livestock, whether actual or in embryo, should perish, and the garments be fit for reissue.

On the 8th October the 10th KRRC (59th Bde. 20th Div.) arrived here from Bernafay Wood. On 5th November the 4th Suffolks (98th Bde. 33rd Div.) were in a canvas camp at the village.

At sometime during the battle a light railway was built that ran from Dernancourt on the original line to Méaulte towards Grove Town and the Loop Line, and also towards Bel Air to the south-west.

The Military Cemetery at Méaulte was designed by Edwin Lutyens and is to the south of the village, on the west side of the road where there are 300 graves. The surrounding country is cultivated, and rises to the south-east from the Ancre Valley.

Sandpit Cemetery was on the Albert–Bray Road, a little east of the village. As already mentioned the Sandpit had been the site of a camp and in early August 'an amazing panorama of flashes, flares and explosions could be seen from dawn to dusk from the hillside there.' It was retaken by the 7th R. Sussex in August 1918. The Cemetery had been made by the 12th Div.

The Méaulte Triangle Cemetery was between a road junction and a light railway crossing on the Morlancourt Road. It was made by the 111 Corps Heavy Artillery and the 12th Div. and contained the graves of 36 soldiers from the United Kingdom who fell on the 23rd-25th August 1918. These last two cemeteries were concentrated in to the Méaulte Military Cemetery.

Méricourt

The village of Méricourt is south-west of Albert on the D 120 road and is to the west of Treux and Morlancourt. It is on the south side of the Ancre River and the Amiens–Albert railway. The nearest station is that of Méricourt–Ribemont and the line is the main Paris–Amiens one.

In the early summer of 1915 the Somme front was taken over by the French and Méricourt–Ribemont became a main railhead for the Somme battlefield. The village was the centre of a vast traffic in both men and materials especially after the battle had begun in July. There were immense stores and endless piles of ammunition stacked up ready for the trenches. In addition it was a main billeting village for the troops. There was a MDS in the village at the beginning of the battle. On the 18th July the 21st Manchesters went from Méaulte to Méricourt Station and on the 19th on to Hangest. On 22nd July the 1st R. Welch Fus. took the train here and also went to Hangest. This was Siegfried Sassoon's Battalion.

A few days later the 8th King's Own attended a church service here in a wooded glade with four battalions present. Private J. Miller of that same battalion gained a posthumous VC at Bazentin le Petit when in action with the 10th R. Warwicks (57th Bde. 19th Div.) on 30th/31st July. He is buried at Dartmoor Cemetery in Bécordel–Bécourt. The 9th KRRC arrived in Méricourt at 12.30 a.m. on 8th August and marched to billets, and left for Fricourt on 12th August. In early August the 9th Suffolks (71st Bde. 6th Div.) moved to the village and the 2nd Suffolks (76th Bde. 3rd Div.) were here for a fortnight before moving up the line to the south-west of Trônes Wood. Later in the month around the 25th the Guards Div. were in the vicinity and they were billeted in a large farm in the centre of the village, with the exception of some officers and one platoon of the Welsh Guards. They used to bathe in the River Ancre. Around the 11th of September the 14th R. Warwicks or 1st Birmingham Pals (13th Bde. 4th Div.) were in the area and used to see the Prince of Wales who was on the staff of the Guards Division going by their camp on a bicycle!

The 10th KRRC marched to Méricourt on 8th August and marched to Ville–sur–Ancre on 11th October.

In his book *The Middle Parts of Fortune* Frederic Manning who was in the 7th King's Shrop. Light Inf. (8th Bde. 3rd Div.) mentioned, but with no date, that they marched from Méaulte to Méricourt and that Bourne, the main character in the book had been set to pull a Lewis gun cart a task that he liked because it enabled him to rid himself of his pack, which he stowed in the cart. The next day they moved on to Mailly–Maillet.

Another book where date is not mentioned is W. V. Tilsley's *Other Ranks* where the central character says that they were billeted at Méricourt before moving on to billets at Saignville. Lastly the 1st Essex (88th Bde. 29th Div.) were billeted in the village for two weeks during November.

Méricourt Communal Cemetery is a little east of the village, and the extension is south of the Communal Cemetery between it and the road to Treux. It lies on the north side of the hills that separate the Ancre and the Somme, in pleasant and well wooded country. The Cemetery had been used mainly by Field Ambulances until 1916, and had been designed by Edwin Lutyens. It contains 407 graves.

Mesnil

The village of Mesnil–Martinsart is on the west bank of the River Ancre between Albert and Beaumont Hamel; it contains two villages. Mesnil the first is to the north of Aveluy Wood and south-east of the village of Engelbelmer. It is in the Department of the Somme and is included with the part of the Commune which includes Martinsart which is south-west of Mesnil and is also divided from the Ancre by Aveluy Wood. The wood was virtually a forest of oak and birch, which was shattered in the war. It is bounded on the east by the main railway line from Albert to Amiens. The road from Albert to Hamel runs through it, and a dump was established there called Lancashire Dump which was later to become a cemetery. There were two particularly well known features in Mesnil, and one was a long communication trench which began there, called Jacob's Ladder, and the other was an artillery observation trench known as Brock's Benefit which was named after Brig. Gen. J. H. Brock of the 36th (Ulster) Div. The area at the beginning of the battle was very much 36th Div. country and there were a number of observation posts in the sector, as it was a good spotting position for the progress of the battle and for the artillery.

The 1/3 Monmouths who were Pioneers to the 49th Div. arrived at Lancashire Dump on 5th July and immediately set about working on the 'business' end of the Trench Railway. In mid July casualties from 'B' Company of the same Battalion were brought to the dump for treatment. Neville Lytton in his book *The Press and the General Staff* mentions without quoting a date that he 'observed' from a hill immediately to the east of Mesnil and had a magnificent view of the Ancre Valley. He was based at Engelbelmer and his Bde. HQ was in a village close by called Vitermont, in French built dugouts. This was probably the 116th Bde. 39th Div. as he was a friend of Edmund Blunden who was in the 11th R. Sussex of that Bde. Lytton and Blunden were in the area on their way to Hamel using the communication trench Jacob's Ladder on the 3rd September. On the same day a VC was gained by Capt. W. B. Allen of the RAMC attached to 246 (West Riding) Bde. RFA close to Mesnil. High explosives were being unloaded from ammunition wagons when the enemy suddenly began to shell the battery position. The first shell fell on one of the limbers, exploded and caused several casualties. Allen with utter disregard for his own safety, ran across the open and tended the wounded. He himself was hit four times by the heavy shelling but went on with his work of dressing the wounds of those wounded. He then went on to another battery to help them before reporting his own wounds.

In a manuscript in the IWM called *Gunner on the Somme* the author a Mr. Price mentioned being at Mesnil high up under a ridge just to the west of the village and directly opposite the village of Thiepval which was in enemy hands. His battery was the 240th and was in this position until mid September. J. Murray of the Hood Battalion in his book says that on the 23rd October that they left Englebelmer for Mesnil where he said that there were no houses or barns left standing. On 30th October they moved back to Hedauville. On the 10th November they were relieved by the Hawke Battalion also of the 63rd Naval Div. and moved to shelters in the railway embankment at Mesnil in cubby holes with corrugated iron sheeting as cover. On the 12th they moved to Hamel. In the history of the Hawke Battalion it says that Mesnil and Engelbelmer will always be associated with the weary period of waiting for the 13th November attack against Beaumont Hamel. Both were deserted by their civilian inhabitants and Mesnil was only a heap of ruins that insecurely covered a handful of cellars where the troops or marines sat and shivered by day and night alike. There was also a RDS of CP in the village.

Mesnil Ridge Cemetery lies about midway between Mesnil and Auchonvillers to the north-west, on the eastern slope of the valley which runs north from Mesnil. It was made by Field Ambulances and fighting units mainly of the 29th and 36th Divs. between August 1915 and August 1916.

Mesnil Community Cemetery is on the road between Mesnil and Martinsart, near the north-west corner of Aveluy Wood, and the Extension is on the south side of it.

The Extension was begun in July 1916, and used again as a front line cemetery in 1918. It was gradually enlarged after the Armistice by the concentration of 244 graves from Mesnil Dressing Station and from the battlefields of 1916 and 1918, north-east of Mesnil. It lies in a valley among cultivated fields. The Dressing Station was to the west of the village across a light railway. It was used from June 1916 until February 1917 and especially by the 63rd Div.

Knightsbridge Cemetery is due north of Mesnil Village, it was named after a communication trench and was begun at the outset of the battle. The 4th

Beds. erected a memorial in the cemetery to seven of their number who were killed on 13th November 1916 during the capture of Beaumont Hamel. This Cemetery also lies in a valley in cultivated fields.

Lancashire Dump Cemetery was begun in June 1916 and was used by fighting units and Field Ambulances until the German withdrawal in February 1917. It stands in Aveluy Wood, and four of the original trees still remain there, covered with climbing roses. The view from it to the south is open and includes Thiepval Wood and Authuille Village.

In 1931 one visitor to the area saw several funk holes and dugouts as well as many battered positions, and in the wood old craters and torn earth. In the wood also could be seen old gun positions, with posts and saps.

In 1985 the author was able to trace very easily after nearly 70 years former trench lines and shell holes to the rear of Aveluy Wood. Also there were Mills bombs still live and hidden amongst the moss on the ground in the wood. Further down the road artillery saps could still be seen quite clearly.

Millencourt

Millencourt is a village to the west of Albert and is on the D 91 road, overlooking Albert. It is south of Senlis and east of Hénencourt. In 1916 Tylers Redoubt was to the east of the village which was to become the home of many brigades during the Somme battle. One of the III Corps MDS was here at the beginning of the battle.

In his published diary Brig. Gen J. L. Jack described the involvement of the 2nd Cameronians (Scottish Rifles) at the beginning of the battle. They were in the 23rd Bde. 8th Div. The 8th Div. was to take the village of Ovillers la Boisselle on the 1st July if all went according to plan. They left the village of Millencourt after sunset on the 30th June. The HQ and four companies of the Cameronians, with some 20 officers and 650 other ranks, filed along the way to Albert where they turned northwards and crossed the River Ancre by a temporary wooden bridge and made their way along the marshy valley to Aveluy. They then climbed the slopes eastwards until they reached Preston Communication Trench for the last part of their five mile walk to their assembly positions in Ribble Street, with Battalion HQ at Ovillers Post close by. At 7 a.m. on the 1st July Jack led two companies up Hodder Street to the rear of the 2nd West Yorks in Houghton Street. The last named together with the assembly trenches had been blasted by the enemy howitzers. On the 2nd after the 8th Division's failure to gain ground at Ovillers the 23rd Bde. returned to Millencourt. During July other brigades came and went and at the end of July Collison of the 11th R. Warwicks recorded in his book, that one evening they moved forward via Millencourt and Albert to a position in reserve that was close to Bécourt Wood.

The 2nd Welch (3rd Bde. 1st Div.) having failed on one of the many attempts to capture High Wood assisted by the 1st Gloster Batt. came back to Millencourt having been in dugouts at the northern end of Mametz Wood. The 2nd Welch had lost 193 men in the attack.

At the beginning of September the 1/4 Green Howards (150th Bde. 50th Div.) were in the area and on the 5th October the 149th Bde. also of the 50th Div. marched here after being in Eaucourt Line.

One night, probably after their success at Martinpuich in mid September, the 12th HLI arrived in Scotts Wood before going on to Millencourt. The 2nd KRRC on 30th September were resting here until 3rd October, then out of the area. There is also a mention of the 7/8 KOSB of the 46th Bde. 15th Div. being in tents at Millencourt Camp. The wood had been turned into a camp and consisted of gaunt tree stumps.

At the other end of October there is mention of troops arriving in the village from the front line direction, in a London bus!

Minden Post

The nearest village to Minden Post was Carnoy which was to the north-east of it. The position of this famous dressing station and headquarters was on the northern side of the Maricourt–Mametz road and just beyond the turning to Carnoy. It was opposite Caftet Wood. In the spring the battalion HQ of the 21st Manchesters was here, and at the beginning of the battle the HQ of the 1st S. Staffs. They were part of the 91st Bde. who attacked the village of Mametz from a position to the north-east, on 1st July. The XIII/XV Corps boundary ran along the eastern boundary of the position.

Geoffrey Malins, if we are to rely on his account, left the 29th Division positions on the morning of 1st July and then drove to Minden Post for more filming. He was joined by Macdowell a colleague who was filming the wounded of both sides, as they were coming out of the line after the first attacks. The 2nd Queen's (91st Bde.) were bivouacked at Minden Post on the 4th July and on the 10th the 115th Bde. of the 38th Div. were in reserve both here and at Mametz. On the next day the 8th Devons were camped in the vicinity and on the 23rd the 30th Div. returned here after their success with the capture of Montauban. Later in the battle the Guards Bde. were in the area before being involved in the September battles against Ginchy and Lesboeufs. The traffic congestion at the time was very great and lorries could scarcely carry out one trip per day from the railhead to the main dump which was at Minden Post.

Miraumont

Miraumont is on the D 107 road, south-east of Puisieux and north-east of Grandcourt. Together with the village of Pys they are adjoining villages and communes in the Department of the Somme. The village was split into two sections by the River Ancre and the railway line on the north bank. It remained in German hands during 1916, and there is not a great deal to say about what happened there. The main event seems to have been that the British Artillery destroyed a German supply base and reserve ammunition store near an old watermill, an explosion so violent that it virtually destroyed the village itself. All this happened on the 5th of August. The Cambridge

Batt. reported seeing from Hamel the activity at a German Dressing Station in early October, with ambulances toing and froing. However the Allied line was halted before Miraumont for many months, and it was not in Allied hands until February 1917.

Philip Gibbs the writer and journalist visited the area in March 1917 and in a despatch dated 12th March he mentioned that the enemy had suffered very considerably in the area of Miraumont, Pys and below Loupart Wood. The land had been destroyed by continuous shell fire and there were many German dead in evidence. Many of whom were half buried by their colleagues or by high explosives. He visited Boom Ravine which Regina Trench leads into between Miraumont and Pys and described it as a 'shambles of German troops'. The Germans had had machine gun emplacements there and also deep dugouts under cover of earth banks. But the Allied artillery had 'found them out'. All the garrison had been killed and shelled to pieces. Their bodies or fragments lay in every shape and shapelessness of death, in puddles of broken trenches or on the edge of deep ponds in shell-craters. Gibbs counted about 850 dead in this small area, the majority being German.[3]

Montauban

Montauban or Monty-Bong as the Tommies used to call it is on the D 64 road between Guillemont in the west and Mametz to the east. To the north are the Bazentin villages and to the south is the village of Maricourt. Bernafay and Trônes Woods are both to the north-east of the village. At the beginning of the battle the village was close to the ridge on which lay the German second line position. A very long communication trench called Montauban Alley ran from Pommiers Redoubt to the north of Montauban and on to the margin of Bernafay Wood.

The Franco/British Army boundary ran from a point south of Bernafay Wood down through Maricourt, cutting the village in half and then southwards towards Cappy and the Somme river. As for the positions of the Divisions at the end of June, the French 39th was to the right of the British 30th whose objective was Montauban, and on their left was the 18th Div. who were to advance west of Montauban. Behind these three Divisions in the same order from right to left were the 11th, 9th and 7th Divisions. As for the Corps the XX was on the right and XIII was on the left.

The *Official History* described the scene in the following way: The front line of the XIII Corps which was on the right of the British line next to the French, extended from Maricourt to beyond Carnoy. It lay near the bottom of the northern slope of the valley between Maricourt and Montauban ridges, in which the village of Carnoy is situated. The German front line was higher up the same slope – Between the Montauban Ridge on whose crest the red roofs of the village were a conspicuous landmark before the bombardment, and the Ginchy–Pozieres Ridge is a long valley, known from the shape of a wood it contains, as Caterpillar Valley. In the Carnoy Valley, known as Railway

Valley, ran a pre-war light railway line and on its steep eastern slope stretched a long plantation called Talus Boise. The level of the attack was in the main a gentle slope upwards. There was splendid observation from the Maricourt Ridge.

The German defences: in the front with a recently dug reserve line Dublin Trench. – Train Valley – Pommiers Trench behind it. The communication trench called Montauban Alley ran from Montauban to Mametz on the reverse slope of Caterpillar Valley. Redoubts in the front line included Glatz Redoubt, Pommiers Redoubt and The Castle. Montauban had been placed in a strong state of defence.

On the 30th June the 9th Div. had assembled in the area about a mile to the east of Billon Wood in a gulley. The enemy gassed the valley which had to be crossed which made the walk 'unpleasant' according to W. D. Croft's *Three Years with the 9th Division.* The French infantry to their right were the 'Iron Corps' from Verdun where they had earned their sobriquet. In Billon Wood according to Croft the French had some extraordinary guns a sort of mixture between a howitzer and a trench mortar. He says that he was never to see anything like them again.

The right brigade of the 30th Div. which was the 89th under Brig. Gen. Hon. F. C. Stanley began from four lines of assembly trenches and at 7.30 a.m. through mist and smoke the two leading battalions the 17/King's and the 20/King's made rapid progress. Casement Trench, Alt Trench and German's Wood were all reached and passed. The wire for a change was well cut and the artillery had done a good job on this particular front as the advancing Allies were to find out as the dugouts were found to be very often blown in. Also many prisoners were taken on the way. Dublin Trench the first objective, which was to the south-west of the Briqueterie was taken at 8.30 a.m. It was empty. Three batteries of the 149th RFA were brought up to the north-west of Maricourt, one was knocked out but two were unscathed. The 89th Bde. had advanced in tandem with the French 39th Div.

To the left of the 89th Bde. the 21st Bde. had had similar success. The leading battalions were the 19th Manchesters and the 18th King's. The enemy held them up in their advance towards Glatz Redoubt and the 2nd Green Howards in support also suffered from machine gun fire. Glatz Redoubt, their first objective, was reached by 8.35 a.m. The capture of the Dublin Trench–Glatz Redoubt–Train Alley Line paved the way for the advance of the 90th Bde. through the 21st Bdes. lines. The 90th Bde. had been at assembly in and around Cambridge Copse which was west of Maricourt. At 8.30 a.m. the leading battalions the 17th and 16th Manchesters moved off supported by the 2nd Scots. The Collecting Post was at Talus Boise and a second one was at Maricourt Avenue. The advance through Talus Boise was sheltered. Lt. Col. H. A. Johnson of the 17th Manchesters was wounded during it. Train Valley was reached ahead of timetable and a German machine gun which had been troublesome was destroyed. There was a delay while the flanking Division caught up and during this time the commanders of the two Manchester Battalions became casualties.

By 11 a.m. part of Montauban Alley was reached and many Germans had surrendered. Many of the enemy could be seen in Caterpillar Valley streaming towards Bazentin le Grand. With Montauban in Allied hands the way was clear to capture the Briqueterie which was a very important German observation post with its chimney stack. The Germans had converted the Brickworks into a place of exceptional strength. It was beside the Maricourt–Longueval Road about half a mile to the south-east of Montauban village and consisted of two large blocks of buildings according to John Masefield in his book *The Battle of the Somme*. The buildings were on either side of the road with outlying offices and furnaces. The Germans had excavated under them and had made an underground fort over which the ruins made excellent cover. The fort was strengthened with concrete and reinforced by iron girders. There was living accommodation for troops, and emplacements for machine guns. As the works were on the top of a plateau and well back from the contour line, there was a good field of fire in all directions.

Philip Gibbs wrote that there had been anxiousness about this German strongpoint and that it had been suggested that the British should just bypass it and not attempt to take it directly. However when the position was approached it was found to have been utterly destroyed by Allied artillery.

The Brickworks were captured by the 20th King's or 4th Liverpool Pals battalion. Due north were the Bernafay and Trônes Woods to which the Brickworks acted as an advance redoubt. Today's chimney is postwar and is within a circle of what was previously a circle of trench works.

In Raleigh/Jones *The War in the Air* it is mentioned that an observer of the 9th Squadron saw the battle for Montauban in the following way. He had watched men of the 30th Div. move forward, with little opposition, towards the line Dublin Trench–Glatz Redoubt, which had been taken at 8.30 a.m. He also saw the 18th Div. take the Pommiers Trench and advance quickly to the capture of Pommiers Redoubt. Another observer could see a line of flashes, reflected from the mirrors which men of the 30th Div. carried on their backs, leaving Glatz Redoubt and moving along the trench known as Train Alley in the direction of Montauban. Suddenly he saw a battery come into action at Bernafay Wood. His pilot flew across at once and attacked the crew with machine gun fire from 700 feet. After the aeroplane left, a company of the King's (Liverpool) Regt. captured the brickfields south-east of Montauban, and this completed the advance of XIII Corps on the first day of the battle.

After lunch, Montauban having fallen about midday Talbot Kelly of the RFA went across the battlefield with his Major and two signallers towards Montauban to reconnoitre a new OP. Glatz Redoubt was a turmoil of brown earth and splintered wood. In Montauban itself there remained no recognisable ruins although there had been 274 houses there before the war began which made the village the largest in the Somme area. Almost immediately Talbot Kelly's battery moved from its second line position into action in the open behind the ruins of the Brickworks, and he experienced wood fighting for the first time. As FOO in Bernafay Wood and later in Trônes Wood he was to endure days of intense terror.

Montauban was the first German held village to fall into British hands and it was one of the few British advances on an otherwise totally disastrous day for the British Army.

The fact that the great dugouts were found to have been smashed by the Allied artillery along with much of the wire helped the advance enormously. Unfortunately no attempt was made to capture Bernafay Wood which would possibly have saved a lot of fighting and casualties over the first two weeks of July. Attempts to take the wood were made a couple of days later. Patrols had been sent out to Bernafay Wood and it was found to be empty except for a few of the enemy. From Montauban Ridge the British could overlook Caterpillar Valley. Although the troops could have gone on, the time was spent in consolidating the important road from Maricourt to Montauban which was repaired to a point close to the old German front line. The village cellars were found to be full of German soldiers who had been killed during the Allied shelling. Major L. P. Walsh of the 2nd R. Dub. Fus. (10th Bde. 4th Div.) and the CO of the 2nd Manchesters (14th Bde. 32nd Div.) were killed or died of wounds at Montauban on the 1st July.

In his book *Three Years with the 9th Division* Lt. Col. W. D. Croft who was commander of the 27th Bde. and then a Divisional Commander reports that on the morning of the 2nd July 'they got it where the chicken got the axe'. The enemy simply blew Bernafay Wood which they were occupying to pieces. And shelling in a wood, 'as everyone knows who has tried it, is far worse than anywhere, not excepting a village'. Montauban being the first German held village to fall to the Allies was an object of considerable interest to the brass-hats who came in swarms according to Croft. After a week in the area the Brigade was relieved by the Black Watch and they went back to Billon Wood, where they had been on the eve of the battle, to recuperate.

General Rawlinson in his diary entry of 2nd July says that as Fricourt had fallen and that the British were getting forward with opposition weakening, it was decided to make a strong line across from la Boisselle to Montauban as a firm basis from which to carry out further attacks.

On the 3rd July the positions held by the 11th R. Scots (27th Bde. 9th Div.) lay along the eastern side of the village; the western being guarded by the 9th Scottish Rifles with the 12th R. Scots in reserve. From the Montauban defences Montauban Alley led towards Bernafay Wood, and to prevent the enemy from closing in on the village, bombing sections from the 11th R. Scots and the 9th Scottish Rifles worked this trench to a strong point known as Triangle Post which they garrisoned easily on the morning of the 3rd July.

John Masefield wrote of this day that on the right the British on the top of the ridge though often sharply attacked and continuously being shelled, were preparing to go down the hill to attack the enemy in the valley below. This was a long valley between chalk cliffs, the eastern end of which ran into the valley which divides Mametz from Fricourt. By the 5th July H. P. Robinson

THE SOMME, 1916.
XIII CORPS ATTACK ON THE 1ST JULY.
THE CAPTURE OF MONTAUBAN.

N.

SCALE

YDS 1000   500   0   1000 YARDS

0   ¼   ½   ¾   MILE

Heights in metres

Bazentin le Pt.

Longueval

De ville Wood

Bazentin le Gd.

Mametz Wood

2 BNS OF 12 R DIV 12·45 p.m.

28 R.

Trones Wd.

Willow Stream

Caterpillar Wood

23   (2 BNS.)

Triangle Pt.

Bernafay Wd

62.

Montauban

12.

White Tr

Alley

Montauban

109 R. & Part of 23.

Briqueterie

Pommiers Rdt.

Loop

Train Alley

Glatz Rdt.

Pommiers Tr.

Warren

Bns. 6 Bav. R.

Dublin Rdt.

Castle

Breslau Tr.

Casino Pt.

Bois Faviere

18.

XIII

21ST

30.

90TH

89.

6 Bav. R.
(Less ¼ Bns.)

Carnoy

7.

British

French

1st Objective	—·—·—
2nd Objective	—··—··
3rd Objective	—···—···
Positions at zero	▬▬▬
Line gained & held at night	●●●●
Brigades	21ST, 89TH 54TH

—o—

●●●●

Maricourt

Fr. French Boundary

XX.

11.

Y Wood

Ordnance Survey, 1929.

in his book *The Turning Point* noted that the Allies had forced their way about a thousand yards beyond the village of Montauban in the direction of Marlborough Wood. This brought them on that side almost abreast of the centre of Mametz Wood.

G. W. Warwick a South African serving with the South African Brigade who were part of the 9th Division wrote a book called *We Band of Brothers* in which he described setting off from Maricourt on the 5th July with the night fatigue party to dig new trenches under machine gun fire at Glatz Redoubt to the south of Montauban. They then camped at Montauban. Of water fatigue Warwick said that they had trouble with a cart in the heavy mud and finished up carrying the water in cans by hand. The quota was two cans of water per platoon, which worked out at about half a bottle per man. He saw Bernafay Wood coming under very heavy German shell fire.

During the period 8th/9th July the HQ of the 89th Bde. (30th Div.) was in dugouts at the Brickworks and on the 9th the 16th Manchesters (90th Bde. 30th Div.) were ordered to the sunken road to attack Trônes Wood from there. Talbot Kelly who it will be remembered was with the RFA says that behind the Brickworks he slept in a slit trench in the side of a large shellhole. On the 13th July he went up with his Major to establish an OP for the next day. They returned slowly back along Montauban Alley and checked their communication wire. The Highlanders were assembling for the battle planned for the 15th July and at dusk these men filed out, to lie all night in quiet lines in no mans land, as close to the German wire as possible. On the 16th Talbot Kelly went as Brigade FOO towards Longueval.

In *A Doctor's War* Geoffrey Keynes wrote that 'gradually our artillery moved forward, and on the 17th July they were in Montauban Alley, a trench just in front of Montauban with a view from Mametz to Delville Wood, of evil memory. At nine thirty that evening we had just finished our supper of bully beef, when suddenly small shells began whistling over our heads at the rate of thirty or forty a minute, making no detonation as they hit the ground.' – 'We were in a shallow trench, and while the other officers were putting on their gas masks, I thought it better to climb up into the open air, where the concentration of gas was much lighter, and so escaped with only a mouthful of gas.'

The 76th Bde. HQ of the 3rd Div. were in the quarry to the north of Montauban and were being heavily shelled on the 19th July. The HQ was too far forward and had to be evacuated to the sunken road that led down from Montauban. This HQ was also shelled and they retreated to a dugout in Montauban itself. Brevet Major William Congreve thought that too little time was being given to the preparation of an attack on Longueval and Delville Wood. Congreve went with Major Stubbs CO of the 2nd Suffolks and was shot dead by a German sniper.

Around the 24th July most of the artillery batteries were still behind Montauban. H. E. Harvey of the Kensington Battalion says that towards the end of July that 'up the long rising slope to the orchard was the great wreckage of Montauban'. They went on despite the 5.9s which crashed down on the rubbish heap ahead, past the overturned water wagon and its slain horses, rotting in the blood stained pond. On, across the road that led down to the quarry and to Caterpillar Valley; when he was on his way back delivering bombs and water, roads were taboo, and his party struck off across the hard fought fields directly towards Montauban, hurrying empty handed through its evil smelling ruins and on to the corner of Bernafay Wood. In the dusk his battalion moved up to the Brigade Reserve position, the dugouts and cellars of mutilated Montauban. They watched a panorama – a long curling wall of smoke, a mile and three quarters distant across the sweeping valley on the high ridge of Contalmaison and the Bazentin Woods to the left; and the smoke palled Longueval, Delville and Trônes Woods on the right, eight to ten miles of bristling, terrifying battle. Harvey continued his description and away below in the valley were the stripped and stunted line of trees once called Caterpillar Wood. To the right of it, the old quarry with its ruined railtrack, and the field guns belching death; away to the left the heavy foliaged Mametz Wood on the further slope; speckled and dotted with white chalk torn up by the 'tornado'. Next morning on the 26th July they were having to dig again under hostile fire byond the Quarry and they were told to draw extra rounds of bombs. In sections by way of the battered trench between Bernafay and Trônes Woods, the 22nd advanced into action, and as Brigade supports found themselves amidst odious destruction.

On the 30th/31st July the 106th Bde. 35th Div. (Bantam) were in the Quarry north of Montauban, when there was an attack on Guillemont. At the end of July a supply line ran from Carnoy to Montauban. On the 11th August the village was surrounded by British batteries and on the 19th August the HQ of the 5th O & BLI (42nd Bde. 14th Div.) were in the village and they had their HQ in the former German blockhouse.

The 9th KRRC (42nd Bde. 15th Div.) were occupying Montauban Alley at this time when they were involved in the fight for Delville Wood. On the 25th August the 4th Suffolks (98th Bde. 33rd Div.) were to attack two hours after the bombardment and in the afternoon the Suffolks entered firstly Montauban Alley and then Carlton Trench.

On the 29th August the R. Welch Fus. (19th Bde. 33rd Div.) moved at 6 a.m. into a trench in front of Montauban which was virtually a ditch. They were on loan to the 99th Bde. at this time.

In his book *The Anatomy of Courage* Lord Moran wrote that 'We hurried on through the silence and desolation of Montauban. On that road which was usually so crowded with troops and transport we seemed that night to be the only living things. It was like being left out in no man's land, wounded, forgotten. Now that I had not the support of numbers, I was full of apprehension. I had a feeling that something was about to happen. I wondered vaguely if it was the cold night air rising up out of the valley that made my teeth chatter.' – 'For some time we had noticed a strange smell and there was something that made our eyes prick; presently tears began to run down our cheeks. The road turned sharply to the left and dipped into a valley and all at once we appeared to be wading through a ground mist. Shells were coming over in great numbers. They detonated almost silently and without the burst of an ordinary shell. We had run into a gas shell barrage. I wanted to ask my servant if his chest felt as if it were being pressed in by an iron band that was gradually getting smaller. I wondered what gas they were using. I remembered we were told that many of the men had heart failure after the last attack'.

'A gunner came by spitting and rubbing his eyes. He said that there was a sunken road a little further on which led to the quarry. He thought that there was an aid post there; this was a landmark we had been told to look out for.' – 'Apparently our batteries were everywhere, it was impossible in the darkness and in the fog to steer through them except by the flash of gun as it fired.'

'Just there the rising ground was fairly clear of gas, it was past three o'clock and we decided to wait for the light. The night lifted reluctantly as if it were loath to let us escape and the cold dawn had passed slowly into the promise of a summer day before we found Carlton Trench. The last companies had just arrived after eight hours pilgrimage in the gas to find that no one expected them or knew why they had come. The Colonels of five battalions were collected in one dug-out and the men were packed in the trench like herrings.'

The road between Montauban and Carnoy was severely cratered. In his book *Other Ranks* W. V. Tilsley wrote that on the 7th September that after Mametz they wheeled past Montauban. The village resembled little more than a series of brickwork heaps and twisted ironwork. Guns lurked around corners and were under camouflage netting and futuristic paint work. Darkness touched the stark tree tops of Bernafay Wood as they dropped down the slope before Longueval. Later they marched back through Montauban.

On 14th September the 12th E. Surreys (122nd Bde. 41st Div.) arrived at night near the Quarry and here they saw tanks for the first time.

On 17th September the 9th KRRC (42nd Bde. 14th Div.) were relieved in Montauban Alley by a Somerset battalion and returned to their former camp at Bécordel. They had been close to the Guards Brigade.

On the 19th September D. V. Kelly of the Leicestershire Regiment who wrote *39 Months* says that they arrived at Montauban which was then packed with heavy artillery and occupied trenches that they had reconnoitred in the afternoon.

On the 5th October the village was the battle HQ of the 29th Div.

On 9th October in *Soldier's Diary* it says that they moved from Citadel Camp by cross country tracks up to the knees in mud, via Bois Caftet, Talus Boise Valley to the Brickworks south-east of Montauban, where they took over from the 169th Bde. 56th Div. At this time at least eight horses were needed to move one limber wagon through the mud. Most of the field gun ammunition was carried up by pack mules. On 15th October they were fired on by the enemy using a long range gun. The 16th KRRC (100th Bde. 33rd Div.) were at the Briqueterie Camp on 19th October in support.

In October John Masefield making his first visit to Montauban described it as being an Iron Gate!

On the 24th October the 4th Suffolks (98th Bde. 33rd Div.) moved to Trônes Wood in very wet weather, and on the 4th November they moved back to hutments on the Montauban–Carnoy Road for a couple of days.

Sidney Rogerson of the 2nd W. Yorks (23rd Bde. 8th Div.) wrote of marching back to Ginchy and arriving at le Briqueterie Camp where they were once again under canvas, in bell tents where originally stood the brick yards which had featured so prominently in the despatches describing the September battles around Montauban.

In November only heavy traffic used the Montauban–Carnoy roads until the weather broke. The Welsh Guards moved for one night to Camp H near Montauban, and from there they took over the line.

Montauban was to remain in British hands until the end of March 1918. The Quarry Cemetery having been an ADS was begun in July 1916 and used until February 1917. It was enclosed by a flint wall, irregular in outline where it borders the quarry. Four cemeteries were concentrated in the Quarry Cemetery and they were Quarry Cemetery Briqueterie No. 3, which contained soldiers mainly from the 1/5th KORL who fell in July and August, Caterpillar Wood Cemetery No. 2 which had been at the east end of Caterpillar Wood and had been begun by the 2nd Suffolks, Green Dump Cemetery Longueval and Quarry Scottish Cemetery Montauban which had been between the quarry and the north end of Bernafay Wood and contained mainly men from the 11th and 12th Royal Scots Fus. from the 9th Division. Not surprisingly owing to the exposed nature of the position a great many of the graves belong to members of the Artillery.

After the war the village was rebuilt half a mile from its railway like so many villages in the area.

Morlancourt

Morlancourt is a village on the D 42 road between Albert and Sailly Laurette which is on the north bank of the Somme river. It is south of Dernancourt, east of Treux and was behind the Allied lines in 1916. It is also on the northern slope of the ridge that separates the Rivers Somme and Ancre close to their junction.

The village in the early part of 1916 was particularly associated with the R. Welch Fus. and Siegfried Sassoon and Bernard Adams both mention it in their books.

In his fictionalised Memoirs, Sassoon in January 1916 says that 'Sherston' his main character, rode with the transport and that they arrived at Morlancourt which was four or five miles from the trenches. It was 'tucked away among the fold of long slopes and bare rides of ploughland'.

In his book *Nothing of Importance* a memoir of life with the 1st Batt. R. Welch Fus. Bernard Adams wrote of 1st February: 'To-day we marched to Morlancourt and are spending the night in huts. It is very cold, and we have a brazier made out of a biscuit tin, but it smokes abominably. We are busy getting trench-kit ready for the next day. From outside the hut I can see star-lights and hear the machine guns tapping. It thrills like the turning up of the footlights'. Between February and June they were often to be billeted in the village. Several roads ran down into the village and Adams described it as a 'cosy spot, and a very jolly thing' after that long, long weary grind up from Méaulte at the end of six weary days, to look down on the snug little village waiting for you below. It was just too far off for shelling.

Sassoon was in the village around 16th March and he too mentions in his diary the friendly convergence of the roads. There was a church with a giant vane, over which birds wheeled and cackled. In the hollow ground, where the five roads met, there was a congregation of farm buildings, round an open space with a pond on one side. The long lines of high ground hid the rest of the world. Sassoon slept in canvas huts close to the transport, as he was transport officer at the time.

In the Spring the 21st Manchesters (91st Bde. 7th Div.) were in the village and were involved in a railway construction between here, Méaulte and Waterloo Junction.

Robert Graves mentioned that his Battalion the 1st R. Welch Fus. (22nd Bde. 7th Div.) were in the village and were in and out of the Fricourt trenches. He wrote in his memoirs that the village was untouched by shellfire and that 'A' Company HQ was a farmhouse kitchen where they slept on the brick floor. In his *Memoirs of an Infantry Officer* Sassoon wrote that after Easter he proceeded to the Fourth Army School for a month's refresher course. He left the centre of Morlancourt and returned there on the 22nd May at the end of a hot day. The bus turned off the bumpy road from Corbie and began to crawl down the steep winding lane. In June Sassoon noted that the Bois des Tailles was full of men from the Border and Devonshire Regiments, and in walking home to Morlancourt he saw the village in the basin with smoke going up and looking very peaceful. On the 9th June he rode down to the village with the Quartermaster in a perfect sunset, the muddy road as they walked away from the Citadel was red before their feet. On 26th June the village was full of troops and supply columns.

On the 21st July the 1st KRRC (99th Bde. 2nd Div.) arrived in the village, and at the time there were five battalions bivouacked in the village. In July the HQ of XIII Corps was in the village and throughout July the village hutments and billets here accommodated troops. There was also a Corps MDS in the village. In early August the 35th Div. (Bantam) were here for a few days and whilst in the village bathed in the river at Ville sur Ancre to the north.

On the 25th August the 1st Scots Guards arrived here from Bus les Artois where they had been training for two weeks. They were now on the east bank of the Ancre. In early September, the 2nd Guards Bde. were billeted in the village, whilst they were training for the battles that they were to take part in later in the month.

Aubrey Smith of the 1st LRB (169th Bde. 56th Div.) who was with the transport wrote that the Guards looked very smart and soldierly when he passed by them on his way to Happy Valley, north-west of Bray. Jack Tucker in *Johnny Get Your Gun* describes how after being with the 1/13th Kensingtons (168th Bde. 56th Div.) at Leuze Wood the battalion was reinforced and marched off past Citadel Camp and on to Morlancourt. There they were billeted in some 'nice dry barns' but not for long as they had to move on to Citadel Camp.

Morlancourt British Cemetery is on the west side of the village. It was made by Field Ambulances in June and July 1916, and stands on the western slope of a long and narrow valley.

Morval

Morval is a village on the D 74 road between Lesboeufs to the north-west and Combles to the south. It is in the extreme south of the Pas-de-Calais, on high ground and was in effect the key to Combles. It had an underground labyrinth and a maze of fortifications above ground, and was a fortress of similar type to Thiepval. At the beginning of the battle the by-road on which the village stands was continuously used by the enemy taking supplies to Combles. With its commanding position and a well fortified line of trenches in front of it facing the Allies it was always going to be a very difficult village to capture. In addition there were numerous sunken roads in the area and timbered ravines which were all carefully fortified for defence which made it even more formidable. Twin trench lines came down from the north-westerly direction in front of Guedecourt, known as Gird Trench and Gird Support, their names altered as they came closer to Lesboeufs and Morval and became known as Cow and Ox with their supports the Bovril, Meat and Mutton Trenches. The comparable German trenches in the Morval area were known as Rainbow, Cloudy, Misty, Zenith etc.

On the 15th September the objective of the 20th Div. was the Blue Line facing Morval and Lesboeufs and about 1,200 yards west of these villages. The second objective skirted Morval on the west and Lesboeufs on the east and ended at the crossroads half way between Lesboeufs and Guedecourt. The 61st Bde. was delayed in their attack on the 15th because the 6th Div. was held up by the Quadrilateral, a German strongpoint about three quarters of a mile to the east of Ginchy.

It was planned that another attempt would be made on the 25th September. The Division chosen to have Morval as its objective was the 5th, and the attacking brigades were the 95th Bde. to the right and the 16th to the left. The attack was part of an offensive along the whole front between Combles and Martinpuich. In fact it was the 15th Bde. the left brigade of the attack who took the village after mopping up the dugouts and cellars in the village. The troops then moved out into the open country to the east of the village. By nightfall the final objective that ran southwards from Morval Windmill was consolidated. Once Morval had fallen the capture of Combles to the south-west was assured. Meanwhile the French Army on the right of the British had captured Frégincourt whilst the 5th Division's 95th Bde. made their way southwards to join up with them.

The whole Morval operation had been very successful and many prisoners in addition to five machine guns were captured. The one thing which didn't help were the tanks! The 5th Div. had been allocated three and one failed to start, the second proceeded some distance and then grounded in the mud in the vicinity of the jumping off line by a sunken road, and the third, after various adventures arrived after the infantry on the southern side of Morval and assisted the 95th Bde. Much of the spotting and observation for the artillery had been done from observation balloons. The capture of Morval was the biggest success since mid July for the Allies in the Somme battle. Private T. A. Jones of the 1st Cheshires (15th Bde. 5th Div.) gained the VC during its capture. He was born in 1880, and on the 25th September he was with his company consolidating the defences of the village when he spied a German sniper some 200 yards away. He went out and although a bullet penetrated his helmet and another penetrated his coat he was able to return the sniper's fire and kill him. He then took on two more Germans who were firing at him although they were displaying the white flag of surrender. He also shot both of these. On reaching the enemy dugouts he found them to be occupied and he proceeded to disarm their occupants and to march them back through a heavy barrage. His haul of prisoners numbered 102 and included three or four officers. Jones had been warned that the Germans were making misuse of the White Flag but insisted on going after them.

Between the 25th and 28th September Morval, Lesboeufs and Guedecourt were the objectives as well as a belt of countryside that was about 1,000 yards deep curving around the north of Flers.

All this was in preparation for the attack against le Transloy to the north-east of Morval. In the period 26th/27th September the 12th KRRC (60th Bde. 20th Div.) gained ground to the right of Morval and joined hands with the French Army. The 2nd R. Welch Fus. (19th Bde. 33rd Div.) on the 23rd October were settled astride a road between Ginchy to the south-west and Morval. It was wintry being misty and cold, and the ground was very soggy. The Field Guns were in what little shelter there was about 60 yards behind them. The Officers' HQ was a sort of shack made out of shell boxes. The battalion had been lent to the 4th Div. which was in action on the Morval–Lesboeuf's front. The idea was to improve the line in readiness for a full scale attack against le Transloy. This attack failed. The 33rd Div. then relieved the 4th Div. The R. Welch Fus. moved closer to Morval and on the 25th of October they were in what was known as Hazy Trench which was for them a sunken road between Morval and Lesboeufs. On the 28th they moved back to Guillemont still very cold. On the 30th they withdrew to trenches between Bernafay and Trônes Woods.

Morval British Cemetery is on the western outskirts of the village and the graves are those of the 38th Welsh Division from the August/September 1918 fighting in the main. It is amongst cultivated fields.

Mouquet Farm

Mouquet Farm (Mucky Farm) was just off to the right of what is now the D 73 road from Pozieres to Thiepval, south of Grandcourt and south-west of Courcelette.

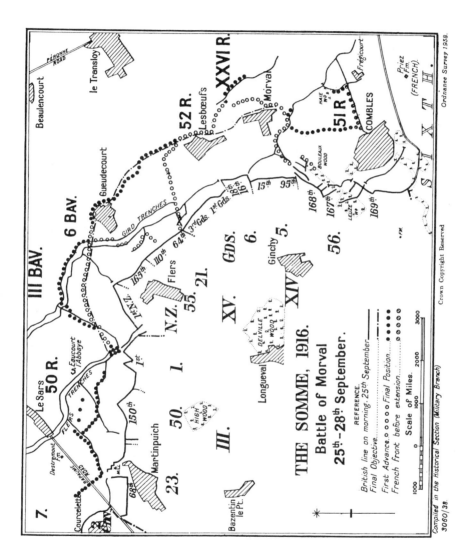

THE SOMME, 1916.
Battle of Morval
25th–28th September.

REFERENCE.
British line on morning. 25th September.
Final Objective.
First Advance. o o o o Final Position.
French front before extension.

Scale of Miles.

Compiled in the Historical Section (Military Branch)
3060/38.

Crown Copyright Reserved

Ordnance Survey 1938.

At the beginning of the battle of the Somme it was a forward advance HQ for the German Army in their second line and on 1st July 1916 the Mouquet Switch which included the Farm was the objective of the 1st Dorsets (14th Bde. 32nd Div.). However the Dorsets were cut down at the Leipzig Salient to the south-west mainly by machine gun fire from the Nord Werk, the machine guns that were concentrated in the Ovillers Spur.

The Leipzig Salient was virtually a bastion that defended Mouquet Farm to the south-east, and all the time that Pozieres was in German hands then the farm was protected from this direction as well. On the night of 10th August patrols of the 4th Australian Division pushed out and established posts in the valley south of the Farm which was already what appeared to be just a mound of rubble. They also established posts to the east. An attack was made however from a seized section of the German Fabeck Trench which was to the north-east. There was an attempt to make the salient deeper in the attacks that were to follow. By the 22nd August the 2nd Australian Division had tried with increased forces to capture the Farm. It had now been realised that the position although just a pile of rubble in appearance was a very superior German strong point with the emphasis on the undergroundness of the position. It contained very large dugouts and passages. On the 3rd September the 13th Bde. of the 4th Australian Div. attacked and captured much of the farm and the neighbouring trenches. There was fierce fighting both above ground and in the underground passages. The 13th Bde. was then forced to withdraw but did manage to cling to part of the Fabeck Trench. During this time the Australian Division had 2,049 casualties.

It was now the turn of the Canadian Divisions. They captured the farm on the 16th September but without totally clearing it, and they were subsequently driven out.

By the 25th September the farm was shared by the two opposing sides but the tunnels under it were still in German hands. On the 26th the farm was attacked and taken by the British 11th Div. with the 34th Bde. finishing the capture with the 33rd Brigade to their left. The Division was on the right of the 18th Division who were busy capturing the stronghold of Thiepval to the west.

The 9th Lancs. Fus. of the 34th Bde. were heavily involved in the fighting in the ruins of the farm. They tried to bomb the exit points and managed to reach their second objective which was the west end of Zollern Trench to the north-west of the farm and where hostile German machine guns had been very active. This confused fighting ended with the surrender of 56 Germans including one officer, after smoke bombs had been flung down into the cellars. Two tanks had been allocated to assist, but they had to be ditched before reaching the objective. And so the farm, Zollern Redoubt and Thiepval were all to fall on the same day. The official War Office photographer Geoffrey Malins saw the farm shortly after its capture and described it in his book as a 'most wonderful defensive point that could possibly be conceived, and chosen by men who made a special study of such positions'. He said that the whole place had been thickly planted with machine guns that were cunningly concealed, and able to cover the ground that attackers would have to cross, which had no vestige of cover. Although the farm and the surrounding area had been shelled continuously, it made little impact on the German garrison which had been in dugouts some forty or fifty feet underground. According to Malins many of the Allied field gun batteries took up their positions in former shell holes near the farm turning them into gun pits. Malins actually entered the underground defences with a guide and found some of it blown in. It was a veritable 'rabbit warren' and his party emerged at a point about 100 yards from their entrance point.

Apart from being a strong point with deep dugouts the farm had also served as a MDS and command position for the German Army.

Munster Alley

Munster Alley was a continuation of Pozieres Trench going in a north-easterly direction. It was parallel to the Pozieres Mill beyond Pozieres. The German OG trenches linked up with the German Switch Line beyond. It was an important point in the enemy's communications with Martinpuich.

On the 3rd July the 68th Bde. 23rd Div. spent one night in trenches at Albert before going, on the 4th, to Bécourt Wood. From the 7th to the 10th they took part in a series of operations, which included an attack on Contalmaison. The 12th and 13th Durham LI succeeded in capturing Bailiff Wood one of the 68th Bde's. main objectives. The 68th were relieved on the 11th and returned to Albert.

During the fighting the British composer George Butterworth, who was serving as an officer with the 13th Durhams, was recommended for the award of the MC. His company commander was wounded which left Butterworth in charge. On the night of 17th July the Bde. which had been lent to another Division was to be involved in the fighting at Pozieres, and made an unsuccessful frontal attack. After consolidating their trenches during the next two days they were relieved by the Australians and reached Albert on the 20th July. They formed up with the 23rd Div. again near Franvilliers. Butterworth was once again recommended for the MC. On the 26th they marched through Contalmaison and joined the right of the Australian Division about half a mile to the east of Pozieres. Munster Alley was the dividing line between the two Divisions. The trench ran at right angles to the British front straight into the enemy's line. On the 27th 70 yards of the trench was secured and consolidated. The Brigade then withdrew to Sausage Valley and Albert. Butterworth wrote what was to be his last letter home, dated the 29th July during a short rest period. The day before his company had succeeded in advancing the line some 200 yards on the right of Munster Alley before being relieved. They had been assisted by a company of the 12th DLI and had gained the ground on the right by digging a trench which was given the name Butterworth. It was almost parallel to the German Switch Trench.

The 68th Bde. went up the line again on the 1st August. It appears that two attacks were made simultaneously on Munster Alley on 4th August one a bombing party under Butterworth up the trench and the other an attack over the top from the loop in Butterworth Trench. The latter failed but Butterworth's party succeeded in gaining some 100 yards of the Alley and in making a block. Butterworth was shot dead through the head on the 5th. He fell close to the section of the line where the 68th Bde. line joined that of the Australians at the southern end of the Alley, behind the modern Radio Station. Private William Short (8th Yorks. Princess of Wales' Own) was awarded the VC for an action at Munster Alley on 6th August.

The Nab

The Nab was a sharp salient at the head of Nab Valley a valley which was to become better known as Blighty Valley. It was in the north-east corner of Authuille Wood. At the beginning of July it was almost on the front line and was virtually a maze of battered trenches. To the south of the Nab ran the reserve line and at one point it ran along what became known as Dead Man's Bank which was the scene of many deaths on 1st July. It was only a few feet high and was half way across no man's land. The two battalions who tried in vain to break out towards Pozieres on that day were the 8th KOYLI and the 8th Y & L (70th Bde. 23rd Div.) The 9th Y & L also had many casualties there. In early September Nab Valley contained many guns of differing calibres and seemed to be safe from counter-shelling.

Ovillers la Boisselle

Ovillers la Boisselle is a village to the north-east of Albert just off to the left of the Albert Bapaume Road. It is north-east of Aveluy, south-west of Pozieres and is twinned with la Boisselle which is across the main road slightly to the south-east. The village lay along a road at right angles to the Allied front line. It was protected by rising ground and enemy parapets hid it from British eyes. To the east was Mash Valley which was also in enemy hands and this complimented Sausage Valley which was on the la Boisselle side of the road. Mash Valley was very broad and the lines went across as they bent south-eastwards, having come down northwards in a relatively north-to-south fashion. Behind Mash Valley was Usna Hill and behind it Usna Valley. Usna Hill was full of reserve and support trenches at the beginning of the battle and from it observers could obtain a view of the extremely powerful looking enemy positions at Ovillers.

It was the 8th Div. who were allocated Ovillers as their objective for 1st July and each of their three Bdes. was to be used in the attack. Right from the start it was known that there would be no chance of success if the flanking Divisions did not make simultaneous progress with the 8th Division attackers. The right Bde. (the 23rd) was to attack up Mash Valley and gain the Albert–Pozieres road due south of Pozieres. The 25th Bde. the centre Bde. was thought to have the easiest task in that it would be out of sight of the German defenders at Ovillers for the first three or four hundred yards. It was to carry the German defences in and around Ovillers village. On their left was the 70th Bde. who were due to attack up the slopes of Nab Valley on to the northern part of Ovillers Spur and to continue on into Pozieres. Their left would then rest on Mouquet Farm. During the final bombardment just before 7.30 a.m. on 1st July the attacking waves began to move forward into no man's land which in many cases was exceptionally wide, as wide as 800 yards and as narrow as 300 yards. They at once came under machine gun and rifle fire. At 7.30 a.m. when the barrage lifted the first waves advanced and despite the appalling fire and very exposed territory that they had to cross, they somehow made enough progress to reach not only the German first line but parties actually reached the second line as well. When the attackers got up close to the German line the German artillery and fire intensified and this resulted in the waves becoming mixed up. The 23rd Bde. had had an appalling stretch of no man's land to traverse with the German garrison at la Boisselle to the right and the fortified village of Ovillers in higher ground to the left. Despite the deadly flanking fire parties of the 2nd Middlsex and 2nd Devons passed through the German defences. They were caught by cross fire and after a time were forced to withdraw. Lt. Col. E. T. F. Sandys CO of the 2nd Middlesex (23rd Bde. 8th Div.) had been concerned before the battle began about uncut German wire and the enemy trenches which were still occupied despite the heavy Allied barrage in the area of Mash Valley. His battalion had 750 yards of no man's land to cross and they were cut down as he had predicted. The disaster so preyed on his mind that he shot himself in September and died a few days later.

The 2nd W. Yorks and the 2nd Scots. Rif. suffered in similar fashion. The brigade orders did not press a further attempt that day to take the village. On the left of the 23rd Bde. the 25th Bde. had a similar story to that of the 23rd Bde. with the 2nd R. Berks. and 2nd Lincolns advancing under the same heavy fire. Though the lines were close together the village provided a terrible obstacle. During the attack Lt. Col. A. M. Holdsworth of the 2nd R. Berks. was mortally wounded and died on the 7th July. In support the 1st R. Irish Rif. also lost heavily and lost their CO Lt. Col. C. C. Macnamara who was killed. To the left of the 25th Bde. the 70th Bde. was in front of Authuille Wood and they lost even more heavily than their two sister Bdes., although the 8th KOYLI and the 8th Y & L did make some progress. In support the 9th Y & L were cut down by gun fire at Thiepval Spur. It is not surprising that in view of this disaster the attack was not renewed that day. There had been little progress on the right flank in the attempts to take la Boisselle. On the left a small lodgement was made in the Leipzig Salient.

There had been mining activity on this front opposite Ovillers and two saps Rivington and Clay were made within 30 feet of the German line and were soon connected to it.

That night 1st/2nd July the 8th Div. was relieved by the 12th Div. by 5.40 a.m. On 2nd July there was no attack on Ovillers but it was bombarded in order to confuse the enemy when the 58th Bde. attacked la Boisselle.

On the 3rd July the bombardment was renewed at 2.15 a.m. by the 12th Div. against the same targets as those of 1st July. Rough assembly trenches had been dug in no man's land in order to make it much narrower. To the right was the 35th Bde. with the 6th R. Berks. and 7th Suffolks in front and on their left was the 37th Bde. with the 6th Queen's and 6th R.W. Kents. The extreme left of the Division's line was held by the 36th Bde. who were to cover the flank with the help of a smoke discharge. The advance began in the dark at 3.15 a.m. and the enemy were very soon to become aware of the attack. The leading waves made progress but on reaching the second line they were met by the enemy who had swarmed out of his dugouts and trenches, with bomb and bayonet. The whole of the 6th R.W. Kents had gone forward with two companies of Buffs acting in support. Three other battalions were held back pending progress, but at 9 a.m. the 12th Div. had to report that the attack had failed except for a small footing in the line that was soon lost. Adequate flank protection and lack of surprise were considered by the Official Historian to be the main reasons for the lack of progress.

On 7th July two battalions of the 36th Bde. of the 12th Div. were involved in the fighting, they were the 8th and 9th Royal Fus. and the 7th R. Sussex was between them in a further attempt to capture Ovillers. The 8th R. Fus. were on the right and the plan was to take the village from the south-west flank. The bombardment had begun at 4.30 a.m. and two leading companies crawled over the parapet into no man's land. The Fusiliers made progress into the German first and second trenches but at a considerable cost in casualties. The 9th R. Fus. fared in similar fashion. Nevertheless the 12th Div. and the 25th Div. did gain part of Ovillers on the 7th.

On the 7th the 13th R. Fus. had moved to the right of the 9th R. Fus. and delivered an attack. One of their members was Arthur Bliss the composer who was in the same battalion as Guy Chapman the writer and historian. The attack began at 8.30 a.m. and Bliss was almost immediately wounded and was picked up by stretcher bearers and soon returned to England. At one point he recollects being transported by barge and this was probably at the Somme end of the journey home as this was a recognised and gentle way of transporting the wounded. Bliss had a brother named Kennard who was with the RGA and who was killed in the Autumn of 1916. After his recovery Bliss returned to France in 1918 and in his autobiography mentions his former trenches at Monchy au Bois and Adinfer Wood which he revisited.

The 12th Div. decided to bomb forward at 3.45 a.m. on the 8th July but the troops were held up by deep and clinging mud. The 36th Bde. were at the edge of Ovillers and were relieved by the 7th E. Surreys of the 37th Bde. and the 9th Essex of the 35th Bde. and they made some progress in the ruins of Ovillers. Major C. I. Ryan of the Essex Battalion was killed and from the valley the 74th and 75th Bdes. bombed forward. At 8 p.m. the 74th Bde. renewed its attacks and were helped by the 13th Cheshires and 2nd R. Irish Rifs. Before morning the 14th Bde. of the 32nd Div. relieved the 12th Div. On 10th July the 13th Batt. of the Rifle Bde. attacked the village to the south-east and captured 200 prisoners.

Bernard Montgomery on the 12th July wrote to his mother. He was never one to censor his own letters, and he told her that they were at Ovillers being heavily shelled and were expected to advance at any moment. He had been over the whole ground and had seen all the recent battlefields including Beaumont Hamel, Hamel, Thiepval, Ovillers, la Boisselle, Contalmaison and Mametz Wood. He describes it as all most interesting! He was living in a very damp dugout at the time.

On the 12th July the 19th Lancs. Fus. (14th Bde. 32nd Div.) were ordered to capture as much of Ovillers as possible and a strong point which was known as Point 18. On 15th July at 2 a.m. the 25th Div. attacked the village from the north-east and south and the 32nd Div. attacked from the south-west but little progress was made. The men of the 32nd Div. were relieved by the 144th Bde. (48th Div.). The 143rd Bde. (48th Div.) attacked without a preliminary bombardment and crossed a thousand yards of open ground and occupied a knot of trenches in the rear of the Ovillers defenders. It fell to Charles Carrington to lead the assault. By such tactics the 48th Div. contained the garrison and compelled it to surrender. North of Ovillers the top of the ridge overlooked Thiepval and the Ancre Valley. The 143rd Bde. attached to the 25th Div. closed in from the north-west. The 74th Bde. 25th Div. with the 144th Bde. pressed in from the south and east. That night the enemy surrendered and the 25th Div. handed over to the 145th Bde. of the 48th Div.

On the 16th the 48th Div. tried to cut off the remainder of the German garrison. The village was virtually surrounded and finally the small German force surrendered. The 144th Bde. had taken over 300 yards of the original German front line.

The historians say that the village was finally taken by the 48th Div. on the 17th July, in the morning. They advanced on the village from three sides and at about 10 a.m. the remnant of the German garrison, which had been reduced to two officers and 124 men of the 3rd Prussian Guard surrendered.

Gerald Brenan comments in his autobiography that around 21st July he went back after crossing again the old front line, the ground torn up by shells and littered with dead bodies from the attack of 1st July. The wounded who could not be brought in had crawled into shell holes, wrapped their waterproof sheets around them, taken out their Bibles, and died like that. Brenan was with the 6th R. Warwicks (143rd Bde. 48th Div.) and between 20th and 23rd July had turned off towards Ovillers, which he decribed as above. He was in search of his friend Ralph Partridge who was in charge of a company. The further end of the trench was occupied by Germans 'What was needed, he said, was to bomb up it so as to reach a machine gun that was holding up our advance, but his men were tired and not out for taking risks.' After the taking of Ovillers Brenan wrote that 'A thing that had happened again and again was that our troops pushed their way up a trench and took a strongpoint without loss and were told to retire in order to consolidate. Two hours later, there having been no change in the meantime, they would be ordered to retake the strongpoint, which was now full of Germans, by a frontal atttack. This might be impossible, but it had to be tried and perhaps fifty men would be killed in the attempt.'

On 7th August the 7th Norfolks (35th Bde. 12th Div.) took over the line at Ovillers. The line was now facing north-west in and behind Ration Trench which ran south-west from Pozieres Trench. The Germans were in Sixth Avenue and trenches on the right (Ridge Trench) during the night 12/13th August. On the 13th August the 12th Div. was relieved and marched towards Arras. Graham Greenwell of the 1/4 O & BLI (145th Bde. 48th Div.) wrote home and said that 'I have just taken over some trenches, such as they are, full of equipment, filth and bodies and am being heavily shelled'. On the 17th he was sitting in Skyline Trench at Ovillers in the bottom of an old German dugout about ten or twelve feet under the earth. The floor was covered with German clothing and filth. The remains of the trench outside was blown to pieces, and full of corpses from the different regiments which had been there, lately Germans and English. The ground was ploughed up by enormous shell holes; there wasn't a single landmark to be seen for miles except a few giant sticks where the trees once were. On 4th September the Church at Ovillers was just a signboard.

On 11th November the 11th Essex rested here under tarpaulin bivouac sheets on the hillside.

The poet Ivor Gurney, who was a member of the Gloster Regiment, probably passed the ruins of Ovillers when on his way to Grandcourt on 21st November.

A poem that he wrote follows:

Ballad of the Three Spectres.
As I went up by Ovillers
In mud and water cold to the knee,
There went three jeering, fleering spectres,
They walked abreast and talked of me.

Ovillers Military Cemetery is a little way south-west of Ovillers village, on the right hand side of the road to Aveluy. It was begun before the capture of Ovillers, as a battle cemetery behind a dressing station, and was used until March 1917. It was enlarged after the Armistice mainly from the battlefields at Pozieres, la Boisselle, Ovillers and Contalmaison. The great majority of the graves belonged to men who fell in July 1916. It was in this valley that so many of the 8th Div. who had to cross 750 yards to reach the German trenches, were killed. Sir Harry Lauder's son Captain John Lauder of the 8th A & SH was killed on 28th December and buried in the cemetery. Other officers buried there include Lt. Col. F. C. Heneker CO of the 2nd Tyneside Scottish and Major L. M. Howard of the 1st Tyneside Irish. In the area of Mash Valley were many craters of the mining warfare of 1915–16. The 22nd R. Fus. erected a wooden memorial in the cemetery to 78 officers and men of the battalion who fell in 1917.

In November 1982 a grave containing the remains of fifty-one men was found twenty yards from the Military Cemetery. Forty-nine of the bodies were from men of British Units from Sussex, Berkshire, Essex and West Yorkshire. The other two bodies were German. All of the remains were taken for re-burial in Terlincthun British Cemetery Wimille.[4]

Pepperbox Hill

In *Salute of Guns* D. Boyd the author wrote that towards the end of August he was here with the Artillery. They were reconnoitering and climbing Pepperbox Hill south of Toutencourt where there were several batteries on the uplands in a disorderly camp of shelters. They returned to Bavelincourt having made contact with the Battery Officer, where they had tents under a crescent of Ilex Trees planted about a crucifix which looked towards the village. The next day they went off along the Albert road. Two or three sections of 9.2 howitzers shot up over their heads. They halted behind Beaucourt Wood close to the D 919 road from Amiens towards Acheux and put up their own lines. They were close to some Australians who were disliked by the British troops in the encampment because despite there being allotted times of watering at the canvas tanks, the Australians galloped down when other horses were in possession which broke down the troughs so that the precious water was wasted and the horses were thrown into disorder.

Boyd said that they went into action on the hill on the 25th August just when light was breaking between Bazentin Wood and Mametz Wood. They used tracks which followed the firm ground amongst shell holes and refuse of the battle. The reserve of the Scottish infantry sat amongst the low mounds which marked the entrance to Welch Alley, which was about four feet deep, its walls were irregular and collapsed, having been blown in. It was full of telephone wire that looped across and under along the walls. There were two OPs, one in 70 Avenue, the front line on the left of Welch Valley, the other in a forward sap that ended in a barricade. The 4.2s had been falling sporadically as they came to these places. They fired their guns and received replies from the enemy. They continued their registration of the front at intervals as the 8 inch guns played continually about 70th Avenue and Welch Valley. He describes the routine in the trench and how he managed to sleep for twelve hours. Ammunition wagons came up and everyone helped with the unloading passing the shells to the pits. The deep German dugout faced the wrong way. His battery's guns were sheltered at the side by walls made of brass 18 pounder cartridge cases that were filled with earth. These costly ramparts supported eight wooden rafters, a roof of corrugated iron and a row of sandbags that were filled with chalk.

Pommier

The village is north-west of Gommecourt and was the home to several battalions including the 5th Lincolns (138th Bde. 46th Div.) who marched from Saulty, a village to the north-west, to Pommier in mid July. At the time of their march the road between Bavincourt and la Cauchie was being shelled. On the 16th and 17th company training was carried out and the officers visited the new trench sector to the north of Monchy, which was to be taken over the next day by the 4th Lincolns of the same brigade.

Pommiers Redoubt

The site of Pommiers Redoubt is on the south side of the road between Montauban and Mametz on the D 64 road. It is just after Danzig Alley, coming to it from Mametz. There is little or nothing to see of it now. The redoubt was well protected by Pommiers Trench which was about 400 yards to the south side of it. Montauban Alley entered the redoubt from the north-east. Beyond the redoubt to the north was Beetle Alley, beyond that White Trench which was to the east of Queen's Nullah and beyond that Mametz Wood.

The Redoubt was one of the objectives of the 18th Div. on 1st July and the assaulting brigades in this sector were the 53rd, to the right and the 54th to the left. It was the latter who were to be mostly involved in the redoubt's capture. The two assaulting battalions of the 54th Bde. were the 7th Bedfords on the right and the 11th R. Fus. on their left. In turn they were supported by the 6th Northamptons with the 12th Middlesex in reserve. Two machine guns went forward with each assaulting battalion. Trench Mortars were in position for a hurricane bombardment according to the history of the 18th Div. The attack pressed forward from the north of Carnoy. They suffered casualties when they reached Emden Trench, defence line in front of Pommiers Trench. Flanking fire from Austrian Trench and wire which was uncut between Bund Trench and Pommiers Trench held the advance up for a time. However Pommiers Trench was captured twenty minutes after the attack began at 7.30 a.m.

On their left the 7th Div. was held up before Danzig Alley whilst the Germans were still in possession of Fritz Trench. However by 9.30 a.m. the redoubt which was a considerable strongpoint and heavily protected by the trenches mentioned above was in the hands of the Bedfords and Fusiliers. The Germans in their dugouts were 'little disposed to surrender'. Beetle Alley to the north of the redoubt was seized by the Fusiliers and the Bedfords and consolidated by the 6th Northamptons. Parties even reached White Trench which was a winding trench nearly a thousand yards beyond the redoubt to the right of Queen's Nullah and within easy distance of Mametz Wood. By 10.20 a.m. the Loop, a trench system that ran eastwards from Pommiers Trench had been captured by the 6th R. Berks. of the 53rd Bde. while by 11 a.m. other parties of the 53rd Bde. were in touch with the 54th Bde. at the north-east corner of the redoubt.

Before midday the 6th R. Berks. found themselves held up within 75 yards of Montauban Alley, and the 8th Norfolks had also to fight hard at the junction of Loop Trench and the Montauban–Mametz Road. The 10th Essex of the 53rd Bde. went up to support the R. Berks. By 1.30 p.m. the 55th Bde. who were attacking to the right of the 53rd Bde. and helped by three companies of the 8th Suffolks were working west along Montbauban Alley towards Loop Trench. Later in the afternoon British patrols reached and probed the German support lines towards Caterpillar Wood Valley.

So the capture of Pommiers Redoubt together with the village of Montauban to the east were part of the successes of the day.

On 3rd July Lt. Col. F. A. Maxwell V.C. commanding officer of the 12th Middlesex reconnoitered nearly two miles of the new line, taking with him a Vickers Gun team for emergencies. By the 8th July the 3rd Div. had taken over the 18th Div. front. The 53rd Bde. settled at Grove Town and the 54th Bde. at the Bois des Tailles. The 55th Bde. rested at Bronfay Farm.

On 19th July the 15th Bde. of the 5th Div. moved into position as Divisional Reserve in the trenches on Pommiers Ridge.

The 2nd KOSB (13th Bde. 5th Div.) retired after the High Wood battles and bivouacked at Pommiers Redoubt and at the same time absorbed a new draft. On the evening of the 29th they left the redoubt and relieved the 95th Bde. of the 5th Div. in Longueval on the west side of Delville Wood. After a long and difficult relief the battered KOSB 'crawled back' in small parties, in the small hours of 31st July to Pommiers Redoubt.

Max Plowman in addition to writing his book *A Subaltern on the Somme* also published a volume of letters called *Over the Bridge* and in this book he 'fills out' some of the material in the first book. He was in 'C' Company of the 10th West Yorks in July and August and in a letter home at the beginning of August he wrote 'Here we are for instance in what is known as divisional reserve, about 3 or 4 miles back and we are entertaining ourselves in what rather more than a month ago was a German Redoubt. As far as my company is concerned it consists of about 150 holes in the ground none more than 3 or 4 feet deep – in fact they are glorified shell holes with a light roof of wood and sandbags over them without any covering and in one of them I slept very comfortably last night with another officer and I am now sitting in the step of it as I write. Here we are just dotted about anywhere while we wait to go farther up, which may be tonight and may be in two or three days time – or we might even go back unwanted. There are some heavy guns behind us and every minute we hear the shell from them travelling over our heads but the nearest I've seen a German shell burst to this place is a good 300 yards away . . .'

After four days opposite High Wood, Plowman and his colleagues returned to Pommiers Redoubt, and Plowman himself was wounded in the neck during this time. He quotes from an order 'Two half companies under the command of two subalterns per half-company will report to the officer of the Royal Engineers for digging on the communication trench at St. Georges Hill this evening.' In the history of the Fifth Div. it gives some information on the origin of the name of Pommiers Redoubt. It says 'that owing to the prominence of a group of apple trees midway along this ridge (Montauban to Mametz) it was known as Pommiers Ridge. For weeks they were used by the British Artillery for registration purposes, until it became a daily habit; one night the Germans felled and removed the trees, and the ensuing consternation of the FOOs, the following morning was most entertaining to those not directly concerned'. The 8th KRRC (41st Bde. 14th Div.) were at the redoubt from the 11th August and on the 12th were in the line opposite Orchard Trench, which was to be their objective. On the 17th August they were back in Pommiers. They were next in an attack on Longueval and the Pommiers area at the time was covered with horses, mules, boxes of shells, with big guns firing in the midst of it all.

They were again in the redoubt on the 12th September whilst taking part in the Delville Wood fighting. On the 14th September the 9th KRRC (42nd Bde. 14th Div.) were moved up to the redoubt from a camp south of Bécordel.

Later on the 73rd Bde. of the 25th Div. was here and according to Lord Moran in mid September the redoubt was being used as a bivouac camp. At the end of September the 7th R. Sussex (36th Bde. 24th Div.) bivouacked here. By then the ground had become a quagmire. The Flers Road was the worst track, the trenches there being completely made up of dead men, mules and horses. Sometimes it took teams of six mules to haul a limber to delivering rations. At the beginning of October the redoubt was used as a 12th Div. Bde. HQ. Towards the end of October the 26th R. Fus. (124th Bde. 41st Div.) bivouacked there.

Pozieres

Pozieres is a village on the main Albert–Bapaume Road the D 929. It is south-east of Mouquet Farm and Thiepval, south-west of Courcelette, north-west of the Bazentin villages, north of Contalmaison and north-east of la Boisselle and Ovillers la Boisselle. It was yet another of the villages that the Germans had fortified extremely strongly and being on a ridge it overlooked the positions of any attackers who advanced from the south-west. The German second line ran behind the village from the direction of Bazentin le Grand in the south-east to the direction of Mouquet Farm at the end of June. There was a windmill on the north-west side of the village which during the battle was to become very well known to the troops who fought for its possession.

John Masefield whom I like to quote from because he developed a very close understanding of the Somme battlefield in the several months that he was stationed in the area when carrying out research for a book on the battle. He wrote two books, one called *The Old Front Line* and the other *The Battle of the Somme.* In the latter book he says that routes which could be used by attackers were overlooked by the Germans who had arranged his trenches and machine guns so that any advance would be impossible especially in daylight. The approach from Sausage and Mash Valleys was commanded by Pozieres Plateau, the one from Mouquet Valley was flanked and enfiladed by points that had not yet been captured and the route by the main road over the central spur was strongly wired, trenched and flanked. There was however some dead ground to the south-east of the main road though much of it could be seen from Pozieres. It was sometimes called Quarry Gulley and in it were two chalk quarries on the eastern bank. The small spur to the east of Quarry Gulley hid the next valley (which Masefield says may have been called Hospital Valley because a dressing station was once there), from the village.

Again, though most of the valley was visible to the enemy trenches at the head of the valley, Masefield wrote that troops who advanced from Bazentin le Petit Wood had a better chance of success than from any other direction. The Quarry Road began from the Albert–Contalmaison road at the top of the rise. Just at the junction it was sunken between two deep banks and here there was a field dressing station, known as Dressing Station Corner. The Quarry Road was forked and close to the fork was a second quarry which was twice the size of the previous one and about half as deep again. It gave better shelter and was deeper as well as being better screened. In the village itself on the extreme south-west of the main road was a position called Gibraltar. Masefield described it as a 'grey concrete fragment'. It stood well up on the bank above the road and overlooked Mash Valley. It was an OP and could be used as a machine gun emplacement. A concrete stair led down to a cellar some 12 to 15 feet below barely large enough to contain two men. The former Blockhouse was opened up in 1986. Beside it were two gun emplacements that were covered or camouflaged with banks of timber. The cellars had been fitted with machine guns as had the windmill, the school and Gibraltar, and these defences were of the strong defensive type. The German second line also known as OG1 and OG2 had been dug to enfilade any attack on the village from th east. At the time of the first attack the Allies held lines to within 600 yards of the village.

Centre Way was a German trench line that ran from close to Pozieres Church in a north-westerly direction towards the OG lines which it reached about three quarters of a mile to the west of the windmill. There were also two orchards to the west of the village.

In his book *Anzac to Amiens* the Australian historian C. E. W. Bean wrote that the breach in the line was only two miles wide and that attempts by the British III Corps to widen it had been prevented by the stubborn German defences. Pozieres protected the German Thiepval flank to the north and also hemmed in the Fourth Army's flank. It was Haig's idea that the Fourth Army should still thrust further forward where they had already been successful and so, went the thinking, the villages of Pozieres and Thiepval would automatically fall. Thus strikes towards Ginchy and Guillemont were continued and the left flank moved slowly forward towards the Pozieres position. In mid July four attacks against Pozieres were made by the British.

The 11th R. Warwicks in the early hours of the morning of the 15th July were informed that the Bde. (the 112th) was to attack Pozieres at 9.20 a.m. The plan was for the 8th E. Lancs. followed by the 6th Bedfords to clear part of the village south and north of the main road. The Warwicks were to act as a back up battalion and assist in consolidating the ground gained. The 10th L.N. Lancs. were to carry bombs and stores etc. The advance was unopposed at first but as the troops went over the crest, above the Chalk Pit, they were met by heavy and continuous machine gun fire. The fire was extremely accurate and this coupled with the Brigade's narrow frontage immobilised the three battalions, who then became intermixed.

C. S. Collison and a fellow officer named Hart walked to the Chalk Pit and found there a 'great gathering'. The majority of the 10th L.N. Lancs. were there, ready to move forward. Well into the small hours of the 16th July the stretcher bearers were still busy evacuating the wounded and moving them to the shelter of the cross-roads, north of Bailiff Wood, to the west of

Contalmaison. On the 15th July the 10th R. Fus. (111th Bde. 37th Div.) the same as for the above Bde. had advanced to Sausage Valley in support of the main attack and about 300 yards from the village were held up by machine gun fire. The Fusiliers reached as far as the orchards on the south-west side of Pozieres when it was obvious to them that the attack had failed, as they found that the hollow road was blocked with troops in the same way as the Chalk Pit.

In *The War in the Air* an Observer reported that the artillery bombardment had wrecked many buildings in the village but had done little damage to the trenches which commanded the village. Once the bombardment lifted, the German infantry and machine gunners came down from their dugouts and cellars and ran to their trenches to the fire steps and opened immediate fire. It appeared to the Observer that the attacking troops got as close to the bombardment as possible but that the enemy had sufficient time to man his positions.

Collison reported that the casualties of the 11th R. Warwicks were 275 and that the casualties of the 6th Bedfords, 8th E. Lancs. and the 10th R. Fus. were probably much greater as they opened the attack. The losses of the 10th L.N. Lancs. were much lighter as they were not heavily engaged. However Collison went on 'the fighting around the Chalk Pit was but an incident in the far-flung battle that raged long on the Franco–British front'. C. E. W. Bean in *Anzac to Amiens* wrote 'the loop trench around the village was twice entered, there was little to show for the effort except the crumpled bodies of British soldiers left hanging in the German wire entanglements.' – 'the second German defence line, an immensely strong system comprising two parallel trenches (and many long approaches) which ran along the actual crest 500 yards behind the village. South-east of Pozieres this line lay on ground seized by the Fourth Army on 14th July, and from that foothold the bombing squads attacked north-westwards'.

In the period 18th to 19th July the Pozieres front was transferred from the responsibility of the Fourth Army to that of the Reserve Army under General Gough renamed the Fifth Army.

On 18th July the 24th Div. of the Fourth Army made a direct attack on Pozieres which failed and Gough in his book on the *Fifth Army* said that in order to relieve Rawlinson (who was of course commander of the Fourth Army) of the necessity of attending to his left flank, and to allow him to concentrate his efforts on pushing his right forward where he had made some progress, Haig had asked Gough to undertake the attacks on Pozieres as well as on Ovillers la Boisselle. This meant that Gough had more territory to look after and he was allocated the 1st Australian Division in order to help out.

The planned attack was launched soon after midnight on the 23rd July at the same time as the left of the 3rd Army made its attack. The village had been heavily bombarded for the four previous days especially on the western side between Bapaume Road and the cemetery as well as on the OG trenches and Pozieres Trench. Also the barrage had been put down on the German line to the west of the village in order to simulate a preparation for an attack from the south-west. The 3rd and 1st Bdes. of the 1st Australian Div. attacked and achieved their objectives except that they didn't take the OG lines on the right

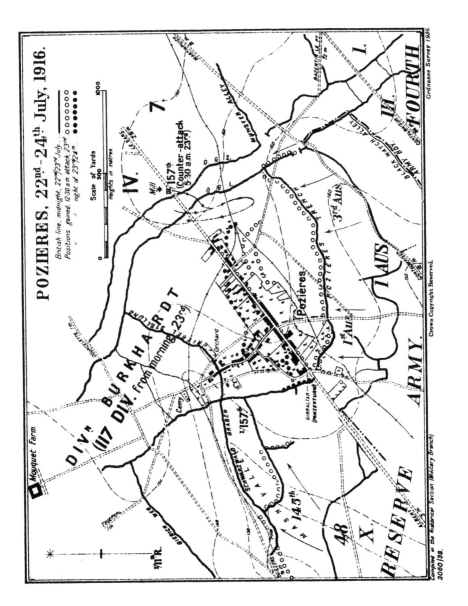

POZIERES, 22nd - 24th July, 1916.

British line, midnight, 22nd/23rd July.
Positions gained, 12:30 a.m. attack 23rd
" " night of 23rd/21st

Scale of Yards

Heights in metres

Moquet Farm

DIVN. BURKHARDT
(117 DIV. from morning 23rd)

IV.

Mill
III/157th
(Counter-attack
5:30 a.m. 23rd)

7.

MUNSTER ALLEY

Pozieres

Orchard

Cemy

1/157th

SCHWARZWALD VALLEY

GIBRALTAR
(PANZERTURM)

14.5th

3rd AUS.

I AUS.

1st AUS

II.

L.

FOURTH

ARMY.

RESERVE

X.

48

Ordnance Survey 1906.

Crown Copyright Reserved.

Compiled in the Historical Section (Military Branch)
3060/38.

completely. The Germans were thus able to fire into the exposed flank of the Australians attacking the eastern end of the village. The enemy was very anxious to maintain their hold on the village and bombarded it methodically as they also did the approach roads to it. During this fighting two Australians gained the VC. A. S. Blackburn, Sec. Lt. of the 10th Batt. AIF received it for the following deed. He was directed with 50 men to drive the enemy from a strongpoint, and with dogged determination they eventually captured the trench. Blackburn personally led four separate parties of bombers against the trench, many of whom became casualties. In the face of fierce opposition he captured 250 yards of it. Then, after crawling forward with a Sergeant to reconnoitre, he returned, attacked and seized another 120 yards of trench, establishing communication with the battalion on the left.

The other VC was Private J. Leak of the 9th Batt. (Queensland). He was born in Queensland and was awarded the VC in the following way: He was one of a party which finally captured an enemy strongpoint. At one assault, when the enemy's bombs were outranging ours, he rushed out of the trench, ran forward under heavy machine gun fire at close range, and threw bombs into the enemy's bombing post. He then jumped into the post and bayoneted three wounded enemy bombers. Later, when the enemy in overwhelming numbers was driving his party back, he was always the last to withdraw at each stage, and kept on throwing bombs. His courage and energy had such an effect on the enemy, that, on arrival of reinforcement, the whole trench was captured.

One of the first points to be captured was the strongpoint called Gibraltar, on the south-west of the village just off the main road. The Hanoverian Fusiliers who were one of the German regiments involved in the fighting wore a regimental badge that represented the Rock of Gibraltar. The 2nd KRRC 2nd Bde. (1st Div.) were all involved in an attack on the south-west trench to the north-east of Pozieres between trips to Scotts Redoubt.

The village was by no means taken on 23rd July and though a foothold was made in it by the Australians, it was several weeks before the whole village and the second line beyond it were to fall into Allied hands, but high ground had been captured which allowed the British to overlook the valleys of Martinpuich and Pys and also the German artillery positions on the high ground to the east. Also the ground gained threatened the flank of the German main fortification around the village of Thiepval.

On the left flank of the Australians the 145th Bde. of the 48th Div. gained some ground in the direction of the cemetery having attacked up Mash Valley. On 24th July the 1st Australian Div. consolidated their positions and the plan for the 25th July was to secure OG1 Trench and to take OG2 Trench. The attacking troops had to file out of Pozieres Trench in the early hours of the 25th and then turn to the right. By 2 a.m. OG1 was taken but attempts to take OG2 failed. During the fighting Private Cooke was to earn the VC. He was born in New Zealand in 1881 and his citation states that after a Lewis gun had been disabled he was ordered to take his own gun team to a dangerous part of the line. Here he did fine work, but came under very heavy

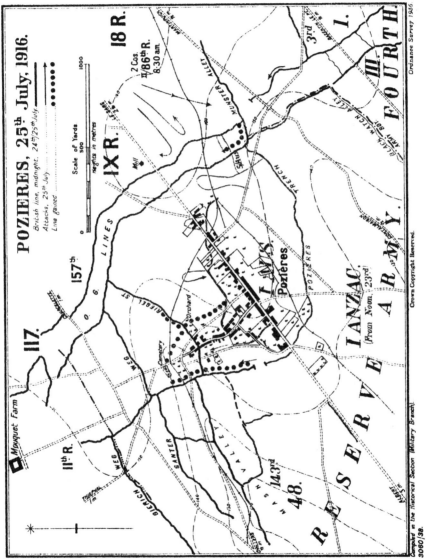

POZIERES, 25th. July, 1916.

British line, midnight, 24th/25th July
Attacks, 25th July
Line gained

Scale of Yards

Heights in metres

Ordnance Survey 1945

Crown Copyright Reserved.

Compiled in the Historical Section (Military Branch)
3060/38.

fire, with the result that finally he was the only man left. He still stuck to his post, and continued to fire his gun. When assistance came he was found dead beside his gun. 'He set a splendid example of determination and devotion to duty'. At night the 2nd Australian Division began to relieve the 1st Div. They moved up Sausage Valley which was full of ingoing and outgoing troops, artillery supply wagons, ammunition limbers and ambulances and into this the enemy fired shells! Whilst the Germans were fighting to keep a hold, however slight on the ridge the 5th Bde. of the 2nd Australian Div. were carrying on a mammoth bomb fight at Munster Alley, to the north-east of the village. The 23rd British Div. who were on the right of the Australians bombed along this communication trench. The enemy counter-attacked. By the end of 26th July the enemy had definitely been driven from Pozieres or at least the northern part as well as from the fortified cemetery to the north-east in the direction of Mouquet Farm. The windmill on Hill 160 being beyond the village to the north had yet to fall.

Sgt. C. C. Castleton of the 5th MGC AIF gained the VC on 28th July, he had been born in England but had joined the AIF. During the attack on the enemy's trenches the infantry was temporarily driven back by the intense machine gun fire. Many wounded were left in no man's land lying in shell holes. Sgt. Castleton went out twice in the face of this intense fire and each time brought in a wounded man on his back. He went out a third time, bringing back another wounded man when he was himself was hit in the back and killed instantly. He is commemorated in Pozieres Cemetery.

The next attempt to take the rest of the Pozieres position was to be made on 29th July. The attack was to begin at 12.15 a.m. and the plan was for the right OG1 between the railway and the Albert road to be captured. Once this was done then the whole of OG2 could be bombed from the direction of Munster Alley. North of the main road the objectives were the continuation of the OG Trenches. Just before midnight the attacking battalions assembled along the line of the railway to the east of the Cemetery. On the left the 23rd Batt. of the 6th Bde. were assembled. Under very heavy enemy shellfire the attack failed although the 23rd Bde. made some progress but without support on their right flank. The Australians took some time to recuperate and plan before their next attack which they made on 3rd August.

But first on the 3rd the British 12th Div. attacked and made progress in that the 8th R. Fus. of the 36th Bde. captured the south-west part of the Fourth Avenue. The 6th Buffs assisted. The attack was made at 11 p.m. Later they were to take Ration Trench on the right, with the 7th R. Sussex and the 9th R. Fus. attacking frontally and the 8th R. Fus. bombing from the left. The Australians had dug new assembly trenches which the enemy was aware of and subsequently bombarded very heavily. South-east of Bapaume Road OG1 and OG2 were taken. On the right the 20th Batt. blocked the entrance to Torr Trench. Between Bapaume Road and the track that led to Courcelette the 7th Bde. fought a very savage battle which resulted in very many dead from both sides. The left flank was checked by machine gun fire but the Windmill was taken, as were many prisoners.

The fighting resulted in more Australians being killed in this sector than in any other part of the Somme battle. The consolidating was very grim because the Germans knew the ground so well themselves. But the crest and the German second line had been finally taken. The Australians were at last able to look over the wide valley beyond the second line. They could see Courcelette in the foreground and the woods that were close to Bapaume about five and a half miles away. German guns could also be seen. The German command were very anxious to retake their lost positions and the Allied plan was not to push on eastwards but northwards towards Mouquet Farm and then on to Thiepval. The 4th Australians replaced the 2nd Australian Div. to carry the attack northwards, the 2nd Aust. Div. had been in the line for eleven days. There were times during the fighting when liquid fire was used and Sgt. C. R. Quinnell in one of the interviews kept at the Imperial War Museum described an incident when a German came over the barricade on the right flank with a canister of liquid fire on his back, squirting the liquid out of the hose, burning twenty three of our chaps to death – but somebody threw a bomb – a Mills bomb – and it burst behind him – he went down. This was on the 5th August, the day that English music lost one of its most talented musicians – George Butterworth of the Durham Light Infantry. He was killed in the Munster Alley fighting (see that entry).[5]

The 4th Div. was bombarded severely but managed to keep the heights and to push northwards towards Mouquet Farm as planned. The farm was camouflaged and was a very well fortified strongpoint. The defences went as much as 30 feet down. Because the Australians had made what was virtually a big bulge in the German lines they were vulnerable to shelling from the German artillery in the rear, in the direction of Thiepval and from both flanks. The enemy even overran the village for a short time before being driven off by the Australians. Private M. O'Meara of the 16th Batt. (4th Bde. 4th Div.) was awarded the VC for conspicuous bravery on 9th/12th August. He was born in Tipperary and had been working in Australia before the war. He was given the award for going out into no man's land over a period of four days and collecting wounded officers and men under artillery and machine gun fire. He also volunteered and carried up ammunition and bombs throughout a heavy barrage.

Pozieres having been a strongly fortified village in the German line had been gradually reduced to just a shapeless mass of rubble and dust. One source said that no fewer than 200 enemy machine guns had been used in its defence. It had now virtually ceased to exist.

On 13th August the Allies made further progress and advanced their line four hundred yards on a front of nearly a mile; casualties were light despite a heavy German gun barrage.

Lt. Cyril W. Winterbotham of the Glosters had published poetry including a volume called *The Muse in Arms*. He had been called to the bar in 1911 and stood as prospective candidate for the Liberals for East Gloucestershire in 1913. He joined the 1/5 Glosters and was killed at Skyline Trench on 27th August south-west of Pozieres, aged 29.

In time the 4th Div. was relieved later in August firstly by the 1st Div. and then by the 2nd, and then it was the 4th's turn again. Little progress was made and the Australians whose 'holy ground' the village had become were finally relieved by the Canadian Army in the first week of September. Sgt. Leo Clarke of the 2nd Batt. 1st Bde. Canadian Div. gained the VC on the 9th September near Pozieres. He was born in 1892 and had been detailed with his bomber section to clear the continuation of a newly captured trench and to cover the building of a 'block'. Most of his section became casualties and in addition they were counter-attacked by a German party of superior numbers. Clarke himself shot five Germans and captured a sixth. He was subsequently ordered to a Dressing Station having been wounded in the leg. He later returned to duty. All this activity took place in the vicinity of Walker Avenue which was a salient that lay between the Canadians and the village of Courcelette. Clarke was to die of wounds on the 19th October.

On the 15th September the stump of the Windmill at Pozieres was a starting point for some of the tanks that were making history in that it was the first time that the machines had been involved in a battle. They helped the British and Canadian infantry to drive the enemy almost to the bottom of the valley that the Australians had previously only looked over. The whole of the fighting for Pozieres had been very slow and extremely costly in terms of casualties. C. E. W. Bean wrote that the casualties of the 1st, 2nd and 4th Australian Divisions were 22,826 and of the 5th Div. in their attack on Frommelles to the north were 5,533. The last named was a battle that was designed to relieve pressure on the Somme battle!

In November there was an ADS or CP in the village.

John Masefield describes Pozieres after the battle as seen from Ovillers–la Boiselle in the following way: 'A clump of small fir and cypress trees stood up dark on the hill at the western end of this row, and behind the trees was a line of green hills topped with the ruins of a windmill. The ruins, now gone, were the end of Pozieres village, the dark trees grew in Pozieres Cemetery and the mill was the famous mill of Pozieres, which marked the crest that was one of the prizes of the battle'.

William Orpen the artist described the village at the same time in the following way: 'On up the hill past the mines to Pozieres. An Army railway was then running through, and the station was marked by a big wooden sign, painted black and white, like you see at any country station in England, with POZIERES in large Roman letters, but that's all there was of Pozieres except a little red in the mud'.

Pozieres British Cemetery is on the west side of the main road on the site of the place which in 1916 was known as Tramway Crossing, or Red Cross Corner. It would have been a place for field ambulances to bring their dead from the battlefield around. The cemetery which was designed by W. H. Cowlish was dedicated in 1932, and includes a Memorial to the Missing. It relates to the months of March and April 1918 or the German breakthrough against the British Fifth Army. The number of officers and men commemorated total more than 14,640 who have no known grave. Pozieres was lost to the Germans in the period 24th/25th March 1918 and the original plots of the cemetery contained the original burials of 1916–1918 by fighting units and field ambulances. The remaining plots were made after the Armistice, by the concentration of graves from the surrounding battlefields. The great majority were men who had been killed in the Autumn of 1916. One of the names on the panels is the poet R. B. Marriott–Watson a Lieutenant in the R. Irish Rif. who was killed on 24th March 1918.

Another literary connection is with the Imagist Poet T. E. Hulme who had been involved in the Pozieres fighting with the 1st Div. and was killed later in the war and buried at Coxde, near Dunkirk.

C. E. W. Bean collected many momentoes and artifacts from the battlefield and these have ended up in the Canberra Museum. They include a bag of debris from the site of the village which was placed in the Cenotaph in the Australian capital. As already stated on 15th September 1916 tanks went into action opposite the site of Pozieres Mill which had been fortified as a German bunker. The mill which is the highest point on Pozieres Ridge is now a grassy mound with a memorial slab that gives details of the Australian stand in the months of July and August in their attempts to capture the Hill whose other name was Hill 160. Opposite across the road is the Tank Corps Memorial which is made up of scale model tanks of the 1916–1918 period.

Puchevillers

The village is on the main road (D 11) between Amiens and Thièvries. It is in the Somme district and is 12 miles north-east of Amiens and three miles south-west of Raincheval. At the beginning of the battle it was one of the principal railheads for ammunition.

It was also one of the places where trains waited to take away the massive number of wounded on 1st/2nd July. The Xth Corps Stations were the No. 3 and No. 44 for the seriously wounded. The Cemetery is a short distance west of the village and was begun in June 1916 and was used by the 3rd and 44th CCS.

On 1st November the Hood Batt. of the RND came here from Hedauville. There was still a CCS in the village in November.

Puisieux

Puisieux is a village between Hébuterne and Achiet le Petit, it is south-west of Bucquoy, north-east of Serre and north-west of Miraumont. It is on the D 919, D 6 and D 27 roads and is a commune in the Department of the Pas de Calais. The road from Mailley–Maillet to Serre and Puisieux in June 1916 entered no man's land about 1,400 yards south-west of Serre and the 31st and 4th Divs. attacked north and south of this road on 1st July 1916. Parties of the 31st Div. reached Serre; but the attack failed, and the 3rd and 31st Divs. attacked again, without success in November.

Puisieux was part of the operations which also entailed the taking of Gommecourt, le Barque, Ligny Thilloy, Serre, and several other villages in the same area. The Germans left the village on 24th February 1917 and the next day the 22nd Manchesters entered it. The village which is in undulating country had been ruined and destroyed by artillery fire and the ground yielded was of significance and importance, as the position had been a strong one. The Germans only gave up the village when they retreated to the Hindenburg Line.

The Church was the last stronghold that the Germans had held on to and in March, 1918 they re-took the village only to lose it in August, 1918.

The Quadrilateral

The Quadrilateral was a German strong point rectangular in shape, that was about 750 yards to the east of Ginchy on a secondary road to Morval, where it bent northwards. It was sheltered by a clump of trees and protected in front by trenches than ran east and west as defence against the Allied direction from the south and also by lines of more trenches on the west side that ran north and south. Just beyond the bend in the road the road ran through a deep ravine with wooded sides. This had been strongly fortified with deep dugouts. The whole position consisted of a veritable redoubt, that formed the southern angle of a V, the two lines of which ran eastwards in the fortified ravine through which passed the continuation of the road. This comprehensive description of the position comes from H. P. Robinson's *Turning Point*.

On 15th September the Quadrilateral held up the attack of the Guards Div. and the 6th Div. whose objectives were Lesboeufs and Morval but after continuous and heavy fighting the position was taken on the 18th and the two villages on the 25th September.

Querrieu

Querrieu is a village on the Amiens to Albert road (D 929) a few miles to the north-east of Amiens. The chateau there was the HQ of General Rawlinson and his Fourth Army. He had been established there since early in 1916 when the Fourth Army took over the line to the south of the Third Army as far as the Somme River where they joined the French Army.

General Rawlinson used what he called 'The Grandstand' from where he observed the progress of the bombardment and later the battle itself. The spot is 200 yards off the main road and closer to Pont Noyelles than Querrieu. On the 27th of June he took Haig there to enable him to observe the barrage.

During this period of the Allied bombardment 150,000 rounds were being fired each day with 50,000 at night. Fifteen hundred guns were being used, four hundred and fifty of them being of a large calibre.

Before the battle began on 1st July General Gough's Fifth Army was billeted behind Rawlinson's HQ and Gough and his troops had been placed at

Rawlinson's disposal. At the time three Cavalry Divisions had been placed under Gough as had the 19th and 49th Divs. in case of a breakthrough. This however didn't materialise and the two Divisions were thrown into the Fourth Army struggle at the beginning of July.

King George V during his visit to the troops in August recorded in his diary that he visited Rawlinson's Chateau after he had been to Fricourt which was about as close to the front line as he was allowed to go. He had lunch there and met the French Generals Fayolle and Balfourier. He presented them with the GCMG award. Generals Pulteney and Horne also attended the luncheon. Haig arrived afterwards and the King decorated some 20 French Artillery Officers at 2.45 p.m. He left for Contay to continue his tour.

Rancourt

Rancourt is a village and commune in the Department of the Somme on the D 944 main road between Peronne to the south, and Bapaume to the north. It is south-east of Combles and south-west of St. Pierre Vaast Wood. It was in the area of French attacks and was just within the captured Somme territory at the end of the battle in mid November 1916. The Military Cemetery is about half a mile south of the village, on the west side of the main road; Rancourt French National German Cemetery with nearly 4,000 burials is to the west.

Rancourt was captured by the French on the 24th September and remained in Allied hands until 24th March 1918. The Military Cemetery was begun by units of the Guards Div. in the winter of 1916–17. It stands on fairly high ground amongst cultivated fields. There is a church adjacent to the cemetery.

Redan Ridge

Redan Ridge was a strong point north of the village of Beaumont Hamel and John Masefield in his book *The Old Front Line* described the situation there during the period before the battle began. He wrote that 'it was a question here, which side should hold the highest point of the spur. Right on top of the spur there is one patch of ground, measuring, it may be, two hundred yards each way, from which one can see a long way in every direction. From this path, the ground droops a little towards the English side and stretches away fairly flat towards the enemy side, but one can see far either way and to have this power of seeing both sides fought desperately.' It was the most northerly point in the line where mining was still in progress in June/July and two mines 57 feet and 62 feet were in active use and in contact with the enemy underground. A series of mines had been fired by both sides.

On 1st July the ridge was one of the objectives of the 4th Div. and it was the 11th Bde. who were most directly involved in the attempt to take it. This Bde. included the 1st Hampshires, 1st E. Lancs., 1st Somerset LI and the 1st Rif.

Brig. They had formed up on either side of Watling Street which was the road that led from Beaumont Hamel village in a north-westerly direction to the Serre Road. Further to the north was another strong point which was known as the Quadrilateral. Fire from the Ridge Redoubt almost wiped out the E. Lancs. and the CO of the 1st Hampshires, Colonel Palk, was killed. The British failed to take command of the Ridge on 1st July and it was not in fact captured until the November battles, and even then it was only partly taken, by the 2nd Division. At the end of the battle the Allied line was consolidated across Waggon Road which was roughly parallel to the still German held Munich Trench and beyond the Frankfurt Trench.

Masefield described 'the whole of the summit (which is called the Redan Ridge) for all its two hundred yards, is blown into pits and craters from twenty to fifty feet deep, and sometimes fifty yards long.' – 'For many weeks, the armies fought for this patch of hill. It was all mined, counter-mined, and re-mined, and at each explosion the crater was fought for and lost and won. It cannot be said that either side won that summit till the enemy was beaten from all that field, for both sides conquered enough to see from. On the enemy side, a fortification of heaped earth was made; on our side, castles were built of sandbags filled with flint. These strongholds gave both sides enough observation. The works face each other across the ponds.'

There is a group of cemeteries here on Redan Ridge and they are as follows: Redan Ridge Cemetery Number 1 is on the top of Redan Ridge, midway between the former front lines. It contains the graves of 154 soldiers who with few exceptions belonged to the 4th Div., which attacked the area on 1st July 1916, or to the 2nd Div. which gained ground here on 13th November. It commands a wide view of the neighbouring villages and Memorials.

Redan Ridge Cemetery Number 2 is on lower ground, about 100 yards to the west of the former German front line. It contains the graves of 279 soldiers who fell, with one exception, in July and November 1916, who belonged to the 4th, 29th and 2nd Divs.

Redan Ridge Cemetery Number 3 is actually amongst the former German front trenches and contains the graves of 67 soldiers. Most of the graves are those of men who fell in November 1916, who were members of the 2nd Div.

Regina Trench

Regina Trench was part of the German line which ran from the north of Courcelette to St. Pierre Divion. It connected up with Stuff Trench which in turn joined Schwaben Redoubt. On the easterly side it ran in a north-easterly direction across the Grandcourt Road, West Miraumont Road, Courcelette Trench and Pys Road towards le Sars.

The fighting for this position is particularly associated with Canadian Battalions who were particularly involved in very hard fighting in the period 8th to 10th October. It was during this time that one of their number, Piper J. C. Richardson of the 16th Batt. 1st Canadian Div., gained the VC. Prior to the start of the attack he had obtained permission to play his company 'over the top'. He had been born in Lanarkshire and was a member of a Canadian Scottish Battalion. As his company approached the objective they found that it was protected by very strong wire, and they subsequently came under intense fire. This caused casualties and demoralised the formation. Piper Richardson strode up and down outside the wire playing his pipes with the greatest coolness. The company were inspired and rushed the wire and overcame the objective. Later Richardson was detailed to take back a wounded man and some prisoners. After proceeding for about 200 yards he remembered that he had left his pipes behind and insisted on returning to fetch them. He was never seen alive again, and his grave is at Adanac Cemetery at Miraumont-Pys.

The trench was reached on 21st October after an effective artillery barrage. The Divisions directly involved were the 18th, the 25th and the 4th Canadian. A defensive flank was formed by the 87th Battalion of the 4th Canadian on the right, which was east of the Pys Road, and posts were established well forward of Regina Trench. On the left were the 10th Essex and the 8th Norfolks of the 53rd Bde. who overcame resistance. 250 Germans were killed and there were over 300 prisoners taken. The conditions here were appalling and as it rained a great deal more in October and November most parts of Regina Trench were to become knee deep in clinging mud. A commentator who visited the area of the trench in 1931 could find no trace of it.

Ribemont

Ribemont is on the River Ancre and is south-west of Buire and south of Bresle. The 16th KRRC (100th Bde. 33rd Div.) were here for one night on 30th August and the 4th King's Own (164th Bde. 55th Div.) were camped in canvas shelters on 13th September.

Rossignol Wood

The wood is famous for fighting later than that of 1916 although it did play a part in the Battle of Gommecourt on 1st July. It was opposite the right of the 56th Div. front and in the afternoon of that day howitzers had fired heavily on the positions of the London Scottish and in addition German batteries had boldly galloped up and opened fire from the slope near to Rossignol Wood. The London Scottish were compelled to withdraw. They had been exposed to enfilade fire from the high ground on the right, and to fire from their immediate front. The impossible position and the lack of counter-battery work rendered it untenable.

Before the battle the enemy had a good point of observation from the wood and was able to bring a very oblique artillery fire from his position between the wood and Gommecourt on any troops attacking from the Allied line. The machine gun site close to Moa Trench was a communication trench that ran from the wood to Puisieux and was later used by Ernst Jünger to get up to the wood against the New Zealanders later in the battle. Close by is the site where Dick Travis was to gain his VC.[6]

Sailly-au-Bois

Sailly-au-Bois is two or three miles to the west of Hébuterne, south-east of Coigneux and Bayencourt and north-east of Courcelles. The road from Hébuterne is the D 27. In the summer of 1916 it was very much a 'behind the scenes village'. Troops were billeted not only in the village but also in the valley between it and Coigneux where there was a pretty dell.

The village had originally been in the lines of the French Army and around the 8th June the 1/5th R. Warwicks were bivouacked in the Dell, Charles Carrington was in the battalion which was part of 143rd Bde. (48th Div.) Hidden batteries were in every copse or farm. The 1/4th R. Berks. of the 145 Bde. in the same Division reported that their billets in the village itself, were in fact 'filthy billets'. They may have been recently vacated by the French who were not always known for their camp cleanliness! The village was full of dumps and camps. On the bare slopes east of Sailly towards Hébuterne and Gommecourt the guns were ranged tier upon tier. In mid June Graham Greenwell's Battalion the 1/4th O & B who were also part of the 48th Div., were camped in the Dell and the 11th Durhams remarked on their camp at the end of July as being the 'filthiest that they had ever seen'. They were Pioneer Battalion to the 20th Div. The London Scottish of the 56th Div. returned to Sailly from Hébuterne on 1st July.

After the battle for Gommecourt the 1/5 Cheshires who were Pioneer Battalion to the 56th Div. were involved in building a new HQ for the 168th Bde. in dugouts at Sailly. Elephant trenches were sunk deep into the ground and covered with earth, trees and bricks.

In mid August the 7th Somerset LI (61st Bde. 20th Div.) were bivouacked in the Dell and in mid October an E. Yorks Battalion was in the village. A few days later the 18th DLI (93rd Bde. 31st Div.) took over support trenches in the 'shattered' village.

The road led westwards from Sailly and ran up the Authuie Valley through Authuie and Coigneux and was fairly sheltered from the enemy shelling, but being situated in the bottom of a valley it was almost impossible to keep in a good state of repair, during the winter. The road between Courcelles and Sailly was very often under enemy fire especially about 500 yards of it south of Sailly, where, before turning up the long road to Hébuterne, 'men often said their prayers'. It was an area where enemy balloons were often seen.

In mid November and in connection with the Ancre battles the 18th DLI and the 18th W. Yorks both of the 93rd Bde. 31st Div. were billeted in huts and sandbag shelters in the Dell.

The Military Cemetery is at the west end of the village on the south side of the road to Coigneux. It was begun in May 1916 and according to the Cemetery Register was opposite the Town Major's Dugout. The Cemetery was used by Field Ambulances until March 1917, and again from April to August in 1918. Many of the graves are of men from the W. Yorks Battalions from the period October/November 1916.

Sailly-le-Sec

Sailly-le-Sec is a village and commune in the Department of the Somme, on the north bank of the Somme river. It is on the D 42 road between the villages of Vaux-sur-Somme and Sailly–Laurette and due south of Treux. The name of the village is given to a cemetery which is as far as a mile away from it, and is called Dive Copse British Cemetery and is just south of the Bray–Corbie Road. In June 1916 before the battle began, the ground to the north of the cemetery was chosen for a concentration of Field Ambulances, which in turn became the XIV Corps MDS. A small wood close by, just south of the main Bray–Corbie Road, was known as Dive Copse after the officer commanding the MDS. The cemetery was made by these Medical Units.

Sailly–Saillisel

Sailly–Saillisel is a village on the D 944 road between Rancourt and le Transloy, east of Morval and north-east of Combles. St. Pierre Vaast Wood is to the south-east. The village was 'shaved' to the ground according to H. A. Taylor in *Goodbye to the Battlefields.* It is in the Department of the Somme and there are two continuous villages of which the western one is called Sailly–Saillisel and the eastern Saillisel. The British Cemetery is south of the former village, on the west side of the road to Rancourt. The Cemetery Register says that the village standing at the north end of the ridge was the object of French attacks in September and October 1916, and was captured on the 18th/19th October by them. The HQ of the 1st Somerset LI (11th Bde. 4th Div.) during the battle for the Transloy Ridges was in an old German mine shaft. The British Cemetery was made after the Armistice, by the concentration of graves from small graveyards and isolated positions chiefly south and east of the two villages. There were four cemeteries originally and all were involved in battles after the first Battle of the Somme. The dates of death are amost exclusively from the period September 1916 to March 1917, and August and September 1918. The British Cemetery stands in cultivated fields, with wide views to the west and south.

St. Amand

St. Amand is a village in the southern part of the Department of the Pas de Calais, and is a little to the north of Souastre and north-east of Hénu. It is west of Foncquevillers and the Gommecourt battle lines. It is also ten miles east of Doullens and four and a half miles from Saulty-L'Arbret Station on the line from Doullens to Arras. It was a village which was mainly associated with the 56th Div. and the period both before the battle and during its beginning. In early May 1916 the London Scottish of the 56th Div. were in reserve in the village and on the 20th they left for Halloy. On the 13th June they were relieved by a Fusilier Battalion and then returned to St. Amand. On the 14th June they left the village for Pas.

The Queen's Westminsters of the 56th Div. had previously been at Halloy, and on the 27th June they moved to St. Amand, prior to taking up positions in the assembly trenches opposite the Gommecourt Salient. Aubrey Smith of the London Rifle Bde. 56th Div. in his book wrote that they were at Halloy until 27th June, when the companies went into huts at Souastre, in the neighbourhood of a twelve inch gun, and the transport, of which Smith was a member, made for St. Amand. There was a narrow valley there which might be called a gully, which was about a mile long, in the neighbourhood of St. Amand where every Division took up its quarters. The bottom of this valley may have been twenty to thirty yards across, and this space was available for horses. On either side were big slopes rising to normal ground level, the easy one being somewhat steep and perhaps a hundred feet high. They put tarpaulin tents near the horses at the bottom of the valley towards the end of June. Smith was still involved in taking up stores by limber to Hébuterne which at this stage of the battle preparation had become a vast dump. At the end of June there were a number of heavy guns here including a battery of 9.2 inch howitzers and there was also one very large gun either a 12 or 15 inch one. On his way to and from Hébuterne Smith had seen vast gunpits, earthworks and ramifications which stretched from north to south. The Transport had contributed a lot to make the battle a success having taken up tons of RE stores, ammunition and reserve rations etc. to the line in the previous few weeks. If all went well the transporting would be continued on the night of 1st/2nd July by taking water, rations and ammunition over the captured German territory. However it was not to be and the first stragglers on the 1st July got back to their lines at about 10 a.m. 'A failure, back again where we started' – Smith wrote in his book that the British had been advertising their intention to attack too much, how obvious had been the digging of jumping off trenches and out beyond the front line and the maze of earthworks on the Hébuterne Plain. That afternoon more survivors of the defeated battalion came down to St. Amand, with the grim look on their faces, of men who had been through a furnace.

The 1/4 Lincolns (148th Bde. 46th Div.) had at one time dug cable trenches and dugouts to serve as Battle HQ at St. Amand.

The British Cemetery is on the northern edge of the village and was begun in April 1916, and used by fighting units and Field Ambulances until August 1918, particularly by the 37th and 56th Divs.

St. Pierre Divion

St. Pierre Divion is north-west of Thiepval between the villages of Grandcourt and Authuille on the D 163 road. On the 1st July it was one of the objectives of the 36th Div. but the Allied troops do not seem to have reached it that day, let alone captured it, and German troops from here were sent to repel the British attack to the south-east at the Schwaben Redoubt. In *Haig's Great Push* it says that by the nature of its fortifications and its situation, it was an important position in itself, and between it and the Allied line lay a maze of new and old trenches. But the chief feature was the subterranean defences which lay on the south side of the Ancre and was the site of an underground labyrinth known as the 'Tunnel' by the Intelligence Officers. There was a perpendicular bank of clay about twenty feet high which showed towards the water-meadows side. German trenches were on the lip of the bank, and under them a vast refuge. The labyrinth was connected by a broad flight of stairs to the ground above and was proof against even the largest shell. The underground shelter had its entrances in the hills of St. Pierre Divion stretching back to Thiepval. Apart from these considerably strong defences the marshy ground of the Ancre Valley also made capture difficult. The enemy also had excellent observation from the Thiepval heights over ground which attackers would have to cross. The 16th Rif. Brig. (117th Bde. 39th Div.) north-west of the village on 3rd September were involved in an unsuccessful attack. After the fall of Thiepval in September it became possible to take the village of St. Pierre Divion from the rear. The 16th Rif. Brig. also were near the River Ancre south of St. Pierre from the 21st to the 23rd October. They took part in another unsuccessful attack on 21st October.

The 39th Division took the village on the 13th November and the Black Watch of the 118th Bde. captured many prisoners in the numerous tunnels. Five men from one tank were recommended for the MM for deeds carried out in the battle. Their tank had been the only one to start and they reached the second support line of the enemy and were able to maintain their position without assistance from the infantry. The latter had got lost in the mist. The officer in charge was killed and his place was taken by Corporal Taffs who drove on for 200 yards and reached a German dugout. The tank then became bogged down and its crew tried for two hours to extricate it until it was finally abandoned, and they then joined the Black Watch in the fighting. An ADS or CP was here in November.

The village was lost to the Germans in March 1918 and was regained by the British in August 1918.

Saulty

Saulty is a small village north-west of Humbercamps just north of the Doullens–Arras road. At the beginning of the battle the HQ of the 139th Bde. 46th Div. was at the chateau, and after their involvement in the Gommecourt fighting the 5th and 6th Sherwood For. returned to the village via Warlincourt. Their cadre had been at la Bazeque Farm.

Schwaben Redoubt

The German position called the Schwaben Redoubt was on the top of a hill that looked down over the village of Thiepval, which was in German hands, and further westwards Thiepval Wood which was in Allied hands and the Ancre Valley where the two sides crossed the river and the marshy area around it. It had a 'face' that stretched about five to six hundred yards and it was about 200 yards in depth. The Redoubt was virtually a parallelogram of trenches. To the north and west the ground fell away steeply and to the east it overlooked German battery positions. On the 1st July the Redoubt was one of the objectives of the 36th (Ulster) Division and three brigades of this Division were all involved in the attack. There were four battalions who at least reached the Redoubt or got a foothold in it. (They had advanced from Thiepval Wood across the Thiepval Road and up hill to the summit). Five hundred prisoners were taken and then the attackers began to advance on the second position, the Grandcourt line. In their enthusiasm they were in front of the Allied barrage which prevented them from taking the line. Also, as the day went on, and despite their progress they found themselves without support from the Allied positions all of which gave the enemy time to recoup and to push the Ulstermen out of the Redoubt. According to *The War in the Air* the position at 4.30 p.m. as reported by No. 4 Squadron was that nowhere was there a massing of troops on this part of the front but that the hold on the Schwaben Redoubt looked insecure.

An hour later an observer reported that the British were still in possession of the Redoubt and the point known as the Crucifix which was to the south-east. The Crucifix was at the point where the roads from Authuille and Thiepval meet at a fork. Having failed to hold the Redoubt on the 1st July the Allies found themselves unable to make any more serious attempts on it until several weeks later and then not until Thiepval had fallen. It was to this village that the Redoubt gave great protection. The enemy was ideally placed to fend off attacks and the position could be enfiladed by machine gun cross fire from Beaucourt Redoubt with St. Pierre Divion and on the south Nord Werk a machine gun stronghold on the Ovillers Spur.

The Pope's Nose was a strong point close to the Redoubt and in early September deadly German cross fire could be brought to bear on the British advance unless it was well protected by Artillery. An attack of the W. Yorks was broken up in this way. But during the battle the 11th Lancs Fus. (74th Bde. 25th Div.) established a block close to the nose.

The battle of Thiepval Ridge lasted for four days between 26th September and the 30th and the Redoubt was half taken during this period. The 18th Division took Thiepval.

T/Sec. Lt. Tom Edwin Adlam was to gain the VC for conspicuous gallantry on the 27th/28th September. In a portion of Thiepval Village which had defied attempts of capture, Adlam of the 7th Bedfords (54th Bde. 19th Div.), realising that the moment was a critical one and with companies held up by menacing rifle and machine gun fire, rushed forward from shell hole to shell hole and collected men and enemy grenades for a sudden rush against the enemy. At this stage he was wounded in the leg but his experience before the war as a schoolmaster stood him in good stead as he had learnt to throw a cricket ball very long distances which is the skill he applied to throwing grenades. The Germans were subjected to a whirlwind attack and he was able to lead his platoon forward and either capture or kill any German who was in their way. He had reached his objective by 8.30 a.m. and went on to gain a further 300 yards. He continued to lead his men all day and was wounded a second time. He had materially assisted in the capture of Schwaben Redoubt (see the Thiepval entry).

Using the history of the 18th Division, the Thiepval position was without doubt one of the main pivots of the whole of the north section of the German defence on the Western Front, and included with it was the Schwaben Redoubt which lay on a ridge about a thousand yards to the north and rear of Thiepval. Four tanks were allotted to the Division, one of which was to do yeoman service in the attack on Thiepval Chateau. The position on the 27th September, as far as the 18th Division was concerned was that the 53rd and 54th Bdes. were lying in a continuous line running north of Thiepval and along Zollern Trench to the point where the 53rd Bde. was in touch with the 11th Div. on the right. In the 53rd Bde. the 8th Norfolks and 10th Essex were very exhausted but the 8th Suffolks and 6th R. Berks were still strong and available for an attack. The 55th Bde. was in support. Zero hour was fixed for 1 p.m. on the 28th September, and there was difficulty in forming up in daylight.

The 8th Suffolks and the 7th Queen's 55th Bde. were assaulting battalions and the 10th Essex were detailed to garrison Zollern Trench. The 8th Norfolks were to provide 'mopping up' companies to attend the assaulting battalions. The 6th R. Berks. who almost entirely were men who had recently joined, were in reserve in Authuille Wood. After very hard fighting a footing was gained in the Redoubt. By the 5th October only a small strip of the Redoubt along the north-west corner was still in enemy hands, and it was not until the 14th October that the 39th Division finally cleared the Germans completely out of the Redoubt.

Edmund Blunden who was with the 11th R. Sussex (116th Bde. 39th Div.) wrote in his book the *Undertones of War* that 'it was now approaching the beginning of November, and the days were melancholy and the colour of clay. We took over that deathtrap known as the Schwaben Redoubt, the way to which lay through the fallen fortress of Thiepval. One had heard the worst accounts of the place and they were true. Crossing the Ancre again, one went up through the scanty skeleton houses of Authuille, and climbing the dirty little road over the steep bank, one immediately entered the land of despair'. At the Schwaben there was always some shelling but on the 31st October they were systematically bombarded and the next day when relieved the tour had cost 32 casualties. The relief was expensive particularly to the Cheshires who the Germans saw coming!

Blunden was back there on the 11th November and his battalion was to take a subsidiary part in the final battle of Grandcourt and Beaumont Hamel. Shortly after the Redoubt was taken the *Illustrated London News* featured a two page panoramic spread of the capture of the Redoubt by an artist called S. Begg. On the 13th November when Blunden was at the Redoubt with the 11th R. Sussex amidst a few deep dugouts and a maze of choked and crushed trenches, the other units of his Division, the 39th, passed through the Sussex positions and over-ran, or over-waded the German fort beyond. Their task should have been to carry and dump wire for the Division in front of its extreme advance, but there was so much shelling that they were allowed off and only had to take the materials as far as the old front line.

The writer Henry Williamson wrote a book about a return visit to the battlefields called *The Wet Flanders Plain* (in 1925). He wrote that one could see still many of the former trenches in the hillside near the Redoubt. On the high ground above Thiepval Wood, where thousands of men perished on the 1st July, stood the Ulster Memorial Tower. The trenches where, for a few hours that hot summer afternoon, the men of the Ulster Division rested and watched eastwards, until the enfilade from the north drove them back to their old trenches like mole-runs, half hidden by the long wild grasses of the years. These former trenches with names such as Wretched Way, Lucky Way, Tea Trench, Coffee Trench and Rum Trench were now half hidden seams in the hillside and filled Williamson with an indescribable emotion − the haunting of ancient sunlight.

It would be very interesting to know just how much of the Redoubt is still intact under the hillside, possibly all of it has by now subsided. One can see though the odd entrance or two, but they are in the fields which are under cultivation.

The Cemeteries in this area are mentioned in the section on Thiepval village itself.

Mill Road Cemetery shows the most obvious post-war association with the Redoubt in that the gravestones have had to be laid flat to avoid subsidence.

Scotts Redoubt

Scotts Redoubt was a strong point to the east of the village of la Boisselle, north-east of Bécourt and south-west of Peake Woods and the village of Contalmaison. It was reached by a trench that ran westwards from the Round Wood and was one of several redoubts in the German first line, made up from a cluster of trenches that contained many shelters grouped around one 'palatial' dugout. To the west between it and the village of la Boisselle were Sausage Redoubt and Heligoland, two more strong points in the German line. On the 1st July Scotts Redoubt was part of the 34th Divisional objectives, and in this area they included Peake Woods and the village of Contalmaison both to the north-east. In fact the Division was to have a disastrous day on the 1st July as they progressed for only about a third of the way towards their objectives. Parties of men had in fact reached as far as Contalmaison but had to withdraw. The attacking battalions advanced from the direction of Bécourt and in the area of Scotts Redoubt; they were the 101st Bde. which included the 15th and 16th Royal Scots and the 24th and 27th North'd. Fus. 103rd (Tyneside Irish) Brigade. In the history of the Royal Scots it says that 'C' Company of the 15th Batt. plodded on and crossed Scotts Redoubt and reached as far as Peake Trench. At Wood Alley the strip of trench adjoining Scotts Redoubt, they met up with a company of the 16th Battalion. Wood Alley had to be retained as security for the 21st Div. who were on the right flank of the 34th Division. It was still held that night but the enemy had regained his hold on his front trench with his strong point the Heligoland. This in turn meant that Wood Alley was cut off from the British front line. The situation according to the history of the Royal Scots was precarious but the enemy didn't press home a counter-attack.

The 24th and 27th North'd. Fus. had gone past to the north of the Redoubt but had then had to withdraw. On the 2nd July the 15th R. Scots attacked and carried the Redoubt along with 50 prisoners. The 16th R. Scots attacked Horseshoe Trench, a long trench which ran down from the direction of Ovillers la Boisselle. They managed to take 150 yards of it. Later communication was established between Scotts Redoubt and the old Allied front line which facilitated the supplies of reinforcements and equipment. On the 3rd July having held their positions at great cost in casualties the R. Scots were relieved by troops of the 33rd Div. and marched back to Scotts Redoubt.

Giles Eyre in his book *Somme Harvest* wrote that in mid July after a few instructions they (the 2nd KRRC 2nd Bde. 1st Div.) went off to meet up with the 1st L.N. Lancs. of the same Brigade, who were lying in Scotts Redoubt. They scrambled down a deep, sandbagged trench and arrived at the HQ of the L.N. Lancs. and settled down in its dugouts. He wrote that the Redoubt trenches were deep and well sandbagged and had stood the past fortnight of fighting pretty well. The 2nd KRRC were in support and liable to go forward at short notice.

After the battles of the first half of July there is little mention of Scotts Redoubt although it is known that the RAMC made full use of the deep dugouts there as accommodation for stretcher bearers.

In the period 4/5th September the 7/8th KOSB who had been in the front line were relieved and withdrawn to Divisional Reserve at Scotts Redoubt in the old German line. On 9th October they went forward to the Redoubt and occupied dugouts there, training and working on roads until in mid October they relieved the 6/7th R. Scots Fus.(45th Bde.) in recently captured trenches west of the north-west of le Sars.

At sometime during the Autumn of 1916 the Redoubt had become a camp and there is mention of the place as being used in early September and towards the end of November, the 5th Glosters and the 1/4th O & BLI (145th Bde. 48th Div.) were both camped there, the latter in Nissen huts.

Senlis

The village of Senlis is to the south-west of the D 938 road, south of Hedauville, north of Hénecourt, west of Bouzincourt and north-east of Warloy Baillon. It was behind the lines, and towards the end of June gave shelter to members of the 49th Div. who on the 1st July were to be in support of the 36th (Ulster) Division, whose objective was the ground between the north-west of Thiepval and the village of St. Pierre Divion above the River Ancre. On the 29th June men of the 1/4th DWR visited the OP at Senlis Mill where they had a very good view of the Allied bombardment. The 15th HLI

(14th Bde. 32nd Div.) were in billets in the village on the 29th June. The 32nd Div. were on the right flank of the 36th Div. on the 1st July, and the 32nd Divisional Wagon Lines were close to the village.

On the 9th July the HQ of the 36th Bde. 12th Div. moved to the village and on the afternoon of 10th August the Brigade was formed up on each side of the road just to the north of Senlis and about a mile to the west of Bouzincourt. They were then inspected by HM King George Vth, the Prince of Wales, General Sir Hubert Gough of the Fifth Army, Lt. Gen. C. Jacob of the 11 Corps and Maj. Gen. A. B. Scott the commanding officer of the 12th Div. itself. The King who had travelled from Warloy Baillon walked down the road between the troops with his party of high ranking officers.

The 7th R. Sussex (36th Bde. 12th Div.) had been in the village in early August before going east to Bouzincourt for two days. Their Division was involved in the battle for Pozieres Ridge at this time. The 1/4th O & BLI (145th Bde. 48th Div.) were in huts in the orchards to the west of Bouzincourt with trenches at Senlis. Not only was the village a camp for infantry battalions but it also housed the Wagon Lines for the Field Artillery. Edmund Blunden of the 11th R. Sussex (116th Bde. 39th Div.) remarks in his book that after their experiences at the Schwaben Redoubt that they rested at Authuille Bluffs before going further back to Senlis. Two days later, and this was in early November, they were back in Thiepval Wood but they soon returned to the barns and estaminets of Senlis. On the 7th November they were carrying our fatigues in the Aveluy Region. It was wintry . . .

A battalion of the KRRC Regiment was in Divisional Reserve in the village from the 29th October to the 2nd November where there was a Divisional Rest Station. There is a Communal Cemetery in the village and Senlis Cemetery has eighty graves in it that date from the period from April to August 1918. There are twenty Australian graves there.

Serre

The village of Serre is on the D 919 road and is between Hébuterne to the north and Beaumont Hamel to the south. It is also south-west of Puisieux and north-east of Mailly–Maillet.

In the summer of 1916 the lines of the two Armies bent south-eastwards from the direction of Hébuterne and Gommecourt, and then began to go in a south-westerly direction in front of Serre and Beaumont Hamel. Serre, Gommecourt to the north-west and Beaumont Hamel to the south were German 'fortress' villages and all three were to hold up the Allied advance on the first day of the battle, and subsequently.

The position mainly in the area of VIII Corps and to the right the 4th Div. was to advance towards the section of Munich Trench which was due south of Serre village itself. The 31st Div. who we will be mostly concerned with, had the position that was opposite Serre itself and the section of Munich Trench immediately to the south. It was planned that they should reach beyond Serre and take in Pendant Copse to the south-east of the village, reaching as far as Pendant Trench and Flank Trench. The focal parts of the Allied line in this area were the four copses which were at the points of assembly on the 1st July and they were from the north – John, Luke, Mark and Matthew.

The trench system here had formerly been in French hands and there were therefore names such as Vercingetorix, du Guesclin and Jean Bart. There is a document written by Sec. Lt. F. P. Roe of the 6th Glosters (114th Bde. 48th Div.) in the Peter Liddle collection at Sunderland Polytechnic which says that at the end of June that he had the job of taking around a group of War Correspondents on a tour of the VIII Corps Trench System and during this time he met up with Gerald Brenan who was an Observer for the Corps Headquarters. Roe also mentioned meeting General Rawlinson and said that he was not as keen as Haig on the prospect of the Somme battle. He also described the 31st Divisional front at this period. His own trenches were at the bottom of a slope and close to them were the 10th and 11th E. Yorks (Hull) Battalions. He was 200 yards west and a little to the north of Matthew Copse. The front line in fact ran roughly along the bottom of a small valley or depression, the ground sloping upwards on the east side towards the German positions and westwards to the British support and reserve trenches. The 31st Div. were to form a defensive flank facing the north-east.

On 1st July the assembly positions were as follows: the 93rd Bde. was to the right of the line and the 94th to the left. The 92nd was to be in reserve all day.

In the 93rd Bde. were the 15th W. Yorks (Leeds Pals) with the 16th W. Yorks (Bradford Pals) immediately behind them. On the right of the Bradford Pals was a company of the 18th DLI (Durham Pals). Behind the Bradford Pals were the 18th W. Yorks (Second Bradford Pals) and behind them the rest of the 18th DLI (Durham Pals).

On the left of the 93rd Bde. the 94th Bde. was as follows: the 11th E. Lancs (Accrington Pals) with the 13th Y & L (1st Barnsley Pals) behind them. On the left of the Accrington Pals were the 12th Y & L (Sheffield Pals) and immediately behind them a half company of the 14th Y & L (2nd Barnsley Pals). Further back beyond the track between la Signy Farm and la Louviere Farm were the rest of the 14th Y & L (Barnsley Pals). It was the 12th Y & L (Sheffield Pals) who were to feature in the novel by John Harris called *Covenant of Death*. As for the 93rd Brigade the 15th W. Yorks (Leeds Pals) began to climb out of their trenches at 7.20 a.m. and to lie down in front of them. They were subsequently annihilated by the German machine guns which had meant to have been dealt with by the British Artillery over the previous few days. The CO of the Battalion, Major R. B. Neill was killed within the first few minutes. The 16th W. Yorks were meant to advance through the line of the 15th Battalion and make their way towards Munich Trench. A great many of this battalion were also killed during the first few minutes of the battle including their CO Maj. C. S. Guyon who was later to be commemorated on the Thiepval Memorial. Part of the problem was that the large number of casualties made the communication trenches very congested and one observer reported that he had never seen a queue like there was on this morning at the RAP. The dead were spread out in thick clumps *behind* their own wire.

The 18th DLI suffered in the same fashion as the Yorkshire Battalions in that their assault was cut down before it had even begun.

On the right flank of the 93rd Bde. (31st Div.) were the 8th R. Warwicks and behind them the 6th R. Warwicks with the 1st King's Own in support. They made some progress and had the German strong point called the Quadrilateral on their right. The latter was very important to the enemy inasmuch as it gave flanking fire along the whole position and bristled with machine guns. The frontage of the Quadrilateral was 400 yards and there was no cover between the German and British trenches. There was however a slight rise in the direction of the German positions. The objective was Pendant Copse to the south-east of Serre village. Brig. Gen. C. B. Prowse of the 11th Bde. was wounded mortally when he was having to move his Bde. HQ forward from the old British line to the German trenches which were taken by the 8th R. Warwicks. He was buried later at Louvencourt Cemetery. The survivors of the Birmingham Battalions were helped by the presence of three large craters which were on the Serre–Mailly road. On the left of the 93rd Bde. the 94th Bde. fared no better. The brigade frontage was about 700 yards from John Copse to the southern part of Matthew Copse. The Sheffield Pals were to the left and the 11th E. Lancs to the right. The Assembly Trenches of the Pals Battalions were between the Copses. The shallow assault trenches had been dug to hold the second, third and fourth waves. Gerald Brenan wrote that he had heard that they were manned in the incorrect order and that this led to confusion when the moment for advancing came. Indeed two of the waves never started at all. In addition a terrible artillery barrage fell on them which churned up the earth all around them. Brenan turned back to his OP which was probably at Observation Wood and in direct line with Serre village. His OP was sprinkled with gas shells. The HQ of the 12th Y & L had to be moved from John Copse to Mark Copse because the former was so full of wounded. The battalions had been told to make for Serre Church steeple but they were cut down by machine gun and shell fire and many of the enemy ignored the British Artillery fire and stood on their parapets firing. The dead and wounded lay in clumps. The CO of the 11th E. Lancs Lt. Col. A. W. Rickman was 'knocked out' by a shell at around 9.40pm and was to die in a tragic accident after the war.

John Harris in his novel *Covenant of Death* has painted a very authentic picture of one of the Pals Battalions from the north of England and his story is based upon the experiences of the Sheffield Pals, although it could probably have been applied to the other New Army Battalions as well. In his novel, the trenches, before the battle began, had been divided into 'up' trenches and 'down' routes for the offensive engineers had erected Divisional signs and bridges had been constructed to be placed across trenches for reserves to pass over, many of them wide enough to carry cavalry. The narrator comments at the beginning of the battle that he thought that he could see Serre just amongst the smoke which was rolling in the hollow in front. Where there had been trees and hedges they were now bare and leafless. Someone said the Y & L had reached Serre village but were then destroyed from behind by

Germans coming up out of deep shelters. All at the end was failure.

According to *The War in the Air* VIII Corps and X Corps met with a similar fate on the 1st July and they were assisted in the air by Nos. 15 and 4 Squadrons. There was an isolated deep penetration into the German defences which air observers alone could report, notably at Pendant Copse where a few of the men of the 18th DLI had succeeded in reaching the Copse.

Gerald Brenan, already referred to, was one of the Corps Observers belonging to VIII Corps Cyclist Battalion and ran an observation post outside Hébuterne. In the period before the battle he wrote in his Autobiography, that every day new batteries would arrive and begin registering, new light railways would spring up, new shell-dumps were laid along the roads, new notice boards made their appearance, while the woods and villages a little way behind filled up with khaki figures. The left of the advance against the hamlet of Serre was opposite his OP and about three quarters of a mile distant from their front trenches, and Brenan's task was to send back reports of how the fighting was going. Corps HQ was at Marieux ten miles behind the line, in a beautiful chateau. Each of the troops carried a triangle on his back that assisted the artillery in their identification, and in the early morning the sun shone on these triangles and made them glitter. But as the hours passed Brenan couldn't see any of them reach the German front line, and later he found out that the bombardment never penetrated the deep dugouts the Germans had excavated in their chalk and their machine gunners had emerged and were mowing down the attackers. The failure of the assault on Serre became obvious, three or four hundred yards of rough ground that lay in front of the Allied lines were thickly sprinkled with silver triangles, only a few of which moved, while the German parapet was bare. And still the pounding of the front line trenches went on. The young men were dead on the Corps front line and not a yard of ground had been gained.

To sum up then; the attempt to take Serre by the British, when the ground sloped upwards to the German trenches which in turn had not been adequately bombarded by the Artillery in the previous few days, was an absolutely disastrous plan; the infantry never had a chance of making any progress in these circumstances. As it was the casualties of five of the front line battalions went well over five hundred each which meant a total number of casualties with these five battalions alone as being over 2,500. The Battalions were the 12th Y & L, the 11th E. Lancs, the 15th W. Yorks, the 16th W. Yorks and the 8th R. Warwicks on the flank of the 31st Div.

Three men who had previously published poetry became casualties on the 1st July in the Serre fighting. Alexander Robertson, born in 1882, a Cpl. with the 12th Y & L, was hit and lost in no man's land coming from the Copses towards Serre. His name is on the Thiepval Memorial. He had been a Lecturer at Sheffield University and published *Comrades: Last Poems* (Erskine Macdonald). Henry Lionel Field a Lt. with the R. Warwicks was also killed on 1st July, by shellfire near the Quadrilateral. (No grave location.) He had published *Poems and Drawings* (Cornish Bros.). He was an Art Student. John William Streets a Sergeant with the 13th Y & L wounded and missing on the 1st July, had published *The Undying Splendour* (Erskine Macdonald). He was a Derbyshire miner. (94th Bde. 31st Div.)

The plan to take Serre later in the year was fixed for the 25th October and was then postponed. Some tunnels which had been bored for the July attempt to take Serre were to be reopened for the next attempt. The two in the area of the 76th Bde. were named Mark and John after two of the four copses. They were dug to within a hundred yards of no man's land and were large enough to take guns and gun teams.

The 3rd Division was chosen for the attack which was finally to take place on 13th November and the two Brigades from right to left in the front line were the 8th and 76th. On the right flank were the 6th and 5th Bdes. of the 2nd Div. and on the left flank were the 92nd and 93rd Bdes. of the 31st Div. The conditions were very bad in that the ground was very muddy and heavy and the weather was cold and likely to be misty. The 8th Bde. had the 2nd R. Scots and 1st R. Scots Fus. in front with instructions to advance as far as Serre, the second objective. The 8th E. Yorks and the 7th KSLI were in the second line. Parties of the 8th Bde. reached the German support line but no further.

It was the 76th Bde. on the left of the 8th Bde. which really bore the brunt of the attack and we are lucky to have a first hand account by Lt. Duffield of the 2nd Suffolks, which is kept at the Regimental Museum at Bury St. Edmunds. He was in charge of machine guns with the battalion and on the 12th November his party had to 'plod' nine miles to the line and to use Mark and John Tunnels which were to be opened up for his gun teams at about 1 a.m. on the 13th, the day of the attack. The machine gun team was accompanied by small bombing parties. HQ had moved up to Rob Roy Trench and occupied dugout No. 213. The attacking infantry formed up in what was virtually a series of swamps and soupy mudholes. By 2 a.m. they had been issued with a rum ration which made some of the men intoxicated and some walked about on top smoking! It should be remembered that the enemy were only 200 yards away. Duffield went up with his team to Mark Tunnel and four British shells from the direction of Hébuterne dropped short amongst his party. Luke Copse to the left of Mark Copse, was virtually a huge crater and used as a large magazine dump. Duffield was to join the team going out of the left hand of John Tunnel at zero hour which was to be 5.45 a.m. He then settled down for a short rest in dugout 214. At 5.40 a.m. he entered the tunnel with his men and with great caution went down 80 yards of it, taking great care not to alert the enemy. All of a sudden there was a terrific rumble and roar. The orders had been changed and the tunnel opened at 5.40 a.m., consequently his men could only go out with the infantry. Through a gaping hole they could see a dense mist, smoke from a thousand shells and all manner of coloured lights. Duffield saw a ladder which his party used to climb up and they discovered waterlogged holes everywhere. The Suffolks were meant to take the enemy's first line and when this was done Duffield was to go in and establish dumps of ammunition for his guns. However the attack miscarried and by 6.15 a.m. most of the battalion had been withdrawn. He saw many casualties some of whom were floundering in an absolute sea of mud and water. Duffield remained with a small party of eight or nine, as to return immediately would be too dangerous and besides the CO would need all the information that he could get. For lunch the small party had two mess sandwiches between them and a small round of whisky from Duffield's flask. They then spent their time reading the *Continental Daily Mail* which the sandwiches had been wrapped in. After 2 p.m. the German artillery began to 'search' no man's land in every direction with high explosives and trench mortars. Duffield himself was hit several times and at 4.45 p.m. his party began to return in twos and threes through the mud and water to the front line which was about 150 yards. He discovered that HQ had gone to Monk Trench which he found after he had had his wounds dressed. By early evening the casualties of the battalion were 273 including 11 officers, and Duffield himself was one of three officers left who wasn't seriously hurt.

The Battle of Serre on the 13th November according to the Suffolk Regimental history was ruefully remembered by those who took part in it as the least successful and most dispiriting engagement of the 2nd Batt. in France. In fact the whole period in the Serre sector was one of unhappy memory. After the war H. A. Taylor in his book *Goodbye to the Battlefields* described the attack of the 2nd Suffolks in a sea of mud, as a futile attempt. The Somme battle had gone better further south where the 63rd Naval Division had reached Beaucourt, and the 51st Div., Beaumont Hamel. On the 14th November a small bunch of the 1st Gordon H. (76th Bde. 3rd Div.) came back to the lines of the 2nd Suffolks and told them how when they were lying exhausted close to the German lines, that a German doctor had tended to their wounds and thus enabled them to return to safety in the early morning. The *War Diary* of the 2nd Suffolks gave the following reasons for the lack of progress on the 13th; mist, early officer casualties, muddy conditions, concertina wire, rifles caked with mud, invisibility of the barrage and the strength of the enemy in their second line as well as machine gun fire. Duffield himself together with another officer and the Adjutant tried to sort out the remains of the battalion and in Rolland Trench he found members of his former gun team. He himself returned to Colincamps for medical attention. On the 15th November he was caught by a German gas attack that seriously affected his eyes, which continued to water badly. On his way back to the front line he mentions Euston Dump as being a huge dump where RE material was kept. He also mentions la Signy Farm which was in ruins, and a few hundred yards back from the front line. He visited Legend Trench where the 13th King's (9th Bde.) were in occupation. Eight or nine snipers who had made themselves comfortable under an elephant shelter had been recently killed by a 5.9 in. shell. Duffield returned with messages to the second in command and to the transport lines at Bus. His next duty was to prepare billets at Vauchelles for the battalion who were to return from the line in lorries from Colincamps. Around the 23rd November a new draft had joined the 2nd Suffolks and lorries took them to Courcelles and then they had a six mile march to Euston Dump where they collected loads of wire and stakes to the area of Rolland and Nairn Trenches. They used the light railway over the top past la Signy Farm, which was behind Serre and housed troops in its cellars. The going was awful and they used trenches where they were up to their knees in water. On the 26th November there was a working party which necessitated wire etc. being taken to Waterloo Bridge which was close to the Euston Batteries. On the 27th November they moved to Courcelles Chateau. He mentions at this time a huge crater at Staff Copse which had previously been a dump. It had blown up with thousands of trench mortar 'puddings' and Mills bombs all going off together. They rode back on trolleys to Euston Dump on the 2nd December and as his eyes were no better he reported sick and went into hospital at Louvencourt.

It is not surprising that in this area where there had been two disastrous attempts to capture the village of Serre there should be several cemeteries which are very close together. Serre Road Cemetery No. 1 is about 1,000 yards west of the village and on the north side of the road. It is in two departments and in three communes, being divided equally between Puisieux and Hébuterne in the Pas de Calais and Beaumont Hamel in the Somme. The cemetery was made by V Corps in 1917 and after the Armistice was greatly enlarged by the concentration of 2,054 graves, which for the most part were from the 1916 Ancre and Somme battlefield. The land above the cemetery is part of the former no man's land ground over which the Leeds and Bradford Pals attacked in July 1916. Above the ridge are the sites of the three contested features that were named after the four evangelists. The cart track leading up the slope opposite the cemetery was used in the actual battle. The cemetery has over 3,300 graves in it. A hundred yards to the west of it is the Hébuterne–Serre French National Cemetery. One of the original burial grounds from which British graves were concentrated was Tree Alley Cemetery No. 1, 700 yards south-east of Serre, which contains the graves of 67 British soldiers who fell on 18th November 1916. The present Ten Tree Alley Cemetery was No. 2.

Serre Road Cemetery No. 2 was designed by Edwin Lutyens and is on the south side of the road, about a mile from Serre village. About two-thirds of it is in the Beaumont Hamel district. It is on the site of the former German Quadrilateral Redoubt. There are 7,067 graves there which makes it the largest of this group of cemeteries. Serre road led from Mailley–Maillet and entered no man's land about 1,400 yards south-west of Serre. The 31st and 4th Divs. had attacked north and south of this road on 1st July. Outside the cemetery is a memorial to Lt. V. A. Braithwaite, M.C. (1st Som. L.I.) who was killed on 2nd July 1916 and is commemorated on the Thiepval Memorial. He was a friend of Compton MacKenzie; they had met in the Turkish Peninsula. Serre Road No. 3 Cemetery is in the fields about 300 yards to the north-east of Serre Road No. 1. A new road now leads to it and originally it was made by V Corps in the spring of 1917. It contains the graves of 81 soldiers from the United Kingdom mainly from the 31st Div. who fell in July and November 1916. It commands extensive views on all sides except for the east. It is in Puisieux.

Railway Hollow Cemetery is on the site of the British Support Line of July 1916 and is 1,300 yards west of Serre and 200 yards west of Mark Copse. It too was made by V Corps in 1917. It contains the graves of 107 soldiers of the 3rd, 19th and 31st Divs. who fell on 1st July or 13th November, men from the Y & L Regiments. It stands in a low lying field, through which formerly a military light railway ran. Adjacent to the cemetery is Sheffield Park, a memorial park, and a portion of the old front line trench can still be traced near the edge of the park by the gate. The Accrington Pals (11th E. Lancs.) attacked from this trench, and there is a separate commemorative plaque dedicated to them which has recently been placed there on a beech tree. A short walk across the field facing the old lines had been no man's land will bring one to the site of the old German front line and one can see the roof of a former concrete machine gun post. Private A. Bull, one of the Sheffield Pals, is commemorated near the entrance to the park where he fell; he was re-buried in Serre Road Cemetery No. 2.

Luke Copse Cemetery is also on the site of the former British front line of July 1916. It was made in February 1917 when the Ancre Battlefields were cleared. The graves belong to members of the 31st and 3rd Divs. who attacked the German line on the 1st July and the 13th November. It is a small cemetery with 72 graves and a Memorial to the 2nd Suffolks.

Queen's Cemetery is also on the line of the old British front line and is south of Mark Copse. It was made by Vth Corps as 'The Queen's' in 1917 and contains the graves of 312 soldiers who were members of the 31st, 3rd and 19th Divs. who fell in July and November 1916 and also in February 1917.

Ten Tree Alley Cemetery is 1,200 yards south of Serre and was made by V Corps as Ten Tree Alley Cemetery No. 2, in 1917. It stood beside a former German trench, captured by the 32nd Div. on the night of 10th/11th February 1917. It contains the graves of 67 soldiers from the United Kingdom who fell on the 18th November 1916 and the 10th/18th February 1917.

Serre was never in fact taken, and in the end the Germans evacuated it on the 24th February 1917, and the 22nd Manchesters entered the village on the following morning.

I would like to end this short history of Serre in 1916/1917 by drawing once again on the novelist John Harris. In his novel *Covenant With Death* he wrote that 'we never did get Serre, and by Christmas the mud was so deep we couldn't have advanced if we'd wanted to' – 'I never fancied going back', one of his characters says 'in spite of the Tours of the Battlefields that they organised in the twenties. I felt I'd left a bit of me behind, there in front of Serre. Everything that seemed to belong to my youth was there'. However he finally did return and drove up the Serre Road and found the Sheffield City Battalion Memorial. 'You can see from the position of the little cemeteries the route we took . . . Down in that little hollow just behind the crest where the machine guns caught us, I found a small cemetery and saw all their names again – Seven hundred and seventeen we lost in those three or four hours between seven thirty and midday when the field finally emptied of human life, and of these most vanished from the earth in the first ten minutes of the battle – Two years in the making. Ten minutes in the destroying. That was our history.'

Shell Valley

Shell Valley was another name for Death Valley to the south of Mametz Wood. After being involved in the fighting for Bazentin Ridge on 15th July the 1/4th Suffolk Battalion (9th Bde. 33rd Div.) went on relief in Shell Valley and dug itself in road trenches for the night. After a day they returned to front line duty, and four days later on the 20th July, they were relieved and returned once again to Shell Valley, but they were shortly afterwards moved up to a position near the cemetery in support of the 19th Bde. also of the 33rd Div. in an attack on High Wood.

Shelter Wood

Shelter Wood is north-west of Fricourt Wood on the west side of the road to Contalmaison. It is mostly associated with the fighting in early July in the Fricourt area. But it was also used later on in the battle, and contained Brigade HQs and was a very congested camp during September.

Snag Trench

In mid October Snag Trench was the scene of fighting in between Eaucourt l'Abbaye and the Butte de Warlencourt to the north-west of it. The trench was a front line one that zigzagged in an irregular line between Martinpuich–Warlencourt–Eaucourt-le Barque Roads.

The fighting here was part of the battle for the Transloy Ridges which lasted from the 7th to the 20th October. In mid October the 9th Division with the 26th Bde. which was a Highland one, on the right and the South African Brigade on the left, attacked. The 68th Bde. (23rd Div.) was in reserve. The Highlanders reached their objective but the South Africans were held up at a place called The Pimple. They were therefore unable to reach their objective, Snag Trench. One of their Companies according to the history of the 9th Division went 'into the blue' and was neither seen or heard of again. Brig. Gen. Croft was under the impression that the 9th Div. was the third division to try to take The Pimple, and the credit for its final capture must according to Croft go to the Borderers, although the South Africans had done most of the spade work. The Pimple absolutely commanded The Snag, so, once the Borderers captured this natural fort, they simply shot the Germans out of it. They were assisted by a heavy concentration of artillery fire, the results of which became evident once The Snag was taken. The 11th Royal Scots (27th Bde. 9th Div.) took the position by a brilliant night attack, and at dawn the next morning there were 300 dead Germans at the junction of Snag Trench and the communication trench, which ran back from it at right angles. They then pushed on to higher ground and were confronted by the Butte de Warlencourt.

At the end of October and in early November Snag Trench was in two feet of mud and was without duckboards.

Souastre

Souastre is a village on the D 6 road between Foncquevillers to the east and Hénu to the west. It is south of St. Amand and to the north of Bayencourt, Coigneux and Couin. In 1916 it was behind the Allied lines by three or four miles and was virtually due west of the northern part of the Somme battlefield. Indeed the hill at Souastre overlooked Gommecourt. The village like several others in the area was to become most associated with the 56th Div. mainly in the build up to the battle and on the first day of the battle when they were involved in the attempt to capture the German stronghold of Gommecourt.

At the end of May a battalion of the City of Londons were in huts in the village and at this time they supplied working parties for roads, light railways, dumps and burying cables. On the 1st of June the London Scottish (68th Bde. 56th Div.) moved from Halloy ten miles to Souastre where they stayed in huts made of corrugated iron and canvas. On the next day they left for the trenches at Hébuterne. In mid June the 'Bow Bells' who were a concert party attached to the 56th Division (which was predominantly a London Division) entertained troops in an old barn in the village. Also in June two large guns were installed in the village which were 15 inch howitzers. Aubrey Smith who was with the transport section of the London Rifle Brigade (169th Bde. 56th Div.) in his Memoirs says that his transport section had made their quarters at Souastre. He also said that the road to Foncquevillers, where they dumped the rations, couldn't be used in day time, and so there was a congestion of traffic after dusk.

Artillery convoys were very numerous as every gun needed reserve supplies of ammunition. And large quantities of stores of all kinds had to be taken up behind the trenches by infantry transports, REs and motor lorries. Smith wrote that tracks seemed to branch both to the right and the left, to one battery or another. The absence of woods meant that the guns were in gun pits in open fields. In addition the heavy guns were hauled up by tractors and in the process frequently held up all the horse traffic till they branched off either to the right or left.

When in Hébuterne frequent burst of gun fire could be heard in the Gommecourt region and there were many casualties amongst the 56th Divisional working parties.

At the end of June the assembly point of the 1/4 Lincolns (138th Bde. 46th Div.) was to be the Corps Line Trench which ran north and south 500 yards to the east of Souastre, between the Souastre–Bienvillers road and the Souastre–Foncquevillers road. Midland Trench was the assembly line for the 46th Div. on 1st July against Gommecourt Wood.

At the end of June Aubrey Smith wrote that he heard the big howitzers at Souastre firing, some heavy guns firing in the vicinity of St. Amand and also guns at Bayencourt. All these guns he wrote were firing their hardest and in addition batteries on the Hébuterne Plain, and around Sailly au Bois and Foncquevillers were contributing their share to the indescribable uproar that was going on. Some reports such as those from Souastre were distinct in themselves, which were firing on more distant objectives, the heavies were firing 9.2s in the direction of the German trenches.

At daybreak on the 1st July the 1/5th Lincolns (138th Bde. 46th Div.) were resting in the Corps Line and they were one of the Brigades who were to be involved in the fighting against Gommecourt Wood later on that day.

After the 1st July fighting at Gommecourt the 1/5th Cheshires who were Pioneer Battalion to the 56th Div. returned to the village. The 16th KRRC (100th Bde. 33rd Div.) came to Halloy on the 9th September and were in reserve billets here for the Hébuterne sector.

In the October/November period the barns in the village were used by the 1/4th DWR (147th Bde. 49th Div.)

Between Souastre and Hébuterne was the Chateau le la Haie which was used as a Divisional HQ. It is now named De la Haye Farm.

Stuff Trench and Stuff Redoubt

Stuff Redoubt was one of several redoubts in the area to the north of Thiepval. It was to the north-west of Zollern Redoubt and due east of its more famous neighbour the Schwaben Redoubt. Beyond the Redoubt was Stuff Trench which on the right became Regina Trench to the north of Courcelette and in the west it came from the Schwaben Redoubt which it met at the junction of an enemy communication trench called Grandcourt Road. The Redoubt in fact lay about midway between Pozieres on the east and Grandcourt to the west and was reached but not completely taken in the Battle of Thiepval Ridge 26th-30th September.

By the 27th September a footing had been made in the Redoubt. This was 24 hours after the Schwaben Redoubt's southern face was captured. Captain A. C. T. White of the 6th Yorkshire Regiment or Green Howards gained the VC between 27th September and 1st October. He was in charge of the troops that held the southern and western faces of Stuff Redoubt and for four nights he held this position under heavy fire of all kinds and fended off several counter-attacks. His party became short of ammunition but despite that fended off a further counter-attack which finally cleared the enemy out of the southern and western faces. On the 12th October in the evening, the north-western corner of the Redoubt was the scene of another counter-attack by the enemy but was driven off by the 8th LN Lancs. (7th Bde. 25th Div.). On the 14th October this Battalion attacked north-westwards from the Redoubt and secured a position called 'the Mounds', which gave observation over Grandcourt. The enemy showed little fight on this occasion. At the same time on the 14th October, the 39th Div. drove the Germans from their last hold on the Schwaben Redoubt.

Edmund Blunden of the 11th R. Sussex (116th Bde. 39th Div.) was involved in an assault that took place on the 21st and 22nd October. The attack was to begin soon after noon, and the attacking force would then have to move forward over a long approach. Stuff Trench was taken and Blunden established 'bombing blocks'. CSM Lee also of the 11th R. Sussex said that they were being steadily blown out of Stuff Trench. On the next day the troops in Stuff Trench were compelled to eat their 'iron rations'. By the time the Trench was in Allied possession the Australian troops to the south held Regina Trench, the continuation of Stuff Trench.[7]

Switch Trench

Switch Trench or Line was a trench hastily dug by the Germans once High Wood became threatened. It ran from the direction of Martinpuich to the north-west of the Wood and went towards the north of Delville Wood. Most importantly however was the section of it that ran through the northern part of High Wood and which considerably helped the Germans to maintain their hold on the Wood for two months. Cavalry had ridden through Switch Trench in mid July but were badly cut down and quickly withdrawn. Their HQ was a former German HQ and was heavily shelled.

The 7/8th KOSB (46th Bde. 15th Div.) although they were only engaged in a secondary role, nevertheless suffered heavy casualties. They were relieved on the 18/19th August by the 10th Scots Rif. of their own Brigade. The 6th Cameron H. were in support on the 19th August. The 7/8th KOSB Battalion withdrew to a camp on the Albert side of the Amiens Road to rest and clean up. It was probably Hénencourt Camp which at that time had the reputation of being one of the worst camps to be billeted in.

In mid September the portion of the German Switch Line in front of the 50th Div. consisted of three lines of trenches known as Hook Trench, behind it Martin Trench and behind that Starfish Line. They all ran east or south-east of Martinpuich. The Switch Line met the Longueval–Flers Road just to the south-west of Flers and it was the first objective of the 2nd New Zealand Bde. on the 15th September when High Wood fell finally into the hands of the Allies. Alexander Aitken of the 2nd Otagos was involved in the attack. He wrote of it in his Memoirs called *Gallipoli to the Somme*.

Fraser-Tyler in his book on the artillery said that the Switch Trench was captured towards mid October and that 'Just before zero hour everybody comes up to Switch Trench. It makes a splendid grandstand, and as the batteries have already all their lifts and alterations in range, we at the OP, are simply spectators'.

Talus Boisé

Talus Boisé was a long strip of woodland in low ground east of Carnoy and north-west of Maricourt about a mile to the north-west. The 90th Bde. was in the wood as part of the 30th Division line on 30th June and the track there formed the line between it and the 30th Division boundary. The 18th King's (21st Bde. 30th Div.) arrived here on the 1st July and the 104th Bde. 35th Div. (Bantam) arrived here on 18th August from Happy Valley. Shells rained down on the wood frequently. Along the track leading north to Montauban was Machine Gun Wood running through the west end of Glatz Redoubt to Montauban. Silesia Trench and support to the north-east of Talus Boisé were formerly part of the German front line.

Thiepval

The village of Thiepval is on the D 73 road from Pozieres in the south-east with Auchonvillers to the north-west, and it is also on the D 151 road from Grandcourt with Authuille to the south-west. Before the battle the village had had 93 houses and was thus the sixth largest village on the Somme at that time.

The *Official History* described the Thiepval Plateau as standing out like a great buttress at the western edge of the Pozieres Ridge. It overlooked the River Ancre towards which the ridge sloped down on the west and north. The three spurs called Ovillers, Thiepval and Thiepval Wood stood out from its southern face. Nab (or Blighty Valley) was a valley between Ovillers and Thiepval and led up towards Mouquet Farm. The front line of X Corps at Authuille Wood ran for about 2,500 yards on the lower slopes of the west face of the Thiepval Spur with the River Ancre behind it, it then passed over the Thiepval Wood spur along the front edge of the Wood and crossed in front of the village of Hamel on the western bank of the river and continued for a thousand yards across the Auchonvillers spur to the right flank of VII Corps.

The enemy defences came down from the Ovillers spur and fell back a little up Nab Valley and then went forward into a sharp salient in order to include the upper slopes of the western edge both of the Thiepval Plateau and Spur, towards St. Pierre Divion a village in the river valley. Thus the German position as a whole overlooked the British position, but Thiepval Wood could be used to conceal Allied troops as indeed it was.

Thiepval itself had been transformed into a fortress and much work had been done by the Germans in order to make it impregnable. Redoubts, block-houses, and concrete vaulted shelters had been built on the surrounding ground and a continuous line of trenches went around the village. Behind the front line was the strongest German position of all, to the north of the forti-fied village and that was the famous Schwaben Redoubt. Stuff and Goat Redoubts were to the east and south-eastwards was Mouquet Farm. There were sub-forts and the entire complex was linked by trenches which were very deep and studded with machine gun pillboxes. Some of the dugouts were thirty feet deep and some of them had trap doors that led to lower chambers. Many of these shelters were shell proof. The Ulstermen had named the Germans Strong Points – Lurgan, Strabane, Duncannon, Lisnakith. (The 1st July was also the anniversary of the Battle of the Boyne.)

The Allied bombardment began seven days before the battle actually began and although it destroyed many of the buildings in the village, this still left the cellars intact. A group of these on the west side of the village were organised for a machine gun defence known as Thiepval Fort as well as the ruins of Thiepval Chateau which was to the south-west of the village. These machine guns were to combine and sweep the entire upper part of the western slope of the Thiepval Spur and could also enfilade to the south from the river valley down as far as Authuille village, and to the north could cover the open ground in front of the Allied trenches along the east side of Thiepval Wood.

In his book *The Old Front Line* John Masefield wrote that but for the stricken Thiepval Wood, the eastern bank of the Ancre was 'a gentle sloping hill, bare of trees'. – 'It is worthwhile' he added to 'clamber up to Thiepval from the Allied lines' (he was writing in 1917). The road ran through a deep cutting, which he says might have once been lovely. There was nothing left of the trench, a big reddish mound of brick, the chateau garden, the village pond . . . Charles Douie in his book *The Weary Road* wrote that the garden of the Chateau was a shell trap of the worst description and in particular in the days that proceeded the opening of the battle. Although the right sector of the division facing the Leipzig Redoubt was comparatively quiet, the chateau trenches such as the Broomielaw, Trongate, Sauchiehall Street and the Hammerhead and Maison Grise saps were of evil omen! One of these saps ran into no man's land and soldiers who ventured to its far end could hear the conversation of the enemy in an outlying post. Behind the chateau lay Douie's Battalion HQ at Johnstone's Post. It was a position in the narrow deep valley which lay along the eastern side of Thiepval Wood and was a point at which many trenches met, but apart from these and a few shelters in the bluff along the edge of the Wood there was no other cover. Douie wrote that the Wood was never silent as shell and rifle fire echoed endlessly amongst the trees. On the edge of the Wood was Paisley Avenue, which was a constant mark for the German artillery, and which led to a high bank above the Ancre. On the Allied side of the wood a safer trench called Hamilton Avenue also led to the bank.

Lancashire Dump was the meeting place for a mass of transport on the 30th June after dark when munitions, rations and stores were brought up for the offensive. Large stores of rations were placed in specially built dugouts on the bank of the river. The work of the 36th Divisional Train was organised by Colonel Bernard the CO of the 10th R. Irish Rif. Transport; wheels were bound with straw and old motor tyres, steel chains were replaced by leather straps, boots, like those used in rolling a cricket pitch, were placed over the horses' hooves.

According to the history of the 36th Div. the most difficult task for the Division before the battle began, was the constructing of two causeways over the River Ancre and the marshes. The only communication with the Allied line on the left bank were some footbridges which had been put up by the French troops who previously occupied the sector. The causeways were built of sandbags filled with chalk. At night the river was constantly swept by machine gun fire. The 16th R. Irish Rif. were the Pioneer Battalion and had made their name in building the Candas–Acheux Railway.

The plan for the battle was that the 36th (Ulster) Div. who had been formed from the Ulster Volunteer Force of Edward Carson's Army should take the Schwaben Redoubt and advance towards Grandcourt. The 32nd Div. who were also part of X Corps were on their right and the 29th Div. who had recently come from Gallipoli were on their left. The 49th Div. were in X Corps Reserve. The HQ of the 36th Div. was at Gordon Castle and the closest transport connection to them was Doncaster Camp.

Thiepval village was the objective of the 32nd Div. who were unable to make any real progress, but the 36th made real progress to their left and since that day have been the Division most associated with Thiepval itself, although they were not allowed Thiepval as a battle honour. The 32nd Div. was in fact broken against the defences of Thiepval on the 1st July whilst the 36th penetrated deep into the German lines. The 16th North'd Fus. (96th Bde.) with the 15th Lancs. Fus. (1st Salford Pals) were hit by machine gun fire from the village as soon as they scrambled out of their trenches at 7.30 a.m. The North'd Fus. followed a football that was kicked off by a famous footballer.

At the beginning of the battle on 1st July the 36th Division's movements were concealed by a smoke screen and the smoke drifted along the northern edge of Thiepval Village and then flooded the Ancre Valley. The smoke had been put down by 4 inch Stokes Mortars. The other thing that concealed their movements was the intensity of the Allied fire. The 109th Bde. (36th Div.) was to emerge from the right of Thiepval Wood and the 108th Bde. (36th Div.) was to emerge on their left. The 107th Bde. began from their points of assembly in the north side of Aveluy Wood and were to proceed across the Ancre soon after 5 a.m. on the 1st July. The 109th Bde. consisted of the 9th, 10th and 11th R. Innis Fus. under Lt. Col. Ricardo and Lt. Col. Macrory respectively, as well as the 14th R. Irish Rif. The 107th of the 8th, 9th, 10th and 15th R. Irish Rif. The 108th of the 11th, 12th, 13th R. Irish Rif. and the 9th R. Irish Fus. The troops formed up in no man's land, facing their objective and their line followed for the most part, the line of the sunken Thiepval–Hamel road. The leading waves reached the German front line trench and were able to move straight across it. They did not suffer heavily but hardly were they across however, when the German barrage fell on no man's land and on the rear companies of the first line battalions and also on the second line. As their barrage lifted, flanking machine gun fire began from the dominant position of Thiepval Cemetery. The 11th R. Innis Fus. and the 14th R. Irish Rif. were literally mown down as they emerged from Thiepval Wood. The enemy was able to come up from the cellars in the village and to pour bullets into the backs of the 109th Bde. as well as the 108th Bde. On the left of the 109th Bde. the 13th R. Irish Rif. (108th Bde.) suffered at this stage of the attack most of all as they were under direct long range fire from the direction of Beaucourt Redoubt across the river. The immediate breakdown of the 32nd Div. which was the flanking Div. on the right of the 36th, resulted in the gravest losses in the ranks of the Ulster Division. The Germans caught the 11th R. Irish Rif. in the rear as they emerged from Thiepval Wood.

The 107th Bde. had moved from Aveluy Wood and across the River Ancre to the western outskirts of Thiepval Wood, almost at the bottom of the valley. At 6.30 a.m. they had assembled at the track known as Speyside. They had an

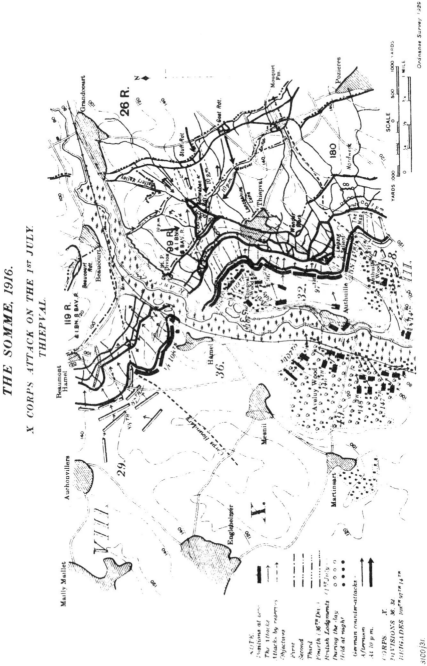

THE SOMME, 1916.

X CORPS ATTACK ON THE 1st JULY.
THIEPVAL.

hour to wait and shells passed over their heads and fell into the marshes beyond. At zero hour led by the 10th R. Irish Rif. under Colonel Bernard they moved to the right for a short distance in order to reach the rides which were to be the paths for their route to the front line. Here the men could see troops of the 32nd Division on the right emerging from their trenches and being gunned down in no man's land by German machine gun fire. The ride or track used by the 10th R. Irish Rif. had been denuded of its foliage by artillery fire and was subsequently in full view. The battalion came under machine gun fire from three directions including the rear. Casualties were high and included Colonel Bernard himself. Lewis guns were brought forward to engage the German machine gunners but their teams were destroyed. Other attacking battalions were not so handicapped as in their rides they were screened and were further away from the Thiepval guns.

It was quite clear to General Nugent in charge of the 36th Division that if the attack went forward in a sort of wedge shape into the enemy lines without support on either flank, the Ulstermen would be simply destroyed. He therefore asked X Corps whether the 107th Bde. could be stopped from advancing to their final line. Corps wanted the attack to continue and then changed their mind. Unfortunately it was too late for the message to get through!

The German bombers poured up from the trenches at St. Pierre Divion to the north of the 36th Division attack but they were beaten off by the 8th and 15th R. Irish Rif. (107th Bde.) and the handful of 13th R. Irish Rif. on the flank of the 109th Bde. In the afternoon the 11th R. Innis Fus. (109th Bde.) reached the Crucifix to the north-east of Thiepval Cemetery and the 9th R. Innis Fus. reached the Schwaben Redoubt. The troops at the Crucifix found that holding the ground there was impossible unless Thiepval was taken.

F. P. Crozier CO of the 9th R. Irish Rif. and Colonel Bernard of the 10th R. Irish Rif. had agreed before the battle to meet up in no man's land, if they were still alive. There they were to supervise the deployment and make any necessary changes to the battle plan. If either of the senior officers became a casualty then the other was to deploy both battalions. If both of them were to become casualties then their seconds in command should carry on. We know that Bernard was killed, when he was at the head of his battalion, by trench mortar fire from Thiepval village which also destroyed his two leading companies who were behind him in columns of four. Crozier had doubled to the sunken road, where he rallied the remnants of the 10th R. Irish Rif. and told his batman at the same time to go to the Battalion HQ in order to help with bringing up ammunition. Most of the stretcher bearers who reached Doncaster Dump were wounded in carrying the wounded. Crozier found that the remaining 10th R. Irish Rif. had gone to ground in desperation and that his own 9th R. Irish Rif. couldn't go forward without their right being guarded, as the ground beyond Thiepval was still held. The two R. Irish Batts. were then given the task of leap-frogging the rest of the Division and of carrying on to the final objective which they actually reached but were unable to hold onto without support from behind.

In mid-afternoon there had been a misunderstanding about the use that the 146th Bde. (49th Div.) was to be put to, and their attack at 3 p.m. failed under terrific machine gun fire. There was a deep valley or re-entrant from the River Ancre half way up to Johnstones Post. The Germans had full view of the 6th West Yorks when they doubled across it.

Cpl. George Sanders 1/7th W. Yorks (146th 49th Div.) born in Leeds on 8th July 1894 gained the VC for most conspicuous bravery. After an advance into the enemy's trenches he found himself isolated with a party of 30 men. He organised his defence, detailed a bombing party, and impressed on his men that his and their duty was to hold the position at all costs. Next morning he drove off an attack by the enemy and rescued some prisoners who had fallen into their hands. Later, two strong bombing attacks were driven off. On the following day he was relieved, after showing the greatest courage, determination and good leadership during 36 hours under very trying conditions. His party was without food and water, having given all their water to the wounded during the first night. After the relieving force was firmly established, he brought in his party, 19 strong. The HQ of the 7th and 8th W. Yorks were at Belfast City in Aveluy Wood and after the disastrous attack the survivors were concealed in trenches near Gordon Castle . As the day wore on it is impossible to imagine the conditions in the woods from which the Ulstermen had launched themselves only a few hours before. Conditions were simply indescribably terrible. At Paisley Dump all the trenches in Thiepval Wood and the tracks to Authuille and across the Ancre met. The wounded lay there in hundreds and the noise was inhuman. The road back to Martinsart behind Aveluy Wood became solid with walking wounded and with ambulances. One sunken road that went in the direction of Hamel became known as 'Bloody Road' because of the massive heaps of dead there at the end of 1st July.

There were two MDS, for stretcher cases and 'walking wounded'. One at Forceville, to the west of Thiepval, that was manned by the 108th Field Ambulance for the 36th Div. and a second at Clairfaye Farm, further west manned by the 110th Field Ambulance. The ADS was situated near the Albert–Arras road to Aveluy Wood.

Evacuation of wounded from Regimental Aid Posts in Thiepval Wood and Authuille would have to take place over Authuille Bridge which connected the village of that name with Aveluy Wood. The alternative would be for the trench tramway which crossed the River Ancre to the north to be used. The motors of the Field Ambulance were to be parked on the Martinsart–Albert road, south of Martinsart itself. For 'walking wounded' there was a collection station to the west of Martinsart, whence horse drawn wagons carried the wounded by cross-country track through Hédauville to Clairfaye Farm. From Hamel evacuation would be simpler, though it had to follow a specially dug trench from Hamel village to a point on the Albert–Hamel road which was screened from enemy observation.

To sum up the deeds of the 36th (Ulster) Div. on this day I would like to quote from H. A. Taylor's *Goodbye to the Battlefields*. He wrote that the 36th

Div. wrote no more glorious chapter of history than it did here at Thiepval. The Ulster Battalions hurled themselves upon Thiepval's underground fortress with such determination that all its wire and all its machine guns, manned by the German regiment which had held the point for two years and had boasted that it was impregnable, could not check the onward rush. On they went, two miles into the enemy system, and though, ultimately, in danger of being cut off, they retired, and brought back with them over five hundred prisoners. The 36th (Ulster) Div. gained two VCs for outstanding bravery on the 1st July. The first VC was awarded posthumously to Private W. F. McFadzean of the 14th R. Irish Rif. (109th Bde.), for action near Thiepval Wood during the attack. While in Concentration Trench and opening a box of bombs for distribution prior to an attack, the box slid down into the trench, which was crowded with men, and two of the safety pins fell out. He instantly realised the danger to his comrades and with heroic courage threw himself on the bombs. The bombs exploded, blowing him to pieces, but only one other man was injured. He knew well the danger, being himself a bomber, but without a moment's hesitation gave his life for his comrades. Temp. Capt. E. N. F. Bell was the other VC which was also awarded posthumously. Bell was in command of a Trench Mortar Battery and advanced with the infantry in the attack. His battalion was the 9th R. Innis. Fus. (109th Bde.) When the Allied line was hung up by enfilading machine gun fire he crept forward and shot dead the machine gunner. Later, on no less than three other occasions, when the Allied bombing parties, which were clearing the enemy's trenches, were unable to advance, he went forward alone and threw trench mortar bombs among the enemy. When he had no bombs available, he stood on the parapet, under intense fire, and used a rifle with great coolness and effect on the enemy advancing to counter-attack. Finally he was killed rallying and reorganising infantry parties which had lost their officers. All this was outside the scope of his normal duties with his battery. He gave his life in his supreme devotion to duty.

On the 2nd July, with over 5,500 casualties, the 36th (Ulster) Division was taken out of the battle. These very high figures promptly threw the Ulster Province into a state of mourning. The 49th Division relieved the 36th and it was during the 2nd July that a force of about 400 men were collected in order to support some small number of British troops who could be seen from Mesnil Ridge to be in the first two lines of enemy trenches.

F. Starrett who was Crozier's batman at the time of the Somme battle and who had helped on the 1st July with bringing up ammunition described the 9th R. Irish Rif. as holding out, before their relief. He also mentions in his unpublished Memoirs that there were three women workers as close to the battlefield as Doncaster Dump. They would have been nurses or drivers. At the time of the 36th's relief Starrett's master F. P. Crozier was promoted to General. Although most of the fighting associated with Thiepval occurred on the 1st July and then nearly three months later, there was still some action on the next few days of July.

Capt. Stevenson-Jones MC. of the 2nd South Lancs. has left a fulsome account of the situation on the 2nd July in the *South Lancs. Regimental Journal*. At about 11 a.m. they received orders to go up to the advance HQ of the 25th Division Commander Sir Guy Bainbridge which was close to two 4.7 inch Naval Guns. At about 2 a.m. they had piled arms in Martinsart Wood, which was a small wood immediately behind Aveluy Wood. They watched the howitzers performing and then had a meal. Just before dusk they fell in and the plan was to move through the wood and then take over trenches in front of Thiepval. The attack was to be at dawn on the 3rd July. On the way there they sang 'Keep the Home Fires Burning'. They went through the wood, along the road at the top of the hill and then down into the Ancre Valley. They had trouble in getting over Blackhorse Bridge owing to a stream of side car ambulances that were crossing the opposite way. They were also shelled at this time. They then went past Ration Dump and the dressing station which was very crowded with rank upon rank of stretchers in front of it. They reached the communication and then the assembly trench. The attack was postponed until 6 a.m. Though the 75th Bde. attacked on a three battalion front, they were blown to pieces and only the 8th South Lancs. who were in reserve, were left to prevent a counter-attack, from getting through to Blackhorse Bridge. Stevenson-Jones said that advance companies were less in danger than those who followed because of the time that it took the Germans to emerge from their dugouts. The 8th Borders were on his right flank and the 11th Cheshires on his left. The Cheshires in particular had been 'mauled' by the enemy and their commander Col. Aspinall was killed. 75th Bde. HQ had been hit by a shell which prevented communication from running properly. Many men got back during the night from no man's land and rested in Campbell Trench. That night they moved back to bivouac at Martinsart Wood. On their return they were passed by the 1st Wiltshires (7th Bde. 25th Div.) who were on their way to have 'another go' for Thiepval. However their attack was called off. Stevenson-Jones informed Bainbridge that their attack had failed because the trenches and no man's land were under direct observation and enfiladed from the high ground on the left, and swept by machine gun fire from high ground well back. He said that Thiepval could never be taken by frontal attack unless Serre and Gommecourt were taken first.

The HQ of the 1/4 Y & L on the 2nd July was at Speyside on the edge of the marsh. However despite this advice another attack was arranged for the 1st Wiltshires for the 4th July and they attacked incurring great losses including their commanding officer Lt. Col. W. S. Brown.

Around the 8th July, in the sunken road at Thiepval Wood, the conditions were ghastly with the bodies of the Ulster Division still there. The Allied trenches had received a fearful hammering and some of them had been obliterated. Some of the dugouts were in fact deep ones but not enough of them were, and the communication trenches that led back to HQ and the crossings over the River Ancre were badly constructed and sited. The main ones lay along or just beside the chief rides in the wood and they could thus be enfiladed by the enemy artillery. Battalion HQ was at Gordon Castle.

By the end of July the actual village of Thiepval which was the objective of the 32 Div. on the 1st of the month was in fact totally destroyed. Communication trenches close to the Battalion HQ at Gordon Castle were Elgin and Inniskillen Avenues and because of enemy shelling HQ was moved 200 yards back from Gordon Castle to Belfast City, which was very well camouflaged. On the 3rd September another attempt was made against the Schwaben Redoubt using the 147th and 146th Bdes (49th Div.). The infantry had assembled at 5.13 a.m. in trenches along the Hamel–Thiepval Road.

The Allied artillery bombarded the enemy lines accurately and gas bombs were used to good effect. However the 1/4th and 1/5th DWR (147th Bde. 49th Div.) to the right, lost direction in part and failed to find and capture a German strong point known as the Pope's Nose. Machine gun fire from the Schwaben Redoubt added to their problems! On their left the 146th Bde. didn't do as well as the 147th Bde., the 1/6th West Yorks were enfiladed from the Pope's Nose and only a few of the 1/8th West Yorks who were next to cross the river even reached the enemy support line. First the 146th Bde. drifted back to their assembly trenches and then the 147th did likewise. Once again the impossibility of a frontal attack against a position such as the Schwaben Redoubt was underlined.

E. Blunden has the following to say in *Undertones of War*. The Black Watch wounded were trailing down the road. They had been wading the marshes of the Ancre, trying to take a machine gun post called Summer House. A few yards ahead on the rising ground, the German front line could not be clearly seen, the water mist and smoke veiling it: The Cheshires took over the front line, the huge throat of the howitzer still being elevated to hurl horror at Thiepval Crucifix. For Thiepval was not yet captured. On 3rd September the 49th Div. could not get twenty yards forward from Thiepval Wood.

There was another Allied plan to capture the stronghold of Thiepval and the redoubts to north and north-east of it. The two British Divisions who were given the task were the 11th on the right or east and the 18th on the left flank. Opposite them the German defence was in the hands of the 7th, 8th and 26th Reserve Division and the line went around the northern face of Courcelette and then westwards past Mouquet Farm and into no man's land. It then continued to the southern side of the ruins of Thiepval village which was about 300 yards behind the line. The line then bent northwards towards St. Pierre Divion. Behind the line Stuff Redoubt and behind it was the Grandcourt Redoubt. These were three lines of defensive systems which included the forts, Schwaben, Zollern and the Stuff Redoubts.

The nose around Thiepval and the village itself was defended by the 180th Wurttemberg Regiment and part of the 77th Reserve Regt. The Schwaben and the front defences to the north-west of St. Pierre Divion were held by the 66th Regt. The enemy had observed the activity of the British in the construction of new assembly trenches and were ready for a fresh attack several days before the 26th September.

The day though was to belong to the Allied Division the 18th (Eastern) Div. On the right flank was the 53rd Bde. whose battalions were the 8th Suffolks, the 8th Norfolks, the 10th Essex and the 6th R. Berks. On their left was the

54th Bde. whose battalions were the 12th Middlesex, 11th R. Fus., 7th Bedfords and 6th Northamptons.

For the view point of the Allies I am going to draw heavily upon the history of the 18th Division itself and the views and letters of the CO of the 12th Middlesex Lt. Col. Maxwell VC. The HQ of the 18th Div. was moved on the 25th September to Hédauville, where it remained until the 6th October. The attack was to be launched from the south instead of from the west and four tanks were allotted to the Division. Dumps had been laid down and trenches had been deepened and improved. Grids too had been put down. One brilliant idea was to clear the road from Authuille to Thiepval and then to erect a brushwood screen along its whole length. The road thus became invaluable for the bringing up of stores and rations and for later taking back wounded troops. The screen had the effect of reducing German shelling. In addition to the enormous range of underground tunnels under the German position, from the centre of Thiepval village there ran a sunken road up as far as the Cemetery which was lined with dugouts. Around the chateau itself the dugouts were immensely strong and deep. According to the Divisional history there were as many as 144 deep dugouts that had been marked on a German map which had fallen into British hands. The Allied bombardment began three days before the battle, the time of which was fixed as 12.35 p.m. on the 26th September. The distance to the trenches was about 250 yards and on the extreme right the 8th Suffolks pushed forward steadily and kept close to the Allied barrage. They found stiffening resistance in Schwaben and Bulgar Trenches. On the left of the Suffolks the 10th Essex had reached their objective as well, which was just beyond Thiepval village. A heavy fire was poured into the assaulting companies from the direction of Martin and Bulgar Trenches. They were also enfiladed by machine guns.

On the left flank in the 54th Bde. attack, the 12th Middlesex under Maxwell had the task of capturing Thiepval village itself. The 11th R. Fus. under Lt. Col. C. C. Carr had the task of clearing the enemy network of trenches and dugouts on the left flank of the Middlesex as well as the dugouts behind the Middlesex Battalion, for which 'C' Company was detailed. The 6th Northamptons under Lt. Col. G. E. Ripley were to move up in close support of the Middlesex and R. Fus. The 7th Bedfords under Lt. Col. G. D. Price were in dugouts in Thiepval Wood and its neighbourhood, so as to be close up when called upon. After the battle had begun there was hard fighting and a fierce barrage. The first waves of the British attacks came under very heavy enemy fire and the 12th Middlesex managed to carry line after line of trenches until they reached the Chateau where they were checked by deadly machine gun fire. At a critical moment in the battle a tank lumbered up from Thiepval Wood and was supported by a third wave of British Infantry. The tank dealt with the enemy machine guns and the leading company of the Middlesex were able to pass around the two flanks of the Chateau. The Brigade itself had been allotted two tanks and the successful one having led the infantry into Thiepval then got bogged down on its way to Schwaben Redoubt. The second tank suffered the same fate. That was the end for the time being of the two tanks which were named 'Crême de Menthe' and 'Cordon Bleu'. In addition to the deeds of the Middlesex Battalion two of their members were to gain the VC on this day.

The local German Telephone HQ which had been identified on a German map was also captured on the 26th September. It was a palatial dugout and was in direct communication with the enemy artillery, and contained twenty operators as well as other staff, who were taken prisoner.

Although the Germans were being pushed back they were by no means beaten and they still had the use of the high ground and directed machine gun fire accurately upon the British. Maxwell sent a message via carrier pigeon from Thiepval Chateau that said although they had been successful, they were exhausted and in need of assistance. Meanwhile the 6th Northamptons, who had moved up in support had been having a tough time as well. Their senior officer joined Maxwell at the Chateau at 5.15 p.m. In the evening the 53rd Bde. to the right were in position, and the Suffolks and the Essex Batts. were consolidating the Zollern Line. The Norfolks were in support in Schwaben Trench. The Berks were being used for carrying parties. On the front of the 54th Bde. Maxwell decided to take command of all the attacking battalions and gathered the scattered units into two defence lines with about 50 yards between them. They provided a defence of the Chateau, which then became a keep.

A strong point was made around one of the stranded tanks. The 7th Bedfords were to relieve the attacking battalions and the 7th R. West Kents (55th Bde.) were to take their place in reserve. The plan was that on the morning of the 26th September, the German rectangle position was to be stormed by two companies and it was then to be cleared in a rush with the use of the bayonet. Maxwell remained at the Chateau in his HQ which was one of the arches with a few steps that led below ground, until the Bedfords attacked in the morning. After that the Schwaben Redoubt was the next objective of the 18th Div. and a small party of the 11th Lancs. Fus. namely their 'D' Company was involved in an attack against the enemy line known as the Pope's Nose, and were successful. (The writer J. R. R. Tolkein was a member of this battalion.)

The German account of the day's battle was that the British had broken against Courcelette on the north-east of the battle and that this had opened the way at Thiepval to Allied progress. They broke through to the east of the village and three front companies of the 77th Regiment were captured almost to a man. The 180th found themselves being attacked by bombers from the rear. The advance at Courcelette had allowed the British to advance on Thiepval and the ground beyond from the south and west simultaneously. The Germans had to evacuate Thiepval and to make a new line astride the Thiepval–Grandcourt Road.

And so the 26th September was a great day for the British and Canadian advance. There were four Divisions involved in an attack on a front of about 5,000 yards and the great fortress of Thiepval had at last fallen.

Private F. J. Edwards of the 12th Middlesex had gained the VC 'for one of

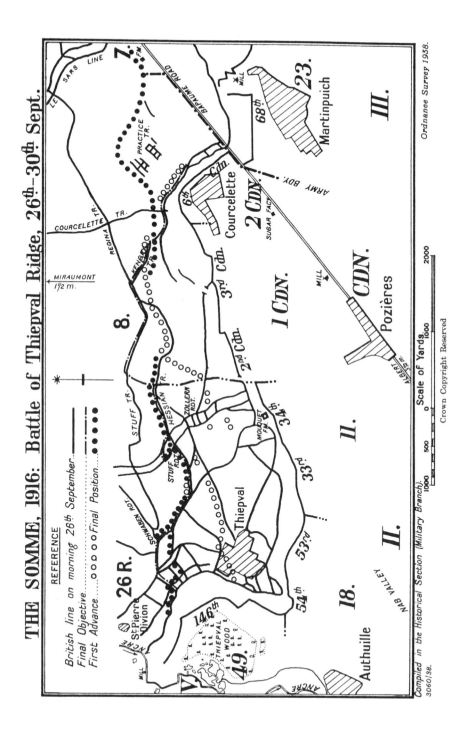

THE SOMME, 1916: Battle of Thiepval Ridge, 26th–30th Sept.

REFERENCE

British line on morning 26th September.
Final Objective
First Advance

Ordnance Survey 1938.

Compiled in the Historical Section (Military Branch).
3060/38.

Crown Copyright Reserved

Scale of Yards

those decisive actions which determine the success or failure of an operation'. His part of the line was held up by a machine gun. The officers had all become casualties. Alone, and on his own initiative, he dashed towards the gun, which he bombed until he succeeded in knocking it out. This made further advance possible. Lt. Col. Maxwell recommended the award. Private R. Ryder also of the Middlesex was awarded the VC. His company was held up by rifle fire, and all of his officers became casualties – Ryder realising the situation dashed absolutely alone at the enemy trench, and by skilful manipulation of his Lewis gun, succeeded in clearing the trench.

Finally for the last comment of the day's events I quote from a letter from Maxwell that is kept in the National Army Museum. It is dated the 27th September. He wrote 'I hadn't personally any hopes of accomplishing it'. The distance of the attack was one mile, which was enormous, over the parapet at an unknown hour. The Prussians and the Württembergers had held the line for a year and were supposed to have left, but were still there. His Regiment (the 12th Middlesex) was accompanied by the 11th R. Fus. It was a very difficult battle – owing to every landmark such as a map shows, being obliterated. He described the trenches at Thiepval as 'white' and the enemy uniforms as being absolutely 'black'.

After Maxwell's success he was given the command of a brigade joining the 27th Bde. of the 9th (Scottish) Div. He was killed on the 21st September 1917 when reconnoitering no man's land.

On the 27th September the battle continued and although the village had been cleared there were pockets of the enemy holding out with fortified nests of machine guns and they also used the underground passages to good effect. In the evening Thiepval Cemetery was completely cleared as well as Zollern Redoubt. Tom Adlam who was a T/Lt. with the 7th Bedfords earned the VC on the 27th September when he organised a bombing party that was equipped with German bombs, after having gone fearlessly from shell hole to shell hole gathering the bombing party together. He himself was a very accurate thrower of bombs and despite being wounded he carried on and also on the next day, despite being severely injured in the arm. Finally he was sent down the line to get his wounds attended to but not before clearing the enemy from a dangerous trench. (See the Schwaben Redoubt Section.) The fighting over the next few days resulted in the British pushing slowly forward using continuous hand grenade fighting. They reached the Schwaben Redoubt and Stuff Redoubt to the north-east of Schwaben. The fighting had been bitter and some positions changed hands several times. Mouquet Farm to the southeast of Thiepval village which had held up the Australians for some weeks had held out until the 26th owing to its deep cellars. It was the 6th East Yorks. Pioneer Battalion who captured the Germans that remained at the Farm – one German officer and 55 men. The remains of a brave garrison.

In early October the 16th Sherwood For. (117th Bde. 39th Div.) had their HQ in deep dugouts in the Chateau and their support company was to the south in Leipzig Redoubt. At the time the most serviceable communication trench which they used was St. Martins Lane. The route to the line that they followed after leaving Aveluy Wood to the south-west was that after passing their Brigade HQ, they crossed the Ancre by a narrow bridge called Passerelle de Magenta and made their way to Paisley Dump. The communication trench then went along the south side of Thiepval Wood and could absorb the main body of a battalion. The area was combed with dugouts. The front line at the time in parts went underground for 30 or 40 yards at a time. The companies lived in them and had periscopes set up at the end of each tunnel. The land on their left flank dropped down to the Ancre.

For the October attack towards the Schwaben Redoubt the points of assembly for troops were Wood Post which was on the main Authuille Road and also Blighty Valley. North Bluff was just behind Thiepval Wood.

Around the 21st October the 8th South Lancs (75th Bde. 25th Div.) were in the centre of an attack against Regina Trench and Stuff Redoubt. Edmund Blunden with the 11th R. Sussex (116th Bde. 39th Div.) wrote − 'Then we went into trenches round about Thiepval Wood (23rd October) which not long before had been so horrible and mad; but now they had assumed a tenderer aspect, were voted a rest-cure sector' . . . 'Occasionally heavy shells blocked up parts of Inniskilling Avenue (which was one of the communication trenches) or the waterside path to Mill Post (opposite our old mill at Hamel)' . . . Blunden saw 'In Paisley Valley, alongside the wood, some tanks were lying veiled with brown nets . . .' The Ancre battle was continuously postponed and a week or two passed without much happening except for rain and fog. Blunden reports that they sheltered in what he called 'a bedroom of corridored chalk bank.' 'Beyond the area he called Thiepval on the map a trench called St. Martin's Lane led forward;' − 'the Schwaben Redoubt ahead was an almost obliterated cocoon' . . . 'and there were deep dugouts, which faced the German guns,' . . . 'The whole zone was a corpse,' − 'Here we were to "hold the line", for an uncertain sentence of days'.

They used tunnels such as Koyli West and Mill Post and they were so small that the men couldn't stand up in them. In the period 25th to 27th October they were back in billets in Pioneer Road. In early November Harrison the 11th R. Sussex Commanding Officer had his HQ at the Thiepval end of St. Martins Lane. The place was deep down and was decorated with German drawings that belonged to the former occupants. The old German front line on its west slope retained its outline despite the number of explosions that it had swallowed up month after month. The Germans had fortified the position with logic and imagination in that they used steel rails and concrete to the best effect. In front of the HQ there were concealed concrete emplacements which had formerly lurked in the weeds and flowers of no man's land. Beneath it their reserve company lived in the prodigious dugouts which were arranged in two storeys, and in the lower storey there was a little door in the wall. If one opened it, it led to steadily descending dark galleries and stacked in them were box after box of explosives. In another great dugout there were elaborate and surgical appliances with medical supplies. Another was a quartermaster's stores. Blunden mentioned the smell of the German dugouts as being peculiar to the German soldier, heavy and clothy.

Blunden also records that on the 13th November that there was a feat of arms that was worth recording in which the enemy was surprised and beaten. From Thiepval Wood the 39th Div. his Division, sprang forth from, passed their old dead, mud-craters and wire and captured the tiny village of St. Pierre Divion with its enormous labyrinth and almost 2,000 Germans in the galleries there.

There was an ADS or CP in Thiepval during November.

According to Michael Hurd, Ivor Gurney's biographer, the poet arranged a setting of a poem by F. W. Harvey a great friend from pre-war days in Gloucestershire, whilst at Crucifix Corner with the 2/5 Glosters in January 1917. It was a 'tender cry of longing for Gloucestershire's fields and rivers'. Harvey himself later became a prisoner of war when captured at Douai in August 1917. His first volume of poetry had been called *A Gloucestershire Lad.*

According to William Orpen's book *An Onlooker in France* Thiepval Chateau, one of the previously largest in northern France was practically flattened and all that was left of it was a mound with flowers on top. In August 1917 a burial party worked in the Thiepval area 'and a sturdy little Scot', a Lt. Clark was in charge of it. During the month or so that they worked there, they dug up, identified and reburied some thousands of bodies. Some of them could not be identified, and what was found on them in the way of money etc. was divided up amongst the burial party. Orpen also mentioned a great colony of Indians being down in the valley of the Ancre close to Thiepval Mill Road. They were all Catholics, and were headed by an old padre who had worked in India for 45 years. Orpen described him as a 'fine old fellow'. Wonderful services were held each Sunday afternoon on the side of Thiepval Mill in the open air. He had put up an altar with wonderful draperies behind it, it hung about 30 feet high. The Indians cleaned up the face of Thiepval in no time at all. In his book *The Wet Flanders Plain* Henry Williamson mentions that after the war the wooden military bridge remained over Mill Causeway. The Thiepval Memorial was designed by Edwin Lutyens and was unveiled by HRH The Prince of Wales on 31st July 1932. He was accompanied by the French President. It is certainly the most important Memorial in France that Lutyens designed and it was mathematically a brilliant exercise. It is designed in a stepped pyramidal form and is made up of a series of intersecting arches which are appropriate in width and height. On the walls of the piers, which number 16 are the names of 73,357 men who at one time had been listed as missing because they had no known graves. Since 1932 many have been found and many of these have in turn been identified and buried. Lutyens himself hoped that his design would convey a sense of 'the eternally tragic'. Unfortunately the Memorial was faced with bricks which have proved to be very brittle and liable to erosion. In recent years this has led to major repairs to the Memorial, which still dominates the Somme landscape. According to H. A. Taylor in his book *Goodbye to the Battlefields,* when the foundations for the Memorial were being excavated, which as it was to stand 140 feet had to be substantial, the workmen struck tunnels and dugouts which were once part of the former German second line. After tunnels had been found, digging was continued to a depth of 10 feet and then there was a 'raft' of concrete laid nine feet seven inches in thickness.

There are of course many famous Somme names mentioned on the walls of the Memorial and these include five VC holders, Capt. E. N. Bell (9th R. Innis), Lt. G. S. Cather (9th R. Irish Rif.), Private W. McFadzean (14th R. Irish Rif.), Lt. T. O. Wilkinson (7th L.N.Lancs Regt.) and H. H. Munro (22nd R. Fus.). Other 'names' are George Butterworth (13th DLI) a promising composer, T. S. Kettle the poet and Donald Hankey who wrote *A Student in Arms*. In the 1930s there was a cafe at Thiepval village run by a former Despatch Rider and he used to show visitors a dais which had been used during the unveiling by the Prince of Wales and the French President. The same man owned the grounds of the chateau at the time.

There is at the memorial an Anglo-French cemetery also designed by Edwin Lutyens which symbolically contains the graves of 300 men each from Britain and France. A little west of north of the memorial is the other imposing memorial in the Thiepval area, a memorial to the 36th (Ulster) Div. which is about 150 feet high and is a stone tower house, a replica of William Burn's 19th century Helen's Tower at Clandeboye. The tower is now looked after by the Somme Association of Belfast and is open to visitors during the summer months. A memorial to 2nd Lt. M. J. Wright (14th RIR) who was killed on 1st July and buried in Thiepval Wood is at present in the tower. His name is commemorated on the Thiepval Memorial.

There is a memorial to the 18th Div. who took the village at the end of September 1916, and owing to their flexible ideas on training and their excellent senior officers they have gained the deserved reputation of being one of the best British divisions who served in the Great War. The memorial is just outside the Thiepval Memorial grounds, between it and the site of Thiepval Chateau and Thiepval Wood. Mill Road Cemetery is to the east of Helen's Tower and some of the graves there have had to be laid flat because of the subsidence of the Schwaben Redoubt tunnels which are directly underneath. Mill Road itself runs south-east from the rail line at Hamel village until it joins the more southerly road from St. Pierre Divion to Thiepval village. The cemetery was at one time called Mill Road Cemetery No. 2 and is a little east of the junction of the two roads, midway between Thiepval village and St. Pierre Divion. After the Armistice it was enlarged by the concentration of 1,038 graves from smaller cemeteries and from the battlefields of Beaumont Hamel and Thiepval. It stands on high ground and has commanding views of the Ancre battlefield.

Connaught Cemetery is roughly between Helen's Tower and Mill Road, and was begun in the early Autumn of 1916, and at the Armistice it contained 228 graves. It was then very greatly increased by the concentration of graves from smaller cemeteries and the battlefield that surrounded it, the great majority being men of the 36th Div. and also of those who fought in the summer and autumn of 1916. A Memorial was erected in the Cemetery by the 1/5th W. Yorks to the men of their battalion who fell on 28th September at the Schwaben Redoubt. It was later moved to the Battalion's Drill Hall at York. The Cemetery stands on high ground overlooking the Ancre Valley. The most important cemeteries which were incorporated in the Connaught Cemetery were Thiepval Village Cemetery which had been on the ridge summit, Thiepval Valley Cemetery which was on the south-east side of Thiepval Wood and Quarry Palace Cemetery, which had been close to the river and a little north-east of the hamlet of St. Pierre Divion. Others that were 'gathered in' included St. Pierre Divion Cemetery No. 1, a little south-east of that Hamlet, Divion Road Cemetery, Small Connaught Cemetery opposite Connaught Cemetery across the road, Battery Valley Cemetery half a mile south-west of Grandcourt, Paisley Hillside Cemetery on the south side of Thiepval Wood and named from Paisley Avenue Trench, Gordon Castle Cemetery just inside the south border of Thiepval Wood and Bluff Cemetery half a mile north of Authuille village.

To add a postscript to Thiepval, Charles Douie who was with the 1st Dorsets (14th Bde. 32nd Div.) was for a time in trenches at the south-east corner of the wood and used to look up the slope towards the village and the former gardens of Thiepval Chateau. That same slope is now bare farm land. A circular drive used to go from the Chateau down the slope and the drive and the paths around the garden disappeared either during or after the War. The entrance to the Chateau is where the entrance to the Memorial is today. The car park is on the ground where the carriages used to turn.

After the War in a book called *We'll Shift Our Ground* Blunden's character Duncan has the following conversation with a Frenchman 'But I am really more interested in the ground than in these new buildings of yours – I suppose there's not a dugout or anything left now? How about Koyli tunnels, or Mills Post, or St. Martins Lane up there? –' Meanwhile he was looking down from the old enemy position into the margins of Thiepval Wood a vast coppice now, and could not detect through the verdant tangle the cliff banks in which he had once slept through midnight's thunderings over his table loaded with telegram forms and typed orders and mugs and maps, grenades and steel hats. – He turned north leaving St. Martins Lane alone; – the road ran past the edge of the wood, whence the old Armies, – 'had come forward to be mauled and murdered by the machine guns'. A cemetery in all its simplicity, – now lay near their places of assembly.

Toutencourt

Toutencourt is on the D 23 road to the west of Harponville and north of Contay, and is most famous as being the HQ of General Gough of the Fifth Army. Rawlinson visited the village on the 7th April. Major Beddington who was GSO Fifth Army July–November stayed at the village from 1st July. In November Gough had his HQ at a farm at one end of the village. 'I gazed out of the poky little window looking on the dull and dirty courtyard and considered what my decision should be, i.e. the November battle'.

The village was used by many units for billeting purposes including the 20th KRRC who arrived here on 30th July and were under canvas under 'great trees close to a small stream'. On 11th August the 52nd Division were in the area.

Trônes Wood

Trônes Wood which is pear-shaped is to the immediate east of Bernafay Wood, east of Montauban, south of Longueval and west of the village of Guillemont. In the period early to mid July it was to be desperately fought for by both sides.

In *Haig's Great Push* there is a good description of the wood on the 8th July when the Somme fighting was principally on the Allied extreme right flank, where Trônes Wood which was some 1,400 yards long from north to south, with a southern frontage of 400 yards was the objective. The Wood was in a position of considerable strategic importance since it was only two miles from the German station at Combles, one of the enemy's most important nerve centres in this region, with roads that branched from it, whereby Peronne could be threatened from the north.

The Germans recognised this and protected the wood by strong trenches, a perfect network of wire entanglements and a small arsenal of machine guns. The problem was not so much to gain Trônes Wood as to hold on to it when it was captured. As it was commanded by artillery from both armies it was to become a death trap for the infantry of both sides.

The centre of Trônes Wood was cut by the Montauban–Guillemont Railway and lay in a dip across the head of Caterpillar Valley. The wood itself was a dense thicket and it had not been cut for two years. This led to there being a very thick undergrowth which made it very difficult to force a way through. Trônes Alley, a German communication trench ran roughly along the top edge of the Montauban Ridge between Trônes and Bernafay Woods. An attack was planned for the 7th and the French on the right flank were to assist; however it was subsequently postponed to 8 a.m. on the 8th July. The southern end of Trônes Wood and Maltz Horn Trench as far as Maltz Horn Farm were to be taken by the Allies. On the right flank the French were to take the remainder of the Maltz Horn Trench and the general line from the farm to Hardecourt Village. The artillery began early and Fraser Tytler in his book *Field Guns of France* said that his guns began at 7.20 a.m. on the 8th July and went on firing until 3.30 p.m. the next day.

The 2nd Yorks were to move through Bernafay Wood and to deploy on the eastern edge facing Trônes Wood. A machine gun from the south-west corner caused heavy loss. The French however had taken Hardecourt knoll and a section of Maltz Horn Trench. This left their left flank exposed and the 2nd Wiltshires (21st Bde. 30th Div.) were detailed to attack at 1 p.m. and thanks to an accurate bombardment the enemy were driven out of the trench and the wood was entered with only a few casualties. A counter-attack from the north was repelled.

The Maltz Horn Trench was on the forward slope of the Hardecourt knoll and the enemy spent some time digging a fresh line about 300 yards beyond, in the hard chalk on the reverse slope. In the small hours the 2nd Royal Scots (90th Bde. 30th Div.) occupied Maltz Horn Farm that lay between the two lines. The 18th Manchesters of the same brigade reinforced the Wiltshires on the southern edge of Trônes Wood and the 17th Manchesters were able to enter the wood without loss. The Central Trench in the wood was connected up to three battery positions and it was taken at about 8 a.m. on the 8th July. However although the wood was in Allied hands it was only to be for a few hours. The 17th Manchesters on the eastern edge of the wood were being badly shelled and signalled for help but the range was too great for the British artillery to be effective. They therefore had no alternative but to withdraw along Trônes Alley westwards to Bernafay Wood. This left the 18th Manchesters in a vulnerable position and they withdrew to the Brickworks at Montauban.

The 2nd R. Scots Fus. did however hang on to Maltz Horn Trench. The 16th Manchesters had sent in parties to assist their sister battalion the 17th Manchesters and they too had to retire.

At 2.30 p.m. on the 9th July the 90th Bde. ordered the 16th Manchesters to attack and to hold on to the southern edge of Trônes Wood. They formed up in the sunken part of the road from Montauban brickworks – Hardecourt Road, south of the wood. The Germans were caught out, expecting an attack on the western side of the wood. The 17th Manchesters were therefore able to reach the southern edge of the wood. However with the presence of German snipers in the trees and of German bombers the Manchesters found that they had to dig a fresh line about 60 yards from the south-west edge which was still parallel to the wood. The Battalion was ordered to prepare for an advance through the wood on the 10th July when they were to be assisted by the 4th South African Regiment who were lent to them by the 9th Div. When it was practicable small parties attempted to go through the wood but the thick undergrowth prevented the patrols from seeing very far either to left or right.

The British began a bombardment at around 3 a.m. on the 10th July. The infantry managed to enter the wood from both ends and this made the centre untenable for the Germans who withdrew to large shell craters which were about 200 yards to the east of Trônes Wood north of the Guillemont road. However the Wood was not in British hands at all and small parties of Germans had hung on at various parts of the wood to the south and especially to the centre. The British 90th Bde. had been replaced by the 89th Bde. who were to endeavour to secure the wood and a company of the 17th Liverpools from Bernafay Wood made an unsuccessful attack which was repulsed.

On the night 10th/11th July there were no British troops in the wood at all. Small German posts held the edge and the main body was along Central Trench in the centre. At 1 a.m. on the 11th July the 20th Liverpools and the 2nd Bedfords formed up along the sunken road immediately east of the brick-works. After a heavy bombardment at 3.27 a.m. the advance began. The 20th Liverpools were to attack the part of the wood which was south of Trônes Alley and then to relieve the 2nd R. Scots Fus. in Maltz Horn Trench. The

2nd Bedfords on their left were to attack between the Alley and the Railway and push on to the eastern edge of the wood.

Machine gun fire from the Trônes Alley Block forced the attackers southwards, but the wood was entered. The fighting continued for some time during the day until the Bedfords were forced out and back to Bernafay Wood. The wood was once again in German hands except for a wedge on the western side, which was occupied by some Bedfords.

The orders for a fresh German attack were found on a German officer which led to the British bringing down a barrage between the wood and Guillemont and the ground to the east of Guillemont was kept under artillery fire. At 10.30 p.m. on the 11th the 17th Liverpools (89th Bde.) set off for a renewed attempt on the wood, and they advanced from the sunken road to the east of the brickworks. They were fortunate as the Germans had been carrying out a relief in the wood which had been held up; this delay coincided with the Liverpools attack and they were able to enter the wood unopposed. At 1 a.m. the relieving Germans were surprised to find the Liverpools in the wood and they were forced back.

On the 12th July a new line was also dug to connect the Liverpools' line with the Bedfords' in the western wedge of the wood. A fresh attempt by the Germans to advance on Maltz Horn Trench and Trônes Wood from an easterly direction was discovered early enough for it to be checked by the combined fire of the British and French artillery. The Germans had to return to their second line trench.

The 90th and 89th Bdes. were relieved after being involed in the wood fighting for three days and their role was taken over by the 18th Div. The 90th Bde. was withdrawn to Bois Celestins and their German opponents, the 182nd Regiment, returned to a sheltered valley between Morval and Ginchy. In the period from the 8th to 12th July the 30th Div. had casualties that totalled 1,934 and these included 250 killed as well as 1,272 wounded and 412 missing.

It was planned that the British Fourth Army Offensive against the German second position would be carried out at 3.20 a.m. on the 14th July, and the capture of Trônes Wood was necessary to the success of this advance in order to secure the right flank of the attack against Longueval, and to allow the British guns to move forward on the northern slope of Caterpillar Valley, this would support the main thrust against the German defences. Rawlinson thus wanted the wood taken at all costs by midnight on the 13th/14th July. The 18th Div. arrived on the evening of the 12th and the 55th Bde. took over the front line trenches, the 7th Buffs to Maltz Horn Trench and the 7th R.W. Kents to the south of Trônes Wood, and the 7th Queen's and 8th East Surreys were to be in support. The attack began at 7 p.m. on the 13th July. The Buffs were to hold Maltz Horn Trench and also capture the German strong point on the Guillemont Road, the R.W. Kents were to push on through the Wood or that part south of the railway and the Queen's were to attack the north part of the wood from the direction of Longueval Alley. The plan then was for the eastern side of the wood which faced Guillemont to be consolidated. The R.W. Kents suffered heavily in going across the sunken road to Trônes Wood, mainly from artillery fire. Nevertheless they entered the wood and went past the newly dug Liverpool–Bedford Trench line. However they were soon checked by the Germans in the centre of the wood around the southern part of Central Trench. Two Companies did manage to get as far as the railway line but lost contact with the remainder of their companies. The HQ of the 7th R.W. Kents at this time was the brickworks at Montauban.

The Germans continued to hold the strong point on the Guillemont Road and the Buffs were unable to capture it. The Queen's attack was met by machine gun and rifle fire from the north-west side of the wood and most of the attack was checked before it even reached the wood. From the British point of view the situation was very unsatisfactory and the attack on the Second Line was in jeopardy. It was therefore decided that the 54th Bde. should replace the 55th Bde. immediately and it was hoped that they would have greater success and gain the wood which meant that the main attack would be unaffected. The plan was now to approach from the south and sweep straight through to the north, and to then establish a defensive flank along the eastern edge facing Guillemont. The 6th Northamptons and the 12th Middlesex had gathered in the sunken road to the south of the wood and the 6th Northamptons reached this edge of the wood despite suffering from shell and rifle fire. They rushed the end of the Central Trench and overcame the Germans in that position. Colonel Maxwell of the 12th Middlesex took command and formed defensive lines drawn from the various units as well as from the parties of the R.W. Kents who had been in the wood all night. This line was then advanced and in its path it drove the remaining Germans out of the wood to the east and north of the railway. They then made for Guillemont. By 9 a.m. the northern part of the wood was reached and the wood was clear of the enemy.

During the attack Sergeant Boulter of the 6th Northamptons was to gain the VC and was the first member of his Regiment to gain this award. He was born in 1892 and the citation says that when one company and part of another company were held up in the attack on Trônes Wood by a hostile machine gunner, causing many casualties, Sergeant Boulter, with utter contempt of danger, and in spite of being severely wounded in the shoulder advanced alone in front of the gun, and bombed the gun team from their position. This very gallant act not only saved many casualties, but was of great military value, as it materially expedited the operation of clearing the enemy out of the wood, thus covering the flank of the whole attacking force. It was during the sweep to the apex of the wood that Boulter gained his VC.

The enemy made no attempt to retake the wood but subjected it to incessant shelling by heavy guns. The 53rd Bde. moved up to support the 54th until the troops of the 30th Div. were relieved on the 17th July at 3.30 a.m. It would be interesting to know if Colonel Maxwell succeeded where others failed simply by the force of his command or if it was simply a case of the enemy being finally worn down by the whole business of the continuous taking of the wood and then losing it. One wonders if they had prepared to withdraw anyway. The action of Maxwell in arranging the attack from the various units is well documented and I would like to quote briefly from his own view of the action which certainly shows us that he was a successful commanding officer. He is talking about the organising of the scattered bodies in order to make a drive through the wood. He had about five officers all told as the others were out of action. He said that the advance through the wood began very slowly and that the men were very shaken and jumpy because of the clamour and continuous shell fire and the problems of even going forward through the debris of the previous fighting and the fallen trees. Instead of organising the attack and controlling it with the use of runners he found that it would only succeed if he led from the front and steadied the men. There was a tendency to go forward in single file behind him but he made the line spread out, the men had fixed bayonets, and he encouraged them by ordering them to also fire ahead which gave them confidence. After dealing with the Germans in the centre of the wood, the extended line continued on slowly driving out the Germans like beaters in a pheasant shoot. When they had got to the north of the wood they didn't show themselves, for fear of reprisals from the German artillery.

Some observers consider the action of the 6th Northamptons and the 12th Middlesex to be one of the finest actions of the War, but I think it true to say that it would not have been the success it was without the personal leadership and example of Maxwell.

Between the 8th and the 14th July the wood had changed hands several times. The terribleness of the conditions in the wood cannot be emphasised too strongly. They were to remain unspeakable for several weeks. A Company of the 11th R. Fus. assisted the 12th Middlesex in their push through the wood and in the early hours of the 15th July they ran into a barrage on the Maricourt–Briqueterie Road. On the 18th July Captain Hoare gained the DSO when he was with two NCO's one of whom was wounded and the other of whom was buried alive. Hoare dug him out and saved his life. On the same day their battalion was relieved and in fact left the Somme area.

A Mr. L. J. Ounsworth (Cpl. Signaller) in an interview recorded with the Imperial War Museum said that on or around the 17th July that they visited Trônes Wood, and that at that time there were no trees intact at all, just stumps of a low height, with tree tops all mixed up with them as was barbed wire. There were dead bodies all over the place from both sides. He saw a concrete emplacement which the Germans would have observed from. The ground was completely open, and even sticking up a flag brought an immediate retaliation from the German artillery. Ounsworth says in his interview 'so we got out of that'.

It was during this period that Bernard Montgomery (in the Second World War the victor at El Alamein), with the 104th Bde. (35th Div.), wrote home on 20th July saying that they were ordered to take part in a suicidal attack, and on the 23rd July they were holding the front line to the east of Trônes Wood. Facing them was Guillemont Farm, with Waterlot Farm to their left. Maltz

Horn Farm he wrote was in no man's land. On the 27th July he wrote home again saying that they had had a hellish time and that on the morning of the 26th July he had gone up to Trônes Wood to extricate one of their battalions who had had a particularly bad time. On the 31st July the 104th Bde. was withdrawn, decimated and exhausted, to Happy Valley. In early August a concrete pillbox just south of the empty sunken road Trônes Wood–Guillemont Road was the cause of many casualties. Around this time one of the Suffolk Battalions moved up into the line to the south-west of Trônes Wood close to Maltz Horn Farm.

Capt. F. C. Hitchcock's Leinster Battalion was still employed in mid August in digging a communication trench called Leinster Avenue that went through Trônes Wood. The Battalion was situated in the ruins of the northern side of Carnoy where they managed to get cover in the cellars. On the 28th August the 21st Manchesters (91st Bde. 7th Div.) were established in a line between Trônes Wood and Delville Wood. Battalion HQ was in the quarry at the north end of Bernafay Wood. On the 31st August they moved to Pommiers Trench and Battalion HQ was to the north of Trônes Wood.

On the 15th September the 9th Norfolks moved back in the evening to trenches close to Trônes Wood after being involved in 'an unfortunate action' according to the regimental history.

In the latter half of September Max Plowman of the 11th West Yorks (69th Bde. 23rd Div.) wrote that they were halted one day at midday on sloping ground above Trônes Wood, waiting while the cooks at their Field Kitchens did their best, in the drizzling rain to make a hot stew. On this slope a number of tarpaulins had been stretched over the ground tentwise in order to provide low shelters, and into these the men scrambled to get out of the wet. Others went off to explore the dugouts in Trônes Wood below them. They later returned and recounted the horrors that they had seen in the wood. At dusk they marched away from the gruesome place through Guillemont and Ginchy.

Geoffrey Malins the War Office Photographer wrote that around 25th September he made his way towards Trônes Wood, on the outskirts of which the Guards had a DS. Many casualties were there lying about on stretchers in all directions, waiting to be taken to CCSs. On the 26th September Dundas of the Scots Guards reported that he was still in Trônes Wood and that his line was behind the front on the forward slope of Flers Road. On the 2nd October Sergeant Skelton of the 3rd Public Schools Battalion reported that they had moved into Nissen huts in the area of Trônes Wood, which was constantly shelled. During this period they were visited by the Prince of Wales. In October Frank Richards of the 2nd R. Welch Fus. says in his book that they returned to the sunken road on the edge of Trônes Wood, where they too were in huts, perhaps the same as those mentioned by the 3rd Public Schools.

Aubrey Smith of the LRB (56th Div.) wrote that in early October he had been taking his water cart beyond Trônes Wood and despite efforts of clearance parties there were still traces of the severe fighting that had gone on in the wood. The wood was really one vast cemetery and by no means had all the bodies been buried. Just inside the hedge on the far side were the remains of what had once been the British front line trench. Beyond lay the land from where many fruitless attempts to take Guillemont had been launched. Smith came across Raymond Asquith's grave which was marked by a wooden cross amongst a handful of other graves by the roadside. At a meeting on 3rd October the DCF (Directeur des Chemins de Fer) suggested that for the sake of uniformity of material and therefore convenience of maintenance the second rail line which it was intended to lay from Plateau to Trônes Wood should itself be laid with British material beyond Trônes Wood station. The main line and any points and crossings on it should be laid with French materials.

The Queen's Westminsters (56th Div.) during the battle for the Transloy Ridges moved at noon on the 7th October across country tracks, to a position to the east of Trônes Wood, where they remained until the evening. The Battalion was then placed at the disposal of the 167th Bde. instead of the 169th Bde. after going forward to a point south of Ginchy.

The 2nd R. Welch Fus. on the 22nd October resumed a march across country tracks that had thawed which made the going very heavy for the men; and the transport skidded on the muddy slopes, and strung out as wagons got stuck. They left it to collect in its allotted part in a vast expanse of mud at Carnoy, and marched across to Trônes Wood, which was a ruin of branches, riven trunks, standing or fallen, amidst shell holes and crumbling trenches. With only little overhead shelter they huddled for warmth for a few hours around green wood fires, blinking and choking.

On the 24th October the 4th Suffolks (98th Bde. 33rd Div.) moved in very wet weather into Trônes Wood and four days later occupied some poor front line trenches on newly gained ground in front of Lesboeufs. In early November the 6th Dorsets (50th Bde. 17th Div.) were in a rest camp in the wood which consisted of shelters of tarpaulins over pits. A few braziers of smoke were the only method of getting dry. There was a covered approach to the wood from the west, called Trench Alley, while the southern part was commanded by the Maltz Horn Ridge.

In early November the 33rd Div. moved to the forward area and on the 2nd bivouacked close to Trônes Wood. The weather had broken and the roads were a morass of treacly mud through which stuck out tree stumps which were supposed to form foundations. Cover of every description had been swept away by shell fire and every yard of ground was pitted by shell holes. Repeated attacks were carried out on the 3rd and 4th November in the area of Hazy Trench, Antelope, German and Brimstones Trenches. The enemy had put out a lot of wire and the thick mists at that time prevented accurate observation. The ground was a quagmire covered with shell holes which made an attack impossible.

General Jack in his diary said that on the 7th November his battalion the 2nd W. Yorks moved forward five miles to bivouacs in Trônes Wood, relieving the 19th Bde. 'At Trônes Wood we found the nearly officerless remnant of the 5th Cameronians, who had just suffered heavily, still in possession of our bivouac'. The Scots refused to vacate this "wretched spot" before the appointed time. They were therefore, forced to sit in the rain for an hour before the Scotsmen had vacated their scraps of shelter and several bell tents. Battalion HQ was housed in an old German trench blocked at one end by a door, roofed with some sheets of corrugated iron, with sandbags filling the cracks. There was a stove also to his joy, which had been 'purloined from Sidney Rogerson's batman.'

Rogerson in his book *Twelve Days* wrote that the camp was situated in an open space of what had once been grassland between the mangled remains of Trônes and Bernafay Woods. The distance was shrouded by rain and mist, from out of which the boom of gunfire came distant and muffled. 'Camp 34' itself was camp only in name and a few forlorn groups of rude tarpaulin-sheet shelters huddled together, as though they shrank from the surrounding desolation. In his book of the Irish Guards Rudyard Kipling said that the trenches to the north of Lesboeufs were reached by interminable duckboards from Trônes Wood and over the battered Flers Ridge. There were no communication trenches.

On the 15th November General Jack was again at the Briqueterie Camp. It had been a very wet morning and the battalion had marched four miles to Citadel Camp, near Fricourt. At Bernafay crossroads a young officer was directing the traffic duties in a most business like manner! On the 18th November the Citadel Camp was dry but 'perishing cold'. The battalion was officially described as resting but at 6 a.m. on the 16th it found 6 officers and 300 other ranks, who proceeding in motor lorries to the Trônes Wood area, were engaged after 3 o'clock in levelling a track for a light railway. It was high time that these lines were laid as the wastage of time and the exhaustion of men and animals was very great. An ADS or CP was at the wood in November.

Lt. Col. Hamilton better known as the 'Master of Belhaven' revisited the Somme battlefield in 1917. His party left their horses and went to Arrow Head Copse, where he noticed that there was a large railway junction at the corner of Trônes Wood.

There is a memorial obelisk dedicated to the 18th Division on the southern side of the wood close to the road.

Even today (1985), there are still several pristine German dugouts in the sunken road close to Trônes Wood.

Vadencourt

Vadencourt is a village adjacent to Contay and is mostly known as a former walking wounded CP. Cases were often taken there by rail.

Varennes

Varennes is a village south of Acheux on the D 74 road. It was much used as a billeting village and there is a cemetery just outside it on the north side of the road to Léalvillers, formed by the 39th CCS in August, which has many graves from burials that came about as a result of its use by mobile field ambulances of several Divisions.

Vauchelles

Vauchelles is right out of the Somme region to the south-west of Doullens and north-west of Flixecourt. Nevertheless it was used as a Divisional Rest Station both at the beginning and at the end of the battle.

Vaux

There are two places of this name, the first is to the east of Corbie on the D 42 road on the north bank of the Somme river. Many battalions spent time there including the 2nd HLI (5th Bde. 21st Div.) who camped on the river bank before going up the line. On 9th July the village was the home of the 6th Cavalry Bde. and on the 13th the village was described as being 'full of cavalry'. This is a reference to their intended use for the High Wood battles in mid July. On the 21st July a battalion belonging to the DLI was camped in the village.

The other Vaux is little more than a small collection of houses and is north-east of Bray between Suzanne and Curlu . . . Fraser-Tytler often mentioned it in his book *Field Guns in France* and noted that in November he rode back to his former position in Vaux Valley only to find that his former 'beautiful gunpits' were now being used as stables by French officers' chargers. His former OP had been blown out but the lower chamber was still intact.

Vecquemenont

The village is due east of Amiens and south of Daours. There was a railway here and at the beginning of the battle five trains were ready to take away the wounded. Fourteen more trains had to be brought up on the 2nd July in order to cope with the enormous number of casualties. The village was mostly used as a CCS and for a time an Indian Field Ambulance was established there.

Vignacourt

Vignacourt was well behind the lines to the west of the Doullens–Amiens road, west of Villers Bocage and between there and Flixecourt. Although it was far from the lines it was used for training and one battalion that was here was the 8th Norfolks (53rd Bde. 18th Div.) between 17th June and 1st July. They then marched eastwards to Hénencourt Wood behind Albert. On 10th July C. E. W. Bean the Australian historian came south and stayed in the village for a short time, and on 25th August the 2nd Scots Gds. were here having previously been at Hem.[8]

Warloy–Baillon

Warloy–Baillon is a village to the west of Albert on the D 91 road to the south of Varennes and a couple of miles to the north of the Amiens–Albert road. It contains a cemetery which is the Communal Cemetery and Extension. The village was always behind the lines and in July there was an emergency hospital established in the village with 62 beds. One of X Corps MDS was also established here.

One of the men buried in the Cemetery is Lt. Col. P. W. Machell who was killed on 1st July in the area of Leipzig Salient with the 11th Border Battalion which he had virtually raised single-handed from the Border Counties between 1914 and 1916. He was 54 and is buried in the Communal Cemetery Extension. There is a bronze wreath at the foot of his grave. Another 'notable' buried in the Cemetery is Maj. Gen. Ingouville-Williams commanding officer of the 34th Div. who was killed by shell fire after reconnoitering in the vicinity of Mametz Wood when walking back from Contalmaison to reach his car which was at Montauban. He was formerly with the Buffs. One of the officers who attended the funeral was C. S. Collison of the 11th Royal Warwicks.

On 9th July the 37th Bde. HQ of the 12th Div. moved to the village and on 10th August King George Vth visited the special hospital for abdominal cases before going on to Senlis. It was an Advanced Operating Centre that had been established by Field Ambulance.

Warlincourt

Warlincourt is south of the Doullens–Arras Road (D 925) and was in the sector used by the 46th Midland Division before the battle began. It was associated in particular with the 4th and 5th Lincoln Battalions (138th Bde.) of this Division. The Divisional HQ was at St. Amand to the south-east. On the 26th June the 4th and 5th Lincolns had moved from Humbercamps to huts at Warlincourt. On 28th June final orders were received for the attack on Gommecourt planned for 1st July. The assembly point was the Corps Line Trench which ran north and south 500 yards east of Souastre, between Bienvillers–Souastre and Foncquevillers–Souastre Roads. After a postponement the men were ready to go at 6 p.m. on 30th June and the advance party proceeded to their stations and at 9 p.m. the 5th Batt. marched off from their huts at Warlincourt, to the strains of the 'Lincolnshire Poacher' from the band. They took up their assembly positions in the Corps Line trench in front of Souastre.

Gommecourt Salient casualties were brought here as well as to Doullens railway halt. The Third Army CCS was established close to the railway.

Bois de Warnimont

The Bois de Warnimont is on the D 176 Road to the east of Bus and south of Couin. It is in a valley, and in mid May there were huts and tents in the wood which were pitched out of sight under tall trees. A Concert Party named 'The Tonics' used to visit the battalions camped here and the wood re-echoed with men's voices singing songs such as 'Nirvana'. In mid May the 12th Y & L, better known as the Sheffield Pals were here in what was described as a 'beautiful resting place'. On one occasion Haig inspected them during their training and had come through the wood with a brilliant cavalcade of Staff Officers, Lancers and Guards.

The wood was used regularly as a hutment camp behind the lines and those battalions who used it included those of the 7th Bde. (25th Div.) in mid July, and the 10th KRRC (59th Bde. 20th Div.) on 26th July before going on to bivouac at Sailly au Bois on the 27th, and Hébuterne Trenches on the 1st August. Also the 1st Scots Gds. were in the wood at the beginning of August, then described as a wooded plateau whose steep sides rose from the eastern side of the Bus–Authie Road. In early September the 1st Bucks. (145th Bde. 48th Div.) were here and in October the Hull Battalions played each other at football and rugger. By this time the camp had become very muddy.

Waterlot Farm

Waterlot Farm was a German strong point in their second line between Longueval and Guillemont. It was called a farm to distinguish it from buildings on the Longueval–Guillemont road, but was really a sugar refinery. The real farm was in the south-west quarter of Ginchy, which in mid July was still in German hands.

In mid July the right of XIII Corps had yet to capture the ruin of the sugar refinery and although troops entered it on the 15th they were forced to withdraw owing to heavy shelling.

The road from the refinery to Guillemont as far as the level railway station and just south then south-east to the cross roads east of the station was a Divisional Boundary. The refinery was captured and consolidated on 17th July. It had been used amongst other things as a base for pigeons for communication between Bernafay Wood and Corbie.

Although once the Allies had taken the sugar refinery they were to use it continuously as a base, there is little mention of it in accounts of the later stages of the battle. It was constantly bombarded by the Germans and by September the reserve trenches were in a very bad state. There were no dugouts and as the year went on conditions grew worse because relentless rain made the position very muddy. After the war the sugar refinery was rebuilt.

Wedge Wood

Wedge Wood is between Ginchy and Maurepas. It is wedge in shape and is north-west of Falfemont Farm. On 3rd September the 1st Bedfords (15th Bde. 5th Div.) took the wood, and part of the battalion reached the Ginchy Road in the area of the 95th Bde. (5th Div.). The 20th Div. which had taken Guillemont had also reached the Wedge Wood–Ginchy road but was in no condition to attack any further. Gunpits ran south of the wood which was under fire from Falfemont Farm. On the 4th the German line ran north-east of the valley close to the wood and Wedge Wood Farm had ceased to exist. Battalion HQ therefore moved to shell holes in the low ground to the south-west of Leuze Wood.

Welcome Woods

Welcome Woods was in the Corbie–Bray area. The 1st South African Infantry was here towards the end of June when they slept in huts. After breakfast they used to march a mile downhill to the Somme Canal where they washed and filled their dixies. Later they left the woods and marched to Sailly le Sec further along the Somme Valley towards Bray.

White City

The White City quarries were behind the British line at Beaumont Hamel and were excavated before the battle began. The position was so named because the excavated chalk appeared to observers as a 'white stroke across the countryside'. The position was on the reverse side of a chalk cliff which was about 40 feet high and could not be ranged accurately by the German artillery. Shells tended to skim over the cliff's edge and burst some 60 or 70 yards back from the cliff. Nevertheless the White City could be a pretty unhealthy spot! It was very important to the British in that they had a relatively secure headquarters very close to the line, and in the caves there was a battle HQ, dressing stations and dumps for the Royal Engineers etc.

On 1st July Lt. Col. C. Howkins of the 1/6 R. Warwicks was severely wounded here. There are many accounts of battalions as being in the White City Trenches and these include the 13th R. Welch Fus. (113th Bde. 38th Div.) in mid July and in the November battles when much of Beaumont Hamel was taken, the 22nd R. Fus., the 17th R. Fus. and the 16th HLI had their HQ here.

Wonderwork

The Wonderwork was behind the Hindenburg Trench which in turn was in front of the Leipzig Salient. It was a strong point that guarded the southern side of the Thiepval, and there was much fighting in order to secure it. On the 3rd September the CO of the 8th South Staffords (51st Bde. 7th Div.) was reported missing and was never found. On 14th September the Wonderwork was taken together with the German front line and in addition 250 yards of the Höhenzollern Trench to the right. The two battalions involved were the 8th DWR and the 9th West Yorks (32nd Bde. 11th Div.).

Y Ravine

Y Ravine is on the south side of Beaumont Hamel and can easily be reached from either Newfoundland Park or from the D 163 Road. In 1916 Station Road which led from Beaumont Hamel village south-eastwards was part of the objective of the 29th Div. for 1st July. The Ravine had steep banks in which numerous deep dugouts could safely stand the heaviest bombardments. In addition to being honeycombed with dugouts, it was crossed with numerous trenches. This meant that the garrison there could be relieved or supported from either Station Road or from the neighbouring trenches. The ravine ran about a half mile south of the village and has two arms that extend outwards at the western end, giving it a Y shape.

In his *The Old Front Line* John Masefield describes the Ravine as giving the British a great deal of trouble. He also says that the enemy sank shafts into the banks of the Ravine, tunnelled living rooms, both above and below the gulley bottom, linked the rooms with galleries, and cut hatchways and bolting holes that lead to the surface as well as to the gulley. In this gulley barracks, and in similar shelters cut in the chalk of the steeper banks near Beaumont Hamel, the enemy could hold ready large numbers of men to repel an attack or make a counter-attack.

On 1st July apart from the attack of the Newfoundlanders the ravine was also attacked by the 2nd SWB (87th Bde. 29th Div.) the 1st Borders and the 1st KOSB (87th Bde.), but with very little success. The starting point of the attacking battalions was St. John's Road between Auchonvillers and Hamel. The 1st Borders followed by the 2nd SWB had made towards the western end of the ravine and reached the area just to the north of the Newfoundlanders' attack. The SWB were wiped out by machine gun fire. Despite this disaster the 1st Borders were ordered to follow up and suffered very heavy losses too, at the hands of the German machine gunners.

Apart from 1st July the other time that Y Ravine comes into prominence is during the mid November attempts to take Beaumont Hamel. One witness at this time is the French liaison officer who worked with the British and who was also a painter, Paul Maze. He wrote in his book *A Frenchman in Khaki* that he made his way towards Y Ravine through destroyed barbed wire over caved-in trenches. The visibility couldn't have been worse. He reached a steep bank that rose before him and ascended to the top, from which he could barely see the bottom or opposite sides, he heard bombs exploding all along this blurred crevasse – the rest of the escort had gone below to inspect a tunnel that communicated with another dugout. He stepped down into darkness. He stretched out his map and located his position in front of Station Road. The fighting continually came from there, as well as from Beaucourt village, lying lost in the fog about a thousand yards away. It was evident to him that enemy troops and the Allies had got mixed up in the fog. Yet 'surprisingly', from all accounts the day had been a great success. Over 5,000 prisoners had been taken! The ravine had been reached by the 153rd Bde. of the 51st Highland Div. on 14th November and consolidated in Beaucourt Trench, north-west of Beaucourt.

After the war Henry Williamson described in his book *The Wet Flanders Plain* a visit to the ravine in 1925. 'The dugouts of the ravine had subsided, the dry-rotted timbers broke with a touch; the pistons and mainshaft and cylinders of an aeroplane rusted in the grasses'. Williamson wrote that he remembered the 'charred framework on the ridge above Station Road, with rifle barrels and holed helmets and burst minewerfer cases. Those dreaded oil drums of the minnies'.

Zollern Redoubt and Trench

Zollern Redoubt was part of the German redoubt system to the north of Thiepval village. Stuff Redoubt was to the immediate north-west. The trench ran from Thiepval village to the Redoubt then towards Courcelette, and the most eastern part was the first objective for the battle of 26th September of Thiepval Ridge. The section of Zollern Trench between Thiepval and Zollern Redoubt was part of the second objective and was reached on that day. The *Official History* notes that it was known that the Germans had withdrawn from the redoubt by 6.30 a.m. on the 27th. In *Haig's Great Push* the action is described in this way: 'on the right, our troops, advancing in three waves, carried the outer defences of Mouquet Farm, and pushing on, penetrated into Zollern Redoubt, which they stormed and proceeded to consolidate.' There is a connection here with Ivor Gurney the poet. He was with the 2nd/5th Glosters, a Territorial battalion, and appears to have been a signaller at the end of the Somme battle. Their Headquarters Office was in Zollern Trench in November. They had come to the Somme from the Laventie Line at the end of October. Gurney wrote songs in the trenches and his 'By a Bierside' is the first one that he was known to have composed in these circumstances. The song deals with a longing for peace and security left behind at home and a troubled concern with the nature of death. The words were written by John Masefield. Later Gurney was to write 'In Flanders' at Crucifix Corner near Thiepval in January 1917. In Gurney's book of poems entitled *Severn To Somme* he wrote 'that those who buy or read the book with the idea of obtaining information about the doings of the 2/5th Glosters would be disappointed'.

A note on the casualties incurred in the Somme battle

I have no wish to enter the controversy over the casualties incurred in the Battle of the Somme in 1916, as the subject has been written about on many occasions. If readers wish to look deeply into the controversy then they should consult the following books or sources: the *Official History* Volumes, the Liddell Hart Archive at King's College, London, the writings of Winston Churchill, Lloyd George, Sir Charles Oman, G. Wynne and M. Williams. All these writers are in the main concerned with the British viewpoint and the continuing re-assessment of the casualty figures.

The main reason for the continuing debate I suppose is firstly to get at the figure which is the most accurate, and secondly with some commentators to show that the Germans suffered more than the Allies. However comparisons are not easy, as the two sides treated their casualties statistically differently. The British took their figures from the daily roll calls recorded at CCSs. This figure was therefore always too high as it included those men missing or taken prisoner who subsequently returned. Thus this figure had always to be adjusted downward. The British casualty figure is now accepted to be in the region of 419,000.

French casualty figures are always quoted as being in the region of 204,000. It is the German figure which is the most difficult figure to agree, and as I write I have twelve sets of German casualty figures in front of me, and this is without going into the subject very deeply. The figure which I prefer is 419,989 which I have taken from the German Medical History, Volume III, and this covers the period of the Allied bombardment from 21st June until the end of November. General Edmonds wrote in the preface to the *Official History* of the Battle of the Somme, Volume II: 'The German Historians seem to be torn between the two conflicting sentiments: first a desire to show how heavily their troops suffered before they gave up, and secondly, a determination to assert that they did not suffer as heavily as their opponents.'

However Edmonds himself had an obsession about the casualty figures on both sides which is probably what the controversy is really about, and he does appear to be clearly guilty of trying to make the figures tell the story in the best light for the Allies, and at the same time show how the Germans lost more men than they owned up to. I am afraid that the reason for this can only be a political one in that he was trying to protect reputations, and if one needs evidence then one only has to look at some of the correspondence between C. E. W. Bean the Official Australian Historian. Bean sent Edmonds the drafts of the volumes that he was compiling and as the letter quoted on page 412 shows he actually took note of what Edmonds said to him and made suitable adjustments to his text.

However it is in the far more revealing second paragraph that the Edmonds case is severely damaged in that Bean quotes John Buchan as saying that the

Commonwealth of Australia,
Historian,
Victoria Barracks,
Sydney

28th August 1928

CONFIDENTIAL

Dear Edmonds,

Many thanks for your final comments upon my Volume III. I have again modified the judgements contained in it by bringing out more clearly the undoubted damage inflicted on the German morale by the Somme offensive, damage which was obvious at the time and which we all recognised.

You ask who was the official who informed me that the authorities recognised that the offensive of 1916 could be maintained until the British had lost 500,000 men. I can of course only give you the name in the strictest confidence. It was John Buchan, then working in the Foreign Office, who told me this on the opening day of the Somme offensive, while we were watching the artillery bombardment. I made a full note in my diary (which is now one of the most important of the Australian records). Buchan was in touch with G.H.Q. and with the British Cabinet and, to some extent, in the confidence both of Ministers and of the staff – which we war correspondents were not. I don't know from which source the information came, but there can be no possible question of its truth, for he was speaking of a conversation of which he had recent personal knowledge, and he was a most reliable man. I don't know if he would remember the matter now, but you have my leave to mention it to him if you care to do so.

Yours sincerely,
C. E. W. BEAN.

Sir James Edmonds, C.B., C.M.G.,
Historical Section (Military Branch),
Committee of Imperial Defence,
Audit House,
Victoria Embankment,
London EC4, England.

Ref. LH/Edmonds VI/2

British Authorities could maintain the Somme Offensive up until a loss of 500,000 men had occurred. This sentence punches a hole right through Edmonds' whole thesis, in that the British were therefore actually allowing for another 80,000 casualties if one accepts that 419,000 is the nearest accurate figure. It is interesting to note here that in 1982 the figure given for maximum casualties for the Task Force to the South Atlantic was 1,000 men*.

For the wounded on the Somme the British figures were close to 316,000 and of these the great majority were evacuated by Ambulance Train, 8,739

*Lord Robert Blake – *Conservative Party from Peel to Thatcher.* Fontana 1985.

were transported by barge and 6,183 by road. In addition to this figure the figures for the sick were 13,766.

To sum up then it is obvious that although the British and Germans might be around the 419,000 figure, it is the French figure of 204,000 casualties that tips the scale in favour of the Germans. It can hardly be surprising that for the first part of the Somme battle at least, that the Allies lost more men than the enemy did. Although initially nearly 30% of our shells were defective the Germans were often well protected by their deep dugouts and their superior positions in defending what was often high ground or the best position on the battlefield.

The officer casualties were approximately 4.8% of the total British casualties which was three or four times the corresponding German figure. However the Germans might have 'economised' on officers but they did not 'economise' on their NCO's who had been very highly trained, and at the beginning of the battle there were still many left in the German Army who had been in at the beginning of the war, but their ranks were savagely depleted by the end of the Somme battle.

THE SOMME, 1916: The end of the Battle.

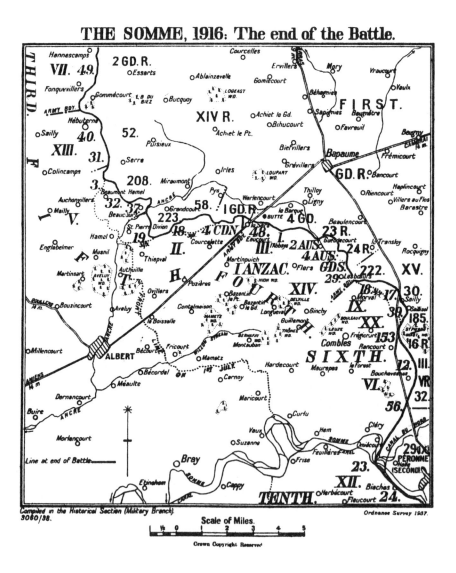

Compiled in the Historical Section (Military Branch). 3060/38.

Ordnance Survey 1937.

Scale of Miles.

½ 0 1 2 3 4 5

Chronology of Events

MM is the daily measurement of rainfall, and the two degree measurements represent the highest and lowest Fahrenheit temperature each day. Trace − minimal rainfall.

June 23rd: Rain 2mm. Temperature 79°-55° windy.

June 24th: Rain 1mm. 72°-52° overcast. Bombardment begins that lasts for 7 days.

June 25th: Rain 1mm. 71°-54° windy.

June 26th: Rain 6mm. 72°-52° cloudy.

June 27th: Rain 8mm. 68°-54° overcast and cloudy. Aeroplane work interfered with. Haig visits Rawlinson, they observe from the Grandstand near Querrieu.

June 28th: Rain 2mm. 68°-50° overcast. The rain was very heavy. Commencement of battle delayed until 1st July at 7.30 a.m., instead of the 29th of June.

June 29th: Some rain. 66°-52° cloudy − low clouds and strong winds all day. If battle had begun on this day then conditions under foot would have been very slippery.

June 30th: 72°-48° overcast, and high wind, but conditions improved towards the evening. Rawlinson noted in his War Diary that the total number of men involved at the start of the battle were about 500,000, that there were 1,500 guns of which 450 were of a large calibre, 150,000 rounds were fired in the day and 50,000 in the night into the enemy front lines.

July 1st: 79°-52° clear sky. Very hazy but the mist lifted at 7.30 a.m. when the Allied attack began. The offensive was a combined Franco−British one on a 25-mile front both north and south of the Somme. The British captured Montauban and Mametz. The French attacked towards Peronne and reached the outskirts of Hardecourt and Curlu. To the north-west of the Albert−Bapaume road the British made little progress against the German defences except for a small gain at the Leipzig Redoubt to the south of Thiepval. They had failed at Gommecourt, Serre, Beaumont Hamel, Thiepval and la Boiselle. Casualties were in the vicinity of 57,000, the highest casualty figure that the British Army ever suffered. There were nine VC awards that stemmed from the day's fighting.

E. N. F. Bell at Thiepval, G. S. Cather near Hamel, J. L. Green at Foncquevillers, W. F. McFadzean at Thiepval, W. P. Ritchie to the north of Beaumont Hamel, G. Sanders near Thiepval, R. Quigg near Hamel, J. Y. Turnbull at the Leipzig Redoubt, and S. W. Loudoun-Shand near Fricourt.

July 2nd: 75°-54° clear sky, fine. Fricourt is surrendered by the Germans. Good deal of cloud in the morning. Rawlinson's estimate of casualties was 30,000. He was visited by Haig and Kiggell. Robertson lunched with him.

July 3rd: Rain 2mm. 68°-55° thunderstorms to the south-east. Fine day with some clouds. La Boisselle was captured and part of Ovillers. T. G. Turrall won the VC at la Boisselle.

July 4th: Rain 17mm. 70°-55° overcast, thunderstorms, windy and cool air. La Boiselle taken, as well as Bernafay Wood.

July 5th: 72°-52° low cloud until evening. Horseshoe Trench taken. D. S. Bell gained the VC there. T. O. L. Wilkinson and Adrian Carton de Wiart both gained the VC at la Boisselle. Many Germans were assembling in Mametz Wood.

July 6th: Rain 2mm. 70°-54° overcast and dull with showers at intervals. Attack on Trônes Wood was delayed for 24 hours. Lloyd George was appointed Secretary of State for War and Lord Derby Under Secretary for War.

July 7th: Rain 13mm. 70°-59° overcast and showery. Contalmaison captured as well as Leipzig Redoubt. Heavy rain in the evening and Contalmaison lost. The British failed to get into Mametz Wood.

July 8th: Rain 8mm. 73°-52° overcast. British penetrate Trônes Wood. Haig visited Rawlinson.

July 9th: 70°-53° cloudy and fine. Large fire reported at Martinpuich and Station. Trônes Wood fighting continues. E. S. Montagu appointed Minister of Munitions.

July 10th: 82°-48° overcast, very hot, no wind, thick cloud bank. Heavy fighting in Trônes Wood. Progress in the fight for Mametz Wood by the 38th Div.

July 11th: 68°-52° overcast. Contalmaison was held against counter-attacks. Fighting still in Trônes and Mametz Woods.

July 12th: Rain-trace. 68°-?? fine but overcast. Mametz Wood totally captured, Contalmaison counter-attacks repulsed. Plans for dawn attacks on the 14th were finalised.

July 13th: Rain-trace. 70°-54° overcast, strong west wind and a little rain. End of the Battle of Albert which began on the 1st July.

July 14th: Fine but overcast. British attack the German second line beginning at 3.25 a.m. under very heavy bombardment. They captured Longueval and Bazentin le Petit and the whole of Trônes Wood where W. E. Boulter gained the VC. The Second Cavalry was sent in to the battle with High Wood as their objective. Haig and Foch came to see Rawlinson to congratulate him on the success of the dawn advance.

July 15th: 72°-47° misty in the morning which turned into a bright clear day. Beginning of the battle for Delville Wood. High Wood not captured.

July 16th: Rain 4mm. 73°-55° dull and overcast. The British consolidate their positions and withdraw from High Wood.

July 17th: 70°-59° misty and overcast. Waterlot Farm taken to the east of Longueval, Ovillers completely cleared of Germans. Battle of Bazentin Ridge ends.

July 18th: 72°-52° overcast. Attack on Fromelles to the north of the Somme battle-field. Germans make strong counter-attacks at Longueval and Delville Wood. W. F. Faulds gains the VC at the last named. Drizzling rain after a dull morning.

July 19th: 70°-50° cloudy. Germans attack Longueval and fighting in Delville Wood continues. Attacks by the enemy on Waterlot Farm and Trônes Wood repulsed by the 35th Div. (Bantam).

July 20th: 75°-52° fine morning, clear skies. Longueval and Delville Wood fighting continues. J. J. Davies and A. Hill both awarded the VC for their role in the Delville Wood fighting and T. W. H. Veale also gained the VC to the east of High Wood. William la Touche Congreve is awarded the VC for actions between July 6th and the 20th. He loses his life to a sniper's bullet.

July 21st: 75°-52° fine day with clear skies. Fighting at High Wood. Haig visits Rawlinson and impresses on him the need to capture the village of Guillemont.

July 22nd: Rain-trace. 77°-55° clear sky although dull early on. Violent fighting on the front Pozieres to Guillemont. New German trench line had been discovered from the air in front of the Switch Line to the north-west of High Wood.

July 23rd: 68°-54° overcast. The second phase of the Somme battle begins and this includes fierce fighting in and around the village of Pozieres. The British recapture the whole of Longueval but the Germans retake the northern part of the village. The outskirts of Guillemont changed hands twice. At Pozieres two men gained the VC. J. Leak and Sec. Lt. Blackburn. Rawlinson noted in his diary that the Germans had not relinquished their attacks in Verdun although they had skimmed their line in order to release troops for the Somme battle.

July 24th: 70°-55° overcast and very hot. Fighting at Pozieres continues and the

Germans counter-attack at High Wood and Guillemont. T. Cooke gained the VC at Pozieres in the dates July 24th/25th.

July 25th: 66°-50° overcast. The current series of attacks against High Wood end. The Germans counter-attack in the Longueval and Bazentin areas. Pozieres is almost entirely in Allied hands and the British push along the Albert–Bapaume road. Rawlinson visited Fricourt which he described as a series of craters.

July 26th: 75°-55° windy day. The whole of Pozieres village in Allied hands.

July 27th: Rain 8mm. 81°-61° hazy day that became a clearer afternoon. Further British attacks and gains in Delville Wood. Fighting continued near Pozieres and at Longueval. A. Gill won the VC at Delville Wood.

July 28th: 77°-59° overcast and hot day. The British captured Longueval and Delville Wood and made further progress near Pozieres. Castleton gained the VC near Pozieres. Haig visited Rawlinson.

July 29th: 81°-57° overcast. German attempts to retake Delville Wood fail. Hand to hand fighting to the north and north-east of Pozieres. The Australians fail to take the Windmill near Pozieres and Munster Alley still in contention.

July 30th: 82°-57° clear day and very hot. The British make progress east of Waterlot Farm and Trônes Wood. Large explosion at Martinpuich. G. Evans won the VC at Guillemont and J. Miller at Bazentin le Petit on the 30th/31st. The attack against Guillemont did not succeed.

July 31st: 82°-59° very hot day and hazy in the morning. Fighting for Guillemont continued. RFC bombed Martinpuich.

August 1st: 86°-61° very hot day. North of Bazentin le Petit the German counter-attack was repulsed. Heavy fighting at Verdun.

August 2nd: 88°-57°. German attack on Delville Wood repulsed. More heavy fighting at Verdun. Hottest day so far in the battle of the Somme.

August 3rd: 84°-57° hot and clear day. The British gained ground to the west of Pozieres and the French progressed at Verdun. An explosion at Courcelette caused smoke to rise 2,000 feet. In Britain Sir Roger Casement was hanged.

August 4th: 79°-52°. The Allies gained the German Second Line system on a front of 2,000 yards to the north of Pozieres. German counter-attacks at Verdun repulsed.

August 5th: 68°-48° clear day. The British advanced their line near Pozieres. Haig visits Rawlinson and is pleased at the Australian success near Pozieres, which included the taking of objectives and the capture of several hundred prisoners.

August 6th: 75°-52°. Slight Allied progress to the east of Pozieres towards Martinpuich. Private W. Short gained the VC at Munster Alley.

August 7th: 73°-50°. The British attacked the outskirts of Guillemont. German attacks to the north and north-east of Pozieres repulsed. The French progress at Verdun. Kiggell wrote to Rawlinson and indicated that reports of British casualties had been exaggerated at home.

August 8th: 77°-52°. British fighting at Guillemont continues. The Station was captured and the northern parts of the village, but not the southern end. G. G. Coury gained the VC near Arrow Head Copse.

August 9th: 84°-54°. Renewed Allied attacks against Guillemont fail. Capt. N. C. Chavasse won the VC at Guillemont and Private O'Meara at Pozieres for work done in the period August 9th/12th.

August 10th: Rain 4mm. 70°-55° heavy rain and low clouds throughout the day. King George Vth visits the front and Rawlinson takes him to the craters at Bois Français. The King tells Rawlinson of a Cabal at home that is out to oust Haig and curb the current offensive. The members of the Cabal include Lord French, Winston

Churchill and F. E. Smith. The British make progress to the north-west of Pozieres.

August 11th: 77°-59° stormy day and misty in the morning.

August 12th: Rain 1mm. 82°-63°. The British advance on a mile front north-west of Pozieres.

August 13th: 81°-59° windy day. Munster Alley was taken by the 15th Division.

August 14th: Rain 2mm. 77°-59° showery day.

August 15th: 75°-57°. The King returned to England after his visit to the Western Front. At night it rains hard.

August 16th: Rain 2mm. 75°-55°. The British advance west and south-west of Guillemont. Albert Ball took on five hostile aeroplanes in his Nieuport Scout.

August 17th: Rain 4mm. 72°-54° showery day with bright intervals.

August 18th: Rain 1mm. 70°-55° overcast day. Ground gained by the British towards Ginchy and Guillemont. Enemy aircraft crashes near High Wood. 33rd Division fail to progress at High Wood.

August 19th: Rain 2mm. 70°-50° overcast day. British gain ground, in Thiepval Ridge area.

August 20th: 72°-54° overcast day. Germans counter-attack near Thiepval.

August 21st: 72°-48°. Progress by the British north-west of Pozieres, Germans counter-attack near Thiepval.

August 22nd: 72°-52°. Two determined counter-attacks by the Germans south of Thiepval were beaten off. Haig visits Rawlinson and chides him about Guillemont still not being in British hands.

August 23rd: 72°-54°. Fighting continues to the south of Thiepval. Strong German attacks at Guillemont repulsed. Rawlinson hears that twelve tanks had arrived.

August 24th: 78°-55°. Further progress by the British towards Thiepval and the north-west part of Delville Wood. German attacks to the west of Ginchy driven off.

August 25th: Rain 8mm. 81°-61° overcast and cloudy day. German attack south of Thiepval repulsed and the enemy driven out of Delville Wood and a line established along the north-east edge.

August 26th: Rain 7mm. 75°-59°. The Germans counter-attacked near Thiepval. Rawlinson saw the tanks in training and was impressed with them but thought that their crews needed much more training for battle conditions.

August 27th: Rain 4mm. 73°-59°. The Third Brigade attacks Grevillers. Italy declares war on Germany.

August 28th: Rain-slight. 73°-59°. Because of the considerable rainfall of the previous few days the conditions were getting worse and some trenches were ankle deep in water. Kiggell visits Rawlinson and they discuss how best to use the tanks in battle. Rawlinson favours caution in their use.

August 29th: Rain-heavy, but no figures. 82°-59°. Since the battle began on July 1st the British have captured 266 German Officers, 15,203 other ranks, 86 guns and 160 machine guns.

Von Hindenburg appointed Chief of General Staff in place of Von Falkenhayn and Von Ludendorff Chief Quarter Master General.

August 30th: Rain 8mm. 63°-48° overcast and very wet day. The trenches at Guillemont are very wet and muddy.

August 31st: 70°-52° fine day. Fierce German attacks between Ginchy and High Wood repulsed. First sight of the German aircraft called the Albatros which was to turn the Air War in Germany's favour. This aircraft had twice the fire power of a British fighter and fired synchronised machine guns between its propellor blades. Albert Ball shoots down two enemy aircraft.

September 1st: 72°-52°. German attacks at High Wood fail but they are back again in the eastern side of Delville Wood.

September 2nd: 75°-52° windy day. Rawlinson inspects the tanks again and is not pleased with their training and handling.

September 3rd: Rain 4mm. 72°-50°. The Battle for Delville Wood ended and also that of Pozieres Ridge. The Battle for Guillemont was won by the British, but Ginchy was first taken and then lost. Four VC's were gained on this day; one by W. B. Allen near Mesnil and three at Guillemont; J. V. Holland, T. Hughes and D. Jones. Continuous fighting towards Falfemont Farm and High Wood.

September 4th: Rain 25mm. 66°-52° low clouds and showers all day. Another attack on Falfemont Farm fails. Haig has tea with Rawlinson and urges on him the necessity of pressing on and is pleased at the taking of Guillemont.

September 5th: 63°-54° overcast and cloudy day. East of Guillemont the Allied line is carried forward 1,500 yards and most of Leuze Wood is captured. The Allies now occupied the whole of the German second line. During the night Falfemont Farm taken.

September 6th: 70°-52° overcast. Guillemont consolidated and the British advance to Ginchy completed. Leuze Wood is secured. H. H. Asquith visits the front and inspects the ruins of Fricourt. He was accompanied by Maurice Hankey and Maurice Bonham-Carter. He lunches with Rawlinson.

September 7th: 70°-54° fine clear day with much aerial activity.

September 8th: 70°-55° fine warm day but overcast, until 1 p.m. The Gloucester Regiment lost heavily in an attack to the west end of High Wood.

September 9th: Rain 5mm. 75°-57°. Ginchy falls to the British. Trenches also taken to the north and east of Leuze Wood. L. Clarke wins the VC near Pozieres.

September 10th: Rain 1mm. 68°-57° overcast day. The Germans counter-attacked at Ginchy but were repulsed. The British line to the east of Guillemont was advanced. Rawlinson attends a conference which features the role of the tanks in the forthcoming battle.

September 11th: Rain-trace. 66°-54° overcast day. British artillery cause fires in German ammunition dump at Grandcourt. Rawlinson takes a break at Boulogne, to be ready for the September 15th attack.

September 12th: 72°-55° fine but dull. The French take the area to the south of Combles as far as the river. Intense British preparatory bombardment.

September 13th: 72°-52° dull and overcast day. The French progress to the south-east of Combles.

September 14th: 61°-41° windy day and cold. British storm trenches to the south-east of Thiepval and take the Wonderwork. Haig visits Rawlinson who is now back from Boulogne. He urges that Martinpuich should be attacked in earnest and that the Cavalry should be pushed out towards le Sars.

September 15th: 59°-43°. This day was one of great progress for the Allies and the British began the third phase of the Battle of the Somme by advancing on a six-mile front to a depth of 2,000 to 3,000 yards. Flers, Martinpuich, Courcelette and High Wood were all captured and tanks made their first ever appearance in battle. The French Army progressed to the south of Rancourt and captured a system of trenches north of le Priez Farm. There were three VC's awarded on this day; D. F. Brown gained his east of High Wood, J. V. Campbell at Ginchy and F. McNess close to Ginchy. During the days from September 15th to the 24th Manfred von Richthofen the future German ace shot down his first aircraft, and Albert Ball shot down four German aircraft in the same period. The day was cool with a morning mist and a slight ground haze. The main delay was that the Guards advancing towards Lesboeufs were held up by the Quadilateral German position. Rawlinson very pleased with the part played by the tanks in the advance.

September 16th: 66°-41° fine sunny day. The Germans counter-attacked at Courcelette but the British gained some territory. Danube Trench and Mouquet Farm were taken by the Allies. J. C. Kerr gained the VC at Courcelette. The New Zealanders made progress to the north and west of Flers.

September 17th: Rain 2mm. 63°-45°. A comparatively quiet day, consolidation at Martinpuich by the 15th Division. Haig visits Rawlinson and congratulates him on the progress of 15th and 16th September.

September 18th: Rain 13mm. 63°-46° continuous rain all day. The Sixth Division took the troublesome Quadrilateral between Ginchy and Bouleux Wood to a depth of a thousand yards.

September 19th: Rain 3mm. 55°-43° wet and windy day which hinders operations. Trenchard takes tea with Rawlinson and tells him that 400 aircraft have been got through since July 1st, from reserves now exhausted. Kiggell reports Haig's views as being that battle should continue until either a shortage of troops or a decline in the weather prevents further fighting.

September 20th: Rain 1mm. 61°-48° showery and unpleasant day. The Germans suffer reversals at the hands of the French close to Combles. Rawlinson delays the next attack to the 23rd of the month. The wind and rain hampered the bringing up of munitions. Haig visits Rawlinson, it is agreed that the Cavalry Division should be withdrawn.

September 21st: Rain-trace. 59°-48° cloudy and showery day. The New Zealanders have taken Cough Drop Alley and a good bit of the Flers Line, whilst the 1st Division captured Starfish Trench. Albert Ball destroys two more enemy aircraft.

September 22nd: 64°-41° fine sunny day with a misty morning. The ground conditions were much improved as a result of a drying day. The British advance to the east of Courcelette. William Robertson has tea with Rawlinson and tells him that Lloyd George is concerned about the number of casualties and Haig's direction of the battle. Battle of Flers–Courcelette ends.

September 23rd: 66°-43° a fine warm day. The operations delayed until the 23rd have been put off until the 25th. A quiet day with the 23rd Division making some ground to the east of Martinpuich.

September 24th: 72°-45° a misty morning that turned into a very fine and warm Autumn day. Enemy attacked unsuccessfully to the west of Lesboeufs.

September 25th: 73°-50° a cloudless day. A very successful day for the British and Lesboeufs and Morval were both captured. The village of Combles was hemmed in by the Allies and the French had progressed at Rancourt, Les Priez Farm, and Frégicourt. The Battle of Morval began. T. Jones gained the VC at Morval. Rawlinson was very pleased with the Allied progress.

September 26th: Rain-trace. 75°-54°. Fine day and another good one for the British advance. Combles fell to the Allies and Thiepval was at last captured. The Battle for Thiepval Ridge began. The British also stormed Guedecourt. R. E. Ryder and F. J. Edwards both gained the VC at Thiepval.

September 27th: Rain-trace. 72°-52° overcast with some showers in the afternoon. The British attack Stuff Redoubt and advance to the north of Flers, to the east of Eaucourt l'Abbaye. T. E. Adlam was awarded the VC for his gallantry during the days the 27th/28th September and A. C. T. White for his at Stuff Redoubt in the period September 27th and October 1st.

September 28th: Rain 1mm. 73°-54° a fine warm day with some showers. The British attack the Schwaben Redoubt on the crest of the Thiepval Plateau, and capture most of it. They advance to the north and north-east of Courcelette, between Martinpuich and Guedecourt. The French make progress at Morval and the Battles of Morval Ridge end. Rawlinson inspects the ground conditions and describes them as appalling. The ground is so completely flattened that the extension of railways is made impossible. The whole ground is covered with troops, guns, lines and bivouacs. 'A German airman could not drop a brick without killing something' he wrote.

September 29th: Rain 17mm. 61°-54° a very wet and windy day. Very poor weather for flying observation and for the condition of the roads. The British captured Destremont Farm which was a strongly defended group of buildings.

September 30th: 63°-41° fine day but overcast at times. The Thiepval Ridge was captured except for part of Schwaben Redoubt. Also an advance made at the south of Eaucourt l'Abbaye.

October 1st: 63°-41° a fine sunny day. The clocks were put back one hour at 1.00 a.m. The Battle of Transloy Ridge and Ancre Heights began. The British attacked on the line Eaucourt-le Sars (on the Albert–Bapaume Road) and captured all their objectives on a front of 3,000 yards. Eaucourt was occupied. R. B. Bradford gained the VC at Eaucourt l'Abbaye and Albert Ball drove down two enemy aircraft near Gommecourt.

October 2nd: Rain 3mm. 57°-45° a wet and misty day. The airmen could not fly in the conditions. The Germans counter-attacked in Eaucourt and the British failed to hold le Sars.

October 3rd: Rain-trace. 70°-50° rainy and misty day. The British recover Eaucourt l'Abbaye. In the afternoon Rawlinson made the first of two visits to local RFC Fighter Squadrons.

October 4th: Rain 4mm. 66°-52° overcast with a very wet morning, finer in the afternoon. The next operations are postponed for 48 hours by Rawlinson because of the poor weather. The roads and tracks are getting into a worse state each day because of the amount of recent rainfall. H. Kelly wins the VC at le Sars. Albert Ball posted back to the United Kingdom.

October 5th: Rain 6mm. 66°-54° overcast, windy with showers. The British advance north-west of Eaucourt and the French make progress east of Morval. The ground dried a little but in the evening it was raining. Ground conditions are increasingly difficut for the collection of casualties and the bringing up of stores and munitions.

October 6th: Rain 2mm. 70°-57° sunny day that turns to rain at night. Rawlinson decides that the operations should go ahead on the 7th. The ground dried out a little owing to sun and wind. Pack horses have been used in carrying ammunition and food for the infantry. Haig visits Rawlinson after lunch. Haig expresses the view that he wants the battle to go on until the winter unless the weather makes it impossible.

October 7th: Rain-trace. 66°-52° fine day, windy and rain at night. The wind and low clouds interfered with flying, but the attack began nevertheless, at 1.45 p.m. The British and French advance on the Albert–Bapaume Road. The British advance a thousand yards and capture le Sars. The French advance to the north-east of Morval and reach to within 200 yards of Sailly. Rawlinson hears that Lord French is to visit the French.

October 8th 64°-54° rain and then fine. North and east of Courcelette, the British line was advanced. The enemy attacked and regained some trenches. The French have success at Sailly–Saillisel. The Canadians capture and then lose Regina

Trench and the Quadrilateral. J. C. R. Richardson gains the VC at Regina.

October 9th: 64°-50° fine day. The British make progress to the east of le Sars towards the Butte de Warlencourt.

October 10th: 68°-46° fine sunny day. French success near Chaulnes. Rawlinson inspects both road and rail and sees roads that have 'simply disappeared'. The desolation he writes 'is appalling'.

October 11th: 66°-50° dull day with slight rain in the morning. The Battle of the Ancre Heights ends and the French repulse German attacks at the Bois de Chaulnes.

October 12th: 61°-55° dull day but dry. The British attack on a four mile front between Eaucourt and Bapaume. As a general undertaking the attack failed.

October 13th: 61°-50° dull day. Rawlinson holds a Corps Conference.

October 14th: 61°-50° overcast day. The French make progress. Rawlinson in his diary considers that the weather will bring the battle to a close soon. The glass is falling and the rain will shortly return. The roads will then become impassable and ammunition will not then be got to the guns. He says that casualties so far since July 1st are 40,000.

October 15th: Rain 3mm. 57°-41° rain in the morning, fine later. The British make progress in the neighbourhood of the Schwaben Redoubt and Thiepval. Rawlinson's diary entry is mainly taken up with a 'plot' against Haig thought up by the Cabal. Rawlinson inspected the ground at Longueval and Delville Wood, as well as High Wood. At this time it seems to Rawlinson that the Germans are reviving themselves in the battle and fighting with greater tenacity.

October 16th: Rain-trace. 54°-36°. There was to be a white frost from the 16th until the 20th of October. Bright sunny day, much colder. No operations.

October 17th: Rain 3mm. 55°-43° fine day, rain at night. Haig confers with Rawlinson about future battle plans.

October 18th: Rain 4mm. 57°-48° rain in the morning but cleared up later. The Battle of the Transloy Ridges ends. The British make progress north of Guedecourt and the French made progress, pushing the Germans out of Sailly. Rawlinson describes the progress during the day as partially successful.

October 19th: Rain 4mm. 57°-37° heavy rain during the day and especially in the morning. The Reserve Army operation was postponed for 48 hours. There was heavy rain the night before as well as in the morning of the 19th, and the roads and ground surface are in a dreadful state.

October 20th: 48°-28° fine day but very, very cold. The lowest temperature so far recorded during the Battle of the Somme. Heavy German attacks against the Schwaben and Stuff Redoubts on the Thiepval Plateau repulsed. An Albatros German aircraft was brought down close to High Wood. Much flying and many photographs taken from the air. Very clear day for observation.

October 21st: 45°-28° fine but very cold day. The British advance on a line between the Schwaben Redoubt and le Sars and take many prisoners. A. J. Balfour visits Rawlinson and is anxious about the number of casualties and the supply of steel not being adequate.

October 22nd: Temp. not known, fine bright day but bitterly cold. The French carry ridge to the west of Sailly.

October 23rd: Rain 3mm. 55°-43° a dull misty morning. The British advance towards le Transloy and capture a thousand yards of enemy trenches. R. Downie gained the VC to the east of Lesboeufs. Kiggell and Gough have tea with Rawlinson and they agree to postpone the planned attack for the 25th to the 26th.

October 24th: Rain 3mm. 54°-45° a dull day with rain. The French have success at Verdun in that they retake Douaumont and capture 3,500 prisoners. Trenchard has tea with Rawlinson and tells him that the enemy is producing a thousand aircraft a month, and that the RFC have lost 660 machines since July 1st.

October 25th: Rain 2mm. 52°-45° rain in the morning which had made the condition of the roads very bad and there were many supply lorries stuck, in particular in the area of Montauban. The shortage of supplies reduced the effectiveness of the artillery.

October 26th: Rain 1mm. 55°-39° a showery day particularly in the morning. Rawlinson postpones the operations due to take place today until the 30th. He then goes away for a short break to Versailles. He says that the weather is as bad as it can be.

October 27th: Rain 1mm. 55°-43° showery and cold day. The conditions are so bad that Rawlinson considers that it would be a physical impossibility for the infantry to advance. Even moving across a short distance would wear the troops out.

October 28th: Rain 8mm. 55°-41° very wet and cold day. The German flying ace Oswald Boelcke was killed in a collision with one of his pilots. He was flying an Albatros D11 and had been credited with 40 'kills'.

October 29th: Rain 7mm. 53°-45° another very wet day. Dewdrop and Hazy Trenches were taken in the morning by the Allies.

October 30th: Rain 7mm. 61°-48° wet and dull cold day. There were deluges of rain which made the condition of the roads worse than ever. The French take trenches north-west of Sailly–Saillisel.

October 31st: 63°-46°. The road and trench conditions are very bad indeed and the area around Guedecourt is waterlogged. Rawlinson despairs of a further advance.

November 1st: Rain 2mm. 59°-46°. German counter-attack against Sailly–Saillisel repulsed. Allies advance north-east of Lesboeufs. Germans evacuate Fort Vaux at Verdun.

November 2nd: Rain 3mm. 57°-43°. The British capture trenches east of Guedecourt.

November 3rd: Rain 1mm. 59°-48°. French advance to the outskirts of Vaux (Verdun).

November 4th: Rain 2mm. 64°-52° a wet and cloudy day. The French occupy Damlup (Verdun). Haig and Foch have conference with Rawlinson.

November 5th: 59°-48° clear day. The French occupy the whole of Vaux (Verdun). The British make some progress at the Butte de Warlencourt and towards le Transloy. The Anzac Corps gain and then lose Bayonet Trench. E. P. Bennett wins the VC at le Transloy.

November 6th: 57°-45° a cloudy day. French progress near St. Pierre Vaast Wood.

November 7th: Rain 12mm. 55°-45°. The British progress to the east of the Butte de Warlencourt.

November 8th: Rain 2mm. 57°-43°. The Germans repulsed at Saillisel.

November 9th: 54°-30° a bright and clear Autumn day, frosty. Large aerial battle near Bapaume with 36 British and 40 Germans involved. Rawlinson says that the British Gunners are complaining that too many German aircraft are now over Allied territory.

November 10th: 50°-30°. The British capture the east portion of Regina Trench to the north of Thiepval. The French capture several German trenches to the north-east of Lesboeufs. Rawlinson tours part of the battlefield and visits Ginchy and Delville Wood. He wants to visit the Orchard at the southernmost corner of Ginchy but is deterred by the German 5.9s dropping into it. He sees for himself how appalling the roads are beyond Ginchy.

November 11th: Rain-trace. 55°-32° misty day with low cloud, also frosty. The British bombard the Germans on the Ancre. German aircraft bombed at night and caused casualties.

November 12th: Rain-trace. 50°-48° a dull overcast day. Henry Wilson visits Rawlinson. It is hoped that the big attack will take place on the next day.

November 13th: 54°-46°. The Battle of the Ancre begins on a foggy morning and Beaumont Hamel is stormed by the British. They capture St. Pierre Divion, and Beaumont Hamel, and over 3,000 prisoners. The beginning of the fourth phase of the Battle of the Somme. J. Cunningham gains the VC opposite Hébuterne and B. C. Freyberg his at Beaucourt. Rawlinson describes the operations as being a great day for Gough and the Fifth Army.

November 14th: 55°-36° overcast day. The British capture Beaucourt and advance to the east of the Butte de Warlencourt. The number of prisoners taken in the two days reaches 5,200. The north-east winds are drying winds. Haig visits Rawlinson on his way to Paris for a conference and is delighted at Gough's success.

November 15th: 46°-37°. German counter-attacks fail.

November 16th: 41°-27° clear but cold day. The British extend their line eastwards from Beaucourt and retreat from part of the ground to the east of the Butte de Warlencourt. Rawlinson takes Lord Milner to Candas aerodrome and Trenchard shows them around. They also watch some flying arranged for them.

November 17th: Rain 2mm. 37°-25° clear day. Further advances on the Ancre.

November 18th: Rain 8mm. 54°-36°. The British advance north and south of the Ancre and reach the outskirts of Grandcourt. The operations end and the Battle of the Somme is over.

NB – I have drawn upon General Rawlinson's *War Diaries* as a basis for this chronology.

The Royal Flying Corps:
Its role in the Battle of the Somme

In March 1916 it had been decided to increase the number of aircraft that were operating in each RFC squadron from twelve to eighteen. At the end of that month with twenty-three squadrons in operation there was an active strength of 270 aircraft. After a 'lightning expansion' the number of aircraft available at the beginning of July for the start of the battle was as high as 637 if machines in reserve and in the aircraft parks were included.

Squadrons consisted of three flights, each flight having four, later six aircraft. Sometimes there was an additional single seater or Scout aircraft that carried out escort duties to protect the BEs (Blériot Experimental). Scouts could be Sopwith Pups, Bristol Scouts, Morane, Nieuports or Martinsydes. They were the 'germ' of the fighter aircraft of later on. They were at a ratio of one to each flight of four or six aircraft. They had rotary engines with a hp of 90 to 105, thus they were minimally faster than the BEs. By mid-1916 several *all*-fighter squadrons were in France.

During the last days of June there was a continuous bombardment on the German positions by the Allied Artillery. During the same period the RFC organised assaults upon the enemy. There was a great increase in the need for more aerial reconnaissance, this being especially of use to the artillery. Strong points could be identified, tracks to hidden or camouflaged batteries could be spotted and new work in the way of new trenches could be seen. During the pre-battle period there had been a 'great rehearsal' some miles behind the lines, which was a rehearsal for the co-operation of the artillery, infantry and the RFC. Of the aircraft themselves the basic type was the BE2 that carried out co-operation with the Army ground forces. It could be used for artillery observation, reconnaissance, photography and bombing. Its maximum speed was 75mph. The single-seater aircraft which were fighters were intended to engage enemy aircraft and thus protect or release the Corps aircraft who were co-operating with the ground forces. They also provided cover for photographic missions and even bombing raids.

The photographic machines were BE2cs and a large camera was strapped to the outside of the fuselage which slowed down the speed of the aircraft. The cameras often had a fixed focal length to suit a height of 4/5000 feet. Their speed was meant to allow them to avoid interception, and the aircraft involved were usually considered as strategic reconnaissance as they often operated over long distances and without armament.

Colonel Robert Macleod wrote that machines fitted with cameras produced much useful material which was both vertical and oblique. He found though, that there was considerable delay in getting copies of the photographs to the batteries, so he arranged for advance copies to be delivered to the artillery concerned. Batteries had to be trained in interpreting the photographs and especially the potential targets highlighted by them. With experience it became possible to identify the particular type of enemy battery i.e. 77mm, 4.2", 5.9", 8" and so on. Also machine gun posts showed up in addition to ventilator shafts as well as tracks that led perhaps to camouflaged batteries already referred to. Sometimes Allied aeroplanes flew over their own batteries and reported on their own visibility. Eventually whole areas of the battlefield were photographed and a mosaic map of the ground was produced which accurately recorded the positions of trenches, battery positions, roads, tracks, decauville railways etc. From these mosaics, maps were built up and produced for daily use throughout the Army. In order to see what changes had been made it was only needed to compare one day's mosiac with the previous day's. Two pictures taken from slightly different angles and placed in a stereoscope could give a good indication of the heights and depths and this way even dummy trenches of only two feet depth could be discovered.

In his autobiography *The Brabazon Story* Lord Brabazon of Tara wrote about the early role of photography in the air. Being one of the first men to fly in Britain he was also especially interested in the possibilities of aerial photography. General Henderson's Chief of Staff, Colonel F. H. Sykes had decided to start up a photographic unit within the RFC. With two colleagues they arrived at No. 1 Wing, which at the time was under command of Colonel Trenchard. They began by experimenting with a bellows camera before others were designed that were more suitable. The cameras had to be mounted in the new machines as they arrived. As a result Brabazon was in touch with every photographic squadron and also operations. When he was with No. 9 Squadron he had also introduced wireless. It was not an operating squadron at the time.

Robert Macleod was also involved with the experiments with wireless in aircraft and wrote that they had a system of wireless listening posts which listened in to signals that the enemy was sending out. They soon found out the code numbers of the batteries and of the targets that they intended to engage. However the Army telephone system was often shot up before the warning arrived. In time they worked out a connection between the German batteries and the areas that they shelled. If, say, German shells were falling in a certain area, they knew it was from a German battery, say N3 or N9. They in turn could be engaged. The primary task of all early squadrons was this Corps reconnaissance and Army co-operation. The scouts developed into fighters and as the occasional bombing raids became more frequent then certain squadrons concentrated on this role. The remaining squadrons developed operation techniques in support of the Army and were known as Corps Reconnaissance units. These squadrons were expected to undertake air obervation, tactical reconnaissance, photography, message and supply dropping and if required light bombing and ground attack. Two-seater aircraft became standard in this role. The air observation squadrons acted as observers for artillery, co-operation with the ground forces and could operate from small fields.

Most of the artillery work was counter-battery, but other targets were also engaged such as columns of infantry, transport, developing counter-attacks, or even stationary targets such as an important cross roads or a railway station. In the year before the Somme battle began there had been various improvements and these included a new system of reporting the fall of shells on their targets, which was known as the 'clock code'.

In Army co-operation duties there were two schools of thought; either the Observer directed the flight course by giving orders to the pilot and sent the wireless contact to the ground etc. Or the pilot chose the flight course himself and operated the wireless signals, the Observer then being no more than a machine gunner. The Germans had a preference for the latter system, the British the former. The success or otherwise of the artillery/air co-operation was a crucial element to the whole campaign.

In Army co-operation techniques the 'clapper break' had been introduced, which varied the Morse key note from each machine and prevented jamming. On Contact Patrol the aircraft made a signal by dropping flares or sounding a klaxon horn for the infantry to put out their signals consisting of a yellow cloth to show their position. The Observer marked the position on a map, flew back and dropped the map at Brigade HQ. The patrol often co-operated by 'shooting up' targets and was sometimes used to enfilade the trenches. The patrol saw the arrows, counted the bars and looked for a target, one thousand yards away in the direction in which the arrow was pointing − it might be a strong point, a mortar or a machine gun. The first bombers were Corps reconnaissance aircraft and from the spring of 1915 the RFC had been called upon to undertake bombing duties. In 1916 as spring began to give way to summer there was an increase in bombing attacks carried out on enemy aerodromes along the southern front. Morane Parasols were mainly used for Army co-operation as were the BE2 cs. The maximum speed of the latter was 75mph at a height of 6,500 feet.

Nieuport single-seaters were fighters as were FE8 Scouts and Sopwith 1½ Strutters which were two-seater fighters; the first British fighters to have a synchronised machine gun as standard equipment. BE12s which were 'ageing' fighters, were used as bombers on occasions. FE 2bs were used for reconnaissance as well as fighters. Martinsyde Scouts better known as Flying Elephants were used for reconnaissance and for bombing. The Nieuport 12 two-seater undertook artillery observation and photography. Other aircraft that played a role in the Somme battle on the Allied side were BE2es, BE2ds, DH2s and RE7s, the last mentioned being used for reconnaissance and the occasional bombing raid.

The Allied balloons had a poor time in France because of the German raiding machines which often destroyed them with incendiary bullets. There was one occasion when ten were shot down in a row. Balloon observers possessed parachutes unlike squadron pilots.

On 1st July a pilot from No. 60 Squadron was forced down owing to engine trouble and had breakfast with Basil Hallam Radford. Better known as 'Gilbert the Filbert' in civilian life, he was a singer and entertainer, a society favourite and one of Lady Diana Cooper's many admirers. Radford was in charge of a balloon section and on 30th August took up a balloon behind Beaumont Hamel from which they looked across the mills and railway stations of the Ancre Valley into Thiepval. He shared the balloon with 2nd

Lt. P. B. Moxon. The wire rope broke and the balloon became freed from its ground anchor and subsequently pointed its nose upward and rose rapidly. Moxon jumped to safety with his parachute but Radford was to fall minus his 'chute onto the Acheux Road. His 'chute was found nearby. Radford's body was truncated and only identified by his cigarette case. He was buried in Couin Military Cemetery.

As a curious postscript to this accident Lord Brabazon engaged Radford's batman who remained with him for the rest of his life as butler etc.

The Order of Battle at the beginning of July was that the operations in the Somme battle were to be the responsibility of the newly formed IV Brigade under the command of Brigadier E. B. 'Splash' Ashmore, consisting of the Third (Corps.) Wing (Artillery) and reconnaissance work and the Fourteenth (Army) Wing (Fighting). These two Wings shared a headquarters in the village of Bertangles and also shared the HQ Mess in the Chateau.

The other Wing involved which completed the RFC concentration, was Ninth Wing under Lt. Col. H. C. T. Dowding and the HQ of this Wing which embraced Nos. 21, 27, 60 Squadrons together with one Flight from No. 70 Squadron arrived at Fienvillers and Vert Galand on 19th June. A second Flight of No. 70 Squadron arrived on 1st July. The 58 aircraft of the Ninth Wing brought the total number of British aircraft involved to 168. This did not include the balloons. At the commencement of the battle, squadrons were not so specialised as they were to later become. Thus it was not unusual for a squadron to play a dual role, and there was often a mixture of aircraft on the strength. In the hangars there could be Moranes (biplanes and scouts), and in addition there might be one or two Nieuports. The squadron would be responsible for all the RFC work in its particular sector. I would like to quote a few statistics and I should say right away that there are different sets of figures available. This does not matter a great deal as they approximately agree.

The sources include *The War in the Air*, the *Statistics of the Military Effort*, and the *AIR Files* kept at the Public Record Office. In addition figures are not always available to cover the Battle of the Somme on its own but rather they cover the situation on the Western Front in its entirety. Nevertheless one knows that most of the action during the summer and autumn of 1916 in France was in the area of the Somme as that is where the major effort to defeat the enemy was attempted. Firstly the number of active British squadrons on the Western Front were as follows:

July	August	September	October	November
27	31	31	34	34

Number of machines at the same time were:

486	558	558	612	612

One should deduct sixty or seventy aircraft as being unserviceable at any one time. The total wastage of aircraft in July was 148. The number of balloons increased from 14 to 22 during the same period.

The total personnel strength of the RFC in July was 35,819 and in November it had risen to 53,345. The number of pilots for the same period was 426 and 585. The number of bombs dropped by Allied aircraft came to approximately 300 tons and the number of hours flown was 84,262. The number of photographs taken was between 19,000 and 21,500. And the number of prints made from them came to 420,000.

The number of hostile aircraft destroyed came to 164 and the number driven down damaged was 205. The number of British aircraft missing in the same period was 190 which included some for part of November when the Battle was officially over.

The number of Allied pilots who were killed, missing or wounded throughout the period was 308 of whom approximately 109 were killed. The number of Observers killed, wounded or missing was 191. The Allies began the battle with the advantage of a numerical superiority gained by the FEs and DH2s from the monoplane Fokkers but lost it to the German Airforce which grew in strength in the period September/October 1916 and was able to introduce new and superior machines in September as a result. Trenchard demanded an increase of fighter squadrons to combat the new threat. In mid November the Allies were fortunate in capturing a German Albatros completely intact.

In the brief squadron histories that follow I am aware that I have only included squadrons that were actually based in the Somme area and were included in the Order of Battle. There were many cases of squadrons based further north joining in the battle.

Candas

Candas was the site of No. 2 Aircraft Depot which was part of IV Brigade and was conveniently near to the airfield at Fienvillers and the RFC HQ. In April General Rawlinson, Commander of the Fourth Army paid a visit to the Depot which was under the supervision of Major R. C. Donaldson. He inspected the stores which he described as being 'large and very important' for they furnished all the spare aircraft parts for the squadrons stationed in the Somme area. Rawlinson commented that he thought that the establishment was run very efficiently. At the beginning of July the Depot had a strength of 89 aircraft which included those which were unserviceable.

Candas also served as a landing ground but according to Lt. Insall it could be blanketed off by a heavy type of thick fog, which could be expected in October. The Candas area was also used for troop training purposes.

The Advanced HQ of Ninth Wing was at the beginning of the battle in the village of Fienvillers and Major General H. M. Trenchard was billeted in the village with his Aide de Camp Maurice Baring who later wrote an excellent account called *Flying Corps Headquarters 1914-1918*. At the end of June, Baring tells us that the village was not far from the No. 2 Aircraft Depot at Candas and that the HQ was in a little square house which stood at the meeting of five cross roads, with three rooms and a kitchen downstairs and six bedrooms upstairs, four of which were turned into offices. Baring himself was billeted in the same village in a notaire's house just opposite the HQ. The Wing was commanded by Hugh Dowding.

Oswald Boelcke

Oswald Boelcke along with Albert Ball were probably the most famous 'personalities' involved in the Somme air fighting, and Boelcke's reputation as an expert flyer was known to friend and foe alike. During the early part of the Somme battle the Allies carried the offensive to the Germans. It was in Boelcke's mind to form a Jasta or fighter Jagdstaffel, and with the help of a new design in aircraft to seize the initiative from the Allies, who had had it all their own way until the autumn of 1916. Thus Boelcke began to collect up pilots from the Eastern Front and Jasta 2 was formed from this group. The first Albatros D1 biplane arrived on 1st September, and by 16th September the Jasta was at Bertincourt, moving to Lagnicourt on 22nd September. Success for the new aeroplane was immediate, and the first victory was scored on the 16th by Lt. Walter Höhne who destroyed a FE2b. On the 17th the Jasta brought down five Allied aircraft from a squadron that was carrying out a bombing raid on Marcoing. This squadron had been equipped with 8 BE2s with six FE2s as escort. At this time Boelcke's 'score' was 25 enemy kills, and one of his victims was Captain George Cruickshank of 70 Squadron who at that time had five 'kills' to his credit. Cruickshank was brought down over Havrincourt Wood. However Boelcke himself was only to live a few more weeks as he was killed in an aerial collision with one of his own pilots on 28th October. His tally at that time was 40 Allied aircraft. He was given a funeral first at Cambrai Cathedral behind the German lines, and then at home in Germany. His success had become legendary, and Von Richtofen (the Red Baron) who was just starting on his career acknowledged Boelcke to be 'the master'.

History of No. 3 Squadron

On 10th April No. 3 Squadron moved to Lahoussoye near Albert and north-east of Querrieu. The squadron had formerly been based at Bertangles, since 1st April. It used Morane Parasols from early in 1916 which were mostly used for artillery spotting duties. The squadron's duties in the main were in Army co-operation reconnaissance.

'C' Flight commenced Contact Patrol in preparation for the forthcoming battle and Cecil Lewis joined the squadron shortly before the battle began. The commanding officer at this time was Major H. D. Harvey-Kelly and in addition to the Parasols the squadron had four Morane Biplanes. Lewis described the aerodrome as standing outside the village of Lahoussoye, right on the arterial road, a single straggling street of tumbledown farm buildings and mud spattered walls. He described his duties in considerable detail in his book *Sagittarius Rising*. His job at first was to go over the front line at 7,500 feet and fly along the German second line trenches from Montauban round the salient at Fricourt and up to la Boisselle, photographing as he went. This section, as the battle drew near, was to be photographed each day, in order that HQ received accurate information on the effects of the Allied bombardment. This artillery fire was meant to destroy the German first and second line trenches and so make the attack easier for the infantry. On 1st July the squadron along with No. 9 Squadron supplied the air co-operation for 111 Corps attack on Ovillers la Boiselle. Lewis said that the drumming of firing and of bursting shells throbbed in their ears. He was ordered to keep clear of la Boiselle itself as a mine was to be detonated there, which was intended to destroy the fortified salient. Once fired, the infantry were to sweep through la Boiselle and on up the road to Pozieres, their first day objective. The whole salient was described by him as having a coverlet of white wool smoking shell burst, a half an hour before the battle commenced. He graphically described the blowing of the mines, but unfortunately the redoubt was not destroyed as the mines had exploded in no man's land. The impregnable machine gun emplacements were intact, and the Germans were able to effectively block the advance. On another occasion Lewis saw north of Thiepval a yellow mist which was gas. He was able to report this and an infantry attack was mounted on Quadrangle along with a two hour bombardment. On 2nd July the squadron observed at la Boiselle and on the 6th it reconnoitred Mametz Wood and the German trenches especially Quadrangle Support. At this time the trees in Mametz Wood were still mostly standing and support was still occupied by the enemy.

On 13th July cavalry were to be put through on the German Third Line between Bazentin le Grand and Longueval, and were massing for an attack on High Wood. On the 15th the squadron observed the Switch Trench as being full of Germans which resulted in an attack on High Wood being very costly. On the 16th Lewis reported that the advance had proceeded and that the Allies occupied most of High Wood. He reported co-operation as being splendid and flares were called for with the use of Klaxons. They flew low in order to draw the German fire and thus give his position away. The squadron located bombing parties from Pozieres to the wood but the squadron cleared up the position and received the congratulations from the General downwards. On 20th July the squadron observed the fighting at Delville Wood and on the 25th mist hampered its work with No. 34 Squadron. On 18th August the squadron reported the progress of the fighting at Delville Wood again, and on the 19th August it reported an enemy readjustment. On 24th August the squadron observed the fighting of XV Corps and on 3rd September it found trenches empty at Ginchy just before it was taken. The Germans were probably hiding. Low flying and trench straffing began in earnest in September. On 15th September the squadron witnessed the first tank attack at Flers, and Cecil Lewis has left us an excellent first hand account of the fighting on that day.

'Hoppy and I were detailed for the first contact patrol with the tanks. It was launched on the 15th September at 6.30 a.m. A systematic heavy bombardment had been carried out, morning and evening, for a week prior to the attack, so that on the morning itself the Hun should not imagine anything was brewing. But at 6.17 a.m. an intense hurricane bombardment was put over from Thiepval to Delville Wood. When we climbed up to the lines, we found the whole front seemingly covered with a layer of dirty cotton-wool, the smoking shell-bursts. Across this were dark lanes' — 'Here no shells were falling. Through these lanes lumbered the tanks in file, four to each lane. By 6.20 a.m. they had reached the front line and the barrage began to roll back as they advanced, the infantry with them. We could see them sitting across the trenches and enfilading the enemy with four-pounders. By eight o'clock the complete network of trenches known as Switch Trench and Flers Line was taken'.

Some of the tanks were put out of action. Some took fire, some suffered direct hits from enemy shell-fire; but later many were still to be seen, refuelling in Flers, the red petrol tin visible on their brown backs. In his log book appears the following entry: 'The Guedecourt Line should have fallen by 10 a.m.; but this failed. It will be attacked tomorrow at dawn. We are at present digging a new front line. Little is known of what happened on our flanks; but it is pretty certain that the cavalry are not through as they intended' — 'I shall never forget the way the tanks waltzed through Flers. There was a little white terrier, a mascot I suppose, following one of the tanks'. — 'The next day we were out again at dawn'.

'A further attack on the third line failed. We were flying very low. No Huns were visible in the trenches and the line very quiet' (Lewis was attacked by a Hun). 'We were right over Guedecourt at the time. We struggled in to the advance landing-ground at Carnoy'. — 'I shall remember for ever the Horse Artillery coming up into action behind Flers, on a road that was mostly shell holes, under a hail of shrapnel. A team of six roan chargers, sweeping up at full gallop, dumping ammunition by the guns, with hardly a pause, galloping back again, the outriders crouching low over the necks of their plunging beasts with their flying manes and terror-struck eyes! There isn't much picturesque or visibly heroic to be seen in this war when you are in the air — but that was it!'

1st October: The fighting towards le Sars was observed by 3 and 34 Squadrons.

Other pilots who flew at one time with the squadron included Whistler and Bell. McCludden was at one time an observer with the squadron.

Sources: *The War in the Air*: C. Lewis — *Sagittarius Rising; History of No. 3 Squadron*, PRO/AIR 1/687).

History of No. 4 Squadron

At the beginning of the battle the squadron was part of Third (Corps) Wing under Maj. T. W. C. Carthew DSO. It possessed 17 BE2c's and 1 BE2d. It arrived at Baizieux on 27th March, 1916 to the west of Albert and its duties consisted mainly of artillery observation, reconnaissance and aerial photography. W. G. Barker, who was later to become an ace, joined the squadron in April having been commissioned as an Observer-Gunner. He served with three different squadrons during the Somme battle before going home to Narborough for pilot training in November 1916. On 1st July together with No. 15 Squadron it assisted in the Serre/Thiepval attack and helped VIII

Corps and X Corps. The squadron reported that a number of enemy batteries were moving back from the ridge between Grandcourt and Courcelette. Thiepval was observed at 600 feet but there was no progress.

2nd July. Together with No. 15 Squadron it was transferred to Fifteenth Wing.

21st July. It recorded new entrenchments around le Sars and Courcelette. On 12th August the squadron saw enemy troops massing at Mouquet Farm about 1,500, and they were subsequently shelled.

Just before the attack on Guillemont on 18th August it took photographs with a view to readjusting artillery fire. On 26th September the squadron observed with No. 7 Squadron and a force was scattered near Miraumont. On 21st October it kept in touch with the attack on Schwaben Redoubt and helped in the capture of Regina Trench by engaging enemy batteries. On 25th October one of the squadron was lost. On 13th November it acted along with 15 Squadron as contact observers on the Battle of Beaumont Hamel.

16th November. Together with Nos. 7 and 15 Squadrons it fired on trenches and on a dump at Miraumont.

(Source: *The War in the Air*.)

History of No. 9 Squadron

From 26th March 1916 the squadron was stationed at Allonville, which is south-east of Bertangles. It had formerly been a bombing squadron and on 1st July was part of Third (Corps) Wing of IV Brigade and was commanded by Major A. B. Burdett. It had 20 pilots and 18 BE2cs. It became an army co-operation squadron and in June most of its sorties were counter-battery ones.

1st July. Machines of the IV Brigade Corps squadrons were mostly involved in counter-battery work and one flight was allotted to each counter-battery area. Aircraft were also involved in contact patrol and trench bombardment work, a flight being told off for each purpose. Many 'excellent shots' were made by the squadron. In *The War in the Air* it was noted that the squadron observed the taking of Pommiers Trench by the 18th Div. and the taking of Dublin Trench—Glatz Redoubt and the entering of Montauban by the 16th Manchesters. The German artillery in Bernafay Wood had been fired on, as well as some Germans who were to the east of that wood.

3rd July. The squadron was unable to see any signs of the enemy as still being in Caterpillar Wood and it was thought that the wood together with Bernafay was in fact empty. This was not so as they were subsequently re-occupied by the enemy. One of the squadron Observers called up the 12th Heavy Artillery to direct fire on German transport on the way to Guillemont, which was coming from the direction of the Bois de Leuze. Seven direct hits were obtained on the column and a number of men were seen to fall and others scattered. A direct hit was also obtained on one of the lorries. The squadron also witnessed some of the fighting at Trônes Wood in July and sometimes there was real danger of the squadron aircraft being hit by the Allied artillery!

15th July. The squadron moved to Chipilly to a site which it shared with a squadron of the French Air Service. According to *The War in the Air* on this same day it photographed Delville Wood and 'observed', reporting progress.

16th July. It was congratulated on the effectiveness of spotting for the artillery which had resulted in havoc in the Mametz Wood/Caterpillar Wood area.

22nd July. It reported new posts at Ginchy and on 28th July it was busy photographing Guillemont. On 19th August it reported enemy readjustments.

3rd September. The squadron was at Morlancourt and according to *The War in the Air* it watched British troops leave and move on to Guillemont and reported that Falfemont Farm as still holding out, and that progress was being made along the Ginchy road north of the Guillemont/Leuze Wood cross roads.

7th September. The taking of Falfemont Farm had thrown the enemy into some confusion as they had to hurriedly produce a new line.

9th September. The squadron observed the fall of Ginchy in detail and of the progress to Leuze Wood.

15th September. It observed the hold up of the 6th Division by the Quadrilateral.

23rd September. With the V Bde. it carried out some bombing raids and used the 112 lb. bomb for the first time in an attack, on Roisel Railway Station.

The squadron casualties: It did not lose any men as killed in direct action, but did lose ten who were presumed to be dead as they were missing and also lost two men as Prisoners of War.

In March 1916 the Canadian William George Barker who was later to became an 'ace' scored his first victory from the back seat of a squadron machine as an NCO aerial gunner.

(Sources: *The War in the Air*, and the *History of Nine Squadron* by T. Mason (Beaumont) 1965 PRO/AIR 1/688).

History of No. 15 Squadron

The squadron was based at Marieux from 27th March 1916 which was southeast of Doullens and seven miles north-east of Vert Galand. It flew Bristol Scouts. On 1st April it became a Corps Squadron, attached to VIII Corps and remained part of Third Wing which in turn became Corps Wing of the Fourteenth (Army Wing) on 14th April.

Its main function was as an artillery co-operation squadron i.e. artillery spotting and photographic reconnaissance. Out of its sixteen aircraft at the end of June it was allocated three for Contact Patrol, eight for counter-battery liaison and three for bombing and reconnaissance.

25th June. It took part in the RFC's large attack on enemy kite balloons when 15 out of 23 were attacked and 6 brought down.

1st July. The squadron together with No. 4 Squadron observed the progress of the Battle around Beaumont Hamel and Serre. It assisted VIII Corps and X Corps. As at 1st July the CO was Major H. le M. Brock.

2nd July. It observed and was transferred along with 4 Squadron from Third (Corps) Wing to Fifteenth Wing of the Reserve Army.

3rd July. It reported considerable train movements in the Cambrai area. This would have been for German reinforcements.

Mid July. The squadron was transferred to V Corps for air liaison work.

18th July. The future Canadian ace William George Barker joined the squadron at Marieux and was an observer. He had already scored the first of his 57 victories at this time.

5th August. The squadron took part in a bombing raid on Grevillers Rail Station. Three out of the bombers which took part in the raid were supplied by the squadron.

12th August. The squadron along with No. 4 Squadron, was inspected by the King who was accompanied by the Prince of Wales. The Prince was a frequent visitor to the squadron whilst it was at Marieux.

In September the squadron took part in further bombing raids and also bombed Miraumont.

2nd October. It moved from its 'comfortable quarters' to a new ground at Clairfaye Farm at Lealvillers. It was four miles south of the former aerodrome and conditions were pretty primitive. It was flying BE2ds by then.

October. It continued carrying out bombing raids which included targets such as Miraumont, Pys and Loupart Wood.

25th October. The squadron was joined by No. 32 Squadron which came from Vert Galand.

28th October. The German ace Boelcke was killed in an accident over the Pozieres area. In less than two months airfighting in the Somme battle he had shot down twenty Allied aircraft.

November. The squadron observed the Beaumont Hamel Battle with No. 4 Squadron. On the 13th William Barker, an Observer for the artillery' reported 300 German infantry as being visible in Y Ravine.

15th November. The squadron was producing valuable battle progress reports although the weather was very misty and the reports had to be obtained by flying at low heights, in grim weather conditions.

16th November. Together with Nos. 7 and 14 Squadrons they fired on trenches and on an ammunition dump at Miraumont.

(Sources: *The War in the Air;* N. J. Roberson and H. J. Stammers *History of the Squadron* privately published in 1972; PRO/AIR 1/689).

History of No. 18 Squadron

Prior to moving to the Somme Battle area the squadron had been with the 10th Wing at Treizennes having moved there from Bruay on 22nd July. On 2nd August it became part of 1st Wing Bde. when it returned to Bruay. On 6th September it left Bruay for Lavieville where it arrived on 8th September. By then it had become part of 9th Wing GHQ and on the 7th joined 14th Wing 4th Brigade.

In mid September the squadron was allotted to the Cavalry Corps which was standing by to exploit any breakthrough. Tactical co-operation was practised with each of the Brigades in turn. Air to ground intercommunication was by dropped message bags. Ground-to-air was by morse code or by ground strips, or by message bags strung between two poles and picked up by a grapple lowered from the aircraft. A very close liaison was built up, but the breakthrough for the cavalry to exploit was not achieved, though the squadron did support the one attempt by low-flying attack and contact patrol. It was from the squadron's attachment to the Cavalry Corps on the Somme in 1916 that the unit's Pegasus badge originated. The squadron was one of the first to use wireless telephone direct with Army HQ with success, whilst flying on reconnaissance.

Its main duties with FE2bs were photography, artillery observation and cavalry contact patrols.

Simultaneously with the preparations for the breakthrough during the Somme battle the squadron held one flight on duty each night for retaliation bombing of active German aerodromes. During the night of 10th/11th November every machine of the squadron carried out reprisal raids for the bombing of Amiens. On 21st October they had bombed Velu and Peronne.

15th December. It moved to St. Leger with its FE2bs and one Scout. The CO was Major G. I. Carmichal.

(Sources: *Yoxall – No. 18 Squadron, Flight,* 27th January 1956 and PRO/AIR 1/689)

History of No. 19 Squadron

BE12s which were unsuitable as fighters were first flown from Filton near Bristol and reached St. Omer on 30th July. On the 1st August they were flown to Fienvillers, south-west of Doullens under Major R. M. Rodwell as part of 9th Wing. The squadron had in 1915, been originally a fighter squadron but in 1916 carried out bombing missions. It had at the beginning of its involvement in the Somme battle 18 of the BE12s. It worked with Nos. 27 and 70 Squadrons, the role of 27 Squadron was chiefly long distance bombing and that of 70 Squadron was long distance photographic reconnaissance.

The squadron was called upon to provide offensive and defensive patrols. The 9th Wing was attached for duty to RFC HQ, then occupying an advanced position in the Chateau in Bertangles which the GOC Maj. Gen. Trenchard used throughout the Somme battles.

12th August. While carrying out familiarisation flights with other squadrons in the 9th Wing, the squadron recorded its first offensive patrol on a line Bapaume–Cambrai–Epeby. The squadron working with No. 21 Squadron was detailed to carry out defence patrols and day and night bombing sorties.

26th August. A force of BE12s, three serving as escorts for those carrying 20lb bombs, bombed objectives at Havrincourt Wood but owing to cloudy stormy conditions five were forced down by the enemy. The wood which was known as 'Mossy' was thought to contain masses of German infantry.

2nd September. The squadron bombed again close to the wood.

15th September. Specially selected pilots carried out a series of low level contact patrols to report the advance of British troops and also of the tanks, which were in action for the first time. The CO had no time for breakfast on that day!

19th September. Together with 21 Squadron it attacked Velu but was involved in heavy fighting.

22nd September. It bombed the airfield at Velu and lost three aircraft with one destroyed.

24th September. It lost two more aircraft over Havrincourt Wood which it was again attacking, with the co-operation of No. 27 Squadron. Dumps at Irles were also bombed. On 1st October it bombed the wood once again and on the 10th it bombed Cambrai during the night. On 12th October it bombed Hermies Station and lost two aircraft shot down, it had previously bombed Havrincourt Wood again.

During the month of October the Spad VII the first 'real' fighter arrived with its Vickers Gun which fired through its screw. The squadron didn't receive its full quota until the end of 1916.

In October/November the squadron bombed Marcoing, Hermies, Ruyalcourt and Arleux. On 9th November together with 27 Squadron it attacked Arleux Station and on the 9th/10th it bombed Havrincourt Chateau in part reply to the German bombing of Lavieville aerodrome.

(Sources: *A Brief History of No. 19 (F) Squadron* by James L. Dixon (Cross and Cockade). *The War in the Air;* PRO/AIR 1/167.).

History of No. 21 Squadron

In May prior to the Battle of the Somme the squadron mainly used RE7s and on 19th June was based at Fienvillers to the south-west of Doullens. At the beginning of the battle its strength was 14 RE7s, 4 BE2cs and 1 BE2e. It was under Major J. R. Campbell-Heathcote and was part of Ninth Wing. The RE7s were used for reconnaissance as well as for occasional bombing raids. Fienvillers was the advanced HQ of the RFC on 27th June, and was not far from the squadron aerodrome. No. 27 Squadron shared the airfield with it.

30th June. The day before the battle began, it bombed railway sheds using the RE7s and on 1st July using the BE2cs. At about midday a group from the squadron bombed Bapaume. One of the BE pilots was Capt. Somerset Leeke.

2nd July. The REs bombed Bapaume in the afternoon and were escorted by Martinsydes of 27 Squadron and Moranes of 60 Squadron. On 3rd July they attacked trains near Cambrai. On the 9th the squadron bombed Cambrai again, using the REs and later the squadron bombed an HQ at le Transloy. Later in the day it also bombed dumps at le Sars. Throughout July the squadron bombed during day and night. On 28th July it moved to Boisdinghem where it was to remain until 25th August, when it moved again, this time to Bertangles. During August the squadron received a delivery of BE12s which were to be used as bombers. This despite the fact that it was fighters that were really needed more! On 19th September it attacked Velu together with 19 Squadron, and was involved in some 'hot' fighting. On 25th October a lone BE12 was shot down. The squadron was to remain at Bertangles until 1917. There are graves of RFC men at Fienvillers. In the future Billy Bishop the Canadian Ace was to fly with the squadron as an Observer.

(Sources: *The War in the Air* and the PRO/AIR 1/690.)

History of No. 22 Squadron

Much of the history of the squadron is lacking in detail as early records had been destroyed by fire which had broken out in the squadron office. The squadron had been formed by Capt. Lord Lucas, who was both a peer and a former Minister of the Crown, in August 1915. Major R. B. Martyn was the squadron commander from October 1915 to February 1917. The squadron went to France in March 1916 and acted as a fighter/reconnaissance squadron over German held territory, fighting, photographing, bombing and ground straffing. It also had to seek our during these trips, camps, railheads and dumps behind their lines. It arrived at Vert Galand in March 1916 and within a few days joined No. 24 Squadron at Bertangles. It flew FE2bs and 24 Squadron flew DH2s. These two squadrons made up the fighter component of IV Bde. RFC of the newly formed Fourth Army. The three flights lived in houses close to the aerodrome. Bertangles in the period 1915/16 had become a teeming RFC centre. It was at all times a much used billeting place.

The HQ of the RFC became in turn the HQ of the Fourth Army under General Rawlinson before it moved to Villers Carbonelle towards Peronne. In June the squadron strength had been raised from 12 to 18 aircraft. On 1st July the Corps Squadrons made their way back and forth as they sent back wireless messages pointing to the centres of resistance and belts of uncut wire. Observers in kite balloons directed counter-battery against the German guns from 4.12 a.m. to dusk. Pairs of 22 Squadron FEs and 24 Squadron DHs maintained protective patrols behind German lines. Some aircraft carried two bombs of 20lb. in weight. On the same day the squadron provided patrols for part of the northern area as well.

In mid-July the squadron was operating in the area of Delville Wood together with No. 9 Squadron.

The use of German ack ack guns or 'Archie' had very much increased by September along with their accuracy. By now the face of the squadron had changed, some men who had been in action with the squadron on 1st July had been killed including two of the three Flight Commanders. In this month Capt. Lord Lucas had rejoined the squadron as a Flight Commander having once more refused the command of the squadron until he had gained sufficient experience in fighting in France. In early November the squadron had spotted the early signs of the construction of the Hindenburg Line.

Both Maurice Baring and John Buchan were friends of Lucas, and Baring reported that Lucas when flying over from St. Omer crashed on the Candas aerodrome and that on 30th October he had gone to Bertangles and saw Lucas there and they walked together across the aerodrome to Major Hawker's

Mess. With Baring at RFC HQ and Buchan a few miles away at Beauquesne Lucas was not short of friends. Buchan mentions that at the end of October and during the first few days of November there were strong gales blowing from the south-west which hampered the flying programme, as the aircraft drifted too far over the enemy lines and had to fight their way back very slowly against a head wind. Buchan rode over to have tea with Bron Lucas during this time and two days later Baring came to see Buchan to tell him that Lucas was missing.

On 3rd November Lucas had been in charge of 'A' Flight leading a photographic reconnaissance of three machines in bad weather conditions and none of the aircraft was to return. Somewhere over the Arras–Bapaume road German Albatroses engaged Lucas who was shot in the head by a m.g. bullet which resulted in his fainting. His Observer managed to land the machine and only broke the undercarriage. Lucas died not having regained consciousness and was to be buried that same day in a little cemetery outside the village of Ecoust St. Mein, north-east of Bapaume. The Observer's name was Lt. Anderson who had been wounded, but who was well looked after by the Germans who also supervised Lucas's burial.

Baring received a telegram on 30th November confirming Lucas' death. Buchan was to base the end of Peter Pienaar (a character in *Mr. Standfast*) on Lucas who despite having a ruined leg, rammed his machine into an enemy aircraft in order to deny him sight of the 'thinness' of the British Army on the ground.

Other flyers with the Squadron at some time or other were Jordan, Gurdon and McKeever. Stuart Wortley was a former Flight Commander and was the author of *Letters From a Flying Officer*.

The squadron's casualties were: 14 killed, 16 wounded and five taken prisoner.

(Sources: PRO/AIR 1/168 Western front. *The War in the Air; Letters From a Flying Officer* and *Pi in the Sky;* Smithers – *Wonder Aces of the Air* and Baring – *Flying Corps HQ, 1914-1918.*)

History of No. 23 Squadron

In 1915 it had been a fighter squadron and at the beginning of the Battle of the Somme was out of the area, being under 13th Wing and based at Izel le Hameau under Major A. Ross-Hume. At this stage it had 14 FE2bs and three Martinsyde Scouts.

1st September. It moved to serve with 9th Wing at Fienvillers near Doullens, to fly FE2b fighters and carry out patrols and reconnaissance missions.

It moved again four days later to Vert Galand to form with No. 32 Squadron 22nd Wing of the newly formed V Bde. The first orders for the squadron on joining this Bde. were issued on 6th September. On the 7th it was to carry out offensive patrols in the area Bucquoy–Achiet le Petit–le Barque, and in the event of the weather being unfavourable for offensive patrols, patrols were to be undertaken on the line Gommecourt–Puisieux–Grandcourt–Martinpuich. Its main role then, during the battle was offensive and reconnaissance patrols. Casualties between June and November were three killed or died of wounds, wounded in action in 1916 and also in 1916 six missing reported dead or presumed dead.

(Sources. *The War in the Air* and PRO/AIR 1/690).

History of No. 24 Squadron

The squadron was formed on 1st September 1915 for fighting duties. Its commanding officer was Major L. G. Hawker who had been awarded the VC in July of that year. The squadron was to become known as Hawker's Squadron. Hawker was born on 30th December 1890, and commissioned in the Royal Engineers in 1910. Whilst training at Woolwich he developed a keen interest in flying and just before the war transferred to the RFC. By the time the squadron had moved to the Somme area he had added the DSO to his VC, and had become one of the leading British aces with nine confirmed kills. On the Somme the squadron was equipped with DH2s which were pusher-fighters, they were 'to be the answer' to the fixed gun Fokker Fighter. This machine gave the RFC the lead in the early stages of the Battle of the Somme, and by mid 1916 the squadron was probably the best known on the Allied side, and registered many victories under Hawker's leadership.

In March the squadron was involved in patrol work and also in April as well as supplying escort to artillery machines and those gathering information from the back area. In May the squadron moved its mess to Bertangles into a large hut on the edge of the aerodrome. For exercise Hawker encouraged his pilots to ride and they borrowed horses from the cavalry. Also a tennis court was established at the aerodrome. In June they carried out further patrol work with artillery especially, and also photograph reconnaissance. On 20th June they patrolled in the Ovillers–Bienvillers area and during the last days of June carried out offensive patrols. On 1st July the first day of the Battle of the Somme the squadron De Havillands were active along the front of the Third and Fourth Armies.

21st July. It was involved in a 'scrap' east of Peronne with fast hostile scouts. During 23rd July victories were registered and it was to destroy 40 German aircraft in the next three months. On 26th August No. 21 Squadron arrived at Bertangles and its 'inadequate' BE12s were housed in a hangar next to the sheds which housed No. 24 Squadron, until on 29th August a gale blew the hangar down which partly destroyed the aircraft inside. The squadron had shot down 25 aircraft by the end of August.

2nd September. A German aircraft was brought down in Delville Wood, north of Lesboeufs and three others were brought down on the same day. During September it carried out further offensive patrols, and troop and train targets in the vicinity of le Transloy and Guedecourt-le-Sars were attacked. On the 15th the squadron shot down an enemy aircraft. At the end of September W. M. Fry joined 60 Squadron for a time, from 24 Squadron. In early October Cowan one of Hawker's most experienced pilots was posted as Flight Commander to No. 29 Squadron who also flew DH2s. On one occasion Cowan's engine had jammed after shooting down an enemy aircraft, and in landing his machine touching the ground was sufficient to release the jammed starter! All this was in German-held territory. On 26th October the squadron fought some Halberstadt fighters with no casualties. Capt. Foot of 60 Squadron engaged the enemy aircraft in his Nieuport but he too crashed. A patrol of 32 Squadron shot down one of the enemy. On 28th October two De Havillands were on patrol near Pozieres, and it was during a scrap with the Germans that Boelcke's aircraft collided with one of his own during a fight with 'C' Flight.

16th November. Six De Havillands engaged the enemy near Cambrai. On 17th November Hawker learnt that Cowan had been killed in a collision while leading 29 Squadron.

A few days before 23rd November Fry met Hawker at the Godbert Restaurant in Amiens which was a meeting place for everyone who could get away from the Somme front for an evening. Usually the RFC were in the majority because their evenings were freer and their transport easier.

23rd November. Hawker himself was shot down by Richthofen whose eleventh victim he became. Hawker's brother who was in the Royal Artillery was in charge of six guns in the shell-ploughed mud near Ginchy Telegraph.

Two and a quarter miles south of Bapaume stood the ruins of Luisenhof Farm in the cellars of which was Major Von Schönberg, commander of the 1st Batt. of the 100th Royal Saxon Reserve Grenadier Regt. Hawker and the 'Red Baron' fought a classic duel and after some time the German managed to get Hawker's aircraft into position for shooting down. The German commander witnessed Hawker's crash 250 yards from the farm, behind the lines at Ligny Thilloy. The area was under fire from Allied machine guns in Guedecourt. Hawker was buried close to his aircraft on 24th November, having received a bullet in the head. Later his grave was lost, but his name appears on Lutyens' designed Air Memorial to the missing of 1914-18 inside the British Military Cemetery on the Fauberg D'Amiens, Arras.

Pilots who at one time flew with the squadron included Hepburn, Johnstone, Gilmore, Fullard, Macdonald, Hazell, Cooper, Lambert and Woollett. The last named was posted to the squadron at the end of November.

(Sources: T. M. Hawker *Hawker VC*, Mitre Press 1966. A. E. Illingworth and V. A. H. Robeson *History of 24 Squadron* and J. D. R. Rawlings *History of 24 Squadron.* W. M. Fry *Air of Battle* and PRO/AIR 1/690).

History of No. 27 Squadron

The squadron had originally been a fighter squadron and Major A. E. Borton had taken command of it on 27th December, 1915, he was formerly an officer of the Black Watch. In February the Martinsyde Scouts began to arrive. The Scout was a biplane with one Lewis gun and it was intended to be used for fighting. The squadron went to France by stages, during February/March 1916 and arrived at Treizennes on 2nd March. It was part of 10th (Army) Wing of 1st Bde. and its duties were those of escort protection. On 7th June it transferred to St. Andre aux-Bois which was six kilometres west of Hesdin, and here it became part of 9th (HQ) Wing under Lt. Col. H. C. T. Dowding. Its number of aircraft was increased to 17 or 18 at this time.

9th June. The 9th Wing moved to Fienvillers near Doullens.

30th June. The squadron bombed St. Sauveur Station, Lille. On 1st July, the first day of the Somme battle, it bombed the German HQ at Bapaume. Special offensive patrols were made by the squadron along with No. 60 Squadron and 27 Squadron continued to bomb the German back areas.

3rd July. It carried out further offensive patrols with No. 60 Squadron. From the 9th the squadron became solely a bomber squadron and on that day the 'Elephants' bombed trains at Bapaume. On 13th July they bombed rail traffic, and on 21st July they bombed the German base at Bertincourt. On 28th July they bombed towards Cambrai. On 29th July on Major Borton's promotion Major Sidney Smith took over the squadron. On the same day the squadron bombed bases at Vélu and Bertincourt. On 30th July Epehy Junction was bombed. On 2nd August Zeppelin sheds near Brussels were bombed and also the railway station at Namur. Bombs were dropped from under 1,000 feet and excellent results were obtained. One machine failed to return. On 7th August the squadron bombed east of Valenciennes and on 23rd August it bombed railway stock. On 31st August in an attack on Havrincourt Wood it lost four aircraft. During the next week there were further raids on enemy bases.

15th September. It twice bombed Gen. von Bulow's HQ at Bourlon Chateau, along with further train bombing, and bombing at Achiet le Grand and at Vélu.

16th September. Cambrai Station was hit and also the rail sidings at Valenciennes. On 22nd September it bombed Quievreche chain railway station and also Havrincourt Wood again, as German infantry were thought to be there.

24th September. There were further attacks on Havrincourt Wood together with No. 19 Squadron, and dumps at Irles were also bombed. In the period 23-27th September it was involved in heavy offensive patrols, and on the 27th bombed Bapaume and was taken on by Boelcke's newly formed Jasta 2.

20th October. Nine aircraft attacked Aulnoye Rail Junction, and on 21st October the squadron was involved in bombing raids with No.12 and 13 Squadrons. On 28th October Boelcke was killed in an accident and on 9th November the squadron bombed Valenciennes, on the 16th it bombed a railway junction at Hirson. Gilmore once flew with the squadron.

(Source: PRO/AIR 1/168. Bowyer, C. *The Flying Elephants. The History of No. 27 Squadron RFC/RAF 1915-1969* and *The War in the Air*).

History of No. 32 Squadron

The squadron was part of Tenth Wing under Maj. L. W. B. Rees, based at Treizennes, well north of the Somme area and it had 12 DH2s fighters. It had been at Treizennes since 7th June and the airfield was close to Aire. The reason for dwelling on this part of its history which is strictly not 'Somme', is that the 'whole line' was involved in the Battle on 1st July. Its task was to deny the enemy the air space over British lines. Also it gives a chance to mention the very famous exploit carried out by Rees for which he was awarded the VC. On 1st July he engaged 8 Albatroses and was wounded and sent to hospital. The incident had arisen from a sortie in which the squadron was escorting raiders on Lille.

15th July. G. H. Lewis shot down a Fokker Monoplane. He was later to write a book called *Wings Over the Somme*. On 21st July the squadron moved to Vert Galand and became part of 9th Wing. On 1st August came under 15th Wing and its duties were to carry out offensive patrols and to provide bomber escort. It patrolled the Bapaume area and provided escort for an attack on Grevillers on 5th August. On the 12th one of its pilots fell to his death over Contalmaison, and on the same day Capt. Gilmour was forced down at Oxford Copse. At the end of August the 15th Wing came under V Bde. On 9th September the DH2s met 5 LVGs over Pozieres and one of the latter was brought down. On 14th September the squadron came under 22nd Wing when formed.

15th September. One of the pilots destroyed a Roland, and Lewis mentions in his book going on a 'jaunt' to Pozieres Mill. On 25th October the squadron moved to Lealvillers. On the 26th a patrol brought down a Halberstadt that was attacking No. 24 Squadron.

(Sources: G. H. Lewis *Wings Over the Somme. A Short History of No. 32 Squadron* by Paratirirtis and PRO/AIR 1/691).

History of No. 34 Squadron

There seems to be uncertainty as to which day in July the squadron moved to Allonville which is near Amiens. It could have been 8th, 10th or 15th July, depending on which source one believes. Allonville was south-east of Bertangles and from the 15th the squadron, under Maj. J. A. Chamier, was flying 18 BE2s and was allotted to 3rd Wing under IV Bde. It was to act as co-operation squadron for the Army and Artillery. The squadron helped to develop artillery co-operation and contact patrol into a system.

22nd July. The squadron discovered a new trench system in advance of the Switch Line and subsequently this line became the first objective instead of the Switch Line. On 25th July it also discovered another new German trench which had been concealed from the air, and had not therefore been photo-graphed. The infantry were held up by an intricate work of trenches. The squadron's work with No. 3 Squadron was hampered by mist. On 19th August along with Nos. 3 and 9 Squadrons they reported on enemy readjust-ments. On 3rd September the squadron observed for III Corps and in mid September it witnessed the use of tanks for the first time. On 1st October the fighting towards le Sars was observed by 34 and 3 Squadrons.

(Sources: *The War in the Air* PRO/AIR 1/691 and AIR 1/173.)

History of No. 45 Squadron

It was a fighter squadron, part of Ninth Wing, and in 1916 flew 12 Sopwith two-seaters (1½ Strutters) in the Somme battle. Under Major W. R. Read it left Britain for France on 12th October 1916, and after landing at St. Omer proceeded to Fienvillers, south-west of Doullens and from there had its baptism of war flying defensive and offensive patrols. The Somme offensive was still in progress and the squadron was heavily involved in the air fighting.

22nd October. Three of its Sopwiths failed to return. On 4th November the squadron went north to Boisdengham near St. Omer, where it remained for about five weeks. At one time Lts. Frew and Howell were members of the squadron.

(Sources: N. Macmillan *Into the Blue* and the PRO/AIR 1/692.)

History of No. 60 Squadron

Major F. F. Waldron formerly of the 19th Hussars was the squadron commander and it was said that three of his Flight commanders were former Etonians. Certainly Smith-Barry who became a Brigadier-General (RAF) was an Etonian. The other two were Captain A. S. M. Summers who *was* an Old Etonian and Captain H. C. A. Tower who wasn't. On 16th June the squadron went to Vert Galand equipped with Morane Bullets, which had their cowls painted red which confused the British Anti-Aircraft Batteries who thought at first that they were Fokkers.

Shortly before Basil Hallam Radford was killed in a kite balloon accident, Major Waldron records having breakfast with him. War patrols were begun very soon after arrival at Vert Galand. The first flights over the line consisted of protection of BE2cs which were bombing rail communications in the Cambrai–Busigny–St. Quentin areas. The scouts worked usually in pairs at the time.

1st July. 60 Squadron along with No. 27 Squadron made special offensive patrols.

2nd July. Its Moranes escorted REs and 27 Squadron Martinsydes on the raid on Bapaume in the afternoon. On 3rd July Waldron was shot down by a Fokker in the Arras–Cambrai road area. He had been leading 'A' flight and died of his wounds that evening. Smith-Barry was in the same attack and took over as squadron commander. Smith-Barry was an Irishman and a brilliant flyer, he was also a stern disciplinarian. During the rest of July the squadron played its part over the area between St. Quentin and Cambrai. The squadron's first kill was by Lt. Vincent in one of the Morane Bullets. On 3rd August the squadron was withdrawn to André-aux-Bois because of high casualty rates, and during this time Lt. Claude Ridley flew over a spy in his 'Parasol', but his engine failed and the aircraft came down in Villers en Couchie in German held territory.

During the early stages of the Somme Battle, partly because of obsolete equipment, the squadron had suffered heavy losses and Smith-Barry was appalled at the high casualty rate and told Dowding who was in charge of the Ninth Wing, that he was not going to allow his pilots to fly without at least seven flying hours over the line. In August the Moranes began to be replaced by Nieuports single-seater fighters. On 16th August the squadron arrived at Izel le Hameau and became a Scout squadron. The squadron was rebuilt from the 'remains' of 11 Squadron. The scouts had come from this squadron and Albert Ball was one of the pilots at the time. Ball was shifted to single-seaters and told to work out his own routine, being permitted to fly lone wolf patrols if he wished. He also developed a new style of airfighting by making the most of a Lewis gun mounted on the upper wing of his Nieuport that could be tilted and aimed at the under side of an enemy aircraft. He was particularly good at trapping German two-seaters in this way. It was his standard that others measured themselves against. He was to go on leave in September.

23rd August. The squadron strength in the line at le Hameau was 15 Nieuports, 2 Moranes and a Spad. The squadron's fighting was mainly over Bapaume, Courcelette, Martinpuich, Busigny, St. Quentin, Cambrai, Havrincourt etc. On 15th September Trenchard and Baring arrived at 60 Squadron Mess and asked for three volunteers to shoot down three German Kite Balloons which might spot tanks, the new weapon.[9]

19th September. Capt H. C. A. Tower in a Morane was shot down. W. M. Fry joined the squadron at the beginning of October. Capt. Foot as well as Ball had come from 11 Squadron. Fry's first flight with the squadron was in a Nieuport on 18th October with 'C' Flight, with whom he flew offensive patrols. On 26th October Capt. Foot engaged some Halberstadts that were attacking No. 24 Squadron but he crashed in his Nieuport. On 9th November one of 60 Squadron escorts was shot down and two from 12 Squadron. Eight Nieuports and eight FE2bs of 11 Squadron went out on new trenches and they sighted the beginnings of the Hindenburg Line. In December 1916 Smith-Barry was sent home to form a training squadron.

Keith Caldwell (Grid) a New Zealander who began his career with the squadron was later to become CO of 74 Squadron. During the Somme offensive the squadron brought down a large number of enemy machines and kite balloons. Many of the squadron papers were burnt in November 1916.

(Sources: Bob Sheldon *A Saga of the Sixty*. History of 60 Squadron. (C & C) *The War in the Air*. A. J. L. Scott *History of 60 Squadron*. Hein. 1920. W. M. Fry *Air of Battle*. Kimber 1974. A. J. Young/D. Warne *60 Squadron RFC* RAF 1966. F. D. Tredrey *Pioneer Pilot – Smith-Barry*. Davies 1976. PRO/AIR 1/173).

History of No. 70 Squadron

The squadron was based at the beginning of July at Fienvillers under Maj. G. A. K. Lawrence and was part of Ninth Wing. At this time it had 8 Sopwith two-seaters and four more were to arrive on 30th July. Flights arrived one at a time on three different dates. 'A' Flight had arrived on 25th May and 'B' Flight on 29th June.

The Sopwiths were one and a half strutters and were two-seaters. This type was to be the first British fighter to have a synchronised machine gun as standard equipment. In addition to fighter patrols, the squadron was also engaged in reconnaissance and bombing missions. On 1st July it was reconnoitering the Cambrai area at 6 a.m. but had nothing to report. It was employed during the Somme battle in taking photographs, carrying out long reconnaissance to Mons, Mauberge, le Cateau and OPs. On 15th September Capt. Cruickshank was shot down and killed by the German ace Boelcke. On the same day the squadron bombed trains near Gouzeaucourt. The Sopwiths brought down a Roland near Havrincourt Wood. 15th September was a very tough day for both sides who suffered a number of casualties.

10th October. The squadron attacked German fighters over Vélu and on 20th October it carried out a long reconnaissance towards Valenciennes and le Quesnoy. It was to bring down 40 enemy aircraft, and casualties included 2nd Lt. Bott, an Observer, who was to write a book called *An Airmen's Outing*. Also Lt. Cousins was killed. A future commanding officer was Major A. W. Tedder, and other names to be associated with the squadron were Quigley, Stewart and Cochrane-Stewart.

(Sources: *The War in the Air*. PRO/AIR 1/176 and AIR 1/694).

History of No. 8 (RNAS) Squadron

During the Battle of the Somme the RFC had maintained a resolute and continuous offensive over the enemy lines, and suffered heavy casualties at a time when the training and construction at home were unable to make good the losses. The Army Council therefore appealed to the Admiralty for help, and after a meeting of the War Cabinet on 17th October, it was decided that a complete naval aeroplane squadron of eighteen fighting machines, together with the necessary personnel should be placed temporarily at the disposal of the GOC in Command BEF from Dunkirk Command. 'A' Flight came from No. 1 Wing at St. Pol, 'B' from No. 5 Wing at Coudekerke and 'C' from No. 4 Wing at Petit Synthe (sic). These three Flights of fighting aeroplanes were withdrawn to form a composite squadron to meet the Army's demand.

The squadron or the 'Naval Eight' as it was called, arrived at Vert Galand on 26th October under G. R. Bromet, their commander, as part of 22nd Wing (V Brigade). 'A' Flight had been using Sopwith Pups under Goble, 'B' Flight under Mackenzie had Le Rhone Nieuports and 'C' Flight had Sopwith 1½ Strutters. After a few days they were all to be using Sopwith Pups. Vert Galand aerodrome was close to the main road between Doullens and Amiens. It was basically a farm, and the aerodrome consisted of seven sheds on the right hand side of the road, and on the other side of the road was No. 23 Squadron with FE2bs. The huts and billets were clustered around the four cross roads to the north of the field and included the farm buildings. HQ Flight messed and slept there. It even had a cinema there to which many Army personnel also came.

V Bde. HQ was at Toutencourt and consisted of 15th and 22nd Wings, 22nd Wing to which it was attached had huts at HQ at Rosel Farm, which was within half a mile of the aerodrome. The squadron after its arrival, practised flying in formation and on 3rd November it carried out its first line patrol. Meanwhile it had numerous visitors including Trenchard, Gough, Baring, Moore-Brabazon and Haig. Haig came to see it on 6th November. Bad weather was holding them up, and it was not until 9th November that it had its first full day's work, and three enemy machines were driven down in damaged condition.

10th November. The squadron claimed its first victim, Flight Sub. M. B. Galbraith attacked a formation of five Roland biplanes at a height of 17,000 feet, and succeeded in shooting one down out of control and in dispersing the remainder. Robert Little, an Australian who was to become an 'ace', and who had volunteered for the RNAS and qualified as a pilot in October 1915, downed his first victim, an Aviatik, on 11th November.

(Sources: PRO/AIR 1/696 and E. G. Johnstone *Naval Eight.)*

Bibliography

I would like to thank the authors and publishers of the following books and articles which have been of the greatest use to me during the preparation of this book:

Adams, B. *Nothing of Importance.* A record of eight months at the front with a Welsh battalion, October 1915 to June 1916. Methuen 1917.

Adcock, A. St. John *For Remembrance:* Soldier Poets who have fallen in the War. Hodder & Stoughton 1920.

Aiken, A. *Courage Past* – A Duty Done. Aiken 1971 Glasgow.

Aitken, A. *Gallipoli to the Somme.* Recollection of a New Zealand Infantryman. OUP 1963.

Army Quarterly. Various Issues.

Ashworth, T. *Trench Warfare, 1914-1918:* Live and Let Live System. Macmillan 1980.

Asquith, R. *Life and Letters.* ed Jolliffe. J. Collins 1980.

Baring, M. *Flying Corps Headquarters, 1914-1918.* Blackwood 1968.

Barrie, A. *War Underground.* Muller 1961.

Bean, C. E. W. *Anzacs to Amiens:* a shorter history of the Australian fighting services in the First World War. Australian War Memorial 1946.

Bean, C. E. W. *Official History of Australia in the War of 1914-1918,* Volume Three. Angus & Robertson 1929.

Becke, Major A. F. *The Order of Battle of Divisions,* I-IV. HMSO 1935-1945.

Bidwell, S. and Graham, D. *Fire Power:* British Army Weapons and Theories of War, 1904-1945. Allen & Unwin 1982.

Blunden, E. *The Mind's Eye* – Essays. Cape 1934.

Blunden, E. *Undertones of War.* Cobden Sanderson 1928.

Blunden, E. and Norman, S. *We'll Shift Our Ground or Two on a Tour.* Cobden Sanderson 1933.

Bott, A. J. *An Airman's Outing.* McClelland, Goodchild & Stewart, Toronto 1917.

Bowyer, C. *The Flying Elephants:* a History of No. 27 Squadron Royal Flying Corps. Royal Air Force 1915-1969. Macdonald 1977.

Boyd, D. *Salute of Guns.* Cape 1930.

Bray, A. T. *The Battle of the Somme, 1916:* A Bibliography. University Microfilms International 1967.

Brenan, G. *A Life of One's Own.* Childhood and Youth. Cape 1975.

Brittain, V. *Testament of Youth.* Arrow/Hutchinson 1960.

Brophy, J. & Partridge, E. *The Long Trail;* What the British soldier sang and said in 1914-1918. Deutsch 1965.

Buchan, J. *The Battle of the Somme.* Nelson (no date).

Buxton, A. R. *Andrew R. Buxton:* A Memoir. Scott 1918.

Cameron, J. *1916* – Year of Decision. Oldbourne 1962.

Carr, C. D. Baker- *From Chauffeur to Brigadier.* Benn 1930.

Carrington, C. *Soldier from the Wars Returning.* Hutchinson 1965.

Chandos, Lord *The Memoirs of Lord Chandos.* Bodley Head 1964.

Chapman, G. *A Kind of Survivor.* Gollanz 1975.

Chapman, G. *A Passionate Prodigality.* MacGibbon and Kee 1965.

Chapman, G. ed. *Vain Glory.* A miscellany of the Great War, 1914-1918. Written by those who fought in it on each side and all fronts. Cassell 1937.

Charteris, J. *AT GHQ.* Cassell 1931.

Churchill, W. S. *The World Crisis 1911-1918.* Thornton Butterworth 1931.

Clayton, C. P. *The Hungry One.* Gomer Press 1978.

Cloete, S. *A Victorian Son.* Collins 1971.

Collier, B. *Brasshat:* A Biography of Field Marshal Sir Henry Wilson. Secker and Warburg 1961.

Congreve, B. *Armageddon Road.* A VC's Diary 1914-1916. ed. Norman T. Kimber 1982.

Cook, A. H. *A Soldier's War.* Molesworth 1957.

Coombs, R. E. B. *Before Endeavours Fades.* A Guide to the Battlefields of the First World War. After the Battle 1976.

Cooper, A. Duff. *Haig,* Two Vols. Faber and Faber 1935.

Coppard, G. *With a Machine Gun to Cambrai.* Imperial War Museum 1969.

Creagh, Sir O'Moore and Humpris, E. M. *The VC and DSO,* 3 Vols. Standard Art Book Company (no date).

Croney, P. *Soldier's Luck.* Stockwell 1965.

Crozier, F. P. *A Brass-hat in No Man's Land.* Cape 1930.

Crozier, F. P. *The Men I Killed.* Cape 1937.

Crutchley, C. E. *Machine Gunner, 1914-1918.* Personal Experiences of the Machine Gun Corps. Bailey Brothers and Swinfen 1975.

Cruttwell, C. R. M. F. *A History of the Great War 1914-1918,* 2nd Edn. OUP 1936.

Cuddeford, D. W. J. *And all for What?* Heath Cranton 1933.

Davson, H. M. *Memoirs of the Great War.* Gale and Polden 1964.

Dewar, G. A. B. and Boraston, J. H. *Sir Douglas Haig's Command,* Vol. I. Constable 1922.

Dolden, A. S. *Cannon Fodder.* An Infantryman's Life on the Western Front, 1914-1918. Blandford Press 1980.

Douie, C. *The Weary Road:* Recollections of a Subaltern of Infantry. Murray 1929.

Doyle, Sir A. Conan *The British Campaign in France and Flanders.* Hodder & Stoughton 1918.

Dundas, H. L. N. *Henry Dundas, Scots Guards:* A Memoir. Blackwood 1921.

Eden, A. *Another World, 1897-1917.* Allen Lane 1976.

Edmonds, Brigadier-General Sir. J. E. (ed.) *Military Operations France and Belgium.* Macmillan and HMSO 1922-1949.

Enser, A. G. S. *A Subject Bibliograhy of the First World War.* Deutsch 1979.

Eyre, G. E. M. *Somme Harvest.* Memories of a PBI in the Summer of 1916. Jarrold 1938.

Feilding, R. *War Letters to a Wife:* France and Flanders 1915-1919. Medici Society 1929.

Fitzgerald, F. Scott *Tender is the Night.* Bodley Head 1959. C. Scribners (New York).

Foley, J. *The Boilerplate War.* Muller 1963.

Foulkes, Major-General C. H. *'Gas!':* the story of the Special Brigade. Blackwood 1934.

Four Years on the Western Front by a Rifleman: Being the experiences of a Ranker in the London Rifle Brigade 4th, 3rd and 56th Divisions. Odhams 1922.

Frankau, G. *Peter Jackson, Cigar Merchant* (a novel). Hutchinson 1919.

Fry, W. *Air of Battle.* Kimber 1974.

Fussell, P. *The Great War and Modern Memory.* OUP 1975.

Gardner, B. *The Big Push.* The Somme 1916. Cassell 1961.

Germains, V. W. *The Kitchener Armies.* Peter Davies 1930.

Gibbs, P. *The Battles of the Somme.* Heinemann 1917.

Gibbs, P. *Now it Can Be Told.* Harper & Brothers 1920.

Gibbs, P. *Realities of War.* Heinemann 1920.

Giles, J. *The Somme Then and Now.* Bailey Brothers & Swinfen 1977.

Gladden, N. *The Somme 1916:* A Personal Account. Kimber 1974.

Glubb, J. *Into Battle:* A Soldier's Diary of the Great War. Cassell 1978.

Gommecourt. *1st July 1916. Report on the Defence of . . .* Royal United Services Journal.

Gough, Sir H. *The Fifth Army.* Hodder & Stoughton 1931.

Graham, S. *The Challenge of the Dead.* Cassell 1921.

Graves, R. *Fairies and Fusiliers* (poems). Heinemann 1917.

Graves, R. *Goliath and David* (poems). Chiswick Press 1916.

Graves, R. *Goodbye to All That.* Cassells 1957.

Graves, R. *In Broken Images* Selected Letters of . . . 1914-1946 ed. by O'Prey. P. Hutchinson 1982.

Greenwell, G. H. *An Infant in Arms.* War Letters of a Company Officer 1914-1918. Allen Lane 1972.

Grieve, W. G. and Newman, B. *Tunnellers.* Jenkins 1936.

Griffith, W. *Up to Mametz.* Faber and Faber 1931.

Gristwood, A. D. *The Somme* (novel). Cape 1927.

Gurney, I. *Severn and Somme* (poems). Sidgwick & Jackson 1917.

Sir Douglas Haig's Great Push: The Battle of the Somme. Hutchinson 1916.

Sir Douglas Haig's Despatches (December 1915-1919) Dent 1919.

The Private Papers of Douglas Haig, 1914-1919. ed. Blake, R., Eyre & Spottiswoode 1952.

Hammerton, Sir J. A. *The Great War:* I Was There. The Amalgamated Press 1938-39.

Hamilton, N. *Monty: The Making of a General 1887-1942.* Hamish Hamilton 1981.

Harris, J. *Covenant with Death* (novel). Hutchinson 1961.

Harris, J. *The Somme:* Death of a Generation. Hodder & Stoughton 1966.

Hart, Sir B. H. Liddell *A History of the First World War.* Faber and Faber 1934.

Hart, Sir B. H. Liddell *Memoirs,* Volume I. Cassell 1965.

Hart, Sir B. H. Liddell *The Tanks:* History of the Royal Tank Regiment, Volume I. Cassell 1959.

Harvey, H. E. *Battle-line narratives, 1915-1918.* Brentano 1928.

Hawker, T. M. *Hawker VC:* The Biography of the late Major Lanoe George Hawker. Mitre Press 1965.

Hawkins, F. *From Ypres to Cambrai:* the diary of an infantryman, 1914-1919. Elmfield 1974.

Hitchcock, Captain F. C. *"Stand To":* A Diary of the Trenches, 1915-1918. Hurst & Blackett 1937.

Hockley, A. H. Farrar-. *The Somme,* Batsford 1964.

Hodson, J. L. *Return to the Wood* (novel). Gollanz 1955.

Hughes, C. *Mametz:* Lloyd George's 'Welsh Army' at the Battle of the Somme. Orion Press 1982.

Hurd, M. *The Ordeal of Ivor Gurney.* OUP 1978.

Hutchison, Lt. Col. G. S. *Footslogger.* An Autobiography. Hutchinson 1931.

Hutchison, Lt. Col. G. S. *Pilgrimage.* Rich & Cowan 1935.

Hutchison, Lt. Col. G. S. *Warrior.* Hutchinson 1932.

James, Brigadier E. A. *British Regiments 1914-1918.* Samson Books 1978.

Johnstone, E. G. *Naval Eight:* A History of No. 8 Squadron RNAS. Signal 1931.

Jones, D. *In Parenthesis.* Faber and Faber 1937.

Jünger, E. *The Storm of Steel.* From the diary of a German storm-troop officer on the Western Front. Chatto & Windus 1929.

Keegan, J. *The Face of Battle.* A study of Waterloo, Agincourt and the Somme. Cape 1976.

Kelly, D. V. *39 Months.* With the 'Tigers', 1915-1918. Benn 1930.

Keynes, G. *The Gates of Memory.* OUP 1981.

Leed, E. J. *No Man's Land.* CUP 1979.

Lewis, C. D. *Sagittarius Rising.* Davies 1936.

Lewis, G. H. *Wings Over the Somme.* Kimber 1976.

Liveing, E. G. D. *Attack:* an Infantry Subaltern's Impressions of July 1st 1916. Heinemann 1918.

Lloyd George, D. *War Memoirs,* Two vols. Odhams Press 1938.

Lytton, N. *The Press and the General Staff.* Collins 1921.

Macdonald, L. *Somme.* Michael Joseph 1983.

Macmillan, H. *Winds of Change 1914-1939.* Macmillan 1966.

Macmillan, N. *Into the Blue.* Jarrold 1969.

Malins, G. H. *How I Filmed The War.* Herbert Jenkins 1920.

Manning, F. *The Middle Parts of Fortune.* Peter Davies 1977.

Masefield, J. *Battle of the Somme.* Heinemann 1919.

Masefield, J. *The Old Front Line.* Or the beginning of the Battle of the Somme. Heinemann 1917.

Mason, T. *History of Nine Squadron.* Beaumont (no date).

Maurice, General Sir F. *The Life of General Lord Rawlinson of Trent.* Cassell 1928.

Maze, P. *A Frenchman in Khaki.* Heinemann 1934.

Michelin Guides: *The Somme Volume One.* Michelin 1919.

Middlebrook, M. *The First Day on the Somme, 1 July 1916.* Allen Lane 1971.

Montague, C. E. *Disenchantment.* Chatto and Windus 1922.

Moore, W. *The Thin Yellow Line.* Leo Cooper 1974.

Moran, Lord *The Anatomy of Courage.* Constable 1945.

Murray, J. *Call to Arms.* Kimber 1980.

Neville, J. E. H. *The War Letters of a Light Infantryman.* Sifton Praed 1930.

Nicholson, G. W. L. *The Fighting Newfoundlander.* Government of Newfoundland 1964.

Norman, T. *Hell they called High Wood:* Somme 1916. Kimber 1984.

Officers Died in the Great War 1914-1919. HMSO 1919.

Oman, Sir C. *The German Losses on the Somme, July-December 1916.* Lord Sydenham of Combe and others, a criticism of 'The World Crisis' by Winston Churchill (no date).

Orpen, Sir W. *An Onlooker in France 1917-1919.* Williams and Norgate 1921.

Palmer, F. *With the New Army on the Somme.* Murray 1917.

Panichas, G. A. (ed.) *Promise of Greatness.* The War of 1914-1918. Cassell 1968.

Plowman, M. *Bridge into the Future, Letters of . . .* Andrew Dakers 1944.

Plowman, M. *A Subaltern on the Somme in 1916.* Dent 1927.

Pound, R. *The Lost Generation.* Constable 1964.

Raleigh, Sir W. and Jones, H. A. *The War in the Air.* Six Vols. OUP 1922-1937.

Repington, C. *The First World War, 1914-1918.* Vol. One. Constable 1920.

Richards, F. *Old Soldiers Never Die.* Faber and Faber 1933.

Robertson, Field-Marshall Sir W. *Soldiers and Statesmen 1914-1918.* Cassell 1926.

Robinson, H. P. *The Turning Point.* The Battle of the Somme. Heinemann 1917.

Rogerson, S. *Twelve Days.* Barker 1933.

Rorie, D. A. *A. Medico's Luck in the War:* being the reminiscences of RAMC work with the 51st Highland Division. Milne and Hutchinson 1929.

Russell, A. *The Machine Gunner.* Roundwood 1977.

Sassoon, S. *Diaries of 1915-1918.* ed. by Hart-Davis R. Faber & Faber 1983.

Sassoon, S. *Memoirs of an Infantry Officer.* Faber and Faber 1930.

Sassoon, S. *Siegfried's Journey.* Faber and Faber 1945.

Scott, S. J. L. *Sixty Squadron.* RAF A History. Heinemann 1920.

Scott, F. G. *The Great War as I Saw It.* Goodchild Toronto 1922.

Seymour-Smith M. *Robert Graves.* His Life and Work. Hutchinson 1982.

Slack, C. M. *Grandfather's Adventures in the Great War 1914-1918.* Stockwell 1977.

Smithers, A. J. *Wonder Aces of the Air:* The Flying Heroes of the Great War. Gordon & Cremonesi 1980.

Sparrow, A. A. H. *The Land-locked Lake.* Barker 1932.

Spears, E. L. *Liaison, 1914.* Heinemann 1930.

Spicer, L. D. *Letters from France 1915-1918.* Robert York 1979.

Statistics of the Military Effort of the British Empire 1914-1920. HMSO 1922.

Tawney, R. H. *The Attack and Other Papers.* Allen and Unwin 1953.

Taylor, A. P. J. *The First World War.* Hamish Hamilton 1963.

Taylor, H. A. *Good-bye to the Battlefields.* To-day and Yesterday on the Western Front. Paul 1928.

Terraine, J. *Douglas Haig:* The Educated Soldier. Hutchinson 1963.

Terraine, J. (ed.) *General Jack's Diary 1914-1918.* The Trench Diary of Brigadier-General J. L. Jack, DSO. Eyre and Spottiswoode 1964.

Terraine, J. *The Smoke and the Fire:* Myths and Anti-myths of War 1861-1945. Sidgwick and Jackson 1980.

Thomas, W. B. *With the British on the Somme* Methuen 1917.

Tilsley, W. V. *Other Ranks.* (a novel) Cobden-Sanderson 1931.

Tomlinson, H. M. *All Our Yesterdays.* Heinemann 1930.

Tredrey, F. D. *Pioneer Pilot:* The Great Smith Barry who taught the World how to Fly. P. Davies 1976.

Tucker, J. F. *Johny Get Your Gun.* A Personal Narrative of the Somme, Ypres and Arras. Kimber 1978.

Turner, P. W. and Haigh, R. H. *Not for Glory.* Maxwell 1969.

Tytler, N. Fraser- *Field Guns in France.* Hutchinson 1922.

Uys, I. *Delville Wood.* Uys, South Africa 1983.

Wade, A. *The War of the Guns.* Western Front, 1917 and 1918. Batsford 1936.

Warwick, G. W. *We Band of Brothers.* Timmins, Cape Town 1962.

The War the Infantry Knew 1914-1919. P. S. King 1938.

The Western Front Then and Now. Pearson 193?

Whinyates, R. *Artillery and Trench Mortar Memories,* 32nd Division. Whinyates 1932.

White, A. S. *A Bibliography of Regimental Histories of the British Army.* The Society for Army Historical Research in conjuction with The Army Museums Ogilby Trust 1965.

Williams, M. *The Treatment of the German Losses on the Somme in the British Official History,* Royal United Service Institutional Journal. February 1966.

Williamson, H. *The Golden Virgin.* (a novel) Macdonald 1957.

Williamson, H. *The Wet Flanders Plain.* Faber and Faber 1929.

Wortley, R. S. *Letters from a Flying Officer.* Alan Sutton 1982.

Winter, D. *Death's Men:* Soldiers of the Great War. Allen Lane 1978.

Wynne, C. W. *If Germany Attacks:* the battle in depth in the West: lessons from the Western Front, 1915-17. Faber and Faber 1940.

I would also like to acknowledge with grateful thanks all the Battalion, Regimental and Divisional Histories that I have used, which unfortunately are too numerous to mention.

Appendix

THE SOMME, 1916

ORDER OF BATTLE OF INFANTRY AND PIONEER BATTALIONS

GUARDS DIVISION

1st Guards Brigade :
2/Gren. Gds.   2/Coldstr. Gds.   3/Coldstr. Gds.   1/Irish Gds.
2nd Guards Brigade :
3/Gren. Gds.   1/Coldstr. Gds.   1/Scots Gds.   2/Irish Gds.
3rd Guards Brigade :
1/Gren. Gds.   4/Gren. Gds.   2/Scots Gds.   1/Welch Gds.
Pioneers : 4/Coldstr. Gds.

1ST DIVISION

1st Brigade :
10/Gloster.   1/Black Watch   8/R. Berks.   1/Camerons.
2nd Brigade :
2/R. Sussex.   1/L. N. Lancs.   1/Northampton.   2/K.R.R.C.
3rd Brigade :
1/S.W.B.   1/Gloster.   2/Welch.   2/R.M.F.
Pioneers : 1/6th Welch.

2ND DIVISION

5th Brigade :
17/R. Fus.   24/R. Fus.   2/O. & B.L.I.   2/H.L.I.
6th Brigade :
1/King's.   2/S. Staffs.   13/Essex.   17/Middlesex.
99th Brigade :
22/R. Fus.   23/R. Fus.   1/R. Berks.   1/K.R.R.C.
Pioneers : 10/D.C.L.I.

3RD DIVISION

8th Brigade :
2/R. Scots.   8/E. Yorks.   1/R. Scots Fus.   7/K.S.L.I.
9th Brigade :
1/North'd Fus.   4/R. Fus.   13/King's.   12/W. Yorks.
76th Brigade :
8/King's Own.   2/Suffolk.   10/R. Welch Fus. 1/Gordons.
Pioneers : 20/K.R.R.C.

4TH DIVISION

10th Brigade :
1/R. Warwick. 2/Seaforth. 1/R. Irish Fus. 2/R. Dub. Fus.

11th Brigade :
1/Somerset L.I. 1/E. Lancs. 1/Hampshire. 1/Rif. Brig.

12th Brigade :
1/King's Own. 2/Lancs. Fus. 2/Essex. 2/D.W.R.

Pioneers : 21/W. Yorks.

5TH DIVISION

13th Brigade :
14/R. Warwick. 15/R. Warwick. 2/K.O.S.B. 1/R. W. Kent.

15th Brigade :
16/R. Warwick. 1/Norfolk. 1/Bedford. 1/Cheshire.

95th Brigade :
1/Devon. 12/Gloster. 1/E. Surrey. 1/D.C.L.I.

Pioneers : 1/6th A. & S. H.

6TH DIVISION

16th Brigade :
1/Buffs. 8/Bedford. 1/K.S.L.I. 2/York & Lanc.

18th Brigade :
1/W. Yorks. 11/Essex. 2/D.L.I. 14/D.L.I.

71st Brigade :
9/Norfolk. 9/Suffolk. 1/Leicester. 2/Sherwood For.

Pioneers : 11/Leicester.

7TH DIVISION

20th Brigade :
8/Devon. 9/Devon. 2/Border Regt. 2/Gordons.

22nd Brigade :
2/R. Warwick. 2/R. Irish. 1/R. Welch Fus. 20/Manchester.

91st Brigade :
2/Queen's. 1/S. Staffs. 21/Manchester. 22/Manchester.

Pioneers : 24/Manchester.

8TH DIVISION

23rd Brigade :
2/Devon. 2/W. Yorks. 2/Middlesex. 2/Sco. Rif.

24th Brigade : [1]
1/Worcs. 1/Sherwood For. 2/Northampton. 2/E. Lancs.

25th Brigade :
2/Lincoln. 2/R. Berks. 1/R. Irish Rif. 2/Rif. Brig.

Pioneers : 22/D.L.I.

9TH (SCOTTISH) DIVISION

26th Brigade :
8/Black Watch. 7/Seaforth. 5/Camerons. 10/A. & S. H.

27th Brigade :
11/R. Scots. 12/R. Scots. 6/K.O.S.B. 9/Sco. Rif.

[1] With 23rd Division until 15th July, in exchange for 70th Brigade.

S.A. Brigade :
  1/Regt. (Cape Prov.)
  2/Regt. (Natal & O.F.S.)
  3/Regt. (Trans. & Rhod.)
  4/Regt. (Scottish).
Pioneers : 9/Seaforth.

11TH DIVISION

32nd Brigade :
| 9/W. Yorks. | 6/Green Howards. | 8/D.W.R. | 6/York & Lanc. |
33rd Brigade :
| 6/Lincoln. | 6/Border Regt. | 7/S. Staffs. | 9/Sherwood For. |
34th Brigade :
| 8/North'd Fus. | 9/Lancs. Fus. | 5/Dorset. | 11/Manchester. |
Pioneers : 6/E. Yorks.

12TH (EASTERN) DIVISION

35th Brigade :
| 7/Norfolk. | 7/Suffolk. | 9/Essex. | 5/R. Berks. |
36th Brigade :
| 8/R. Fus. | 9/R. Fus. | 7/R. Sussex. | 11/Middlesex. |
37th Brigade :
| 6/Queen's. | 6/Buffs. | 7/E. Surrey. | 6/R. W. Kent. |
Pioneers : 5/Northampton.

14TH (LIGHT) DIVISION

41st Brigade :
| 7/K.R.R.C. | 8/K.R.R.C. | 7/Rif. Brig. | 8/Rif. Brig. |
42nd Brigade :
| 5/O. & B.L.I. | 5/K.S.L.I. | 9/K.R.R.C. | 9/Rif. Brig. |
43rd Brigade :
| 6/Somerset L.I. | 6/D.C.L.I. | 6/K.O.Y.L.I. | 10/D.L.I. |
Pioneers : 11/King's.

15TH (SCOTTISH) DIVISION

44th Brigade :
| 9/Black Watch. | 8/Seaforth. | 8th/10th Gordons. | 7/Camerons. |
45th Brigade :
| 13/R. Scots. | 6th/7th R. Scots Fus. | 6/Camerons. | 11/A. & S. H. |
46th Brigade :
| 10/Sco. Rif. | 7th/8th K.O.S.B. | 10th/11th H.L.I. | 12/H.L.I. |
Pioneers : 9/Gordons.

16TH (IRISH) DIVISION

47th Brigade :
| 6/R. Irish. | 6/Conn. Rangers. | 7/Leinster. | 8/R.M.F. |
48th Brigade :
| 7/R. Irish Rif. | 1/R.M.F. | 8/R. Dub. Fus. | 9/R. Dub. Fus. |
49th Brigade :
| 7/R. Innis. Fus. | 8/R. Innis. Fus. | 7/R. Irish Fus. | 8/R. Irish Fus. |
Pioneers : 11/Hampshire.

17TH (NORTHERN) DIVISION

50th Brigade :
  10/W. Yorks.   7/E. Yorks.   7/Green Howards. 6/Dorset.

51st Brigade :
  7/Lincoln.   7/Border Regt.   8/S. Staffs.   10/Sherwood For.

52nd Brigade :
  9/North'd Fus.   10/Lancs. Fus.   9/D.W.R.   12/Manchester.

Pioneers : 7/York & Lanc.

18TH (EASTERN) DIVISION

53rd Brigade :
  8/Norfolk.   8/Suffolk.   10/Essex.   6/R. Berks.

54th Brigade :
  11/R. Fus.   7/Bedford.   6/Northampton. 12/Middlesex.

55th Brigade :
  7/Queen's.   7/Buffs.   8/E. Surrey.   7/R. W. Kent.

Pioneers : 8/R. Sussex.

19TH (WESTERN) DIVISION

56th Brigade :
  7/King's Own.   7/E. Lancs.   7/S. Lancs.   7/L. N. Lancs.

57th Brigade :
  10/R. Warwick.   8/Gloster.   10/Worcs.   8/N. Staffs.

58th Brigade :
  9/Cheshire.   9/R. Welch Fus. 9/Welch.   6/Wiltshire.

Pioneers : 5/S.W.B.

20TH (LIGHT) DIVISION

59th Brigade :
  10/K.R.R.C.   11/K.R.R.C.   10/Rif. Brig.   11/Rif. Brig.

60th Brigade :
  6/O. & B.L.I.   6/K.S.L.I.   12/K.R.R.C.   12/Rif. Brig.

61st Brigade :
  7/Somerset L.I. 7/D.C.L.I.   7/K.O.Y.L.I.   12/King's.

Pioneers : 11/D.L.I.

21ST DIVISION

62nd Brigade :
  12/North'd Fus. 13/North'd Fus. 1/Lincoln.   10/Green
                                                            Howards.

63rd Brigade : [1]
  8/Lincoln.   8/Somerset L.I. 4/Middlesex.   10/York & Lanc.

64th Brigade :
  1/E. Yorks.   9/K.O.Y.L.I.   10/K.O.Y.L.I.   15/D.L.I.

Pioneers : 14/North'd Fus.

23RD DIVISION

68th Brigade :
  10/North'd Fus. 11/North'd Fus. 12/D.L.I.   13/D.L.I.

---

[1] Exchanged with 110th Bde. of 37th Division, 7th July.

69th Brigade :
11/W. Yorks. 8/Green Howards. 9/Green Howards. 10/D.W.R.

70th Brigade [1] *:*
11/Sherwood For. 8/K.O.Y.L.I. 8/York & Lanc. 9/York & Lanc.

Pioneers : 9/S. Staffs.

24TH DIVISION

17th Brigade :
8/Buffs. 1/R. Fus. 12/R. Fus. 3/Rif. Brig.

72nd Brigade :
8/Queen's. 9/E. Surrey. 8/R. W. Kent. 1/N. Staffs.

73rd Brigade :
9/R. Sussex. 7/Northampton. 13/Middlesex. 2/Leinster.

Pioneers : 12/Sherwood For.

25TH DIVISION

7th Brigade :
10/Cheshire. 3/Worcs. 8/L. N. Lancs. 1/Wiltshire.

74th Brigade :
11/Lancs. Fus. 13/Cheshire. 9/L. N. Lancs. 2/R. Irish. Rif.

75th Brigade :
11/Cheshire. 8/Border Regt. 2/S. Lancs. 8/S. Lancs.

Pioneers : 6/S.W.B.

29TH DIVISION

86th Brigade :
2/R. Fus. 1/Lancs. Fus. 16/Middlesex. 1/R. Dub. Fus.

87th Brigade :
2/S.W.B. 1/K.O.S.B. 1/R. Innis. Fus. 1/Border Regt.

88th Brigade :
4/Worcs. 1/Essex. 2/Hampshire. R.Newfoundland Regt.

Pioneers : 2/Monmouth.

30TH DIVISION

21st Brigade :
18/King's. 2/Green Howards. 2/Wiltshire. 19/Manchester.

89th Brigade :
17/King's. 19/King's. 20/King's. 2/Bedford.

90th Brigade :
2/R. Scots Fus. 16/Manchester. 17/Manchester. 18/Manchester.

Pioneers : 11/S. Lancs.

31ST DIVISION

92nd Brigade :
10/E. Yorks. 11/E. Yorks. 12/E. Yorks. 13/E. Yorks.

93rd Brigade :
15/W. Yorks. 16/W. Yorks. 18/W. Yorks. 18/D.L.I.

94th Brigade :
11/E. Lancs. 12/York & Lanc. 13/York & Lanc. 14/York & Lanc.

Pioneers : 12/K.O.Y.L.I.

[1] With 8th Division until 15th July, in exchange for 24th Bde.

32ND DIVISION

14th Brigade :
19/Lancs. Fus.[1]   1/Dorset.   2/Manchester.   15/H.L.I.

96th Brigade :
16/North'd Fus.   15/Lancs. Fus.   16/Lancs. Fus.   2/R. Innis. Fus.

97th Brigade :
11/Border Regt.   2/K.O.Y.L.I.   16/H.L.I.   17/H.L.I.

Pioneers : 17/North'd Fus.[2]

33RD DIVISION

19th Brigade :
20th R. Fus.   2/R. Welch Fus.   1/Cameronians.   5/Sco. Rif.

98th Brigade :
4/King's.   1/4th Suffolk.   1/Middlesex.   2/A. & S. H.

100th Brigade :
1/Queen's.   2/Worcs.   16/K.R.R.C.   1/9th H.L.I.

Pioneers : 18/Middlesex.

34TH DIVISION

101st Brigade :
15/R. Scots.   16/R. Scots.   10/Lincoln.   11/Suffolk.

102nd (Tyneside Scottish) Brigade[3] :
20/North'd Fus.   21/North'd Fus.   22/North'd Fus.   23/North'd Fus.

103rd (Tyneside Irish) Brigade[4] :
24/North'd Fus.   25/North'd Fus.   26/North'd Fus.   27/North'd Fus.

Pioneers : 18/North'd Fus.[5]

35TH (BANTAM) DIVISION

104th Brigade :
17/Lancs. Fus.   18/Lancs. Fus.   20/Lancs. Fus.   23/Manchester.

105th Brigade :
15/Cheshire.   16/Cheshire.   14/Gloster.   15/Sherwood For.

106th Brigade :
17/R. Scots.   17/W. Yorks.   19/D.L.I.   18/H.L.I.

Pioneers : 19/North'd Fus.

36TH (ULSTER) DIVISION

107th Brigade :
8/R. Irish Rif.   9/R. Irish Rif.   10/R. Irish Rif.   15/R. Irish Rif.

108th Brigade :
11/R. Irish Rif.   12/R. Irish Rif.   13/R. Irish Rif.   9/R. Irish Fus.

109th Brigade :
9/R. Innis. Fus.   10/R. Innis Fus.   11/R. Innis. Fus.   14/R. Irish Rif.

Pioneers : 16/R. Irish Rif.

[1] Replaced by 5th/6th R. Scots, 29th July.
[2] Replaced by 12/L. N. Lancs., 19th October.
[3] Attached to 37th Division 7th July-21st Aug.   Replaced by 111th Bde.
[4] Attached to 37th Division 7th July-21st Aug.   Replaced by 112th Bde.
[5] Attached to 37th Division 7th July-21st Aug.   Replaced by 9/N. Staffs.

37TH DIVISION

110th Brigade [1] :
6/Leicester.   7/Leicester.   8/Leicester.   9/Leicester.
111th Brigade [2] :
10/R. Fus.   13/R. Fus.   13/K.R.R.C.   13/Rif. Brig.
112th Brigade [2] :
11/R. Warwick.   6/Bedford.   8/E. Lancs.   10/L. N. Lancs.
Pioneers : 9/N. Staffs.[2]

38TH (WELSH) DIVISION

113th Brigade :
13/R. Welch Fus. 14/R. Welch Fus. 15/R. Welch Fus. 16/R. Welch Fus.
114th Brigade :
10/Welch.   13/Welch.   14/Welch.   15/Welch.
115th Brigade :
10/S.W.B.   11/S.W.B.   17/R. Welch Fus. 16/Welch.
Pioneers : 19/Welch.

39TH DIVISION

116th Brigade :
11/R. Sussex.   12/R. Sussex.   13/R. Sussex.   14/Hampshire.
117th Brigade :
16/Sherwood For. 17/Sherwood For. 17/K.R.R.C.   16/Rif. Brig.
118th Brigade :
1/6th Cheshire.   1/1st Cambs.   1/1st Herts.   4th/5th Black
                                                         Watch.
Pioneers : 13/Gloster.

41ST DIVISION

122nd Brigade :
12/E. Surrey.   15/Hampshire.   11/R. W. Kent.   18/K.R.R.C.
123rd Brigade :
11/Queen's.   10/R. W. Kent.   23/Middlesex.   20/D.L.I.
124th Brigade :
10/Queen's.   26/R. Fus.   32/R. Fus.   21/K.R.R.C.
Pioneers : 19/Middlesex.

46TH (NORTH MIDLAND) DIVISION (T.F.)

137th Brigade :
1/5th S. Staffs.   1/6th S. Staffs.   1/5th N. Staffs.   1/6th N. Staffs.
138th Brigade :
1/4th Lincoln.   1/5th Lincoln.   1/4th Leicester.   1/5th Leicester.
139th Brigade :
1/5th Sherwood   1/6th Sherwood   1/7th Sherwood   1/8th Sherwood
   For.   For.   For.   For.
Pioneers : 1/Monmouth.

[1] Exchanged with 63rd Bde., 21st Division, 7th July.
[2] Attached 7th July–21st Aug. to 34th Division *q.v.*

47TH (1/2ND LONDON) DIVISION (T.F.)

140th Brigade :
1/6th London (City of London).   1/8th London (P.O. Rifles).
1/7th London (City of London).   1/15th London (C.S. Rifles).

141st Brigade :
1/17th London (Poplar &   1/19th London (St. Pancras).
   Stepney Rifles).   1/20th London (Blackheath &
1/18th London (London   Woolwich).
   Irish Rifles).

142nd Brigade :
1/21st London (1st Surrey Rifles).   1/23rd London.
1/22nd London (The Queen's).   1/24th London (The Queen's).

Pioneers : 1/4th R. Welch Fus.

48TH (S. MIDLAND) DIVISION (T.F.)

143rd Brigade :
| 1/5th R. War-
wick. | 1/6th R. War-
wick. | 1/7th R. War-
wick. | 1/8th R. War-
wick. |

144th Brigade :
| 1/4th Gloster. | 1/6th Gloster. | 1/7th Worcs. | 1/8th Worcs. |

145th Brigade :
| 1/5th Gloster. | 1/4th O. & B.L.I. | 1/1st Bucks. | 1/4th R. Berks. |

Pioneers : 1/5th R. Sussex.

49TH (W. RIDING) DIVISION (T.F.)

146th Brigade :
| 1/5th W. Yorks. | 1/6th W. Yorks. | 1/7th W. Yorks. | 1/8th W. Yorks. |

147th Brigade :
| 1/4th D.W.R. | 1/5th D.W.R. | 1/6th D.W.R. | 1/7th D.W.R. |

148th Brigade :
| 1/4th K.O.Y.L.I. | 1/5th K.O.Y.L.I. | 1/4th York &
Lanc. | 1/5th York &
Lanc. |

Pioneers : 3/Monmouth. (Replaced by 19/Lancs. Fus. 6th Aug.)

50TH (NORTHUMBRIAN) DIVISION (T.F.)

149th Brigade :
| 1/4th North'd
Fus. | 1/5th North'd
Fus. | 1/6th North'd
Fus. | 1/7th North'd
Fus. |

150th Brigade :
| 1/4th E. Yorks. | 1/4th Green
Howards. | 1/5th Green
Howards. | 1/5th D.L.I. |

151st Brigade :
| 1/5th Border
Regt. | 1/6th D.L.I. | 1/8th D.L.I. | 1/9th D.L.I. |

Pioneers : 1/7th D.L.I.

51ST (HIGHLAND) DIVISION (T.F.)

152nd Brigade :
1/5th Seaforth.   1/6th Seaforth.   1/6th Gordons.   1/8th A. & S. H.

153rd Brigade :
1/6th Black   1/7th Black   1/5th Gordons.   1/7th Gordons.
Watch.   Watch.

154th Brigade :
1/9th R. Scots.   1/4th Seaforth.   1/4th Gordons.   1/7th A. & S. H.

Pioneers : 1/8th R. Scots.

55TH (W. LANCS.) DIVISION (T.F.)

164th Brigade :
1/4th King's   1/8th King's.   2/5th Lancs. Fus. 1/4th L. N.
Own.   Lancs.

165th Brigade :
1/5th King's.   1/6th King's.   1/7th King's.   1/9th King's.

166th Brigade :
1/5th King's   1/10th King's.   1/5th S. Lancs.   1/5th L. N.
Own.   Lancs.

Pioneers : 1/4th S. Lancs.

56TH (1/1ST LONDON) DIVISION (T.F.)

167th Brigade :
1/1st London   1/3rd London   1/7th Middlesex. 1/8th Middlesex.
(R.F.).   (R.F.).

168th Brigade :
1/4th London   1/12th London   1/13th London   1/14th London
(R.F.).   (Rangers).   (Kensington).   (Lon. Scot.).

169th Brigade :
1/2nd London   1/5th London   1/9th London   1/16th London
(R.F.).   (L.R.B.).   (Q.V.R.).   (Q.W.R.).

Pioneers : 1/5th Cheshire.

63RD (R.N.) DIVISION

188th Brigade :
Anson Bn.   Howe Bn.   1/R. Marine Bn.   2/R. Marine Bn.

189th Brigade :
Hood Bn.   Nelson Bn.   Hawke Bn.   Drake Bn.

190th Brigade :
1/H.A.C.   7/R. Fus.   4/Bedford.   10/R. Dub. Fus.

Pioneers : 14/Worcs.

1ST AUSTRALIAN DIVISION

1st (N.S.W.) Brigade :
1st Bn.   2nd Bn.   3rd Bn.   4th Bn.

2nd (Victoria) Brigade :
5th Bn.   6th Bn.   7th Bn.   8th Bn.

3rd Brigade :
9th (Q'land) Bn.   11th (W. Austr.) Bn.
10th (S. Austr.) Bn.   12th (S. & W. Austr., Tas.) Bn.

Pioneers : 1st Austr. Pioneer Bn.

2ND AUSTRALIAN DIVISION

5th (N.S.W.) Brigade :
  17th Bn.   18th Bn.   19th Bn.   20th Bn.

6th (Victoria) Brigade :
  21st Bn.   22nd Bn.   23rd Bn.   24th Bn.

7th Brigade :
  25th (Q'land) Bn.   27th (S. Austr.) Bn.
  26th (Q'land, Tas.) Bn.   28th (W. Austr.) Bn.

Pioneers : 2nd Austr. Pioneer Bn.

4TH AUSTRALIAN DIVISION

4th Brigade :
  13th (N.S.W.) Bn.   15th (Q'land, Tas.) Bn.
  14th (Vic.) Bn.   16th (S. & W. Austr.) Bn.

12th Brigade :
  45th (N.S.W.) Bn.   47th (Q'land, Tas.). Bn.
  46th (Vic.) Bn.   48th (S. & W. Austr.) Bn.

13th Brigade :
  49th (Q'land) Bn.   51st (W. Aust.) Bn.
  50th (S. Austr.) Bn.   52nd (S. & W. Austr., Tas.) Bn.

Pioneers : 4th Aust. Pioneer Bn.

5TH AUSTRALIAN DIVISION

8th Brigade :
  29th (Vic.) Bn.   31st (Q'land, Vic.) Bn.
  30th (N.S.W.) Bn.   32nd (S. & W. Austr.) Bn.

14th (N.S.W.) Brigade :
  53rd Bn.   54th Bn.   55th Bn.   56th Bn.

15th (Victoria) Brigade :
  57th Bn.   58th Bn.   59th Bn.   60th Bn.

Pioneers : 5th Austr. Pioneer Bn.

1ST CANADIAN DIVISION

1st Brigade :
  1st (Ontario) Bn.   3rd Bn. (Toronto Regt.).
  2nd (E. Ontario) Bn.   4th Bn.

2nd Brigade :
  5th (Western Cav.) Bn.   8th Bn. (90th Rif.).
  7th Bn. (1st Br. Columbia).   10th Bn.

3rd Brigade :
  13th Bn. (R. Highlanders).   15th Bn. (48th Highlanders).
  14th Bn. (R. Montreal Regt.).   16th Bn. (Canadian Scottish).

Pioneers : 1st Canadian Pioneer Bn.

2ND CANADIAN DIVISION

4th Brigade :
18th (W. Ontario) Bn.
19th (Central Ontario) Bn.
20th (Central Ontario) Bn.
21st (E. Ontario) Bn.

5th Brigade :
22nd (Canadien Français) Bn.
24th Bn. (Victoria Rif.).
25th Bn. (Nova Scotia Rif.).
26th (New Brunswick) Bn.

6th Brigade :
27th (City of Winnipeg) Bn.
28th (North-West) Bn.
29th (Vancouver) Bn.
31st (Alberta) Bn.

Pioneers : 2nd Canadian Pioneer Bn.

3RD CANADIAN DIVISION

7th Brigade :
P.P.C.L.I.
R. Cdn. Regt.
42nd Bn. (R. Highlanders).
49th (Edmonton) Bn.

8th Brigade :
1st Cdn. M.R.   2nd Cdn. M.R.   4th Cdn. M.R.   5th Cdn. M.R

9th Brigade :
43rd Bn. (Cameron Highlanders).
52nd (New Ontario) Bn.
58th Bn.
60th Bn. (Victoria Rif.).

Pioneers : 3rd Canadian Pioneer Bn.

4TH CANADIAN DIVISION

10th Brigade :
44th Bn.
46th (S. Saskatchewan) Bn.
47th (Br. Columbia) Bn.
50th (Calgary) Bn.

11th Brigade :
54th (Kootenay) Bn.
75th (Mississauga) Bn.
87th Bn. (Canadian Grenadier
  Guards).
102nd Bn.

12th Brigade :
38th (Ottawa) Bn.
72nd Bn. (Seaforth Highlanders).
73rd Bn. (R. Highlanders).
78th Bn. (Winnipeg Grenadiers).

Pioneers : 67th Canadian Pioneer Bn.

NEW ZEALAND DIVISION

1st N.Z. Brigade :
1/Auckland.   1/Canterbury.   1/Otago.   1/Wellington.

2nd N.Z. Brigade :
2/Auckland.   2/Canterbury.   2/Otago.   2/Wellington.

3rd N.Z. Rifle Brigade :
1/N.Z.R.B.   2/N.Z.R.B.   3/N.Z.R.B.   4/N.Z.R.B.

Pioneers : N.Z. Pioneer Bn.

THE SOMME, 1916

ORDER OF BATTLE OF GERMAN INFANTRY

3rd Guard Division :	Guard Fus.; Lehr Regt.; Gren. Regt. No. 9.
4th Guard Division :	5th Gd. Ft.; 5th Gd. Gren.; Res. Regt. No. 93.
5th Division :	Gren. Regts. Nos. 8, 12 ; Regt. No. 52.
6th Division :	Regts. Nos. 20, 24, 64.
7th Division :	Regts. Nos. 26, 27,[1] 165.
8th Division :	Regts. Nos. 72, 93, 153.
12th Division :	Regts. Nos. 23, 62, 63.
16th Division :	Regts. Nos. 28, 29, 68, 69.
24th Division :	Regts. Nos. 133, 139, 179.
26th Division :	Gren. Regt. No. 119 ; Regts. Nos. 121, 125.
27th Division :	Regt. No. 120 ; Gren. Regt. No. 123 ; Regts. Nos. 124, 127.
38th Division :	Regts. Nos. 94, 95, 96.
40th Division :	Regts. Nos. 104, 134, 181.
52nd Division :	Regts. Nos. 66, 169, 170.
56th Division :	Fus. Regt. No. 35 ; Regts. Nos. 88, 118.
58th Division :	Regts. Nos. 106, 107 ; Res. Regt. No. 120.
111th Division :	Fus. Regt. No. 73 ; Regts. Nos. 76, 164.
117th Division :	Regt. No. 157 ; Res. Regts. Nos. 11, 22.
183rd Division :	Regts. Nos. 183, 184 ; Res. Regt. No. 122.
185th Division [2] :	Regts. Nos. 185, 186, 190.
208th Division :	Regts. Nos. 25, 185 ; Res. Regt. No. 65.
222nd Division :	Regts. Nos. 193, 397 ; Res. Regt. No. 81.
223rd Division :	Regts. Nos. 144, 173 ; Ersatz Regt. No. 29.
1st Guard Reserve Div. :	Gd. Res. Regts. Nos. 1, 2 ; Res. Regt. No. 64.
2nd Guard Reserve Div. :	Res. Regts. Nos. 15, 55, 77, 91.
7th Reserve Division :	Res. Regts. Nos. 36, 66, 72.
12th Reserve Division :	Res. Regts. Nos. 23, 38, 51.

[1] Replaced by Regt. No. 393 for second tour.
[2] Reorganized for second tour, composition being Regts. Nos. 65, 161 and Res. Regt. No. 28.

17th Reserve Division :	Regts. Nos. 162, 163 ; Res. Regts. Nos. 75,[1] 76.
18th Reserve Division :	Res. Regts. Nos. 31, 84, 86.
19th Reserve Division :	Res. Regts. Nos. 73, 78, 79, 92.
23rd Reserve Division :	Res. Gren. Regt. No. 101 ; Res. Regts. Nos. 101, 102 ; Regt. No. 392.
24th Reserve Division :	Res. Regts. Nos. 101, 107, 133.
26th Reserve Division :	Res. Regts. Nos. 99, 119, 121 ; Regt. No. 180.
28th Reserve Division :	Res. Regts. Nos. 109, 110, 111.
45th Reserve Division :	Res. Regts. Nos. 210, 211, 212.
50th Reserve Division :	Res. Regts. Nos. 229, 230, 231.
51st Reserve Division :	Res. Regts. Nos. 233, 234, 235, 236.
52nd Reserve Division :	Res. Regts. Nos. 238, 239, 240.
4th Ersatz Division :	Regts. Nos. 359, 360, 361, 362.
5th Ersatz Division :	Landwehr Regts. Nos. 73, 74 ; Res. Ersatz Regt. No. 3.
2nd Bavarian Division :	Bav. Regts. Nos. 12, 15, 20.
3rd Bavarian Division :	Bav. Regts. Nos. 17, 18, 23.
4th Bavarian Division :	Bav. Regts. Nos. 5, 9 ; Bav. Res. Regt. No. 5.
5th Bavarian Division :	Bav. Regts. Nos. 7, 14, 19, 21.
6th Bavarian Division :	Bav. Regts. Nos. 6, 10, 11, 13.
10th Bavarian Division :	Bav. Regt. No. 16 ; Bav. Res. Regts. Nos. 6, 8.
6th Bavarian Res. Div. :	Bav. Res. Regts. Nos. 16, 17, 20, 21.
Bav. Ersatz Division :	Bav. Res. Regts. 14, 15 ; Ersatz Regt. No. 28.
89th Reserve Brigade :	Res. Regts. Nos. 209, 213.
Marine Brigade :	Marine Regts. Nos. 1, 2, 3.

[1] Left division before second tour.

FOURTH ARMY

FORMATION.

Fourth Army Headquarters began to form at Tilques on the 5th February, 1916, and nineteen days later Army Headquarters moved to Querrieu. A week later the Fourth Army took over the right sector of the B.E.F. front, a 15-mile stretch from Curlu on the Somme to Hébuterne. The Fourth Army was in touch on the south with the French Sixth Army and to the north with the right of the British Third Army. Fourth Army took over this front with the XIII and X Corps, in the line, and the VIII Corps in Army Reserve.*

BATTLES AND ENGAGEMENTS.

1916

BATTLES OF THE SOMME [III, VIII, X, XIII, XIV, XV, and Cav. Corps; with C and D Tank Cos.].

1–13 July	**Battle of Albert** [III, VIII,** X,** XIII, and XV Corps].
1 July	**Capture of Montauban** [30th Div.: XIII Corps].
1 July	**Capture of Mametz** [7th Div.: XV Corps].
2 July	**Capture of Fricourt** [17th Div.: XV Corps].
2–4 July	**Capture of La Boisselle** [19th Div.: III Corps].
3 July	**Capture of Bernafay Wood** [9th Div.: XIII Corps].
7–11 July	**Mametz Wood** [38th Div.: XV Corps].
10 July	**Capture of Contalmaison** [23rd Div.: III Corps].
7–13 July	**Fighting in Trônes Wood** [30th Div.: XIII Corps].
14–17 July	**Battle of Bazentin Ridge** [III, XIII, and XV Corps].
14 July	**Capture of Trônes Wood** [54th Bde. (18th Div.): XIII Corps].
14–18; and 29 July ...	**Capture of Longueval** [*14–18/7*—3rd and 9th Divs.: XIII Corps; and on *29/7*—5th Div.: XV Corps].
15 July–3 September	**Battle of Delville Wood** [XIII Corps, until *Mn. 16/8/16*; then XIV Corps; also from *31/8/16*, XV Corps].

---

* X Corps had 32nd, 36th, 48th, and 49th Divs., and XIII Corps had 7th, 18th, and 30th Divs., VIII Corps (at that time in Army Reserve) had only the 31st Div.

** On 4/7/16 the Reserve (later Fifth) Army took over (in the line) VIII Corps (4th, 29th, 31st, and 48th Divs.) and X Corps (25th, 32nd, 36th, and 49th Divs.) from the Fourth Army.

20–30 July	Attacks on High Wood* [19th Div.: III Corps; and 5th, 7th, 33rd, and 51st Divs.: XV Corps].
27 and 28 July	Capture and consolidation of Delville Wood [2nd Div.: XIII Corps].
8 and 9 August ...	Attack of Waterlôt Farm—Guillemont [2nd Div.: XIII Corps].
23 July–3 September	Battle of Pozières Ridge [III Corps].
3–6 September	Battle of Guillemont [XIV and XV Corps].
9 September	Battle of Ginchy [XIV and (part) XV Corps].
15–22 September ...	Battle of Flers-Courcelette [III, XIV, and XV Corps, and 1st Cav. and 5th (Ind.) Cav. Divs. (Cav. Corps); with 42 tanks (C Coy.—17 tanks, and D Coy.—25 tanks). 17 tanks C Coy. with XIV; 17 tanks D Coy. with XV; and 8 tanks D Coy. with III].
15 September	Capture of Flers [41st and N.Z. Divs., with 1 tank: XV Corps].
15 September	Capture of Martinpuich [15th Div., with 4 tanks: III Corps].
25–28 September ...	Battle of Morval [III, XIV, and XV Corps, and Cav. Corps; with, on 25/9, 2 tanks D Coy. with III; and, on 26/9, 2 tanks C Coy. with XIV, and 1 tank D Coy. with XV].
25 September	Capture of Lesbœufs [Gds. and 6th Divs.: XIV Corps].
26 September	Capture of Combles [56th Div., with 2 tanks C Coy.: XIV Corps.]
26 September	Capture of Gird Trench* and Gueudecourt [21st Div., with 1 tank D Coy.: XV Corps].
1–18 October	Battle of the Transloy Ridges [III, XIV, and XV Corps; with 5 tanks C and D Cos.—3 with XIV and 2 with XV].
1–3 October	Capture of Eaucourt l'Abbaye [47th Div.: III Corps].
7 October	Capture of Le Sars [23rd Div.: III Corps].
7 October–5 November	Attacks on the Butte de Warlencourt [9th, 23rd, 47th, 48th, and 50th Divs.: III Corps].
3–11 November	Battle of the Ancre Heights [Part of III Corps].
13–18 November ...	Battle of the Ancre [Part of III Corps].

* High Wood was finally captured by 47th Div., III Corps, on 15/9/16.
* The first instance of the co-operation of tank and aeroplane in the field.

FIFTH ARMY*

FORMATION.

Headquarters of the Reserve Corps (then at Regnière Écluse—5 miles W.N.W. of Crécy en Ponthieu) became the Headquarters of the Reserve Army on the 22nd May, 1916 (p. 265).   Three weeks later Reserve Army H.Q. moved to Daours (6 miles east of Amiens) ; and on the 2nd July, 1916, preparatory to taking over the northern part of the Somme battle-front, Reserve Army H.Q. was installed at Toutencourt (10 miles S.E. of Doullens).

Two days later the Reserve Army took over (from the Fourth Army) the left of the Somme battle-front from la Boisselle to Hébuterne (8 miles), and with it the X and VIII Corps.**   At the outset of this change of command, the immediate attack of this sector of the German position was postponed and on this part of the front trench-warfare tactics were adopted ; though the X Corps fought on to extend the two footings it had already gained to the north and south of Thiepval.

BATTLES AND ENGAGEMENTS.

1916

BATTLES OF THE SOMME [II, V, VIII, X XIII, Cdn., and I Anzac Corps ; with A, C, and D Tank Cos.].

4–13 July	**Battle of Albert** [VIII and X Corps].***
14–17 July	**Battle of Bazentin Ridge** [X Corps].
17 July	**Capture of Ovillers** [48th Div. : X Corps].
23 July–3 September	**Battle of Pozières Ridge** [X (until 24/7) ; then II Corps ; and, from 28/7, I Anzac Corps].
6 August–3 September	**Fighting for Mouquet Farm** [12th, 25th, and 48th Divs. : II Corps ; and 1st Aus., 2nd Aus., and 4th Aus. Divs : 1 Anzac Corps].
14 September	**Capture of the Wonder Work** [11th Div. : II Corps].
15–22 September ...	**Battle of Flers-Courcelette** [II and Cdn. Corps ; with 6 tanks C Coy. with 2nd Cdn. Div.].
26–28 September ...	**Battle of Thiepval Ridge** [II, V (part), and Cdn. Corps ; with, on 26/9, 8 tanks C Coy.—6 tanks with II, and 2 tanks with Cdn. Corps].

* Reserve Army was renamed Fifth Army on 30/10/1916.
** At this time X Corps comprised the 25th, 32nd, 36th, and 49th Divs., and in VIII Corps were the 4th, 29th, 31st, and 48th Divs.
*** VIII and X Corps were taken over (in the line) from Fourth Army on 4/7/16.

26 September   ...   ...   **Capture of Mouquet Farm** [11th Div.: II Corps ; with 2 tanks C Coy.].

1–18 October   ...   ...   **Battle of Transloy Ridges** [Cdn. Corps].

1 Oct.–11 Nov. ...   ...   **Battle of the Ancre Heights** [II, V (part), and Cdn. Corps ; with 4 tanks A Coy. with 18th Div.: II Corps].

9 October ...   .   **Capture of Stuff Redoubt** [25th Div.: II Corps].

14 October ...   .   **Capture of Schwaben Redoubt** [39th Div.: II Corps].

21 October ...   .   **Capture of Regina Trench and Redoubt** [18th and 25th Divs.: II Corps ; with 4 tanks A Coy. with 18th Div.].

21 October ...   .   **Capture of Stuff Trench** [39th Div.: II Corps].

On 30/10/1916, Reserve Army was renamed Fifth Army.

13–18 November   ...   **Battle of the Ancre** [II, V, and XIII* Corps ; with, on *13/11*, 3 tanks A Coy. with 39th Div. (II), and 2 tanks D Coy. with 51st Div. (V) ; on *14/11*, 3 tanks D Coy. with 63rd Div. (V) ; on *16/11*, 2 tanks D Coy. with 2nd Div. (V) ; and, on *18/11*, 5 tanks D Coy. with 32nd (4) and 51st (1) : V Corps ; and 3 tanks A Coy. with 19th Div. (II)].

13 November   ...   ...   **Capture of Beaumont Hamel** [51st Div.: V Corps ; with 2 tanks D Coy.].

14 November   ...   ...   **Capture of Beaucourt** [190th Bde., 63rd Div.: V Corps ; with 2 tanks D Coy.].

---

* On 4/10/16 XIII Corps took over the left of Reserve (later Fifth) Army, from opposite Serre to Hébuterne.

Additional Material

Most of the new material has been added to the relevant sections of the text, but where that has proved impossible the superior numbers in the text refer to the notes here.

1. Major R. G. Raper (8th South Staffs.) was killed on 2nd July 1916. He is regarded as a local hero and a street is named after him in the village. For years his body lay outside the walls of Fricourt British Cemetery, but was taken into it during the 1960s.

2. There is a cross to the memory of Major C. C. Dickens (see p. 146) to the north-west of the wood, and although it is in good condition the 'garden approach' is overgrown. It can be assumed that Dickens' body is somewhere close by, although it was not found when a search was made. His name is therefore commemorated on the Thiepval Memorial.

3. Adanac Military Cemetery is on the east side of the road between Miraumont and Courcelette; it contains the graves of 3,172 men including some from the 31st Division, killed on 1st July. Piper Richardson VC is buried here (see pp. 358-9) and Sgt. S. Forsyth, a New Zealand VC winner from 1918.

4. Pargny
Although this village was three miles south of Péronne, casualties from the Serre Road fighting were buried here in the British Cemetery.

5. On the 8th the 7th Suffolks (35th Bde. 12th Div.) lost very heavily when the enemy temporarily took the possession of Ration Trench from them.

6. Halfway along the Gommecourt–Puisieux road, on the south side, lies Rossignol Wood Cemetery, begun in March 1917.

7. Suzanne
To the east of Bray is the very pretty village of Suzanne which is on the Somme river. The Communal Cemetery and the British Extension is close to the village with many graves from 1915, 1916 and 1918. On the road to Maricourt, north of the village, lies the Military Cemetery No. 3 which contains the bodies of men killed on 1st July 1916.

8. Ville-sur-Ancre
The Communal Cemetery and Extension have the graves of about twenty British casualties. The village is south-west of Dernancourt and north-east of Treux.

9. Capt. Summers was killed when attacking German Kite Balloons during this operation and is buried at Beaulencourt British Cemetery, three miles south of Bapaume.

Index to Formations and Units

Index to Personal Names